DEVELOPMENTAL PSYCHOLOGY

DEVELOPMENTAL PSYCHOLOGY Fourth Edition

Elizabeth B. Hurlock

McGraw-Hill Book Company

New York
St. Louis
San Francisco
Düsseldorf
Johannesburg
Kuala Lumpur
London
Mexico
Montreal
New Delhi
Panama
Paris
São Paulo
Singapore
Sydney
Tokyo
Toronto

DEVELOPMENTAL PSYCHOLOGY

4567890   DODO   798

Library of Congress Cataloging in Publication Data

Hurlock, Elizabeth Bergner, date
  Developmental psychology.

  Includes bibliographies
  1. Developmental psychology. I. Title.
[DNLM: 1. Psychology. BF701 H965d]
BF713.H87 1975   155   74-8604
ISBN 0-07-031444-6

This book was set in Century Expanded by Progressive Typographers.
The editors were John Hendry and James R. Belser; the designer was
Merrill Haber; the production supervisor was Thomas J. LoPinto. The
photo editor was Gabriele Wunderlich. The drawings were done by
Vantage Art, Inc.

To my daughter,
Gail McKnight Beckman

CONTENTS

PREFACE

When *Developmental Psychology* first appeared in 1953, it was customary in most colleges and universities to teach developmental psychology as a two-semester course, the first semester covering the childhood years and the second semester covering adolescence, adulthood, and old age. Today, however, most colleges and universities offer only a one-semester course in developmental psychology.

Research in all stages of the life span has increased greatly since the first edition appeared. This poses a serious dilemma for the textbook author: How can substantial new material be incorporated in a textbook without increasing its size beyond what can be covered in a one-semester course? In the fourth edition of *Developmental Psychology,* I have tried to resolve this problem without eliminating any important material, old or new. This effort has taken three major forms.

First, boxes are extensively used to summarize and highlight important subject matter. Because of their concise format, they enable the reader to grasp important points quickly and easily, thus gaining space for other material.

Second, in spite of all the new studies that have been reported since the third edition of this book appeared, the number of references has been kept down by omitting many older studies. This was done not because newer reports are necessarily better, but because they themselves contain references to the older studies which the reader can investigate if he or she wishes to pursue the topic further.

Third, unless variations in patterns of development at different ages are marked or unless they have a pronounced effect on the individual's personal and social adjustments, they have been touched on briefly or omitted. While this may give the reader the impression that all people develop in the same way at the same ages or that patterns of interests, values, and behavior are similar, a careful study of the material presented will show that this is not so. Instead, the typical patterns of development in American culture today are noted, and any marked variations from these patterns are reported or commented on.

Some other changes in this edition deserve mention.

Adolescence is now covered in one chapter instead of two. The lowering of the age of legal maturity from 21 to 18 years has made anachronistic the third edition's separate chapter on "late adolescence" (17 to 21 years). In the new single chapter on adolescence, emphasis has been placed on changes in interests, values, and behavior patterns that occur as the individual progresses from the early to the latter part of adolescence.

The fourth edition contains fewer graphs from research studies. This change was made in the belief that such material is not very meaningful to the reader unless the conditions and results of the studies are reported in detail. But new line drawings and cartoons have been added to exemplify and reinforce points made in the text discussion.

Topics of current interest and controversy—among them death, sexual mores among the young and the elderly, and attitudes toward work, unemployment, and retirement—are given more detailed treatment in this edition.

Each chapter concludes with a brief list of "Chapter Highlights." These highlights call to the reader's attention the most important topics discussed in the chapter. They are more selective than conventional chapter summaries.

Finally, it should be noted that the chapter bibliographies contain works not specifically cited in the text discussion—another departure from earlier editions of this book. Only when a direct quotation from an author or a summary of the findings of a particular study has been given do I include a reference to it in the text discussion. However, every work cited in the bibliography has contributed to my thinking, and thus—however indirectly—to my presentation. In this way I hope I have acknowledged my debt to all, and at the same time given the interested reader the chance to range beyond those works specifically mentioned in the text discussion.

I thank my professional colleagues for their helpful criticisms of the third edition of this book and of the manuscript for this edition. This help has been invaluable to me, and I say "thank you" for it.

Elizabeth B. Hurlock

CHAPTER ONE

GROWTH AND DECLINE

Developmental psychology is the branch of psychology that studies the development of the human being from conception to death.

Developmental psychologists have six major objectives: (1) to find out what are the common and characteristic age changes in appearance, in behavior, in interests, and in goals from one developmental period to another; (2) to find out when these changes occur; (3) to find out what causes them; (4) to find out how they influence behavior; (5) to find out whether they can be predicted or not; and (6) to find out whether they are individual or universal.

In its early years, as Siegel has pointed out, ". . . developmental psychology was preoccupied with ages and stages. Investigators sought to learn the typical age at which various stages of development occurred" (92). The areas selected for research were those considered significant for human evolutionary adaptation, such as upright locomotion and speech. These early studies showed that some individuals reach some of these stages earlier than others; for example, some babies begin to walk at eight months, some at ten, and some at twelve. However, because the focus of interest among developmental psychologists has changed over the years, there are gaps in our knowledge of the different developmental phenomena characteristic of the different age periods. There are two major reasons for the uneven emphasis of developmental psychology. First, the motivation to study a particular period in the developmental pattern has been greatly influenced by a desire to solve some practical problem or problems associated with that period. Research in the area of childhood, for example, was designed first to throw light on educational problems and, later, to deal with problems related to child-training methods. The latest focus of research attention, middle age, is the outgrowth of the realization that good adjustment in the latter years of life depends on how well one has adjusted to the physical and psychological changes that normally occur in the middle years.

The second reason for the uneven emphasis of developmental psychology is that it is harder to study people at some stages of their life than at others. These difficulties will be discussed in detail later in this chapter.

MEANING OF DEVELOPMENTAL CHANGES

The term *development* means *a progressive series of changes that occur in an orderly, predictable pattern as a result of maturation and experience.* Development does not consist merely of adding inches to one's height or improving one's ability. Instead, development is a complex process of integrating many structures and functions (4).

Two essentially antagonistic processes in development take place simultaneously throughout life—*growth,* or evolution, and *atrophy,* or involution. Both begin at conception and end at death. In the early years, growth predominates, even though atrophic changes occur as early as embryonic life. In the latter part of life, atrophy predominates, though growth does not stop; hair continues to grow, and cells to be replaced, for example. With aging, some parts of the body and mind change more than others.

The human being is never static. From conception to death, change is constantly taking place in his physical and psychological capacities. As Piaget has explained, structures are "far from being static and

given from the start." Instead, a maturing organism undergoes continued and progressive changes in response to experiential conditions, and these result in a complex network of interaction (82).

Often the pattern of change resembles a bell-shaped curve, rising abruptly at the start and then flattening out during the middle years, only to decline slowly or abruptly in old age. It is important to recognize that at no time can this pattern be represented by a straight line, though plateau periods of short or long duration may occur in the development of different capacities.

Goal of Development

The goal of development is to enable the individual to adapt to the environment in which he lives. To achieve this goal, self-realization—or, as Maslow has labeled it, "self-actualization"—is essential. This goal, like the person himself, is never static. It may be thought of, in fact, as an urge—the urge to do what one is fitted to do, the urge to become the best person, both physically and psychologically, that he can (71). How

Will she have the chance to become "the best person, physically and psychologically, that she can be"? (Suzanne Szasz)

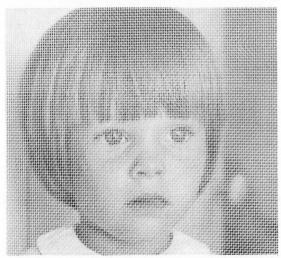

each of us expresses this urge depends on our innate abilities and the training we receive—not only during the early, formative years but also as we grow older and come under ever-greater pressures to conform to social expectations.

Because self-actualization plays an important role in mental health, the individual should have opportunities to express his interests and desires in ways that give him satisfaction, while at the same time conforming to social expectations.

Attitudes toward Developmental Changes

Although changes of a physical or psychological nature are constantly taking place, the individual may not be aware of them. The changes of old age occur at a much slower pace than those of childhood and adolescence. They still require readjustments on the individual's part, but because he can make these readjustments more slowly, neither he nor others may recognize them.

When changes are rapid, on the other hand, the individual is only too well aware of them, as are others. During the puberty growth spurt at the end of childhood and the beginning of adolescence, such comments as "My, how you have grown since I last saw you!" are evidence of how others notice these changes.

Likewise, in senescence, when the downward movement begins to accelerate, the individual is aware of the fact that his health is "failing" and his mind is "slipping." These changes necessitate constant readjustments in the scheduled pattern of his life. He must slow down as the incapacities and infirmities of old age catch up with him.

When the individual is aware of the changes that are taking place, he develops definite attitudes toward them. Whether his attitudes will be favorable or unfavorable depends on a number of factors, the three most important of which are described in Box 1-1. How many young children view developmental changes is illustrated in Figure 1-1.

Box 1-1. FACTORS INFLUENCING ATTITUDES TOWARD DEVELOPMENTAL CHANGES

Behavior
Changes that affect behavior adversely, such as the awkwardness or irritability of puberty, are difficult for the individual to accept.

Appearance
The individual welcomes changes that improve his looks, while those which make him less attractive are unwelcome.

Cultural Attitudes
Society's attitudes toward the changes that take place at different times in the life span have a marked influence on the individual's own feelings. Older people, for example, may do all they can to camouflage the telltale signs of aging.

Figure 1-1 How many young children view developmental changes. (Hank Ketcham. "Dennis the Menace." Courtesy Publishers-Hall Syndicate, Oct. 11, 1973.)

"That's what growin' up means, Joey . . . ya just keep gettin' BIGGER and OLDER and BIGGER and OLDER. . . ."

SIGNIFICANT FACTS
ABOUT DEVELOPMENT

Certain fundamental and predictable facts are central to a proper understanding of the pattern of development. These are listed and explained in Box 1-2. Each of these facts has important implications for development.

Early Foundations Because early foundations are likely to be persistent, it is important that they be of the kind that will lead to good personal and social adjustments as the individual grows older. As James warned many years ago, "Could the young but realize how quickly they will become mere walking bundles of habits, they would give more heed to their conduct while still in the plastic state" (51).

Early patterns do tend to persist, but they are not unchangeable. There are three conditions under which change is likely to occur. First, change may come about when the individual receives help and guidance in making the change. Some parents, for example, may succeed in training a child to use his right hand in preference to his left.

Second, change is likely to occur when significant people in the individual's life treat him in new and different ways. A child whose parents believe that children should be "seen but not heard" can be encouraged to express himself more freely by a teacher who makes him feel that he has something to contribute to the group.

Box 1-2. IMPORTANT FACTS ABOUT DEVELOPMENT

Childhood Is the Foundation Period of Life
Attitudes, habits, and patterns of behavior established during the early years determine, to a large extent, how successfully the individual will adjust to life as he grows older.

Development Results from Maturation and Learning
Maturation is the unfolding of the individual's inherent traits. It provides the raw material for learning and determines the more general patterns and sequences of behavior. Learning is development that comes from exercise and effort on the individual's part.

Development Follows a Definite and Predictable Pattern
There are orderly patterns of physical, motor, speech, and intellectual development. The pattern of physical and motor development is illustrated in Figure 1-2. Within these patterns there is marked correlation between physical and psychological development.

All Individuals Are Different
Each individual follows his developmental pattern in his own way; some develop smoothly and gradually, while others move in spurts.

Each Phase of Development Has Characteristic Traits
The developmental pattern is marked by periods of equilibrium, when the individual adapts easily to environmental demands, and periods of disequilibrium, when he experiences difficulties in adaptation.

There Are Developmental Hazards at Every Age
Some of the hazards that interfere with good adjustment are environmental in origin, while others originate from within. These hazards may affect physical, psychological, or social adjustments.

There Are Traditional Beliefs about Individuals of Different Ages
Traditional beliefs have grown up about the physical and psychological characteristics of individuals of all ages. These affect the judgments others make of a person as well as his self-evaluations.

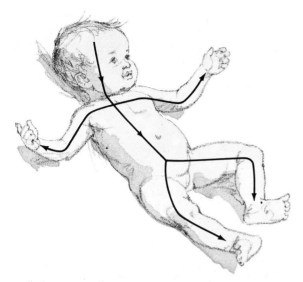

Figure 1-2 The pattern of physical and motor development follows the laws of developmental direction, which hold that development proceeds from head to foot and from trunk to extremities. (Adapted from E. L. Vincent & P. C. Martin. *Human psychological development.* New York: Ronald Press, 1961. Used by permission.)

The third condition which can bring about changes in the foundations laid early in life is a strong motivation on the part of the individual to make the change. When behavior is rewarded by social approval, there is little motivation to make a change. When, on the other hand, behavior meets with social disapproval, there will be a strong motivation to change.

Maturation and Learning Three important facts emerge from our present knowledge of the interrelationship of maturation and learning as the cause of development. First, because human beings are capable of learning, variation is possible. Individual differences in personality, attitudes, interests, and patterns of behavior come not from maturation alone but from maturation and learning. Second, maturation sets limits beyond which development cannot progress, even with the most favorable learning methods and the strongest motivation on the part of the learner. Cattell et al. stressed this point when they said, "All learning and adjustment is limited by inherent properties of the organism" (31).

The third important fact about the interrelation between maturation and learning is that it suggests a "timetable" for learning. The individual cannot learn until he is ready. "Developmental readiness," or readiness to learn, determines the moment when learning can and should take place. Harris has emphasized the importance of providing an opportunity to learn when the individual is ready: "It is possible, indeed likely, that a person who comes late to his training will never realize the full measure of his potential" (48).

Individual Differences Because all individuals are different, no two people can be expected to react in the same manner to the same environmental stimuli. What one person perceives as humorous, for example, will depend on his past experiences as well as upon the level of his intellectual development. Another person of the same intellectual development may not find the same thing humorous because his past experiences have been different. Because no two individuals ever have identical hereditary endowments and the same environmental experiences, one can never predict with accuracy how a person will react to a situation, even when there is ample information about his inherited abilities and even when it is known how the *average* person behaves in similar situations. Nor should one expect the same achievement from people of the same age and intellectual development. Children of the same mental age, for example, will not necessarily be ready to read or do other types of schoolwork at the same time. And, finally, individual differences are significant because they are responsible for individuality in personality makeup. Not only does individuality make people interesting, but it also makes social progress possible.

Characteristic Behavior While it is unquestionably true that some stages of growing up are marked by more difficult behavior than others, there is no stage when the characteristic behavior is not "problem behavior" if it is judged by adult standards. Only when an individual's behavior is atypical for his age and leads to poor adjustment may it justly be considered problem behavior. In most instances, such behavior is infantile in that it is characteristic of an earlier age level. The child has not learned to act his age either because no one has taught him how to do so or because he derives more satisfaction from infantile behavior.

Many of these difficult, unsocial, and often hard-to-understand forms of behavior which appear at different times during the growing-up years will gradually wane and disappear, only to be replaced by other forms of behavior as difficult to understand and live with as the ones that have just been outgrown.

However, it is never safe to assume that all difficult behavior will disappear as the child grows older. Such behavior may be a warning of possible future trouble and should not be disregarded. When it persists beyond the age at which it is normally found, difficult behavior suggests that the individual's needs, both personal and social, are not being satisfactorily met.

Developmental Hazards Each period in the life span has associated with it certain developmental hazards — whether physical, psychological, or environmental in origin — and these inevitably involve adjustment problems. As Lawton has pointed out (62):

Throughout the life span, people develop techniques of handling each of their difficulties. Some of these techniques are suitable and efficient, others are inappropriate and wasteful, or a method may be suitable for one age period and not another.

It is important to be aware of the hazards commonly associated with each period in the life span because the way in which the individual copes with them has an important effect on his personal and social adjustments.

Traditional Beliefs and Stereotypes Traditional beliefs and stereotypes influence the individual's behavior and his attitudes both toward others and toward himself. In our culture, for example, commonly held stereotypes relating to old age can lead to unfavorable treatment of individuals in the latter years of their lives. Acceptance of these stereotypes by those who are growing old is responsible for much unhappiness during old age and also is an important factor in physical and mental decline.

THE LIFE SPAN

Today, American men and women, on the average, live longer than men and women of any other country and longer than

---

Box 1-3. CONDITIONS INFLUENCING LONGEVITY

Heredity.

General physical condition.

Underweight or overweight. People whose body builds more closely approximate the norm tend to live longer.

Sex. Women, as a group, outlive men.

Race. In this country, blacks, Puerto Ricans, and other minority-group members have a shorter life expectancy than whites.

Socioeconomic level. The higher the individual's socioeconomic level, the longer his life span tends to be.

Education. People who are better educated tend to live longer.

Occupation. The kind of work the individual does affects the length of his life span. See Figure 1-3.

Geographic location. People who live in urban and suburban areas tend to live longer than those who live in rural areas.

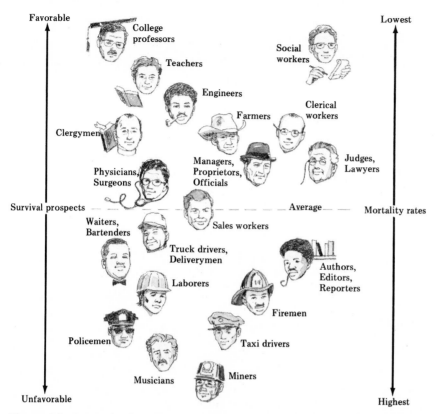

Figure 1-3 Longevity in people is related to occupation. (Adapted from A. Scheinfeld. *Your heredity and environment.* Philadelphia: Lippincott, 1965. Used by permission.)

men and women in the United States in past generations. In 1900, for example, the life expectancy for white males was 48.2 years; for white females, it was 51 years. By 1970, the life expectancy for white males had risen to 67.5 years, and for white females it had risen to 74.1 years. For blacks and other minority groups, the life expectancy for both males and females was several years less. It has been estimated that by 1990, 9.4 percent of the entire American population will be over sixty-five years of age (54, 113).

Many factors influence the length of the life span; the most important of these are given in Box 1-3.

How long a given individual will live is impossible to predict. However, Scheinfeld has suggested that if three factors are taken into consideration, a general prediction is possible. According to him (90):

How long you, personally, may expect to live depends on these principal influences: First, environment—the way in which you were started off in life and the conditions under which you lived thereafter and live now. Second, your inherited vigor or weakness (as applied both to specific diseases and defects and to general resistance factors), with particular attention to your sex. And, third, luck.

Regardless of how short or long the total life span may be, it is divided into ten stages or periods, each of which is characterized by certain developmental and behavioral patterns. These are shown in Box 1-4.

Box 1-4.   STAGES IN THE LIFE SPAN

Prenatal period: conception to birth
Infancy: birth to the end of the second week
Babyhood: end of the second week to end of the second year
Early childhood: two to six years
Late childhood: six to ten or twelve years
Puberty or preadolescence: ten or twelve to thirteen or fourteen years
Adolescence: thirteen or fourteen to eighteen years
Early adulthood: eighteen to forty years
Middle age: forty to sixty years
Old age or senescence: sixty years to death

The remaining chapters of this book will discuss in detail the characteristic patterns of behavior for each of these age periods and the reasons for any deviations from the predictable patterns. They will also explain the meanings of the names applied to each of the major periods in the life span.

All cultures divide the life span into periods, although different names are applied to them from culture to culture and the age levels encompassed by the different stages vary. As Neugarten and Moore have explained (76):

In all societies, age is one of the important factors in determining the way people behave toward each other. Certain biological and social events come to be regarded as significant punctuation marks in the life line and to signify the transition from one age stage to the next. . . . In all societies, age-status systems emerge in which duties, rights and rewards are differentially distributed to age groups which themselves have been socially defined.

DIFFICULTIES IN STUDYING THE LIFE SPAN

To understand the pattern of development from conception to death, one must have a picture of this that is based on the results of scientific studies, not on traditional beliefs and stereotyped ideas. However, as was pointed out earlier, many obstacles confront the developmental psychologist in his study of the various stages in the life span, and as a result there are gaps in our knowledge. As Bromley has said (22):

We spend about one quarter of our lives growing up and three quarters growing old. It is strange, therefore, that psychologists and others have devoted most of their efforts to the study of childhood and adolescence.

While Bromley's criticism may suggest that this concentration on childhood and adolescence is deliberate, this is far from the truth. There is almost as much scientific interest in the later years of life as there is in the early years, but attempts to study the later years have been blocked, in part at least, by obstacles which are only now being minimized and in some instances eliminated.

Interest in the latter part of the life span is not of recent origin. Hippocrates treated illnesses of old age, and there are also historic references to beauty aids for the elderly and to attempts at rejuvenation (1, 64). However, until the turn of the present century too few people lived long enough to make the latter part of life a serious problem. Now an increasing percentage of the population lives longer, and this has created many problems for the individuals themselves and for their families, their employers, and society in general.

As a result, two new areas of scientific research have been developed—gerontology and geriatrics. *Gerontology* is the science of aging. It is derived from the Greek *geron,* meaning "old man," and *ology,* meaning "the study of," and it is concerned with all facets of aging. *Geriatrics,* on the other hand, is that branch of medicine concerned with the diseases of old age. It deals with the health of the aged, just as pediatrics deals with the health of infants and children.

The major goal of studies in the area of

gerontology is to gather data to disprove traditional beliefs about the aged and to show how they can function successfully in a youth-oriented culture.

To prolong the usefulness and happiness of old people through better health has been the goal of geriatrics. While improvement in the health of old people may and often does add years to their life span, this is of little value unless the individual is able to enjoy and make use of this added time not only for his own enjoyment but also to aid society. The goal of geriatrics is therefore to add life to the years of the elderly, not just years to their lives.

Middle age, until recently one of the least explored periods in the life span, has come under scientific investigation. As Archer has explained, "Traditionally, social science research on human development has concentrated on childhood, adolescence, and to a lesser extent old age. Concerning the years stretching between early adulthood and advanced age, there has been virtual silence" (5).

The reason for this "virtual silence" is that few problems related to middle age seemed important enough to engage the attention of the psychologist, who was already preoccupied with studies relating to children, adolescents, young adults, and old people.

Not only has there been increasing scientific interest in the latter years of life, but there is also a strong popular interest in the subject, as evidenced by the appearance of many books and articles dealing with the problems of middle and old age. An article in *Time* magazine emphasized the important role that popular literature has played in this increase in interest (107):

In 1932, Walter B. Pitkin wrote Life Begins at Forty *and it became an overnight inspirational bestseller precisely because people thought life ended at 40 and there was nothing left to do but wait around for retirement and death.*

Obstacles to Studying Development

The most common obstacles that confront the scientist in his study of development are given in Box 1-5. All studies of the life span are beset by these obstacles in varying degrees. For example, it is relatively easy to get representative samplings of subjects from among schoolchildren and college students. In the case of newborn infants, however, researchers often meet with strong parental objections. Getting older adolescents and young adults who are not attending school to volunteer as subjects is also difficult because they may not be available for study at any one particular place.

Obtaining information from subjects of any age is extremely difficult because most resent having a stranger pry into their personal affairs. Even schoolchildren and college students, who often take tests or give information as part of their classroom work, show their resentment by being uncoopera-

---

Box 1-5. COMMON OBSTACLES TO STUDYING DEVELOPMENT

Subjects
It is difficult to obtain a large, representative sample of an age group.

Obtaining Information
Even when a large, representative sample of an age group has been obtained, there is no guarantee that the scientist will be able to elicit the information he is seeking.

Methodology
No one method can be used successfully to study people of all ages or to investigate all areas of development, and some of the methods that must be resorted to, for lack of better ones, are of dubious scientific value.

Accuracy of Data Obtained
Data about an area of development may be inaccurate as a result of poor methodology or because subjects are uncooperative or give false information.

Because so many people resent being treated as "guinea pigs," it is difficult for developmental researchers to get adequate information from subjects of any age. Elderly people are often the most uncooperative. (Bruce Roberts from Rapho Guillumette)

study persons in homes for the aged, hospitals, or on pension lists. The retired, the rejected, the isolated, and the sick are most likely to be the subjects of aging research. Our generalizations about older persons are then made upon the basis of a sample not necessarily reflective of the older part of our population.

Finding a satisfactory method for studying development has also proved to be a stumbling block to research. Because of the wide age range and the variety of different areas of development that must be studied to give a composite picture, many methods have had to be used. Some have been borrowed from medicine, from the physical sciences, and from related social sciences, especially anthropology and sociology. Some have made use of laboratory settings, and others of the naturalistic settings of the home, school, community, or work environment. Some are regarded as reliable, while others, especially the retrospective and introspective techniques, are of questionable value.

Regardless of the method used, most of the studies of development have been cross-sectional comparisons of the same abilities at different stages of development. As such, they do not give evidence about developmental trends or about intraindividual variability. Nor is it possible, when using cross-sectional comparisons, to assess the relative behavior constellations of individuals at an early age and similar behavior in adult life.

One of the most serious problems connected with the cross-sectional approach to the study of developmental changes is that it is almost impossible to get comparable groups of subjects for study at different age levels. This can bias the results of studies, especially studies of old age. When mental abilities are studied using the cross-sectional approach, mental decline is reported to be far greater than when the same mental abilities are studied using the longitudinal approach (88, 89). This, in turn, has given sci-

tive or even by falsifying the information they give.

This difficulty increases with advancing age, which is why so many of the studies relating to the latter years of life have been made on men and women living in institutions, people who unquestionably are not representative of the general population. In commenting on this sampling bias, Breen has pointed out (19):

Studies of older people are all too frequently devised to maximize the use of available persons and data. As a result, researchers

entific backing to the popular belief that mental decline in old age is not only great but also universal. This matter will be discussed in more detail in Chapter 13.

Another serious problem associated with the use of the cross-sectional approach is that it does not take into consideration cultural changes which always play a major role in the patterns of physical and mental development. This results in a tendency to interpret *any* change that may appear as an age change.

Cultural changes affect values, among other things. A comparison of adolescents of today with members of the older generation showed that the latter tend to disapprove more strongly of extravagance than adolescents do. This might be interpreted to mean that members of the older generation have become rigid with age. In reality, the difference is one of cultural values. When members of the older generation were growing up, high value was placed on a prudent spending of money and on having a nest egg for the proverbial rainy day. Today, adolescents are growing up in a culture dominated by the philosophy of "keeping up with the Joneses" and of "letting Uncle Sam take care of you when you can't take care of yourself" (60). Because of the rapid change in cultural values taking place at the present time, children often consider their parents' values old-fashioned. See Figure 1-4.

Inaccuracy obtained from studies of development is unquestionably the most serious stumbling block the developmental psychologist must cope with. Inaccuracies may result when a biased sampling of subjects gives a false picture of the normal developmental pattern at a particular age, as when institutionalized persons are used for the study of old age; when a subject tries to present as favorable a picture of himself as he can and, either consciously or unconsciously, distorts his introspective or retrospective reports; or when the only method available for the study of a particular area of development is less than satisfactory.

Even though the longitudinal approach has a methodological advantage over the cross-sectional approach, the problem of accuracy is still ever present. Unless such studies are started when the subjects are very young, information about their earlier lives must be supplied by the subjects themselves or by parents, teachers, and peers, who tend to interpret the data they report in terms of their own attitudes and experiences.

The obstacles discussed above have resulted in a paucity or absence of scientific evidence about some areas of development. This has two serious consequences. First, it leads to a distortion of the picture we have of normal development. For example, lack of adequate evidence about the learning capacities of newborns and about their sensory development encourages acceptance of

Figure 1-4 Rapid changes in cultural values make many parental values seem "old fashioned" to their children. (M. O. Lichty. "Grin and Bear It." Publishers-Hall Syndicate, Nov. 17, 1965. Used by permission.)

"I'm glad we had this man-to-man talk, Pop . . . Some of your ideas were pretty old-fashioned!"

the traditional belief that they are completely helpless. In time, new evidence may show that the newborn infant is less helpless than he appears.

Second, a lack of adequate information leads to the continued acceptance of old wives' tales, especially in regard to old age. People are conditioned to think unfavorably about this phase of life, and this affects not only the personal and social adjustments older people make but also the treatment they receive from the social group.

Attempts to Cope with Obstacles

Many attempts have been made, with varying degrees of success, to cope with the obstacles that confront the scientist in his study of development. Whenever possible, animal subjects are being replaced by human subjects for research studies. To obtain more representative samplings of subjects at different age levels, especially in the case of middle-aged and old subjects and in the case of the newborn, cooperation has been encouraged by offering guidance and counseling in exchange for participation in research.

To increase the accuracy of the data obtained, research studies are made in naturalistic settings (such as the home, school or community), whenever possible, rather than in laboratories. Moving pictures and other measuring devices have been substituted for observations by experimenters. Even more important, training laboratories have been established to train experimenters in observation and in handling children and subjects of other age levels in experimental settings.

A growing number of studies, using the longitudinal rather than the cross-sectional approach, have been appearing. Some of these cover only small segments of the life span, while others cover large segments. However, they give a picture of developmental changes over a span of years, and when they are combined with other studies covering other age spans, the composite result serves to give a fairly accurate picture

of the normal pattern of development. Bijou has commented on how much confidence one can have in the results of these studies (14):

Confidence can be expected to remain high, if after a reasonable period the productions clearly advance basic knowledge of the historical-developmental component of psychological events in the form of the concepts and principles they generate and if they establish new guidelines to applied problems in the form of demonstrated empirical relationships. On the other hand, confidence can be expected to wane, if the field continues to yield products which are peripheral to general psychological theory and offers solutions which turn out to be fads, gimmicks, and verbal prescriptions with only captivating face validities.

DEVELOPMENTAL TASKS

Every culture expects its members to master certain essential skills and acquire certain appropriate behavior patterns at various ages during the life span. As Neugarten has explained (75):

Every society is age-graded, and every society has a system of social expectations regarding age-appropriate behavior. The individual passes through a socially-regulated cycle from birth to death as inexorably as he passes through the biological cycle; and there exists a socially prescribed timetable for the ordering of major life events . . . Although the norms vary somewhat from one socioeconomic, ethnic, or religious group to another, for any social group it can easily be demonstrated that norms and actual occurrences are closely related.

Meaning of Developmental Tasks

Society expects individuals to exhibit certain behavior patterns at various stages in their lives; Havighurst has labeled these *developmental tasks.* According to him, a developmental task is "a task which arises at or about a certain period in the life of the individual, successful achievement of which leads to his happiness and to success with later tasks, while failure leads to unhappiness and difficulty with later tasks." Some tasks arise mainly as a result of physical maturation, such as learning to walk; others develop primarily from the cultural pres-

---

Box 1-6. DEVELOPMENTAL TASKS DURING THE LIFE SPAN

Babyhood and Early Childhood
Learning to walk
Learning to take solid foods
Learning to talk
Learning to control the elimination of body wastes
Learning sex differences and sexual modesty
Achieving physiological stability
Forming simple concepts of social and physical reality
Learning to relate oneself emotionally to parents, siblings, and other people
Learning to distinguish right and wrong and developing a conscience

Late Childhood
Learning physical skills necessary for ordinary games
Organizing one's knowledge of physical and social reality
Learning to work well in the peer group
Becoming an independent person
Building wholesome attitudes toward oneself as a growing organism
Learning to get along with age-mates
Learning an appropriate sex role
Developing fundamental skills in reading, writing, and calculating
Developing concepts necessary for everyday living
Developing conscience, morality, and a scale of values
Developing attitudes toward social groups and institutions

Adolescence
Accepting one's physique and accepting a masculine or feminine role
Establishing new relations with age-mates of both sexes
Gaining emotional independence from parents and other adults
Achieving assurance of economic independence

Selecting and preparing for an occupation
Developing intellectual skills and concepts necessary for civic competence
Desiring and achieving socially responsible behavior
Preparing for marriage and family life
Building conscious values in harmony with an adequate scientific world picture

Early Adulthood
Selecting a mate
Learning to live with a marriage partner
Starting a family
Rearing children
Managing a home
Getting started in an occupation
Taking on civic responsibility
Finding a congenial social group

Middle Age
Achieving adult civic and social responsibility
Establishing and maintaining an economic standard of living
Assisting teen-age children to become responsible and happy adults
Developing adult leisure-time activities
Relating oneself to one's spouse as a person
Accepting and adjusting to the physiological changes of middle age
Adjusting to aging parents

Old Age
Adjusting to decreasing physical strength and health
Adjusting to retirement and reduced income
Adjusting to death of spouse
Establishing an explicit affiliation with members of one's age group
Meeting social and civic obligations
Establishing satisfactory physical living arrangements

sures of society, such as learning to read; and still others grow out of the personal values and aspirations of the individual, such as choosing and preparing for a vocation. In most cases, however, developmental tasks arise from these three forces working together (50). The important developmental tasks for different phases in the life span as outlined by Havighurst are shown in Box 1-6.

Although each culture expects the members of that culture to master certain developmental tasks, cultural values change. Some of the old developmental tasks may be eliminated and replaced by new ones, or their relative importance may be lessened. When, for example, it became apparent that the Russians were ahead of us in science, after the launching of Sputnik I, one of the tasks the American schools put great emphasis on was the learning of mathematics and science. Although this had always been a part of the American school curriculum, its relative importance changed radically. After about a decade, it became apparent that other subjects were of more practical value to the majority of students, and the emphasis on mathematics and science was lessened.

Purposes of Developmental Tasks

Developmental tasks serve three very useful purposes. First, they are guidelines to enable the individual to know what society expects of him at a given age. Parents of a young child, for example, can be guided in teaching him different skills by the knowledge that society expects him to master them at certain ages and that his adjustments will be greatly influenced by how successfully he does so.

Second, developmental tasks motivate the individual to do what the social group expects him to do at certain times during his life. As Neugarten et al. have said (77):

Expectations regarding age-appropriate behavior form an elaborated and pervasive system of norms governing behavior and in-

teraction. . . . There exists what might be called a prescriptive timetable for the ordering of major life events. Age norms and age expectations operate as prods and brakes upon behavior, in some instances hastening an event, in others delaying it. . . . For a great variety of behaviors, there is a span of years within which the occurrence of a given behavior is regarded as appropriate. When the behavior occurs outside that span of years, it is regarded as inappropriate and is negatively sanctioned.

Third, developmental tasks serve to show the individual what lies ahead and what he will be expected to do when he reaches the next stage of development in the life span.

Adjustment to a new situation is always difficult and is always accompanied by varying degrees of emotional tension; however, much of this difficulty and stress can be eliminated if the individual knows what will come next and prepares gradually for it. Just as the child who learns some of the social skills needed for the new social life of adolescence will find adjustment to members of the opposite sex easier when he reaches adolescence, so will the young adult find the transition into middle age easier and less stressful if he gradually cultivates adult leisure-time activities as his parental responsibilities lessen.

Potential Hazards Related to Developmental Tasks

Because developmental tasks play such an important role in setting guidelines for normal development, anything that interferes with their mastery may be regarded as a potential hazard. There are three very common potential hazards related to developmental tasks. The first is inappropriate expectations; either the individual himself or the social group may expect the development of behavior that is impossible at the time because of physical or psychological limitations. As Norton has explained (79):

Expectations which were entirely appropriate to a prior stage will be grossly inappropriate to a present one. . . . Expectations which will become appropriate to a future stage are grossly misused when applied prematurely.

Norton has suggested a second potential hazard related to developmental tasks — the bypassing of a stage of development as a result of failure to master the developmental tasks for that stage (79):

No stage of growth can be bypassed but each must be lived through if it is to be transcended. This means that neglect or suppression of a stage inevitably results in development arrest. And this condition is frought with further jeopardy, for the suppressed stage is ever afterward liable to erupt, always disjunctively.

The crises that the individual experiences when he passes from one stage of development to another are the third common potential hazard arising from developmental tasks.

Even though he may have mastered the developmental tasks for one stage satisfactorily, having to master a new set of tasks appropriate for the next stage inevitably brings with it tension and stress — conditions which can lead to a crisis. For example, a man whose working life has come to an end — and with it the prestige and personal satisfaction associated with the job — experiences a "retirement crisis."

Effects of Developmental Tasks on Attitudes and Behavior

Sooner or later, everyone becomes aware that he is expected to master certain developmental tasks at various periods during his life, and each person also becomes aware of being "early," "late," or "on time" with regard to these tasks (75). It is this awareness that affects his attitudes and behavior as well as the attitudes of others toward him.

While most people would like to master developmental tasks at the appropriate time, some are unable to do so, while others are ahead of schedule. Box 1-7 gives some of the most important factors that influence mastery of developmental tasks.

Regardless of the cause, there are two serious consequences of a failure to master developmental tasks. First, unfavorable social judgments are inevitable; members of the individual's peer group regard him as immature, a label which carries a stigma at any age. This leads to unfavorable self-judgments, which in turn lead to an unfavorable concept of self. Gordon emphasized the seriousness of this when he said that "Negative self-views may be as damaging as physical illness or actual physical handicap" (47).

The second consequence of failure to master developmental tasks is that the foundations for the mastery of later developmental tasks will be inadequate. As a result, the individual continues to lag behind his peers, which increases his feelings of inadequacy. Equally serious, the individual must try to master developmental tasks appropriate for the next stage of development at the same

---

Box 1-7. FACTORS INFLUENCING MASTERY OF DEVELOPMENTAL TASKS

Handicaps to Mastery
A retarded developmental level
Lack of opportunity to learn the developmental tasks or lack of guidance in their mastery
Lack of motivation
Poor health
Physical defects
A low intellectual level

Aids to Mastery
A normal or accelerated developmental level
Opportunities to learn the developmental tasks and guidance in mastering them
Motivation
Good health and the absence of physical defects
A high level of intelligence
Creativity

Expressing anger and frustration by biting mother's foot *might* be considered age-appropriate behavior in a two-year-old. But flying into a rage at age thirty is inappropriate behavior in most situations. (Tim Kantor from Rapho Guillumette; Jan Lukas from Rapho Guillumette)

time he is trying to complete the mastery of the tasks appropriate for the age level he has just emerged from. A child who is unprepared to enter school, for example, will find that his attempts to catch up to his age-mates only intensify his feelings of inadequacy and reinforce social judgments of his immaturity. In time, if the struggle to catch up proves too difficult for him, he may stop trying and continue to behave immaturely, or he may build up defenses to justify his behavior to himself and others. The building up of defenses is never a satisfactory solution to social or personal problems and results in the intensification of unfavorable social judgments as well as self-judgments, causing the child further unhappiness.

HAPPINESS AND UNHAPPINESS DURING THE LIFE SPAN

Because happiness and unhappiness are subjective states, information about them must, of necessity, come from introspective reports; only the person himself can say whether he is happy or unhappy. Introspective reports, however, are not always accurate. An unhappy person may want to put up a cheerful front, or a person who says he is unhappy may be only temporarily depressed. In retrospect, a person can get a clearer perspective and see how one stage in his life compares with another. Retrospective reports, however, are subject to error; people tend to forget things and to minimize the unhappiness of some periods of their lives and exaggerate the unhappiness of others.

Freud believed that people tend to remember more happy experiences than unhappy experiences. Repression of unhappy experiences, he maintained, is a form of ego-defense (41). Studies have since substantiated this. While it is true that some unhappy memories are reported at every period in the life span, there is a tendency to report more happy than unhappy memories.

Because of the many difficulties involved in making long-term longitudinal studies, as previously discussed, most studies of happiness have been made through the use of the cross-sectional approach. The few that have used the longitudinal approach have covered only relatively short periods of the life span.

Significant Facts about Happiness

Inadequate and inaccurate as introspective and retrospective data are, they give clues about what contributes to happiness and unhappiness at different ages, what is responsible for variations in happiness and unhappiness not only between people but also in the same person at different age levels, and what are most likely to be happy and unhappy periods in the life span. The results of these studies are discussed below.

Relative Happiness It is doubtful that such a state as 100 percent happiness or 100 percent unhappiness exists. Instead, happiness is a relative matter. At every age level, and at all times during every age level, there are times of happiness and times of unhappiness. If the pleasant experiences outweigh the unpleasant ones, the individual will regard himself as happy. If, on the other hand, the unpleasant experiences outweigh the pleasant ones, he will judge himself as being unhappy.

Essentials to Happiness Three things are essential to happiness, or a state of well-being and contentment: acceptance, affection, and achievement, often called the "three A's of happiness." If they are present, the individual can accept himself, makes reasonably good adjustments to life, and is satisfied and contented.

Acceptance by others depends largely on self-acceptance, which comes from good personal adjustments as well as good social adjustments. Thus acceptance by others is a circular matter. Affection is a normal accompaniment of acceptance by others. The better accepted a person is, the more he can count on the affection of others. Achievement relates to reaching a goal the

individual has set for himself. If this goal is unrealistically high, the result will be failure instead of achievement, and the individual will be dissatisfied and consequently unhappy. Affection and achievement, like acceptance by others, contribute to self-acceptance, which in turn affects the degree of adjustment the individual makes.

Happiness Varies at Different Times in the Life Span Retrospections covering the whole life span or large segments of it reveal the degree of happiness at different ages. Many adults remember puberty and early adolescence as so unhappy that they claim they would not want to return to childhood even if they could. In a study reported by Meltzer and Ludwig, even the adult years were found to vary in degree of happiness, with the subjects describing the years before middle age as happier than those after middle age. This is shown in Figure 1-5. Pleasant memories were focused on family, marriage, good health, and achievements, while unpleasant memories were associated with illness, physical injuries, death of a loved one, unsuccessful work experiences, and failure to reach goals (72).

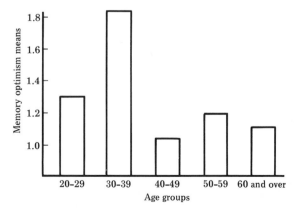

Figure 1-5 Age differences in memory optimism, or pleasant memories. (Adapted from H. Meltzer and D. Ludwig. Age differences in memory optimism and pessimism in workers. *J. genet. Psychol.,* 1967, **110,** 17–30. Used by permission.)

Happiness at One Age Does Not Guarantee Happiness at Other Ages There is no evidence that once happy, always happy. Instead, happiness at one age may be followed by unhappiness at later ages, or vice versa. Whether or not happiness or unhappiness will be persistent depends upon how successfully the individual adjusts to the new roles and social expectations of each phase in the life span and how quickly and satisfactorily his environment enables him to meet his needs, especially those for achievement, acceptance, and affection.

At Every Age There Are Sex Differences in Happiness During the early years of life and up to middle age, females tend to be happier than males. After forty, the reverse is true. The reason for this sex difference can be traced to the fact that females gain their happiness mainly from interpersonal relationships, while males gain theirs from successful achievements.

At Every Age There Are Obstacles to Happiness Some obstacles to happiness are subjective, and others are environmental. Poor health, mental limitations, and unrealistic aspirations are the most common subjective obstacles. It is difficult for a person of any age to be happy if he feels he is a failure, even if others regard him as a success. Likewise, it is hard for a person to be happy if poor health prevents him from doing what his peers do.

There may also be environmental obstacles to happiness at any age. For example, a child who grows up in a neighborhood where he is discriminated against because of his race, religion, socioeconomic status, or any other reason will lack social acceptance, affection from peers, and an opportunity to achieve success in peer-prized activities. His unhappiness may affect his performance in school and thus jeopardize his chances for success in later life.

Many Factors Influence Happiness At every period in the life span, happiness is influenced by a number of factors. This is in part responsible for the variation in happiness at different ages and also for the fact, discussed above, that happiness at one age does not necessarily guarantee happiness at

---

Box 1-8. FACTORS INFLUENCING HAPPINESS

Material Possessions
It is not material possessions per se that influence a person's happiness, but the way he feels about them. See Figure 1-6.

Emotional Adjustment
The well-adjusted, happy person expresses negative emotions, such as fear, anger, and jealousy, less often, with less intensity, and with more focus and direction than the poorly adjusted, unhappy person.

Attitude toward an Age Period
How happy a person will be at a particular age may be determined by his own childhood experiences with people of that age and by cultural stereotypes. People also tend to regard previous ages as happier than their present age. The adult, for example, looks back to the "carefree" days of childhood.

Unrealistic Self-Concepts
The person who believes his abilities to be greater than they actually are becomes unhappy when he fails to reach his goals; he feels inadequate, misunderstood, and mistreated.

Unrealistic Role Concepts
People tend to romanticize a role they will play at a later age. If the new role does not live up to the person's expectations, he may be unhappy until he learns to accept the realities of his new situation.

"Happiness comes from within, my boy . . . from within a safety deposit box full of blue-chip stocks and tax-free investments."

Figure 1-6 Happiness comes not from material possessions per se, but from how one feels about them. (George Clark. "The Neighbors." Chicago Tribune–New York News Syndicate, Feb. 19, 1973. Used by permission.)

other ages. The most common and important of these factors are given in Box 1-8.

Importance of Happiness and Unhappiness

The significant fact about the unhappiness that occurs throughout a person's life span is that it affects his attitudes and in turn leaves its mark on his personality. In addition, it reduces his efficiency in whatever work he may undertake. Whether he be a schoolchild, a factory worker, or a business executive, his chances of making the most of his potentialities are greatly reduced by his unhappy mental state.

Equally serious is the fact that unhappiness may and often does become a habit. And, like all habits, the longer it persists, the more deeply rooted and resistant to change it becomes.

Because unhappiness can play such havoc with personal and social adjustments throughout life, an attempt will be made throughout the remainder of the book to discuss the causes of unhappiness at each age level and to suggest what might be done to prevent or to minimize it. In addition, emphasis will be placed on the factors that contribute to happiness at each developmental age and on how they might be strengthened to counteract any unhappiness that is inevitable.

Chapter Highlights

1 Developmental psychology is the study of the development of the human being from conception to death. Its objectives are to find out the characteristic changes that take place, when they occur, what causes them, how they influence behavior, whether they are universal or individual, and whether they can be predicted.

2 The focus of interest in developmental psychology has been uneven for two reasons: the motivation to study a particular developmental period is greatly influenced by the desire to solve some practical problem associated with it, and many difficulties are encountered in the study of any period in the life span.

3 Attitudes toward developmental changes are greatly influenced by changes in the individual's appearance and behavior and by cultural attitudes and values associated with these changes.

4 There are seven significant facts about development: Childhood is the foundation period of life; development is the result of maturation and learning; development follows a definite and predictable pattern; all individuals are different; certain characteristic traits are associated with each phase of development; each period involves hazards; and traditional beliefs exist about individuals of different ages.

5 The length of the life span varies from individual to individual, depending on such factors as health, race, sex, childhood activities, kind of work done during adult life, and living environment.

6 The life span is commonly divided into ten stages: the prenatal stage, infancy, babyhood, early childhood, late childhood, puberty, adolescence, early adulthood, middle age, and old age.

7 To date, the major emphasis in the scientific study of the life span has been on childhood, adolescence, and early adulthood. Only recently has interest spread to other periods, especially middle and old age.

8 In spite of scientific interest in all periods of the life span, certain obstacles have hindered researchers in their study of some periods. The most important of these are difficulties in getting representative samples of subjects and then eliciting the desired information from them, finding a method that is both applicable and reliable for different age levels, and ensuring the accuracy of the data obtained.

9 Developmental tasks, or certain behavior patterns that are expected to develop at certain ages, act as guidelines for the individual and motivate him to do what the social group expects him to do at each stage in his life span.

10 There are certain handicaps to the mastery of developmental tasks and certain aids. The most important handicaps are lack of motivation and opportunity to learn, and the most important aids are a high level of intelligence and a normal or accelerated developmental level.

11 Reports about happiness at different periods during the life span must, of necessity, be either introspective or retrospective; both types of reports are subject to distortion by the individual.

12 At any age, acceptance by others, affection (which is a normal accompaniment of acceptance), and achievement that comes up to the individual's expectation are essential to happiness.

Bibliography

1 Alvarez, W. C. History of geriatrics goes back to 2500 B.C. *Geriatrics*, 1964, **19**, 701–704.

2 Ames, L. B., & Ilg, F. L. The developmental point of view with special reference to the principle of reciprocal neuromotor interweaving. *J. genet. Psychol.*, 1964, **105**, 195–209.

3 Anandakshmy, S., & Grinder, R. E. Conceptual emphasis in the history of developmental psychology, evolutionary theory, theology, and the nature-nurture issue. *Child Develpm.*, 1970, **41**, 1113–1123.

4 Anderson, J. E. Child development research: The next 25 years. *Child Develpm.*, 1950, **31**, 191–199.

5 Archer, D. The male change of life. *Yale Alumni Mag.*, March 1968, 33–35.

6 Baer, D. M. An age-irrelevant concept of development. *Merrill-Palmer Quart.*, 1970, **16**, 238–245.

7 Bayley, N. The life span as a frame of reference in psychological research. *Vita hum., Basel*, 1963, **6**, 125–139.

8 Bell, R. Q., Weller, G. M., & Waldrop, M. F. Newborn and preschooler: Organization of behavior and relations between periods. *Monogr. Soc. Res. Child Develpm.*, 1971, **36** (1 and 2).

9 Beller, E. K. The concept readiness and several applications. *Read. Teacher*, 1970, **23**, 727–737.

10 Bernard, H. W., & Huckins, W. C. Hazards of development. In H. W. Bernard & W. C. Huckins (Eds.), *Readings in human development*. Boston: Allyn and Bacon, 1967. Pp. 403–404.

11 Bernard, H. W., & Huckins, W. C. Self-realization: The goal of development. In H. W. Bernard & W. C. Huckins (Eds.), *Readings in human development*. Boston: Allyn and Bacon, 1967. Pp. 427–428.

12 Bernard, H. W., & Huckins, W. C. Developmental perspectives. In H. W. Bernard & W. C. Huckins (Eds.), *Exploring human development: Interdisciplinary readings*. Boston: Allyn and Bacon, 1972. Pp. 1–8.

13 Bettelheim, B. Where self begins. *Child & Family*, 1968, **7** (1), 5–9.

14 Bijou, S. W. Ages, stages and the naturalization of human development. *Amer. Psychologist*, 1968, **23**, 419–427.

15 Birns, B., & Golden, M. Prediction of intellectual performance at 3 years from infant tests and personality measures. *Merrill-Palmer Quart.*, 1972, **18**, 53–58.

16 Birren, J. E. Principles of research on aging. In B. L. Neugarten (Ed.), *Middle age and aging: A reader in social psychology*. Chicago: University of Chicago Press, 1968, Pp. 545–551.

17 Bischof, L. J. *Adult psychology*. New York: Harper & Row, 1969.

18 Boyd, R. D., & Koskela, R. N. A test of Erikson's theory of ego-stage development by means of a self-report instrument. *J. exp. Educ.*, 1970, **38**, 1–14.

19 Breen, L. Z. Some problems of research in the field of aging. *Sociol. soc. Res.*, 1957, **41**, 412–416.

20 Bringmann, W., & Rieder, G. Stereotyped attitudes toward the aged in West Germany and the United States. *J. soc. Psychol.*, 1968, **76**, 267–268.

21 Brockman, L. M., & Riccuti, H. A. Severe protein-calorie malnutrition and cognitive development in infancy and early childhood. *Develpm. Psychol.*, 1971, **4**, 312–319.

22 Bromley, D. B. *The psychology of human aging*. New York: Penguin, 1966.

23 Bronson, W. C. Adult derivatives of emotional expressiveness and reactivity-control: Developmental continuities from childhood to adulthood. *Child Develpm.*, 1967, **38**, 801–817.

24 Brooks, J. B., & Elliott, D. M. Prediction of psychological adjustment at age thirty from leisure time activities and satisfactions in childhood. *Hum. Develpm.*, 1971, **14**, 51–61.

25 Bühler, C. The life cycle: Structural determinants of goal-setting. *J. humanist. Psychol.,* 1966, **6,** 37–52.

26 Bühler, C. The course of human life as a psychological problem. In W. R. Looft (Ed.), *Developmental psychology: A book of readings.* Hinsdale, Ill.: Dryden Press, 1972. Pp. 68–84.

27 Butler, R. N. The life review: An interpretation of reminiscence in the aged. In B. L. Neugarten (Ed.), *Middle age and aging: A reader in social psychology.* Chicago: University of Chicago Press, 1968. Pp. 486–496.

28 Caldwell, B. M. The effects of psychosocial deprivation on human development in infancy. *Merrill-Palmer Quart.,* 1970, **16,** 260–277.

29 Caldwell, B. M., & Richmond, J. B. The impact of theories of child development. *Children,* 1962, **9,** 73–78.

30 Cameron, P. Age parameters of young adult, middle-aged, old, and aged. *J. Gerontol.,* 1969, **24,** 201–202.

31 Cattell, R. B., Stice, G. F., & Kristy, N. F. A first approximation to nature-nurture ratios for eleven primary personality factors in objective tests. *J. abnorm. soc. Psychol.,* 1957, **54,** 143–159.

32 Charlesworth, W. R. Developmental psychology: Does it offer anything distinctive? In W. R. Looft (Ed.), *Developmental psychology: A book of readings.* Hinsdale, Ill.: Dryden Press, 1972. Pp. 1–22.

33 Cohler, B. J. The role of retrospective accounts in the study of intergenerational attitudes. *Merrill-Palmer Quart.,* 1972, **18,** 59–60.

34 Dennis, W. (Ed.) *Historical readings in developmental psychology.* New York: Appleton Century Crofts, 1972.

35 Douglass, J. H. The child, the father of the man. *Family Coordinator,* 1969, **18,** 3–8.

36 English, H. B. Chronological divisions of the life span. *J. educ. Psychol.,* 1957, **48,** 437–439.

37 Erikson, E. H. *Childhood and society.* (Rev. ed.) New York: Norton, 1964.

38 Foulds, M. L. Effects of a personal growth group on a measure of self-actualization. *J. humanist. Psychol.,* 1970, **10,** 33–38.

39 Fowler, W. Problems of deprivation and developmental learning. *Merrill-Palmer Quart.,* 1970, **16,** 141–161.

40 Frank, L. K. The beginnings of child development and family life education in the twentieth century. *Merrill-Palmer Quart.,* 1962, **8,** 207–227.

41 Freud, S. *The standard edition of the complete psychological works of Sigmund Freud.* London: Hogarth Press, 1953–1962, 21 vols.

42 Furth, H. G. On language and knowing in Piaget's developmental theory. *Hum. Develpm.,* 1970, **13,** 241–257.

43 Gardner, R. W. Individuality in development. In W. R. Looft (Ed.), *Developmental psychology: A book of readings.* Hinsdale, Ill.: Dryden Press, 1972. Pp. 402–414.

44 *Geriatric Focus* article. Physical, mental, social predictors of longevity. *Geriatric Focus,* 1969, **8**(16), 1–5.

45 Ginsburg, B. E. Developmental genetics of behavioral capacities: The nature-nurture problem re-evaluated. *Merrill-Palmer Quart.,* 1971, **17,** 187–202.

46 Gollin, E. S. An organism-oriented concept of development. *Merrill-Palmer Quart.,* 1970, **16,** 246–252.

47 Gordon, I. J. The beginnings of self: The problem of the nurturing environment. *Phi Delta Kappan,* 1969, **50,** 375–378.

48 Harris, D. B. The development of potentiality. *Teachers Coll. Rec.,* 1960, **61,** 423–428.

49 Hauser, P. M. The census of 1970. *Scient. American,* 1971, **225**(1), 17–25.

50 Havighurst, R. J. *Human development and education.* New York: Longmans, 1953.

51 James, W. *Talks to teachers on psychology.* New York: Holt, 1899.

52 Jensen, A. R. How much can we boost IQ and scholastic achievement? *Harv. educ. Rev.,* 1969, **39,** 1–123.

53 Jewett, S. P. Longevity and the longevity syndrome. *Gerontologist,* 1973, **13,** 91–99.

54 Johnson, W. Whatever happened to the baby bust? *The New York Times,* July 15, 1972.

55 Jordon, T. J. Longitudinal study of preschool development. *Except. Children,* 1971, **37,** 509–512.

56 Kagan, J. Future of child development research. *Hum. Biol.,* 1972, **44,** 277–287.

57 Kagan, J., & Moss, H. A. *Birth to maturity: A study in psychological development.* New York: Wiley, 1962.

58 Kaplan, H. B., & Pokorny, A. D. Sex-related correlates of adult self-derogation: Reports of childhood experiences. *Develpm. Psychol.,* 1972, **6,** 536.

59 Kreitler, H., & Kreitler, S. Unhappy memories of "the happy past": Studies in cognitive dissonance. *Brit. J. Psychol.,* 1968, **59,** 157–166.

60 Kuhlen, R. G. Age and intelligence: The significance of cultural change in longitudinal vs. cross-sectional findings. In B. L. Neugarten (Ed.), *Middle age and aging: A reader in social psychology.* Chicago: University of Chicago Press, 1968. Pp. 552–557.

61 Kuhlen, R. G., & Thompson, G. G. (Eds.) *Psychological studies of human development.* (3rd ed.) New York: Appleton Century Crofts, 1969.

62 Lawton, G. *Aging successfully.* New York: Columbia University Press, 1951.

63 Lefrancois, G. R. Jean Piaget's developmental model: Equilibrium through adaptation. In W. R. Looft (Ed.), *Developmental psychology: A book of readings.* Hinsdale, Ill.: Dryden Press, 1972. Pp. 297–307.

64 Leon, E. F. Cicero on geriatrics. *Gerontologist,* 1963, **3,** 128–130.

65 Lerner, R. M., & Korn, S. J. The development of body-build stereotypes in males. *Child Develpm.,* 1972, **43,** 908–920.

66 Linn, M. W. Perceptions of childhood: Present functioning and past events. *J. Gerontol.,* 1973, **28,** 202–206.

67 Lipsitt, L. P., & Eimas, P. D. Developmental psychology. *Annu. Rev. Psychol.,* 1972, **23,** 1–50.

68 Looft, W. R. Perceptions across the life span of important informational sources for children and adolescents. *J. Psychol.,* 1971, **78,** 207–211.

69 Looft, W. R. (Ed.) *Developmental psychology: A book of readings.* Hinsdale, Ill.: Dryden Press, 1972.

70 Mahrer, A. R. Childhood determinants of adult functioning: Strategies in clinical research use of the personal-psychological history. *Psychol. Rec.,* 1969, **19,** 39–46.

71 Maslow, A. H. *Motivation and personality.* New York: Harper & Row, 1954.

72 Meltzer, H., & Ludwig, D. Age differences in memory optimism and pessimism in workers. *J. genet. Psychol.,* 1967, **110,** 17–30.

73 Montagu, A. *The direction of human development.* (Rev. ed.) New York: Hawthorn, 1970.

74 Nadelman, L. Training laboratories in developmental psychology. *Psychol. Rep.,* 1968, **23,** 923–931.

75 Neugarten, B. L. Continuities and discontinuities of psychological issues into adult life. *Hum. Develpm.,* 1969, **12,** 121–130.

76 Neugarten, B. L., & Moore, J. W. The changing age-status system. In B. L. Neugarten (Ed.), *Middle age and aging: A reader in social psychology.* Chicago: University of Chicago Press, 1968. Pp. 5–21.

77 Neugarten, B. L., Moore, J. W., & Lowe, J. C. Age norms, age constraints, and adult socialization. In B. L. Neugarten (Ed.), *Middle age and aging: A reader in social psychology.* Chicago: University of Chicago Press, 1968. Pp. 22–28.

78 *New York Times* article. Ratio of women among aged is up. *The New York Times,* Feb. 15, 1973.

79 Norton, D. L. The rites of passage from dependence to autonomy. *School Review,* 1970, **79,** 19–41.

80 Oden, M. H. The fulfillment of promise: 40-year follow-up of the Terman gifted group. *Genet. Psychol. Monogr.,* 1968, **77,** 3–93.

81 Palmore, E. B., & Stone, V. Predictors of longevity: A follow-up of the aged in Chapel Hill. *Gerontologist,* 1973, **13,** 88–90.

82 Piaget, J. Piaget's theory. In P. H. Mussen (Ed.), *Carmichael's manual of child psychology.* (3rd ed.) Vol. 1. New York: Wiley, 1970. Pp. 703–732.

83 Piaget, J. Intellectual evolution from adolescence to adulthood. *Hum. Develpm.,* 1972, **15,** 1–12.

84 Pressey, S. L. Most important and most neglected topic: Potentials. *Gerontologist,* 1963, **3,** 69–70.

85 Read, M. S. Malnutrition and learning. In H. W. Bernard & W. C. Huckins (Eds.), *Exploring human development: Interdisciplinary readings.* Boston: Allyn and Bacon, 1972. Pp. 240–247.

86 Rosenthal, J. Fertility level in nation close to zero growth. *The New York Times,* Sept. 24, 1972.

87 Sanford, N. Will psychologists study human problems? *Amer. Psychologist,* 1965, **20,** 192–202.

88 Schaie, K. W. Age changes and age differences. In B. L. Neugarten (Ed.), *Middle age and aging: A reader in social psychology.* Chicago: University of Chicago Press, 1968. Pp. 558–562.

89 Schaie, K. W., Labouvie, G. V., & Barrett, T. J. Selective attrition effects in a fourteen-year study of adult intelligence. *J. Gerontol.,* 1973, **28,** 328–334.

90 Scheinfeld, A. *Your heredity and environment.* Philadelphia: Lippincott, 1965.

91 Scott, J. P. Critical periods in behavioral development. *Science,* 1962, **138,** 949–958.

92 Siegel, A. E. Current issues in research on early development. *Hum. Develpm.,* 1969, **12,** 86–92.

93 Simonson, E. The concept and definition of normality. *Ann. N.Y. Acad. Sci.,* 1966, **134,** 541–558.

94 Skeels, H. M. Adult status of children with contrasting early life experiences: A follow-up study. *Monogr. Soc. Res. Child Develpm.,* 1966, **31**(3).

95 Smith, A. C., Flick, G. L., Ferris, G. S., & Sellmann, A. H. Prediction of developmental outcome at seven years from prenatal, perinatal and postnatal events. *Child Develpm.,* 1972, **43,** 495–507.

96 Sontag, L. W. Implications of fetal behavior and environment for adult personalities. *Ann. N.Y. Acad. Sci.,* 1966, **132,** 782–786.

97 Staats, A. W., Brewer, B. A., & Gross, M. C. Learning and cognitive development: Representative samples, cumulative-hierarchical learning and experimental-longitudinal methods. *Monogr. Soc. Res. Child Develpm.,* 1970, **35**(8).

98 Stein, Z., Susser, M., Saenger, G., & Marolla, F. Nutrition and mental performance. *Science,* 1972, **178,** 708–713.

99 Stevenson, H. W. Learning in children. In P. H. Mussen (Ed.), *Carmichael's manual of child psychology.* (3rd ed.) Vol. 1. New York: Wiley, 1970. Pp. 849–938.

100 Stone, J. L., & Church, J. Some representative theoretical orientations in developmental psychology. In W. R. Looft (Ed.), *Developmental psychology: A book of readings.* Hinsdale, Ill.: Dryden Press, 1972. Pp. 35–59.

101 Sullivan, W. Study finds increase in life expectancy at birth. *The New York Times,* July 6, 1972.

102 Sutton-Smith, B. Developmental laws and the experimentalist's ontology. *Merrill-Palmer Quart.,* 1970, **16,** 253–259.

103 Taeuber, C. Population changes to 1975. *Ann. Amer. Acad. pol. soc. Sci.,* 1957, **131,** 25–31.

104 Thomas, A., Chess, S., & Birch, H. G. The origin of personality. *Scient. American,* 1970, **223**(8), 102–109.

105 Thomas, H. Psychological assessment instruments for use with human infants. *Merrill-Palmer Quart.,* 1970, **16,** 179–223.

106 Thompson, W. P., & Grusec, J. E. Studies of early experience. In P. H. Mussen (Ed.), *Carmichael's manual of child psychology.* (3rd ed.) Vol. 1. New York: Wiley, 1970. Pp. 565–654.

107 *Time* article. The command generation. *Time,* July 29, 1966, 50–54.

108 Tizard, G. New trends in developmental psychology. *Brit. J. educ. Psychol.,* 1970, **40,** 1–7.

109 Tomlinson-Keasey, C. Formal operations in females from eleven to fifty-four years of age. *Develpm. Psychol.,* 1972, **6,** 364.

110 Tuddenham, R. D. The constancy of personality ratings over two decades. *Genet. Psychol. Monogr.,* 1959, **60,** 3–29.

111 Tulkin, S. R. An analysis of the concept of cultural deprivation. *Develpm. Psychol.,* 1972, **6,** 326–339.

112 Tyler, L. E. Human abilities. *Annu. Rev. Psychol.,* 1972, **23,** 177–206.

113 U.S. Bureau of the Census. *Population report,* ser. B. Washington: GPO, 1966.

114 *U.S. News & World Report* article. The age mix of America is changing. *U.S. News & World Report,* Jan. 17, 1972, 16–19.

115 Vedder, C. B. (Ed.) *Problems of the middle-aged.* Springfield, Ill.: Charles C Thomas, 1965.

116 Wattana-Kasetr, S., & Spiers, P. S. Geographic mortality rates and rates of aging: A possible relationship? *J. Gerontol.,* 1973, **28,** 374–379.

117 Wenar, C., & Coulter, J. B. A reliability study of developmental histories. *Child Develpm.,* 1962, **33,** 453–462.

118 White, S. H. The learning-maturation controversy: Hall to Hull. *Merrill-Palmer Quart.,* 1968, **14,** 187–196.

119 Whiting, J., & Whiting, B. Contribution of anthropology to the methods of studying child rearing. In P. H. Mussen (Ed.), *Handbook of research methods in child development.* New York: Wiley, 1970. Pp. 918–944.

120 Wilson, W. Correlates of avowed happiness. *Psychol. Bull.,* 1967, **67,** 294–306.

121 Yarrow, M. R., Campbell, J. D., & Burton, R. V. Recollections of childhood: A study of the retrospective method. *Monogr. Soc. Res. Child Develpm.,* 1970, **35**(5).

122 Zaccaria, J. S. Developmental tasks: Their implications for the goals of guidance. *Personnel Guid. J.,* 1965, **44,** 372–375.

CHAPTER TWO

HOW LIFE BEGINS

The first major developmental period in the life span is next to the shortest of all, but it is in many respects the most important. This period, which begins at conception and ends at the time of birth, is approximately 280 days long or nine calendar months.

The prenatal period, in spite of its relatively short length, is important for four reasons:

1 The hereditary endowment which serves as the foundation for later development is fixed, once and for all, at this time.

2 Favorable conditions in the mother's body can foster the development of hereditary potentials, while unfavorable conditions can stunt their development, even to the point of distorting the pattern of future development.

3 Proportionally greater growth and development take place during this period than at any other time throughout the individual's entire life.

4 This is the time when significant people in the individual's life are forming attitudes toward him. These attitudes will have a marked influence on the way they treat him, especially during the early, formative years of his life.

Knowing what happens before birth is essential to a complete understanding of the normal pattern of development and to a realization of what can happen to distort this pattern. In the remaining sections of this chapter, an attempt will be made to explain the major happenings during the nine months before birth and to show how each affects the course of human life from the time of birth until the end of the life span.

THE BEGINNING

New life begins with the union of a male sex cell and a female sex cell. These sex cells are developed in the reproductive organs, the *gonads*. The male sex cells, the *spermatozoa* (singular: *spermatozoon*), are produced in the male gonads, the *testes*, while the female sex cells, the *ova* (singular: *ovum*), are produced in the female gonads, the *ovaries*.

Male and female sex cells are similar in that they contain chromosomes. There are twenty-three *chromosomes* in each sex cell, and each chromosome contains *genes*, the true carriers of heredity. A gene is a minute particle which is found in combination with other genes in a stringlike formation within the chromosome. It has been estimated that there are approximately 3,000 genes in each chromosome. These are passed on from parent to offspring (56, 68).

Before new life can begin, all sex cells, whether male or female, must go through preliminary stages of development. Male sex cells go through two preliminary stages—maturation and fertilization—and female sex cells must go through three stages—maturation, ovulation, and fertilization.

Maturation

Maturation is the process of chromosome reduction through cell division: one chromosome from each pair goes to a subdivided cell, which in turn splits lengthwise and forms two new cells. The mature cell, which contains twenty-three chromosomes, is known as a *haploid cell*. Maturation of sex cells does not occur until sex maturity has been attained, following the onset of puberty in both boys and girls. In the case of the spermatozoon, there are four new cells, the *spermatids*, each of which is capable of fertilizing an ovum.

In the division of the ovum, one chromosome from each pair is pushed outside the cell wall and forms a *polar body*. Three polar bodies are formed in the process of division. Unlike the spermatids, the polar bodies cannot be fertilized, while the fourth cell, the *ovum*, can. If, however, the ovum is not fertilized, it disintegrates and passes from the body with the menstrual flow.

Division of the chromosomes during the maturational process is a matter of chance. Any possible combination of chromosomes from the male and female may be found in a new cell after division. It has been estimated that there are 16,777,216 possible combinations of the twenty-three chromosomes from the male and the twenty-three from the female sex cells (56, 68).

Ovulation

Ovulation is a preliminary stage of development limited to the female sex cells. It is the process of escape of one mature ovum during the menstrual cycle. It is believed that the two ovaries alternate in producing a ripe ovum during each menstrual cycle.

After being released from one of the follicles of the ovary, the ovum finds its way to the open end of the Fallopian tube nearest the ovary from which it was released. Once it enters the tube, it is propelled along by a combination of factors: cilia, or hairlike cells which line the tube; fluids composed of estrogen from the ovarian follicle and a mucus from the lining of the tube; and rhythmic, progressive contractions of the walls of the tube. When the length of the menstrual cycle is normal, approximately twenty-eight days, ovulation occurs between the fifth and the twenty-third days of the cycle, with the average on the eleventh day.

Fertilization

Fertilization, which occurs at the time of conception, is the third stage of development preliminary to the beginning of a new life. It normally occurs while the ovum is in the Fallopian tube. More specifically, it is generally believed that fertilization takes place within twelve to thirty-six hours and usually within the first twenty-four hours after the ovum has entered the tube. During coitus, or sexual intercourse, spermatozoa are deposited at the mouth of the uterus. Through strong hormonic attraction, they are drawn into the tubes, where they are aided in making their way up by rhythmic muscular contractions.

After a spermatozoon has penetrated the ovum, the surface of the ovum changes in such a way that no other spermatozoon can enter. After the sperm cell penetrates the wall of the ovum, the nuclei from the two cells, each containing twenty-three chromosomes, approach each other. There is a breakdown in the membrane surrounding each nucleus, and this allows the two nuclei to merge. Thus the species number of chromosomes, forty-six, is restored, with one half coming from the female cell and the other half coming from the male cell.

IMPORTANCE OF CONCEPTION

At the moment of conception, four important things are determined that influence the individual's later development. These are listed in Box 2-1 and discussed in the following sections.

Hereditary Endowment The individual's hereditary endowment, determined once and for all at the moment of conception, affects his later development in two ways. First, heredity places limits beyond which the indi-

---

> **Box 2-1. CONDITIONS DETERMINED AT CONCEPTION**
>
> **Hereditary Endowment**
> The individual's hereditary endowment is determined once and for all at conception. See Figure 2-1.
>
> **Sex**
> The individual's sex is determined at the moment of conception.
>
> **Number of Offspring**
> Whether the birth will be a single birth or a multiple birth is determined at the moment of conception.
>
> **Ordinal Position**
> The individual's position in the family into which he will be born is determined at the time of conception. Whether he is a firstborn, second-born, or later-born child is an important factor in the molding of his personality and behavior patterns.

---

vidual cannot go. If prenatal and postnatal conditions are favorable and if the individual is strongly motivated, he can develop his inherited physical and mental traits to their maximum potential, but no further. As Montagu has stressed, "Where we control the environment, we to some extent control heredity. Heredity, it has been said, determines what we *can* do, and environment what we *do* do" (56).

The second important thing about hereditary endowment is that it is entirely a *matter of chance*: there is no known way to control the number of chromosomes from the maternal or paternal side that will be passed on to the child. As Scheinfeld has pointed out, the birth of a given individual depends on the union of a particular ovum with a particular sperm. The probability that this particular union will occur is only 1 in 300,000,000,000,000 (68).

Sex. Two kinds of mature spermatozoa are produced in equal numbers. The first contains twenty-two matched chromosomes

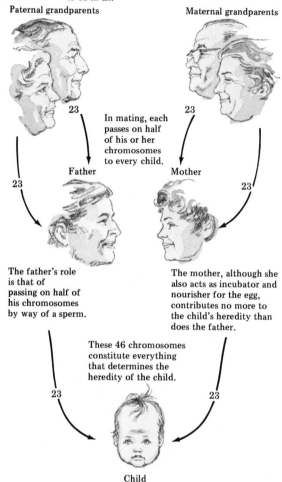

Every man and every woman at conception received 23 chromosomes from each parent or 46 in all.

Paternal grandparents

Maternal grandparents

23

23

In mating, each passes on half of his or her chromosomes to every child.

Father

Mother

23

23

The father's role is that of passing on half of his chromosomes by way of a sperm.

The mother, although she also acts as incubator and nourisher for the egg, contributes no more to the child's heredity than does the father.

These 46 chromosomes constitute everything that determines the heredity of the child.

23

23

Child

Figure 2-1 The hereditary process. (Adapted from A. Scheinfeld. *The new you and heredity.* Philadelphia: Lippincott, 1961. Used by permission.)

plus one X chromosome; the second contains twenty-two matched chromosomes plus one Y chromosome. The X and Y chromosomes are the sex-determining chromosomes. The mature ovum always contains an X chromosome. If it is fertilized by a Y-bearing spermatozoon, the offspring will be a boy; if it is fertilized by an X-bearing spermatozoon, the

offspring will be a girl. Figure 2-2 shows how sex is determined.

Once the male and female cells have united, nothing can be done to change the sex of the newly formed individual, and whether this individual is male or female will have a lifelong effect on his patterns of behavior and his personality.

Each year, the child comes under increasing cultural pressures from parents, teachers, the peer group, and society at large to develop attitudes and behavior patterns that are sexually appropriate. The child who learns to behave in a way that is considered appropriate for his sex is assured of social acceptance; the child who fails to conform is subjected to criticism and social ostracism.

The learning experiences of the individual are determined by his sex. In the home, at school, and in play groups, the child is given an opportunity to learn what members of his or her sex consider appropriate. A boy who learns to play girls' games, for example, is labeled a "sissy," just as a girl who enjoys boys' games and sports is known as a "tomboy."

The most important influence stemming from the sex of the individual is the attitude of parents. Studies of sex preferences for offspring have revealed that the traditional preference for a boy, especially for the first-born, still persists. Strong preferences for a child of a given sex have marked influences on parents' attitudes, which in turn affect their behavior toward the child and their relationships with him (31, 40).

Number of Offspring When a ripe ovum is fertilized by one spermatozoon, the result will be a *singleton*, unless the fertilized ovum (*zygote*) splits into two or more distinct parts during the early stages of cell cleavage. When this happens, the result will be identical (uniovular) twins, triplets, or other multiple births. If two or more ova are released simultaneously and are fertilized by different spermatozoa, the result will be *nonidentical* (also called *biovular* or *fra-*

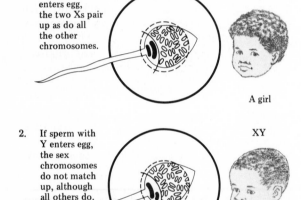

Father produces sperms of two kinds, in equal numbers:

Mother produces eggs all of one kind, each with a large X sex chromosome.

(a) With large X sex chromosome.

(b) With small Y sex chromosome.

(Note that all 22 other chromosomes in sperms or eggs are of corresponding types).

1. If sperm with X enters egg, the two Xs pair up as do all the other chromosomes.

XX

A girl

2. If sperm with Y enters egg, the sex chromosomes do not match up, although all others do.

XY

A boy

Figure 2-2 How sex is determined. (Adapted from A. Scheinfeld. *The new you and heredity*. Philadelphia: Lippincott, 1961. Used by permission.)

ternal) twins, triplets, or other multiple births.

Approximately one-third of all twins are identical. Because the chromosomes and genes of the two or more zygotes from which individuals of nonidentical multiple birth develop are not the same, their mental and physical makeups are different. By contrast, those of identical multiple birth come from the same zygote, and consequently they have the same assortment of chromosomes and genes. Children of identical multiple birth are always of the same sex, while those of nonidentical multiple birth may be of the same or opposite sex.

Both the prenatal environment and the postnatal environment of singletons are very different from those of children of multiple birth. This contributes to different patterns of development, different patterns of behavior, and differences in personality.

Before birth, the singleton has the mother's uterus to himself, and thus his development is not affected by crowding, a factor in multiple births that will be discussed more fully in the following chapter.

There are also differences in the postnatal environments of singletons and those of multiple birth. While the mother can give her undivided attention to the care of a singleton, those of multiple birth must share it. Thus during the early years, when the foundations of the personality pattern are laid, babies of multiple birth receive less mothering than singletons, and consequently they may feel unloved or actually rejected.

Many parents, especially mothers, feel that children of multiple birth should be dressed alike and share the same friends and engage in the same play activities. This is particularly true when the children are of the same sex.

Most studies of the effects of multiple birth on development have been limited to twins for the reason that triplets, quadruplets, and other multiple births occur very infrequently and the mortality rates among them are much higher than among twins. It has been reported, for example, that in the United States, twins occur in 1 out of every 95 births, triplets in 1 out of every 10,593 births, and quadruplets in 1 out of every 910,481 births. There are more multiple births among blacks, and fewer among Chinese, Japanese, and other Mongoloid-race groups, than among whites (67).

There is reason to assume that the effects of multiple birth on twins are the same as the effects on children of other multiple

If twins receive less mothering than a singleton, they may feel unloved and rejected. (Suzanne Szasz)

births; the latter, however, feel these effects to a greater extent. Box 2-2 lists characteristics of twins. It should be apparent that hereditary factors are by no means alone responsible for these characteristics; environmental factors, especially in the form of social pressures, play an even more important role. As Koch has concluded from her extensive studies of twins: "It does seem to me that the play of forces, biological and social, upon twins is rather different in many respects from that which molds singletons" (42).

Ordinal Position The individual's ordinal position has an effect in terms of the role he will play in the family and also in terms of the way significant people in his life—parents and siblings—will treat him during the early, formative years and the attitudes they will have toward him. Since roles, attitudes, and treatment are far more likely to persist than to change, the individual constantly receives reinforcement which will result in firmly established habits.

A firstborn girl, for example, who is expected to help with the housework and with the care of younger siblings may become resentful when she finds that the boys in the family have fewer duties and are granted privileges and given opportunities that are denied to her. Such resentment is likely to persist and to become more pronounced. Box 2-3 gives some common characteristics associated with ordinal position. Because there have been few longitudinal studies of ordinal position, it is impossible to say how

---

Box 2-2. CHARACTERISTICS OF TWINS

Developmental Lag
In physical, mental, motor, and speech development, twins tend to lag behind singletons of the same age.

Mental Characteristics
Mental similarities between identical twins are much greater than between nonidentical twins, and this persists into senescence. Identical twins also show strong similarities in terms of special abilities, such as musical or artistic aptitude. During the early years of life, twins lag markedly behind singletons in language ability.

Social Development
Twins tend to compete for adult attention, to imitate each other's behavior, and to depend on each other for companionship during the preschool years. As they grow older, sibling rivalry and competition develop. One twin is likely to take on the role of leader, and this affects their relationships with other family members and outsiders.

Personality Development
Some twins have difficulty developing a sense of personal identity, especially identical twins and nonidentical twins of the same sex. This can lead to frustration, resentment, and feelings of inferiority. Others enjoy the close relationship and like the attention they receive as a result of the similarity in their appearance, and this leads to feelings of satisfaction and self-confidence.

Box 2-3. COMMON CHARACTERISTICS ASSOCIATED WITH ORDINAL POSITION

Firstborn

Behaves in a mature fashion because of his association with adults and because he is expected to assume responsibilities.

Resents not having free time to do what his peers do.

Tends to conform to group wishes and pressures as a carryover of conformity to parental wishes.

Has feelings of insecurity as a result of being replaced as the center of attention by a second child.

Is often spoiled and may become petulant when he receives less attention and is subjected to more parental demands and expectations.

Tries to achieve success in some area in order to win back parental approval if he sees it shifting to younger siblings.

Middle-born

When compared unfavorably with an older sibling, becomes resentful or tries to emulate the other's behavior.

Resents privileges an older sibling is granted.

Acts up and breaks rules to attract parental attention to himself and away from siblings.

Attacks younger siblings who get more parental attention than he.

Develops the habit of being an underachiever as a result of fewer parental expectations and less pressure to achieve.

Has fewer responsibilities than the firstborn, which he may resent if the firstborn tries to "boss" him.

Tends to turn to outsiders for peer companionship, which leads to better social adjustments than firstborns make.

Last-born

Tends to be willful and demanding as a result of more relaxed parental treatment and less strict discipline.

Is spoiled by parents and siblings.

Has fewer resentments and a greater feeling of security as a result of never being replaced by a younger sibling.

Is usually protected by parents from physical or verbal attacks from siblings, which encourages dependency and irresponsibility.

Tends to underachieve because of fewer parental expectations and demands.

Experiences good social relationships outside the home.

---

long the effects persist or whether they are limited to the childhood years, when the major influences on development come from the home environment.

PERIODS OF PRENATAL DEVELOPMENT

The normal prenatal period is ten lunar months or nine calendar months long. However, this period can vary greatly in length, ranging from 180 to 334 days, the legal limit of postmaturity. There are approximately three times as many babies born prematurely as postmaturely.

Prenatal development is orderly and predictable, and hence it is possible to give a timetable of the important developments taking place during this period. The prenatal period is generally divided into three stages, each characterized by a particular kind of development. These are outlined in Box 2-4. If anything prevents these developments from taking place at the proper time, the individual will begin his postnatal life with a handicap that may plague him for the remainder of his life.

ATTITUDES OF SIGNIFICANT PEOPLE

Until the early 1940s, psychological interest in the prenatal period was concentrated on the physical conditions in the mother's body that might affect development and on the persistence of these effects into

Box 2-4. TIMETABLE OF PRENATAL DEVELOPMENT

Period of the Ovum (fertilization to end of second week)

The size of the zygote—that of a pinhead—remains unchanged because it has no outside source of nourishment; it is kept alive by yolk in the ovum.

As the zygote passes down the Fallopian tube to the uterus, it divides many times and separates into an outer and an inner layer.

The outer layer later develops into the placenta, the umbilical cord, and the amniotic sac, and the inner layer develops into a new human being.

About ten days after fertilization, the zygote becomes implanted in the uterine wall.

Period of the Embryo (end of the second week to end of the second lunar month)

The embryo develops into a miniature human being.

Major development occurs, in the head region first and in the extremities last. See Figure 2-3.

All the essential features of the body, both external and internal, are established.

The embryo begins to turn in the uterus, and there is spontaneous movement of the limbs.

The placenta, the umbilical cord, and the amniotic sac develop; these protect and nourish the embryo.

Period of the Fetus (end of the second lunar month to birth)

Changes occur in the actual or relative size of the parts already formed and in their functioning. No new features appear at this time.

By the end of the third lunar month, some internal organs are well enough developed to begin to function. Fetal heartbeat can be detected by about the fifteenth week.

By the end of the fifth lunar month, the different internal organs have assumed positions nearly like the ones they will have in the adult body.

Fetal activity increases rapidly up to the end of the ninth lunar month, when it slows down because of crowding in the amniotic sac and pressure on the fetal brain.

By the end of the seventh lunar month, the fetus is well enough developed to survive, should he be born prematurely.

By the end of the eighth lunar month the fetal body is completely formed, though smaller than that of a normal, full-term infant.

---

postnatal life. The work of Sontag and his associates, for example, called attention to the fact that the mother's emotional state can affect the development of the unborn child (72, 73).

Now, however, psychologists are interested in finding out what is responsible for maternal and other family-member attitudes toward the developing child, how persistent these attitudes are, and what effects they have on the relationships of different family members with the child during his postnatal life, especially during the early, formative years when the significant people in his world are the members of his family. While relatively recent in origin, these studies have revealed important information, summarized briefly below.

Effects of Attitudes

The mother's attitudes can have an effect on her unborn baby—not through the umbilical cord, which is the only direct connection between the two—but as a result of endocrine changes which can occur if she is subjected to severe and prolonged stress.

After birth, the mother's attitudes toward the baby—most of which were formed before he was born—have an influence on him since they are reflected in her treatment of him. Although these attitudes may change, they more commonly tend to persist. For example, a mother who wanted a boy will have a more favorable attitude toward a son than she would toward a daughter. If a daughter is born and she is disappointed, she

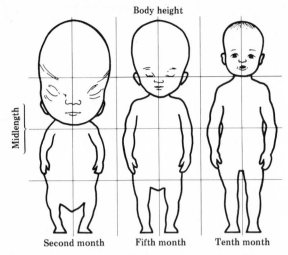

Figure 2-3 Body proportions at the end of different lunar months during the prenatal period. (Adapted from C. Murchison (Ed.). *A handbook of child psychology.* (2d ed.) Worcester, Mass.: Clark University Press, 1933. Used by permission.)

may feel guilty and compensate for this by being overprotective and overindulgent. If a later child should be the hoped-for son, either consciously or unconsciously she may show favoritism toward him, and her treatment of her daughter will be colored by rejection.

The attitudes of other family members—the father, siblings, and grandparents—can also affect the child. Before his birth, they may affect him indirectly through the mother, for example, if family members let her know that they do not welcome the idea of his birth and thus cause her to become nervous and upset. By contrast, favorable attitudes on the part of other family members reinforce the mother's favorable attitudes or lessen any emotional stress she may be under if her attitudes are not favorable.

Like maternal attitudes, the attitudes of other family members tend to persist, though they may change slightly, depending partly on whether the child conforms to their expectations and partly on how he treats them. Grandparents, for example, may have favorable attitudes toward a very

young child, but then feel differently about him if he treats them with less respect and affection as he grows older. This will be reflected in their treatment of him.

Origin of Attitudes

Attitudes toward children and parenthood are usually formed early in life, though they may crystallize when the individual knows that he or she will soon become a parent.

Many factors influence the formation of attitudes toward children. First, a person's earlier experiences with children have a marked effect on how he feels about them in general and about his own impending parenthood. A woman who had to help care for her younger brothers and sisters when she was a girl may have an unfavorable attitude toward children, or a woman who grew up as an only child may want many children to make up for the loneliness she felt when she was young.

Second, the experiences of friends, either in the past or at present, color the individual's attitudes. For example, a young man who hears his friends complain about the financial burdens of parenthood may decide that he would rather not have children.

Third, a parent or grandparent who loves children and who pities people who are childless can influence a person's attitudes favorably. Fourth, a person's attitude toward the sex of his unborn child can be influenced by stereotyped ideas—that boys are "a handful," for example.

Fifth, the mass media tend to glamorize family life and the parental role. The attitudes of an adult whose own experiences with children have been limited may be profoundly influenced by "family shows" on television.

Conditions Influencing Attitudes

Many conditions affect the attitudes —both favorably and unfavorably—of parents, siblings, and grandparents toward

---

Box 2-5. CONDITIONS AFFECTING ATTITUDES OF SIGNIFICANT PEOPLE

Mother's Attitude
Love of children
Desire for companionship
Desire to please her husband or improve a poor marital relationship
Desire to be like her friends who have children
Feelings of inadequacy for the parental role
Resentment at having to give up a career
Fear of childbirth or of having a defective child
Resentment at the physical discomforts and weight gain associated with pregnancy
Resentment at being overworked or tied down

Father's Attitude
Desire for a son to carry on the family name or be associated with him in business
A need to prove his virility to himself and others
Feelings of inadequacy for the parental role
Resentment at interference with educational or vocational plans

Worry about the financial burdens of raising a child
Resentment at being tied down

Siblings' Attitudes
Desire for a playmate
Desire to have as many siblings as their friends
Fear of losing parental affection and attention
Fear of having to share a room or toys with the new sibling or having to help care for it
Desire for sympathy from friends who complain about their own siblings

Grandparents' Attitudes
Desire for a grandchild to carry on the family name
Love of children
Desire to feel useful by helping care for the grand-child
Fear of being imposed on for financial or other help

---

the child. The most commonly reported of these are given in Box 2-5.

Persistence of Attitudes

As is true of likes, dislikes, and prejudices, attitudes, once formed, tend to persist, though slight changes are possible. The changes that do occur are usually in the form of modifications of existing attitudes; the attitudes become less or more favorable than they originally were. Thus changes in attitudes are *quantitative* rather than *qualitative*. For example, a teen-ager's hero worship of a well-known football player may diminish when he discovers that his idol has faults not readily apparent at first. Similarly, a person's dislike for someone of a different race, religion, or socioeconomic background may mellow somewhat with personal contacts. Such changes are modifications of already-existing attitudes.

Attitudes tend to persist because they are based on beliefs the individual considers valid and justified. After all, the hero-worshiping teen-ager contends, his idol certainly must be someone special if he has become a hero to others too.

Siblings and other significant people in the life of the unborn child have reasons for wanting or not wanting him, and they consider these reasons valid. Hence their attitudes, like those of parents, tend to persist, though they too may be modified.

To date, relatively few studies have been made of the persistence of attitudes toward family members, partly because of the problems inherent in making such studies—such as the difficulty of getting accurate reports of attitudes, especially when they are unfavorable—and partly because of the difficulty of following the same group of subjects for a long enough period of time to assess whether their attitudes have persisted or changed over a span of time.

A study by Schaefer and Bayley concentrated on the persistence of maternal behavior toward boys from birth through the preadolescent years. Because behavior is greatly influenced by attitudes, the results of this study help to throw light on the persistence of attitudes. These researchers reported little change in maternal behavior through the years, suggesting that attitudes likewise change little (66).

Effects of Attitudes on Family Relationships

The attitudes of different family members toward the child, formed before and after his birth, have a profound influence on him and on his relationship with his family. This influence may be favorable or unfavorable, depending not on the attitude of one family member but on the attitudes of *all* family members.

If favorable attitudes toward a new baby could be counted on to persist and if unfavorable attitudes could be counted on to become less unfavorable or even favorable, they would not represent a threat to family relationships. Unfortunately, favorable attitudes often become less favorable after the child's birth, and unfavorable attitudes tend to persist, even though they may be so cloaked that they appear to have changed for the better.

Sooner or later, the child becomes aware of the way different members of his family feel about him, and this influences his attitude toward them and toward himself, as well as his behavior. Feeling loved and wanted will motivate him to behave in a way that will intensify these favorable family attitudes. If, on the other hand, he senses, suspects, or knows that he is a disappointment to his father, a burden to his already-overworked mother, and a nuisance to his siblings, he will show his resentment of these attitudes by behaving in ways that intensify them and consequently worsen the family relationships. This may be and often is the starting point of personality maladjustments and problem behavior which can plague the child for years to come—often throughout his life.

HAZARDS DURING THE PRENATAL PERIOD

At no other time during the life span are there more serious hazards to development—or hazards of a more serious nature—than during the relatively short period before birth. These may be physical or psychological. Physical hazards have received more scientific attention because they are more easily recognized.

However, psychological hazards are often as serious as physical hazards, and sometimes more serious, since they affect the attitudes of significant people toward the developing child. Furthermore, they often intensify physical hazards.

Even before development begins, there is the hazard that fertilization will not occur. Conditions are not always favorable to conception. Failure to produce an offspring, or sterility, may result from a number of unfavorable conditions, the four most common of which are briefly explained in Box 2-6.

Box 2-6. CONDITIONS AFFECTING FERTILIZATION

An unfavorable condition in the female reproductive organs, such as excessive acidity of the vaginal secretions, which kills the spermatozoa, or obstruction in the Fallopian tube due to inflammation or some foreign substance.

Lengthening of the menstrual cycle as a result of a glandular deficiency. This delays the release of the ripened ovum or prolongs its passage down the Fallopian tube. Even if fertilized, it may not have enough yolk to keep it alive until it becomes embedded in the uterine wall.

An unfavorable condition of the ovum due to poor maternal health, malnutrition, glandular or vitamin deficiency, or old age.

An unfavorable condition of the spermatozoa due to poor health, malnutrition, vitamin or glandular deficiency, or old age. The spermatozoa do not have the strength to swim up the Fallopian tube or to penetrate the wall of the ovum.

Physical Hazards

Each of the three major subdivisions of the prenatal period involves particular physical hazards. While these do not affect all individuals by any means, they do occur with some frequency and can be serious enough to affect the development of the individual throughout his life. As Davis and Havighurst have pointed out (19):

What happens to the fetus in the womb, and in the process of its birth; the adequacy of its uterine nutrition; its good or ill fortune at birth with regard to infection or injury, all these often prove as important as its heredity.

Box 2-7 gives the common physical hazards associated with each of the three prenatal periods.

Certain conditions have been found to increase the likelihood that these hazards will occur or to accentuate them. Maternal age is an important factor. Women approaching the menopause in their late thirties or early forties frequently have endocrine disorders which slow down the development of the embryo and fetus, causing such developmental irregularities as cretinism, mongolism, heart malformations, and hydrocephalus, all of which involve physical and mental defects. Older women also tend to have smaller babies and to have more complications at birth (56, 61).

For reasons as yet unknown, female em-

Box 2-7. COMMON PHYSICAL HAZARDS DURING THE PRENATAL PERIOD

Period of the Ovum

Starvation
The ovum will die of starvation if it has too little yolk to keep it alive until it can lodge itself in the uterine wall or if it remains too long in the tube.

Lack of Uterine Preparation
Implantation cannot occur if, as a result of glandular imbalance, the uterine walls are not prepared in time to receive the zygote.

Implantation in the Wrong Place
If the zygote becomes attached to a small fibroid tissue in the uterine wall or to the wall of the Fallopian tube, it cannot get nourishment and will die.

Period of the Embryo

Miscarriages
Falls, emotional shocks, malnutrition, glandular disturbances, vitamin deficiency, and serious diseases, such as pneumonia and diabetes, can cause the embryo to become dislodged from its place in the uterine wall, resulting in a miscarriage. Miscarriages that are due to unfavorable conditions in the prenatal environment are likely to occur between the tenth and eleventh weeks after conception.

Developmental Irregularities
Maternal malnutrition; vitamin and glandular deficiencies; excessive use of drugs, alcohol, and tobacco; and diseases, such as diabetes and German measles, interfere with normal development, especially that of the embryonic brain.

Period of the Fetus

Miscarriages
Miscarriages are always possible up to the fifth month of pregnancy; the most vulnerable time is when the woman's menstrual period would normally occur.

Prematurity
Fetuses who weigh less than 2 pounds 3 ounces have less chance of surviving than heavier fetuses and a greater chance of developing malformations.

Complications of Delivery
Maternal stress affects uterine contractions and is likely to lead to complications during birth.

Developmental Irregularities
Any of the unfavorable environmental conditions present during the period of the embryo will also affect the development of fetal features and retard the whole pattern of fetal development.

bryos have a better chance of survival than male embryos. For example, for every 100 females lost through miscarriage, 160 males are lost. Developmental irregularities have also been found to be more common among males than among females (56, 68).

Multiple births are more hazardous than single births. Fetuses of multiple birth are crowded during the prenatal period, and this inhibits the normal fetal activity essential for development. Prematurity is also more likely in the case of multiple births, as is the possibility of developmental irregularities. Because multiple births are more common among blacks than among whites, as was pointed out earlier, this may account in part for the higher infant mortality rate and the greater incidence of developmental irregularities among blacks than among whites.

Long-term Effects If developmental irregularities are serious and if the embryo or fetus does not miscarry or die at birth or shortly afterward, the individual will be deformed in some way. One of the serious aspects of developmental irregularities is that they are often not diagnosed as such until months or even years after birth. Epilepsy, cerebral palsy, and mental deficiency, for example, may not show up until babyhood or even early in childhood.

Parents who believe that their baby is normal at birth find it difficult to accept a defective child and often blame themselves for having caused the defect. This leads to strong feelings of guilt and a tendency to overprotect the defective child or to refuse to accept the fact that he is as defective as he is.

It is now known that malnutrition during pregnancy may damage the developing fetal brain, causing learning difficulties in school, especially reading disabilities. Damage to the fetal brain, whatever the cause, will have effects on the individual's behavior that become more and more apparent as he grows older and is compared with other children of the same age.

A chromosomal abnormality, especially in an X chromosome, has been found to lead to physical abnormalities that can predispose the individual to abnormal behavior if they make it difficult for him to adjust to social expectations (12, 25).

Studies of the long-term effects of twinning have revealed that prenatal crowding, which influences development during that time, carries over into postnatal life and affects patterns of personal and social adjustment (59). Because the firstborn twin is likely to be bigger and stronger, he makes better academic and social adjustments than the smaller, weaker twin. In addition, the smaller twin tends to have a lower IQ, which accounts, in part, for his usually poorer academic performance (42, 67). Twins also are usually born prematurely and suffer from the physical and psychological effects of prematurity. This will be discussed in detail in the following chapter.

Excessive smoking—to the point where the mother-to-be shows nervousness, wakefulness, and irregular heartbeat—has been shown to have some effect on the fetal heart and circulatory system as well as on the other organs. By the time they are seven years old, children whose mothers smoked excessively during pregnancy have been found to be shorter and generally less well developed than the mean for their age. This is illustrated in Figure 2-4. In addition, they are less well adjusted socially and read less well than children born to nonsmoking or moderately smoking mothers (9, 30).

Psychological Hazards

Like the physical hazards associated with the prenatal period, the psychological hazards can have persistent effects on the individual's development and can influence his postnatal environment and the treatment he receives from the significant people in his life during the early, formative years. The three most important psychological hazards are traditional beliefs about prenatal development, maternal stress during the

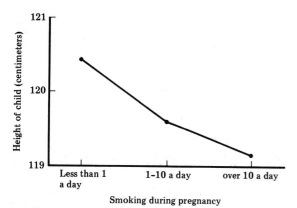

Figure 2-4 The relationship of maternal smoking during pregnancy and the height of children up to seven years of age: mean scores for a group of boys and girls. (Adapted from H. Goldstein. Factors influencing the height of seven-year-old children: Results of the National Child Development Study. *Hum. Biol.,* 1971, **43**, 92–111. Used by permission.

prenatal period, and unfavorable attitudes toward the unborn child on the part of people who will play a significant role in his life.

Traditional Beliefs Perhaps there are more traditional, and more damaging, beliefs about the prenatal development period than about any other period in the life span. Such beliefs can affect the parents' treatment of the child and often have an effect on their attitudes toward each other. See Figure 2-5.

In spite of scientific evidence to the contrary, many people still believe that it is within their power to control the sex of their offspring. The effects of such a belief are more serious than most people realize. When parents are convinced that they can produce an offspring of the sex they want, they are generally bitterly disappointed when the child turns out to be of the opposite sex. This disappointment may wane and disappear in time, but it frequently leaves its imprint upon the parents' attitudes toward the child. Furthermore, many men feel that it is the woman who has the power to control the sex of her child, and if

she does not produce an offspring of the sex her husband wants, his attitude toward her may be seriously affected.

There are also many traditional beliefs about the causes of developmental irregularities. Some of these emphasize heredity, but most stress the role played by maternal impressions. There are two lines of medical evidence to disprove these beliefs about maternal impressions. First, there is evidence that the same types of abnormalities found in humans are also found in the lower animals whose low level of mental development would make them incapable of maternal impressions. Second, there is no direct nervous connection between the mother and the embryo. There are no nerves in the umbilical cord, and thus the mother's thoughts, feelings, and emotions could have no direct influence on the embryo.

Acceptance of these beliefs can lead to strong feelings of guilt on the part of the

Figure 2-5 Acceptance of the traditional belief that the mother's behavior during pregnancy will affect the child's development often leads to husband-wife conflicts. (Drawn by Art Gates. *Atlanta Journal & Constitution,* Oct. 28, 1973. Used by permission.)

"I warned Janet about eating all of those sour pickles!"

mother, resentments toward her on the part of the father, and a tendency for the mother to overprotect the child as a form of compensation for the harm she believes she has brought him. The more handicapped a child is by a developmental irregularity, the more unfavorable these feelings and attitudes will be.

In the past, twins were believed to be caused by evil spirits and thus were feared and rejected by the social group. Today, only the most uncivilized cultures hold such beliefs, although many people still think that it is "animal-like" to have twins and that twins are less desirable and less acceptable than singletons.

Such unfavorable beliefs will inevitably color the attitudes of family members and also of significant outsiders toward twins. For example, if parents believe that twins always cause trouble in terms of work, expense, family friction, or unfavorable attitudes on the part of relatives, friends, and neighbors, their attitudes toward their twins and their treatment of them will be less favorable than if they were uninfluenced by such beliefs.

Maternal Stress The second important psychological hazard associated with the prenatal period is maternal stress—heightened general emotionality over a prolonged period of time. Stress can be the result of feelings of fear, anger, grief, jealousy, or envy.

Maternal stress affects the developing child both before and after birth. Before birth, severe and persistent glandular imbalance due to stress may result in developmental irregularities in the developing child and complications of delivery or even prematurity. Maternal anxiety affects uterine contractions, with the result that labor lasts longer and the chances of complications are greater because the fetus must often be delivered by instruments. Furthermore, anxiety often leads to overeating and excessive weight gain in pregnancy, which further complicates birth.

Sporadic, less severe maternal stress is less likely to lead to developmental irregularities, though it does increase fetal activity. If this increase is slight, the effect is favorable because the fetus will get the exercise necessary for healthy muscular development. If stress leads to excessive fetal activity, however, the fetus will be underweight and nervous to the point where early postnatal adjustments will be seriously affected.

Although relatively few studies have been made of the effects of maternal stress on the child after birth, it has been shown that when prolonged emotional strain affects endocrine balance, anxieties may carry over into the period of the newborn and seriously affect the infant's adjustments to postnatal life. He may show hyperactivity, which prevents him from adjusting to feeding and sleep patterns, or he may cry excessively (72, 73).

It has been noted that newborn infants and young babies who were most active as fetuses show certain motor performances at an earlier age than those who were less active (72, 77). On the other hand, excessive fetal activity causes infants to be considerably underweight and often to be slower in acquiring skills postnatally, a result of excessive nervousness. In addition, as Sontag has reported, they often become "hyperactive, irritable, squirming, crying" infants who suffer from a "prenatally produced neurosis" which makes their adjustment to life outside the mother's body difficult (72). Research studies of animals hint that excessive maternal stress can curb masculinity in boys (10).

Prolonged and extreme maternal stress during the period of the fetus frequently causes more illness during the first three years of the child's life than is experienced by children who had a more favorable fetal environment. Children whose mothers were under great stress during pregnancy also show more "free-floating anxiety"; although they can still perform their daily routines, such anxiety has an adverse effect on their ability to remember and to reason to their full capacity. As a result, they seem to be less bright than they actually are (72).

There are many causes of maternal stress during pregnancy, the most common of which are the following: not wanting a child because of marital or economic difficulties or because having a child will interfere with educational or vocational plans; physical discomforts that are severe and frequent enough to make the mother-to-be nervous, irritable, and generally emotionally disturbed; feelings of inadequacy for the parental role; and fears that the child will be physically deformed or mentally deficient—fears that are often heightened by mass-media reports of the frequency of birth defects and of specific causes of birth defects, such as rubella and thalidomide. Some women have fantasies and dreams about giving birth to deformed babies which intensify such fears (29).

Unfavorable Attitudes on the Part of Significant People The third common psychological hazard—unfavorable attitudes on the part of significant people in the child's life—is in many respects the most serious because these attitudes tend to persist. Many unfavorable attitudes toward the child begin to develop when his potential arrival becomes known to his parents, family members, and other significant people in his life. The most common and the most serious of these are given in Box 2-8.

On the surface, attitudes toward the child's sex and attitudes influenced by a "dream-child" concept do not seem unfavorable. However, because they are unrealistic, they are likely to lead to disappointment or even resentment which will be expressed in intolerance toward the child or even rejection. If the child is not wanted, or at least not wanted at this time, attitudes are unfavorable from the start, and often little or no attempt is made to cloak them. A father-to-be may blame his wife for being careless and make her feel guilty about not preventing the pregnancy. This will lead to

Unrealistic parental expectations can result in resentful, intolerant parental behavior. If this little boy is unfairly punished too often, his psychological development may suffer. (Suzanne Szasz)

marital friction and resentment toward the child when he is born. If older children do not want the baby, they will show their resentment toward it when it arrives and also toward their parents for having had it. On the basis of observations of the adjustment difficulties that unwanted children experience, Ferreira has commented: "The psychiatric and social implications of these observations suggest a sober reappraisal of the current attitudes toward the unwanted pregnancy" (26).

Unfavorable attitudes toward children of multiple birth are often stronger and more persistent than those toward singletons. These unfavorable attitudes are intensified when multiple births come unex-

Box 2-8. COMMON UNFAVORABLE ATTITUDES TOWARD THE UNBORN CHILD

Not Wanting the Child

The mother may not want the child because it is illegitimate, because it will interfere with her career, because it will tie her down, or because she is already overworked caring for other children. The father may not want the child because he does not want to be forced to marry the mother, because of the financial burden the child will represent, because he does not want to be tied down, or because he does not want his wife to be preoccupied with child care and neglect him. Siblings may not want the child because they resent the restrictions a baby will place on their activities or because they do not want to share their possessions or their mother's time and attention with him.

Not Wanting the Child at This Time

The parents may not want the child now because it will interfere with their educational and vocational plans, because they feel they are too young and inexperienced to care for a child, because they cannot afford it, or because they do not want to assume parental responsibilities so soon. Grand-

parents may feel that the young couple cannot afford the baby and may fear that they will have to provide financial and other help.

Preference for a Child of a Particular Sex

The father and the grandparents usually want the firstborn to be a boy; if there are already boys in the family, they may want a girl. The mother may want a boy to please her husband, or she may prefer a girl, who she feels will be more of a companion to her. Siblings generally prefer a child of their own sex, whom they regard as more likely to be a playmate.

Dream-Child Concept

All family members have a dream-child concept that colors their attitudes toward the unborn baby. Parents and grandparents want him to be perfect mentally, emotionally, and physically—bright, obedient, beautiful—and siblings want an ideal playmate, one who will do whatever *they* want to do and who will never rival or outstrip them.

---

pectedly and parents have not had time before the births to adjust to them. Even when parents welcome the idea of a multiple birth, their attitudes may become unfavorable when they are faced with the realities of the babies' care and the expense involved. An anonymous writer, quoted by Scheinfeld (67), has described such feelings:

The Joy (?) of Twins

Drudgery that's double or more
Laundering till your hands are sore;
Tangle of lines with soggy things drying,
Day and night chorus of yelling and
*   crying,*
Endless chores and no end of expenses.
Worries that drive you out of your senses,
Everyone bothering you with questions,
Everyone giving you crazy suggestions,

Husband complaining you're no kind of
*   wife,*
Everything mixed up in your life.
If I knew whom to blame for twins, I'd sue
*   'em.*
Those who want twins are welcome to
*   'em.*

Chapter Highlights

1 The prenatal period is important for four reasons: the hereditary endowment is fixed at this time; the development of hereditary potentials is affected either favorably or unfavorably by conditions within the mother's body; there is proportionally greater growth and development during this period than at any other time; and the attitudes of significant people are formed then.

2 Before new life can begin, there must be maturation and fertilization on the part of the male and maturation, ovulation, and fertilization in the female.

3 At the moment of conception, four important things are determined that affect the individual's later development: hereditary endowment, sex, number of offspring, and ordinal position.

4 There are three subdivisions of the prenatal period: the period of the ovum, the period of the embryo, and the period of the fetus.

5 The period of the ovum lasts for approximately two weeks; during this time there is no increase in size, but marked internal development occurs. The period of the embryo extends from the end of the second week until the end of the second lunar month. All internal and external features are established at this time. The period of the fetus lasts from the end of the second lunar month until birth and is marked by further development of these features.

6 The attitudes formed by significant people —mother, father, siblings, and grandparents—during the prenatal period determine how they will treat the child during the early, formative years of his life.

7 The attitudes of significant people affect the developing individual indirectly through the mother if they cause stress that produces endocrine disturbances.

8 Many conditions influence the attitudes of significant people in the child's life, and these differ for the mother, father, siblings, and grandparents.

9 Once formed, attitudes tend to persist, though minor changes can and do occur. It is the persistence of attitudes that makes them important factors in the development of the new individual as well as in the quality of family relationships.

10 Even before conception, there is a hazard that fertilization will not take place. An unfavorable condition in the female reproductive organs, lengthening of the menstrual cycle, and an unfavorable condition of the ovum or sperm are the most common causes of failure to produce an offspring.

11 Common physical hazards are associated with each of the periods of prenatal development, any of which may result in malformations of the developing individual or in its death.

12 Psychological hazards associated with the prenatal period are traditional beliefs, maternal stress, and unfavorable attitudes on the part of significant people.

Bibliography

1 Allen, M. G., Pollin, W., & Hoffer, A. Parental, birth, and infancy factors in infant twin development. *Amer. J. Psychiat.,* 1971, **127,** 1597–1604.

2 Altman, L. K. Physicians urge exercise of caution in prescribing drugs during pregnancies. *The New York Times,* June 26, 1970.

3 Altus, W. D. Birth order and its sequelae. *Science,* 1966, **151,** 44–49.

4 Auerbach, A. B. Meeting the needs of new mothers. *Children,* 1964, **11,** 223–233.

5 Bakwin, H., & Bakwin, R. M. *Clinical management of behavior disorders in children.* (3rd ed.) Philadelphia: Saunders, 1966.

6 Bench, J., & Parker, A. Hyper-responsivity to sound in the short-gestation baby. *Develpm. Med. child Neurol.,* 1971, **13,** 15–19.

7 Blatz, W. E. *The five sisters.* New York: Morrow, 1938.

8 Bowes, W. A., Brackbill, Y., Conway, A., & Steinschreider, A. The effects of obstetrical medication on fetus and infant. *Monogr. Soc. Res. Child Develpm.,* 1970, **35**(4).

9 Brody, J. E. Study finds smoking can imperil fetus. *The New York Times,* Apr. 11, 1970.

10 Brody, J. E. Study hints prenatal stress can curb masculinity. *The New York Times,* Jan. 13, 1972.

11 Brown, A. M., Stafford, R. E., & Vandenberg, S. G. Twins: Behavioral differences. *Child Develpm.,* 1967, **38,** 1055–1064.

12 Brown, W. M. C., Price, W. H., & Jacobs, P. A. Further information on the identity of 47 XYY males. *Brit. med. J.,* 1968, **2,** 325–328.

13 Carmichael, L. The onset and early development of behavior. In P. H. Mussen (Ed.), *Carmichael's manual of child psychology.* (3rd ed.) Vol. 1. New York: Wiley, 1970. Pp. 447–563.

14 Conniff, J. C. G. The world of the unborn. *The New York Times,* Jan. 8, 1967.

15 Coursin, D. B. Nutrition and brain development in infants. *Merrill-Palmer Quart.,* 1972, **18,** 177–202.

16 Dales, R. J. Motor and language development of twins during the first three years. *J. genet. Psychol.,* 1969, **114,** 263–271.

17 Davids, A. A research design for studying maternal emotionality before childbirth and after social interaction with the child. *Merrill-Palmer Quart.,* 1968, **14,** 345–354.

18 Davids, A., & Holden, R. H. Consistency of maternal atti-

tudes and personality from pregnancy to eight months following childbirth. *Develpm. Psychol.,* 1970, **2**, 364–366.

19 Davis, A., & Havighurst, R. J. *Father of the man.* Boston: Houghton Mifflin, 1947.

20 Demarest, R. J., & Sciarra, J. J. *Conception, birth, contraception: A visual presentation.* New York: McGraw-Hill, 1969.

21 Edwards, D. DeA., & Edwards, J. S. Fetal movement: Development and time course. *Science,* 1970, **169**, 95–97.

22 Engstrom, L., Geijerstam, G., Holmberg, N. G., & Uhrus, K. A prospective study of the relationship between psychosocial factors and course of pregnancy and delivery. *J. psychosom. Res.,* 1964, **8**, 151–155.

23 Ernhart, C. B., Graham, F. K., Eichman, P. L., Marshall, J. M., & Thurston, D. Brain injury in the preschool child: Some developmental considerations. II. Comparison of brain injured and normal children. *Psychol. Monogr.,* 1963, **77**(11).

24 Felig, P., & Lynch, V. Starvation in human pregnancy: Hypoglycemia, hypoinsulinemia and hyperketonemia. *Science,* 1970, **170**, 990–992.

25 Ferdon, N. K. Chromosomal abnormalities and antisocial behavior. *J. genet. Psychol.,* 1971, **118**, 281–292.

26 Ferreira, A. J. Emotional factors in prenatal environment. *J. nerv. ment. Dis.,* 1965, **141**, 108–118.

27 Flapan, M. A paradigm for the analysis of childbearing motivations of married women prior to the birth of the first child. *Amer. J. Orthopsychiat.,* 1969, **39**, 402–417.

28 Gebhard, P. H., Pomeroy, W. B., Martin, C. E., & Christenson, C. V. *Pregnancy, birth, and abortion.* New York: Harper & Row, 1958.

29 Gillman, R. D. The dreams of pregnant women and maternal adaptation. *Amer. J. Orthopsychiat.,* 1968, **38**, 688–692.

30 Goldstein, H. Factors influencing the height of seven-year-old children: Results of the National Child Development Study. *Hum. Biol.,* 1971, **43**, 92–111.

31 Hartley, R. E. Children's perceptions of sex preference in four culture groups. *J. Marriage & Family,* 1969, **31**, 380–387.

32 Heinstein, M. I. Expressed attitudes and feelings of pregnant women and their relations to physical complications. *Merrill-Palmer Quart.,* 1967, **13**, 217–236.

33 Helper, M. M., Cohen, P. L., Beitenman, E. T., & Eton, L. F. Life events and acceptance of pregnancy. *J. psychosom. Res.,* 1968, **12**, 183–188.

34 Hill, O. W. A twin study. *Brit. J. Psychiat.,* 1968, **114**, 175–179.

35 Hooker, D. The development of behavior in the human fetus. In W. Dennis (Ed.), *Readings in child psychology.* (2nd ed.) Englewood Cliffs, N.J.: Prentice-Hall, 1963. Pp. 1–10.

36 Horstmann, D. M., Banalava, J. E., Riorden, J. T., Payne, N. C., Whittemore, R., Opton, E. M., & Floray, C. diV. Maternal rubella and the rubella syndrome in infants. *Amer. J. Dis. Children,* 1965, **110**, 408–415.

37 Howard, R. G., & Brown, A. M. Twinning: A marker for biological insults. *Child Develpm.,* 1970, **41**, 519–530.

38 Hytten, F. E. Smoking in pregnancy. *Develpm. Med. child Neurol.,* 1973, **15**, 355–357.

39 Joesting, J., & Joesting, R. Birth order and desired family size. *J. indiv. Psychol.,* 1973, **29**, 34.

40 Khatri, A. A., & Siddiqui, B. B. "A boy or a girl?" Preferences of parents for sex of offspring as perceived by East Indian and American children: A cross-cultural study. *J. Marriage & Family,* 1969, **31**, 388–392.

41 Kim, C. C., Dales, R. J., Connor, R., Walters, W., & Witherspoon, R. Social interaction of like-sexed twins and singletons in relation to intelligence, language and physical development. *J. genet. Psychol.,* 1969, **114**, 203–214.

42 Koch, H. L. *Twins and twin relations.* Chicago: University of Chicago Press, 1966.

43 Kuhlen, R. G., & Thompson, G. G. (Eds.) *Psychological studies of human development.* (3rd ed.) New York: Appleton Century Crofts, 1969.

44 Lewis, M., Wilson, C. D., Ban, P., & Baumel, W. H. An exploratory study of resting cardiac rate and variability from last trimester of prenatal life through the first year of postnatal life. *Child Develpm.,* 1970, **41**, 799–811.

45 Liebenberg, B. Expectant fathers. *Child & Family,* 1969, **8**, 265–278.

46 *Life* article. Drama of life before birth. *Life,* Apr. 30, 1965.

47 Lunneborg, P. W. Birth order, aptitude and achievement. *J. consult. clin. Psychol.,* 1968, **32**, 101.

48 MacDonald, A. P. Manifestations of differential levels of socialization by birth order. *Develpm. Psychol.,* 1969, **1**, 485–492.

49 Martin, P. C., & Vincent, E. L. *Human development.* New York: Ronald Press, 1960.

50 Matheney, A. P., & Brown, A. M. The behavior of twins: Effects of birth weight and birth sequence. *Child Develpm.,* 1971, **42**, 251–257.

51 McClearn, G. E. Genetic influences on behavior and development. In P. H. Mussen (Ed.), *Carmichael's manual of child psychology.* (3rd ed.) Vol. 1. New York: Wiley, 1970. Pp. 39–76.

52 McDonald, R. L. The role of emotional factors in obstetric complications: A review. *Psychosom. Med.,* 1968, **30**, 222–237.

53 McKeown, T. Prenatal and early postnatal influences on measured intelligence. *Brit. med. J.,* 1970, **3**, 63–67.

54 Mead, M. *Male and female.* New York: Dell, 1968.

55 Meyerowitz, J. H. Satisfaction during pregnancy. *J. Marriage & Family,* 1970, **32**, 38–42.

56 Montagu, A. *The direction of human development.* (Rev. ed.) New York: Hawthorn, 1970.

57 Newberry, H. H., Freeman, F. N., & Holzinger, K. J. *Twins: A study of heredity and environment.* Chicago: University of Chicago Press, 1966.

58 Nisbet, R. E. Birth order and participation in dangerous sports. *J. Pers. soc. Psychol.,* 1968, **8**, 351–353.

59 Ounsted, M. Fetal growth and mental ability. *Develpm. Med. child Neurol.,* 1970, **12**, 222–224.

60 Page, E. W., Villee, C. A., & Villee, D. B. *Human reproduction: The core content of obstetrics, gynecology and perinatal medicine.* Philadelphia: Saunders, 1972.

61 Pasamanick, B., & Knobloch, H. Prospective studies on the epidemiology of reproductive casualty: Methods, findings and some implications. *Merrill-Palmer Quart.,* 1966, **12**, 27–43.

62 Pohlman, E. Unwanted conceptions: Research on undesirable consequences. *Child & Family,* 1969, **8**, 240–253.

63 Reid, D. E., Ryan, K. J., & Benirschksi, K. (Eds.) *Principles and management of human reproduction.* Philadelphia: Saunders, 1972.

64 Rothbart, M. K., & Maccoby, E. E. Parents' differential reactions to sons and daughters. *J. Pers. soc. Psychol.*, 1966, **4**, 237–243.

65 Scarr, S. Environmental bias in twin studies. *Eugen. Quart.*, 1968, **15**, 34–40.

66 Schaefer, E. S., & Bayley, N. Consistency of maternal behavior from infancy to preadolescence. *J. abnorm. soc. Psychol.*, 1960, **61**, 1–6.

67 Scheinfeld, A. *Twins and supertwins.* Philadelphia: Lippincott, 1967.

68 Scheinfeld, A. *Heredity in humans.* (Rev. ed.) Philadelphia: Lippincott, 1971.

69 Schooler, C. Birth order effects: Not here, not now! *Psychol. Bull.*, 1972, **78**, 161–175.

70 Shrader, W. K., & Leventhal, T. Birth order of children and parental report of problems. *Child Develpm.*, 1968, **39**, 1165–1175.

71 Smith, J. A., Renshaw, D. C., & Renshaw, R. H. Twins who want to be identified as twins. *Diseases of the Nervous System,* 1968, **29**, 615–618.

72 Sontag, L. W. Implications of fetal behavior and environment for adult personalities. *Ann. N.Y. Acad. Sci.*, 1966, **134**, 782–786.

73 Sontag, L. W., Steele, W. G., & Lewis, M. The fetal and maternal cardiac response to environmental stress. *Hum. Develpm.*, 1969, **12**, 1–9.

74 Taussig, H. B. The thalidomide syndrome. *Scient. American,* 1962, **207**, 29–35.

75 Vockell, E. L., Felker, D. W., & Miley, C. H. Birth order literature 1967–1971: Bibliography and index. *J. indiv. Psychol.,* 1973, **29**, 39–53.

76 Walters, C. E. Reliability and comparison of four types of fetal activity and total activity. *Child Develpm.*, 1964, **35**, 1249–1256.

77 Walters, C. E. Prediction of postnatal development from fetal activity. *Child Develpm.*, 1965, **36**, 801–808.

78 Willerman, L., & Churchill, J. A. Intelligence and birth weight in identical twins. *Child Develpm.*, 1967, **38**, 623–629.

79 Williamson, D. A. J. A syndrome of congenital malformations possibly due to maternal diabetes. *Develpm. Med. child Neurol.,* 1970, **12**, 145–152.

80 Wilson, R. S., & Harpring, E. B. Mental and motor development in infant twins. *Develpm. Psychol.*, 1972, **7**, 277–287.

81 Winestine, M. C. Twinship and psychological differentiation. *J. Amer. Acad. child Psychiat.*, 1969, **8**, 436–455.

CHAPTER THREE

INFANCY

Infancy, or the period of the newborn, is the shortest of all the developmental periods. It begins at birth and ends when the infant is approximately two weeks old. This is the time when the fetus must adjust to life outside the uterine walls of the mother, where he has lived for approximately nine months.

According to medical criteria, the adjustment is completed with the fall of the umbilical cord from the navel; according to physiological criteria, it is completed when the infant has regained the weight lost after birth; and according to psychological criteria, it is completed when he begins to show signs of developmental progress in behavior. Although most infants complete this adjustment in two weeks or slightly less, those whose birth has been difficult or premature require more time.

Infancy is generally subdivided into two periods: the period of the partunate and the period of the neonate. These are described in Box 3-1.

CHARACTERISTICS OF INFANCY

Each period in the life span is characterized by certain developmental phenomena that distinguish it from the periods that precede and follow it. This is true of infancy, in spite of its shortness. While some of these phenomena may be associated with other periods, they appear in distinctive forms in infancy.

Traditional Beliefs about Birth

Traditional beliefs about birth color the attitudes of significant people in the infant's life toward him. For example, there are

> **Box 3-1. SUBDIVISIONS OF INFANCY**
>
> **Period of the Partunate** (*birth to fifteen to thirty minutes after birth*)
> The infant continues to be a parasite and makes no adjustments to the postnatal environment.
>
> **Period of the Neonate** (*from the cutting of the umbilical cord to the end of the second week*)
> The infant is now a separate, independent individual who must make adjustments to his new environment.

many beliefs about auspicious and inauspicious times to be born. There is also the belief that the ease or difficulty of birth affects postnatal adjustments and the belief that a premature baby will never be as strong as one born at full term or make as successful an adjustment to life.

Infancy Is a Time of Radical Adjustments

Although the human life span legally begins at the moment of birth, birth is merely an interruption of the developmental pattern that started at the moment of conception. It is the graduation from an internal to an external environment. Like all graduations, it requires adjustments on the individual's part. It may be easy for the infant to make these adjustments or so difficult that he will fail to do so. As Miller has commented, "In all the rest of his life, there will never be such a sudden and complete change of locale" (65). Even in the case of difficult births, it seldom takes more than forty-eight hours for the fetus to emerge from the mother's body. By contrast, it requires approximately two weeks to adjust to his new environment.

Infancy Is a Plateau in Development

The rapid growth and development which took place during the prenatal period suddenly come to a stop with birth. In fact, there is often a slight regression, such as loss of weight and a tendency to become less strong and healthy than at birth. Normally, this slight regression lasts for several days to a week; then the infant begins to improve, and by the end of the period of infancy, he is back to where he was at the time of birth.

The halt in growth and development, characteristic of this plateau, is due to the necessity for making radical adjustments to the postnatal environment. Once these adjustments have been made, the infant resumes his growth and development.

While a plateau in development during infancy is normal, many parents, especially those of firstborn children, become concerned about it and fear that something is wrong with their child. Consequently, the infancy plateau may become a psychological hazard, just as it is a potential physical hazard.

Infancy Is a Preview of Later Development

It is not possible to predict with even reasonable accuracy what the individual's future development will be on the basis of the development apparent at birth. However, the newborn's development provides a clue as to what to expect later on. As Bell et al. have said (12):

Newborn behavior is more like a preface to a book than like a table of its contents yet to be unfolded. Further, the preface is itself merely a rough draft undergoing rapid revision. There are some clues to the nature of the book in the preface but these are in code form and taking them as literally prophetic is likely to lead to disappointment.

Infancy Is a Hazardous Period

Infancy is a hazardous period, both physically and psychologically. Physically, it is hazardous because of the difficulties of making the necessary radical adjustments to the totally new and different environment. The high infant mortality rate is evidence of this.

Psychologically, infancy is hazardous because it is the time when the attitudes of significant people toward the infant are crystallized. Many of these attitudes were established during the prenatal period and may change radically after the infant is born, but some remain relatively unchanged or are strengthened, depending on conditions at birth and on the ease or difficulty with which the infant and his parents adjust during the infancy period.

MAJOR ADJUSTMENTS OF INFANCY

The infant must make four major adjustments before he can resume his developmental progress. If he does not make them quickly, his life will be threatened. While these adjustments are being made, there is no developmental progress. Instead, the infant remains on a plateau or may even regress to a lower stage of development. These adjustments are described in Box 3-2.

Every newborn infant finds adjustment to postnatal life difficult at first. Some have

---

Box 3-2. ADJUSTMENTS OF INFANCY

Temperature Changes
There is a constant temperature of 100°F in the uterine sac, while temperatures in the hospital or home may vary from 60 to 70°F.

Breathing
When the umbilical cord is cut, the infant must begin to breathe on his own.

Sucking and Swallowing
The infant must now get nourishment by sucking and swallowing, instead of receiving it through the umbilical cord. These reflexes are imperfectly developed at birth, and the infant often gets less nourishment than he needs and thus loses weight.

Elimination
The infant's organs of elimination begin to work soon after birth; formerly, waste products were eliminated through the umbilical cord.

Box 3-3. INDICATIONS OF THE DIFFICULTY OF ADJUSTMENT TO POSTNATAL LIFE

Loss of Weight
Because of difficulties in adjusting to sucking and swallowing, the newborn infant usually loses weight during the first week of postnatal life.

Disorganized Behavior
For the first day or two of postnatal life, all infants show relatively disorganized behavior, such as irregularities in breathing rate, frequent urinations and defecations, wheezing, and regurgitation. This is due partly to pressure on the brain during birth, which results in a stunned state, and partly to the undeveloped state of the autonomic nervous system, which controls body homeostasis.

Infant Mortality
Even today, the rate of infant mortality during the first two days of postnatal life is high. The causes of infant mortality are many and varied.

---

trouble adjusting to temperature changes and develop colds, which often turn into pneumonia. Others find breathing difficult and must be given oxygen. Most choke when they attempt to suck and swallow, and many regurgitate more than they are able to retain, in which case they get less nourishment than they need to grow or even to retain their birth weight. Few have any real trouble eliminating urine, but many have difficulties with fecal elimination.

Three common indications of the difficulty of adjusting to postnatal life are given in Box 3-3.

FACTORS INFLUENCING ADJUSTMENT TO POSTNATAL LIFE

Many factors influence the infant's success in making the necessary adjustments to postnatal life. These include the kind of prenatal environment he had, the kind of birth he has experienced and its ease or difficulty, the length of the gestation period, parental attitudes, and postnatal care.

Prenatal Environment

Many kinds of intrauterine disturbance may cause an infant to be born, as Schwartz has pointed out, "with severe injuries and then be subject to a miserable life" (89). Inadequate prenatal care of the mother, as a result of either poverty or neglect, is often responsible for the development of unfavorable conditions in the intrauterine environment which affect the developing child and lead to complications during childbirth, both of which affect the kind of adjustment the infant makes.

Malnutrition of the mother during pregnancy has been found to be responsible for premature births, stillbirths, and infant mortality during the early days of life. Infants whose mothers suffer from diabetes have more difficulties in adjustment and a higher incidence of mortality than infants whose mothers are nondiabetic (66, 73).

Unquestionably one of the most important factors that contribute to difficulties in postnatal adjustment is a prenatal environment characterized by prolonged and intense maternal stress. As was mentioned earlier, this leads to complications during pregnancy and childbirth. Maternal stress also causes the fetus to become hyperactive during the last months of pregnancy, and this condition tends to persist after birth, manifesting itself in feeding difficulties, failure to gain weight, sleep problems, general irritability, distractibility, and a host of other conditions that make adjustment to postnatal life difficult. In commenting on the effects of maternal stress during pregnancy on the infant's later adjustment, Sontag has emphasized (95):

To all intents and purposes, a newborn infant with such a background is a neurotic infant when he is born—the result of an unsatisfactory fetal environment. In this instance, he does not have to wait until childhood for a bad home situation or other cause to make him neurotic. It was done for him before he even saw the light of day.

Birth

Birth has been described as hazardous. As Jeffcoate has pointed out, the "most dangerous journey made by any individual is

Figure 3-1 In a natural or spontaneous birth (a) the infant emerges from the mother's body headfirst while in a breech birth (b) the buttocks emerge first and the head last. (Adapted from N. J. Eastman & L. M. Hellman. *Williams obstetrics.* (13th ed.). New York: Appleton Century Crofts, 1966. Used by permission)

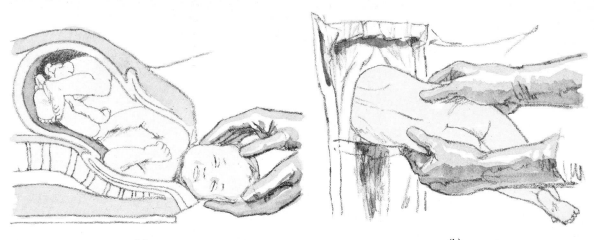

(a)   (b)

through the four inches of the birth canal" (45). Schwartz further emphasized the hazardous nature of birth when he said, "Birth is almost without exception a brutal process which endangers the life and health of the child" (89).

There are five kinds of birth, each with its distinctive characteristics. These are explained in Box 3-4. Figure 3-1 illustrates two of the five—natural (or spontaneous birth) and breech birth.

The infant who has been born spontaneously usually adjusts more quickly and more successfully to his postnatal environment than one whose birth has been difficult enough to require use of instruments or caesarean section.

More hazards are associated with instrument births and caesarean sections than with spontaneous births. The more difficult the birth, the greater the chance of damage and the more severe the damage. Small women show a relatively high stillbirth rate as compared with larger women, often because instruments must be used to aid in delivery. Motor disabilities, paralysis, cerebral palsy, and mental deficiency are frequently reported as aftermaths of difficult births, especially when instruments have had to be used (32, 66).

Babies born by caesarean section are the quietest, crying less than those born spontaneously or with the aid of instruments and showing greater lethargy and decreased reactivity. As a result, they normally make better adjustments to their postnatal environment unless they have had difficulty establishing respiration, which may cause temporary or permanent brain damage. Neonatal deaths are more frequent among those born by caesarean section than among those born spontaneously or with the aid of instruments (8, 32).

Factors Associated with Birth Regardless of the kind of birth, two factors have a major effect on postnatal adjustment: the extent to which the mother is medicated and the ease with which respiration is established.

Infants whose mothers are heavily medicated during labor show drowsiness and disorganized behavior for three or more days after birth, as compared with one or two days for those whose mothers are lightly medicated or receive no medication at all. Furthermore, infants whose mothers are heavily medicated lose more weight and take longer to regain their lost weight than infants whose mothers have less medication (18, 53).

The ease or difficulty with which the infant starts to breathe after birth affects his postnatal adjustment. When there is interruption of the oxygen supply to the brain before or during birth—*anoxia*—the infant may die. Even those infants who do not die may be temporarily or permanently brain-damaged, although this may not be apparent for months or even years after birth.

Box 3-4. KINDS OF BIRTH

Natural, or Spontaneous, Birth
In a natural birth, the position of the fetus and its size in relation to the mother's reproductive organs allow it to emerge in the normal, headfirst position.

Breech Birth
In a breech birth, the buttocks appear first, followed by the legs and finally the head.

Transverse Birth
In a transverse presentation, the fetus is positioned crosswise in the mother's uterus. Instruments must be used for delivery unless the position can be changed before the birth process begins.

Instrument Birth
When the fetus is too large to emerge spontaneously or when its position makes normal birth impossible, instruments must be used to aid in delivery.

Caesarean Section
If x-rays taken during the latter part of pregnancy indicate that complications will result if the infant emerges through the birth canal, he is brought into the world through a slit made surgically in the mother's abdominal wall.

Precipitate labor—labor lasting less than two hours—is an important factor in the establishment of respiration. When this occurs, the infant is introduced to oxygen too suddenly and is not yet ready to start to breathe. How much brain damage there will be and how permanent its effects will be depend largely on how quickly the infant can establish respiration.

Length of Gestation Period

Very few infants are born exactly 280 days after conception. Those who arrive ahead of time are known as *prematures*—often referred to in hospitals as "premies"—while those who arrive late are known as *postmatures*, or *postterm babies*.

Postmaturity occurs less often than in the past because it is now possible to induce labor when x-rays show that the fetus is large enough and well-enough developed to adjust successfully to postnatal life. Induced labor is also used as a means of preventing possible birth complications and birth injuries, especially brain damage, which can result if the fetal head is allowed to grow too large. The number of prematurely born babies has increased, however. It is possible to prevent miscarriages, but medical science has not yet solved the problem of keeping an infant from arriving ahead of schedule.

A baby is considered postmature if he is born two or more weeks late, and premature if he is born two or more weeks early. However, because the length of the gestation period cannot always be estimated accurately, birth weight and size are more commonly used as criteria for determining postmaturity and prematurity. When an infant is 20 or more inches long and weighs 8 or more pounds, he is considered postmature. If he is less than 19 inches long and weighs 5 pounds 8 ounces or less, he is regarded as premature. The more he deviates from the norm for his sex and racial group on the plus side, the more postmature he is considered; the more he deviates on the minus side, the more premature he is judged to be.

Unless he is damaged at birth, the postmature infant usually adjusts more quickly and more successfully to his postnatal environment than the infant born at full term. However, because the chances of birth damage increase as postmaturity increases, the advantages that come from the speed and ease of adjustment are far outweighed by the possibilities of birth damage.

Prematurely born babies usually experience complications in adjusting to the postnatal environment, and these may have a serious effect on future adjustment. Furthermore, every difficulty that the normal, full-term infant faces in adjusting to his new environment is magnified in the case of the premature baby. This will be discussed more fully later in connection with the hazards of infancy.

Parental Attitudes

How quickly and how successfully the infant will adjust to postnatal life is greatly influenced by his parents' attitudes toward him. When parental attitudes are unfavorable, for whatever reason, they are reflected in treatment of the infant that militates against his successful adjustment to postnatal life.

By contrast, parents whose attitudes are favorable treat the infant in ways that encourage good adjustment. Parent-infant interactions are not characterized by the emotional tension and nervousness that are normally present when parental attitudes are unfavorable. A relaxed mother, for example, usually produces more milk than one who is tense and nervous, and this helps the infant adjust to a new method of taking nourishment.

Postnatal Care

The newborn infant, accustomed to a stable environment before birth in which his bodily needs were automatically met with no effort on his part, must now depend on the people in his new environment to meet these needs for him. Because of his neurophysiological immaturity, these needs will not necessarily arise at given times. Furthermore, he cannot tell those around him what he wants: all he can do is cry to let them know that he needs their attention.

In the modern hospital, the infant is placed in a nursery with other infants. Unless he has been damaged at birth or is premature, he will not have a nurse to take care of him exclusively. Instead, he must wait his turn for an overworked nurse to come to him when he cries. She will not have time to "mother" him, but will go to the next infant when he has been fed or turned around or bathed. Furthermore, different nurses tend to him at different times, and thus he must constantly adjust to different kinds of handling.

Adjusting to postnatal life is difficult enough for the infant without complicating it with inadequate attention and shifts in the type of attention given. Although the newborn infant stays in the hospital only five to six days, these are critical days in the period of adjustment to postnatal life. While most healthy, normal, full-term infants suffer no serious or lasting effects as a result of this impersonal care, there is evidence that it delays their adjustment to postnatal life (32, 77).

CHARACTERISTICS OF THE INFANT

Because some infants are born prematurely and some postmaturely, it is obvious that not all infants will show the same level of physical and mental development. The following description of the neonate, however, deals with the normal, full-term infant. Exceptions will be noted and explained.

Physical Development

Infants differ greatly in appearance and physiological functions at birth and in their early adjustments after birth.

Size At birth, the average infant weighs 7½ pounds and measures 19½ inches in length. Weight in relation to height is less at birth, on the average, in the more active fetuses than in those who have been less active during the latter part of the fetal period. Boys, on the whole, are slightly longer and heavier than girls. There are marked individual differences, however, in infants of both sexes.

Infantile Features The muscles of the newborn infant are soft, small, and uncontrolled. At the time of birth, less development has taken place in the muscles of the neck and legs than in those of the hands and arms. The bones, like the muscles, are soft and flexible because they are composed chiefly of cartilage or gristle. Because of their softness, they can readily be misshapen. The skin is soft and often blotchy. The flesh is firm and elastic.

Frequently, soft downy hair is found on the head and back, though the latter soon disappears. The eyes of white newborns are usually a bluish gray, though they gradually change to whatever their permanent color will be. Infants with dark skin have dark brown eyes but they also change, becoming darker in time. Natal teeth occur approximately once in every 2,000 births. They are the "baby" type and are usually lower central incisors.

Physical Proportions The newborn is not a miniature adult. This is illustrated in Figure 3-2. The head is approximately one-fourth of the body length; the adult head, by comparison, is approximately one-seventh of the total body length. The cranial region, the area over the eyes, is proportionally much larger than the rest of the head, while the chin is proportionally much too small. By contrast, the eyes are almost mature in size. The nose is very small and almost flat on the face, while the tiny mouth may look like a slit if the lips are narrow.

The neck is so short that it is almost invisible, and the skin covering it lies in thick folds or creases. In the trunk, the shoulders are narrow, while the abdomen is large and bulging. Proportionally, the arms and legs of the infant are much too short for his head and trunk. The hands and feet are miniature.

Physiological Functions Because of the undeveloped state of the autonomic nervous system at birth, the infant is unable to maintain homeostasis, which is one of the causes of the high mortality rate at this time.

With the birth cry, the lungs are inflated and respiration begins. The respiration rate at first ranges from forty to forty-five breathing movements per minute. By the end of the first week of life, it normally drops to approximately thirty-five per minute and is more stable·than it was at first.

Neonatal heartbeat is more rapid than that of the adult because the infant's heart is small compared with the arteries. When body movements are restricted by means of swaddling the infant's body, there is an increase in stability of the heartbeat. As a result, the infant is quieter, sleeps more, and has a lower heart rate. Even in a healthy infant, the temperature is higher and more variable than in the adult.

Reflex sucking movements occur when the infant is hungry or when the lips are touched. There is an increase in the rate of sucking and in the amount of nutrients consumed with each passing day, partly because of maturation and partly because of learning.

The hunger rhythm does not develop until several weeks after birth. The hunger demands of the newborn are therefore irregular, not only in regard to intervals between feedings but also in regard to amounts. Because the hunger contractions of the infant are more vigorous than those of the adult, the infant experiences real pain when he is hungry.

Elimination of waste products begins a few hours after birth. Many voidings occur during periods of wakefulness and when the infant is quiet, usually within an hour after feeding. Defecations likewise occur when the infant is awake and quiet, shortly after feeding.

Figure 3-2 The body proportions of the newborn infant and the adult. (After Stratz, from K. Bühler. *Mental development of the child*. New York: Harcourt, Brace, 1930. Used by permission.)

In no physiological function is lack of homeostasis more apparent than in sleep. Neonatal sleep is broken by short waking periods which occur every two or three hours, with fewer and shorter waking periods during the night than during the day. Throughout the neonatal period, there is a general increase in bodily movements during sleep as well as during the time the infant is awake.

There are marked variations in infant posture during sleep. However, the characteristic posture, when prone, is similar to that of the fetus during intrauterine life. By the end of the first month of life, this posture is generally outgrown, owing to the tonus of the baby's musculature.

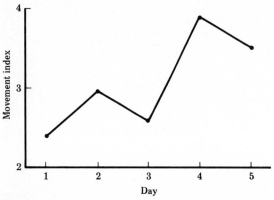

Figure 3-3 Increase in mass activity during the first five days of life. (Adapted from W. Kessen, E. J. Williams, & J. P. Williams. Selection and test of response measures in the study of the human newborn. *Child Develpm.*, 1961, **32,** 7–24. Used by permission.)

Activities of the Infant

Movements of the body appear as soon as the fetus emerges from the mother's body. Because of the neurophysiological immaturity of the infant, one could not expect his movements to be coordinated or meaningful. Nor are they related to events in his environment or under his voluntary control.

Box 3-5. CATEGORIES OF INFANT ACTIVITY

Mass Activity
Mass activity occurs throughout the entire body when any area is stimulated, though the activity is most pronounced in the stimulated area.

Specific Activities
Specific activities involve certain limited areas of the body. They include *reflexes,* which are definite responses to specific sensory stimuli and which remain unchanged with repetition of the same stimulus, and *generalized responses,* which use larger groups of muscles than are involved in reflexes and which may be aroused by either external or internal stimuli.

This is one cause of the helplessness of the newborn infant.

In spite of their random, meaningless nature, movements of the infant can be classed, roughly, into two general categories. These are explained in Box 3-5.

Mass Activity Normally, mass activity increases in intensity and frequency with each passing day. Figure 3-3 shows the increases during the first five days after birth. Mass activity also varies during the day. The greatest activity generally occurs early in the morning, when the infant is rested after a relatively long sleep, and is lowest at noon, when he is apt to be fatigued as a result of having been bathed and dressed during the morning.

The prenatal and birth experiences of the infant influence his activity after birth. Infants who have been most active as fetuses tend to be most active during the period of the newborn. A long and difficult labor or heavy medication of the mother can cause the infant to be relatively inactive for the first few days of life. Infants delivered by caesarean section have been found to be the least active of all (16, 62).

The condition of the infant's body has a marked influence on mass activity. Hunger, pain, and general discomfort give rise to great activity, while limited activity follows nursing. When clothing and covers are removed from the infant's body, activity increases. The greatest amount of activity is in the trunk and legs, and the head moves the least. The greatest amount of movement occurs when the infant is awake and crying.

Environmental conditions also influence the amount of neonatal activity. All light is disturbing and becomes increasingly so with added intensity. Sounds likewise produce an increase in the infant's activity.

Reflexes Most of the important reflexes of the body, such as the pupillary reflexes, reflexes of the lips and tongue, sucking, flexion, knee jerk, sneezing, and others, are present at birth. The first reflexes to appear have distinct survival value. The others appear within a few hours or days after birth. With practice, the reflexes become stronger.

Generalized Responses Some of the most common generalized responses which appear during the neonatal period are visual fixation on light; spontaneous eye movements; shedding of tears; feeding responses such as tongue, cheek, and lip movements; sucking of the fingers; yawning; hiccuping; rhythmic mouthing movements; frowning and wrinkling of the brow; turning and lifting the head; turning the trunk; body jerk; hand and arm movements; prancing and kicking; and leg and foot movements. All these are uncoordinated, undefined, and aimless. However, they are important because they are the basis from which skilled, highly coordinated movements will develop as a result of learning.

Vocalization of the Newborn

The vocalizations of the newborn infant can be divided into two categories: crying and explosive sounds. During infancy and the early months of babyhood, crying is the dominant form of vocalization. However, from the long-term point of view, explosive sounds are the more important kind of vocalization because speech eventually develops from them.

Crying Normally, crying begins at birth or shortly afterward. Occasionally, in a long and difficult birth, the fetus will cry even while in the uterus. Prebirth cries are rare and dangerous, for there is always the possibility that the fetus will be choked by the fluid in the uterus.

The birth cry is a purely reflex activity which results when air is drawn over the vocal cords, causing them to vibrate. Its purpose is to inflate the lungs, thus making breathing possible, and to supply the blood with sufficient oxygen.

Shortly after birth, the infant's cry shows variations in pitch, intensity, and con-

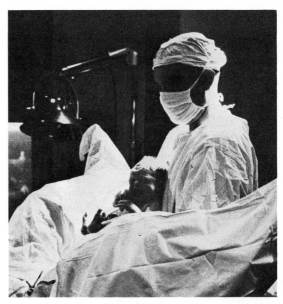

The birth cry is a purely reflex activity. (Suzanne Szasz)

tinuity. It is then possible to tell, within limits, what he wants. Ostwald has described the social value of infant crying (70):

The infant cry is the very first piece of human behavior which has social value. It indicates a shift from total silent dependency upon a single being—the pregnant woman—to the possibility of communicating with groups of people in the environment. . . . Survival of the human species hinges to a certain degree on infants properly emitting and mothers correctly perceiving the cry.

As the infant recovers from the shock of birth, he is awake more and cries more than he did at first. While crying may occur at any time, it is most frequent and most intense from 6 P.M. until midnight, as may be seen in Figure 3-4.

Mass activity almost always accompanies the infant's crying. The more vigorous the crying, the more widespread the

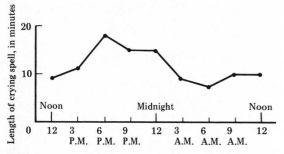

Figure 3-4 The characteristic twenty-four-hour pattern of crying during the first ten days of life. (Adapted from J. Bernal. Crying during the first 10 days of life, and maternal responses. *Develpm. Med. child Neurol.,* 1972, **14,** 362–372. Used by permission.)

activity. Bodily activity that accompanies crying is a signal that the infant needs attention. It is thus a form of language.

Explosive Sounds In addition to crying, the newborn infant occasionally makes explosive sounds similar to heavy breathing. They are uttered without meaning or intent and occur purely by chance whenever the vocal muscles contract. They are commonly called "coos," "gurgles," or "grunts." These are gradually strengthened and develop into babbling, which later develops into speech.

Sensitivities of the Newborn Infant

The best criterion that can be used to determine the presence or absence of sensory capacity is the motor response to sensory stimuli that would normally arise when these sense organs are stimulated. However, it is often difficult to tell whether a motor response is made to a stimulus or whether the reaction is a part of general mass activity.

Furthermore, absence of response does not necessarily mean absence of sensitivity. It may mean only that the stimulus used was too weak to elicit a response. Present knowledge about sensory reactions in the newborn is somewhat limited, although it is believed that infants have a greater capacity for sensory discrimination than was

---

Box 3-6. SENSORY CAPACITIES OF INFANTS

Vision
The infant's visual field is small. The muscles that control the movement of the eyes are often so undeveloped at birth that the infant cannot focus both eyes on the same object and hence sees everything as a blur.

Hearing
At birth, hearing is the least well developed of all the sensory capacities owing to the stoppage of the middle ear with amniotic fluid. Low-frequency tones can be heard sooner than those of high frequency. Hearing improves within four to seven days after birth, and the infant can then determine the direction from which a sound comes.

Smell
The sense of smell is well developed at birth, and the ability to distinguish odors is also present.

Taste
Because taste is markedly influenced by smell, it too is well developed at birth. The infant has generally positive reactions to sweet tastes and negative reactions to salty, sour, and bitter tastes.

Skin Sensitivities
The skin of the lips is especially sensitive to touch in the newborn, while the skin on the trunk, thighs, and forearms is less sensitive. The infant's sensitivity to cold is more highly developed than his sensitivity to heat. Sensitivity to pain is weak for the first day or two and then improves rapidly. Pain responses develop earlier in the anterior than in the posterior end of the body.

Organic Sensitivities
Sensitivity to hunger is fully developed at birth, and hunger contractions occur every ten or fifteen minutes.

formerly thought. There are, of course, marked variations in the sensory abilities of infants, just as there are in other areas of their development. What is known about the sensory capacities of newborn infants is summarized in Box 3-6.

State of Consciousness

Because of the relatively undeveloped state of the most important sense organs, the eyes and the ears, one could not logically expect the newborn infant to be keenly aware of what goes on around him. His awareness is more likely to be "one great, blooming, buzzing confusion," as James has said (44).

As was pointed out earlier in the chapter, *all* infants experience some disorganization for the first day or two after birth. This would suggest that they are not entirely conscious of what goes on around them. Gradually, as the shock of birth wears off and their sense organs begin to function better, they become more conscious of their surroundings.

The consciousness of the infant is markedly influenced by the depressant effects of drugs used during labor, and these effects persist longer than in adults. Prematurely born infants take longer to adjust to the ordeal of birth than full-term infants whose birth has been difficult. Consequently, it takes them even longer to become conscious of what goes on around them.

Capacity for Learning

To learn, the individual must be aware of what he is expected to do. Furthermore, the brain and nerves must be developed enough to make learning possible. These conditions do not exist in newborn infants, especially during the first few days of postnatal life. Newborn infants are often incapable of even the simplest form of learning—conditioning or learning by association. With the possible exception of the feeding situation, conditioned responses are

difficult to elicit. When they do appear, they are unstable and of little permanent value.

Emotions of the Newborn

In view of the incoordination that characterizes the activities of the newborn infant, it would be illogical to expect specific, identifiable emotions to be present at birth.

The outstanding characteristic of the infant's emotional makeup is the complete absence of gradations of responses showing different degrees of intensity. Whatever the stimulus, the resultant emotion is intense and sudden.

Beginnings of Personality

Children are born with characteristic temperamental differences that are reflected in activity rates and sensitivities. It is these differences from which the individual's personality pattern will develop. Individual differences are apparent at birth and are shown in responses to food, in crying, and in motor activities.

Personality, like other physical and mental traits, results from the maturation of hereditary traits. Thomas et al. have commented on the importance of the interrelationship between maturation of hereditary traits and experiences in the development of personality thus: "If the two influences are harmonized, one can expect healthy development of the child; if they are dissonant, behavioral problems are almost sure to ensue" (101).

As early as the neonatal period, a number of factors influence the infant's developing personality. A disturbed prenatal environment, which can result if the mother is subjected to severe or prolonged stress, for example, may cause a modification of the newborn infant's behavior pattern. Such disturbances are especially important if they occur during the latter part of intrauterine life and may cause a state of hyperactivity and irritability in the newborn (20, 95).

There is little evidence that the *birth trauma*, or psychological shock that results when the infant is separated from the mother, has any lasting effects on his personality, as Rank claimed (75). There is evidence, however, that infants who are separated from their mothers after birth do not make as good an adjustment to postnatal life as infants who remain with their mothers (107).

There is also evidence that the mother's attitude toward the infant, which is reflected in her behavior, influences the development of his personality. For example, if the mother suspects that something may be wrong with the baby, her reaction to him may be confused and unstable, shifting from day to day or even from hour to hour.

HAZARDS OF INFANCY

In spite of its short duration, infancy is one of the most hazardous periods in the life span. Hazards at this time may be physical, psychological, or both, and they can affect both present and future adjustment. In the case of the plateau in development, discussed earlier, the physical adjustments may take place too slowly, thus threatening the infant's life. Psychologically, this plateau is hazardous because it may cause parents to become anxious and fearful about the infant's development, feelings that can persist and lead to overprotectiveness in later years.

Physical Hazards

Some of the physical hazards of infancy are of only temporary significance, while others can affect the individual's entire life pattern. The most important physical hazards of infancy are those relating to an unfavorable prenatal environment, a difficult and complicated birth, a multiple birth, postmaturity and prematurity, the time of birth, and conditions leading to infant mortality.

Unfavorable Prenatal Environment As a result of unfavorable conditions in the prenatal environment, discussed in the preceding chapter, the infant may have difficulty adjusting to postnatal life. Excessive smoking on the part of the mother, for example, can affect the development of the fetus. Prolonged and intense maternal stress is another important factor, causing the infant to be tense and nervous and experience difficulty adjusting to the postnatal environment (88, 95).

Difficult and Complicated Birth As was stressed earlier, a difficult birth or one requiring surgery or the aid of instruments frequently results in temporary or permanent brain damage. Severe and persistent brain damage will have an adverse effect on all adjustments during infancy and childhood, resulting in uncoordinated behavior, hyperactivity, learning difficulties, or emotional problems (79, 91).

Multiple Birth Children of multiple birth are usually smaller and weaker than singletons as a result of crowding during the prenatal period, which inhibits fetal movements. Furthermore, these babies tend to be born prematurely, which adds to their adjustment problems.

Postmaturity Postmaturity is hazardous only when the fetus becomes so large that the birth requires the use of instruments or surgery, in which case the hazards are due to the conditions associated with birth rather than to postmaturity per se. One study of babies born more than three weeks after term reported that they experienced neonatal adjustment problems and were also socially maladjusted and required special schooling by the age of seven (95).

Prematurity Prematurity causes more neonatal deaths than any other condition. This will be discussed in more detail in the section on infant mortality. Prematurely born infants are also especially susceptible to brain damage at birth because the skull is not yet developed enough to protect the brain from pressures experienced during birth. Anoxia is another common problem since the premature baby's respiratory mechanism is not fully developed.

The problems of adjustment that a normal newborn infant must face are exaggerated in the case of a premature baby. For example, he requires nearly three times as much oxygen as a full-term infant because his breathing is characterized by jerks and gasps. He often has difficulty expanding his lungs, and muscular weakness makes breathing hard.

Because his sucking and swallowing reflexes are underdeveloped, he will require special feeding with a medicine dropper or tube. The premature infant's body temperature is not yet properly controlled, and special equipment is needed to duplicate as nearly as possible the constant temperature of intrauterine life.

Prematurity affects adjustments not only during infancy but also for many years thereafter. Some of these effects are the direct result of the fact that the brain and the nervous system have not had time to develop fully, and others are due to neurological disorders resulting from birth injuries and anoxia, which are more common among premature infants than among those born at full term. Other effects are the indirect result of unfavorable attitudes on the part of significant people in the infant's life, which will be discussed in the section dealing with psychological hazards.

While few studies of the long-term effects of prematurity have been carried beyond childhood, there is evidence that some of the lag in development experienced by children who were born prematurely is due to protectiveness on the part of parents. Whether this developmental lag persists as the children grow older and parental overprotection is relaxed is still unknown. However, if there has been brain damage, it is

---

Box 3-7. LONG-TERM EFFECTS OF PREMATURITY

Physical Development
Prematures are smaller than those born at full term, even after the growth spurt of puberty. They are more prone to illness, and to more serious illness, and they often have more physical defects, especially eye defects.

Developmental Status
Prematures are slow to sit, stand, and walk.

Motor Control
Prematures are frequently awkward and have poor posture. Cerebral palsy is also common, a result of brain damage.

Speech Development
Speech is slower to develop in prematures than in those born at full term. Baby talk persists longer, and they have more speech defects, especially stuttering. They also tend to have smaller vocabularies and to make more mistakes in sentence structure.

Intelligence
Prematures as a group have lower IQs than those born at full term, and they have more serious mental defects due to brain injury. Their scores on reading and arithmetic tests tend to be lower, and their grade placement is below that which would be normal for their age.

Socialization
Prematures make poorer social adjustments than those born at full term. This persists into adolescence and may be due in part to parental overprotectiveness. They also have more behavior problems at all ages.

Emotional Behavior
Some prematures tend to be emotionally apathetic, but more often they are petulant, irascible, and negativistic. Emotional disorders are common, as are nervous traits, such as irritability, temper outbursts, and thumb-sucking.

likely that such children continue to lag behind their age-mates as they grow older.

The long-term effects of prematurity are given in Box 3-7.

Time of Birth There is little scientific evidence to substantiate the many traditional beliefs about the significance of time of birth. However, the mother's health plays an extremely important role during the prenatal period, and unfavorable conditions during these months can affect her physical condition and thus prove hazardous to her unborn child.

The infant who is conceived during the winter months, for example, reaches the critical time in his development—the first trimester of the prenatal period—when

Attitudes of parents and siblings toward the infant usually persist as the child grows older. So it is important that the attitudes of "significant persons" be favorable. (Suzanne Szasz)

childhood diseases are most prevalent, rubella, for example, which the mother may contract.

A baby who is born within a year after the birth of a sibling is subject to a less favorable prenatal environment than would have been the case had the interval between births been longer. The mother has not had time to recover fully from the previous birth, and such an infant tends to be lethargic at birth which affects his postnatal adjustments. Throughout the early years of life he is likely to receive less attention and less stimulation than he needs for good development because of the other demands on his mother's time (48, 103).

Infant Mortality The most critical time in terms of the infant's survival is the day of birth, when approximately one-third of all neonatal deaths occur; the second and third days are the next most critical period.

The causes of infant mortality are numerous and varied. Some neonatal deaths are due to conditions that detrimentally affected the prenatal environment and thus impaired normal development. Some are the result of difficult and complicated births, such as those requiring the use of instruments or caesarean section. Some are the result of brain damage, anoxia, or excessive medication of the mother during labor. And some—but fewer than in the past—are due to unfavorable conditions in the postnatal environment; a radical temperature change may cause pneumonia, for example, or a substitute for the mother's milk may cause diarrhea or other digestive disturbances.

Psychological Hazards

Even though psychological hazards tend to have less effect on the infant's adjustment to postnatal life than physical hazards, they are nonetheless important because of their long-term effects. Psychological scars acquired during infancy can cause the individual lifelong adjustment problems.

Two of the many potential psychological

hazards of infancy have received special attention in scientific research: unfavorable attitudes toward the infant on the part of the significant people in his life and the name or nickname given to him at birth.

Unfavorable Attitudes on the Part of Significant People Even though parents, siblings, and grandparents may have favorable attitudes toward the unborn baby during most of the pregnancy, their feelings may change as the birth draws nearer and they become increasingly aware of the new responsibilities they will soon have to face.

The mother's attitudes are especially important because they may directly affect the care the baby receives when he comes home from the hospital. Attitudes of the father, siblings, grandparents, and other relatives are important because they are likely to persist after the period of infancy, when their contacts with the child will increase.

There are a number of reasons for the development of unfavorable attitudes toward infants; the most common ones are given in Box 3-8. Although it is primarily parents who develop unfavorable attitudes, other significant people in the infant's life may react negatively to him because of his appearance and behavior or because of the extra demands he makes on the mother's time. The other family members may resent her preoccupation with the infant and her changed behavior toward them.

While any newborn infant may be regarded unfavorably by the significant people in his life, the most usual targets for such attitudes are firstborns, those who are damaged at birth, those who are born prematurely, and those of multiple birth. Parents of later-born children are more realistic in their hopes and expectations than parents of firstborns, and they accept the infant more philosophically. In the case of

---

Box 3-8. SOME CAUSES OF UNFAVORABLE ATTITUDES TOWARD THE INFANT

Appearance
Even a normal, full-term infant is anything but a thing of beauty at first, and thus, in terms of looks at least, he may be a disappointment to parents, siblings, and other relatives.

Behavior
Excessive crying, wakefulness, and difficulties in nursing cause many parents to become worried and anxious.

Sex
Parents who strongly desired a child of one sex are likely to be bitterly disappointed when it turns out to be of the other sex.

Birth Experience
If a difficult birth means that the mother can have no more children, the parents may either resent the infant or be overprotective of him.

Helplessness
Parents, especially those of firstborns, are often frightened by the infant's extreme helplessness and feel inadequate to assume its care after the hospital stay.

Multiple Births
Parents may feel that a multiple birth will overtax them, both physically and financially. If the babies are born prematurely, as is usually the case, these feelings are intensified.

"New-Parent Blues"
New-parent blues—feelings of depression and anxiety—affect most parents shortly after the infant's birth. In the mother, these feelings are partly physiological and partly psychological in origin. She may suffer from fatigue or feel inadequate to meet the challenges of motherhood. The father, while not physically affected, may worry about the extra financial burden and the fact that he will have to share his wife's time and attention with the baby.

prematures and those of multiple birth, traditional beliefs are apt to affect attitudes unfavorably.

Unfavorable parental attitudes affect the infant more than unfavorable attitudes on the part of other significant people, although, as was pointed out earlier, their attitudes may persist and affect their treatment of the child as he grows older. Unfavorable attitudes on the part of the mother have the greatest impact on the infant because she has the closest contact with him. Only in emergencies, when the father must assume the care of the infant, are his attitudes likely to affect him directly or even indirectly, unless they affect the mother's attitudes.

Studies of the effects of unfavorable maternal attitudes have emphasized how markedly they affect the infant's adjustments to postnatal life. When the mother is tense, nervous, or rejectant, this is quickly reflected in her treatment of the infant. Should she become worried about whether the infant is normal or if she feels she may be responsible for what she regards as abnormal behavior on his part, the mother-infant relationship will be adversely affected, thus further complicating the infant's adjustments (17, 80).

Unfavorable maternal attitudes are often reinforced by the infant's disturbing behavior—some of which, in turn, is the result of the unfavorable maternal attitudes. As Moss has pointed out, "The amount of time the infant is awake and crying is a potent modifier of maternal treatment since wakefulness and crying are likely to lead to greater maternal surveillance and contact" (67). Thus the infant's behavior influences the mother's behavior; if this is unfavorable to begin with, it will become increasingly so, with the result that the infant's adjustment problems are worsened.

Names Names are only potential psychological hazards during infancy. They do not become real hazards until the child is old enough to understand how others outside the home react to his name, usually during the preschool years. Of course, a child's name is a psychological hazard only if it causes him embarrassment or humiliation—if his friends think his name is funny, for example, or if he has a sex-inappropriate name.

However, because the child's name is legally established shortly after birth, it can be classified as one of the important potential psychological hazards of infancy. Although it is possible to change a child's name legally, this usually meets with strong opposition from family members. Hartman et al. have emphasized the potential hazard of a name (41):

A child's name, like his somatotype, is generally a settled affair when his first breath is drawn, and his future personality must then grow within its shadow. A powerful mesomorphic boy must experience a different world from his puny counterpart; and, similarly, a boy who answers to a unique, peculiar, or feminine name may well have experiences and feelings in growing up that are quite unknown to John or William. We would expect these childhood experiences to be reflected in the subsequent personality. It is plausible, and confirmed by clinic experience, to assume also that some individuals are seriously affected in their adjustment as a result of a peculiar name.

While it is impossible to predict during infancy how the individual will react to his name as he grows older, certain kinds of names are almost universally hazardous in our culture. The most common of these are listed in Box 3-9.

Because of the potential psychological damage that the infant's name can cause, Allen et al. were correct in saying that "an unfortunate selection may doom him to recurring embarrassment or even unhappiness" (2). As McDavid and Harari have warned, a "parent might appropriately think twice before naming his offspring for Great Aunt Sophronia" (60).

Box 3-9. **NAMES THAT ARE POTENTIAL PSY-CHOLOGICAL HAZARDS**

Names that are so common that the individual feels he lacks personal identity

Names that are so unusual that the individual feels he is conspicuous

Names that are used for both sexes and thus are sex-inappropriate

Names that are associated with comic-strip characters or unpopular characters in television series, for example

Names that identify the individual with a racial, religious, or ethnic group against which there is prejudice

Names that are difficult to pronounce or spell

Names that lend themselves to embarrassing nicknames

Old-fashioned names

Chapter Highlights

1   Infancy is subdivided into two periods: the period of the partunate (birth to fifteen to thirty minutes after birth) and the period of the neonate (from the cutting of the umbilical cord to the end of the second week).

2   There are many traditional beliefs about infancy. While it is a time of radical adjustments, a plateau in development may occur. Infancy is also a preview of development that will take place later, and it is a time of physical and psychological hazards.

3   The major adjustments the infant must make are to temperature changes, breathing, sucking, swallowing, and elimination.

4   How well the infant makes these difficult adjustments is influenced by many factors, the most important of which are his prenatal environment, the kind of birth he experienced and the ease or difficulty of his birth, the length of the gestation period, parental attitudes toward him, and the postnatal care he receives.

5   In addition to his small size, infantile features, and top-heavy proportions, the homeostasis of the newborn is poor as a result of the undeveloped state of the autonomic nervous system.

6   The infant's activities are of two types: mass activity, which involves the whole body, and specific activities (such as reflexes and generalized responses), which involve certain limited areas of the body.

7   Vocalization of the newborn infant consists of crying and explosive sounds; both are forms of communication, but only the latter is the forerunner of speech.

8   Because the infant's sensitivities are unevenly developed at birth, with vision and hearing the least well developed, he is not entirely conscious of what goes on around him.

9   Emotional states at birth are general rather than specific because of the uncoordinated state of the infant's activity and his limited capacity for learning.

10   Temperamental differences at birth are the foundation for later personality development.

11   The major physical hazards of infancy are the aftereffects of an unfavorable prenatal environment, a difficult and complicated birth, prematurity or postmaturity, and conditions leading to infant mortality.

12   The major psychological hazards of infancy are unfavorable attitudes toward the infant on the part of people who are significant to him and the potentially harmful effect of the name given to him at birth.

Bibliography

1   Albott, W. L., & Bruning, J. L. Given names: A neglected social variable. *Psychol. Rec.*, 1970, **20**, 527–533.

2   Allen, L., Brow, L., Dickinson, L., & Pratt, K. C. The relation of first name preferences to the frequency in the culture. *J. soc. Psychol.*, 1941, **14**, 279–293.

3   Allport, G. W. *Pattern and growth in personality.* New York: Holt, 1961.

4   Altus, W. D. Birth order and its sequelae. *Science,* 1966, **151**, 44–49.

5   Ashton, R. Behavioral sleep cycles in the human newborn. *Child Develpm.,* 1971, **42**, 2098–2100.

6   Ashton, R. The state variable in neonatal research: A review. *Merrill-Palmer Quart.,* 1973, **19**, 3–20.

7   Bailar, J., & Gurian, J. The medical significance of date of birth. *Eugen. Quart.,* 1967, **14**, 89–102.

8   Baird, D. Perinatal mortality. *Develpm. Med. child Neurol.,* 1970, **12**, 368–369.

9 Banham, K. M. Senescence and the emotions: A genetic theory. *J. genet. Psychol.,* 1951, **78,** 175–183.

10 Bauman, J. D., & Searls, D. Head shape and size of newborn infants. *Develpm. Med. child Neurol.,* 1971, **13,** 572–573.

11 Behrman, R. E. Fetal and neonatal mortality in white middle class infants. *Amer. J. Dis. Children,* 1971, **121,** 486–489.

12 Bell, R. Q., Weller, G. M., & Waldrop, M. F. Newborn and preschooler: Organization of behavior and relations between periods. *Monogr. Soc. Res. Child Develpm.,* 1971, **36**(1, 2).

13 Bernal, J. Crying during the first 10 days of life, and maternal responses. *Develpm. Med. child Neurol.,* 1972, **14,** 362–372.

14 Boshier, R. Attitudes toward self and one's proper names. *J. indiv. Psychol.,* 1968, **24,** 63–66.

15 Bowes, W. A., Brackbill, Y., Conway, E., & Steinschneider, A. The effects of obstetrical medication on fetus and infant. *Monogr. Soc. Res. Child Develpm.,* 1970, **35**(4)

16 Brazelton, T. B. Psychophysiologic reactions in the neonate. II. Effect of maternal medication on the neonate and his behavior. *J. Pediat.,* 1961, **58,** 513–518.

17 Brody, J. E. New mothers get advice on "blues." *The New York Times,* Feb. 25, 1968.

18 Brody, J. E. Risk for baby and mother seen in the use of anesthesia at birth. *The New York Times,* Apr. 17, 1970.

19 Broussard, E. R., & Hartner, M. S. S. Maternal perception of the neonate as related to development. *Child Psychiat. & Hum. Develpm.,* 1970, **1,** 16–25.

20 Caldwell, B. M. Assessment of infant personality. *Merrill-Palmer Quart.,* 1962, **8,** 71–81.

21 Caputo, C. V., & Mandell, W. Consequences of low birth weight. *Develpm. Psychol.,* 1970, **3,** 363–383.

22 Catton, W. R. What's in a name: A study of role inertia. *J. Marriage & Family,* 1969, **31,** 15–18.

23 Churchill, J. A., Willerman, L., Grisell, J., & Ayers, M. A. Effect of head position at birth on WISC verbal and performance IQ. *Psychol. Rep.,* 1968, **23,** 495–498.

24 Connolly, K., & Stratton, P. An exploration of some parameters affecting classical conditioning in the neonate. *Child Develpm.,* 1969, **40,** 431–441.

25 Coursin, D. B. Nutrition and brain development in infants. *Merrill-Palmer Quart.,* 1972, **18,** 177–202.

26 Crelin, E. L. *Anatomy of the newborn: An atlas.* Philadelphia: Lea & Febiger, 1969.

27 Davids, A., & Holden, R. H. Consistency of maternal attitudes and personality from pregnancy to eight months following childbirth. *Develpm. Psychol.,* 1970, **2,** 364–366.

28 deHirsch, K., Jansky, J. J., & Langford, W. S. Comparisons between prematurely and maturely born children at three age levels. *Amer. J. Orthopsychiat.,* 1966, **36,** 616–628.

29 Demarest, R. J., & Sciarra, J. J. *Conception, birth, contraception: A visual presentation.* New York: McGraw-Hill, 1969.

30 Drillien, C. M. Studies in mental handicap. II. Some obstetric factors of possible aetiological significance. *Arch. Dis. Childh.,* 1968, **43,** 283–294.

31 Dubignon, J., Campbell, D., Curtis, M., & Partington, M. W. The relation between laboratory measures of sucking, food intake and perinatal factors during the newborn period. *Child Develpm.,* 1969, **40,** 1107–1120.

32 Eastman, N. J., & Hellman, L. M. *Williams obstetrics.* (13th ed.) New York: Appleton Century Crofts, 1966.

33 Edwards, N. The relationship between physical condition immediately after birth and mental and motor performance at age four. *Genet. Psychol. Monogr.,* 1968, **78,** 257–289.

34 Emde, R. N., McCartney, R. D., & Harmon, R. J. Neonatal smiling in REM states. IV. Premature study. *Child Develpm.,* 1971, **42,** 1657–1661.

35 Falkner, F. Infant mortality: An urgent national problem. *Children,* 1970, **17,** 83–87.

36 Farley, F. H. Season of birth, intelligence and personality. *Brit. J. Psychol.,* 1968, **59,** 281–283.

37 Fisichelli, V. R., & Karelitz, S. The effect of stimulus intensity on induced crying activity in the neonate. *Psychonomic Sci.,* 1969, **16,** 327–328.

38 Fitzgerald, H. E., & Porges, S. W. A decade of infant conditioning and learning research. *Merrill-Palmer Quart.,* 1971, **17,** 79–117.

39 Gilliom, B. No more baby-care blues. *Parents' Mag.,* February, 1973, pp. 35–37, 86.

40 Hammond, J. Hearing and response in the newborn. *Develpm. Med. child Neurol.,* 1970, **12,** 3–5.

41 Hartman, A. A., Nicolay, R. C., & Hurley, J. Unique personal names as a social adjustment factor. *J. soc. Psychol.,* 1968, **75,** 107–110.

42 Horowitz, F. D. Infant learning and development: Retrospect and prospect. *Merrill-Palmer Quart.,* 1968, **14,** 101–120.

43 Hunt, E. Infant mortality trends and infant care. *Children,* 1970, **17,** 88–90.

44 James, W. *The principles of psychology.* New York: Holt, 1890.

45 Jeffcoate, T. N. A. Prolonged labor. *The Lancet.* Pt 2., 1961, **281,** 61–67.

46 Johnson, P. A., & Staffieri, J. R. Stereotypic affective properties of personal names and somatotypes in children. *Develpm. Psychol.,* 1971, **5,** 176.

47 Kant, I. *Critique of practical reason and other works on the theory of ethics.* (6th ed.) London: Longmans, 1963.

48 Karabenick, S. A. On the relationship between personality and birth order. *Psychol. Rep.,* 1971, **28,** 258.

49 Karelitz, S., Fisichelli, V. R., Costa, J., Karelitz, R., & Rosenfeld, L. Relation of crying activity in early infancy to speech development and intellectual development at age three years. *Child Develpm.,* 1964, **35,** 769–777.

50 Kessen, W., Haith, M. M., & Salapatek, P. M. Human infancy: A bibliography and guide. In P. H. Mussen (Ed.), *Carmichael's manual of child psychology.* (3rd ed.) Vol. 1. New York: Wiley, 1970. Pp. 287–445.

51 Korner, A. F. Individual differences at birth: Implications for early experience and later development. *Amer. J. Orthopsychiat.,* 1971, **41,** 608–619.

52 Korner, A. F., & Thoman, E. B. The relative efficacy of contact and vestibular-proprioceptive stimulation in soothing neonates. *Child Develpm.,* 1972, **43,** 443–453.

53 Kraemer, H. C., Korner, A. F., & Thoman, E. B. Methodological considerations in evaluating the influence of drugs used during labor and delivery on the behavior of the newborn. *Develpm. Psychol.,* 1972, **6,** 128–134.

54 Lamper, C., & Eisdorfer, C. Prestimulus activity level and responsivity in the neonate. *Child Develpm.*, 1971, **42**, 465–473.

55 Lewis, M. State as an infant-environment interaction: An analysis of mother-infant interaction as a function of sex. *Merrill-Palmer Quart.*, 1972, **18**, 95–121.

56 Lipsitt, L. P. Learning processes of human newborns. *Merrill-Palmer Quart.*, 1966, **12**, 45–71.

57 Martin, P. C., & Vincent, E. L. *Human development.* New York: Ronald Press, 1960.

58 Martindale, C., & Black, F. W. Season of birth and intelligence. *J. genet. Psychol.*, 1970, **117**, 137–138.

59 Matheney, A. P., & Hull, K. An apparatus for the measurement of a neonate's general activity. *Psychosom. Med.*, 1969, **31**, 437–440.

60 McDavid, J. W., & Harari, H. Stereotyping of names and popularity in grade-school children. *Child Develpm.*, 1966, **37**, 453–459.

61 McDonald, R. L. The role of emotional factors in obstetric complications: A review. *Psychosom. Med.*, 1968, **30**, 222–237.

62 McGrade, B. J. Newborn activity and emotional response at eight months. *Child Develpm.*, 1968, **39**, 1247–1252.

63 Meredith, H. V. Body height at birth of viable human infants: A worldwide comparative treatise. *Hum. Biol.*, 1970, **42**, 217–264.

64 Meyerowitz, J. H. Satisfaction during pregnancy. *J. Marriage & Family*, 1970, **32**, 38–42.

65 Miller, V. L. *The miracle of growth.* Urbana: University of Illinois Press, 1950.

66 Montagu, A. *Prenatal influences.* Springfield, Ill.: Charles C Thomas, 1962.

67 Moss, H. A. Methodological issues in studying mother-infant interaction. *Amer. J. Orthopsychiat.*, 1965, **35**, 482–486.

68 Nesmith, J. Child's name may affect performance in school. *Atlanta Journal & Constitution*, Sept. 3, 1973.

69 Orme, J. E. Ability and season of birth. *Brit. J. Psychol.*, 1965, **56**, 471–475.

70 Ostwald, P. The sounds of infancy. *Develp. Med. child Neurol.*, 1972, **14**, 350–361.

71 Page, E. W., Villee, C. A., & Villee, D. B. *Human reproduction: The core content of obstetrics, gynecology and perinatal medicine.* Philadelphia: Saunders, 1972.

72 Pasamanick, B., & Knobloch, H. Brain and behavior. 2. Brain damage and reproductive casualty. *Amer. J. Orthopsychiat.*, 1960, **30**, 298–305.

73 Peckos, P. S. Nutrition during growth and development. *Child Develpm.*, 1957, **28**, 273–285.

74 Pohlman, E. Timing of first births: A review of effects. *Eugen. Quart.*, 1968, **15**, 252–263.

75 Rank, O. *The trauma of birth.* New York: Harcourt, Brace, 1929.

76 Rebelsky, F., & Black, R. Crying in infancy. *J. genet. Psychol.*, 1972, **121**, 49–57.

77 Reid, D. E., Ryan, K. J., & Benirschke, K. (Eds.) *Principles and management of human reproduction.* Philadelphia: Saunders, 1972.

78 Richman, N. Individual differences at birth. *Develpm. Med. child Neurol.*, 1972, **14**, 400–402.

79 Rosenblith, J. F. Prognosis value of neonatal assessment. *Child Develpm.*, 1966, **37**, 623–631.

80 Ross, A. O. *The exceptional child in the family.* New York: Grune & Stratton, 1964.

81 Rovee, C. K. Psychological scaling of olfactory response to aliphatic alcohols in human neonates. *J. exp. Child Psychol.*, 1969, **7**, 245–254.

82 Ruja, H. The relation between neonate crying and the length of labor. *J. genet. Psychol.*, 1948, **73**, 53–55.

83 Ruskell, G. L. Some aspects of vision in infants. *J. Amer. Optom. Ass.*, 1969, **40**, 434.

84 Sameroff, A. J. Can conditioned responses be established in the newborn infant: 1971? *Develpm. Psychol.*, 1971, **5**, 1–12.

85 Scarr-Salapatek, S., & Williams, M. L. The effects of early stimulation on low-birth-weight infants. *Child Develpm.*, 1973, **44**, 94–101.

86 Schaefer, E. S., & Bayley, N. Consistency of maternal behavior from infancy to preadolescence. *J. abnorm. soc. Psychol.*, 1960, **61**, 1–6.

87 Scheinfeld, A. *Heredity in humans.* (Rev. ed.) Philadelphia: Lippincott, 1971.

88 Schmeck, H. M. Women smokers warned of fetal and infant risks. *The New York Times*, Jan. 18, 1973.

89 Schwartz, P. Birth injuries of the newborn. *Arch. Pediat.*, 1956, **73**, 429–450.

90 Self, P. A., Horowitz, F. D., & Paden, L. Y. Olfaction in newborn infants. *Develpm. Psychol.*, 1972, **7**, 349–363.

91 Shipe, D., Vandenberg, S., & Williams, R. D. B. Neonatal Apgar ratings as related to intelligence and behavior in preschool children. *Child Develpm.*, 1968, **39**, 861–866.

92 Simner, M. L. Newborns' response to the cry of another infant. *Develpm. Psychol.*, 1971, **5**, 136–150.

93 Siqueland, E. R. Reinforcement patterns and extinction in human newborns. *J. exp. Child Psychol.*, 1968, **6**, 431–442.

94 Smith, C. A. The first breath. *Scient. American*, 1963, **209**, 27–35.

95 Sontag, L. W. Implications of infant behavior and environment for adult personalities. *Ann. N.Y. Acad. Sci.*, 1966, **132**, 782–786.

96 Sostek, A. M., Sameroff, A. J., & Sostek, A. J. Evidence for the unconditionability of the Babkin reflex in newborns. *Child Develpm.*, 1972, **43**, 509–519.

97 Steinschneider, A. Sound intensity and respiratory responses in the neonate. *Psychosom. Med.*, 1968, **30**, 534–541.

98 Stern, E., Parmelee, A. H., Akiyama, Y., Schultz, M. A., & Wenner, W. H. Sleep cycle characteristics in infants. *Pediatrics*, 1969, **43**, 65–70.

99 Stone, F. H. Psychological aspect of mother-infant relationships. *Brit. med. J.*, 1971, **4**, 224–226.

100 Thoman, E. B., Leiderman, P. H., & Olson, J. P. Neonate-mother interaction during breast feeding. *Develpm. Psychol.*, 1972, **6**, 110–118.

101 Thomas, A., Chess, S., & Birch, H. G. The origin of personality. *Scient. American*, 1970, **223**(2), 102–109.

102 Turkewitz, G., Birch, H. G., & Cooper, K. K. Patterns of response to different auditory stimuli in the human newborn. *Develpm. Med. child Neurol.*, 1972, **14**, 487–491.

103 Waldrop, M. F., & Bell, R. Q. Effects of family size and density on newborn characteristics. *Amer. J. Orthopsychiat.*, 1966, **36**, 544–550.

104 Wickelgren, L. W. The ocular response of human new-borns to intermittent visual movement. *J. exp. Child Psychol.,* 1969, **8,** 469–482.

105 Wiener, G., Rider, R. V., Oppel, W. C., & Harper, P. A. Correlates of low birth weight: Psychological status at eight to ten years of age. *Pediat. Res.,* 1968, **2,** 110–118.

106 Wilson, R. S. Twins: Early mental development. *Science,* 1972, **175,** 915–917.

107 Yarrow, L. J. Research in dimensions of early maternal care. *Merrill-Palmer Quart.,* 1963, **9,** 101–114.

108 Zelazo, P. R., Zelazo, N. A., & Kolb, S. "Walking" in the newborn. *Science,* 1972, **176,** 314–315.

CHAPTER FOUR

BABYHOOD

Traditionally, the term *infant* has been used in medical circles to refer to a person who is incapable of speech and thus helpless. Many psychological research studies refer to the first two years of life as *infancy* and to the individual who has not yet reached his second birthday as an *infant*. Legally, a person is regarded as an infant until he reaches the age of eighteen. A minor, according to the law, is thus an infant.

In this book, however, the term *babyhood* will be used to refer to that period extending from the end of the second week after birth until the end of the second year of life. By that time, the average baby is relatively independent and can do many things for himself which formerly had to be done for him. Although many babies attain relative independence before their second birthday, the average baby is two years old before he reaches this stage in his development.

The term *baby* means an extremely young individual, but it does not carry the connotation of helplessness that *infant* does.

CHARACTERISTICS OF BABYHOOD

Certain characteristics of babyhood, while similar to characteristics of other periods, are of particular importance during these years.

Babyhood Is an Age of
Rapid Growth and Change

Babies grow rapidly, physically and psychologically. With this rapid growth comes a change not only in appearance but also in capacities. The baby gradually becomes less top-heavy than he was as an infant, and the trunk and limbs seem to be more in proportion to the large head. The random mass movements of the infant give way to more coordinated movements which make it possible for him to do things for himself which formerly he had to rely on others to do for him. Perhaps in no area is change more apparent than in the baby's ability to recognize and respond to people and objects in his environment.

Babyhood Is an Age of
Decreasing Dependency

The decrease in dependency on others results from the rapid development of body control, which enables the baby to sit, stand, walk, and manipulate objects at will. Independence also increases as the baby becomes better able to communicate his needs and wishes to others in forms they can understand. Perhaps the most significant thing about increased independence is that it permits the baby to develop along lines suited to his interests and abilities. As a result, the individuality apparent at birth increases as he grows older.

Babyhood Is the Foundation Age

Babyhood is the true foundation period of life because, at this time, the foundations of many behavior patterns, many attitudes toward others and toward the self, and many patterns of emotional expression are being established. While these foundations are not so firmly established at the end of babyhood that they cannot be changed should they prove inefficient or socially unacceptable, they are nevertheless firmly enough established so that change entails relearning, with its accompaniment of emotional tension and confusion.

Babyhood Is a Hazardous Age

Certain hazards are more common during babyhood than at other ages. Among the physical hazards, illnesses and accidents are the most serious. Because behavior patterns, interests, and attitudes are established during babyhood, serious psychological hazards can result if poor foundations are laid at this time.

Babyhood Is an Appealing Age

Adults as well as older children find the small baby appealing because of his helplessness and dependency. Furthermore, he is easy to manage, and this adds to his appeal. Gradually, as his dependency is replaced by the ability to do things for himself, the baby becomes less easy to manage and more resistant to adult help, qualities which make him less appealing than he was earlier.

DEVELOPMENTAL TASKS
OF BABYHOOD

All babies are expected to learn to walk, to take solid foods, to have their organs of elimination under partial control, to achieve reasonable physiological stability (especially in hunger rhythm and sleep), to learn the foundations of speech, and to relate emotionally to their parents and siblings to some extent instead of being completely self-bound, as they were at birth (41). Most of these developmental tasks will not, of course, be completely mastered when babyhood draws to a close, but the foundations for them should be laid.

When babyhood ends, for example, all normal babies have learned to walk, though with varying degrees of proficiency. They have also learned to take solid foods and have achieved a reasonable degree of physiological stability. The major tasks involving the elimination of body wastes are well under control and will be completely mastered within another year or two.

While most babies have built up a useful vocabulary, can pronounce the words they use reasonably correctly, can comprehend the meaning of simple statements and commands, and can put together several words into meaningful sentences, their ability to communicate with others and to comprehend what others say to them is still on a low level. Much remains to be mastered before they enter school.

The rapid development of the nervous system, the ossification of the bones, and the strengthening of the muscles make it possible for the baby to master the developmental tasks of babyhood. However, his success in this regard depends to a large extent upon the opportunities he is given to master them and the help and guidance he receives.

PHYSICAL DEVELOPMENT

Babyhood is one of the two periods of rapid growth during the life span; the other comes at puberty. During the first six months of life, growth continues at the rapid rate characteristic of the prenatal period and then begins to slow down. In the second year, the rate of growth decelerates rapidly. During the first year of life, the increase in weight is proportionally greater than the increase in height; during the second year, the reverse is true.

The pattern of physical growth in babyhood is much the same for boys and girls. However, within the sex groups, there are marked variations. Throughout the first year of life, there is no difference in height and weight between black babies and white babies from comparable economic levels. Differences begin to appear in the second year, however, because the black child is typically of a more slender build than the white child (59).

Variations continue throughout the ba-

byhood years, with variations in weight always greater than variations in height. Variations in weight are dependent partly on body build and partly on the baby's eating habits. In spite of variations, it is possible to get a general picture of the pattern of growth during the babyhood years. The highlights of this picture are given in Box 4-1.

PHYSIOLOGICAL FUNCTIONS

Babyhood is the time when the fundamental physiological patterns of eating, sleeping, and elimination should be established, even though the habit formation may not be completed when babyhood ends.

Sleep Patterns During the first year of babyhood, the mean duration of night sleep increases from 8½ hours at three weeks to 10 hours at twelve weeks and then remains constant during the rest of that year. During the first three months, the decline in day sleep is balanced by an increase in night sleep. Throughout the first year, wakefulness-sleep cycles of approximately one hour in length occur in both day and night sleep, with deep sleep lasting only about twenty-three minutes (89).

Eating Patterns From birth until four or five months of age, all eating is in the infantile form of sucking and swallowing. Food, as a result, must be in a liquid form. Chewing generally appears in the developmental pattern a month later than biting. But, like biting, it is in an infantile form and requires much practice before it becomes serviceable.

Food dislikes, which begin to develop during the second year, are frequently the result of the prolongation of infantile eating patterns. After becoming accustomed to food in liquid form, it is difficult for the baby to adjust to it in a semisolid form. This adds to the baby's revolt against his food, even though he may like its taste.

Box 4-1. PATTERNS OF PHYSICAL DEVELOPMENT DURING BABYHOOD

Weight
At the age of four months, the baby's weight has normally doubled; at one year, he weighs three times as much as he did at birth, or approximately 21 pounds. At age two, the typical American baby weighs 25 pounds. Weight increases in babyhood come mainly from an increase in fat tissue.

Height
At four months, the baby measures between 23 and 24 inches; at one year, between 28 and 30 inches; and at two years, between 32 and 34 inches.

Physical Proportions
Head growth slows down in babyhood, while trunk and limb growth increases. Thus the baby gradually becomes less top-heavy and appears more slender and less chunky by the end of babyhood. See Figure 4-1.

Bones
The number of bones increases during babyhood. Ossification begins in the early part of the first year, but is not completed until puberty. The fontanel, or soft spot on the skull, has closed in approximately 50 percent of all babies by the age of eighteen months, and in almost all babies by the age of two years.

Teeth
The average baby has four to six of his twenty temporary teeth by the age of one, sixteen by the age of two. The first teeth to cut through are those in the front, the last to appear are the molars.

Nervous System
Growth in the nervous system consists primarily of the development of immature cells present at birth, rather than the formation of new cells. Approximately one-fourth of the adult brain weight is attained at birth.

Sense-Organ Development
By the age of three months, the baby's eye muscles are well-enough coordinated to enable him to see things clearly and distinctly; he can also distinguish colors. Hearing, smell, and taste are well developed at birth. The baby is highly responsive to all skin stimuli because of the thin texture of his skin and because all sense organs relating to touch, pressure, pain, and temperature are present.

Figure 4-1 How physical proportions change as the person grows older: The same boy at six different ages. (Adapted from N. Bayley. Individual patterns of development. *Child Develpm.,* 1956, **27,** 45–74. Used by permission.)

    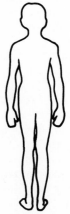 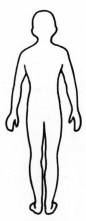

15 months 30 months 6 years 11 years 14 years 18 years

Patterns of Elimination Bowel control begins, on the average, at six months, and bladder control begins between the ages of fifteen and sixteen months. In the case of the former, habits of control are established by the end of babyhood, though temporary lapses may be expected when the baby is tired, ill, or emotionally excited. Bladder control, on the other hand, is in a rudimentary state at the close of babyhood. Dryness during the daytime can be expected for a major part of the time except when deviations from the scheduled routine of the day, illness, fatigue, or emotional tension interfere. Dryness at night cannot be achieved in the average child until several years later.

MUSCLE CONTROL

Development of control over the muscles follows a definite and predictable pattern governed by the *laws of developmental direction.* See Figure 1-2. According to these laws, muscle control sweeps over the body from head to foot and from trunk to extremities. This means that the muscles in the head region come under voluntary control first, and those in the leg region last.

At first, the baby's body is in more or less constant motion similar to the mass activity of the newborn infant. This is true even during sleep. Gradually this random, meaningless motility becomes more coordinated.

Box 4-2. PATTERN OF MOTOR CONTROL

Head Region

Eye Control
Optic nystagmus, or the response of the eyes to a succession of moving objects, begins about twelve hours after birth; ocular pursuit movements, between the third and fourth weeks; horizontal eye movements, between the second and third months; vertical eye movements, between the third and fourth months; and circular eye movements, several months later.

Smiling
Reflex smiling, or smiling in response to a tactual stimulus, appears during the first week of life; social smiling, or smiling in response to the smile of another person, begins between the third and fourth months.

Head holding
In a prone position, the baby can hold his head erect at one month; when lying on his back, at five months; and when held in a sitting position, between four and six months.

Trunk Region

Rolling
The baby can roll from side to back at two months and from back to side at four months; at six months he can roll over completely.

Sitting
The baby can pull to a sitting position at four months, sit with support at five months, and sit without support momentarily at seven months and for ten or more minutes at nine months.

Arm and Hand Region

Hands
Thumb opposition—the working of the thumb in opposition to the fingers—appears in grasping between three and four months and in picking up objects between eight and ten months.

Arms
The baby can reach for objects by six or seven months and can pick up a small object without random movements by one year.

Leg Region
Shifting of the body by kicking occurs by the end of the second week. Hitching, or moving in a sitting position, appears by six months. Crawling and creeping appear between eight and ten months, and at eleven months the baby walks on "all fours." The baby can pull himself to a standing position at about ten months, stand with support at eleven months, stand without support at one year, walk with support at eleven months or one year, and walk without support at fourteen months.

Maturation and learning work together in the development of muscle control. As a result of maturation of the muscles, bones, and nerve structures and because of a change in body proportions, the baby becomes able to use his body in a coordinated manner. He must, however, be given an opportunity to learn how to do this. Until this state of readiness is present, teaching will be of little or no value.

The approximate ages at which muscle control appears in the different areas of the body and the usual pattern of development are given in Box 4-2. There are, of course, individual differences in these ages and, to a lesser extent, in the pattern of development.

There is evidence that the age at which the baby starts to walk is consistent with the rate of his total development. Babies who sit early, for example, walk earlier than babies who start to sit later. It is possible to predict with a fair degree of accuracy when a baby will start to walk if one knows what the rate of his development in other motor coordinations is. A fairly accurate way to predict the age at which he will start to walk alone is to multiply the age at which he begins to creep by 1½ or the age at which he sits alone by 2 (14).

Babyhood Skills

The baby develops skills—fine coordinations in which the smaller muscles play a major role—from the foundations laid during maturation. Given an opportunity for practice, an incentive to learn, and a good model to copy, the baby will acquire many skills that will be useful to him in his daily activities. None of these skills will, of course, be perfected in the relatively short span of babyhood.

The skills a baby can be expected to learn can be divided into two major categories—hand skills and leg skills. Box 4-3 lists the common hand and leg skills of baby-

---

Box 4-3. SOME COMMON SKILLS OF BABYHOOD

Hand Skills

Self-feeding
At eight months the baby can hold his bottle after it has been placed in his mouth; at nine months he can put it in and take it out without help. At twelve months he can drink from a cup when he holds it with both hands; several months later he can drink using one hand. At thirteen months he begins to feed himself with a spoon, and a month or two later he spears food with a fork and carries it to his mouth with much spilling. By his second birthday he can use a spoon and fork without too much spilling.

Self-dressing
At the end of the first year most babies can pull off their socks, shoes, caps, and mittens. By the middle of the second year the baby attempts to put on his cap and mittens, and by the end of babyhood he can pull off all his clothes and put on a shirt or dress.

Self-grooming
Self-bathing is limited mainly to running a cloth or sponge over the face and body. Before they are two, most babies try to brush their hair and teeth.

Play Skills
At twelve months the baby can scribble with a pencil or crayon, and several months later he can throw or roll a ball, open a box, unscrew a lid from a bottle, turn the leaves of a book, build with a few blocks, insert pegs in a pegboard, string large beads, and cut a gash in paper with scissors.

Leg Skills
The baby learns to jump and also to climb stairs, which he does first by crawling and creeping. After he can walk alone, he goes up and down steps in an upright position, placing one foot on a step and then drawing the other up to it. Very few babies are able to ride a tricycle, and then only when they are held on the seat. They swim by slashing the arms and kicking the legs.

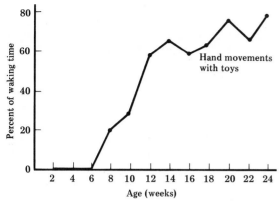

Figure 4-2 There is a rapid increase in the use of the hands during the early weeks of babyhood. (Adapted from J. Dittrichova & V. Lápačková. Development of the waking state in the young child. *Child Develpm.*, 1964, **35**, 365–370. Used by permission.)

Step climbing is one of the important skills developed in babyhood. (Suzanne Szasz)

hood and the ages at which they are usually acquired.

Because there is a rapid increase in the use of the hands during the early weeks of life, as shown in Figure 4-2, hand coordinations develop rapidly. As each new hand skill develops, it absorbs the baby's interest and activity, and he devotes much of his waking time to the use of his hands. This further increases his control over them. By contrast, because the major part of babyhood is devoted to developing the ability to walk, leg skills are in only a rudimentary state of development by the end of this period. The few leg skills acquired during babyhood are learned mainly during the last part of the second year.

Learning to use one hand in preference to the other—*handedness*—is an important aspect of the development of hand skills during babyhood. During the early months of life, a baby is ambidextrous, with no preference for either hand. By the time they are eight months old, babies who are above average in mental and motor development show a greater degree of hand preference than those who are less well advanced, and this preference is usually for the right hand. However, most babies shift from the use of one hand to the other, depending largely on the position of the person or object they want to reach. If the object is closer to the right hand, that is the hand the baby will use.

Shifting likewise occurs during the second year but not as frequently as during the first. Thus, during babyhood, the individual is neither dominantly left- nor dominantly right-handed, though he shows, especially in the second year, a tendency to use one hand more than the other (3, 63).

SPEECH DEVELOPMENT

Because learning to talk is a long and laborious task and because the baby is not maturationally ready for such complicated learning during the first year of life, nature provides substitute forms of communication to be used until he is ready to learn to speak. Many babies try to make known their wants and needs by these means.

If these prespeech forms of communication prove to be extremely satisfactory and effective substitutes for speech, the baby's motivation to learn to speak will be weakened. He will then continue to use infantile forms of communication even after he is capable of learning to speak.

Prespeech Forms

Three prespeech forms normally appear in the developmental pattern: crying, babbling, and gesturing. Crying is the most frequently used of the three during the early months of life, though from the long-range point of view, babbling is the most important because real speech eventually develops from it.

Crying The cries of the newborn baby gradually become differentiated, so that by the third or fourth week of life it is possible to tell what the cry signifies from its tone and intensity and from the bodily movements accompanying it. Pain, for example, is expressed by shrill, loud cries, interrupted by groaning and whimpering. Hunger cries are loud and interrupted by sucking movements. Cries from colic are accompanied by a peculiar, high-pitched scream, with alternate and forceful flexion and extension of the legs. Before he is three months old, the baby has learned that crying is a sure method of gaining attention.

Babbling As the baby's vocal mechanism develops, he becomes capable of producing a larger number of explosive sounds than he could at birth. Some of these sounds are retained and will develop into babbling or lalling. In time, some will form the basis of real speech. The number of sounds produced in babbling gradually increases. The baby can, by the time he is six months old, combine certain vowel and consonant sounds such as "ma-ma," "da-da," or "na-na." Babbling begins during the second or third month of life, reaches its peak by the eighth month, and then gradually gives way to real speech.

Gestures The baby uses gestures as a substitute for speech. Even after he is able to say a few words, the baby will continue to use gestures, combining them with the words he knows to make his first sentence. By outstretching his arms and smiling, for example, the baby readily communicates the idea that he wants to be picked up; when he pushes away his plate, at the same time saying "no," he is obviously indicating that he does not want the food that has been placed before him. No gestures are more expressive than facial gestures, and the baby uses these to communicate his emotional state to others—happiness, fear, or anger, for example.

Comprehension

At every age, a child comprehends the meaning of what others say more readily than he can put his own thoughts and feelings into words. This is true of babyhood also. The facial expression, tone of voice, and gestures of the speaker help him to understand the meaning of what is being said. Pleasure, anger, and fear can be comprehended as early as the third month of life.

Until the baby is eighteen months old, words must be reinforced with gestures, such as pointing to an object, if he is to understand the meaning. By the age of two, according to the Terman-Merrill Scale of Intelligence Tests, the average baby should comprehend well enough to respond correctly to two out of six simple commands, such as "Give me the kitty" or "Put the spoon in the cup," when the objects are within easy reach (93).

Learning to Speak

Learning to speak involves the tasks of learning how to pronounce words so that they will be understandable to others, asso-

Box 4-4. TASKS INVOLVED IN LEARNING TO SPEAK

Pronunciation

The baby learns to pronounce words partly by trial and error but mainly by imitating adult speech. Consonants and consonant blends are more difficult for babies to pronounce than vowels and diphthongs. Much of the baby's speech is incomprehensible up to the age of eighteen months, after which there is gradual but marked improvement.

Vocabulary Building

The baby learns the names of people and objects first, and then verbs such as "give" and "take." Just before babyhood ends, he learns a few adjectives such as "nice" and "naughty," as well as a few adverbs. Prepositions, conjunctions, and pronouns are generally not learned until early childhood. Vocabulary increases with age. Figure 4-3 shows how words are learned.

Sentences

The baby's first "sentences," which appear between twelve and eighteen months, generally consist of one word accompanied by a gesture. Gradually more words creep into the baby's sentences, but he continues to use gestures well into childhood.

---

ciating meanings with words and thus building a vocabulary of usable words for communication, and combining these words into sentences. These tasks involve not only control over the vocal mechanism but also the ability to comprehend meanings and to associate them with words which act as symbols for meanings. These tasks are explained in Box 4-4.

EMOTIONAL BEHAVIOR IN BABYHOOD

At birth, the emotions appear in simple, almost completely undifferentiated forms. With age, however, emotional responses become less diffuse, less random, and more differentiated, and they can be aroused by a wide variety of stimuli.

There are two distinctive characteristics of babyhood emotions. First, they are accompanied by behavior responses that are proportionally too great for the stimuli that gave rise to them, especially in the case of anger and fear. They are brief in duration, though intense while they last. They appear frequently, but are transitory and give way to other emotions when the baby's attention is distracted.

Second, emotions are more easily conditioned during babyhood than at later ages. Because the baby's intellectual ability is limited, he responds easily and quickly to stimuli that have given rise to an emotional response in the past; he may be reluctant to enter a doctor's office, for example, if he had an inoculation during his last visit.

Figure 4-3 A baby learns to associate meaning with an object, and then a word becomes a symbol or label for the object. (Adapted from M. E. Breckenridge & E. L. Vincent. *Child development: Physical and psychologic development through adolescence.* (5th ed.) Philadelphia: Saunders, 1965. Used by permission.)

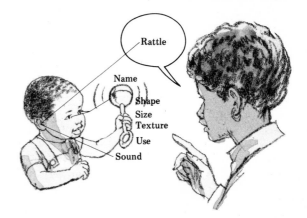

Box 4-5. COMMON EMOTIONAL PATTERNS IN BABYHOOD

Anger

The common stimuli that give rise to anger in babyhood are interference with the movements the baby wants to make, thwarting of some wish, not being able to do what he sets out to do, and not being able to make himself understood. Typically, the angry response takes the form of screaming, kicking the legs, waving the arms, and hitting or kicking anything within reach. During the second year, babies may also jump up and down, throw themselves on the floor, and hold their breath.

Fear

The stimuli most likely to arouse fear in babies are loud noises; strange persons, objects, and situations; dark rooms; high places; and animals. Any stimulus which occurs suddenly or unexpectedly or which is different from what the baby is accustomed to gives rise to fear. The typical fear response in babyhood consists of an attempt to withdraw from the frightening stimulus, accompanied by whimpering, crying, temporary holding of the breath, and checking of the activity he was engaged in when he became frightened.

Curiosity

Anything new or unusual acts as a stimulus to curiosity, unless the newness is so pronounced that it gives rise to fear. As fear wanes, it is replaced by curiosity. Young babies express curiosity mainly through their facial expressions—tensing the facial muscles, opening the mouth, and protruding the tongue. Later, the baby grasps the object that aroused his curiosity and handles, shakes, bangs, or sucks it.

Joy

Joy is stimulated at first by physical well-being. By the second or third month the baby reacts to being played with, being tickled, and watching and listening to others. He expresses this by smiling, laughing, and moving his arms and legs. When joy is intense, the baby coos, gurgles, or even shouts with glee, and all bodily movements are intensified.

Affection

Anyone who plays with the baby and takes care of his bodily needs or shows him affection will be a stimulus for the baby's affection. Later, his toys and the family pet may also become love objects. Typically he expresses his affection by hugging, patting, and kissing the loved object or person.

Box 4-5 lists the common emotional responses which develop in babyhood and the usual stimuli that give rise to them. However, as was pointed out above, since the baby's emotions are especially susceptible to conditioning, there are variations in these patterns as well as in the stimuli that evoke them. Different babies respond emotionally to different stimuli, depending to a certain extent upon their past experiences. For example, babies who are exposed to few people outside the home or who are cared for almost exclusively by members of their family are far more likely to experience a pronounced "shy age" than those who are exposed to many outsiders and who are cared for by grandparents and baby-sitters as well as parents and siblings. Figure 4-4 shows the percentage of a group of babies showing fear of strangers at different ages.

Variations in emotional responses begin to appear in babyhood and are influenced by a number of factors, mainly the baby's physical and mental condition at the time the stimulus occurs and how successful a given response formerly was in meeting his needs. If, in the past, he was punished for pulling, biting, or tearing something, he will satisfy his curiosity by a more hands-off approach, merely looking at an object and touching it.

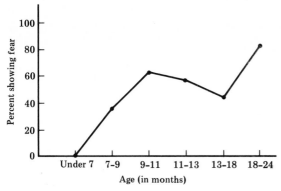

Figure 4-4 The development of the fear response: percentage of a group of babies showing fear of strangers at different ages. (Adapted from S. Scarr and P. Salapatek: Patterns of fear development during infancy. *Merrill-Palmer Quart.*, 1970, **16**, 53–90. Used by permission.)

One of the most important variations in emotional responses involves the dominance of pleasant or unpleasant emotions. Some babies experience many more pleasant than unpleasant emotions, while the reverse is true for others, depending mainly on the baby's physical condition and conditions in his environment. A baby who cries from anger or fear more often than he smiles or shows other pleasant emotions may be sickly or may live in an environment where he is neglected or treated punitively. By contrast, the baby whose dominant emotions are pleasant may be in better physical condition and live in an environment which stimulates pleasant emotions and in which he is protected from stimuli that would normally give rise to fear and anger.

DEVELOPMENTS IN SOCIALIZATION

Early social experiences play a dominant role in determining the baby's future social relationships and the pattern of his behavior toward others. And because the baby's life is centered around the home, it is here that the foundations for later social behavior and attitudes are laid. There is little evidence that a person is inherently social or antisocial. Instead, whether he becomes outer- or inner-bound—extroverted or introverted—depends mainly on his early social experiences.

Studies of the social adjustments of older children and even adolescents show the importance of the social foundations laid in babyhood. Social behavior has been found to remain consistent as children grow older; those who cried excessively during babyhood tend to become aggressive and exhibit other attention getting behavior, while friendly, happier babies become socially better adjusted.

Early social behavior follows a fairly predictable pattern, though variations can occur as a result of the baby's health or emotional state or because of conditions in his environment. At birth, the infant is nongregarious in the sense that it makes no difference to him who attends to his physical needs. In fact, a young baby can be soothed as well by a hot-water bottle or a soft pillow as by human caresses. At around the age of six weeks, a true social smile—or a smile in response to a person rather than to a tactile stimulus applied to the lips, which produces a reflex smile—appears, and this is regarded as the beginning of socialization.

The pattern of social responses to adults differs from that of social responses to other babies, and these are described separately in Box 4-6. The first social responses are to adults, while those to other babies appear slightly later.

During the first year of babyhood, the baby is in a state of equilibrium, which makes him friendly, easy to handle, and pleasant to be with. Around the middle of the second year, equilibrium gives way to disequilibrium, and the baby becomes fussy, uncooperative, and difficult to handle. Before babyhood is over, however, equilibrium

---

Box 4-6. PATTERN OF EARLY SOCIALIZATION

Social Responses to Adults

Two to three months
The baby distinguishes people from inanimate objects and discovers that people supply his needs. He is content when he is with people and discontented when left alone. At this age babies show no preferences for any one person.

Four to five months
The baby wants to be picked up by anyone who approaches him, and he reacts differently to scolding and smiling and to friendly voices and angry ones.

Six to seven months
The baby differentiates between "friends" and "strangers" by smiling at the former and showing fear in the presence of the latter. This is the beginning of the "shy age." He becomes strongly attached to his mother and displays a waning of indiscriminate friendliness.

Eight to nine months
The baby attempts to imitate the speech, gestures, and simple acts of others.

Twelve months
The baby reacts to the warning "no-no."

Sixteen to eighteen months
Negativism, in the form of stubborn resistance to requests or demands from adults, is manifested in physical withdrawal or angry outbursts.

Twenty-two to twenty-four months
The baby cooperates in a number of routine activities, such as being dressed, fed, and bathed.

Social Responses to Other Babies

Four to five months
The baby tries to attract the attention of another baby or a child by bouncing up and down, kicking, laughing, or blowing bubbles.

Six to seven months
The baby smiles at other babies and shows an interest in their crying.

Nine to thirteen months
The baby attempts to explore the clothes and hair of another baby, to imitate his behavior and vocalization, and to cooperate in the use of toys, although he may become upset when the other baby takes one of his toys.

Thirteen to eighteen months
Fighting over toys decreases, and the baby shows more cooperation during play and a willingness to share.

Eighteen to twenty-four months
The baby shows more interest in playing with other babies and uses play materials to establish social relationships with them.

---

is restored, and the baby again becomes more pleasant and social in his behavior (3).

BEGINNINGS OF INTEREST IN PLAY

As it is at every other age, play during babyhood is influenced by physical, motor, intellectual, and social development. This is true in regard to the form of play as well as in regard to the amount of play the individual engages in. The play of babies is, of course, simple as compared with the play of older children, adolescents, and adults.

There are certain distinctive characteristics of babyhood play. First, play is free and spontaneous, and there are no rules or regulations. The baby plays how and when he wishes without any preparation for, or restrictions on, the way he plays.

Second, throughout babyhood, play is more often solitary than social. Even when playing with his mother, as Stone has explained, the baby is "often a plaything, while the mothering one is the player. In time,

Because the play of very young children is more solitary than social, the baby is often a plaything and the mothering one the player. (Suzanne Szasz)

both the child and the mothering one are mutually players and playthings" (90). When he is with other babies or children, there is little interaction or cooperation. Instead, it is "onlooker play," in which the baby watches what the other is doing, or "parallel play," in which each baby plays in his own way without regard to what the other is doing. When there is any interaction, it consists mainly of grabbing and snatching the other baby's toys; there is little or no social give-and-take.

Third, because play is dependent on the baby's physical, motor, and intellectual development, the kinds of play he engages in depend on his patterns of development in these areas. As these patterns unfold, his play becomes more complex and varied.

Fourth, toys and other play equipment are less important than they will be later. And fifth, the play of babyhood is characterized by much repetition and little variation, since the baby lacks the skills which make

the wider repertoire of play activities of the preschooler and the older child possible.

Certain patterns of play among babies are found more or less universally, regardless of environment. These are given in Box 4-7.

DEVELOPMENT OF UNDERSTANDING

Because a baby begins life with no comprehension of the things he sees in his environment, he must acquire, through maturation and learning, an understanding of the meaning of what he observes. What meanings he acquires will depend partly on the level of his intelligence and partly on his previous experiences. And as new meanings are acquired, he will interpret new experiences in terms of memories of previous ones. The association of ideas with objects and situations results in the development of *concepts*.

Box 4-7. COMMON PLAY PATTERNS OF BABYHOOD

Sensorimotor Play

This is the earliest form of play and consists of such things as kicking, bouncing, wiggling, moving fingers and toes, climbing, babbling, and rolling.

Exploratory Play

As hand and arm coordinations develop, the baby begins to explore his body by pulling his hair, sucking his fingers or toes, pushing his finger in his navel, and manipulating his sex organs. He shakes, throws, sucks, bangs, and pulls at his toys and explores by pulling, banging, or tearing any object within his reach.

Imitative Play

During the second year, the baby tries to imitate the actions of those around him, such as reading a newspaper, sweeping the floor, or writing with a pencil or crayon.

Games

Before the baby is a year old, he plays such traditional games as peekaboo, pat-a-cake, pigs to market, and hide-and-seek.

Amusements

Babies like to be sung to, talked to, and read to. Most are fascinated by radio and television and enjoy looking at pictures.

The baby's behavior shows that, at an early age, concepts develop rapidly. For example, he shows his recognition of familiar persons and objects in his environment through his pleasurable responses, just as he regards strange persons and objects with fear. At first, he responds to the total situation rather than to any one part of it. As a result, he responds to objects and situations that have elements in common as if they were the same.

That is why, as was pointed out earlier, conditioning of emotions is so easy and so common in babyhood. In a classic experiment, Watson conditioned a baby to fear a rabbit by associating a loud, harsh noise with it; the baby later showed fear of white stuffed animals, a white muff, and even a person in a Santa Claus costume with a flowing white beard (104).

How Understanding Develops

The baby's earliest perceptions come through sensory exploration. He looks at, listens to, touches, smells, and tastes anything he can. Later, as muscle coordination develops, he is able to acquire more meanings through handling whatever is within his reach. Handling causes the baby's attention to be fixed, and this gives him an opportunity to discover meanings. While a baby of about six months may be held back in his exploratory behavior by fear of new and strange stimuli, by the end of the first year manipulation begins, and he tries to discover meanings in new and strange objects or persons. Piaget has labeled this the *sensorimotor stage* in conceptual development, lasting from birth to two or three years (70).

Toward the end of babyhood, the baby begins to put words together into sentences, generally sentences beginning with "who," "what," and "why." While he cannot understand all that is said in explanation, he derives enough meaning from the words he hears and the accompanying demonstrations to build on the meanings he has already discovered through sensory exploration and motor manipulation. At no time does he abandon the simpler forms of discovering

The baby's earliest perceptions come through sensory exploration. She "touches, smells, and tastes anything she can get into her hands." (Suzanne Szasz)

meanings, even when he is capable of using more advanced forms.

By the time he is two years old, the baby is capable of making simple generalizations based on similar experiences in which he has observed relationships. His limited knowledge and experience, however, make it difficult for him to distinguish between living and inanimate objects. As a result, he believes that all objects are animate and have the same attributes as living things.

Many of the important concepts needed for adjustment to life are learned in rudimentary form in the babyhood years. As the baby's social horizons broaden during childhood and adolescence, new meanings will be added to the foundations laid at this time. Emotional weighting, characteristic of all concepts, begins to become an important element of the developing concepts during the babyhood years. The most important concepts that begin to develop during babyhood are given in Box 4-8.

BEGINNINGS OF MORALITY

The baby has no conscience and no scale of values. He is therefore neither moral nor immoral, but *nonmoral* in the sense that his behavior is not guided by moral standards. Eventually he will learn moral codes from his parents and later from his teachers and playmates, as well as the necessity for conforming to these codes.

Learning to behave in a socially approved manner is a long, slow process. However, the foundations are laid in babyhood, and on these foundations the child builds a moral code which guides his behavior as he grows older.

Because of his limited intelligence, the baby judges the rightness or wrongness of an act in terms of the pleasure or pain it brings him, rather than in terms of its good or harmful effect on others. He therefore perceives an act as wrong only when it has some ill effect on him. He has no sense of guilt because he lacks definite standards of right and wrong. He does not, for example, feel guilty when he takes things that belong to others because he has no concept of personal property.

The baby is in a stage of moral development which Piaget has called *morality by constraint*—the first of three stages in moral development. This stage lasts until the age of seven or eight and is characterized by automatic obedience to rules without reasoning or judgment (70). This stage will be discussed more fully in the following chapter.

Role of Discipline in Babyhood

The major purpose of discipline is to teach the child what the group with which he is identified regards as right and wrong and then to see to it that he acts in accordance with this knowledge, first by means of external controls over his behavior and later by means of internal controls, when he assumes responsibility for his own behavior.

Throughout babyhood, the baby must

Box 4-8. CONCEPTS THAT DEVELOP IN BABYHOOD

Concepts of Space
During the second year, babies rarely reach for objects that are more than 20 inches away, indicating that they are able to estimate distance; the direction of their reach is usually correct.

Concepts of Weight
Concepts of weight are inaccurate during babyhood; babies perceive a small object as light and a large object as heavy.

Concepts of Time
A baby has no idea of how long it takes to eat his dinner, for example, nor has he any concept of the passage of time. Only when he is on a fairly rigid daily schedule does he know morning from afternoon or night.

Concepts of Self
The baby develops a *physical* self-concept by looking at himself in the mirror and handling the different parts of his body. *Psychological* self-concepts develop later and are based mainly on what the significant people in his life think of him. Before babyhood is over, most babies know that they are either boys or girls.

Social Concepts
By eight months the baby responds to the emotions of others as revealed in their facial expressions, though there is little evidence that, even by the end of babyhood, he understands exactly what these emotions are.

Concepts of Beauty
Between the ages of six and twenty-four months babies begin to respond to different colors. They are also apt to say that something is "pretty," for example, and they like music with a definite tune.

Concepts of the Comic
At four months the baby perceives vocal play or babbling as comic, and he enjoys blowing bubbles in his milk and splashing his bath water. At six months he derives enjoyment from dropping things that are handed to him, and at one year he likes to make funny faces. The two-year-old laughs at his own stunts, such as squeezing through a narrow space.

---

learn to make correct, specific responses to specific situations in the home and in the neighborhood. Acts that are wrong should be wrong at all times, regardless of who is in charge. Otherwise, the baby will be confused and will not know what is expected of him.

With strict discipline, involving emphasis on punishment for wrongdoing, even a young baby can be forced into a pattern of behavior that makes him less troublesome to his parents during the second year of life, when his exploratory behavior and tendency to refuse to comply with parental wishes make him less easy to handle than he was during the first year.

But before the baby is punished for wrongdoing, he must *learn* what is wrong.

This he cannot do overnight. Therefore, during babyhood, the emphasis should be on the educational aspect of discipline—teaching the baby what is right and what is wrong—and on rewarding him with approval and affection when he does what is right, rather than on punishing him.

Many parents assume that a baby cannot understand words of praise and therefore refrain from telling him that he has done something good. Although few babies are able to understand what is said in praise, they do understand the accompanying facial expressions, which are pleasanter than those accompanying scolding or other forms of punishment and thus motivate the baby to repeat the act that brought such a favorable response.

FAMILY RELATIONSHIPS

Because the baby's early environment is limited primarily to the home, family relationships play a dominant role in determining the future pattern of his attitudes toward others. Although this pattern will unquestionably be changed and modified as he grows older and as his environment broadens, the core of the pattern is likely to remain with little or no modification.

Evidence of Importance of Family Relationships

Studies of family relationships have shown that *all* family relationships are important factors in the individual's development. However, during the babyhood years, parent-child relationships are more important than any other. For example, a baby who is institutionalized and thus is deprived of normal opportunities to express love becomes quiet, listless, and unresponsive to the smiles of others; he shows extreme forms of temper, as if seeking attention, and he gives the general appearance of unhappiness (13, 38).

The baby needs the continuous care of one person—usually the mother or a satisfactory mother substitute—for the first nine to twelve months of his life. Such care gives him a feeling of security, and the lack of it can have a profound influence on his development, psychological as well as physical (20).

Equally important evidence of the influence of family relationships on the baby's development comes from studies of babies from different-sized families. Babies from large families in which the children are closely spaced have fewer contacts with their mothers, who are preoccupied with other responsibilities; as a result, they suffer from some of the usual effects of maternal deprivation. Lack of attention and stimulation can cause them to become lethargic, for example (66).

On the other hand, there is little evidence that satisfying experiences during babyhood will be adequate to compensate for unfavorable parent-child relationships that develop as the child grows older or for the effects of economic privation, for example. Although it is true that the foundations of attitudes, behavior patterns, and personality structure are laid in babyhood, events of childhood and the later years are of great importance in reinforcing or even changing the personality structure tentatively formed in the early years of life.

Changes in Family Relationships

At no time in his life do the individual's relationships with his family remain static. Sometimes these relationships change slowly, and sometimes rapidly. Babyhood is one of the times when the changes are rapid, for the better or for the worse. In babyhood, the changes tend to be for the worse.

Many things are responsible for changes in family relationships, but one of the most important is the fact that every member involved in the relationship undergoes changes of his own. Davids and Holden have discussed the changes that take place in the mother-child relationship during the early months of the baby's life (25):

Such changes in maternal characteristics might well be a function of the infant's physical and/or temperamental attributes. That is, whether the infant is healthy or sickly, unusually attractive or obviously handicapped, usually calm and contented or generally fussy and irritable, especially responsive to maternal contacts or somewhat rejecting of her—these are the kinds of infant variable that could well play a prominent role in modifying the mother's attitudes and personality during the first few months after childbirth. Then again, it might be that the infant's physical or emotional makeup has little to do with the mother's changed outlook or behavior. Rather, in certain cases, it might be that changes in the mother's physi-

cal condition, or changes in the husband-wife relationship (in either a positive or negative direction) or changes in the family's socio-economic situation (for better or worse) are responsible for differences in maternal char-acteristics found during pregnancy and sev-eral months after childbirth.

Normally, family relationships during most of the baby's first year are favorable. It has been said that "everyone loves a baby," and this holds true not only for parents but also for siblings, grandparents, and other relatives. However, before the baby's first birthday, some of this love has been tempered with annoyance, anger, frus-tration, and other unpleasant emotions, and the baby himself may have become nega-tivistic in some respects, exhibiting behavior

that is in sharp contrast to the docile compliance of early babyhood. With these changes comes a deterioration in the baby's relationships with different family members. Some of the most common causes of such deterioration are given in Box 4-9.

PERSONALITY DEVELOPMENT IN BABYHOOD

As we have seen, the potential for per-sonality development is present at birth. As Thomas et al. have emphasized, "Personality is shaped by the constant interplay of tem-perament and environment" (94). And, be-cause no two individuals have the same physical or mental endowments or the same environmental experiences, no two persons

---

Box 4-9. COMMON CAUSES OF CHANGES IN FAMILY RELATIONSHIPS DURING BABYHOOD

Dream-Child Concept
If the baby lives up to the dream-child concepts of parents and siblings, in terms of appearance and behavior, family relationships will become increas-ingly more favorable. If he does not, they will dete-riorate.

Degree of Dependency
As the baby's complete dependency—one of his most appealing features—decreases, he becomes more troublesome and demanding and thus less appealing.

Parental Anxiety
Parents may become nervous about how well they are performing their parental roles, or they may worry if the baby behaves differently from the way an older sibling did, for example. Such feelings are communicated to the baby, and he may react by becoming resentful and negativistic and by crying excessively, which makes him seem less appealing than before.

Child-Training Methods
Most child-training methods during babyhood center on sleeping, eating, and going to the toilet.

How authoritarian or permissive these methods are will influence the character of the parent-child rela-tionship. Corporal punishment is very damaging to this relationship.

Arrival of New Sibling
The arrival of a new sibling may cause the baby to feel displaced and neglected, leading to fussiness, crying, and a tendency to revert to infantile behav-ior, all of which is upsetting to the family.

Relationships with Older Siblings
Older siblings may begin to think of the baby as a pest when they must be quiet while he naps, share their mother's time and attention with him, and help with his care.

Preference for Certain Family Members
Even before his first birthday, the baby shows definite preferences for certain family mem-bers—usually his mother or an older sister. Other family members tend to resent this and to com-municate their feelings to the baby, thus intensify-ing his preferences.

will ever develop identical personality patterns.

Babyhood is often referred to as a "critical period" in the development of personality because at this time the foundations are laid upon which the adult personality structure will be built.

A number of lines of evidence show how critical a time babyhood is in the development of personality. First, studies of emotional deprivation due either to neglect in the home or to institutionalization have revealed that personality changes are an almost inevitable accompaniment (13, 109).

Second, because the baby's environment is limited almost exclusively to the home and because the mother is the baby's most constant companion, the kind of person she is and the kind of relationship she has with her baby will have a profound influence on his personality.

Third, there is evidence that functions which are in an active stage of development when something unfavorable occurs in the environment are most subject to damage. For example, when the baby is developing independence, overprotectiveness on the part of the parents is especially harmful (91).

Fourth, sex differences in personality begin to appear as early as the first year of life. There is little evidence that these differences are due to heredity and much that they are the result of environmental pressures, which are different for boys and for girls. These environmental pressures are likely to increase with time, and thus the foundations laid in babyhood will persist (2).

Fifth, and most important, genetic studies of the persistence of personality traits over a period of years have revealed that patterns established early in life remain almost unchanged as the child grows older (5, 64). As Thomas et al. have pointed out, "A child's temperament is not immutable. In the course of his development the environmental circumstances may heighten, diminish or otherwise modify his reactions and behavior" (94).

Certain personality traits do change, and these changes may be either quantitative, in that there is a strengthening or weakening of a trait already present, or qualitative, in that a socially undesirable trait, for example, is replaced by one that is socially more desirable. For the most part, personality changes tend to be quantitative in nature. For example, a young child who has been shy since babyhood will seek the kind of environment that will encourage the development of this trait, avoiding situations that would make him feel ill at ease or self-conscious. As a result, his shyness will likely become stronger rather than weaker with age.

The core of the personality pattern—the self-concept—remains fundamentally the same. As time goes on, this core becomes less and less flexible. Then a change in personality traits may upset the personality balance. Thus early experiences are extremely important in shaping the personality pattern.

HAZARDS OF BABYHOOD

Because babyhood is the foundation age, it is an especially hazardous time. The hazards may be physical, psychological, or both, as is true of infancy. For example, excessive crying is both physically and psychologically damaging to the baby and to the home atmosphere. It leads to gastrointestinal disturbances, regurgitation of food, night waking, and general nervous tension. Furthermore, excessive crying leads to feelings of insecurity, which affect the baby's developing personality. In addition, excessive crying affects his relationships with his parents and other family members unfavorably. This, in turn, indirectly affects his personality development.

In the first year of babyhood, physical hazards tend to be more numerous and more serious than psychological ones, while the reverse is true during the second year. Both are serious, however, and thus it is important that they be prevented from occur-

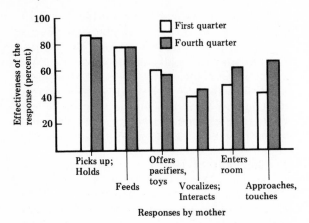

Figure 4-5 Effectiveness of various maternal responses to crying in young babies. (Adapted from S. M. Bell & M. D. S. Ainsworth. Infant crying and maternal responsiveness. *Child Develpm.*, 1972, **43**, 1171–1190. Used by permission.)

ring whenever possible and that everything be done to minimize their severity should they happen to occur. For example, certain patterns of maternal responsiveness during the first and fourth quarters of the first year of life can be effective in coping with excessive crying. See Figure 4-5. Since much of the crying that occurs during the first year is social in origin, different forms of social reactions on the part of the mother are most effective in dealing with the crying (8).

Physical Hazards

Of the many physical hazards of babyhood, those leading to death are unquestionably the most serious. Two-thirds of all deaths during the first year of life occur in the first month. After that, the mortality rate decreases rapidly. Deaths are usually caused by a serious illness, although apparently normal, healthy babies can be the victims of "crib death." During the second year, deaths are more often due to accidents than to illness. Boys, throughout babyhood, die more often than girls (79, 100).

Vaccination and inoculation during the early months of life can prevent the occurrence of serious illnesses. However, minor illnesses such as colds and digestive upsets are common. Prompt diagnosis and proper medical care can keep these from causing serious harm, but if they are neglected, as frequently happens in the case of colds, serious disturbances can develop rapidly, especially ear infections.

Although accidents are infrequent during the first year of life, owing to the fact that the baby is carefully protected in his crib and carriage, they are far more frequent during the second year, when he begins to move around more freely and cannot be as well protected as he was earlier. Some of these accidents, such as bruises and cuts, are minor and have no harmful effect. Others are serious and may even prove fatal.

Stress—a prolonged unpleasant emotional state, such as fear or anger—is a less common physical hazard of babyhood. Stress can cause endocrine changes which upset body homeostasis, and this is reflected in eating and sleeping difficulties, in nervous mannerisms such as excessive thumb-sucking, and in excessive crying. There are many causes of stress—poor health, parental neglect, and poor environmental conditions that interfere with proper sleeping and eating—but constant and close association with a nervous, tense mother is a particularly important factor.

A more common physical hazard of babyhood is poor nutrition. This may take the form either of overeating or of eating a poorly balanced diet. The way in which a mother feeds her baby during the first year of his life may be crucial in determining how healthy he will be not only during babyhood but also throughout the growth years.

Fat babies, for example, tend to have obesity problems as they grow older, while thin babies do not. This is because the number and size of the fat cells of the body are established early in life. Thus, even though a fat child slims down later, he still has the same large number of cells capable of storing fat—a built-in potential for becoming obese. Similarly, babies who are fed large amounts of carbohydrates not only are overweight as babies but also are more subject to diabetes and heart disease as they grow older (11).

Malnutrition, as a result of either inadequate food intake or a lack of some of the nutrients essential for normal growth and development, can play havoc not only with physical development but also with mental development. Because the brain grows and develops at such an accelerated rate during babyhood, it can be seriously impaired by malnutrition (11, 26).

The foundations of the important physiological habits—eating, sleeping, and eliminating—are established during babyhood, and thus a common physical hazard of this period is the establishment of unfavorable attitudes on the baby's part toward these habits. Box 4-10 gives some of the common hazards that arise in relation to the establishment of physiological habits.

Psychological Hazards

The most serious psychological hazards of babyhood involve the baby's failure to master the developmental tasks for that age. Mastery of these tasks is important for two reasons. First, the sooner the baby gains control over his body, the sooner he can become independent of help from others. Second, mastery of these tasks provides the foundation on which mastery of later developmental tasks will be built. The better the baby masters the tasks of babyhood, the more easily and quickly he will master those of early childhood.

The baby who fails to master the developmental tasks of babyhood is subject to serious psychological hazards. Because later skills depend upon the development of control over different areas of the body, a baby whose motor development is delayed, for example, will be at a great disadvantage when he begins to play with other children. The more he lags behind the group in the acquisition of body control, the slower he is likely to be in acquiring the skills other children possess. Furthermore, because the desire to be independent makes its appearance early in the second year, a baby whose motor development lags becomes frustrated when he tries to do things for himself and fails.

Almost as handicapping to good adjustment is parental pressure to achieve motor control and learn motor skills before the

---

Box 4-10. HAZARDS IN ESTABLISHING PHYSIOLOGICAL HABITS

Eating Habits

A baby who sucks for long periods shows signs of tenseness; he engages in more nonnutritive sucking (such as thumb-sucking), has more sleep difficulties, and is more restless than one whose sucking periods are shorter. If weaning is delayed, the baby is likely to resist the new kind of food and substitute thumb-sucking for the nipple. He will also resist semisolid foods if they are introduced too early, not because of their taste, but because of their texture.

Sleep Habits

Crying, strenuous play with an adult, or noise in the environment can make the baby tense and keep him from falling asleep. Sleep schedules that do not meet the baby's individual requirements make him tense and resistant to sleep.

Habits of Elimination

These habits cannot be established until the nerves and muscles have developed adequately. Trying to train a baby too early will make him uncooperative about establishing these habits when he is maturationally ready. Delay in toilet training results in habits of irregularity and lack of motivation on the baby's part. Enuresis—bed-wetting—is common when training is not timed according to the baby's developmental readiness.

baby is maturationally ready to do so. The baby may develop a resistant, negativistic attitude that will stifle his motivation and cause a delay in learning tasks that he is otherwise ready to master.

Delayed speech, like delayed motor control, is serious in babyhood because, at this age, the foundations are being laid for the development of the tools of communication that the baby will need as his social horizons broaden. In early childhood, when interest in people outside the home begins to awaken, the child whose speech lags markedly behind that of other children finds himself in the role of an outsider. Twins, it has been reported, are especially susceptible to this hazard (24).

Baby talk—childish mispronunciations—is frequently regarded as "cute" by parents and relatives, who may permit it to continue or even encourage it by using it themselves. As a result, an incorrect auditory image is developed. Continued mispronunciation of a word results in the formation of a word habit which may be difficult to replace with a habit of correct pronunciation when the baby emerges into childhood and discovers that his playmates cannot understand him or ridicule him because he "talks like a baby."

Three common psychological hazards frequently arise in relation to the baby's emotional development. These are given in Box 4-11.

The major social hazard of babyhood is lack of opportunity and motivation to learn to become social. This encourages the prolongation of egocentrism, which is characteristic of all babies, and leads to the development of introversion. Being deprived of opportunities for social contacts is detrimental at any age, but it is especially so from the ages of six weeks to six months—the critical time in the development of attitudes which affect the pattern of socialization. While social attitudes can and do change, many individuals who formed unfavorable social attitudes as babies continue to be socially less well adjusted as they grow older.

Box 4-11. COMMON EMOTIONAL HAZARDS OF BABYHOOD

Emotional Deprivation
The baby who is not given the opportunity to experience the normal emotions of babyhood—especially affection, curiosity, and joy—does not thrive physically, is backward in motor and speech development, and does not learn how to establish social contacts or show affection. He usually becomes listless and apathetic and often develops nervous mannerisms, such as thumb-sucking.

Too Much Affection
Parents who are oversolicitous or overdemonstrative encourage the baby to focus his affection on himself and to become self-bound and selfish, rather than show affection for others.

Dominant Emotions
Conditions in the baby's environment encourage the development of certain emotions to the exclusion of others, and these eventually become the dominant ones in his life unless conditions change and the development of other emotions is encouraged. Timidity may persist long after babyhood, for example, if a shy or fearful child is exposed to too many strangers or too many frightening situations.

Play in babyhood is potentially hazardous, both physically and psychologically. Many toys can inflict cuts and bruises or cause the baby to choke on a part that has come loose. The major psychological hazard is that the child may come to rely too much on the toys themselves for amusement, instead of learning to play in ways that involve interaction with others. Television, used as a built-in baby-sitter, also discourages the baby from taking an active role in play. When playing games, the adult may allow the baby to win, with the result that he will find competition with other children difficult as he grows older and not be able to lose graciously.

Even though understanding is in a rudimentary stage of development in babyhood, it presents one serious psychological hazard. In the development of concepts, it

A deterioration in family relationships is a hazard of babyhood. If the parents quarrel a great deal, for example, the baby may feel unloved and rejected—and it may develop feelings of resentment and insecurity. (Suzanne Szasz)

is relatively easy to replace wrong meanings associated with people, objects, or situations with correct meanings. However, all concepts have some emotional weighting, and this is where the potential hazard lies. If, for example, the baby learns to associate sweets with rewards for good behavior and to think of vegetables as a form of punishment, the emotional weighting of these concepts may lead to persistent food likes and dislikes.

Because the family constitutes the baby's main social environment, any unfavorable condition in family relationships leads to psychological hazards with serious and far-reaching consequences. The four given in Box 4-12 are the most common.

The developing self-concept is in large part a mirror image of what the baby believes significant people in his life think of him. As family relationships deteriorate during the second year of babyhood, the baby's self-concept reflects the unfavorable attitudes he thinks family members have toward him. He then expresses this unfa-

vorable self-concept in aggressive, resentful, negativistic, or withdrawn behavior, all of which make him seem less desirable to family members than he did earlier. Their changed attitudes are reflected in their treatment of him, and this reinforces his unfavorable self-concept.

HAPPINESS IN BABYHOOD

Normally, the first year of life can be one of the happiest of the life span. As was pointed out earlier in the chapter, the dependency of the young baby makes him appealing to children as well as to adults. Most children like to play with him, and adults not only want to cuddle and love him, but also are tolerant toward his crying and the disruption his care brings into their lives.

For almost all babies, the second year of life is far less happy than the first. There are many reasons for this, the most important of which are given in Box 4-13.

Box 4-12. FAMILY—RELATIONSHIP HAZARDS IN BABYHOOD

Separation from Mother
Unless a satisfactory and stable substitute is provided, the baby who is separated from his mother develops feelings of insecurity which are expressed in personality disturbances that lay the foundations for later maladjustments.

Deterioration in Family Relationships
The deterioration in family relationships that almost always occurs during the second year of the baby's life is psychologically hazardous because he notices that family members have a changed attitude toward him and treat him differently. He may feel unloved and rejected and develop feelings of resentment and insecurity.

Overprotection
A baby who is overprotected and prevented from doing what he is capable of doing becomes overdependent and afraid to do what other babies of his age can do. This is likely to lead to an abnormal fear of school and excessive shyness in the presence of strangers.

Inconsistent Training
Inconsistent child-training methods—which can be the result of permissiveness or of parents' feelings of inadequacy for the parental role—provide poor guidelines for the baby, and this slows down his learning to behave in approved ways.

Not all babies have reason to be unhappy as babyhood draws to a close, nor is the baby who has one or more reasons for unhappiness *always* unhappy. There are times when he is happy, just as there are times when he is not. Which will dominate will depend on how many reasons he has to be unhappy and how frequently the causes of unhappiness occur. In general, however, most babies have more reasons to be unhappy during the second year of babyhood than during the first.

Box 4-13. CAUSES OF UNHAPPINESS DURING BABYHOOD

Teething
Teething causes periodic discomfort, if not actual pain, and the baby tends to be irritable, fretful, and negativistic.

Desire for Independence
The baby now has increased control over his body and may resent adult assistance or interference. He shows his resentment by being balky or having a temper tantrum.

Increased Need for Maternal Attention
As dependency decreases and waking time increases, the baby wants more attention from his mother. If she cannot give him the attention he craves, he may become angry, causing her to behave punitively and the baby to feel that he has lost her love.

Beginning of Discipline
Many parents' initial attempts at discipline consist of slaps, spankings, harsh words, and angry expressions. The baby interprets this to mean that the parent is angry at *him,* not at the thing he has done, and this makes him feel unloved and unwanted.

Increased Sibling Resentment
Siblings may now regard the baby as a nuisance, especially when he takes their own belongings or when they must help care for him. If he senses that *everyone* in his environment is against him, he may have strong feelings of resentment and insecurity.

Chapter Highlights

1 Babyhood, which extends from the end of the period of the newborn to the end of the second year of life, is a time of increasing independence due to rapid physical and psychological development.

2 Babyhood is a foundation age and a very appealing age, but it is also a hazardous age, both physically and psychologically.

3 The major developmental tasks of babyhood involve learning to be independent.

4 Babyhood is a period of rapid physical growth accompanied by changes in body proportions. As a result of maturation and learning, the major physiological functions—eating, sleeping, and elimination—are brought under control.

5 Muscle control follows the laws of developmental direction. When babyhood ends, control is more developed in the arm than in the leg region, and thus arm and hand skills are superior to leg skills.

6 Prespeech forms of communication—crying, babbling, and gesturing—predominate during the first year of life, after which rapid strides are made in learning to talk.

7 There are two outstanding characteristics of emotional development during babyhood: All emotional responses are proportionally too great for the stimuli that gave rise to them, and emotions are more easily conditioned than will be possible later.

8 The foundations for social behavior are laid during babyhood. Whether the baby will become socially well adjusted or socially maladjusted depends on his social experiences both in the home and outside the home.

9 There are five major categories of babyhood play: sensorimotor play, exploratory play, imitative play, games, and amusements. Proficiency in all types of play develops rapidly at this age.

10 Concepts develop rapidly during babyhood as a result of sensory exploration and motor manipulation. Concepts are usually specific in form, however, especially concepts of right and wrong and self-concepts.

11 Because family relationships play a dominant role in shaping the baby's concept of self, changes in these relationships often result in unhappiness and in unfavorable self-concepts as babyhood draws to a close.

12 On the whole, physical hazards are more serious than psychological hazards during the first year of life, while the reverse is true during the second year. This is one of the major reasons for a decrease in happiness as babyhood progresses.

Bibliography

1 Ainsworth, M. D. S., Bell, S. N., & Stayton, D. J. Individual differences in the development of some attachment behaviors. *Merrill-Palmer Quart.,* 1972, **18,** 123–143.

2 Allport, G. W. *Pattern and growth in personality.* New York: Holt, 1961.

3 Ames, L. B., & Ilg, F. L. The developmental point of view with special reference to the principle of reciprocal neuromotor interweaving. *J. genet. Psychol.,* 1964, **105,** 195–209.

4 Bayley, N. *Bayley's Scales of Infant Development.* New York: Psychological Corporation, 1968.

5 Bayley, N. Development of mental abilities. In P. H. Mussen (Ed.), *Carmichael's manual of child psychology.* (3rd ed.) Vol. 1. New York: Wiley, 1970. Pp. 1163–1209.

6 Beckwith, L. Relationships between infants' social behavior and their mothers' behavior. *Child Develpm.,* 1972, **43,** 397–411.

7 Bell, R. Q. A reinterpretation of the direction of effects in studies of socialization. *Psychol. Rev.,* 1968, **75,** 81–95.

8 Bell, S. M., & Ainsworth, M. D. S. Infant crying and maternal responsiveness. *Child Develpm.,* 1972, **43,** 1171–1190.

9 Benjamin, L. S., Serdahely, W., & Geppert, T. V. Night training through parents' use of operant conditioning. *Child Develpm.,* 1971, **42,** 963–966.

10 Bernstein, P., Emde, R., & Campos, J. REM sleep in four-month infants under home and laboratory conditions. *Psychosom. Med.,* 1973, **35,** 322–329.

11 Blakeslee, S. A pediatrician at Stanford says the diet given infants helps shape the adult. *The New York Times,* Oct. 31, 1972.

12 Bossard, J. H. S., & Boll, E. S. *The sociology of child development.* (4th ed.) New York: Harper & Row, 1966.

13 Bowlby, J., Ainsworth, M., Boston, M., & Rosenbluth, R. The effects of mother-child separation: A follow-up study. *Brit. J. med. Psychol.,* 1956, **29,** 211–247.

14 Breckenridge, M. E., & Vincent, E. L. *Child development: Physical and psychologic development through adolescence.* (5th ed.) Philadelphia: Saunders, 1965.

15 Brown, R. Development of the first language in the human species. *Amer. Psychologist,* 1973, **28,** 97–106.

16 Caldwell, B. M. The effects of psychosocial deprivation on human development in infancy. *Merrill-Palmer Quart.,* 1970, **16,** 260–277.

17 Cameron, J., Livson, N., & Bayley, N. Infant vocalizations and their relationship to mature intelligence. *Science,* 1967, **157,** 331–333.

18 Chase, H. P., & Martin, H. P. Undernutrition and child development. *New Eng. J. Med.,* 1970, **282,** 933–939.

19 Clarke, A. D. B. Consistency and variability in the growth of human characteristics. *Develpm. Med. child Neurol.,* 1972, **14,** 668–683.

20 Coates, B., Anderson, E. P., & Hartup, W. W. Interrelations in the attachment behavior of human infants. *Develpm. Psychol.,* 1972, **6,** 218–230.

21 Corter, C. M., Rheingold, H. L., & Eckerman, C. O. Toys delay the infant's following of his mother. *Develpm. Psychol.,* 1972, **6,** 138–145.

22 Coursin, D. B. Nutrition and brain development in infants. *Merrill-Palmer Quart.,* 1972, **18,** 177–202.

23 Cruickshank, W. M., & Johnson, G. O. (Eds.) *Education of exceptional children and youth.* (2nd ed.) Englewood Cliffs, N.J.: Prentice-Hall, 1967.

24 Dales, R. J. Motor and language development of twins during the first three years. *J. genet. Psychol.,* 1969, **114,** 263–271.

25 Davids, A., & Holden, R. H. Consistency of maternal attitudes and personality from pregnancy to eight months following childbirth. *Develpm. Psychol.,* 1970, **2,** 364–366.

26 Dayton, D. H. Early malnutrition and human development. *Children,* 1969, **16,** 210–217.

27 deHirsch, K. A review of early language development. *Develpm. Med. child Neurol.,* 1970, **12,** 87–97.

28 Dodd, B. J. Effects of social and vocal stimulation on infant babbling. *Develpm. Psychol.,* 1972, **7,** 80–83.

29 DuBois, F. S. Rhythms, cycles, and periods in health and disease. *Amer. J. Psychiat.,* 1959, **116,** 114–119.

30 Eichorn, D. H. Physiological development. In P. H. Mussen (Ed.), *Carmichael's manual of child psychology.* (3rd ed.) Vol. 1. New York: Wiley, 1970. Pp. 157–283.

31 Ely, K. P., Healey, A., & Smidt, G. L. Mothers' expectations of their child's accomplishments of certain gross motor skills. *Develpm. Med. child Neurol.,* 1972, **14,** 621–625.

32 Emmerich, W. Personality development and concepts of structure. *Child Develpm.,* 1968, **39,** 671–690.

33 Escalona, S. Basic modes of social interaction: Their emergence and patterning during the first two years of life. *Merrill-Palmer Quart.,* 1973, **19,** 205–232.

34 Ferguson, L. R. Origins of social development in infancy. *Merrill-Palmer Quart.,* 1971, **17,** 119–137.

35 Fleener, D. E., & Cairns, R. B. Attachment behaviors in human infants: Discriminative vocalization on maternal separation. *Develpm. Psychol.,* 1970, **2,** 215–223.

36 Gagné, R. M. Contributions of learning to human development. In J. Eliot (Ed.), *Human development and cognitive processes.* New York: Holt, 1971. Pp. 111–128.

37 Garai, J. E., & Scheinfeld, A. Sex differences in mental and behavioral traits. *Genet. Psychol. Monogr.,* 1968, **77,** 169–299.

38 Gardner, D. B., Hawkes, G. R., & Burchinal, L. G. Noncontinuous mothering in infancy and development in later childhood. *Child Develpm.,* 1961, **32,** 225–234.

39 Goldberg, S., & Lewis, W. Play behavior in the year-old infant: Early sex differences. *Child Develpm.,* 1969, **40,** 21–31.

40 Hall, J. W. Word recognition by children of two age levels. *J. educ. Psychol.,* 1968, **59,** 420–424.

41 Havighurst, R. J. *Human development and education.* New York: Longmans, 1953.

42 Herron, R. E., & Sutton-Smith, B. (Eds.) *Child's play.* New York: Wiley, 1971.

43 Hoffman, M. L. Conscience, personality and socialization techniques. *Hum. Develpm.,* 1970, **13,** 90–126.

44 Horowitz, F. D. Infant learning and development: Retrospect and prospect. In J. Eliot (Ed.), *Human development and cognitive processes.* New York: Holt, 1971. Pp. 96–110.

45 James, W. *Principles of psychology.* New York: Holt, 1890.

46 Jones, S. J., & Moss, H. A. Age, state and maternal behavior associated with infant vocalization. *Child Develpm.,* 1971, **42,** 1039–1051.

47 Kagan, J., & Kogan, N. Individual variation in cognitive processes. In P. H. Mussen (Ed.), *Carmichael's manual of child psychology.* (3rd ed.) Vol. 1. New York: Wiley 1970. Pp. 1273–1365.

48 Kagan, J., & Moss, H. A. *Birth to maturity: A study in psychological development.* New York: Wiley, 1962.

49 Kaplan, E., & Kaplan, G. The prelinguistic child. In J. Eliot (Ed.), *Human development and cognitive processes.* New York: Holt, 1971. Pp. 358–381.

50 Koch, H. L. The relation of certain formal attributes of siblings to attitudes held toward each other and their parents. *Monogr. Soc. Res. Child Develpm.,* 1960, **25**(4).

51 Kravitz, H., & Boehm, J. J. Rhythmic habit patterns in infancy: Their sequence, age of onset, and frequency. *Child Develpm.,* 1971, **42,** 399–413.

52 Lewis, M. Infants' responses to facial stimuli during the first year of life. *Develpm. Psychol.,* 1969, **1,** 75–86.

53 Lipsitt, L. P. Learning processes of human newborns. *Merrill-Palmer Quart.,* 1966, **12,** 45–71.

54 Macnamara, J. Cognitive basis of language learning in infants. *Psychol. Rev.,* 1972, **79,** 1–13.

55 Marshall, H. R. Relations between home experiences and children's use of language in play interactions with peers. *Psychol. Monogr.,* 1961, **75**(5).

56 Martin, P. C., & Vincent, E. L. *Human development.* New York: Ronald Press, 1960.

57 McCall, R. B. Smiling and vocalization in infants as indices of perceptual-cognitive processes. *Merrill-Palmer Quart.,* 1972, **18,** 341–347.

58 McNeill, D. The development of language. In P. H. Mussen (Ed.), *Carmichael's manual of child psychology.* (3rd ed.) Vol. 1. New York: Wiley, 1970. Pp. 1061–1161.

59 Meredith, H. V. Body size of contemporary groups of one-year-old infants studied in different parts of the world. *Child Develpm.,* 1970, **41,** 551–600.

60 Messer, S. B., & Lewis, M. Social class and sex differences in the attachment and play behavior of the year-old infant. *Merrill-Palmer Quart.,* 1972, **18,** 295–306.

61 Meyer, J. W., & Sobieszek, B. L. Effect of a child's sex on adult interpretations of its behavior. *Develpm. Psychol.,* 1972, **6,** 42–48.

62 Miklasheŏskaya, N. N. Sex differences in growth of the head and face in children and adolescents. *Hum. Biol.,* 1969, **41,** 250–262.

63 Miller, E. Handedness and the pattern of human ability. *Brit. J. Psychol.,* 1971, **62,** 111–112.

64 Mischel, W. Continuity and change in personality. *Amer. Psychologist,* 1969, **24,** 1012–1018.

65 Moerk, E. Principles of interaction in language learning. *Merrill-Palmer Quart.,* 1972, **18,** 229–257.

66 Moss, H. A. Methodological issues in studying mother-infant interaction. *Amer. J. Orthopsychiat.,* 1965, **35,** 482–486.

67 *New York Times* article. Crying of an infant is called important in diagnosing "ills." *The New York Times,* July 16, 1972.

68 Parry, M. H. Infants' responses to novelty in familiar and unfamiliar settings. *Child Develpm.,* 1972, **43,** 233–237.

69 Peterson, R. A. The natural development of nocturnal bladder control. *Develpm. Med. child Neurol.,* 1971, **13,** 730–734.

70 Piaget, J., & Inhelder, B. *The psychology of the child.* New York: Basic Books, 1969.

71 Pikler, E. Some contributions to the study of the gross motor development of children. *J. genet. Psychol.,* 1968, **113,** 27–39.

72 Ramey, C. T., & Ourth, L. L. Delayed reinforcement and vocalization rates in infants. *Child Develpm.,* 1971, **42,** 291–297.

73 Rebelsky, F., & Black, R. Crying in infancy. *J. genet. Psychol.,* 1972, **121,** 49–57.

74 Rees, N. S. The role of babbling in the child's acquisition of language. *Brit. J. Disord. Commun.,* 1972, **7,** 17–23.

75 Rheingold, H. L., & Eckerman, C. O. The infant separates himself from his mother. In W. R. Looft (Ed.), *Developmental psychology: A book of readings.* Hinsdale, Ill.: Dryden Press, 1972. Pp. 271–288.

76 Sachs, J. The status of developmental studies of language. In J. Eliot (Ed.), *Human development and cognitive processes.* New York: Holt, 1971. Pp. 381–394.

77 Scarr, S., & Salapatek, P. Patterns of fear development during infancy. *Merrill-Palmer Quart.,* 1970, **16,** 53–90.

78 Schaefer, E. S., & Bayley, N. Maternal behavior, child behavior, and their intercorrelations from infancy through adolescence. *Monogr. Soc. Res. Child Develpm.,* 1963, **28**(3).

79 Scheinfeld, A. *Heredity in humans.* (Rev. ed.) Philadelphia: Lipponcott, 1971.

80 Schneiders, A. A. The nature and origins of guilt. *Trans. N.Y. Acad. Sci.,* 1968, **30,** 705–713.

81 Schneirla, T. C. The concept of development in comparative psychology. In J. Eliot (Ed.), *Human development and cognitive processes.* New York: Holt, 1971. Pp. 55–78.

82 Seagoe, M. V. Children's play as an index of socialization. *Proc. 77th Annu. Convent. APA,* 1969, **4,** 683–684.

83 Seth, G. Eye-hand coordination and "handedness": A developmental study of visuo-motor behavior in infancy. *Brit. J. educ. Psychol.,* 1973, **43,** 35–49.

84 Siegelman, M. "Origins" of extraversion-introversion. *J. Psychol.,* 1968, **69,** 85–91.

85 Spock, B. *The pocket book of baby and child care.* (Rev. ed.) New York: Pocket Books, 1968.

86 Sroufe, L. L., & Wunsch, J. P. The development of laughter in the first year of life. *Child Develpm.,* 1972, **43,** 1326–1344.

87 Starr, R. H. Cognitive development in infancy: Assessment, acceleration and actualization. *Merrill-Palmer Quart.,* 1971, **17,** 153–186.

88 Stayton, D. J., Hogan, R., & Ainsworth, M. D. Infant obedience and maternal behavior: The origin of socialization reconsidered. *Child Develpm.,* 1971, **42,** 1057–1069.

89 Stern, E., Parmelee, A. H., Akiyama, Y., Schultz, M. A., & Wenner, W. H. Sleep cycle characteristics of infants. *Pediatrics,* 1969, **43,** 65–70.

90 Stone, G. P. The play of little children. In R. E. Herron & B. Sutton-Smith (Eds.), *Child's play.* New York: Wiley, 1971. Pp. 4–14.

91 Stone, L. J., & Church, J. *Childhood and adolescence.* (3rd ed.) New York: Random House, 1973.

92 Tanner, J. M. Physical growth. In P. H. Mussen (Ed.), *Carmichael's manual of child psychology.* (3rd ed.) Vol. 1. New York: Wiley, 1970. Pp. 77–165.

93 Terman, L. M., & Merrill, M. A. *Stanford-Binet Intelligence Scale.* Boston: Houghton Mifflin, 1960.

94 Thomas, A., Chess, S., & Birch, H. G. The origin of personality. *Scient. American,* 1970, **223**(2), 102–109.

95 Tomlinson-Keasey, C. Conditioning of infant vocalizations in the home environment. *J. genet. Psychol.,* 1972, **120,** 75–82.

96 Touwen, B. C. L. A study on the development of some motor phenomena in infancy. *Develpm. Med. child Neurol.,* 1971, **13,** 435–446.

97 Tryon, A. F. Thumb-sucking and manifest anxiety: A note. *Child Develpm.,* 1968, **39,** 1159–1163.

98 Tulkin, S. R., & Kagan, J. Mother-child interaction in the first year of life. *Child Develpm.,* 1972, **43,** 31–41.

99 Turnure, C. Response to voice of mother and stranger by babies in the first year. *Develpm. Psychol.,* 1971, **4,** 182–190.

100 Ubell, E. Crib death: 10,000 victims in year, cause unknown. *The New York Times,* Jan. 30, 1972.

101 Uzgiris, I. C. Patterns of cognitive development in infancy. *Merrill-Palmer Quart.,* 1973, **19,** 181–204.

102 Valadian, I., Stuart, H. C., & Reed, R. B. Studies of illness of children followed from birth to eighteen years. *Monogr. Soc. Res. Child Develpm.,* 1961, **26**(3).

103 Vincent, E. L., & Martin, P. C. *Human psychological development.* New York: Ronald Press, 1961.

104 Watson, J. B. *Behaviorism.* New York: People's Institute Publishing Co., 1925.

105 Weiner, B., & Goodnow, J. J. Motor activity: Effects on memory. *Develpm. Psychol.,* 1970, **2,** 448.

106 Wener, C. Executive competence and spontaneous social behavior in one-year-olds. *Child Develpm.,* 1972, **43,** 256–260.

107 Wilson, J. S. Smiling, cooing and "the game." *Merrill-Palmer Quart.,* 1972, **18,** 323–339.

108 Wingerd, J. The relation of growth from birth to two years to sex, parental size and other factors, using Rao's method of transformed time scale. *Hum. Biol.,* 1970, **42,** 105–131.

109 Yarrow, L. J. Research in dimensions of early maternal care. *Merrill-Palmer Quart.,* 1963, **9,** 101–114.

110 Yourglich, A. Explorations in sociological study of sibling systems. *Family Life Coordinator,* 1964, **13,** 91–94.

111 Zelazo, P. R. Smiling and vocalizing: A cognitive emphasis. *Merrill-Palmer Quart.,* 1972, **18,** 349–365.

112 Zern, D. The relationship between mother-infant contact and later differentiation of the social environment. *J. genet. Psychol.,* 1972, **121,** 107–117.

EARLY CHILDHOOD

Childhood begins when the relative dependency of babyhood is over, at approximately the age of two years, and extends to the time when the child becomes sexually mature, at approximately thirteen years for the average girl and fourteen years for the average boy. After the child has become sexually mature, he is known as an *adolescent*.

During this long period of time—roughly eleven years for girls and twelve years for boys—marked changes take place in the child both physically and psychologically. Because cultural pressures and expectations to learn certain things at one age are different from the pressures and expectations at another age, a child in the early part of

childhood is quite different from a child in the latter part of the period.

Today, it is widely recognized that childhood should be subdivided into two separate periods—early and late childhood. Early childhood extends from two to six years, and late childhood extends from six to the time the child becomes sexually mature. Thus early childhood begins at the conclusion of babyhood—the age when dependency is practically a thing of the past and is being replaced by growing independence—and ends at about the time the child enters first grade in school.

This dividing line between early and late childhood is significant because, as the child leaves the home environment and enters school, new pressures and new expectations result in marked changes in his patterns of behavior, attitudes, interests, and values. He becomes, as a result, a "different" person.

CHARACTERISTICS OF EARLY CHILDHOOD

Just as certain characteristics of babyhood make it a distinctive period in the life span, so certain characteristics of early childhood set it apart from other periods. These characteristics are reflected in the names that parents, educators, psychologists, and sociologists commonly apply to this period.

Names Used by Parents

Most parents consider early childhood a *problem age* or a *troublesome age*. While babyhood presents problems for parents, most of these center around the baby's physical care. With the dawn of childhood, behavior problems become more frequent and more troublesome than the physical-care problems of babyhood. The young child is developing a distinctive personality and is demanding an independence which, in most cases, he is incapable of handling successfully. A young child is often an obstinate, stubborn, disobedient, negativistic, antagonistic individual. He has frequent temper tantrums, he is bothered by nightmares at night and irrational fears during the day, and he suffers from jealousies.

Because of these problems, early childhood seems a less appealing age than babyhood to many parents. The dependency of the baby, so endearing to his parents as well as to older siblings, is now replaced by a resistance on the child's part to their help and a tendency to reject demonstrations of their affection. Furthermore, few young children are as cute as babies, which also makes them less appealing.

Parents also refer to early childhood as the *toy age* because the young child spends much of his waking time playing with his toys. Interest in toys begins to decrease rapidly after the child reaches school age, but during early childhood they play a dominant role.

Names Used by Educators and Psychologists

Educators, doctors, sociologists, and psychologists have given early childhood a number of names, each of which describes an important aspect of the young child's development. Educators refer to it as the *preschool age*, even though the young child may be in nursery school or kindergarten, because the pressures and expectations he is subjected to now are very different from those he will experience when he enters first grade.

To the psychologist, early childhood is the *pregang age*, the time when the child is learning the foundations of social behavior which will prepare him for the more highly organized social life he will be required to adjust to when he enters first grade.

Because the major development that occurs during early childhood concerns gaining control over the environment, psychologists call it the *exploratory age*. The child wants to know what his environment is, how it works, how it feels, and how he can be a part of it. This includes people as well as inanimate objects. One common way of exploring in early childhood is by asking questions; thus this period is also called the *questioning age*.

At no other time in the life span is imitation of the speech and actions of others more pronounced than it is during early childhood. For this reason, it is also known as the *imitative age*. However, in spite of this tendency, most children show more creativity in their play during early childhood than at any other time in their lives. For that reason, psychologists also regard it as the *creative age*.

DEVELOPMENTAL TASKS OF EARLY CHILDHOOD

Although the foundations of some of the developmental tasks the child is expected to master before he enters school are laid in babyhood, much remains to be learned in the relatively short four-year span of early childhood. See page 13 for a complete list of developmental tasks.

When babyhood ends, all normal babies have learned to walk, though with varying degrees of proficiency; have learned to take solid foods; and have achieved a reasonable degree of physiological stability. The major task of learning to control the elimination of body wastes has been almost completed and will be fully mastered within another year or two.

While most babies have built up a useful vocabulary, have reasonably correct pronunciation of the words they use, can comprehend the meaning of simple statements and commands, and can put together several words into meaningful sentences, their ability to communicate with others and to comprehend what others say to them is still on a low level. Much remains to be mastered before they enter school.

Similarly, they have some simple concepts of social and physical realities but far too few to meet their needs as their social horizons broaden and as their physical environment expands. Few babies know more than the most elementary facts about sex differences, and even fewer understand the meaning of sexual modesty. It is questionable whether any babies, as they enter early childhood, actually know what is sex-appropriate in appearance, and they have only the most rudimentary understanding of sex-appropriate behavior.

This is equally true of concepts of right and wrong. What knowledge they have is limited to home situations and must be broadened to include concepts of right and wrong in their relationships with people outside the home, especially in the neighborhood, in school, and on the playground.

Even more important, the young child must lay the foundations for a conscience as a guide to right and wrong behavior. The conscience serves as a source of motivation to do what he knows is right and to avoid doing what he knows is wrong when he is too old to have the watchful eye of a parent or a parent substitute constantly focused on him.

One of the most important and, for most young children, one of the most difficult of the developmental tasks of early childhood is to learn to relate emotionally to parents, siblings, and other people. The emotional relationships that existed during babyhood must be replaced by more mature ones. The baby's relationships to others is based on his dependence on them to meet his emotional needs, especially his need for affection. The young child, however, must learn to give as well as to receive affection. In short, he must learn to be outer-bound instead of self-bound.

PHYSICAL DEVELOPMENT

Growth during early childhood proceeds at a slow rate as compared with the rapid rate of growth in babyhood. Early childhood is a time of relatively even growth, though there are seasonal variations; July to mid-December is the most favorable time for increases in weight, and April to mid-August is most favorable for height increases.

The major aspects of physical development are summarized in Box 5-1. Compare the development that takes place in early childhood with that which takes place in babyhood, as summarized in Box 4-1.

In spite of the predictable pattern described in Box 5-1, there are individual differences in all aspects of physical development. Children of superior intelligence, for example, tend to be taller in early childhood than those of average or below-average intelligence and to shed their temporary teeth sooner. While sex differences in height and weight are not pronounced, ossification of the bones and shedding of the temporary teeth are more advanced, age for age, in girls than in boys. Because children from higher socioeconomic groups tend to be better nourished and receive better prenatal and postnatal care, variations in height, weight, and muscular development are in their favor (13, 41, 86).

PHYSIOLOGICAL HABITS

During early childhood, the physiological habits whose foundations were laid in babyhood become well established. It is no longer necessary to provide specially prepared food for the child, and he learns to eat his meals at regular times. However, his appetite is not as ravenous as it was in babyhood, partly because his growth rate has slowed down and partly because he has now developed marked food likes and dislikes.

There are daily variations in the amount of sleep a young child needs, depending on such factors as the amount of exercise he has had during the day and the kinds of activities he has engaged in. Three-year-olds sleep approximately twelve out of the twenty-four hours. Each successive year during childhood, the average daily amount of sleep is approximately one-half hour less than in the previous year.

As was pointed out in the preceding chapter, bowel control is generally well es-

---

Box 5-1. PHYSICAL DEVELOPMENT IN EARLY CHILDHOOD

Height
The average annual increase in height is 3 inches. By the age of six, the average child measures 46.6 inches.

Weight
The average annual increase in weight is 3 to 5 pounds. At age six, the child should weigh approximately seven times as much as he did at birth. The average girl weighs 48.5 pounds, and the average boy weighs 49 pounds.

Body Proportions
Body proportions change markedly, and the "baby look" disappears. Facial features remain small but the chin becomes more pronounced and the neck elongates. There is a gradual decrease in the stockiness of the trunk, and the body tends to become cone-shaped, with a flattened abdomen, a broader and flatter chest, and shoulders that are broader and more square. The arms and legs lengthen and may become spindly, and the hands and feet grow bigger. Refer to Figure 4-1.

Body Build
Differences in body build become apparent. Some children have an *endomorphic,* or heavy, body build; some have a *mesomorphic,* or sturdy, muscular body build; and some have an *ectomorphic,* or relatively thin, body build.

Bones and Muscles
The bones ossify at different rates in different parts of the body, following the laws of developmental direction. The muscles become larger, stronger, and heavier, with the result that children look thinner as early childhood progresses, even though they weigh more.

Fat
Children who tend toward endomorphy have more adipose than muscular tissue; those who tend toward mesomorphy have more muscular than adipose tissue; and those with an ectomorphic build have both small muscles and little adipose tissue.

Teeth
During the first four to six months of early childhood, the last four baby teeth—the back molars—erupt. During the last half year of early childhood, the baby teeth begin to be replaced by permanent teeth. The first to come out are the front central incisors—the first baby teeth to appear. When early childhood ends, the child generally has one or two of his permanent teeth in front and some gaps where permanent teeth will eventually erupt.

tablished when babyhood ends. By the time the child is three or four years old, bladder control at night should be achieved. By the time the child is ready to enter school, bladder control should be so complete that even fatigue and emotional tension will not interfere with it.

SKILLS OF EARLY CHILDHOOD

Early childhood is the ideal age to learn skills. The young child enjoys repetition and is therefore willing to repeat an activity until he has acquired the ability to do it well. He is adventuresome and hence is not held back by fear of hurting himself or of being

It will be some time before this five-year-old is a good carpenter but practicing with hammer and nails helps him develop other hand skills. (Alice Kandell from Rapho Guillumette)

ridiculed by his associates, as older children often are. He learns easily and quickly because his body is still very pliable and because he has acquired so few skills that they do not interfere with the acquisition of new ones.

Typical Skills

What skills the young child will learn depends partly upon his maturational readiness to learn but mainly upon the opportunities he has to learn them and the guidance he receives in mastering them quickly and efficiently. Children from poorer environments, it has been reported, generally master skills earlier and in larger numbers than children from more favored environments, not because they are maturationally more advanced but because their parents are too busy to wait on them when it is no longer necessary (13).

There are sex differences in the kinds of skills children learn. Early in childhood, boys come under pressure to learn play skills that are culturally approved for members of their own sex and to avoid mastering those which are considered more appropriate for girls. They are, for example, encouraged to learn skills involved in ball play, just as girls are encouraged to learn skills related to homemaking.

In spite of variations, all young children learn certain common skills, though the time they learn them may vary somewhat and the proficiency with which they learn them may be different. These common skills can be divided into two major categories: hand skills and leg skills.

Hand Skills Self-feeding and dressing skills, begun in babyhood, are perfected in early childhood. The greatest improvement in dressing skills generally comes between the ages of 1½ and 3½ years. Brushing the hair and bathing are skills which can be acquired easily in early childhood. By the time the child reaches kindergarten age, he should be able to bathe, dress, tie his shoes, and comb his hair with little or no assistance.

Between the ages of five and six, most children can become proficient in throwing and catching balls. They can use scissors and can mold with clay, make cookies, and sew. Using crayons, pencils, and paints, young children are able to color outlined pictures, draw or paint pictures of their own, and make a recognizable drawing of a man.

Leg Skills Once the young child has learned to walk, he turns his attention to learning other movements requiring the use of his legs. He learns to hop, skip, gallop, and jump by the age of five or six years. Climbing skills are likewise well established in early childhood. Between the ages of three and four, tricycling and swimming can be learned. Other leg skills acquired by young children include jumping rope, balancing on rails or on the top of a wall, roller skating, ice skating (on double-runners), and dancing.

IMPROVEMENTS IN SPEECH DURING EARLY CHILDHOOD

Learning to speak in early childhood is important because speech is an essential tool in socialization. The child who can communicate easily with his peers makes better social contacts and is more readily accepted as a member of the play group than the child whose ability to communicate is limited. Unless he speaks as well as his classmates in school, the child will be handicapped both educationally and socially.

Role of Comprehension

To be able to communicate with others, the child must understand what they say to him. Otherwise, his speech will be unrelated to what they say, and his social contacts will be jeopardized. This is well illustrated in the case of bilingual children whose dominant language is different from that of their playmates. They fail to understand what their playmates say, and as a result they become socially isolated.

Comprehension is greatly influenced by how attentively the child *listens* to what is said to him. Listening to the radio and watching television can be helpful in this regard because they encourage attentive listening.

Tasks in Learning Speech Skills

Early childhood is normally a time when rapid strides are made in the major tasks of learning to speak—building up a vocabulary, mastering pronunciation, and combining words into sentences. Box 5-2 describes how these tasks are mastered. Compare the pattern of speech development in early childhood with that in babyhood, as outlined in

---

Box 5-2. TASKS INVOLVED IN LEARNING TO SPEAK IN EARLY CHILDHOOD

Vocabulary Building
The young child's vocabulary increases rapidly as he learns new words and new meanings for old ones. See Figure 5-1. He learns a general vocabulary of words, such as "good" and "bad," as well as many specific words, such as numbers and the names of colors.

Pronunciation
Certain sounds and sound combinations are especially difficult for a young child to learn to pronounce, such as the consonants *z, w, d, s,* and *g* and the consonant combinations *st, str, dr,* and *fl.* Listening to radio and television can be an aid in learning correct pronunciation.

Forming Sentences
Three- or four-word sentences are used as early as two years of age and commonly at three. Many of these sentences are incomplete, consisting mainly of nouns and lacking verbs, prepositions, and conjunctions. After age three, the child forms six- to eight-word sentences containing all parts of speech.

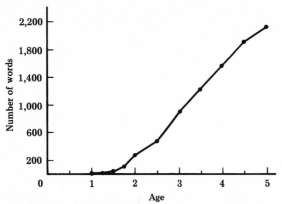

Figure 5-1 Vocabulary increases rapidly during early childhood. (Adapted from L. P. Lipsitt. Learning processes of human newborns. *Merrill-Palmer Quart.,* 1966, **12**, 45–71. Used by permission.)

Box 4-4. Most young children today speak better than children in past generations. McCarthy has explained this improvement as follows (89):

Several possibilities account for this. Among those I would list are the advent of radio and television, fewer foreign-born and bilingual children, the rise of nursery schools affording more opportunities for language stimulation outside the home for formerly underprivileged groups of children, more leisure time for parents to spend with their children, reduced amount of time that children are cared for by nursemaids of limited verbal ability, better economic conditions allowing parents even in lower income brackets to provide more stimulating environments for their children, and finally the somewhat greater tendency for children to be treated more permissively and to find greater acceptance in the modern home.

Content of Speech

At first, the young child's speech is egocentric in the sense that he talks mainly about himself, his interests, his family, and his possessions. Toward the end of early childhood, socialized speech begins, and the child talks about other people as well as himself. However, much of this early socialized speech is unsocial in that it is heavily weighted with criticism of others, and it may take the form of tattling or complaining. Most young children also make unkind, derogatory comments about other people and about their actions and their possessions. They also engage in name-calling, especially when they are angry. Boasting, especially about material possessions, is very common at this age.

As the size of the child's play group becomes larger, his language becomes more sociable and less egocentric. He is also slightly less critical, asks fewer questions, and gives more commands. Small social groupings are most favorable for the development of speech in young children.

The most frequent topics of conversation among young children are themselves and their activities. When a second person is the subject of a remark, the remark is generally a command for that person to do something. Topics such as personal likes and dislikes, clothes, where one lives, and matters of everyday routine predominate in the young child's conversation.

Amount of Talking

Some children talk incessantly, once they are able to speak with ease, while others are relatively silent—the nontalkers. How much the child talks depends upon a number of factors. The brighter the child, the more quickly he will master speech skills and the easier it is for him to talk. Children who grow up in homes where permissive discipline is used talk more than those whose parents are authoritarian and believe that "children should be seen but not heard." Firstborn and only children are encouraged to talk more than later-born children or children from large families, where the discipline is likely to be authoritarian.

In lower-class families, family activities tend to be less organized than those in middle- and upper-class families, and there is less conversation among the family members and less encouragement for the child to talk.

The poorer quality of speech and of conversational skills of many young black children may be due in part to the fact that they have grown up in homes where the father is absent or where family life is disorganized because there are many children or because the mother must work outside the home.

While children from bilingual homes may talk as much at home as children from monolingual homes, their speech is very limited when they are with members of their peer group.

EMOTIONS OF EARLY CHILDHOOD

Emotions are especially intense during early childhood. This is a time of disequilibrium, and the child is "out of focus" in the sense that he is easily aroused to emotional outbursts and, as a result, is difficult to live with and guide. This is true of the major part of early childhood; it is especially true of children aged 2½ to 3½ and 5½ to 6½ (2).

Although any emotion may be "heightened" in the sense that it occurs more frequently and more intensely than is normal for that particular individual, heightened emotionality in early childhood is characterized by temper tantrums, intense fears, and unreasonable outbursts of jealousy. Part of the intense emotionality of children at this age may be traced to fatigue due to strenuous and prolonged play, rebellion against taking naps, and the fact that they may eat too little.

Much of the heightened emotionality characteristic of this age is psychological rather than physiological in origin. Most young children feel that they are capable of doing more than their parents will permit them to do and revolt against the restrictions placed upon them. In addition, they become angry when they find they are incapable of doing what they think they can do easily and successfully. The child whose parents expect him to measure up to unrealistically high standards will experience more emotional tension than the child whose parents are more permissive.

Common Emotional Patterns

Young children experience most of the emotions normally experienced by adults. However, the stimuli that give rise to them and the ways in which children express these emotions are markedly different. Box 5-3 gives the common emotional patterns of early childhood.

Many factors influence the intensity and frequency of emotions in early childhood. Emotions are intense at certain ages and less so at others. Temper tantrums, for example, reach their peak of severity between the ages of two and four, after which they become shorter in duration and give way to sulking, brooding, and whining. Fear follows much the same pattern, partly because the child realizes that there is nothing frightening about situations he formerly feared and partly because of social pressures that make him feel he must conceal his fears. By contrast, jealousy usually begins around the age of two and increases as the child grows older.

Young children vary greatly in the amount of curiosity they experience and in the way they express it. Bright children, it has been found, are more active in exploring their environment and ask more questions than those of lower intellectual levels (88). Sex differences in emotions come mainly from social pressures to express emotions in sex-appropriate ways. Because temper tantrums are considered more sex-appropriate for boys than for girls, boys throughout early childhood have more tantrums, and more violent tantrums, than girls (41). On the other hand, fear, jealousy, and affection are considered less sex-appropriate for boys than for girls, and thus girls express these emotions more strongly than boys (24).

Box 5-3. COMMON EMOTIONS OF EARLY CHILDHOOD

Anger
The most common causes of anger in young children are conflicts over playthings, the thwarting of wishes, and vigorous attacks from another child. Children express anger through temper tantrums, characterized by crying, screaming, stamping, kicking, jumping up and down, or striking.

Fear
Conditioning, imitation, and memories of unpleasant experiences play important roles in arousing fears, as do stories, pictures, radio and television programs, and movies with frightening elements. See Figure 5-2. At first, a child's response to fear is panic; later, his responses become more specific and include running away and hiding, crying, and avoiding frightening situations.

Jealousy
A child becomes jealous when he thinks parental interest and attention are shifting toward someone else in the family, usually a new sibling. He may openly express his jealousy, or he may show it by reverting to infantile behavior (such as bed-wetting), pretending to be ill, or being generally naughty. All such behavior is a bid for attention.

Curiosity
Children are curious about anything new that they see and also about their own bodies and the bodies of others. Their first responses to curiosity take the form of sensorimotor exploration; later, as a result of social pressures and punishment, they respond by asking questions.

Envy
A young child may become envious of the abilities or material possessions of another person and may express his envy by complaining about what he has, by verbalizing a wish to have what another has (see Figure 5-3), or by appropriating the object he envies.

Joy
The young child derives joy from such things as a sense of physical well-being, incongruous situations, sudden or unexpected noises, slight calamities, playing pranks on others, and accomplishing what seems to him a difficult task. He expresses his joy by smiling, laughing, clapping his hands, jumping up and down, or hugging the object or person that has made him happy.

Grief
The child is saddened by the loss of anything that he loves or is important to him, and he typically expresses his grief by crying and losing interest in his normal activities, including eating.

Affection
The young child learns to love the things—people, pets, or objects—that give him pleasure, and he expresses his affection either verbally or physically.

Family size influences the frequency and intensity of jealousy and envy. Jealousy is more common in small families, where there are two or three children, than in larger families, where none of the children can receive much attention from their parents. Envy, on the other hand, is more common in large than in small families; the larger the family, the fewer material possessions the child will have, and therefore the more likely he is to envy those of his siblings. Within a family, firstborn children display jealousy more often and more violently than their later-born siblings.

The social environment of the home plays an important role in the frequency and intensity of the young child's anger. For example, temper tantrums are more frequent in homes where there are many guests or where there are more than two adults. Similarly, the child with siblings has more temper outbursts than the only child. The kind of discipline and the child-training methods used also influence the frequency and intensity of the child's angry outbursts. The more authoritarian the parents are, the more likely the child is to respond with anger.

"**But being in the woods SCARES us! Goldilocks met the bears there, Red Riding Hood met the wolf, Snow White met the witch . . .**"

Figure 5-2 Many fears of young children come from the mass media. (Bil Keane. "The Family Circus." Register and Tribune Syndicate, Aug. 5, 1965. Used by permission.)

PATTERN OF EARLY SOCIALIZATION

One of the important developmental tasks of early childhood is acquiring the preliminary training and experience needed to become a member of a "gang" in late childhood. Thus early childhood is often called the *pregang age.* The foundations for socialization are laid as the number of contacts young children have with their peers increases with each passing year. Not only do they play more with other children, but they also talk more with them (85). This is illustrated in Figure 5-4.

However, the *kind* of social contacts the young child has is more important than the number of such contacts. If he enjoys his contacts with others, even if they are only occasional, his attitude toward future social

contacts will be more favorable than if he has many social contacts of a less favorable kind. Furthermore, the advantage he takes of the opportunities offered him for social contacts will be greatly influenced by how pleasurable his past social contacts have been.

Early Forms of Behavior in Social Situations

The most important forms of social behavior necessary for successful social adjustment appear and begin to develop at this time. In the early years of childhood, they are not developed well enough to enable the child to get along successfully with others at all times. However, this is a crucial stage in their development because it is at this time that the basic social attitudes and the patterns of social behavior are established. These are given in Box 5-4. Note that many of these patterns appear to be unsocial or even antisocial rather than social, but each

Figure 5-3 Children learn at an early age to express their envy. (Bil Keane. "The Family Circus." Register and Tribune Syndicate, July 21, 1972. Used by permission.)

"**I wish you'd buy us a swing like THEIRS!**"

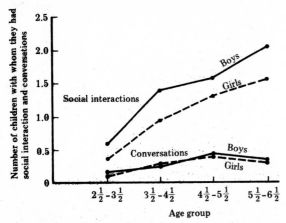

Figure 5-4 Children play more with, and talk more to, other children as they grow older. (Adapted from H. R. Marshall. Relations between home experiences and children's use of language in play interactions with peers. *Psychol. Monogr.,* 1961, **75**(5). Used by permission.)

is important as a learning experience that will enable the child to know what the social group approves and disapproves and what it will and will not tolerate.

Companions in Early Childhood

Between the ages of two and three, the child shows a decided interest in watching other children, and he attempts to make social contacts with them. *Parallel play*, in which the child plays independently beside other children rather than with them, is his earliest form of social activity with his contemporaries.

Following this comes *associative play*, in which the child engages in similar, if not identical, activities with other children, and *cooperative play*, in which he is a part of a group. Frequently children play the role of an onlooker, watching other children at play. By the time the child is four years old, he understands the rudiments of team play, is conscious of the opinions of others, and tries to gain attention by showing off.

Companions of the same age and level of maturity are important at this time. Because young children are relatively unaware of socioeconomic differences, this factor is of little importance in their choice of companions.

Leaders in Early Childhood

In early childhood, the leader is characteristically larger, more intelligent, and usually older than the other members of the group. The fact that he is older and more intelligent makes it possible for him to offer suggestions for play which the other children, because of their habitual reliance upon adult suggestions, are willing to follow. The big child has an advantage over smaller ones in that children tend to respect size as a result of their habits of obedience to adult requests.

Most leaders in early childhood are tyrannical bosses who show little consideration for the wishes of others. When his tyranny becomes too great, the leader loses status and is replaced by another. Some leaders in early childhood are "diplomats" who lead others by indirect and artful suggestions or by bargaining. Girls at this age frequently assume the role of leadership in groups containing boys.

PLAY IN EARLY CHILDHOOD

The play interests of young children conform more or less closely to a pattern which is markedly influenced by their maturational readiness for certain forms of play and by the environment in which they are growing up. However, there are variations in this pattern. Highly intelligent children, for example, show a preference for dramatic play and creative activities and for books which inform rather than merely amuse. In their constructions, they make more complicated and original designs than children who are less bright.

Even in the preschool years, children become aware of the fact that certain kinds of

Box 5-4. SOCIAL AND UNSOCIAL BEHAVIOR PATTERNS

Social Patterns

Imitation
To identify himself with the group, the child imitates the attitudes and behavior of a person whom he especially admires and wants to be like.

Rivalry
The desire to excel or outdo others is apparent as early as the fourth year. It begins at home and later develops in play with children outside the home.

Cooperation
By the end of the third year, cooperative play and group activities begin to develop and increase in both frequency and duration as the child's opportunities for play with other children increase.

Sympathy
Because sympathy requires an understanding of the feelings and emotions of others, it appears only occasionally before the third year. The more play contacts the child has, the sooner sympathy will develop.

Social Approval
As early childhood draws to a close, peer approval becomes more important than adult approval. Young children find that naughty and disturbing behavior is a way of winning peer approval.

Unsocial Patterns

Negativism
Negativism, or resistance to adult authority, reaches its peak between three and four years of age and then declines. Physical resistance gradually gives way to verbal resistance and pretending not to hear or understand requests.

Aggressiveness
Aggressiveness increases between the ages of two and four and then declines. Physical attacks begin to be replaced by verbal atacks in the form of name-calling, tattling, or blaming others.

Ascendant Behavior
Ascendant behavior, or "bossiness," begins around the age of three and increases as opportunities for social contacts increase. Girls tend to be bossier than boys.

Selfishness
While the child's social horizons are limited mainly to the home, he is selfish and egocentric. As his social horizons broaden, selfishness gradually wanes, but generosity is still very undeveloped.

Sex Antagonism
Until they are four years old, boys and girls play together harmoniously. After that, boys come under social pressures that lead them to shun play activities that might be regarded as "sissyish." Many engage in aggressive behavior which antagonizes girls.

Prejudice
Most preschool children show a preference for playmates of their own race, but they seldom refuse to play with children of another race. (See Figure 5-5.) Racial prejudice begins sooner than religious or socioeconomic prejudice, but later than sex prejudice.

play and certain kinds of toys are considered more appropriate for one sex than for the other. This influences the kind of play equipment they use and the way they play with it. Boys are more aware of the sex appropriateness of toys than girls are. Boys also, throughout early childhood, show a wider range of play interests than girls.

The amount of play equipment children have and the amount of space they have to play in—both of which are influenced by the socioeconomic status of the family—will also influence the patterns of their play. Socioeconomic status likewise influences the amount of supervision they have in their play. This is well illustrated in the case of television watching. Children from families of lower socioeconomic status spend more time watching television, and their parents exert less control over what they watch,

"Me 'n' Jackson are exactly the same age. Only he's different. He's LEFT-HANDED!"

Figure 5-5 Among preschool children, there is little refusal to play with children of another race. (Hank Ketcham. "Dennis the Menace." Courtesy Publishers-Hall Syndicate, Jan. 6, 1970.)

extends from about two or three years of age to seven or eight years (97).

Because of his limited experiences with people and things and his limited vocabulary, it is understandable that many of the young child's concepts are inaccurate or actually faulty. Furthermore, when concepts are heavily weighted with emotional accompaniments, there is resistance to change even when new knowledge would increase the accuracy of the formerly learned concepts.

Children develop many of the same concepts because of common learning experiences. Other concepts are individual and depend upon the learning opportunities of the particular child. For example, a young child who has traveled to other countries will develop concepts of people and patterns of life unlike those of a child whose experi-

than is the case in middle-class families (85).

In spite of these variations, certain patterns of play are found almost universally among children of preschool age in the American culture of today. The most common of these are given in Box 5-5.

DEVELOPMENT OF UNDERSTANDING

New experiences lead to new meanings which are associated with meanings established in babyhood. The child now begins to notice details which formerly escaped his attention. As a result, he is not so apt to confuse objects, situations, or people that have elements in common, as he formerly did. His concepts thus become more specific and meaningful to him. Piaget has called this the *preoperational stage* of thinking; it

Television watching: one of the most common play patterns of early childhood. (Suzanne Szasz)

Box 5-5. PLAY PATTERNS IN EARLY CHILDHOOD

Toys

Interest in toys begins to lag somewhat toward the end of early childhood. The child no longer endows his toys with living qualities, and his interest in solitary play is replaced by interest in group play.

Dramatizations

At around age three, dramatization consists of playing with his toys in ways that imitate life experiences. Later, the child plays make-believe games with his friends—cops and robbers, for example—many of which are based on stories that have been read to him or movies and television shows he has seen.

Constructions

The young child makes many things with blocks, sand, mud, clay, beads, paints, crayons, scissors, and paints. Most of his constructions are in imitation of what he sees in daily life—people and houses, for example.

Games

During the fourth year the child begins to prefer games played with peers to those played with adults. These games can have any number of players and involve few rules. Games that test skills, such as throwing and catching balls, are also popular.

Reading

The young child likes to be read to and to look at pictures in books. Fairy tales, nursery rhymes, and stories about animals and everyday occurrences appeal to him.

Movies, Radio, and Television

Most young children attend movies infrequently, but they do like cartoons, movies about animals, and home movies of family members. They also enjoy listening to the radio, but are especially fond of television watching. They like programs meant for older children as well as those aimed at the preschooler. Since they watch in the security of their own homes, they are not upset by frightening elements in the programs.

---

ences have been more limited. Box 5-6 shows the important categories of concepts that commonly develop during early childhood.

MORAL DEVELOPMENT IN EARLY CHILDHOOD

The young child's intellectual development has not yet reached the point where he can learn or apply abstract principles of right and wrong. He must learn moral behavior in specific situations. And, because his retention is still poor, the learning is a slow process. If he is told not to do something one day, he may forget and do it again the next day, or the day after that.

Early childhood is characterized by what Piaget has called "morality by constraint."

The child obeys rules automatically, without using reason or judgment, and he regards adults in authority as omnipotent. He also judges all acts as right or wrong in terms of their consequences rather than in terms of the motivations behind them. A "wrong" act results in punishment, which is dealt out either by other human beings or by natural or supernatural forces (97).

Because of his mental immaturity, the child cannot understand the whys and wherefores of behavior. He merely learns how to act without knowing why he does so. As early childhood comes to an end, habits of obedience should be established, provided the child has had consistent discipline. However, the young child does not feel guilty when he is caught doing something he knows is wrong. Rather, he may become frightened at the prospect of punishment, or he may rationalize his action.

Box 5-6. COMMON CATEGORIES OF CONCEPTS THAT DEVELOP DURING EARLY CHILDHOOD

Life

Children tend to ascribe living qualities to inanimate objects—dolls and stuffed animals, for example. Adults may encourage this by pointing out similarities between animate and inanimate objects, such as a cloud formation that resembles a dog or a horse.

Death

The young child tends to associate death with anything that goes away or disappears, although he is unable to comprehend the finality of death.

Bodily Functions

The young child has very inaccurate concepts of bodily functions and of birth. This remains the case even after he enters school.

Space

Four-year-olds can judge short distances accurately, but the ability to judge long distances does not develop until late childhood.

Weight

Before the child learns that different materials have different weights—which does not occur much before the school age—he estimates weight exclusively in terms of size.

Numbers

Children who attend nursery school or kindergarten usually understand numbers up to 5, but have only vague concepts about numbers higher than that.

Time

Young children have no idea of the duration of time—how long an hour is, for example—nor can they estimate time in terms of their own activities. Most four- or five-year-olds know the day of the week, and by the age of six they know the month, season, and year.

Self

By the time the child is three, he knows his sex, his full name, and the names of the different parts of his body. When he starts to play with other children, his self-concept begins to include facts about his abilities and his race but not his socioeconomic level.

Sex Roles

Clear concepts of appropriate sex roles are developed by the time the child is five years old.

Social Awareness

Before early childhood ends, most children are able to form definite opinions about others—whether a person is "nice" or "mean," for example.

Beauty

The young child prefers music with a definite tune or rhythm, and he likes bright, gaudy colors.

Comic

Among the things most often perceived as comic by the young child are funny faces made by himself or others, socially inappropriate behavior, and the antics of domestic animals.

Discipline

Regardless of the kind of discipline used, almost all young children are punished at some time. Common forms of punishment are spanking, isolating the child in his room, sending him to bed, making him sit on a chair, withdrawing a privilege, threatening to leave or to cease to love the child, comparing him unfavorably with siblings, nagging, and harping on the misdemeanor. Today there is a swing back to the use of corporal punishment in the form of spanking. See Figure 5-6.

Rewards in the form of toys, candy, or being taken somewhere or given a special treat are used, somewhat sparingly, by parents of young children, even by those who favor democratic discipline. They are afraid they will spoil the child, or they regard the reward as a form of bribery, which they have been told is a bad disciplinary technique.

Discipline affects young children in different ways. The common effects of discipline on children's behavior, attitudes, and personalities are given in Box 5-7.

Misdemeanors

Young children learn that willful disobedience of a minor sort will generally bring them more attention than good behavior. Thus a child who feels he is being ignored may misbehave frequently in the hope of getting the attention he craves.

Desire for adult attention is by no means the only cause of misdemeanors in early childhood. The young child may misbehave through ignorance of what is expected of him; he may have forgotten what he was told to do; he may be confused because rules change from day to day; or he may want to test adult authority and see how much he can get away with without being punished.

While young children engage in every conceivable kind of misdemeanor, the most common forms are capriciousness—"orneriness"—thumb-sucking, bed-wetting, boisterous attempts to get attention, temper tantrums, lying, destructiveness, cheating in games, and dawdling. Most of these are as-

"It's a new way of disciplining children . . . I just read about it."

Figure 5-6 Spanking as a form of punishment is coming back into style. (George Clark. "The Neighbors." Chicago Tribune–New York News Syndicate, Dec. 11, 1972. Used by permission.)

Box 5-7. EFFECTS OF DISCIPLINE ON YOUNG CHILDREN

Effects on Behavior

Children of permissive parents become selfish, disregard the rights of others, and are aggressive and unsocial. Those who are subjected to strict, authoritarian training are overly obedient in the presence of adults but aggressive in peer relationships. Children brought up under democratic discipline learn to restrain behavior they know is wrong, and they are more considerate of the rights of others.

Effects on Attitudes

Children whose parents are either authoritarian or permissive tend to resent those in authority. In the former case, they feel they have been treated unfairly; in the latter case, they feel their parents

should have warned them that not all adults will accept undisciplined behavior. Democratic discipline may lead to temporary anger, but not to resentment. The attitudes formed as a result of child-training methods tend to become generalized, to spread to all persons in authority, and to persist.

Effects on Personality

The more physical punishment is used, the more likely the child is to become sullen, obstinate, and negativistic. This results in poor personal and social adjustments, which are also characteristic of children brought up permissively. Those brought up with democratic discipline make the best personal and social adjustments.

sociated with immaturity and appear less and less frequently as the child grows older.

COMMON INTERESTS IN EARLY CHILDHOOD

Some interests are almost universal among young children in the American culture today. These include interest in religion, in the human body, in sex, and in clothes.

Interest in Religion

Religious beliefs are, for the most part, meaningless to a young child, although he may show some interest in religious observances. However, because so many of the mysteries centered around birth, death, growth, and the elements are explained to him in religious terms, his curiosity about religious matters is great, and he asks many questions relating to religion. He accepts what he is told without questioning or doubting.

The young child's religious concepts are realistic in the sense that he interprets what he hears in terms of what he knows. To him, God is a man who wears clothes different from the clothes of the persons he knows and who has a flowing white beard and long white hair. God is all-knowing, all-powerful. He is really a "watcher" who observes what people do and punishes those who are evil, though he is kind and merciful to those who try to be good. Angels are men and women with white wings, and heaven is a place where every human wish is gratified.

Early childhood is the "fairy-tale stage" of religious belief. That is why religious stories have such a strong appeal to young children and also why they find the pageantry of religious services so awe-inspiring. Even home religious observances inspire awe and reverence in the young child.

The young child's interest in religion is egocentric, however. Prayer, for example, is a way of gaining childish desires. He thinks of God as a person who can and will do things for him, just as his parents do when he asks them. The egocentrism of religion in childhood is best illustrated by the young child's attitude toward Christmas, which he does not think of as a day to celebrate the birth of Christ, but rather as the day when Santa Claus will bring him all the things he has asked for.

Interest in the Human Body

The young child expresses his interest in his body by commenting on the various parts and asking questions about them, examining parts of his body and calling attention to them, and occasionally engaging in exhibitionism. Children are also curious about elimination, though their attitude toward it is matter-of-fact and unconcerned (43).

While young children recognize anatomical differences between boys and girls, they regard these as incidental characteristics. They are curious about germs and how they cause the body to become sick and about how medicine cures sickness. When a person dies, they are curious about what happens to the body and how it gets to heaven.

Interest in Sex

Young children are extremely curious about where babies come from and ask many questions about this matter. Some children believe that babies come from heaven, but most believe that they come from a hospital or a store or that a stork brings them.

Many children show their interest in sex by talking about it to their playmates when adults are not present, by looking at pictures of adult men and women in amorous poses, by engaging in sex play with members of their own sex or of the opposite sex, and by masturbating. However, because many parents regard sex play and masturbation as naughty, if not actually wicked, such activities are usually carried out in private.

Interest in Clothes

The young child has little interest in his appearance—whether he is clean or dirty, for example—but he does have a strong interest in his clothes. At an early age, he discovers that his clothing attracts attention. Adults make favorable comments about his clothes, and his playmates often admire them or even envy him because of them.

The young child is well aware of the sex appropriateness of clothes and wants to be sure that his clothes conform to the approved styles for his sex. Boys, for example, regard being dressed up as a sign of a sissy, and they prefer playclothes to dressy clothes.

FAMILY RELATIONSHIPS IN EARLY CHILDHOOD

The young child's attitudes toward people, things, and life in general are patterned by his home life. Although no one method of child training can guarantee good or poor adjustment, the child who is brought up in a democratic home generally makes better adjustments to outsiders than the child from an authoritarian home. As Chittenden et al. have pointed out, the firstborn "is brought up; the others grow up" (21). Thus the firstborn generally makes better social adjust-

ments than his later-born siblings, though not necessarily better personal adjustments.

Child-training methods alone are not responsible for the effects of family relationships on the young child's personal and social adjustments. If the child feels closer to one parent than the other, he will imitate the attitudes, emotions, and behavior patterns of that parent.

Changes in parent-child relationships, which begin during the second year of babyhood, continue throughout early childhood, usually at a more rapid rate. Many conditions are responsible for these changes, the most important of which are given in Box 5-8.

Sibling Relationships

Siblings are important aids to the socialization of the young child. From his siblings, the young child learns to evaluate his behavior as others do and to think of himself as others think of him. Older siblings serve as role models for him to imitate, and in this way he learns not only socially approved behavior patterns but also those which are considered appropriate for his sex.

Box 5-8. CONDITIONS CONTRIBUTING TO CHANGED PARENT-CHILD RELATIONSHIPS

Changes in the Child
The soft, cuddly baby has now become a rebellious, mischievous, self-assertive individual who is constantly into everything, demanding attention, and refusing to do as he is told.

Changes in Parental Attitudes
As the young child becomes more independent, parents feel that he needs less care and attention than he did when he was a baby, and the child resents this. See Figure 5-7.

Parental Concept of a "Good" Child
When a child does not come up to his parents' expectations, they become critical and punitive, and the child reacts to this treatment by being even more negativistic and troublesome.

Parental Preference
Because the mother spends more time with the child than the father and because most mothers understand the troublesome behavior of young children better than fathers do, the child may not only prefer his mother but also show it plainly. The father may resent this and become critical of the child and his behavior, thus widening the gap between them.

Preference for Outsiders
A young child who goes to nursery school, for example, may develop a preference for his teacher over his parents, and they may feel hurt and resentful.

"Why CAN'T you play cards with us, Mommy? Grandma always does."

Figure 5-7 When parental behavior does not come up to children's expectations, it leads to unfavorable parent-child relationships. (Bil Keane. "The Family Circus." Register and Tribune Syndicate, Jan. 10, 1966. Used by permission.)

Whether his siblings are older or younger than he, they contribute to his emotional security and teach him how to show his affection for others. Every child learns, in a family where there are siblings, to play a certain role, depending on his sex, his ordinal position in the family, and the age differential between him and his siblings. This is also an important aid to his socialization because, in the peer group, he will be expected to play the role of leader or follower.

Even sibling quarrels provide a valuable learning experience for the young child. He discovers what other children will and will not tolerate, and he learns how to be a good loser as well as a gracious winner. The only child, deprived of this learning experience, often has difficulty in making good social adjustments during the gang age of late childhood.

PERSONALITY DEVELOPMENT IN EARLY CHILDHOOD

The pattern of the child's personality, the foundations of which were laid in babyhood, begins to take form in early childhood. Because parents, siblings, and relatives constitute the child's social world for the most part, how they feel about him and how they treat him are important factors in the shaping of his self-concept—the core of the personality pattern. That is why Glasner has said that the child's concept of himself as a person is "formed within the womb of family relationships" (45).

Conditions Shaping the Self-Concept

Many conditions within the family are responsible for shaping the self-concept during the early childhood years. The child's general relationship with his family is important, as are specific parental attitudes—toward his appearance, for example.

The *child-training* method used in the home is important in shaping the young child's developing concept of self. Strict, authoritarian discipline, accompanied by frequent and harsh corporal punishment, for example, tends to build up resentments against all persons in authority and feelings of martyrdom—feelings which can and often do develop into a martyr complex.

The *aspirations* parents have for the child play an important role in his developing self-concept. When these are unrealistically high, the child is doomed to failure. Regardless of how children react, failure leaves an indelible mark on their self-concepts and lays the foundation for feelings of inferiority and inadequacy.

The child's *ordinal position* in the family has an effect on his developing personality. This may be explained in part by the fact that each child in the family learns to play a specific role, in part by differences in child-training methods used by the parents with the different children, and in part by the child's success or failure in competing with his siblings.

Even though young children are infrequently aware of *minority-group* identification, those who have such an awareness are influenced unfavorably if their peers neglect or reject them. As was pointed out earlier, young children tend to show a preference for playmates of their own race and to neglect, though not discriminate against, those of other racial groups.

As Inselberg and Burke have pointed out, as early as the late preschool years "Appropriate *sex-role identification* in boys is associated with favorable personality characteristics." Boys with masculine physiques are more successful in interacting with other boys, and this reinforces overt masculine behavior, which in turn leads their peers to judge their actions as sex-appropriate (57).

Environmental insecurity, whether due to death, divorce or separation, or social mobility, affects the young child's self-concept unfavorably because he feels insecure and different from his peers. Children whose parents are upwardly mobile, it has been reported, may learn to be independent and ambitious, but they tend to become nervous, tense, anxious, and highly competitive and aggressive in their peer relationships (11, 74).

Beginnings of Individuality

By the time the young child enters school, the pattern of his personality can be readily distinguished. Some children are leaders, and some are followers; some are despotic, while others are meek; some are sociable, while others are solitary; some like to show off and be the center of attention,

Young children are often unaware of minority-group identification, such as race or ethnicity. (Hella Hammid from Rapho Guillumette)

while others prefer to shun the limelight.

Thomas et al. have identified three personality syndromes among young children: There are "easy children," who are well adjusted both physically and psychologically; "difficult children," who are irregular in bodily functions, intense in their reactions, and slow to adapt to change; and "slow-to-warm-up children," who have a low activity level and do not adapt quickly. These syndromes show up in children's characteristic adjustive behavior during the preschool years (115).

Individuality is greatly influenced by early social experiences outside the home. When these experiences are unfavorable, the child is likely to become unsocial in his relationships with people and to compensate in unsocial ways, such as spending his playtime watching television or imagining himself a martyr who is picked on by others.

HAZARDS OF EARLY CHILDHOOD

Like the hazards of babyhood, those of early childhood can be physical, psychological, or both. Poor nutrition, for example, may stunt physical and mental growth, just as excessive family friction can lead to stress, which can also stunt growth. However, the psychological hazards of early childhood are more numerous than the physical hazards and are more damaging to the child's personal and social adjustments.

Physical Hazards

The physical hazards of early childhood have psychological as well as physical repercussions, especially such hazards as illness, accidents, and awkwardness. These will be discussed in more detail in the following sections.

Mortality Deaths start to decline rapidly in the latter part of babyhood and decline even more rapidly during early childhood. Deaths in early childhood are more often the result of accidents than of illness, and because boys have more accidents than girls, deaths in early childhood are more frequent among boys than among girls.

Illness Young children are highly susceptible to all kinds of illness, though respiratory illnesses are the most common. While most illnesses are physiological in origin, some are psychosomatic and result from family tensions.

Because of the "wonder drugs" available today, children's illnesses are shorter in duration and less severe than in the past and are far less likely to result in permanent physical defects. However, they are psychologically damaging for two reasons. First, a child who is sick for an extended period falls behind in his learning of the skills needed for play with his peers; as a result, he may lag behind them when he returns to the play group. Second, if parents consider the child's illness a family calamity and blame him for the inconvenience it causes, he will become tense and nervous; this not only prolongs his illness but also damages his relationships with his parents.

Accidents Most young children experience cuts, bruises, infections, burns, broken bones, strained muscles, or similar minor disturbances resulting from accidents. Others have more serious accidents that disable them temporarily or permanently. As was pointed out above, boys have more accidents than girls, and they tend to be more serious.

Although most accidents in early childhood are not fatal, many of them leave permanent physical or psychological scars. Many disabilities of childhood, for example, are the result of accidents. A disability can cause the child to develop feelings of inferiority and martyrdom that permanently distort his personality pattern. Even if an accident leaves no permanent physical scar, it may make the young child timid and fearful to the point where these feelings will predominate in his adjustment to life.

Unattractiveness As early childhood progresses, children become increasingly unattractive, reaching a low point as they emerge into late childhood. There are a number of reasons for this. First, as the body changes shape, the child begins to look skinny and gawky; second, his hair becomes coarser and less manageable, and this gives him an unkempt appearance; third, there are gaps in his mouth where baby teeth have fallen out, and the permanent teeth which have erupted seem proportionally too large; and fourth, the child cares more about having a good time than about keeping neat and clean, and thus he does not always look tidy and well groomed.

The young child's less attractive appearance, added to his changed behavior, makes him less appealing to his parents and other adults than he was as a baby, and he interprets this as a rejection of him.

Awkwardness The child who is hampered by overprotective parents, by fear engendered by accidents or warnings to "be careful," by environmental obstacles, or by lack of opportunity to practice becomes awkward as compared with other children of his age. He cannot keep up with them, and as a result he is left out of their play. He soon comes to think that they are better than he is—a feeling which in time may become generalized and develop into an inferiority complex.

Left-Handedness Left-handedness becomes a hazard when a child attempts to learn a skill from a right-handed person; he becomes confused, and this confusion may worsen as the child grows older and skills play a more important role in his life. Left-handedness can affect the child's educational success and later his vocational success or his social adjustments. A self-conscious adolescent, for example, may shun social situations in which eating with his left hand would embarrass him and make him feel conspicuous.

While children are relatively ambidex-trous during babyhood, between the ages of four and six they develop a preference for one hand over the other. Many parents try to force a left-handed child to use his right hand. This can be hazardous because it emphasizes the child's differentness, which he interprets as inferiority, especially when parents use punitive approaches. Ames and Ilg have sounded a word of caution about putting too much pressure on the young child to learn to use his right hand in preference to his left. According to them (2):

If nature is working out something so complex, it seems obvious that, in all probability, best results will be obtained if parents do not interfere with the child's natural expression of handedness other than, perhaps, to present objects nearest to his right hand.

Psychological Hazards

Every major area of the child's behavioral development has associated with it potential hazards which can affect his personal and social adjustments adversely. The most common of these are discussed below.

Speech Hazards Because speech is a tool for communication and because communication is essential to social belonging, the child who cannot communicate with others as well as his age-mates can will be socially handicapped, and this will lead to feelings of inadequacy and inferiority.

Three common hazards are associated with the young child's communicative ability. First, he may be unable to comprehend what others are saying because they use words he does not understand, because they use pronunciations that are unfamiliar to him, or because they speak too fast. An even more common cause is the child's own failure to listen. Because most young children are egocentric and are more interested in what they want to say to others than in what others are saying to them, they often do not listen attentively enough to comprehend what is being said. As a result, their

"Dad, you're always correcting my grammar. But when we met them, you said 'Hi, folks—long time no see!'"

Figure 5-8 Because the young child's speech is greatly influenced by the model he imitates, it is essential that parents speak correctly. (George Clark. "The Neighbors." Chicago Tribune–New York News Syndicate, May 6, 1967. Used by permission.)

speech is unrelated to what others are saying, and this jeopardizes their social contacts.

Second, when the quality of the young child's speech is so poor that what he says is unintelligible to others, his ability to communicate with them is even more jeopardized than when he has not listened to what they said to him. Poor speech quality may be due to mispronunciation of words or grammatical errors, often the result of imitating a poor model (see Figure 5-8); speech defects such as lisping, slurring, or stuttering; or bilingualism.

The third serious speech hazard in early childhood, and in many respects the most serious one, concerns the content of the child's speech. While others will overlook poor speech, assuming that he will learn to speak more correctly as he grows older, they

are far less likely to be tolerant if his speech is largely egocentric and if the comments he does make about others are critical and derogatory. Because the child derives temporary ego-satisfaction from hurting others, he is likely to get into the habit of speaking in an unsocial way, and this will play havoc with his social adjustments.

Emotional Hazards The major emotional hazard of early childhood is the dominance of the unpleasant emotions, especially anger. If the child experiences too many of the unpleasant emotions and too few of the pleasant ones, it will distort his outlook on life and encourage the development of an unpleasant disposition. In addition, he soon acquires a facial expression that makes him look surly, sullen, or generally disagreeable—an expression that contributes to the decline in his appealingness.

Almost as great a hazard to good personal and social adjustments in early childhood is the child's inability to establish the *empathic complex*, or an emotional linkage with significant people in his life. The child who does not receive affection from others is likely to become self-bound, and this prevents him from having an emotional exchange with them. Almost as serious is the development of too strong an affection for one person—usually the mother—because this makes the child feel insecure and anxious whenever the loved person's behavior seems threatening to him—reproval for misbehavior, for example—or when the loved one pays attention to another. Both the inability to establish emotional linkages with others and the development of an emotional overdependence on one person make it difficult for the child to establish friendly relationships with his peers.

Social Hazards There are three common hazards to good social development in early childhood. First, if the child's speech or behavior makes him unpopular with his peers, not only will he be lonely but, even more important, he will be deprived of opportunities to learn to behave in a peer-approved manner. His socially unacceptable speech or behavior will become habitual, and his chances of winning acceptance will worsen as time goes on.

Second, a child who is placed under strong pressure to play in a sex-appropriate way may overdo it and make himself obnoxious to his peers. For example, a boy may try to be so masculine and aggressive in his play that he antagonizes not only the members of his family but also his friends.

The third social hazard of early childhood is the use of imaginary companions and pets to compensate for a lack of real companions. Having an imaginary companion is a temporary solution to the lonely-child problem, but it does little to socialize the young child. He is likely to acquire the habit of dominating his friends, which is possible with an imaginary playmate but frequently not possible with a real one. When he discovers that the technique that worked so successfully with his imaginary playmate does not work with real children, the child is likely to become a maladjusted member of the group.

While pets meet the social needs of a child to some extent, they lack the socializing influence that the child should have. A pet that is considered suitable for a young child is usually so docile that it will take *any* treatment from the child without protest. This encourages the child to be aggressive in his relationships with the pet, even though he may at times show affection. As was stressed earlier, in order for a child to be an accepted member of the play group, his aggressive reactions must give way to friendly, affectionate ones.

Play Hazards The child who lacks friends is forced to engage in solitary forms of play. Because socialization in early childhood comes mainly through play activities with peers, the lonely child is deprived of opportunities to learn to be social.

Because most young children enjoy watching television more than other forms of solitary play, the child who lacks playmates may spend proportionally too much of his playtime in this way and may come to think of it as the best form of solitary play. See Figure 5-9.

Studies of television watching by young children recognize that it has some beneficial effects, but emphasize the harmful ones, such as nervous tension, nightmares, and increased aggressiveness in play with other children. This is especially true when parents exercise little or no control over the programs the child sees (38, 76). Furthermore, while many parents claim that television watching is not harmful to young children because they do not "understand what they see," they fail to realize that children are less critical than adults and therefore are more influenced by what they see on the screen than adults are. They may not un-

Figure 5-9 Many young children learn to think of television watching as the best way to spend their playtime. (George Clark. "The Neighbors." Chicago Tribune–New York News Syndicate, Nov. 6, 1971. Used by permission.)

"They're for people who don't have TV."

derstand what a particular program is about, but they often have a distorted impression or misconception of what they have seen. Thus even a harmless program can be harmful to the young child. Even more important, young children remember details of frightening programs better than those of programs that arouse less fear, which reinforces their harmful effects (95).

Toys can present another play hazard in early childhood. Toys that offer little opportunity for creativity, such as fully equipped dollhouses or sets of soldiers, will stifle the child's creative urge. The child's creativity can also be stifled if parents or nursery school teachers provide too much supervision and direction concerning the use of toys.

Concept Hazards Because concept development is a long, complicated, and arduous task, young children cannot be expected to have well-developed concepts. However, if the child's concepts are less well developed than those of his peers, this can greatly affect his social adjustments. For example, the child who has limited opportunities to associate with people outside the home does not learn to behave as well with strangers as children who have more such opportunities. As a result, he may say things that seem tactless or rude.

The emotional weighting of concepts can present an even more serious hazard. The young child, for example, whose concept of Christmas has been built up around Santa Claus, with its pleasurable emotional weighting, will be resistant to changing his concept about Christmas when he discovers that there is no Santa Claus. Instead of revising it to include its religious meaning, he will claim that "Christmas doesn't mean anything now" (25).

Moral Hazards There are four common hazards in moral development during early childhood. First, inconsistent discipline slows down the process of learning to con-

form to social expectations. When different people require that the child behave differently under similar circumstances, he understandably becomes confused about why something he did was all right yesterday but not today. This not only complicates learning for the child but also may encourage him to be sly and to lie if threatened with punishment.

Second, if the child is not reprimanded for misdemeanors and if he is permitted to get temporary satisfaction from the admiration and envy of his peers when he misbehaves, this is likely to encourage him to persist in his misbehavior. As Glueck has pointed out, it is possible to spot potential delinquents as early as two or three years of age, not just by their behavior, but—even more important—by their attitudes toward their misbehavior (46).

Third, too much emphasis on punishment for wrongdoing and too little emphasis on rewards for good behavior can lead to unfavorable attitudes. Children who are punished more than they are rewarded are less apt to be repentant than to be angry, rebellious, and determined to "get even" with the person who punished them.

Fourth, and most serious of all from the long-term point of view, young children who are subjected to authoritarian discipline, which puts major emphasis on external controls, are not encouraged to develop the internal controls over their behavior that form the foundations for the later development of a conscience. Development of these internal controls must begin early, and it is best accomplished through democratic discipline which encourages the child to *want* to learn to conform to group expectations.

Family-relationship Hazards Deterioration in any human relationship is hazardous to good personal and social adjustments, but this is especially so in the case of the relationship between the young child and his parents, who are the most significant people in his life. The conditions that bring about deterioration in the parent-child relationship are the major source of feelings of insecurity, and they are different for boys and girls.

Girls who feel that their parents prefer the boys in the family will resent their parents and also their brothers. This resentment may grow as early childhood draws to a close if a girl's brothers, who have learned that sex-appropriate behavior involves not playing with girls or girls' toys, adopt an attitude of smug superiority.

For boys the major threat to parent-child relationships during early childhood is the lack of a father to identify with or the lack of emotional warmth between father and son, which encourages continuation of the child's identification with his mother and the acquiring of interests and behavior patterns which may cause his peers to regard him as a sissy.

An often-overlooked family hazard in early childhood is sibling quarreling, which can be caused by jealousy or by differences in interests among siblings. Quarreling among siblings is serious because it can deprive them of companionship at an age when their social world is limited mainly to the family and when the rudiments of social behavior should be learned. Equally important, sibling quarreling can become such a habitual pattern of adjustment to peers that the child will carry it to the play group. This can jeopardize his chances for making friends which he needs to fill the companionship gap created by the poor sibling relationships that have developed in the home.

Personality Hazards Unfavorable self-concepts develop easily in early childhood and are hard to overcome. Unfortunately, far too many parents either fail to recognize that the child is developing an unfavorable self-concept, or else they believe that he is having only a temporary problem.

Genetic studies of the same children over a period of time have shown that the pattern of personality remains persistently uniform. However, during early childhood it

Punishment often results in a desire to "get even" rather than in repentance. (Suzanne Szasz)

is possible to eliminate habits and attitudes which predispose the child to act in a socially unacceptable manner (1, 9, 115).

Certain aspects of the young child's personality do change as a result of advancing maturity, experience, the social and cultural environment in which he lives, and factors within himself, such as emotional pressures or identification with another person. A difficult child may, for example, become more tractable, just as a happy, contented child may develop into a sullen one as he grows older. Changes, however, are usually quantitative rather than qualitative; for example, an undesirable trait is more likely to worsen than to disappear and be replaced by a new one. As Emmerich has pointed out, "Salient personality dimensions have high stability from ages 3 to 5, supporting the view that personality differences arise early in life and are maintained in essentially their original form" (32).

HAPPINESS IN EARLY CHILDHOOD

Early childhood can and should be a happy period in life, and it is important that it be so. Otherwise, the habit of being unhappy can readily develop. Once it does, it will be hard to change.

As is true of every age, happiness in early childhood depends partly on what happens to the individual—such as the loss of friends or the breakup of his family—and partly on things that go on within him—such as a physical defect that prevents him from doing what his age-mates do or the failure to meet a goal he has set for himself.

Because the young child spends most of his time at home, his happiness depends mainly on how the different members of his family treat him and on what he believes they think of him. Not until the latter part of early childhood are the young child's contacts with people outside the home frequent enough, close enough, or prolonged enough to have any appreciable influence on his happiness. It is thus the family's responsibility to see that the child has the three A's of happiness—acceptance by others, affection, and acceptance of self through achievement.

Certain basic wants and needs must be fulfilled if the child is to be happy. Box 5-9 gives some of the conditions that contribute to happiness in early childhood.

Box 5-9. CONDITIONS CONTRIBUTING TO HAPPINESS IN EARLY CHILDHOOD

Good health, which enables the child to enjoy whatever he undertakes and carry it out successfully.

A stimulating environment in which he has the opportunity to use his abilities to their maximum.

Parental acceptance of annoying childish behavior and guidance in learning to behave in a socially more acceptable way.

A disciplinary policy that is well planned and consistently adhered to. This lets the child know what is expected of him and prevents him from feeling that he is being punished unfairly.

Developmentally appropriate expressions of affection, such as showing pride in the child's achievements and spending time with him doing things he enjoys.

A reasonable number of successes. Parents can guide the child's aspirations in accordance with his capacities and can show him how to make a success of what he undertakes, thus fostering a favorable self-concept.

Acceptance by siblings and playmates, which parents can help him achieve by giving him guidance in how to get along in play situations.

A general atmosphere of happiness in the home, which will help the child to tolerate temporary unpleasantness.

Chapter Highlights

1 Early childhood, which extends from two to six, is called the *problem age*, the *troublesome age*, and the *toy age* by parents and the *preschool age*, the *pregang age*, the *exploratory age*, the *questioning age*, the *imitative age*, and the *creative age* by educators and psychologists.

2 The major developmental tasks of early childhood are centered on laying the foundations for adjustments to people and situations outside the home.

3 Physical development proceeds at a slower rate in early childhood than in babyhood, and the major physiological habits, whose foundations were laid in babyhood, become well established at this time.

4 Skills are of great advantage to a young child, both personally and socially, and there are rapid advances in the mastery of hand and leg skills, as well as in those related to speech.

5 The content and quantity of speech in early childhood play important roles in the child's adjustments to peers as well as to adults.

6 The common emotional patterns of early childhood are similar to those of babyhood, though young children show more control over the overt expression of their emotions with each passing year.

7 As judged by adult standards, young children's patterns of behavior in social situa-

tions are often more unsocial than social. This is especially true of such patterns as negativism, aggressiveness, selfishness, and the beginning of sex antagonism.

8 The typical play activities of young children include toy play, dramatizations, constructions, games, being read to, watching movies, listening to the radio, and watching television.

9 The common categories of concepts developed by young children include concepts of life and death, bodily functions, space, weight, numbers, time, self, sex roles, other people, right and wrong, beauty, and the comic. These concepts have a profound influence on the child's personal and social adjustments.

10 As the young child's social horizons broaden, he acquires many new interests, especially in religion, the human body, sex, and clothes.

11 Deterioration in parent-child and in sibling relationships, which begins at the end of babyhood, affects the developing self-concepts of young children differently and this contributes to the development of individuality.

12 The physical hazards of early childhood, especially illness and accidents, have a less profound influence than the psychological hazards—speech defects, lack of social acceptance, and conceptual errors—in determining the kind of personal and social adjustments the young child will make and, as a result, the degree of happiness or unhappiness he will experience.

Bibliography

1 Allport, G. W. *Pattern and growth in personality.* New York: Holt, 1961.
2 Ames, L. B., & Ilg, F. L. The developmental point of view with special reference to the principle of reciprocal neuromotor interweaving. *J. genet. Psychol.,* 1964, **105,** 195–209.
3 Annett, M. The growth of manual preference and speed. *Brit. J. Psychol.,* 1970, **61,** 545–558.
4 Baldwin, A. L., Baldwin, C. P., Hilton, I. R., & Lambert, N. W. The measurement of social expectations and their development in children. *Monogr. Soc. Res. Child Develpm.,* 1969, **34**(4).
5 Bandura, A. Social learning of moral judgments. *J. Pers. soc. Psychol.,* 1969, **11,** 275–279.
6 Bar-Adon, A., & Leopold, W. F. (Eds.) *Child language: A book of readings.* Englewood Cliffs, N.J.: Prentice-Hall, 1971.
7 Barnes, K. E. Preschool play norms: A replication. *Develpm. Psychol.,* 1971, **5,** 99–103.

8 Baumrind, D. Current patterns of parental authority. *Develpm. Psychol. Monogr.,* 1971, **4**(1).
9 Bayley, N. Research in child development: A longitudinal perspective. *Merrill-Palmer Quart.,* 1965, **11,** 183–208.
10 Birnie, L., & Whitely, J. H. The effects of acquired meaning on children's play behavior. *Child Develpm.,* 1973, **44,** 355–358.
11 Bossard, J. H. S., & Boll, E. S. *The sociology of child development.* (4th ed.) New York: Harper & Row, 1966.
12 Brainerd, C. J. The origin of number concepts. *Scient. American,* 1973, **228**(3), 101–109.
13 Breckenridge, M. E., & Vincent, E. L. *Child development: Physical and psychologic development through adolescence.* (5th ed.) Philadelphia: Saunders, 1965.
14 Bronson, W. C. Central orientations: A study of behavior organization from childhood to adolescence. *Child Develpm.,* 1966, **37,** 125–155.
15 Brown, L. B. Egocentric thought in petitionary prayer: A cross-cultural study. *J. soc. Psychol.,* 1966, **68,** 197–210.
16 Bryan, J. H., & Walbek, N. H. The impact of words and deeds concerning altruism upon children. *Child Develpm.,* 1970, **41,** 747–757.
17 Burnett, C. N., & Johnson, E. W. Development of gait in childhood. I. Method. *Develpm. Med. child Neurol.,* 1971, **13,** 3–8; II, 207–215.
18 Busse, T. V. Child-rearing antecedents of flexible thinking. *Develpm. Psychol.,* 1969, **1,** 584–591.
19 Carrow, Sister M. A. The development of auditory comprehension of language structure in children. *J. speech hear. Disord.,* 1968, **33,** 99–111.
20 Childers, P., & Wimmer, M. The concept of death in early childhood. *Child Develpm.,* 1971, **42,** 1299–1301.
21 Chittenden, E. A., Foan, M. W., Zweil, D. M., & Smith, J. R. School achievement of first- and second-born siblings. *Child Develpm.,* 1968, **39,** 1223–1228.
22 Clifford, E. Discipline in the home: A controlled observational study of parental practices. *J. genet. Psychol.,* 1959, **95,** 45–82.
23 Cowan, P. A., Langer, J., Heanenrich, J., & Nathanson, M. Social learning and Piaget's cognitive theory of moral development. *J. Pers. soc. Psychol.,* 1969, **11,** 261–274.
24 Croake, J. W. Fears of children. *Hum. Develpm.,* 1969, **12,** 239–247.
25 Cummins, S., Garns, N., & Zusne, L. Another note on Santa Claus. *Percept. mot. Skills,* 1971, **32,** 510.
26 Dare, M. T., & Gordon, N. Clumsy children: A disorder of perceptive and motor organisation. *Develpm. Med. child Neurol.,* 1970, **12,** 178–185.
27 Denzin, N. K. The genesis of self in early childhood. *Sociol. Quart.,* 1972, **13,** 291–315.
28 Deur, J. L., & Parke, R. D. Effects of inconsistent punishment on aggressiveness in children. *Develpm. Psychol.,* 1970, **2,** 403–411.
29 Dewing, K. Family influences on creativity: A review and discussion. *J. spec. Educ.,* 1970, **4,** 399–404.
30 D'Heurle, A., & Fiemer, J. N. On play. *Elem. Sch. J.,* 1971, **72,** 118–124.
31 Dickie, J., & Bagur, J. S. Considerations for the study of language in young low-income minority group children. *Merrill-Palmer Quart.,* 1972, **18,** 25–38.
32 Emmerich, W. Continuity and stability in early social

development. II. Teacher ratings. *Child Develpm.,* 1966, **37,** 17–27.

33 Erikson, E. H. *Childhood and society.* (Rev. ed.) New York: Norton, 1964.

34 Estvan, F. J. The social perception of nursery-school children. *Elem. Sch. J.,* 1966, **66,** 377–385.

35 Eveloff, H. H. Some cognitive and affective aspects of early language development. *Child Develpm.,* 1971, **42,** 1895–1907.

36 Feigenbaum, K. D., Geiger, D., & Crevoshay, S. An exploratory study of the 3-, 5-, and 7-year-old female's comprehension of cooperative and uncooperative social interaction. *J. genet. Psychol.,* 1970, **116,** 141–148.

37 Feldman, C., & Shen, M. Some language-related cognitive advantages of bilingual five-year-olds. *J. genet. Psychol.,* 1971, **118,** 235–244.

38 Feshbach, S. Aggression. In P. H. Mussen (Ed.), *Carmichael's manual of child psychology.* (3rd ed.) Vol. 2. New York: Wiley, 1970. Pp. 159–259.

39 Flavell, J. H. Concept development. In P. H. Mussen (Ed.), *Carmichael's manual of child psychology.* (3rd ed.) Vol. 1. New York: Wiley, 1970. Pp. 983–1059.

40 Fling, S., & Manosevitz, M. Sex typing in nursery school children's play interests. *Develpm. Psychol.,* 1972, **7,** 146–152.

41 Garai, J. E., & Scheinfeld, A. Sex differences in behavioral and mental traits. *Genet. Psychol. Monogr.,* 1968, **77,** 169–299.

42 Gardner, H. Children's sensitivity to musical styles. *Merrill-Palmer Quart.,* 1973, **19,** 67–77.

43 Gellert, E. Children's conceptions of the content and function of the human body. *Genet. Psychol. Monogr.,* 1962, **65,** 293–405.

44 Gergen, K. J. *The concept of self.* New York: Holt, 1971.

45 Glasner, Rabbi S. Family religion as a matrix of personal growth. *Marriage fam. Living,* 1961, **23,** 291–293.

46 Glueck, E. T. A more discriminative instrument for the identification of potential delinquents at school entrance. *J. crim. Law Criminol. police Sci.,* 1966, **57,** 27–30.

47 Gnagey, T. Let's individualize discipline. *Adolescence,* 1970, **5,** 101–108.

48 Govatas, L. A. Motor skill learning. *Rev. educ. Psychol.,* 1967, **37,** 583–598.

49 Graebner, O. S. Child concepts of God. *Relig. Educ.,* 1964, **59,** 234–241.

50 Grusec, J. E., & Ezrin, S. A. Techniques of punishment and the development of self-criticism. *Child Develpm.,* 1972, **43,** 1273–1288.

51 Guilford, J. P. Creativity: Yesterday, today and tomorrow. *J. creat. Behav.,* 1967, **1,** 3–14.

52 Hatch, E. The young child's comprehension of time connectives. *Child Develpm.,* 1971, **42,** 2111–2113.

53 Havighurst, R. J. How the moral life is formed. *Relig. Educ.,* 1962, **57,** 432–439.

54 Haynes, E. D. Imaginary companions. Unpublished master of home economics thesis, Colorado State University, 1970.

55 Henry, J. Permissiveness and morality. *Ment. Hyg., N.Y.,* 1961, **45,** 282–287.

56 Hoffman, M. L. Father absence and conscience development. *Develpm. Psychol.,* 1971, **4,** 400–406.

57 Inselberg, R. M., & Burke, L. Social and psychological cor-

relates of masculinity in young boys. *Merrill-Palmer Quart.,* 1973, **19,** 41–47.

58 Irish, D. P. Sibling interaction: A neglected aspect in family life research. *Soc. Forces,* 1964, **42,** 279–288.

59 Irwin, M., & Moore, S. G. The young child's understanding of social justice. *Develpm. Psychol.,* 1971, **5,** 406–410.

60 Jakobson, R. Verbal communication. *Scient. American,* 1972, **227**(3)**,** 73–80.

61 Jersild, A. T. *Child psychology.* (6th ed.) Englewood Cliffs, N.J.: Prentice-Hall, 1969.

62 Joffee, C. Sex role socialization and the nursery school: As the twig is bent. *J. Marriage & Family,* 1971, **33,** 467–475.

63 Jones, P. A., & McMallin, W. B. Speech characteristics as a function of social class and situational factors. *Child Develpm.,* 1973, **44,** 117–121.

64 Kagan, J., & Kogan, N. Individual variation in cognitive processes. In P. H. Mussen (Ed.), *Carmichael's manual of child psychology.* (3rd ed.) Vol. 1. New York: Wiley, 1970. Pp. 1273–1365.

65 Kagan, J., & Moss, H. A. *Birth to maturity: A study in psychological development.* New York: Wiley, 1962.

66 Kircher, M., & Furby, L. Racial preferences in young children. *Child Develpm.,* 1971, **42,** 2076–2078.

67 Koch, H. L. The relation of certain formal attributes of siblings to attitudes held toward each other and toward their parents. *Monogr. Soc. Res. Child Develpm.,* 1960, **25**(4).

68 Krauss, R. M. Language as a symbolic process in communication: A psychological perspective. In W. R. Looft (Ed.), *Developmental psychology: A book of readings.* Hinsdale, Ill.: Dryden Press, 1972. Pp. 387–407.

69 Kreitler, H., & Kreitler, S. Children's concepts of sexuality and birth. *Child Develpm.,* 1966, **37,** 363–378.

70 Langlois, J. H., Gottfried, N. W., & Seay, B. The influence of sex of peer on the social behavior of preschool children. *Develpm. Psychol.,* 1973, **8,** 93–98.

71 Lazar, E. Children's perception of other children's fears. *J. genet. Psychol.,* 1969, **114,** 3–14.

72 Leithwood, K. A., & Fowler, W. Complex motor learning in four-year-olds. *Child Develpm.,* 1971, **42,** 781–792.

73 Lerner, R. M., & Schroeder, C. Physique identification: Preference and aversion in kindergarten children. *Develpm. Psychol.,* 1971, **5,** 538.

74 Levinson, B. M. The inner life of the extremely gifted child as seen from the clinical setting. *J. genet. Psychol.,* 1961, **99,** 83–88.

75 Levinson, B. M. *Pets and human development.* Springfield, Ill.: Charles C Thomas, 1972.

76 Liebert, R. M., & Baron, R. A. Some immediate effects of televised violence on children's behavior. *Develpm. Psychol.,* 1972, **6,** 469–475.

77 Liebert, R. M., McCall, R. B., & Hanratty, M. A. Effects of sex-typed information on children's toy preferences. *J. genet. Psychol.,* 1971, **119,** 133–136.

78 Lipsitt, L. P. Learning processes of human newborns. *Merrill-Palmer Quart.,* 1966, **12,** 45–71.

79 Looft, W. R., & Bartz, W. H. Animism revived. In W. R. Looft (Ed.), *Developmental psychology: A book of readings.* Hinsdale, Ill.: Dryden Press, 1972. Pp. 309–336.

80 Love, J. M., & Parker-Robinson, C. Children's imitation of grammatical and ungrammatical sentences. *Child Develpm.,* 1972, **43,** 309–319.

81 Maccoby, E. E., & Masters, J. C. Attachment and dependency. In P. H. Mussen (Ed.), *Carmichael's manual of child psychology.* (3rd ed.) Vol. 2. New York: Wiley, 1970. Pp. 73–157.

82 Manosevitz, M., Prentice, N. M., & Wilson, F. Individual and family correlates of imaginary companions in preschool children. *Develpm. Psychol.,* 1973, **8,** 72–79.

83 Margolin, E. What do group values mean to young children? *Elem. Sch. J.,* 1969, **69,** 250–258.

84 Marshall, H. H. The effect of punishment on children: A review of the literature and a suggested hypothesis. *J. genet. Psychol.,* 1965, **106,** 23–33.

85 Marshall, H. R. Relations between home experiences and children's use of language in play interactions with peers. *Psychol. Monogr.,* 1961, **75**(5).

86 Martin, P. C., & Vincent, E. L. *Human development.* New York: Ronald Press, 1960.

87 Maurer, A. What children fear. *J. genet. Psychol.,* 1965, **106,** 265–277.

88 Maw, W. H., & Maw, E. W. Self-concepts of high- and low-curiosity boys. *Child Develpm.,* 1970, **41,** 123–129.

89 McCarthy, D. Language development. *Monogr. Soc. Res. Child Develpm.,* 1965, **25**(3), 5–14.

90 Mehrabian, A. Measures of vocabulary and grammatical skills for children up to age six. *Develpm. Psychol.,* 1970, **2,** 439–446.

91 Meredith, H. V. Body size of contemporary groups of preschool children studied in different parts of the world. *Child Develpm.,* 1968, **39,** 335–377.

92 Moore, J. E., & Kendall, D. G. Children's concepts of reproduction. *J. sex Res.,* 1971, **7,** 42–61.

93 Mueller, E. The maintenance of verbal exchanges between young children. *Child Develpm.,* 1972, **43,** 930–938.

94 Neidhart, W. What the Bible means to children and adolescents. *Relig. Educ.,* 1968, **63,** 112–119.

95 Osborn, D. K., & Endsley, R. C. Emotional reactions of young children to TV violence. *Child Develpm.,* 1971, **42,** 321–331.

96 Patton, W. F., & Edwards, E. School readiness skills, personality characteristics and popularity in kindergarten children. *Percept. mot. Skills,* 1970, **31,** 689–690.

97 Piaget, J. *Psychology and epistemology.* New York: Grossman, 1971.

98 Pulaski, M. A. S. Play as a function of toy structure and fantasy predisposition. *Child Develpm.,* 1970, **41,** 531–537.

99 Rand, C. W. Copying in drawing: The importance of adequate visual analysis versus the ability to utilize drawing rules. *Child Develpm.,* 1973, **44,** 47–53.

100 Richmond, B. O., & Weiner, G. P. Cooperation and competition among young children as a function of ethnic grouping, grade, sex, and reward condition. *J. educ. Psychol.,* 1973, **64,** 329–334.

101 Rosenbloom, L., & Horton, M. E. The maturation of fine prehension in young children. *Develpm. Med. child Neurol.,* 1971, **13,** 3–8.

102 Rosenfeld, H. M., & Gunnell, P. Effects of peer characteristics on preschool performance of low-income children. *Merrill-Palmer Quart.,* 1973, **19,** 81–94.

103 Rubin, K. H. Relationship between egocentric communication and popularity among peers. *Develpm. Psychol.,* 1972, **7,** 364.

104 Ryan, M. S. *Clothing: A study in human development.* New York: Holt, 1966.

105 Schroeer, R. S., & Flapan, D. Assessing aggressive and friendly behavior in young children. *J. Psychol.,* 1971, **77,** 193–202.

106 Shantz, C. U., & Wilson, K. E. Training communication skills in young children. *Child Develpm.,* 1972, **43,** 693–698.

107 Siegel, L. S. The sequence of development of certain number concepts in preschool children. *Develpm. Psychol.,* 1971, **5,** 357–361.

108 Singer, J. L. *The child's world of make-believe.* New York: Academic Press, 1973.

109 Snow, C. E. Mothers' speech to children learning language. *Child Develpm.,* 1972, **43,** 549–565.

110 Stabler, J. R., Johnson, E. E., & Jordon, S. E. The measurement of children's self-concepts as related to racial membership. *Child Develop.,* 1971, **42,** 2094–2097.

111 Steuer, F. B., Applefield, J. M., & Smith, R. Televised aggression and interpersonal aggression of preschool children. *J. exp. Child Psychol.,* 1971, **11,** 442–447.

112 Sutton-Smith, B. Child's play: Very serious business. *Psychology Today,* 1971, **5**(7), 66–69, 87.

113 Sutton-Smith, B., & Rosenberg, B. G. Peer perceptions of impulsive behavior. *Merrill-Palmer Quart.,* 1961, **7,** 233–238.

114 Taylor, B. J., & Howell, R. J. The ability of three-, four-, and five-year-old children to distinguish fantasy from reality. *J. genet. Psychol.,* 1973, **122,** 315–318.

115 Thomas, A., Chess, S., & Birch, H. G. The origin of personality. *Scient. American,* 1970, **223**(2), 102–109.

116 Turnure, J. E., & Rynders, J. E. Effectiveness of manual guidance, modeling and trial and error learning procedures on the acquisition of new behaviors. *Merrill-Palmer Quart.,* 1973, **19,** 49–65.

117 Valadian, I., Stuart, H. C., & Reed, R. B. Studies of illness of children followed from birth to eighteen years. *Monogr. Soc. Res. Child Develpm.,* 1961, **26**(3).

118 Vincent, E. L., & Martin, P. C. *Human psychological development.* New York: Ronald Press, 1961.

119 Wallach, M. A. Creativity. In P. H. Mussen (Ed.), *Carmichael's manual of child psychology.* (3rd ed.) Vol. 1. New York: Wiley, 1970. Pp. 1211–1272.

120 Williams, R. Theory of God-concept readiness: From the Piagetian theories of child artificialism and the origin of religious feelings in children. *Relig. Educ.,* 1971, **66,** 62–66.

121 Witryol, S. L., Lowden, L. M., Fagan, J. F., & Bergen, T. C. Verbal versus material rewards as a function of schedule and set in children's discrimination preference choice behavior. *J. genet. Psychol.,* 1968, **113,** 3–25.

122 Wolman, R. N. A developmental study of the perception of people. *Genet. Psychol. Mongr.,* 1967, **76,** 95–140.

123 Zuger, B. The role of familial factors in persistent effeminate behavior in boys. *Amer. J. Psychiat.,* 1970, **126,** 1167–1170.

CHAPTER | SIX

LATE CHILDHOOD

Late childhood extends from the age of six to the time the individual becomes sexually mature. It is marked, at the beginning, by the child's entrance into first grade. This is a milestone in his life and is responsible for many of the changes that take place in his attitudes and behavior. Marked physical changes take place during the last year or two of childhood, and these also cause changes in attitudes and behavior.

Although it is possible to mark off the beginning of late childhood fairly accurately, one cannot be so precise about the time this period comes to an end because sexual maturity—the criterion used to divide childhood from adolescence—comes at varying ages.

There are marked variations in the ages at which both boys and girls become sexually mature. As a result, some children have a longer-than-average late childhood, while for others it is shorter than average. For the average American girl, late childhood extends from six to thirteen, a span of seven years; for boys, it extends from six to fourteen, a span of eight years.

CHARACTERISTICS OF LATE CHILDHOOD

Educators and psychologists apply various names to late childhood, and these reflect the most important characteristics of this period.

Name Used by Educators Educators call late childhood the *elementary school age.* It is the time when the child is expected to acquire the rudiments of knowledge that are considered essential for successful adjustment to adult life. It is also the time when he is expected to learn certain essential skills, both curricular and extracurricular.

Names Used by Psychologists To the psychologist, late childhood is the *gang age*—the time when the child's major concern is acceptance by his age-mates and membership in a "gang." This concern leads the older child to be a conformist in terms of the appearance, speech, and behavior that are approved by the gang. As Church and Stone have pointed out (25):

For a 7- or 8-year old the worst "sin" is to be in any way different from other children. . . . He apes the dress and mannerisms of older children and subscribes to the group code, even when it runs sharply counter to his own, his family's, and the school's.

Late childhood is frequently called the *play age* by psychologists, not because more time is devoted to play than at any other age—which would be impossible after the child enters school—but rather because there is an overlapping of play activities characteristic of the younger years and those characteristic of adolescence.

DEVELOPMENTAL TASKS OF LATE CHILDHOOD

To achieve a place in the social group, the older child must master the developmental tasks that society expects him to master at this time. Failure to do so will result in an immature pattern of behavior, which will militate against acceptance in the peer group, and in an inability to keep up with his age-mates who have mastered these developmental tasks. See page 13 for a list of the developmental tasks of late childhood.

No longer is the mastery of developmental tasks the sole responsibility of parents, as it was during the preschool years. It now becomes the responsibility also of the child's teachers and, to a lesser extent, the members of his peer group. For example, developing fundamental skills in reading, writing, and calculating and developing attitudes toward social groups and institutions becomes as much the responsibility of teachers as of parents. Although parents can help to lay the foundation of the child's learning to get along with age-mates, being a member of the peer group provides the major part of this learning experience.

Because boys mature sexually later than girls and, as a result, have a slightly longer childhood, it is logical to assume that they would master the developmental tasks of late childhood better than girls and therefore be more mature. There is little evi-

Late childhood is the time when the major concern of every normal boy or girl is to be accepted by his age-mates. (Georg Gerster from Rapho Guillumette)

dence that this is the case. In fact, evidence points to the greater maturity of girls of the same ages. The reason for this is that girls have more adult guidance and supervision than boys, which provides them with better opportunities to master the developmental tasks.

PHYSICAL GROWTH IN LATE CHILDHOOD

Late childhood is a period of slow and relatively uniform growth until the changes of puberty begin, approximately two years before the child becomes sexually mature, at which time growth speeds up markedly. Box 6-1 shows the important physical changes that take place before the puberty growth spurts begin. Compare these physical changes with those of babyhood (Box 4-1) and of early childhood (Box 5-1).

Physical growth follows a predictable pattern, although variations do occur. Body build affects both height and weight in late childhood. The ectomorph, who has a long, slender body, can be expected to weigh less than a mesomorph, who has a heavier body.

Bright children tend to be taller and heavier than those who are average or below average in intelligence. However, when very bright children are compared with their less bright siblings, this difference ceases to exist. As Laycock and Caylor have explained, "The gifted child probably comes from a home where all the children grow bigger" because of better nutrition and health care (74).

Sex differences in physical growth, relatively slight in earlier years, become more pronounced in late childhood. Because boys begin their puberty growth spurt approximately a year later than girls, they tend to be slightly shorter and lighter in weight than girls of the same age until they too become sexually mature. Girls also get their permanent teeth slightly earlier than boys, while boys' heads and faces grow larger than girls'.

SKILLS OF LATE CHILDHOOD

At the beginning of late childhood the child has a remarkably large repertoire of skills that he learned during the preschool

---

Box 6-1. PHYSICAL DEVELOPMENT IN LATE CHILDHOOD

Height
The annual increase in height is 2 to 3 inches. The average eleven-year-old girl is 58 inches tall, and the average boy of the same age is 57.5 inches tall.

Weight
Weight increases are more variable than height increases, ranging from 3 to 5 or more pounds annually. The average eleven-year-old girl weighs 88.5 pounds, and the average boy of the same age weighs 85.5 pounds. Fat tissue accounts for only approximately 25 percent of the total body weight.

Body Proportions
Although the head is still proportionally too large for the rest of the body, some of the facial dispro-portions disappear as the mouth and jaw become larger, the forehead broadens and flattens, the lips fill out, the nose become larger and acquires more shape. The trunk elongates and becomes slimmer, the neck becomes longer, the chest broadens, the abdomen flattens, the arms and legs lengthen (although they appear spindly and shapeless because of undeveloped musculature), and the hands and feet grow larger, but at a slow rate.

Teeth
By the onset of puberty, the child normally has twenty-eight of his thirty-two permanent teeth. The last four, the wisdom teeth, erupt during adolescence.

Box 6-2. **CATEGORIES OF LATE-CHILDHOOD SKILLS**

Self-Help Skills
The older child should be able to eat, dress, bathe, and groom himself with almost as much speed and adeptness as an adult, and these skills should not require the conscious attention that was necessary in early childhood.

Social-Help Skills
Skills in this category relate to helping others. At home, they include making beds, dusting, and sweeping; at school, they include emptying waste-baskets and washing blackboards; and in the play group, they include helping to construct a tree house or lay out a baseball diamond.

School Skills
At school, the child develops the skills needed in writing, drawing, painting, clay modeling, dancing, singing, sewing, cooking, and woodworking.

Play Skills
The older child learns such skills as throwing and catching balls, riding bicycles, skating, and swimming in connection with his play.

years. What skills the older child learns will depend partly on his environment, partly on the opportunities he is given for learning, partly on his body build and previously developed skills, and partly on what is in vogue among his age-mates. Marked sex differences, for example, exist not only in play skills at this age but also in the level of perfection of these skills. Girls, as a rule, surpass boys in skills involving finer muscles, such as painting, sewing, weaving, and hammering, while boys are superior to girls in skills involving the grosser muscles, such as throwing a basketball, kicking a soccer ball long distances, and doing broad jumps (39).

The skills of late childhood can be divided roughly into four categories: self-help skills, social-help skills, school skills, and play skills. These are given in Box 6-2. All the different skills of late childhood contrib-ute either directly or indirectly to the child's socialization. For example, although social-help skills learned in the home, such as dusting and doing dishes, will not help the child directly to make better adjustments to his peers in school and in the neighborhood, indirectly they help him by teaching him to be cooperative, which will contribute greatly to his acceptance by the peer group.

SPEECH IMPROVEMENT IN LATE CHILDHOOD

As the child's social horizons broaden, he discovers that speech is an important tool for gaining acceptance into a group, and this gives him a strong incentive to learn to speak better. He also learns that the simpler forms of communication, such as crying and gesturing, are socially unac-ceptable. This gives him an added incen-tive to improve his speech.

Help in improving speech in late child-hood comes from three sources. First, parents from middle and upper socioeco-nomic groups may feel that speech is es-pecially important and thus motivate their children to speak better by correcting faulty pronunciation and grammatical errors and by encouraging them to participate in gen-eral family conversations. Second, radio and television provide good models for speech for older children, as they do for chil-dren during the preschool years. And third, after the child learns to read, he adds to his vocabulary and becomes familiar with cor-rect sentence formation. Mispronounced words and wrong meanings associated with words are usually quickly corrected by the teachers in school.

Areas of Improvement

In spite of the fact that all children are given similar opportunities to improve their speech in school, there are marked varia-tions in the improvements made. There are also variations in the amount of improvement that takes place in the different tasks involved in learning to speak. An analysis of these tasks will show where the improvement occurs.

Vocabulary Building Throughout late childhood, the child's general vocabulary grows by leaps and bounds. From his studies in school, his reading, his conversations with others, and his exposure to radio and television, he builds up a vocabulary which he uses in his speech and writing. It has been estimated that the average first grader knows between 20,000 and 24,000 words, or 5 to 6 percent of the words in a standard dictionary. By the time he is in the sixth grade, he knows approximately 50,000 words (8, 10).

Not only does the older child learn many new words, but he also learns new meanings for old ones, thus further enlarging his vocabulary. Children from better-educated families increase their vocabularies more than those from families in which the parents have less education, and girls, on the whole, build up larger vocabularies than boys.

Words with special meanings and limited uses are also learned at this age. Box 6-3 gives the most common of the special vocabularies learned by older children.

Sex differences are marked in these special vocabularies. Girls have larger color vocabularies than boys because of their greater interest in clothes and in activities involving the use of color—decorating a dollhouse, for example. Boys, on the other hand, have larger and rougher slang-word and swearword vocabularies than girls because they regard such words as signs of their masculinity, while girls have larger secret vocabularies. Socioeconomic differences in slang-word and swearword vocabularies are apparent in both sex groups, with boys and girls from the lower socioeconomic groups using such words more

---

Box 6-3. SPECIAL VOCABULARIES OF LATE CHILDHOOD

Etiquette Vocabulary
By the end of the first grade, the child who has had training at home in using such words as "please" and "thank you" has as large an etiquette vocabulary as that of the adults in his environment.

Color Vocabulary
The child knows the names of all the common colors and many of the less common ones shortly after he enters school.

Number Vocabulary
The older child learns the names and meanings of numbers from his study of arithmetic at school.

Money Vocabulary
Both in school and at home, the older child learns the names of the different coins and understands the value of the various denominations of bills.

Time Vocabulary
The older child's time vocabulary is as large as that of the adults with whom he comes in contact.

Slang-word and Swearword Vocabularies
Children learn slang words and swearwords from older siblings or older children in the neighborhood. Using such words makes the child feel "grown-up."

Secret Vocabularies
Older children use secret vocabularies to communicate with their intimate friends. These can be *written,* consisting of codes formed by symbols or the substitution of one letter for another; *verbal,* consisting of distortions of words—pig Latin, for example; or *kinetic,* consisting of gestures and the use of the fingers to communicate words. Most children start to use one or more of these forms at the time they enter the third grade, and their use reaches a peak just before puberty.

frequently, and using more offensive words, than those of the same ages from higher socioeconomic groups. Children of both sexes in the lower socioeconomic groups also have larger money vocabularies because they are more apt to run errands for their mothers and thus become accustomed to handling money.

Pronunciation Errors in pronunciation are less common at this age than earlier. A new word may be incorrectly pronounced the first time it is used, but after the child hears the correct pronunciation once or twice, he is generally able to pronounce it correctly. This, however, is less true of children of the lower socioeconomic groups, who hear more mispronunciations in their homes than children from more favored home environments, and it is even less true of children from bilingual homes.

Forming Sentences The six-year-old child should have command of nearly every kind of sentence structure. From six until the age of nine or ten, the length of his sentences will increase. These long sentences are generally rambling and loosely knit. Gradually, after the age of nine, the child begins to use shorter and more compact sentences.

Content of Speech

The older child's speech is less egocentric than that of the preschool child. Just when he will shift from egocentric to socialized speech will depend not so much upon his age as upon his personality, the number of social contacts he has had and the satisfaction he has derived from them, and the size of the group to which he is speaking. The larger the group, the more socialized the speech. When the child is with his contemporaries, his speech is generally less egocentric than when he is with adults.

Although children may talk about anything, their favorite topics of conversation, when with their peers, are their own experiences, their home and family, games, sports, movies, television programs, their gang activities, sex, sex organs and functions, and the daring of a contemporary that led to an accident. When he is with an adult, it is the latter who usually determines the topic of conversation (2, 44).

When the older child talks about himself, it is usually in the form of boasting. He boasts less about material possessions than about his superior skill and strength in games. Boasting, as a rule, is very common between the ages of nine and twelve years, especially among boys.

The older child also likes to criticize and make fun of other people. Sometimes he criticizes people openly, and sometimes behind their backs. When criticizing adults, the child generally puts his criticism in the form of a suggestion or complaint, such as "Why don't you do so-and-so?" or "You won't let me do what my friends do." Criticism of other children frequently takes the form of name-calling, teasing, or making derogatory comments.

How much improvement there will be in the content of the older child's speech and in the way he presents what he has to say will depend not so much on his intelligence as on the level of his socialization. Children who are popular have a strong incentive to improve the quality of their speech. They learn, from personal experience, that words can hurt and that the popular children are those whose speech adds to the enjoyment of their contact with their peers.

EMOTIONS AND EMOTIONAL EXPRESSIONS IN LATE CHILDHOOD

The older child soon discovers that violent expressions of emotions, especially unpleasant emotions, are socially unacceptable to his contemporaries. They regard temper outbursts as babyish, withdrawal reactions to fear as cowardly, and hurting another in jealousy as poor sportsmanship. Hence a child acquires a strong incentive to learn to control the outward expressions of his emotions.

At home, however, there is not the same strong incentive to control emotions. As a result, the child frequently expresses his emotions as forcibly as he did when he was younger. Under such circumstances, it is not surprising that parents criticize or punish him for "not acting his age."

Characteristically, emotional expressions in late childhood are pleasant ones. The child giggles or laughs uproariously; squirms, twitches, or even rolls on the floor; and in general shows a release of pent-up animal spirits. Even though these emotional expressions are immature by adult standards, they indicate that the child is happy and making good adjustments.

Not all emotionality at this age, however, is of a pleasant sort. Numerous outbursts of temper occur, and the child suffers from anxiety and feelings of frustration. Girls often dissolve into tears or have temper outbursts reminiscent of their preschool days; boys are more likely to express their annoyances or anxieties by being sullen and sulky.

The common emotions of late childhood differ from those of early childhood (1) in terms of the kind of situation that gives rise to them and (2) in terms of the form of emotional expression. These changes are the result of broadened experience and learning, rather than maturation. From experience, the child discovers how others feel about various forms of emotional expression. In his desire to win social approval, he tries to curb the forms of expression that he has discovered are socially unacceptable. As he grows older, he begins to express his anger through moodiness, sulkiness, and general orneriness. For example, temper tantrums become less frequent as the child discovers that they are considered babyish.

Children who are popular tend to be less anxious and less jealous than those who are less popular. Boys, at every age, express the emotions that are regarded as sex-appropriate, such as anger and curiosity, more overtly than girls, while girls are likely to experience more fears, worries, and feelings of affection than boys—emotions that are regarded as sex-appropriate for them.

Periods of Heightened Emotionality

There are times during late childhood when the child experiences more frequent and more intense emotions than he does at others. Because these emotions tend to be unpleasant rather than pleasant, periods of heightened emotionality become periods of disequilibrium—times when the child is out of focus and difficult to live or work with.

Heightened emotionality in late childhood may come from physical or environmental causes or from both. When a child is ill or tired, he is likely to be irritable, fretful, and generally difficult. Just before childhood ends, when the sex organs begin to function, heightened emotionality is normally at its peak. This will be discussed in detail in the following chapter.

Adjustments to new situations are always upsetting for a child. Heightened emotionality is almost universal at the time the child enters school, for example. Generally, however, late childhood is a period of relative emotional calm, which lasts until the puberty growth spurt begins. There are several reasons for this. First, the roles of the older child are well defined, and he knows how to play them; second, games and sports provide a ready outlet for pent-up emotional energy. Finally, because of improvement in his skills, the child is less often frustrated in his attempts to accomplish various tasks.

SOCIAL GROUPINGS AND SOCIAL BEHAVIOR

Late childhood is often referred to as the *gang age* because it is characterized by interest in peer activities, an increasingly strong desire to be an accepted member of the gang, and discontentment on the part of the child when he is not with his friends. The older child is no longer satisfied to play at home alone or to do things with members of his family. Even one or two friends are not enough for him. He wants to be with the gang because only then will there be a sufficient number of individuals to play the games he now enjoys and to give excitement to his play. From the time the child enters school until puberty, the desire to be with, and to be accepted by, the gang becomes increasingly strong. This is just as true of girls as of boys. Box 6-4 gives the outstanding characteristics of children's gangs.

Insecure about his status and often afraid that he will be rejected by the gang unless he conforms wholeheartedly to its standards, the child tends to bend over backward to be like his gang-mates in dress, behavior, and opinions, even when this means going against parental standards. It is upon this slavish conformity that socialization in late childhood is based. Figure 6-1 shows some of the important aspects of socialization that come from membership in a gang.

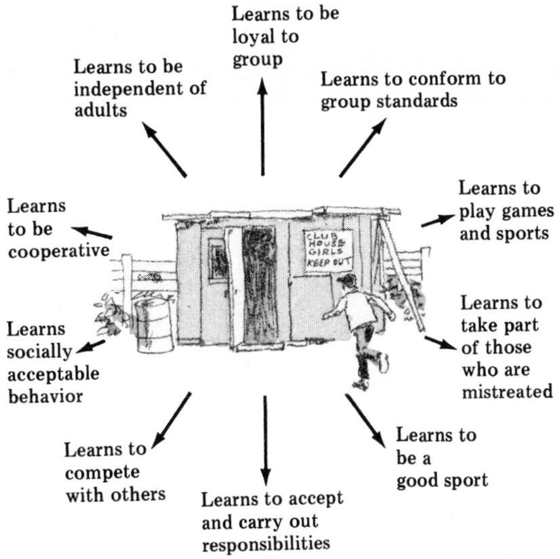

Friendships in Late Childhood

While the older child may have a closer relationship with some of the gang members than with others, he regards them all as his

Figure 6-1 Some ways in which gang belonging leads to improved socialization in late childhood.

Box 6-4. CHARACTERISTICS OF CHILDREN'S GANGS

Children's gangs are play groups.
To belong to a gang, a child must be invited.
Members of a gang are of the same sex.
At first gangs consist of three or four members, but this number increases as children grow older and become interested in sports.
Boys' gangs more often engage in socially unacceptable behavior than girls' gangs.
Popular gang activities include games and sports, going to the movies, and getting together to talk or eat.
The gang has a central meeting place, usually away from the watchful eyes of adults.
Most gangs have insignia of belonging; the members may wear similar clothes, for example.
The gang leader represents the gang's ideal and is superior in most respects to the other members.

---

friends. The gang is made up of members of the same sex, though the child may occasionally like a member of the opposite sex and may even prefer that individual as a friend.

The more usual pattern, however, is for antipathy toward members of the opposite sex to reach a high point just before puberty, at which time girls' attitudes toward boys are more emotionally toned than boys' attitudes toward girls. There is reason to believe that the unfavorable attitude of girls toward boys at this age stems partly from their resentment at the greater freedom boys are permitted and partly from the fact that, as girls reach puberty, the greater social maturity that accompanies their early sexual maturity makes the typical behavior of boys of their own age seem immature.

Many factors influence the older child's choice of friends. As a rule, he chooses those he perceives as similar to himself and those who meet his needs. Propinquity in the school or neighborhood is important because the child is limited to a relatively small area from which to select his friends. There is a strong tendency for children to choose friends from their own grades in school.

Personality traits are an important factor in the choice of friends; children value cheerfulness, friendliness, cooperativeness, kindness, honesty, generosity, even temperedness, and good sportsmanship in their friends. As childhood draws to a close, the child shows a preference for friends with similar socioeconomic, racial, and religious backgrounds.

Treatment of Other Children

Once older children have formed a group of friends, they are often cruel to others whom they do not regard as their friends. Much of the secrecy that surrounds gangs is designed to keep out children the members do not want as friends. The tendency to be cruel and callous toward all who are not gang-mates generally reaches a peak around the eleventh year.

While any child may have difficulty making friends and being accepted by a gang, a child who is new to a neighborhood or school has an especially difficult problem. It is the new child who must initiate the contacts if he wants to have friends. This he does by trying to talk to or play with members of one of the already-formed groups, by observing and imitating their play, and by trying to attract their attention to himself.

At first, he is usually ignored or rebuffed. If he is willing to try again and again, he may succeed in getting one member of the group interested in him, and through this contact he may eventually win a place in the gang.

Even though gangs are tightly knit social units, shrouded in secrecy to keep out newcomers or others who are not wanted as members, there is a great deal of fighting within the ranks. Often children in a gang are not on speaking terms with some of their friends. Many of these quarrels are made up and the friendships reestablished; others are not.

As a result, children's friendships are rarely static. The child shifts from best friend to enemy, or from casual acquaintance to close friendship, quickly and often for little reason. Quarreling, bossiness, disloyalty, underhandedness, conceit, and incompatibility are the reasons most often given by children for changing friends. However, as children grow older, their friendships become more stable. Children who are popular have been found to change their friends almost as often as unpopular children. Girls, at all ages in late childhood, are slightly more stable in their friendships than boys (93).

PLAY INTERESTS AND ACTIVITIES IN LATE CHILDHOOD

The play activities the older child will engage in and the amount of time he will devote to these activities will depend on how popular he is and on whether he belongs to a gang. The child who lacks acceptance in a gang will be forced to spend much of his playtime in solitary activities, such as making things or amusing himself in other ways.

Both boys and girls are keenly aware of the sex appropriateness of different types of play, and they shun play activities that they know are regarded as inappropriate for their sex, regardless of personal preference.

Bright children, especially as they grow older, are more solitary than social in their play, and they participate in fewer activities that involve strenuous physical play than children who are less bright. The kind of neighborhood in which the child lives also determines what opportunities there will be for play.

Regardless of these variations, for most children play becomes less active as childhood progresses, and such amusements as movies, radio, television, and reading gain in popularity. This shift is due partly to increased schoolwork and partly to additional home duties. The favorite play activities of late childhood are discussed in the following sections.

Constructive Play

Making things just for the fun of it, with little thought given to their eventual use, is a popular form of play among older children. Construction with wood and tools appeals to boys, while girls prefer finer types of construction, such as sewing, drawing, painting, clay modeling, and jewelry making.

Drawing, painting, and clay modeling gradually decrease in popularity as childhood advances, not so much because the child loses interest in these activities, but rather because he feels self-conscious if he is criticized by his classmates and teachers. Many children enjoy these activities at home, however. The drawings that older children do make are likely to be cartoons of their teachers, their friends, or people in the news. This kind of drawing is generally done during school hours when they are bored.

Singing is another form of creative play the older child enjoys. He does not like to sing at school, during the music period, for example, but rather with his friends when he is away from the listening ears of teachers and parents. Boys make little attempt to sing well; they derive their fun just from making a noise or from making up a silly version of a song they already know.

As children grow older, they become more self-conscious about their drawing and painting. Criticism by classmates and teachers often causes them to lose interest in these activities. (Suzanne Szasz)

Collecting

Collecting as a form of play increases in popularity as childhood progresses. The older child is more selective in his collections than he was when he was younger. He now collects only a few things—stamps or shells, for example. He chooses things that he thinks will give him prestige in the eyes of his friends, and he tries to get a wide variety of each item.

Games and Sports

The young child's games are the simple, undifferentiated type characteristic of early childhood. However, he is anxious to play the games of older children, and he begins to practice basketball, football, baseball, and hockey. By the time the child is ten or eleven years old, his games are largely competitive in spirit. His interest is now concentrated on skill and excellence, rather than on merely having fun.

During late childhood, most children who belong to gangs start to play indoor games when the weather is too poor to allow them to play outdoors. Many of these are games they played with family members when they were younger, while others, such as simple card games and craps, they learn from older siblings or from watching adults play them. Boys prefer games with an element of gambling.

Amusements

When the child is not with his friends—during the evening, for example—he spends what time he has free from schoolwork and from home responsibilities amusing himself by reading, listening to the radio, watching television, or daydreaming. These amusements are described in Box 6-5.

Because amusements are, for the most part, a solitary form of play, individual preferences are more apparent than in group play activities, where the child's preferences are overshadowed by those of the group. Regardless of individual preferences, there are predictable age differences; children show a preference for more serious reading and less interest in comic books as they grow older, for example. Sex differences in amusements, especially reading, television watching, and moviegoing, are even more marked than in other forms of play. Children of the lower socioeconomic groups spend more time watching television than those of the middle and upper groups and less time reading. The more popular the child, the less he will daydream and the more he will prefer amusements, such as going to the movies or watching television, that can be carried out as group activities.

INCREASE IN UNDERSTANDING

As the child's world expands with his entrance into school, so do his interests. And with this broadening of interests comes an understanding of people and things which formerly had little or no meaning for him. He enters what Piaget calls the *stage of concrete operations* in thinking; the vague and nebulous concepts of early childhood now become specific and concrete (107).

After the child enters school, he associates new meanings with old concepts on the basis of what he learns at school. In addition, he derives new meanings from the mass media, especially movies, radio, and television. In building up social concepts, for example, he associates cultural stereotypes with people of different racial, religious, sex, and socioeconomic groups.

Box 6-5. FAVORITE AMUSEMENTS DURING LATE CHILDHOOD

Reading
The older child prefers books and children's magazines which stress adventure and in which he may read about a heroic person with whom he can identify. He also enjoys cartoons and comic strips in adult magazines and newspapers.

Comic Books and Comic Strips
Regardless of intellectual level, almost all children enjoy comic books and comic strips, whether humorous or adventure-oriented. Their appeal comes from the fact that they are amusing, exciting, easy to read, and a stimulus to the child's imagination.

Movies
Movie attendance is one of the favorite gang activities of late childhood, although some children at-

tend alone or with family members. They enjoy cartoons, adventure movies, and movies about animals.

Radio and Television
Radio is less popular than television among older children, although they do enjoy listening to music or tuning into a sports event that is not presented on television. Watching television is one of the favorite amusements of most older children. They enjoy cartoon shows and other programs geared toward their age level, as well as many adult shows.

Daydreaming
The child who is lonely at home or who has few friends amuses himself by daydreaming, typically imagining himself as a "conquering hero."

Even elementary reading textbooks, Zimet has pointed out, present people as living in a "falsely glamorized fantasy world" (137).

In the development of concepts, new emotional weightings are often added to old concepts. Children who watch movies and television shows involving death or who see pictures of dead people in magazines or newspapers develop concepts of death that are colored by these vicarious experiences. As Barclay has stressed (11):

The way that life is lived today children are exposed continually to ersatz examples of

---

Box 6-6. COMMON CATEGORIES OF CONCEPTS IN LATE CHILDHOOD

Life
While some older children find it difficult to understand that many things that move—a river, for example—are not alive, they become increasingly aware that movement is not the sole criterion of life.

Death
Children who experience the death of a family member or pet have a good understanding of the meaning of death, and the emotional weighting of their concept of death is colored by the reactions of those around them.

Life after Death
The child's concept of life after death depends mainly on the religious instruction he receives and on what his friends believe.

Bodily Functions
Until the child begins to study health in elementary school, many of his concepts about bodily functions are inaccurate and incomplete. See Figure 6-2.

Space
By using scales and rulers, the child learns the meaning of ounces, pounds, inches, feet, and even miles; from reports of space exploration in the mass media, he develops concepts about outer space.

Numbers
Numbers take on new meanings as the older child uses money and works with arithmetic problems. By the time he is nine years old, he understands number concepts to 1,000 or beyond.

Money
The child begins to understand the value of the various coins and bills when he starts to use money himself. Opportunities to use money vary markedly in different families.

Time
The rigid schedule of the school day enables the child to develop concepts of what he can accomplish in a given period of time. Social studies in school and mass media help him to develop concepts of historical time.

Self
The child's concept of himself becomes clarified when he sees himself through the eyes of his teachers and classmates and when he compares his abilities with those of his peers.

Sex Roles
Not only do boys and girls develop clear concepts of approved sex roles, but before childhood is over they may also learn that the male role is apt to be considered more prestigious than the female role.

Social Roles
The older child is aware of his peers' social, religious, racial, and socioeconomic status, and he accepts cultural stereotypes and adult attitudes toward these statuses. This leads to group consciousness and in some cases to social prejudice.

Beauty
The older child tends to judge beauty in terms of group standards, rather than according to his own aesthetic sensibilities.

The Comic
The older child's concept of the comic is based largely on what he has observed others to perceive as funny.

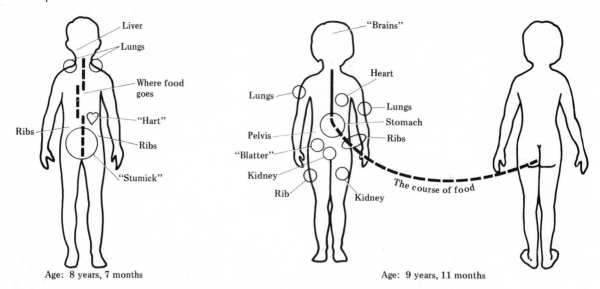

Figure 6-2 Some examples of the older child's concept of the digestive process and of the location of different bodily organs. (Adapted from E. Gellert. Children's conceptions of the content and function of the human body. *Genet. Psychol. Monogr.,* 1962, **65,** 293–405. Used by permission.)

death on television which are either cold, bloodless, and unmourned, or violently reacted to in the most melodramatic manner possible. At the same time, news programs, newspapers and picture magazines show them graphic evidences of real death and of real reactions to it—some stricken, some apparently emotionless, a few smirkingly self-conscious. . . . If the child is upset by death in a movie or television show, his parents reassure him that the upsetting incident was just "make believe." But he knows that at other times and other places it is surely real.

Because older children's experiences are more varied than those of preschoolers, it is understandable that their concepts change in different directions and become increasingly more varied. However, certain concepts are commonly found among older children in the American culture of today. The concepts that change most and the new ones most commonly developed in late childhood are given in Box 6-6. Compare these concepts with those of early childhood, given in Box 5-6.

MORAL ATTITUDES AND BEHAVIOR

No longer are the child's moral concepts narrow and specific, as they were when he was younger. He gradually generalizes his concepts so that they refer to *any* situation rather than to a specific one. In addition, he discovers that the social group attaches different degrees of seriousness to different acts, and this knowledge is incorporated in his concepts. Between the ages of five and twelve, as Piaget has explained, the child's concept of justice changes. His rigid and inflexible notion of right and wrong, learned from parents, becomes modified, and he begins to take into account the specific circumstances surrounding a moral violation. Thus moral relativism replaces moral inflexibility. For example, to a five-year-old lying is always "bad," while an older child realizes that in some situations a lie is justified and therefore necessarily not bad (107).

The child's moral code develops from these generalized moral concepts. However, his moral code is greatly influenced by that of the group to which he belongs. This does not, of course, mean that he rejects the family moral code in favor of that of the gang; it means simply that if he must make a choice, he will go along with the group standards *when he is with the group* as a means of maintaining his status there.

As the child reaches the end of childhood, his moral code gradually approaches that of the adults with whom he is associated, and his behavior conforms more closely to their standards. Children with high IQs tend to be more mature in their moral judgments and behavior than those of lower intellectual levels, and girls tend to form more mature moral judgments than boys (113).

Role of Discipline in Moral Development

Discipline plays an important role in the development of a moral code. In spite of the child's need for discipline, it becomes a serious problem with older children. Continuing use of the disciplinary techniques that proved to be effective when the child was younger is likely to lead to strong resentments on the part of the older child. If discipline is to fill its role as a developmental need of the child, it must be suited to the child's level of development. Box 6-7 gives the essentials of effective discipline for older children.

Development of Conscience

The kind of discipline used also plays an important role in the development of conscience—one of the important developmental tasks of late childhood. The term *conscience* means a conditioned anxiety response to certain kinds of situations and actions which has been built up by associating certain acts with punishment. It is an "internalized policeman" which motivates the child to do what he knows is right and thus avoid punishment (34).

Guilt is a "special kind of negative self-evaluation which occurs when an individual

---

> **Box 6-7. ESSENTIALS OF DISCIPLINE FOR OLDER CHILDREN**
>
> **Aid in Building a Moral Code**
> In the case of the older child, the teaching of right and wrong should emphasize the reasons why certain patterns of behavior are acceptable while others are not, and it should be directed toward helping him broaden specific concepts into more generalized, abstract ones.
>
> **Rewards**
> Rewards, such as praise or a special treat, for handling a difficult situation well, have a strong educational value in that they show the child he has behaved correctly, and they also motivate him to repeat the approved behavior. However, if they are to be effective, rewards must be appropriate to the child's age and level of development.
>
> **Punishment**
> Like rewards, punishment must be developmentally appropriate and administered fairly; otherwise, it may arouse resentment on the child's part. Punishment must also motivate him to conform to social expectations in the future.

---

acknowledges that his behavior is at variance with a given moral value to which he feels obligated to conform" (34). *Shame,* by contrast, is an "unpleasant emotional reaction of an individual to an actual or presumed negative judgment of himself by others, resulting in self-depreciation vis-à-vis the group" (34). Shame thus relies on external sanctions alone, though it may be accompanied by guilt. Guilt, by contrast, relies on *both* internal and external sanctions.

Misdemeanors in Late Childhood

Like those of younger children, some of the misdemeanors of older children are due to ignorance of what is expected of them or to a misunderstanding of the rules. Most, however, are a result of the child's testing of authority and his attempt to assert his independence. What misdemeanors the child will commit will depend on what rules he breaks. Because home rules are, of necessity, different from school rules, home misdemeanors are different from school misdemeanors. Box 6-8 lists some of the most commonly reported misdemeanors of late childhood.

As the child grows older, he tends to violate more rules both at home and in school. At home this is due in part to the fact that he wants to assert his independence and in part to the fact that he feels the home rules are unfair and the punishment he receives for violating them unjust. At school his increased misbehavior may be explained by the fact that he likes school less than he did earlier, that he is more likely to dislike his teacher, that he finds some school subjects boring, and that he is often less well accepted by the peer group than he was earlier or than he hoped to be.

At home, in school, and in the neighborhood, boys break more rules than girls. There are two reasons for this sex difference: First, boys are given more freedom than girls and are less often punished for misbehavior on the grounds that "boys will be boys"; and second, boys feel that they must defy rules to show their masculinity and thus win peer approval.

Box 6-8. COMMON MISDEMEANORS OF LATE CHILDHOOD

Home Misdemeanors
Fighting with siblings
Breaking possessions of other family members
Being rude to adult family members
Dawdling over routine activities
Neglecting home responsibilities
Lying
Being sneaky
Pilfering things belonging to other family members
Spilling things intentionally

School Misdemeanors (See Figure 6-3.)
Stealing
Cheating
Lying
Using vulgar and obscene language
Destroying school property and materials
Being truant
Annoying other children by teasing them, bullying them, and creating a disturbance
Reading comic books or chewing gum during school hours
Whispering, clowning, or being boisterous in class
Fighting with classmates

Figure 6-3 Percent of boys and girls, six to eleven years of age, found to commit different kinds of school misdemeanors in a nationwide sample. (Adapted from J. Roberts & J. T. Baird. *Behavior patterns of children in school: United States.* Rockville, Md.: U.S. Department of Health, Education and Welfare, 1972. Used by permission.)

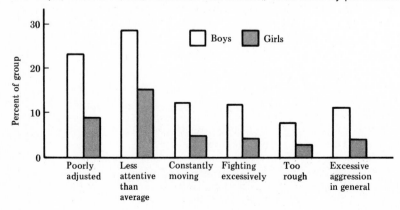

Problem behaviors in school

INTERESTS IN
LATE CHILDHOOD

Because of differences in abilities and experiences, the interests of older children vary more than those of younger children. Although each child will develop certain individual interests, every child in a particular culture develops other interests that are almost universally found among children of that culture. Box 6-9 summarizes the interests that are common among children in this country.

The interests the older child develops have a powerful influence on his behavior, not only during childhood, but also as he grows older. They influence the form and intensity of his aspirations. A girl who is interested in matters of health or in the functioning of the human body may aspire to be a nurse or doctor when she grows up, while a boy who has a strong interest in sports may want to become an athletic coach. Interests also serve as a strong motivating force. The child who is interested in being as autonomous as his gang-mates

---

Box 6-9. COMMON INTERESTS OF LATE CHILDHOOD

Appearance
The child is interested in his looks only if he is so homely or so different in appearance from his age-mates that he feels conspicuous.

Clothes
Older children are interested in new clothing, but it must be like that worn by their friends. They also have definite color preferences in clothing.

Names and Nicknames
The child's name interests him only if it is very different from his friends' names. He also becomes aware that the nickname his friends give him reflects their judgment of him, and he does not want one that implies ridicule.

Religion
Older children who attend Sunday school may have less interest in it than they did earlier, although they still enjoy seeing their friends there. However, they often become skeptical about religious teaching and about the efficacy of prayer.

The Human Body
Since he is unable to observe most bodily functions directly, the older child tries to satisfy his curiosity about them by asking questions and reading books.

Health
Only when children are ill or have a chronic illness such as asthma are they interested in health.

Boys, especially, regard this interest as a sign of a sissy.

Sex
The older child wants to know more details about the relations between the sexes, the father's role in reproduction, and the birth process. He tries to get such information from books and from his friends, with whom he exchanges "dirty" stories and jokes.

School
Typically, the child is greatly enthusiastic about school at first, but by the end of the second grade he may have developed a bored, antagonistic, critical attitude toward the academic work, though he may still like the nonacademic aspects.

Future Vocation
The child's early interest in his future vocation is centered on jobs that are glamorous, exciting, and prestigious, and he gives little consideration to his capacities. (See Figure 6-4.)

Status Symbols
The older child has a growing realization of the importance of socioeconomic status, and he becomes interested in visible symbols of his own family's status.

Autonomy
How much autonomy the older child is interested in having depends on how much his friends have. If he has as much or more, he is satisfied.

Figure 6-4 Boys frequently are encouraged to aspire unrealistically high while girls are brainwashed to aspire below their capacities. (Morris Turner, "Wee Pals." King Features Syndicate, July 6, 1970. Used by permission.)

will strive hard to be mature in his behavior in the hopes of winning the autonomy he craves.

Achievements are always influenced by the kind and intensity of the individual's interests. The child who is interested in mathematics, for example, will work hard to get good grades in that subject, while the child who lacks interest in math will become an underachiever in this area. Because interests lead to satisfaction, the child is likely to repeat actions related to his interests, and thus these interests may persist throughout his life. Interests in painting or music in adulthood, for example, usually originated during childhood.

CHANGES IN FAMILY RELATIONSHIPS

The far-reaching effects of the child's relationships with his family are apparent in many areas of his life. His work in school and his attitude toward it are greatly in-

fluenced by these relationships; wholesome family relationships lead to motivation to achieve, while unwholesome relationships cause emotional tension, which may have a very detrimental effect on the child's ability to learn.

When family relationships are favorable, the child's social adjustments to people outside the home are better than when family relationships are stressful. The role the child learns to play in the home and the kind of relationships he has with his siblings form the basis of his relationships with peers outside the home and influence the pattern of his behavior toward them.

When authoritarian child-training methods are employed in the home, the child learns to be a follower—often a discontented follower, as he is in his relationships with his parents—while democratic training encourages the development of leadership ability. How well he performs approved sex roles outside the home will depend on the home training he receives for these roles.

The child's aspirations and achievements in different areas of his life are greatly influenced by his parents' attitudes. Firstborn and only children usually come under more pressure to achieve than later-born children and are given more aid and encouragement to achieve the goals their parents set for them. Whether the child will be creative or conformist in his outlook and behavior is likewise influenced by his home training; democratic child-training methods encourage creativity, and authoritarian methods tend to foster conformity.

In no area of the child's development do family relationships play a more important role than in his developing personality. What he thinks of himself as a person is a direct reflection of what he *believes* the different family members think of him as judged by the way they treat him.

Deterioration in
Family Relationships

Because of the strong influence of the family on the older child's personal and social adjustments, the deterioration in family relationships, which began during the latter part of babyhood and continued through early childhood, becomes increasingly detrimental to his development as childhood progresses. Many conditions are responsible for this deterioration; some are carryovers of earlier conditions, and some are new.

The conditions contributing to changed parent-child relationships in early childhood, given in Box 5-8 (page 109), still exert their influence in late childhood. In addition, new conditions develop in late childhood that contribute to the deterioration in family relationships. These are described in Box 6-10.

There are, of course, times of peace and harmony in the home. And there are times when older children show real affection for, and interest in, their siblings, even to the point of helping in the care of younger brothers or sisters and following the advice and pattern of behavior set by those older than he. But these favorable relationships are outweighed in number and frequency by less favorable ones.

There are times when older children show real interest in and affection for their younger siblings. (Bob Kreuger from Rapho Guillumette)

Similarly, there are times when the older child is on the best of terms with his parents and relatives and even seems to enjoy family gatherings. However, he more frequently shows a definite preference for his friends and a critical, resentful attitude toward his parents and relatives. The more pronounced these unfavorable attitudes and behavior patterns are, the more the family relationships will deteriorate.

PERSONALITY CHANGES IN
LATE CHILDHOOD

As the child's social horizons broaden with his entrance into school, new factors begin to influence the development of his

---

Box 6-10. CONDITIONS CONTRIBUTING TO DETERIORATION IN FAMILY RELATIONSHIPS

Attitudes toward Parenthood
Parents who perceive their roles unfavorably and feel that the time, effort, and money expended on their children are unappreciated tend to have poor relationships with their children.

Parental Expectations
By the time the child enters school, many parents have high expectations about the quality of his schoolwork and the amount of responsibilities he will assume in the home. When he fails to meet these expectations, parents often criticize, nag, and punish.

Child-Training Methods
Authoritarian child training, commonly used in large families, and permissive discipline, used mainly in small families, both lead to friction in the home and to feelings of resentment on the child's part. Democratic discipline fosters good family relationships.

Socioeconomic Status
The child may feel that his home and possessions compare unfavorably with his peers' and may blame and criticize his parents if he thinks he has less than other children have.

Parental Occupations
How his peers feel about his father's occupation influences the child's feelings about it and about his father. If the mother works, his attitudes toward her are colored by how his friends feel about this

and by how many home responsibilities he is expected to assume.

Changed Attitude toward Parents
From his contacts with his friends' parents and as a result of what he reads in books or sees on television and in movies, the child builds up concepts of an ideal mother and father. If his own parents fall short of these ideals, as they invariably do, he may become critical of them.

Sibling Friction
Older siblings frequently criticize the appearance and behavior of the child, while he in turn likes to tease and bully younger siblings. If parents attempt to put a stop to this, they are accused of playing favorites, and the children may gang up against them and the sibling whom they regard as the parental pet.

Changed Attitudes toward Relatives
The child enjoys being with relatives less than he did when he was younger. He may regard them as "too old" or "too bossy" and put up a protest when he is expected to be a part of a family gathering. Relatives often resent this attitude and reprove him for it.

Stepparents
Older children who remember a real parent who is no longer in the home usually resent a stepparent and show it by critical, negativistic, and generally troublesome behavior. This leads to friction in the home.

---

personality, and thus he must frequently revise his self-concept. Since he has seen himself almost exclusively through the eyes of his parents up until now, it is not surprising if his concept of himself is biased. Now he sees himself as his teachers, his classmates, and his neighbors see him. Even his parents react differently toward him now, and this helps to shatter the foundations upon which his concept of himself was based.

As childhood draws to a close and the child begins his hero worship of characters in history and in fiction, on the stage or on the screen, or in the world of sports or national affairs, he forms a concept of the *ideal self*, the kind of person he would like to be. At first, this ideal is patterned along the lines set by parents, teachers, and others from his immediate environment. Later, as his horizons broaden, people he does not know but has heard or read about form the nucleus of this ideal self (56). From these many sources, the older child builds an ego-ideal, which, as Van den Daele has pointed out, "serves as a general internalized standard of the self's behavior" (130).

This ego-ideal includes traits which are admired by the group. Because the two sexes are widely separated at this age, it is not surprising that boys and girls admire different personality traits.

Factors Affecting the Self-Concept

Many of the factors that influenced the self-concept in early childhood continue to do so as childhood progresses. These are discussed in Chapter 5 under "Personality Development in Early Childhood." Even

though the older child's social environment has broadened, family relationships continue to exert a marked influence on his developing personality. The quality of his relationships with his parents, siblings, and relatives and the way he feels about the child-training methods used all play a role in determining the sort of individual he will become. His ordinal position in the family is even more important now than when he was younger because his attitudes toward the role associated with this position have a greater effect on the way he feels about himself. If he is the oldest child and is now expected to help with the care of younger siblings, he may feel either self-important

---

Box 6-11. FACTORS AFFECTING THE OLDER CHILD'S SELF-CONCEPT

Physical Condition
Poor health or a physical defect that cuts the child off from play with his peers makes him feel inferior and martyred.

Body Build
A child who is overweight or very short for his age, for example, may be unable to keep pace with his peers and thus develop feelings of inferiority.

Names and Nicknames
Names which cause the child to be ridiculed or which suggest minority-group status can lead to feelings of inferiority. Also, nicknames that make fun of a physical or personality trait lead to feelings of inferiority and resentment.

Socioeconomic Status
If the child feels that he has a better home and more toys, for example, than his friends, he will feel superior to them; if he senses that his socioeconomic status is lower than that of his friends, he is likely to feel inferior.

School Environment
Competent, understanding teachers do much to bring about good adjustment in their pupils, while teachers who use discipline the child considers

unfair or who otherwise antagonize him have the opposite influence.

Social Acceptance
Acceptance or the lack of it on the part of peers influences the child's personality through its effect on his self-concept. Very popular children and isolates are especially affected, and others less so.

Success and Failure
Success in the tasks the child sets out to achieve leads to a feeling of confidence and self-acceptance, while failure makes him feel inadequate. The more prestigious the activity, the greater the effect of success or failure on the self-concept. Repeated failures have a damaging effect on the child's personality.

Intelligence
The child's personality is adversely affected if his intelligence deviates markedly from the norm. The child who is duller than average senses his inferiority and the rejectant attitude of the group toward him, and he may become shy, introverted, and apathetic or else aggressive and hostile toward those who reject him. The very bright child not only feels superior to the group but may also become smug and intolerant toward those less bright than he.

or martyred. Only children may become increasingly dependent or increasingly more mature than children with siblings, depending on how their parents treat them.

When a child from a minority group enters school, he becomes more aware of prejudice against him than he was earlier. This gradually builds up a feeling of inferiority which may be expressed in poor social adjustments and antisocial behavior and which may color the child's whole outlook on life.

An unstable home environment has less effect on the personality development of the older child than on that of the younger child, but an unstable social environment has a greater effect. When geographic or upward social mobility brings a radical change in the older child's social world, this affects him in much the same way that instability in the home environment affected him when he was younger. A feeling of rootlessness and of not belonging makes him insecure, and this encourages overconformity and a curbing of individuality.

A number of new factors influence the child's self-concept when he enters school, and the pattern of his life changes as a result of his expanding social world. All these are related, either directly or indirectly, to the new environmental conditions that are part of his expanded social horizons. Box 6-11 lists these new factors.

HAZARDS OF LATE CHILDHOOD

The real impact of failure to master earlier developmental tasks is felt in late childhood, when the child is constantly in a position to compare himself with his age-mates. Failure to master the developmental tasks relating to skills and to social and sex-role behavior, for example, is especially damaging to the child's personal and social adjustments because it cuts him off from the group and deprives him of opportunities to master the new developmental tasks his age-mates are mastering, many of which depend on acceptance by his peers.

Some of the common hazards of late childhood are carryovers from earlier years, though they often take new forms now. Others are new, arising from changes in the child's life pattern after he enters school.

As is true of earlier ages, the hazards of late childhood are both physical and psychological. However, during late childhood the psychological repercussions of many of the physical hazards are especially serious, and major emphasis will be placed on these.

Physical Hazards

As a result of new medical techniques for diagnosing, preventing, and treating illnesses, mortality during late childhood occurs much less frequently than in the past. However, accidents still cause death among older children.

While many of the physical hazards of the earlier years persist into late childhood, their effects on the child's physical well-being tend to be less severe and less far-reaching than they were earlier. On the other hand, their psychological effects are greater and more persistent. The major physical hazards of late childhood are discussed below.

Illness Since vaccines against most childhood diseases are now available, older children suffer mainly from occasional colds and stomach upsets, which rarely have any lasting physical effects.

The psychological effects of illness in late childhood, however, can be serious. Illness upsets the body's homeostasis, which in turn makes the child irritable, demanding, and difficult to live with. If he is sick for a long period, his schoolwork may suffer and he may fall behind in his learning of various play skills. Equally serious, parents may be intolerant in their attitudes toward the child's illness, complaining about the extra work and expense it entails.

While most illnesses of late childhood are real, some are imaginary or "faked."

The child has learned that when he is ill he is not expected to carry out his usual activities, home discipline is relaxed, and he receives more attention than usual. As a result, he may feign illness—or actually believe he is ill—as a way of avoiding an unpleasant task or situation. If this tactic works, he will repeat it and thus lay the foundation for a proneness to imaginary illness.

Obesity The child who is markedly overweight—due more often to overeating than to a glandular condition—loses out in active play, and as a result he misses the opportunity to acquire the skills so essential to social success. In addition, his playmates often tease and taunt him, calling him "Fatso" or other names that make him feel inferior and martyred.

Sex-inappropriate Body Build Girls with masculine body builds and boys with girlish physiques are likely to be ridiculed by their peers and pitied by adults. This leads to personal and social maladjustment, though more so for boys than for girls. By contrast, a sex-appropriate body build aids good adjustment. In speaking about boys, Biller and Borstelmann have explained (14):

The tall and husky or mesomorphic boy may, even without the encouragement of parents, find success easier in masculine activities so that he is seen by others, and consequently learns to see himself, as very masculine. The frail ectomorph or pudgy endomorph may find such success difficult so that he may be seen by others, and learn to see himself, as unmasculine.

Accidents Even when accidents leave no permanent physical scar, they can and often do leave psychological scars. The older child, like the younger one, who experiences more than his share of accidents usually learns to be more cautious. In time, this may lead to timidity concerning all physical

The child who is markedly overweight loses out in active play, which makes it harder for him to develop some of the skills that are essential to social success. (Sherry Suris from Rapho Guillumette)

activities, which may spread to other areas of his behavior and develop into a generalized shyness that will affect his social relationships, his work, and his personality.

Physical Disabilities Many physical disabilities are the aftereffect of an accident and thus are more common among boys than girls. The seriousness of the aftereffect depends on the degree of the disability and on the way others treat the child, especially members of the peer group. While some children may show marked sympathy and consideration for a disabled child, others may ignore, reject, or even ridicule him. It is not uncommon for a child to discover that a handicap is a way of avoiding unpleasant situations and hence develop an imaginary handicap or even pretend that a real handicap is more disabling than it actually is.

Homeliness Unlike the adolescent or adult who develops feelings of personal inadequacy when he knows he is considered

---

Box 6-12. PSYCHOLOGICAL HAZARDS OF LATE CHILDHOOD

Speech Hazards
A smaller-than-average vocabulary handicaps the child in his schoolwork as well as in his communications with others. Speech errors, such as mispronunciations and grammatical mistakes, and speech defects, such as stuttering or lisping, may make the child so self-conscious that he will speak only when necessary. Egocentric speech, critical and derogatory comments, and boasting antagonize his listeners.

Emotional Hazards
The child may be considered immature by both age-mates and adults if he still exhibits unacceptable patterns of emotional expression, such as temper tantrums, or if he is generally disagreeable and unpleasant to be with.

Social Hazards
Being rejected or neglected by the peer group deprives the child of opportunities to learn to be social. Voluntary isolates, who have little in common with the group, come to feel that they are "different" and have no chance for acceptance. Followers who want to be leaders become resentful and disgruntled group members.

Play Hazards
The child who lacks social acceptance is deprived of opportunities to learn the games and sports essential for gang belonging. He may also devote much of his playtime to watching television, rather than to wholesome amusements, such as reading.

Conceptual Hazards
The child who has an idealized self-concept is dissatisfied with himself as he is and with the way others treat him. If his social concepts are based on stereotypes, he may become prejudiced and discriminatory in his treatment of others. Because such concepts are emotionally weighted, they tend to persist and to continue to affect the child's social adjustments unfavorably.

Moral Hazards
Four hazards are commonly associated with the development of moral attitudes and behavior: (1) the development of a moral code based on peer or mass-media concepts of right and wrong, which may not coincide with adult codes; (2) a failure to develop a conscience as an inner control over behavior; (3) intolerance of the wrongdoings of others; and (4) finding peer approval of misdemeanors so satisfying that such behavior becomes habitual, and leads to an unfavorable reputation and perhaps juvenile delinquency.

Hazards Associated with Interests
The child who is uninterested in the things his age-mates consider important may experience poor personal as well as social adjustments. (See Figure 6-5.)

Family-Relationship Hazards
Friction with family members often leads to a habitual unfavorable pattern of adjustment to people and problems which is carried outside the home.

unattractive, the homely child is relatively unconcerned about his appearance and is not likely to be rejected by his age-mates because of his looks.

However, homeliness can be a hazard if other people react unfavorably to it and communicate their feelings to the child through their treatment of him. The older child is less appealing than a baby and even a young child, and thus adults may be more critical of him and less tolerant of his normal, but often annoying, behavior. The older child interprets this as rejection, an interpretation that can have a harmful effect on the developing self-concept.

Awkwardness The older child now begins to compare himself with his age-mates. If clumsiness or awkwardness prevents him from keeping pace with them, he will start to think of himself as inferior. And because skills play such an important role in school and at play, the clumsy child finds himself in many situations where his awkwardness is apparent to himself and to others, and thus his feelings of inadequacy are constantly reinforced.

Psychological Hazards

The psychological hazards of late childhood are mainly the ones that affect the child's social adjustments, around which the major developmental tasks of late childhood are centered. Thus they have a powerful influence on his personal adjustments and on his developing personality. The most important psychological hazards of late childhood are given in Box 6-12.

The child who is less well accepted by the group than he would like to be may become dissatisfied with himself and envy those who are more popular. Personality maladjustments can begin in this way, usually early in the child's school career, when he first begins to compare himself with his age-mates and to consider his own achievements in light of theirs. Common signs of future trouble are habitual with-

drawal, excessive excitability, excessive resentment against authority, chronic depression, self-enhancement through derogation of others, diffuse hyperactivity, excessive egocentrism, and chronic anxiety or emotional "deadening."

Children who are dissatisfied with themselves commonly use defense mechanisms such as rationalization to explain their shortcomings or projection of blame on others; they may also resort to escape mechanisms, especially daydreaming and imaginary illness. Although these may alleviate the child's unhappiness temporarily, they are only stopgap measures. With each passing year he will have to use such mechanisms more frequently and in more exaggerated forms. In time they may lose their effectiveness and cease to work for him altogether.

Maladjustment stemming from lack of

Figure 6-5 The child's attitude toward school can be adversely affected by an unfavorable personal experience. (Bil Keane. "The Family Circus." Register and Tribune Syndicate, Nov. 2, 1972. Used by permission.)

"You should do better than this in art. I had your brother and he was VERY good!"

acceptance by the social group tends to persist. The shy, retiring, self-effacing child, for example, continues his characteristic patterns of behavior even though he knows they lessen his chances of acceptance.

Some children who are unhappy and dissatisfied with themselves because of lack of social acceptance take matters into their own hands and try to "buy" their way into the group. See Figure 6-6. While this may produce the desired results temporarily, it rarely results in permanent acceptance.

Because of the psychological damage that persistent lack of social acceptance does to a child, clinicians and educators are now trying to find ways to help children who are experiencing such difficulties. However, making an unacceptable child more acceptable to his age-mates is difficult for three reasons. First, he may have acquired a reputation as a "bully," a "crybaby," or a "tattler," for example, and this reputation is likely to cling; second, by the time the child

reaches first grade, the patterns of behavior that make him unpopular are so much a part of his personality that changing them is difficult; and third, the way the child treats other children will determine their reaction to him. If, for example, he is bossy and domineering, other children will resent him, and such attitudes are hard to change.

This, of course, does not mean that there is no hope for the unpopular child. With guidance, he can acquire socially acceptable patterns of behavior; for example, he can learn to say pleasant instead of unpleasant things, to talk about things other than himself, and to consider the wishes of the group, rather than just his own. Equally important, he must learn that what makes him popular at one age does not guarantee popularity later. Consequently, he must be willing to change his patterns of behavior to conform to those of the group as its members become more socially mature.

HAPPINESS IN LATE CHILDHOOD

Late childhood can and should be a happy period in the life span. While it cannot be a completely carefree time, since the child is expected to assume added responsibilities in school and at home, success in handling these responsibilities, especially those which significant people consider important, will add to, instead of detracting from, his happiness.

Many factors contribute to the older child's happiness. Some of these were also important factors in early childhood, though now they affect him differently because his interests and pattern of life have changed and because he wants to spend increasingly more time with his friends.

For example, because most of his skills have improved greatly, the child is less dependent; he can do many things himself without relying on the help of others. Similarly, speech skills have developed to the point where he no longer experiences the

Figure 6-6 The child who craves social acceptance by his peers may try to "buy" it. (George Clark, "The Neighbors." Chicago Tribune–New York News Syndicate, July 21, 1972. Used by permission.)

"I believe it's called 'cookie jar diplomacy.'"

frustrations of not understanding what others are talking about or not being understood when he communicates with them.

Unless some unusual conditions exist in his family life, he will have ample opportunity for play and the equipment he needs to play as his peers play. If he enjoys reasonable social acceptance, his play can be a source of daily happiness to him.

As school begins to occupy an increasingly large part of the older child's time, how he feels about school can be a source of real happiness. The child who does well academically, who gets along well with his teacher and his classmates, and who enjoys learning new things will have an added reason to be happy.

Even though the older child spends increasingly more time outside the home, the home climate and the relationships he has with different family members are two vitally important factors in his happiness. If he has a warm and affectionate relationship with his family, even though there may be occasional friction and occasional punishment for intentional misbehavior, he will feel that his family loves him and treats him fairly. His happiness will be greatly increased if the home climate is relaxed and cheerful when he is there.

While happiness in the closing years of childhood will not guarantee happiness for the remainder of the child's life, the conditions that contribute to happiness then will likewise contribute to happiness as he grows older. Even though new values are used in the selection of friends in adolescence and adulthood, the individual who learned to be socially acceptable to others when he was young has a foundation on which to build new patterns of behavior to conform to the new values.

Similarly, a child who has learned to see himself realistically and whose failures either motivate him to find better ways of achieving his goals or cause him to modify his aspiration in accordance with his capabilities will, as he grows older, be spared the unhappiness that comes from repeated failures and the feelings of inadequacy and inferiority that accompany them. This is just as true in the case of social failures as in the case of academic or business failures.

When it is apparent that one or more of the three A's of happiness—achievement, acceptance by others, and affection from others—are not present in a child's life, this should be regarded as a danger signal of future trouble. If an individual is not happy at a time when conditions are favorable to happiness, it suggests that he is poorly equipped to face later periods when conditions will be less favorable.

Chapter Highlights

1 Late childhood, which extends from the age of six to the time the individual becomes sexually mature, is called the *elementary school age* by educators and the *gang age* or the *play age* by psychologists.

2 The major developmental tasks of late childhood are concentrated on learning to achieve social acceptance by acquiring patterns of behavior that are approved by members of the group.

3 Because late childhood is a period of relatively slow and uniform growth, it is possible for the child to acquire a large repertoire of skills during this time and to improve his speech, both of which aid in his personal and social adjustments.

4 As the child's social horizons broaden, he learns to express his emotions in ways that are approved by members of the social group, even at times of heightened emotionality.

5 During late childhood, membership in a gang of peers plays an important role in the child's socialization. He also learns to engage in play activities which give him satisfaction and also win the approval of others.

6 The older child acquires new interests and comes in contact with a wide range of people of different backgrounds and abilities. As a result, he associates new meanings with previously developed concepts and also develops new concepts.

7 Even though the older child has a better un-

derstanding of right and wrong than he did when he was younger, he often misbehaves at home, in school, and in the neighborhood, partly to win peer approval and partly to assert his independence of adult authority.

8 Because of differences in abilities and experience, older children's interests vary more than those of younger children. However, almost all are interested in such things as clothes, religion, the human body, sex, their future vocations, status symbols, and achieving autonomy.

9 A deterioration in family relationships during late childhood has a markedly unfavorable influence on the child's adjustments to his schoolwork and to people outside the home, as well as on his self-concept.

10 The physical hazards of late childhood are less serious than the psychological ones, although obesity or a physical disability, for example, can make a child feel different from his peers and thus have an adverse effect on his self-concept.

11 Most of the important psychological hazards of late childhood involve failure to master the appropriate developmental tasks for that age.

12 Because social acceptance plays such an important role in the older child's life, the degree to which he is accepted by the group has a great effect on how happy or unhappy he will be.

Bibliography

1 Adams, R. L., & Phillips, B. N. Motivational and achievement differences among children of various ordinal birth positions. *Child Developm.*, 1972, **43**, 155–164.

2 Alvy, K. T. Relation of age to children's egocentric and cooperative communications. *J. genet. Psychol.*, 1968, **112**, 275–286.

3 Annett, M. The growth of manual preference and speed. *Brit. J. Psychol.*, 1970, **61**, 545–558.

4 Anthony, E. J. The behavior disorders of childhood. In P. H. Mussen (Ed.), *Carmichael's manual of child psychology.* (3rd ed.) Vol. 2. New York: Wiley, 1970. Pp. 667–764.

5 Armentrout, J. A. Sociometric classroom popularity and children's reports of parental child-rearing behaviors. *Psychol. Rep.*, 1972, **30**, 261–262.

6 Armsby, R. E. A reexamination of the development of moral judgments in children. *Child Developm.*, 1971, **42**, 1241–1248.

7 Aspy, D. N. Better self concepts through success. *J. Negro Educ.*, 1970, **40**, 369–372.

8 Baldwin, T., McFarlane, P. T., & Garvey, C. J. Children's communication accuracy related to race and socioeconomic status. *Child Developm.*, 1971, **42**, 345–357.

9 Bank, I. M. Children explore careerland through vocational role-models. *Vocat. Guid. Quart.*, 1969, **17**, 284–289.

10 Bar-Adon, A., & Leopold, W. F. (Eds.) *Child language: A book of readings.* Englewood Cliffs, N.J.: Prentice-Hall, 1971.

11 Barclay, D. Questions of life and death. *The New York Times,* July 15, 1962.

12 Bayley, N. Research in child development: A longitudinal perspective. *Merrill-Palmer Quart.*, 1965, **11**, 183–208.

13 Berlyne, D. E. Children's reasoning and thinking. In P. H. Mussen (Ed.), *Carmichael's manual of child psychology.* (3rd ed.) Vol. 1. New York: Wiley, 1970. Pp. 939–981.

14 Biller, H. B., & Borstelmann, L. J. Masculine development: An integrative review. *Merrill-Palmer Quart.*, 1967, **13**, 253–294.

15 Blain, M. J., & Ramirez, M. Increasing sociometric rank, meaningfulness and discriminability of children's names through reinforcement and interaction. *Child Developm.*, 1968, **39**, 949–955.

16 Blau, B., & Rafferty, J. Changes in friendship status as a function of reinforcement. *Child Developm.*, 1970, **41**, 113–121.

17 Blazer, J. A. Fantasy and daydreams. *Child & Family,* 1966, **5**(3), 22–28.

18 Bonney, M. E. Assessment of efforts to aid socially isolated elementary school pupils. *J. educ. Res.*, 1971, **64**, 359–364.

19 Boshier, R. Self-esteem and first names in childhood. *Psychol. Rep.*, 1968, **22,** 762.

20 Bossard, J. H. S., & Boll, E. S. *The sociology of child development.* (4th ed.) New York: Harper & Row, 1966.

21 Bruning, J. L., & Husa, F. T. Given names and stereotyping. *Develpm. Psychol.*, 1972, **7**, 91.

22 Bryan, J. H., Redfield, J., & Mader, S. Words and deeds about altruism and the subsequent reinforcement power of the model. *Child Developm.*, 1971, **42**, 1501–1508.

23 Carey, R. G. Influence of peers in shaping religious behavior. *J. scient. Stud. Relig.*, 1971, **10**, 157–159.

24 Cavior, N., & Lombardi, D. A. Developmental aspects of judgment of physical attractiveness in children. *Develpm. Psychol.*, 1973, **8**, 67–71.

25 Church, J., & Stone, L. J. The early school years. *Children,* 1960, **7**, 113–114.

26 Clifford, E. Discipline in the home: A controlled observational study of parental practices. *J. genet. Psychol.*, 1959, **95**, 45–82.

27 Clifford, M. M., & Walster, E. The effect of physical attractiveness on teacher expectations. *Sociology of Education,* 1973, **46**, 248–258.

28 Cruickshank, W. M., & Johnson, G. O. (Eds.) *Education of exceptional children and youth.* (2nd ed.) Englewood Cliffs, N.J.: Prentice-Hall, 1967.

29 DeFleur, M. L., & DeFleur, L. B. The relative contribution of television as a learning source for children's occupational knowledge. *Amer. sociol. Rev.*, 1967, **32**, 777–789.

30 Eifermann, R. R. Social play in childhood. In R. E. Herron & B. Sutton-Smith (Eds.), *Child's play.* New York: Wiley, 1971. Pp. 270–297.

31 Elliott, F. Shy middle graders. *Elem. Sch. J.*, 1968, **69**, 296–300.

32 Emans, R. What do children in the inner city like to read? *Elem. Sch. J.*, 1968, **69**, 118–122.

33 Erikson, E. H. *Childhood and society.* (Rev. ed.) New York: Norton, 1964.

34 Eysenck, H. J. The development of moral values in children. VII. The contribution of learning theory. *Brit. J. educ. Psychol.,* 1960, **30,** 11–21.

35 Feldhusen, J. F., & Hobson, S. K. Freedom and play: Catalysts for creativity. *Elem. Sch. J.,* 1972, **73,** 148–155.

36 Feshbach, S. Aggression. In P. H. Mussen (Ed.), *Carmichael's manual of child psychology.* (3rd ed.) Vol. 2. New York: Wiley, 1970. Pp. 159–259.

37 Flanders, N. A., Morrison, B. M., & Brode, E. L. Changes in pupil attitudes during the school year. *J. educ. Psychol.,* 1968, **59,** 334–338.

38 Friend, R. M., & Neale, J. M. Children's perceptions of success and failure: An attributional analysis of the effects of race and social class. *Develpm. Psychol.,* 1972, **7,** 124–128.

39 Garai, J. E., & Scheinfeld, A. Sex differences in mental and behavioral traits. *Genet. Psychol. Monogr.,* 1968, **77,** 169–299.

40 Gardner, H. Children's sensitivity to musical styles. *Merrill-Palmer Quart.,* 1973, **19,** 67–77.

41 Gellert, E., Gircus, J. S., & Cohen, J. Children's awareness of their bodily appearance: A developmental study of factors associated with the body percept. *Genet. Psychol. Monogr.,* 1971, **84,** 109–179.

42 Gesell, A., Ilg, F. L., & Ames, L. B. *Youth: The years from ten to sixteen.* New York: Harper & Row, 1956.

43 Glavia, J. P. Persistence of behavior disorders in children. *Except. Children,* 1972, **38,** 367–376.

44 Glucksberg, S., & Krauss, R. M. What do people say after they have learned to talk? Studies of the development of referential communication. *Merrill-Palmer Quart.,* 1967, **13,** 309–316.

45 Goldstein, H. Factors influencing the height of seven-year-old children: Results from the National Child Development Study. *Hum. Biol.,* 1971, **43,** 92–111.

46 Grusec, J. E., & Ezrin, S. A. Techniques of punishment and the development of self-criticism. *Child Develpm.,* 1972, **43,** 1273–1288.

47 Hardeman, M. Children's moral reasoning. *J. genet. Psychol.,* 1972, **120,** 49–59.

48 Harris, D. B., & Roberts, J. *Intellectual maturity of children: Demographic and socioeconomic factors.* Rockville, Md.: U.S. Department of Health, Education, and Welfare, 1972.

49 Harris, L. J. Discrimination of left and right, and development of the logic of relations. *Merrill-Palmer Quart.,* 1972, **18,** 307–322.

50 Harrison, C. W., Rawls, J. E., & Rawls, D. J. Differences between leaders and nonleaders in six-to-eleven-year-old children. *J. soc. Psychol.,* 1971, **81,** 269–272.

51 Hartman, A. A., Nicolay, R. C., & Hurley, J. Unique personal names as a social adjustment factor. *J. soc. Psychol.,* 1968, **75,** 107–110.

52 Hartup, W. W. Peer interaction and social organization. In P. H. Mussen (Ed.), *Carmichael's manual of child psychology.* (3rd ed.) Vol. 2. New York: Wiley, 1970. Pp. 361–456.

53 Haskett, G. J. Modification of peer preferences of first-grade children. *Develpm. Psychol.,* 1971, **4,** 429–433.

54 Helper, M. M., & Quinlivan, M. J. Age and reinforcement of value of sex-role labels in girls. *Develpm. Psychol.,* 1973, **8,** 142.

55 Herron, R. E., & Sutton-Smith, B. (Eds.). *Child's play.* New York: Wiley, 1971.

56 Hess, A. L., & Bradshaw, H. L. Positiveness of self-concept and ideal self as a function of age. *J. genet. Psychol.,* 1970, **117,** 57–67.

57 Hess, R. D. Social class and ethnic influences upon socialization. In P. H. Mussen (Ed.), *Carmichael's manual of child psychology.* (3rd ed.) Vol. 2. New York: Wiley, 1970. Pp. 457–557.

58 Hindelang, M. J. Educational and occupational aspirations among working class Negro, Mexican-American and white elementary school children. *J. Negro Educ.,* 1970, **39,** 351–353.

59 Hirt, M., Ross, W. D., Kurtz, R., & Gleser, G. C. Attitudes to body products among normal subjects. *J. abnorm. Psychol.,* 1969, **74,** 486–489.

60 Hoffman, M. L. Moral development. In P. H. Mussen (Ed.), *Carmichael's manual of child psychology.* (3rd ed.) Vol. 2. New York: Wiley, 1970. Pp. 261–359.

61 Hundleby, J. D., & Cattell, R. B. Personality structure in middle childhood and the prediction of school achievement and adjustment. *Monogr. Soc. Res. Child Develpm.,* 1968, **33**(5).

62 Jacobs, J. C. Teacher attitude toward gifted children. *Gifted Child Quart.,* 1972, **16,** 23–26.

63 Jacobsen, R. B. An exploration of parental encouragement as an intervening variable in occupational-educational learning of children. *J. Marriage & Family,* 1971, **33,** 174–182.

64 Jenkins, R. L. Classification of behavior problems of children. *Amer. J. Psychiat.,* 1969, **125,** 1032–1039.

65 Kaspar, J. C., & Lowenstein, R. The effect of social interaction on activity levels in six- to eight-year-old boys. *Child Develpm.,* 1971, **42,** 1294–1298.

66 Keasey, C. B. Social participation as a factor in the moral development of preadolescents. *Develpm. Psychol.,* 1971, **5,** 216–220.

67 Kessel, F. S. The role of syntax in children's comprehension from ages six to twelve. *Monogr. Soc. Res. Child Develpm.,* 1970, **35**(6).

68 Kiener, F., & Nitschke, H. An investigation of nicknames. *Child Develpm. Abstr.,* 1972, **46,** No. 233.

69 Kogan, N., & Pankove, E. Creative ability over a five-year span. *Child Develpm.,* 1972, **43,** 427–442.

70 Kohn, M. The child as a determinant of his peers' approach to him. *J. genet. Psychol.,* 1966, **109,** 91–100.

71 Koslin, S. C., Amarel, M., & Ames, N. The effect of race on peer evaluation and preference in primary grade children: An exploratory study. *J. Negro Educ.,* 1970, **39,** 346–350.

72 Krieger, L. H., & Wells, W. D. The criteria for friendship. *J. soc. Psychol.,* 1969, **78,** 109–112.

73 Krogman, W. M. Growth of head, face, trunk, and limbs of Philadelphia white and Negro children of elementary and high school age. *Monogr. Soc. Res. Child Develpm.,* 1970, **35**(3).

74 Laycock, F., & Caylor, J. S. Physique of gifted children and their less gifted siblings. *Child Develpm.,* 1964, **35,** 63–74.

75 Leff, R. Effects of punishment intensity and consistency on the internalization of behavioral suppression in children. *Develpm. Psychol.,* 1969, **1,** 345–356.

76 Lerner, R. M. The development of stereotyped expectancies of body build–behavior relations. *Child Develpm.,* 1969, **40,** 137–141.

77 Levinson, B. M. *Pets and human behavior.* Springfield, Ill.: Charles C Thomas, 1972.

78 Levitin, T. E., & Chananie, J. D. Responses of primary school teachers to sex-typed behaviors in male and female children. *Child Develpm.,* 1972, **43,** 1309–1316.

79 Liebert, R. M., & Baron, R. A. Some immediate effects of televised violence on children's behavior. *Develpm. Psychol.,* 1972, **6,** 469–475.

80 Liebert, R. M., McCall, R. B., & Hanratty, M. A. Effects of sex-typed information on children's toy preferences. *J. genet. Psychol.,* 1971, **119,** 133–136.

81 Long, D., Elkind, D., & Spilka, B. The child's conception of prayer. *J. scient. Stud. Relig.,* 1967, **6,** 101–109.

82 Lorber, N. M. Concomitants of social acceptance: A review of research. *Psychology,* 1969, **6,** 53–59.

83 Lott, A. J., Lott, B. E., & Matthew, G. M. Interpersonal attraction among children as a function of vicarious reward. *J. educ. Psychol.,* 1969, **60,** 274–283.

84 Love, J. M., & Parker-Robinson, C. Children's imitation of grammatical and ungrammatical sentences. *Child Develpm.,* 1972, **43,** 309–319.

85 Marshall, H. H. The effect of punishment on children: A review of the literature and a suggested hypothesis. *J. genet. Psychol.,* 1965, **109,** 23–33.

86 Marshall, H. H. Behavior problems in normal children: A comparison between lay literature and developmental research. In W. R. Looft (Ed.), *Developmental psychology: A book of readings.* Hinsdale, Ill.: Dryden Press, 1972. Pp. 85–95.

87 Martin, P. C., & Vincent, E. L. *Human development.* New York: Ronald Press, 1960.

88 Maw, W. H., & Magoon, A. J. The curiosity dimension of fifth-grade children: A factorial discriminant analysis. *Child Develpm.,* 1971, **42,** 2023–2031.

89 McCracken, J. H. Sex typing of reading by boys attending all male classes. *Develpm. Psychol.,* 1973, **8,** 148.

90 McDavid, J. W., & Harari, H. Stereotyping of names and popularity in grade-school children. *Child Develpm.,* 1966, **37,** 453–459.

91 McGhee, P. E. Development of the humor response: A review of the literature. *Psychol. Bull.,* 1971, **76,** 328–348.

92 McIntyre, W. G., & Payne, D. C. The relationship of family functioning to school achievement. *Family Coordinator,* 1971, **20,** 265–268.

93 McKinney, J. P. The development of choice stability in children and adolescents. *J. genet. Psychol.,* 1968, **113,** 79–83.

94 Merchant, R. L., & Rebelsky, F. Effects of participation in rule formation on the moral judgments of children. *Genet. Psychol. Monogr.,* 1972, **85,** 287–304.

95 Meredith, H. V. Body size of contemporary groups of eight-year-old children studied in different parts of the world. *Monogr. Soc. Res. Child Develpm.,* 1969, **34**(1).

96 Minturn, L., & Lewis, M. Age differences in peer ratings of socially desirable and socially undesirable behavior. *Psychol. Rep.,* 1968, **23,** 783–791.

97 Mischel, W. Sex-typing and socialization. In P. H. Mussen (Ed.), *Carmichael's manual of child psychology.* (3rd ed.) Vol. 2. New York: Wiley, 1970. Pp. 3–72.

98 Mussen, P. H., Rutherford, E., Harris, S., & Keasey, C. B. Honesty and altruism among preadolescents. *Develpm. Psychol.,* 1970, **3,** 169–194.

99 Nelson, M. O. The concept of God and feelings toward parents. *J. indiv. Psychol.,* 1971, **27,** 46–49.

100 Nelson, P. D. Similarities and differences among leaders and followers. *J. soc. Psychol.,* 1964, **63,** 161–167.

101 Nias, D. K. B. The structuring of social attitudes in children. *Child Develpm.,* 1972, **43,** 211–219.

102 Nighswander, J. K., & Mayer, G. R. Catharsis: A means of reducing elementary school students' aggressive behavior. *Personnel Guid. J.,* 1969, **47,** 461–466.

103 Nordberg, R. B. Developing the idea of God in children. *Relig. Educ.,* 1971, **66,** 376–379.

104 Palermo, D. S., & Molfese, D. L. Language acquisition from age five onward. *Psychol. Bull.,* 1972, **78,** 409–428.

105 Pederson, D. R., & McEwan, R. C. Children's reactions to failure as a function of instructions and goal distance. *J. exp. Child Psychol.,* 1970, **9,** 51–58.

106 Phillips, B. N. Problem behavior in the elementary school. *Child Develpm.,* 1968, **39,** 895–903.

107 Piaget, J. *Science of education and psychology of the child.* New York: Orion Press, 1970.

108 Reese, H. W. Attitudes toward the opposite sex in late childhood. *Merrill-Palmer Quart.,* 1966, **12,** 157–163.

109 Richardson, S. A., & Royce, J. Race and physical handicap in children's preference for other children. *Child Develpm.,* 1968, **39,** 467–480.

110 Robbins, P. R. Personality and psychosomatic illness: A selective review of research. *Genet. Psychol. Monogr.,* 1969, **80,** 51–90.

111 Roberts, J., & Baird, J. T. *Behavior patterns of children in school: United States.* Rockville, Md.: U.S. Department of Health, Education, and Welfare, 1972.

112 Rothberg, C., & Harris, M. B. "Right" and "wrong" and discrimination learning in children. *J. genet. Psychol.,* 1972, **120,** 275–286.

113 Rubin, K. H. Egocentrism in children: A unitary construct? *Child Develpm.,* 1973, **44,** 102–110.

114 Ryan, M. S. *Clothing: A study in human behavior.* New York: Holt, 1966.

115 Scarlett, H. H., Press, A. N., & Crockett, W. H. Children's descriptions of peers: A Wernerian developmental analysis. *Child Develpm.,* 1971, **42,** 439–453.

116 Seagoe, M. V. Children's play in three American subcultures. *Journal of School Psychology,* 1971, **9,** 167–172.

117 Sears, R. R. Relation of early socialization experiences to self-concepts and gender role in middle childhood. *Child Develpm.,* 1970, **41,** 267–289.

118 Senn, M. J. E., & Solnit, A. J. *Problems in child behavior and development.* Philadelphia: Lea & Febiger, 1968.

119 Singer, J. L. *Daydreaming: An introduction to the experimental study of inner experience.* New York: Random House, 1966.

120 Sontag, L. W. Somatopsychics of personality and body function. In D. C. Charles & W. R. Looft (Eds.), *Readings in psychological development through life.* New York: Holt, 1973. Pp. 91–99.

121 Staffieri, J. R. A study of social stereotypes of body image in children. In W. R. Looft (Ed.), *Developmental psychology: A book of readings.* Hinsdale, Ill.: Dryden Press, 1972. Pp. 289–296.

122 Stein, G. M., & Bryan, J. H. The effect of a television model upon rule adoption behavior of children. *Child Develpm.,* 1972, **43,** 268–273.

123 Steward, M. A. Hyperactive children. *Scient. American,* 1970, **222**(4), 94–98.

124 Sweetser, D. A. The structure of sibling relationships. *Amer. J. Sociol.,* 1970, **76,** 47–58.

125 Tuckman, J., & Regan, R. A. Size of family and behavioral problems in children. *J. genet. Psychol.,* 1967, **111,** 151–160.

126 Tudor, J. F. The development of class awareness in children. *Soc. Forces,* 1971, **49,** 470–476.

127 Tyler, L. E. The antecedents of two varieties of vocational interests. *Genet. Psychol. Monogr.,* 1964, **70,** 177–227.

128 Utech, D. A., & Hoving, K. L. Parents and peers as competing influences in the decisions of children of different ages. *J. soc. Psychol.,* 1969, **78,** 267–274.

129 Valadian, I., Stuart, H. C., & Reed, R. B. Studies of illness of children followed from birth to eighteen years. *Monogr. Soc. Res. Child Develpm.,* 1961, **26**(3).

130 Van den Daele, L. A developmental study of the ego-ideal. *Genet. Psychol. Monogr.,* 1968, **78,** 191–256.

131 Vincent, E. L., & Martin, P. C. *Human psychological development.* New York: Ronald Press, 1961.

132 Warner, L. G., & Dennis, R. M. Prejudice versus discrimination: An empirical example and theoretical extension. *Soc. Forces,* 1970, **48,** 473–484.

133 Werry, J. S., & Quay, H. C. The prevalence of behavior symptoms in younger elementary school children. *Amer. J. Orthopsychiat.,* 1971, **41,** 136–143.

134 Williams, R. L., Cormier, W. H., Sapp, G. L., & Andrews, H. B. The utility of behavior management techniques in changing interracial behaviors. *J. Psychol.,* 1971, **77,** 127–138.

135 Zax, M., Cowan, E. L., Rappaport, J., Beach, D. R., & Laird, J. D. Follow-up study of children identified early as emotionally disturbed. *J. consult. clin. Psychol.,* 1968, **32,** 369–374.

136 Ziller, R. C. The alienation syndrome: A triadic pattern of self-other orientation. *Sociometry,* 1969, **32,** 287–300.

137 Zimet, S. F. American elementary reading textbooks: A sociological review. *Teachers Coll. Rec.,* 1969, **70,** 331–340.

CHAPTER | SEVEN

PUBERTY

Puberty is the period in the developmental span when the individual changes from an asexual to a sexual being. The word *puberty* is derived from the Latin word *pubertas*, meaning "age of manhood." It is the time when the individual becomes sexually mature and capable of producing offspring.

Puberty was recognized as a distinct period in the life span as far back as the time of Aristotle, who wrote in his *Historia Animalium*:

For the most part males begin to produce sperm when 14 years have been completed. At the same time pubic hair begins to appear. . . . At the same time in females a swelling of the breasts begins and the menses begin to flow and this fluid resembles fresh blood. . . . In the majority the menses are

first noticed after the breasts have grown to the height of two fingers' breadth.

Of even greater significance was Aristotle's emphasis on behavioral changes. He described pubescent girls as being irritable, passionate, ardent, and in need of constant surveillance because of their developing sexual impulses.

Primitive peoples observe various rites in recognition of the fact that the child is emerging from childhood into maturity and is thus approaching the age when he or she should be granted the rights and privileges and assume the responsibilities that accompany adulthood.

While few civilized peoples engage in formal rites of puberty to mark the transition from childhood to adolescence, except the bar mitzvah for Jewish boys, social expectations change at this time, and the child becomes aware that he is entering a new phase in his life.

CHARACTERISTICS OF PUBERTY

Puberty is a unique and distinctive period and is characterized by certain developmental changes that occur at no other time in the life span. The most important of these are discussed below.

Puberty Is an Overlapping Period

Puberty must be regarded as an overlapping period because it encompasses approximately one-third of the closing years of childhood and one-half of the beginning of adolescence, as shown in Figure 7-1. Until he is sexually mature, the child is *pubescent;* after he becomes sexually mature, he is a *young adolescent.*

Puberty Is a Short Period

Puberty is a relatively short period, lasting from two to four years, and it is customarily divided into three stages, as shown in Box 7-1.

Puberty Is a Time of Rapid Change

Puberty is one of the two periods in the life span that are characterized by rapid growth and marked changes in body propor-

> **Box 7-1. STAGES OF PUBERTY**
>
> **Prepubescent Stage**
> During the prepubescent (or immature) stage, the secondary sex characteristics begin to appear, but the reproductive organs are not yet fully developed.
>
> **Pubescent Stage**
> During the pubescent (or mature) stage, the secondary sex characteristics continue to develop. Sex cells are produced in the sex organs at this time.
>
> **Postpubescent Stage**
> During the postpubescent stage, the secondary sex characteristics become well developed, and the sex organs function in a mature manner.

tions. The other is the prenatal period and the first half of the first year. The rapid growth that occurs during puberty is generally referred to as the *adolescent growth spurt.* In reality, however, it is a preadolescent rather than an adolescent spurt because it precedes slightly or occurs simultaneously with the other physical changes of puberty. This growth spurt lasts for a year or two before the boy or girl becomes sexually mature and continues for six months to a year afterward. Thus the entire period of rapid growth lasts for about three years.

The rapid changes that take place during puberty lead to confusion, to feelings of inadequacy and insecurity, and in many

Figure 7-1 Puberty overlaps the end of childhood and the beginning of adolescence.

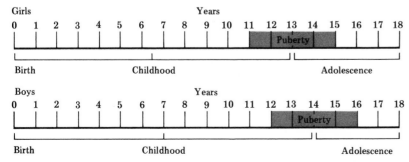

cases to unfavorable behavior. In discussing these changes, Dunbar has said (23):

During this period the developing child experiences changes in body, changes in status including appearance and clothes, possessions and range of choice, and changes in attitude toward sex and the opposite sex, all of which by necessity involve a changed child-parent relationship and changes in the rules and regulations to which the youngster is subjected.

Puberty Is a Negative Phase

Many years ago, Charlotte Bühler labeled puberty the *negative phase* (11). The term *phase* suggests a period of short duration; *negative* suggests that the individual takes an "anti" attitude toward life or that he seems to be losing some of the good qualities he previously developed. There is evidence that negative attitudes and behavior are characteristic mainly of the early part of puberty and that the worst of the negative phase is over when the individual becomes sexually mature (72).

Puberty Is a Variable Age

Puberty can occur any time between the ages of three and nineteen; however, the average girl becomes sexually mature at thirteen, and the average boy a year later. These variations in the age at which puberty occurs create many personal as well as social problems for both boys and girls.

CRITERIA OF PUBERTY

The criteria most often used to determine the onset of puberty and to pinpoint a particular stage of puberty that the child has reached are the menarche, nocturnal emissions, and evidence derived from chemical analysis of the urine and x-rays of bone development.

The *menarche,* or the first menstruation, is commonly used as a criterion of sexual maturity among girls, but it is neither the first nor the last of the physical changes that occur during puberty. When the menarche occurs, the sex organs and secondary sex characteristics have all started to develop, but none of them have yet reached a state of maturity. The menarche is more correctly considered a midpoint in puberty.

Among boys, a popularly used criterion of puberty is *nocturnal emissions*. During sleep, the penis sometimes becomes erect, and semen, or the fluid containing sperm cells, is released. This is a normal way for the male reproductive organ to rid itself of excessive amounts of semen. However, not all boys experience this phenomenon, and not all realize what it is. Furthermore, nocturnal emissions, like the menarche, occur after some puberty development has taken place and therefore cannot be used as an accurate criterion of the onset of puberty.

Chemical analysis of the first urine passed by boys in the morning has proved to be an effective technique for determining sexual maturity, as has analysis of girls' urine to see whether the female gonadotropic hormone, estrogen, is present. However, the practical difficulty of obtaining specimens of the early-morning urine of boys and girls limits the use of this method.

X-rays of different parts of the body, but especially the hands and knees, during the preadolescent growth spurt can reveal whether puberty has begun and the rate at which puberty is progressing. To date, this has proved to be the most dependable method of determining sexual maturity, though it, like the chemical analysis of early-morning urine, involves certain practical difficulties that make its widespread use unfeasible.

CAUSES OF PUBERTY

About five years before the child becomes sexually mature, there is a small excretion of the sex hormones in both boys and girls. The amount of hormones excreted increases as time passes, and this eventually leads to the maturing of the structure and function of the sex organs.

It has been established that there is a close relationship between the pituitary gland, located at the base of the brain, and the gonads, or sex glands. The male gonads are the *testes*, and the female gonads are the *ovaries*. The roles they play in bringing about the changes of puberty are described in Box 7-2.

AGE OF PUBERTY

Approximately 50 percent of all girls mature between 12.5 and 14.5 years, with the average maturing at 13. The average boy becomes sexually mature between the ages of 14 and 16.5, with 50 percent of all boys maturing between 14 and 15.5 years. The remaining 50 percent in each sex group is about evenly divided between those who mature earlier and those who mature later than average—the *early maturers* and the *late maturers*.

Between the ages of twelve and fourteen, differences between the sexes are especially marked, with many more girls having become mature than boys. This difference is reflected in the larger and more mature bodies of the girls and in their more mature, more aggressive, and more sex-conscious behavior.

There is evidence that boys and girls in the United States are reaching puberty earlier now than in past generations. This is true also in Europe and especially in the Scandinavian countries. The explanation for this is better health, better prenatal and postnatal medical care, and better nutrition (72, 92).

The total time needed to become sexually mature is approximately three years for girls and two to four years for boys. Boys show less uniformity in this process than girls. Approximately one to two years are required for the preliminary changes from an asexual to a sexual state, the prepubescent stage, and one to two years for the changes to be completed after the individual's sex organs have become mature.

The child who is slow in starting to mature usually matures more rapidly than the average child, once he gets started, and often even more rapidly than those who entered puberty earlier than average. The *fast ma-*

Box 7-2. CONDITIONS RESPONSIBLE FOR PUBERTY CHANGES

Role of the Pituitary Gland
The pituitary gland produces two hormones: the *growth* hormone, which is influential in determining the individual's size, and the *gonadotropic* hormone, which stimulates the gonads to increased activity. Just before puberty, there is a gradual increase in the amount of the gonadotropic hormone and an increased sensitivity of the gonads to this hormone; this initiates puberty changes.

Role of the Gonads
With the growth and development of the gonads, the sex organs—the primary sex characteristics—increase in size and become functionally mature, and the secondary sex characteristics, such as pubic hair, develop.

Interaction of the Pituitary Gland and the Gonads
The hormones produced by the gonads, which have been stimulated by the gonadotropic hormone produced by the pituitary gland, act in turn on this gland and cause a gradual reduction in the amount of growth hormone produced, thus stopping the growth process. The interaction between the gonadotropic hormone and the gonads continues throughout the individual's reproductive life, gradually decreasing as women approach the menopause and men approach the climacteric.

turer has greater spurts of rapid growth, his periods of accelerated and halted growth come abruptly, and he attains adult proportions very quickly. There is an early development of the sex organs and the secondary sex characteristics, and the osseous development comes earlier than average.

The *slow maturer*, by contrast has less intense periods of accelerated growth; his growth is more even and gradual, and it continues for a longer time. The sex organs and secondary sex characteristics develop later than average, and the osseous development is also late.

Individual differences in age and rate of maturing are more common that similarities, even among children in the same family. As Johnston has pointed out, "The time clock which governs the developmental process in children is an individual one" (40).

THE PUBERTY GROWTH SPURT

The growth spurt for girls begins between 8.5 and 11.5 years, with a peak coming, on the average, at 12.5 years. From then on, the rate of growth slows down, until growth gradually comes to a standstill between 17 and 18 years. Boys experience a similar pattern of rapid growth except that their growth spurt starts later and continues for a longer time. For boys, the growth spurt starts between 10.5 and 14.5 years, reaches a peak between 14.5 and 15.5 years, and is then followed by a gradual decline until 20 or 21 years, when growth is completed. Increases in height, weight, and strength come at approximately the same time.

The rapid growth and development that occur during puberty depend partly on hereditary factors, as they influence the endocrine glands, and partly on environmental factors, of which nutrition has been found to be the most important. Poor nutrition in childhood causes a diminished production of the growth hormone. Good nutrition, on the other hand, speeds up the production of this hormone. Emotional disturbances can affect growth by causing an overproduction of the adrenal steroids, which have an adverse effect on the growth hormone.

When the growth spurt of puberty is interfered with by illness, poor nutrition, or prolonged emotional tension, there will be delayed fusion of the bones, and the child will not attain his full height. However, if such disturbances are detected in time and corrected, growth can be speeded up to three or four times its normal rate and continue at that rate until the child reaches his hereditary potential (76, 92).

BODY CHANGES AT PUBERTY

During the puberty growth spurt, four important physical changes occur which transform the child's body into that of an adult: changes in body size, changes in body proportions, the development of the primary sex characteristics, and the development of the secondary sex characteristics.

Changes in Body Size

Changes in body size come from increased height and weight, and both types of growth follow a predictable pattern. The period of most rapid increase in height comes in the early part of puberty. Among girls, the average annual increase in the year preceding the menarche is 3 inches, though a 5- to 6-inch increase is not unusual. Two years preceding the menarche, the average increase is 2.5 inches, making a total increase of 5.5 inches in the two years preceding the menarche. After the menarche, the rate of growth slows down to about 1 inch a year, coming to a standstill at around eighteen years.

For boys, the onset of the period of rapid growth in height comes, on the average, at 12.8 years and ends, on the average, at 15.3 years, with a peak occurring at 14 years. The greatest increase in height comes in the year following the onset of puberty. After that, growth decelerates and continues at a slow rate until the age of 20 or 21. Because of this longer growth period, boys achieve greater height by the time they are mature than girls do.

Weight gain during puberty comes not only from an increase in fat but also from an increase in bone and muscle. Thus, even though pubescent boys and girls gain weight rapidly, they often look thin and scrawny. Girls experience the greatest weight gain just before and just after the menarche. Only slight increases in weight occur after that. For boys, the maximum gain in weight comes a year or two later than for girls and reaches its peak at sixteen years, after which the gain is small.

It is not uncommon for both boys and girls to go through a fat period during puberty. Between the ages of ten and twelve, at or near the onset of the growth spurt, children tend to accumulate fat on the abdomen, around the nipples, in the hips and thighs, and in the cheeks, neck, and jaw. This fat usually disappears after pubertal maturing and rapid growth in height are well started, though it may remain for two more years during the early part of puberty.

Changes in Body Proportions

Certain areas of the body, which in the early years of life were proportionately much too small, now become proportionately too big because they reach their mature size sooner than other areas. This is particularly apparent in the nose, feet, and hands. It is not until the latter part of adolescence that the body attains adult proportions in all areas, although the most pronounced changes take place before puberty is over.

The thin, long *trunk* of the older child begins to broaden at the hips and shoulders, and a waistline develops. This appears high at first because the legs grow proportionately more than the trunk. As the trunk lengthens, the waistline drops, thus giving the body adult proportions. The broadness of the hips and shoulders is influenced by

The physical changes of puberty: rapid physical growth, changes in body proportions, and development of the sex characteristics. (Hella Hammid from Rapho Guillumette)

the age of maturing. Boys who mature early usually have broader hips than boys who mature late and girls who mature late have slightly broader hips than early-maturing girls.

Just before puberty, the *legs* are disproportionately long in relation to the trunk and continue to be so until the child is approximately fifteen. In late-maturing children, the leg growth continues for a longer time than in early maturers. The result is that the late maturer is a long-legged individual at maturity, while the early maturer is short-legged. The legs of the early maturer tend to be stocky, while those of the late maturer are generally slender.

Much the same pattern occurs in the *arms*, whose growth precedes the rapid spurt of growth in the trunk, thus making them seem disproportionately long. As is true of leg growth, the growth of the arms is affected by the age of maturing. Early maturers tend to have shorter arms than late maturers, just as the early maturer is shorter-legged than the late maturer. Not until the growth of the arms and legs is nearly complete do they seem to be in the right proportion to the hands and feet, both of which reach their mature size early in puberty. Figure 7-2 shows the changes in body proportions of boys and girls after they have completed the puberty growth spurt.

Primary Sex Characteristics

The male gonads, or *testes*, which are located in the *scrotum*, or sac, outside the body, are only approximately 10 percent of their mature size at the age of fourteen years. Then there is rapid growth for a year or two, after which growth slows down; the testes are fully developed by the age of twenty or twenty-one.

Shortly after the rapid growth of the testes begins, the growth of the penis accelerates markedly. The first growth is in length, followed by a gradual increase in circumference.

When the male reproductive organs have become mature in function, nocturnal emissions generally begin to occur, usually when the boy is having a sexually exciting dream, when he has a full bladder or is constipated, when he is wearing tight pajamas, or when he is too warmly covered. Many boys are unaware of what is taking place until they see the telltale spot on their bedclothes or pajamas.

All parts of the female reproductive apparatus grow during puberty, though at

Figure 7-2 Changes in body proportions of boys and girls (a) before and (b) after puberty changes have been completed. (Adapted from J. M. Tanner. Growing up. *Scient. American,* 1973, **229**(3), 35–43. Used by permission.)

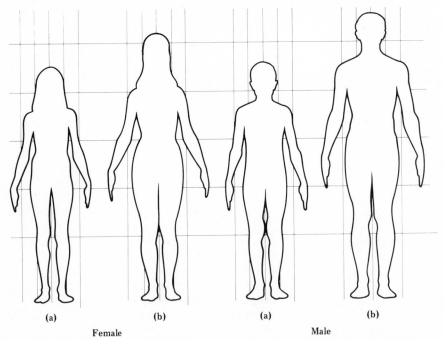

(a) (b) (a) (b)

Female Male

different rates. The uterus of the average eleven- or twelve-year-old girl, for example, weighs 5.3 grams; by the age of sixteen, the average weight is 43 grams. The Fallopian tubes, ovaries, and vagina also grow rapidly at this time.

The first real indication that a girl's reproductive mechanism is becoming mature is the menarche, or first menstrual flow. This is the beginning of a series of periodic discharges of blood, mucus, and broken-down cell tissue from the uterus that will occur approximately every twenty-eight days until she reaches the menopause, in the late forties or early fifties.

The girl's menstrual periods generally occur at very irregular intervals and vary markedly in length for the first year or so. This period is known as the *stage of adolescent sterility*. During this time ovulation, or the ripening and release of a ripe ovum from a follicle in the ovary, does not occur, and the girl is therefore sterile. Even after several menstrual periods, it is questionable whether the girl's sex mechanism is mature enough to make conception possible.

Secondary Sex Characteristics

As puberty progresses, boys and girls become increasingly dissimilar in appearance. This change is caused by the gradual development of the secondary sex characteristics—the physical features that distinguish members of the two sexes. They are called "secondary" because they are not directly related to reproduction, as the primary sex characteristics are. They have an indirect relation to reproduction, however, because they make members of one sex appealing to members of the other sex. As long as the body remains childish in appearance, there is no "sex appeal"; this changes when the secondary sex characteristics appear.

Like other development at puberty, that of the secondary sex characteristics follows a predictable pattern. The pattern of development of several of the important secondary sex characteristics, in relation to growth

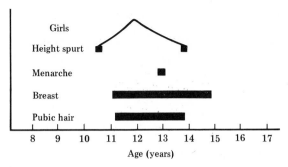

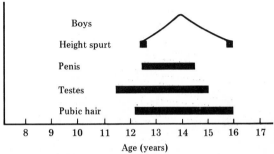

Figure 7-3 Sequence of events of puberty for girls and boys and predictable patterns of development of the secondary sex characteristics. (Adapted from W. A. Marshall & J. M. Tanner. Variations in the pattern of pubertal changes in boys. *Arch. Dis. Childh.,* 1970, **45,** 13–23. Used by permission.)

in height, is shown in Figure 7-3, which diagrams the sequence of events at puberty for boys and for girls and indicates the range of ages at which these developments take place. The secondary sex characteristics of boys and girls are summarized in Box 7-3.

EFFECTS OF PUBERTY CHANGES

The physical changes of puberty affect every area of the pubescent's body, both externally and internally, and thus it is not surprising that they also affect his physical and psychological well-being. Even though these effects are normally only temporary, they are severe enough while they last to bring about a change in habitual patterns of behavior, attitudes, and personality.

Box 7-3. SECONDARY SEX CHARACTERISTICS

Boys

Hair
Pubic hair appears about one year after the testes and penis have started to increase in size. Axillary and facial hair appear when the pubic hair has almost completed its growth, as does body hair. At first, all hair is scanty, lightly pigmented, and fine in texture. Later it becomes darker, coarser, more luxuriant, and slightly kinky.

Skin
The skin becomes coarser, less transparent, and sallow in color, and the pores enlarge.

Glands
The sebaceous, or oil-producing, glands in the skin enlarge and become more active, which may cause acne. The apocrine glands in the armpits start to function, and perspiration increases as puberty progresses.

Muscles
The muscles increase markedly in size and strength, thus giving shape to the arms, legs, and shoulders.

Voice
Voice changes begin after some pubic hair has appeared. The voice first becomes husky and later drops in pitch, increases in volume, and acquires a pleasanter tone. Voice breaks are common when maturing is rapid.

Breast Knots
Slight knobs around the male mammary glands appear between the ages of twelve and fourteen. These last for several weeks and then decrease in number and size.

Girls

Hips
The hips become wider and rounder as a result of the enlargement of the pelvic bone and the development of subcutaneous fat.

Breasts
Shortly after the hips start to enlarge, the breasts begin to develop. The nipples enlarge and protrude, and as the mammary glands develop, the breasts become larger and rounder.

Hair
Pubic hair appears after hip and breast development is well under way. Axillary hair begins to appear after the menarche, as does facial hair. Body hair appears on the limbs late in puberty. All hair except facial hair is straight and lightly pigmented at first and then becomes more luxuriant, coarser, darker, and slightly kinky.

Skin
The skin becomes coarser, thicker, and slightly sallow, and the pores enlarge.

Glands
The sebaceous and apocrine glands become more active as puberty progresses. Clogging of the sebaceous glands can cause acne, while the apocrine glands in the armpits produce perspiration, which is especially heavy and pungent just before and during the menstrual cycle.

Muscles
The muscles increase in size and strength, especially in the middle of puberty and toward the end, thus giving shape to the shoulders, arms, and legs.

Voice
The voice becomes fuller and more melodious. Huskiness and breaks in the voice are rare among girls.

Effects on Health

Rapid growth and bodily changes are likely to be accompanied by fatigue, listlessness, and other unfavorable symptoms. These discomforts are frequently made worse by an increase in duties and responsibilities, just at the time when the individual is least able to cope with them successfully.

Digestive disturbances are frequent, and appetite is finicky. The prepubescent child is upset by glandular changes and changes in the size and position of the internal organs. These changes interfere with the normal functions of digestion. Anemia is common at this period, not because of marked changes in blood chemistry, but because of erratic eating habits, which in turn increase the already-present tendency to be tired and listless.

During the early menstrual periods, girls frequently experience headaches, backaches, cramps, and abdominal pain, accompanied by fainting, vomiting, skin irritations, and even swelling of the legs and ankles. As a result, they feel tired, depressed, and irritable at the time of their periods. As menstruation becomes more regular, the physical and psychological disturbances which accompany its early appearances tend to diminish.

Headaches, backaches, and a general feeling of achiness occur at other times besides during menstruation, and both boys and girls suffer intermittently from them, the frequency and severity depending to a large extent upon how rapidly the pubescent changes are occurring and upon how healthy the individuals were when puberty began.

While puberty may be regarded as a "sickly age" when the individual is not up to par, relatively few diseases are characteristic of this period. If the pubescent child were actually ill, he would be treated with more sympathy and understanding than he usually is, less would be expected of him, and much of his unsocial behavior would be understood and tolerated, which it rarely is.

Effects on Attitudes and Behavior

The changes in attitudes and behavior that occur are more the result of social than of glandular changes, though the latter unquestionably play some role through their

---

Box 7-4. COMMON EFFECTS OF PUBERTY CHANGES ON ATTITUDES AND BEHAVIOR

Desire for Isolation
When the puberty changes begin, the child usually withdraws from peer and family activities and often quarrels with friends and members of his family. He may spend much time alone, daydreaming about how misunderstood and mistreated he is or experimenting with sex through masturbation.

Boredom
The pubescent child is bored with the play he formerly enjoyed, with schoolwork, with social activities, and with life in general, and he does as little work as he can at school and at home.

Incoordination
Rapid and uneven growth affects habitual patterns of coordination, and the pubescent child is clumsy and awkward for a time. As growth slows down, coordination gradually improves.

Social Antagonism
The pubescent child is often uncooperative, disagreeable, and antagonistic. Open hostility between the sexes, expressed in constant criticism and derogatory comments, is common at this age.

As puberty progresses, the child becomes friendlier, more cooperative, and more tolerant of others.

Heightened Emotionality
Moodiness, sulkiness, temper outbursts, and a tendency to cry at the slightest provocation are characteristic of the early part of puberty. It is a time of worry, anxiety, and irritability, as may be seen in Figure 7-4. As the pubescent child becomes more mature physically, he grows less tense and exhibits more mature emotional behavior.

Loss of Self-Confidence
The pubescent child, formerly so self-assured, becomes lacking in self-confidence and fearful of failure. This is due partly to lowered physical resistance and partly to the constant criticism of adults and peers. Many boys and girls emerge from puberty with the foundations of an inferiority complex.

Excessive Modesty
The bodily changes that take place during puberty cause the child to become excessively modest for fear that others will notice these changes and comment unfavorably on them.

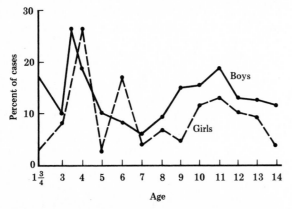

Figure 7-4 Irritability tends to increase early in puberty and then to decline. (Adapted from J. Macfarlane, L. Allen, & M. P. Honzik. *A developmental study of the behavior problems of normal children between twenty-one months and fourteen years.* Berkeley: University of California Press, 1954. Used by permission.)

influence on body homeostasis. The less sympathy and understanding the pubescent child receives from parents, siblings, teachers, and peers and the greater the social expectations at this time, the greater the psychological effects of the physical changes.

The most common, serious, and persistent of the many effects of puberty changes on attitudes and behavior are given in Box 7-4. Although all children exhibit some of these attitudes and behavior patterns, they are more marked before sexual maturity is attained, or during the so-called "negative phase."

Girls, as a general rule, are more seriously affected by puberty than boys, partly because they usually mature more rapidly than boys and partly because more social restrictions begin to be placed on their behavior, just at a time when they are trying to free themselves from such restrictions. More has discussed the reason why boys are not as greatly affected by puberty changes as girls (65):

Puberty appears to have been a more gradual affair. It did not burst on them with the rapidity of development that the girls experienced. The impulses aroused may have been just as strong or stronger for the male but he had more chance to adjust to them as they grew.

Because they reach puberty earlier, girls show signs of disruptive behavior sooner than boys do. However, girls' behavior stabilizes earlier than that of boys, and they begin to act more as they did before the onset of puberty, just as boys will do later.

How seriously puberty changes will affect the pubescent's behavior will be greatly influenced by his ability and willingness to communicate his concerns and anxieties to others and thus get a new and better perspective on them. As Dunbar has explained, "The affective reaction to change is largely determined by the capacity to communicate. . . . Communication is a means of coping with anxiety which inevitably accompanies stress" (23). Pubescent children who find it difficult or impossible to communicate with others exhibit more negative behavior than those who can and will communicate.

The psychological effects of puberty are also complicated by the social expectations of parents, teachers, and other adults. A boy or a girl is expected to act according to certain standards appropriate for his age, and he finds this relatively easy if his behavior patterns are at the appropriate developmental level. However, the child who is maturationally unready to fulfill the social expectations for his age is likely to have problems.

Those whose behavior is most affected are the *deviant maturers*—those whose sexual maturation varies by a year or more from the norm for their sex group. For boys, early maturing is advantageous, especially in the area of sports, from which they derive much of their prestige and status in the peer group. It is from the ranks of the early maturers that most of the leaders in boys' groups come, and this gives them added prestige in the eyes of girls also.

By contrast, boys who are late maturers tend to be restless, tense, rebellious, and attention-seeking. Because of these unsocial patterns of behavior, they are less popular with both peers and adults and are far less often selected for leadership roles by their peers than early maturers are. In commenting on the disadvantages of late maturing for boys, Weatherley has pointed out the following problems (102):

The later maturer must cope with the developmental demands of the junior high and high school period with the liability of a relatively small, immature appearing physical stature. His appearance is likely to call out in others at least mild reactions of derogation and the expectation that he is capable of only ineffectual, immature behavior. Such reactions constitute a kind of social environment which is conducive to feelings of inadequacy, insecurity and defensive "small-boy" behavior. Such behavior once initiated may well be self-sustaining, since it is likely to only intensify the negative environmental reactions which gave rise to it in the first place.

Early maturing is less advantageous to girls than it is to boys. Early-maturing girls are more grown-up and sophisticated in their behavior, but their appearance and actions may lead to a reputation of being "sexually promiscuous." In addition, early-maturing girls are more out of step with their peers than early-maturing boys, and this adds to their social problems. In commenting on the social problems the early-maturing girl is confronted with, Jones and Mussen have pointed out (43):

The early-maturing girl quite naturally has interests in boys and in social usages and activities more mature than those of her chronological age group. But the males of her own age are unreceptive, for while she is physiologically a year or two out of step with the girls in her class, she is three or four years out of step with the boys—a vast and terrifying degree of developmental distance.

Girls who are late maturers are less damaged psychologically than late-maturing boys. They are less likely to engage in status-seeking behavior than boys, though they are concerned about their normalcy, which they reflect in shy, retiring, diffident behavior. Because this is considered sex-appropriate behavior for girls, it is not as damaging to their reputations as similar behavior in boys would be.

A study of social attitudes among members of the peer group toward early- and late-maturing boys and girls revealed that early-maturing boys were mentioned much more often in the school newspaper than late maturers, while the reverse was true for girls (41).

SOURCES OF CONCERN

One of the developmental tasks of growing up is that of accepting the newly developed body and recognizing that nature has endowed the individual with certain physical characteristics that he can do little to change. Many children enter puberty with childhood ideals of what they will look like when they are grown up. Because these ideals rarely take into consideration the realities of the child's physical endowment, they must be markedly revised.

Furthermore, most children enter puberty with little foreknowledge of the time needed to mature or the pattern that maturing takes. As a result, they may become deeply concerned as they watch their bodies change, often so slowly that they wonder whether they will ever grow up. The pubescent child's concern about his developing body is heightened by his growing realization of the important role appearance plays in social acceptance.

Different children worry about different parts of their bodies. Usually they consider one physical characteristic to be particularly homely, out of proportion, or sexually inappropriate and magnify its seriousness out of all reasonable proportion. Girls, as a rule, are more concerned about their physical appearance than boys.

In general, pubescent children are concerned (1) about whether certain physical characteristics are normal and (2) about whether they are sexually appropriate.

Concerns about Normalcy

As Havighurst has pointed out, "It is a rare youngster who is never worried during this period with the question: Am I normal?"

(37). Because boys and girls are very conscious of every change that takes place in their bodies and because they have definite ideas about how they would like to look, they become concerned if they feel that they are unattractive or that their appearance is sexually inappropriate.

Since boys and girls undergo very different changes in appearance during puberty, they are naturally concerned about

---

Box 7-5. COMMON CONCERNS ABOUT NORMALCY DURING PUBERTY

Boys' Concerns

Nocturnal Emissions
If the boy has not been told about nocturnal emissions, his first such experience is likely to be traumatic.

Secondary Sex Characteristics
Boys are disturbed mainly by the slow growth of facial hair, the huskiness and cracking that accompany voice changes, and the slow development and strengthening of their muscles.

Lack of Interest in Girls
When they see older or sexually mature boys showing an interest in girls and in dating, boys wonder whether they are normal because they have no such interests.

Girls' Concerns

The Menarche
Even with some foreknowledge, the menarche is often a traumatic experience, especially if accompanied by vomiting and cramps. Many girls wonder whether they will "bleed to death."

Menstruation
Many girls wonder whether the cramps, headaches, and backaches they experience during their periods are normal.

Secondary Sex Characteristics
Because the breasts have a conical shape when they begin to develop, girls wonder whether they will eventually be normal in appearance. They also worry about whether their hips will be too large for the rest of their bodies and whether the down on their faces will turn into a beard or moustache.

Lack of Sex Appeal
Many girls worry if they are unable to attract the attention and win the favor of boys.

Concerns of Boys and Girls

Sex Organs
The pubescent child may fear that his enlarged sex organs will show through his clothing.

Body Disproportions
His large hands, feet, and nose; his long and lanky arms and legs; his small shoulders; and perhaps a slightly receding chin—all characteristics of early puberty—make the pubescent child wonder whether he will ever look like a normal person.

Awkwardness
The child becomes awkward and clumsy during puberty and may worry that he is losing skills acquired earlier. His concern is heightened if he is ridiculed or reproved for his awkwardness.

Age of Maturing
Earlier maturers may feel like misfits, while those who are slow to mature are embarrassed by their undeveloped bodies and concerned about their lack of interest in the things that absorb their more mature age-mates.

Masturbation
Tension and discomfort in the developing sex organs often lead the pubescent to handle them. Most children have been told that masturbation is wrong, and they feel guilty and ashamed. Their concern is heightened if they have heard old wives' tales—that masturbation leads to insanity, for example.

the normalcy of different physical characteristics. Some concerns, however, are shared
by all pubescents. Box 7-5 gives the usual
concerns of boys and of girls as well as those
common to both sexes.

Concern about Sex Appropriateness

From the movies he sees, the television
programs he watches, and the books he
reads, as well as from his observations of
adults, the pubescent child builds up a clear
concept of what constitutes masculine and
feminine appearance and behavior.

The sudden increase in size that occurs
during the pubertal growth spurt is likely to
disturb girls because they are afraid their
size will make them unattractive to boys.
Boys, on the other hand, become disturbed
when they see girls of their own age literally
towering over them.

Children frequently gain weight during
the early part of puberty, and this is a
source of great concern. In our culture, fat
is considered unattractive, and the overweight girl who compares herself with movie
stars and cover girls, for example, may be
very distressed by her own appearance.

For a boy, fat is considered sexually
inappropriate, especially on the thighs,
around the waist, and in the mammary
region. While this generally disappears as
puberty progresses, it may affect personality
development unfavorably for many years.

There is a widespread belief that small
genitalia mean lack of normal sexual development. When the boy's penis is developing,
he is greatly concerned by its thinness.
Growth in circumference follows growth in
length, and thus for awhile the boy may feel
that his penis is not developing normally and
that he will be sexually inadequate.

Until the breasts become curved and
filled out as a result of the development of
the mammary glands and subcutaneous
tissue, the girl worries that they are un-
feminine in appearance. Broad hips are
regarded as sexually inappropriate for both
sexes, but especially so for boys, and can also
be a source of concern during the early
stages of puberty.

The pubescent child has clear concepts of masculinity and femininity in appearance and behavior.
(Suzanne Szasz)

Secondary sex characteristics that are
late in developing are likely to be the sources
of greatest concern, especially those which
differentiate the two sexes most clearly. In
the case of boys, facial hair, the development
of large muscles in the shoulder and arm
regions, and voice changes come late in puberty. As the boy watches hair appear on
other areas of his body but not on his face,
he wonders whether he will always have the
smooth skin of a girl and anxiously awaits
the time when he can begin to shave. The
breast knots, which develop early in puberty
and then gradually disappear, add to his concern about his sex-appropriate appearance.

Typically, a feminine woman is supposed
to have a beautiful complexion. As puberty
progresses, acne usually gets worse rather
than better, and facial hair is darker and
more profuse than in the early stages of
puberty, which frequently alarms the girl.

HAZARDS OF PUBERTY

The hazards of puberty are generally
serious mainly in terms of their long-range
consequences. This contrasts with the ear-

lier stages of development, when the hazards themselves tend to be more important than their long-term effects.

As is true of late childhood, the psychological hazards of puberty are more numerous and more far-reaching in their effects than the physical ones. Furthermore, only a small percentage of pubescent children are affected by the physical hazards, while *all* are affected by the psychological ones, though to varying degrees.

Physical Hazards

Even though most pubescent children do not feel up to par physically, actual illness is less common during this period than at earlier ages. Mortality also occurs infrequently among pubescent children. Since they rarely suffer from illnesses severe enough to lead to death and since they are so inactive and socially withdrawn that accidents—a common cause of death in the years preceding and following puberty—are infrequent, there is less likelihood of mortality at this time than in the earlier or even the post-pubescent years. Actually, many deaths reported as due to accidents are the result of suicide, which a pubescent child may attempt if he becomes severely depressed.

The major physical hazards of puberty are due to slight or major malfunctioning of the endocrine glands that control the puberty growth spurt and the sexual changes that take place at this time. Box 7-6 describes the effect of glandular malfunctioning on development.

Psychological Hazards

The psychological hazards of puberty are those which prevent the pubescent child from mastering two of the most important developmental tasks for that age: acceptance of his changed body and acceptance of the sex role he is now expected to play as a near-adult. Many conditions interfere with this acceptance, although three are particularly important.

First, if the pubescent child is not informed about, or is psychologically unprepared for, the physical changes that take place at puberty, undergoing these changes may be a traumatic experience for him, and he is likely to develop an unfavorable attitude toward them—an attitude that is more apt to persist than to disappear.

There are many reasons why the child is often unprepared for puberty. Parents may lack adequate knowledge, or they may be

---

Box 7-6. EFFECTS OF ENDOCRINE IMBALANCE AT PUBERTY

Insufficient Growth Hormone
An insufficient amount of growth hormone in late childhood and early puberty causes the individual to be smaller than average at maturity.

Insufficient Gonadal Hormones
If the gonadal hormones are not released in adequate amounts soon enough to check the growth hormone, growth of the limbs continues too long, and the individual becomes larger than average. Insufficient amounts of gonadal hormones also affect the normal development of the sex organs and the secondary sex characteristics, with the result that the individual remains childish in appearance

or takes on characteristics of the opposite sex, depending on when the interruption in the developmental cycle occurs.

Excessive Supply of Gonadal Hormones
An imbalance in the functioning of the pituitary gland and the gonads can cause production of an excessive amount of gonadal hormones at a very young age, resulting in the onset of puberty sometimes as early as five or six years of age. While the child is sexually mature in that his sex organs have begun to function, he is still small in stature, and the secondary sex characteristics are not as well developed as in those who mature at the usual age.

held back by modesty and embarrassment. The gap that develops between the pubescent child and his parents often prevents him from asking them about the changes that are taking place in his body, or, to avoid embarrassment, he may pretend that he already knows all he needs to know and thus rebuff his parents' attempts to give him the information he wants.

Unless the school gives courses in sex hygiene or provides information about puberty in connection with a physical hygiene course, the child will not get the information he needs at school, nor will he turn to a teacher for help, partly because of embarrassment and partly because his attitudes toward school and toward his teachers are more likely to be unfavorable at this time. Even though his classmates or friends may have received information from their parents that they could impart to him, pride keeps him from turning to them. He does not want to admit that he knows less than they.

Regardless of the reason for inadequate preparation, it is a serious psychological hazard, especially in the case of the early or late maturer, because it encourages him to imagine that something is wrong with him or that his development is so abnormal that he will never again look like his peers. Being different is always a concern to children and young adolescents, and the more they deviate in ways that are apparent to all, the more concerned they become and the more likely they are to feel abnormal and consequently inferior.

Second, traditional beliefs about sex-appropriate appearance tend to color the pubescent child's attitudes in ways that interfere with his acceptance of his changed body and the new sex role he must assume. For example, since being flat-chested is generally considered unattractive in a woman, the girl whose breasts are developing slowly may become concerned about her femininity.

Third, it is difficult for the pubescent child to be acceptant about anything that makes him different and thus—in his view—inferior. Deviations in sexual ma-

turing, regardless of the form they take, are therefore a potential psychological hazard. The child feels that there is something wrong with him and also that he is inferior to his age-mates. The early maturer, who looks older than he actually is, may be expected to act in accordance with his appearance, and if he fails to do so, he may develop feelings of inadequacy and inferiority. All the normal effects of puberty changes—awkwardness, heightened emotionality, and so on—are accentuated in the early maturer, and this intensifies his feelings of inferiority. The late maturer, who looks younger than he is, may be treated accordingly by his friends and by adults, and this makes him doubt his ability to do what his age-mates do. The slow maturer has more time to adjust to the physical changes of puberty than rapid maturers or those who mature at a normal rate, but concern about whether he will ever grow up counteracts this favorable effect and encourages him in his belief that he is inferior to his age-mates.

Long-term Effects Unfortunately, the psychological effects of puberty changes can be persistent, extending far beyond this relatively short period in the life span. Unfavorable attitudes toward menstruation, for example, developed at puberty, often continue throughout life, causing women to become even more depressed at the time of their period than would be justified on the basis of the physical discomforts involved. For example, attempts at suicide among women occur more frequently during the menstrual period than at other times (96). Similarly, a disinclination to work, developed when rapid physical changes sap the pubescent child's strength, often persists, and he may develop into an underachiever, both academically and, later, vocationally.

Studies have documented the long-term effects on behavior of deviations in sexual maturing. In the case of the slow maturer, the damage results from the fact that he has a longer-than-average time during which to develop the undesirable patterns of behavior normally associated with puberty, although this need not necessarily be permanently handicapping to him.

Some, it is true, may develop into habitual daydreamers; some may develop a hypercritical, frictional attitude toward others; and some may develop into restless people who find it difficult to concentrate on any task. But if their desire for social acceptance is strong enough and if they are able to achieve a reasonable amount of social acceptance, they will be sufficiently motivated to break these habits and replace them with more socially acceptable patterns of behavior.

Not all those who deviate from the norm—the early and late maturers—are damaged permanently by this. Some, in fact, benefit, not only during puberty, but in later years as well. Although studies of the long-term effects on behavior have so far been limited to boys, evidence from these studies and knowledge of the effects of reinforcement through repetition enable us to hazard a guess concerning what the long-term effects on girls might be.

Early-maturing boys normally become socially active and popular, holding leadership roles in the peer group. They have assets that are valued in the peer group, and as a result of repetition, these develop into habitual patterns of behavior. Follow-up studies of subjects into their mid-thirties and early forties have shown these patterns of behavior to be persistent. As a result, the early maturers are more successful vocationally and socially as adults, just as they were during adolescence. Their success stems from the fact that they make better impressions on others than the normal or late maturers.

By contrast, middle-aged men who were late maturers were found to cling to the "little-boy" patterns of behavior which caused them to be unpopular when they were younger. Thus late maturers tend to be less active socially, less successful in business, and less likely to be selected for leadership roles than might be expected on the basis of their abilities (2, 42).

Speculation about the long-term effects of deviant maturing on girls leads one to believe that early maturers who were embarrassed about being larger than their contemporaries and who often developed aggressive patterns of behavior to attract the attention of boys will continue to show similar patterns of behavior as adult women. Late maturers, by contrast, who were better adjusted personally and socially in adolescence, are likely to continue to be so during adulthood, unless conditions unrelated to sexual maturing interfere with this pattern.

UNHAPPINESS AT PUBERTY

One essential of happiness is self-acceptance. It is difficult for a pubescent child to be self-acceptant when he is anxious and concerned about his changing body and dissatisfied with his appearance.

Furthermore, the realization of the increasingly important role that appearance plays in social acceptance adds to his worries. The more concerned the pubescent child becomes about social acceptance, the more concerned he will be about his appearance. Girls tend to worry more about their looks than boys because they realize that appearance plays a more important role in their social acceptance than it does in boys'.

Studies of pubescent children who are dissatisfied with their looks have pinpointed the areas of greatest concern. Girls, for example, want to have a good figure. Boys want to be tall, since they associate this with masculinity, and very tall girls want to be shorter to conform to the stereotype for their sex. Boys want to be heavier than they are, and girls want to be lighter. Boys want broader shoulders and thicker arms and legs, while girls want smaller hips and waists, thinner arms and legs, and larger busts. Boys are usually dissatisfied with their chins—they want more prominent ones—while girls and boys both wish their noses were less prominent and better shaped (12, 45). As Calden et al. have pointed out,

Girls want to have a good figure so that they will conform to the cultural stereo-type—often represented by the "beauty queen"—of a feminine girl. (Jason Lauré from Rapho Guillumette)

"Females desire changes from the waist down and wish for smallness and petiteness of body parts (except for bust). Males are dissatisfied with body dimensions from the waist up, desiring bigness of body parts" (12).

Concern about appearance is not the only cause of unhappiness during puberty. The pubescent child's behavior is so unsocial that parents, teachers, siblings, and peers—the most significant people in his life—may be rejectant in their attitudes toward him. In addition, pubescent children's achievements usually fall far short of their potentials, and they feel guilty about this. Even worse, their temper outbursts and restlessness create the impression that they are not acting their age—an impression that further jeopardizes their social acceptance and consequently their self-acceptance.

Not all phases of puberty are unhappy to the same degree; the early part—the "negative phase"—is usually the most unhappy. After sexual maturing occurs and growth slows down, the pubescent child has more energy. This results in better achievements and better social relationships. Furthermore, he is less concerned about his appearance because he realizes that many of the conditions that worried him were only temporary. As he more closely approximates his ideal and as he becomes more sex-appropriate in appearance, some of his anxiety wanes. Even more important, he learns that there are ways in which he can improve his appearance—girls may try dieting or may experiment with different hairstyles, for example—and thus increase his chances for social acceptance.

Because unhappiness at any age is serious, especially if it persists long enough to become habitual, it is important to keep the unhappiness of the pubescent child at a minimum. Parents and teachers can do this by making sure he is as healthy as possible, telling him what he needs to know about the process of sexual maturing, helping him to improve his appearance, lightening the work load during periods of rapid growth, overlooking drops in the quality of his work at such times, and accepting his moodiness and orneriness as only a temporary condition.

Children usually look forward to the time when they will be grown up, and this attitude can be maintained if steps are taken to prevent unhappiness from developing during puberty. This is important for the pubescent child's mental health, but even more important, it increases his motivation to learn adult patterns of behavior. The developmental tasks of adolescence are difficult, and learning them is a long, laborious task at best. A strong motivation to do so, resulting from happy anticipation of achieving adult status in society, will go a long way toward easing the burden of these tasks and toward guaranteeing a successful end result.

Chapter Highlights

1 During puberty, the individual becomes sexually mature. Marked behavioral as well as physical changes occur at this time.

2 Puberty overlaps the end of childhood and the beginning of adolescence and is subdivided into three stages: the prepubescent stage, the pubescent stage, and the postpubescent stage. The rapid changes that take place have mainly unfavorable effects on behavior, and thus puberty has been called a *negative phase*.

3 Puberty changes are caused by an interrelationship between the hormones produced by the pituitary gland and the gonads.

4 The average girl reaches puberty at thirteen and the average boy, approximately a year later. However, there are marked variations in the age of onset of puberty and also in the time needed to complete the puberty changes.

5 The puberty growth spurt is due to a combination of hereditary and environmental factors. This growth involves four major kinds of body changes: changes in body size, changes in body proportions, development of the primary sex characteristics, and development of the secondary sex characteristics.

6 These changes have their major effects on health and on attitudes and behavior.

7 Body changes at puberty cause the child to become concerned about the normalcy and sex appropriateness of his development.

8 The major physical hazards of puberty come from three sources—an insufficient amount of growth hormone, an insufficient amount of gonadal hormones, and an excessive supply of gonadal hormones.

9 The psychological hazards of puberty are those which prevent the pubescent child from mastering the important developmental tasks for his age, thus making him unprepared for the personal and social demands of adolescence.

10 Failure to master the developmental tasks of puberty are mainly the result of the child's reaching sexual maturity either too early or too late as compared with his age-mates.

11 Unhappiness at puberty, which is common, results from the pubescent child's dissatisfaction with his appearance and also from the unfavorable effects of his behavior on his social adjustments.

12 Because unhappiness at puberty can develop into a persistent pattern of behavior that may color the individual's attitudes toward his social role for many years to come, parents and teachers should do all they can to make this a less stressful period of development.

Bibliography

1 Adams, P. L. Puberty is a biosocial turning point. *Psychosomatics,* 1969, **10**, 343–349.

2 Ames, R. Physical maturing among boys as related to adult social behavior. *Calif. J. educ. Res.,* 1957, **8**, 69–75.

3 Andersen, H. The influence of hormones on human development. In F. Falkner (Ed.), *Human development.* Philadelphia: Saunders, 1966. Pp. 184–221.

4 Bayley, N. Consistency of maternal and child behavior in the Berkeley Growth Study. *Vita Hum., Basel,* 1964, **7**, 73–95.

5 Bayley, N. Research in child development: A longitudinal perspective. *Merrill-Palmer Quart.,* 1965, **11**, 183–208.

6 Blank, L., Sugerman, A. A., & Roosa, L. Body concern, body image and nudity. *Psychol. Rep.,* 1968, **23**, 963–968.

7 Bojlen, K., & Bentzon, M. W. The influence of climate and nutrition on age at menarche: A historical review and a modern hypothesis. *Hum. Biol.,* 1968, **40**, 69–85.

8 Broderick, C. B. Sexual behavior among pre-adolescents. *J. soc. Issues,* 1966, **22**(7), 7–21.

9 Brŏzek, J. (Ed.) Physical growth and body composition. *Monogr. Soc. Res. Child Develpm.,* 1970, **35**(7).
10 Bruch, H. Psychological aspects of obesity in adolescence. *Amer. J. publ. Hlth.,* 1958, **48,** 1349–1353.
11 Bühler, C. *Das Seelenleben der Jungendlichen.* Stuttgart: Gustav Fischer Verlag, 1927.
12 Calden, G., Lundy, R. M., & Schlafer, R. J. Sex differences in body concepts. *J. consult. Psychol.,* 1959, **23,** 378.
13 Calderone, M. S. Sex education and the roles of school and church. *Ann. Amer. Acad. pol. soc. Sci.,* 1968, **376,** 53–60.
14 Clarke, H. H., & Degutis, E. W. Comparison of skeletal age and various physical and motor factors with the pubescent development of 10, 13, and 16 year old boys. *Res. Quart. Amer. Ass. Hlth. Phys. Educ. Recr.,* 1962, **33,** 356–368.
15 Compton, M. H. Body build, clothing and delinquent behavior. *J. Home Econ.,* 1967, **49,** 655–659.
16 Corboz, R. J.: Psychological aspects of retarded puberty. *Adolescence,* 1966, **1,** 141–143.
17 Cruickshank, W. M., & Johnson, G. O. (Eds.) *Education of exceptional children and youth.* (2nd ed.) Englewood Cliffs, N. J.: Prentice-Hall, 1967.
18 Damon, A., Damon, S. T., Reed, R. B., & Valadian, I. Age at menarche of mothers and daughters, with a note on accuracy of recall. *Hum. Biol.,* 1969, **41,** 161–175.
19 Dreyer, A. S., Hulac, V., & Rigler, D. Differential adjustment to pubescence and cognitive style patterns. *Develpm. Psychol.,* 1971, **4,** 456–462.
20 Dubois, F. S. Rhythms, cycles, and periods in health and disease. *Amer. J. Psychiat.,* 1959, **116,** 114–119.
21 Duffy, R. J. Description and perception of frequency breaks (voice breaks) in adolescent female speakers. *Lang. Speech,* 1970, **13,** 151–161.
22 Duffy, R. J. Fundamental frequency characteristics of adolescent females. *Lang. Speech,* 1970, **13,** 14–24.
23 Dunbar, F. Homeostasis during puberty. *Amer. J. Psychiat.,* 1958, **114,** 673–682.
24 Eichorn, D. H. Biological correlates of behavior. *62nd Yearb. Nat. Soc. Stud. Educ.* I. 1963, 4–61.
25 Eisenberg, L. A developmental approach to adolescence. *Children,* 1965, **12,** 131–135.
26 Faterson, H. F., & Witkin, H. A. Longitudinal study of development of the body concept. *Develpm. Psychol.,* 1970, **2,** 429–438.
27 Faust, M. S. Developmental maturity as a determinant in prestige of adolescent girls. *Child Develpm.,* 1960, **31,** 173–184.
28 Frisancho, A. R., Garn, S. M., & Rohmann, C. G. Age at menarche: A new method of prediction and retrospective assessment based on hand X-rays. *Hum. Biol.,* 1969, **41,** 42–50.
29 Frisch, R. E., & Revelle, R. The height and weight of adolescent boys and girls at the time of peak velocity of growth in height and weight: Longitudinal data. *Hum. Biol.,* 1969, **41,** 536–559.
30 Frisch, R. E., & Revelle, R. The height and weight of boys and girls at the time of initiation of the adolescent growth spurt in height and weight and the relationship to menarche. *Hum. Biol.,* 1971, **43,** 140–159.
31 Frisch, R. E., Revelle, R., & Cook, S. Height, weight and age at menarche of the "critical weight" hypothesis. *Science,* 1971, **174,** 1148–1149.
32 Garrison, K. C. Physiological changes in adolescence. In

J. F. Adams (Ed.), *Understanding adolescence: Current developments in adolescent psychology.* Boston: Allyn and Bacon, 1968. Pp. 43–69.
33 Hanseman, C. F., & Maresh, M. M. A longitudinal study of skeletal maturation. *Amer. J. Dis. Children,* 1961, **101,** 305–321.
34 Harms, E. Puberty: Physical and mental. *Adolescence,* 1966, **1,** 293–296.
35 Harper, J. F., & Collins, J. K. The effects of early or late maturation on the prestige of the adolescent girl. *Austral. & New Zeal. J. Sociol.,* 1972, **8,** 83–88.
36 Hart, M., & Sarnoff, C. A. The impact of the menarche: A study of two stages of organization. *J. Amer. Acad. child Psychiat.,* 1971, **10,** 257–271.
37 Havighurst, R. J. *Human development and education.* New York: Longmans, 1953.
38 Heald, F. P., Dangela, M., & Brunschyber, P. Physiology of adolescence. *New Eng. J. Med.,* 1963, **268,** 192–198, 243–252, 299–307, 361–366.
39 Israel, S. L. Normal puberty and adolescence. *Ann. N.Y. Acad. Sci.,* 1967, **142,** 773–778.
40 Johnston, F. E. Individual variations in the rate of skeletal maturation between five and eighteen years. *Child Develpm.,* 1964, **35,** 75–80.
41 Jones, M. C. A study of socialization patterns at the high school level. *J. genet. Psychol.,* 1958, **93,** 87–111.
42 Jones, M. C. Psychological correlates of somatic development. *Child Develpm.,* 1965, **36,** 899–911.
43 Jones, M. C., & Mussen, P. H. Self-conceptions, motivations, and interpersonal attitudes of early- and late-maturing girls. *Child Develpm.,* 1958, **29,** 491–501.
44 Joseph, W. Vocal growth measurements in male adolescents. *J. Res. music Educ.,* 1969, **17,** 423–426.
45 Jourard, S. M., & Secord, P. F. Body-cathexis and the ideal female figure. *J. abnorm. soc. Psychol.,* 1955, **50,** 243–246.
46 Krogman, W. M. Growth of head, face, trunk, and limbs in Philadelphia white and Negro children of elementary and high school age. *Monogr. Soc. Res. Child Develpm.,* 1970, **35**(3).
47 Kurtz, R. M. Sex differences and variations in body attitudes. *J. consult. clin. Psychol.,* 1969, **33,** 625–629.
48 Larsen, V. L. Sources of menstrual information: A comparison of age groups. *Family Life Coordinator,* 1961, **10,** 41–43.
49 Lavine, L. S., Moss, M. L., & Noback, C. R. Digital epiphyseal fusion in adolescence. *J. Pediat.,* 1962, **61,** 571–575.
50 Levy, E. Toward understanding the adolescent. *Menninger Quart.,* 1969, **23,** 14–21.
51 Livson, N., & McNeill, D. Physique and maturation rate in male adolescents. *Child Develpm.,* 1962, **33,** 145–152.
52 Lucas, C. J., & Ojha, A. B. Personality and acne. *J. psychosom. Res.,* 1963, **7,** 41–43.
53 Macfarlane, J., Allen, L., & Honzik, M. P. A developmental study of the behavior problems of normal children between twenty-one months and fourteen years. Berkeley: University of California Press, 1954.
54 Marshall, W. A., & Tanner, J. M. Variations in pattern of pubertal changes in girls. *Arch. Dis. Childh.,* 1969, **44,** 291–303.
55 Marshall, W. A., & Tanner, J. M. Variations in the pattern of pubertal changes in boys. *Arch. Dis. Childh.,* 1970, **45,** 13–23.
56 Martin, P. C., & Vincent, E. L. *Human development.* New York: Ronald Press, 1960.

57 Masters, W. H., & Johnson, V. E. *Human sexual response.* Boston: Little, Brown, 1965.

58 Masterson, J. G. True precocious puberty. *Ann. N.Y. Acad. Sci.,* 1967, **142,** 779–782.

59 McNeill, D., & Livson, N. Maturation rate and body build in women. *Child Develpm.,* 1963, **34,** 25–32.

60 Meredith, H. V. Body size of contemporary youth in different parts of the world. *Monogr. Soc. Res. Child Develpm.,* 1969, **34**(7).

61 Miller, A. C. Role of physical attractiveness in impression formation. *Psychonomic Sci.,* 1970, **19,** 241–243.

62 Money, J., & Ehrhardt, A. A. *Man and woman, boy and girl.* Baltimore: Johns Hopkins Press, 1973.

63 Money, J., & Walker, P. A. Psychosexual development, maternalism, nonpromiscuity, and body image in 15 females with precocious puberty. *Arch. sexual Behav.,* 1971, **1,** 45–60.

64 Montagu, A. *Human heredity.* New York: Harcourt, Brace & World, 1959.

65 More, D. M. Developmental concordance and discordance during puberty and early adolescence. *Monogr. Soc. Res. Child Develpm.,* 1953, **18,** 1–128.

66 Morgan, C. T. *Physiological psychology.* (3rd ed.) New York: McGraw-Hill, 1964.

67 Mussen, P. H., & Bouterline-Young, H. Relationships between rate of physical maturing and personality among boys of Italian descent. *Vita Hum., Basel,* 1964, **7,** 196–200.

68 Muuss, R. E. Adolescent development and the secular trend. *Adolescence,* 1970, **5,** 267–284.

69 Muuss, R. E. Puberty rites in primitive and modern societies. *Adolescence,* 1970, **5,** 109–128.

70 Newton, M., & Issekutz-Wolsku, M. The effect of parental age on the rate of female maturation. *Gerontologia,* 1969, **15,** 328–331.

71 Owen, G. M., & Brŏzek, J. Influence of age, sex, and nutrition on body composition during childhood and adolescence. In F. Falkner (Ed.), *Human development.* Philadelphia: Saunders, 1966. Pp. 222–238.

72 Parker, E. *The seven ages of woman.* Baltimore: Johns Hopkins Press, 1960.

73 Peckos, P. S., & Heald, F. F. Nutrition of adolescents. *Children,* 1964, **11,** 27–30.

74 Poppleton, P. K. The secular trend in puberty: Has stability been achieved? *Brit. J. educ. Psychol.,* 1966, **36,** 95–100.

75 Poppleton, P. K. Puberty, family size and the educational progress of girls. *Brit. J. educ. Psychol.,* 1968, **38,** 286–292.

76 Prader, A., Tanner, J. M., & vonHarnack, G. E. Catch-up growth following illness or starvation. *J. Pediat.,* 1963, **62,** 646–659.

77 Rakoff, A. E. Menstrual disorders of the adolescent. *Ann. N.Y. Acad. Sci.,* 1967, **142,** 801–806.

78 Roche, A. F., French, N. Y., & Davila, G. H. Areola size during pubescence. *Hum. Biol.,* 1971, **43,** 210–223.

79 Schachter, S. Obesity and eating. *Science,* 1968, **161,** 751–756.

80 Schauffler, G. C. Dysmenorrhea in and near puberty. *Ann. N.Y. Acad. Sci.,* 1967, **142,** 794–800.

81 Scheinfeld, A. *Heredity in humans.* (Rev. ed.) Philadelphia: Saunders, 1971.

82 Schonfeld, W. A. Body-image disturbances in adolescents. *Arch. gen. Psychiat.,* 1966, **15,** 16–21.

83 Shipman, G. The psychodynamics of sex education. *Family Coordinator,* 1968, **17,** 3–12.

84 Shipman, W. G. Age of menarche and adult personality. *Arch. gen. Psychiat.,* 1964, **10,** 155–159.

85 Sigurjonsdotter, T. J., & Hayles, A. B. Precocious puberty. *Amer. J. Dis. Children,* 1968, **115,** 309–321.

86 Smith, S. L., & Sander, C. Food craving, depression and premenstrual problems. *Psychosom. Med.,* 1969, **31,** 281–287.

87 Stephens, W. N. A cross-cultural study of menstrual taboos. *Genet. Psychol. Monogr.,* 1961, **64,** 385–416.

88 Stokes, W. R. Intelligent preparation of children for adolescence. *J. Marriage & Family,* 1965, **27,** 163–165.

89 Sullivan, W. Boys and girls are now maturing earlier. *The New York Times,* Jan. 24, 1971.

90 Talwar, P. P. Adolescent sterility in an Indian population. *Hum. Biol.,* 1965, **37,** 256–261.

91 Tanner, J. M. *Growth at adolescence.* (2nd ed.) Oxford: Blackwell, 1962.

92 Tanner, J. M. Physical growth. In P. H. Mussen (Ed.), *Carmichael's manual of child psychology.* (3rd ed.) Vol. 1. New York: Wiley, 1970. Pp. 77–155.

93 Tanner, J. M. Sequence, tempo and individual variation in the growth and development of boys and girls aged twelve to sixteen. *Daedalus,* 1971, **100,** 907–930.

94 Tanner, J. M. Growing up. *Scient. American,* 1973, **229**(3), 35–43.

95 Tejmar, J. Achievement, body weight and blood pressure in preadolescent girls. *Adolescence,* 1970, **5,** 345–352.

96 Tonks, C. M., Rack, P. H., & Rose, M. J. Attempted suicide and the menstrual cycle. *J. psychosom. Res.,* 1968, **11,** 319–323.

97 Valadian, I., Stuart, H. C., & Reed, R. B. Studies of illness of children followed from birth to eighteen years. *Monogr. Soc. Res. Child Develpm.,* 1961, **26**(3).

98 Valsık, J. A. The seasonal rhythm of the menarche: A review. *Hum. Biol.,* 1965, **37,** 75–90.

99 Vamberova, M. P., & Tefralova, J. The effect of puberty on the development of obesity. *Child Develpm. Abstr.,* 1963, **38,** No. 36.

100 Verinis, J. S., & Roll, S. Primary and secondary male characteristics: The hairiness and large penis stereotypes. *Psychol. Rep.,* 1970, **26,** 123–126.

101 Vincent, E. L., & Martin, P. C. *Human psychological development.* New York: Ronald Press, 1961.

102 Weatherley, D. Self-perceived rate of physical maturation and personality in late adolescence. *Child Develpm.,* 1964, **35,** 1197–1210.

103 Weiland, R. G., Cohen, J. C., Zorn, E. M., & Hallberg, M. C. Correlation of growth, pubertal staging, growth hormone, gonadotropins, and testosterone levels during the pubertal growth spurt in males. *J. Pediat.,* 1971, **79,** 999.

104 Wiggins, J. S., Wiggins, N., & Conger, J. C. Correlates of heterosexual somatic preference. *J. Pers. soc. Psychol.,* 1968, **10,** 82–90.

105 Wolanski, N., & Pyzuk, M. A new graphic method for the evaluation of sexual maturity in girls. *Develpm. Med. child Neurol.,* 1971, **13,** 590–596.

106 Young, H. B., Zoli, A., & Gallagher, J. R. Events of puberty in 111 Florentine girls. *Amer. J. Dis. Children,* 1963, **106,** 568–577.

CHAPTER EIGHT

ADOLESCENCE

The term *adolescence* comes from the Latin word *adolescere*, meaning "to grow" or "to grow to maturity." Primitive peoples—as was true also in earlier civilizations—do not consider puberty and adolescence to be distinct periods in the life span; the child is regarded as an adult when he is capable of reproduction. As it is used today, the term *adolescence* has a broader meaning and includes mental, emotional, and social as well as physical maturity. Legally, in the United States, the individual is mature at age eighteen.

Until recently, adolescence was regarded as beginning when the individual becomes sexually mature and ending when he reaches legal maturity. However, studies of changes in behavior throughout adolescence have revealed not only that these changes are more rapid in the early than in the latter part of adolescence but also that behavior and attitudes in the early part of the period are markedly different from those in the latter part. As a result, it has become a widespread practice to divide adolescence into two periods, *early* and *late* adolescence.

The dividing line between early and late adolescence is somewhat arbitrarily placed at around seventeen years, the age when the average boy or girl enters the senior year of high school. He then is usually recognized by his parents as nearly grown up and on the verge of entering the adult world of work, going to college, or receiving vocational training of some kind. His status in school likewise makes him conscious of responsibilities he has never before been expected to assume, and his awareness of this new and formally recognized status, both at school and at home, motivates him to behave in a more mature manner.

Because boys mature, on the average, later than girls, they have a shorter period of early adolescence, although they are regarded as adults when they reach eighteen, just as girls are. As a result, they frequently seem more immature for their age than girls. However, as they are accorded, along with girls, a more mature status in the home and school, they usually settle down quickly and show a maturity of behavior which is in marked contrast to that of the younger adolescent.

Early adolescence extends roughly from thirteen to sixteen or seventeen years, and late adolescence covers the period from then until eighteen, the age of legal maturity. Late adolescence is thus a very short period.

Early adolescence is usually referred to as the "teens," sometimes even the "terrible teens." Although the older adolescent is a teen-ager until he reaches twenty, this label, which has become closely associated with the characteristic patterns of behavior of the young adolescent, is rarely applied to him. Instead, older adolescents are usually referred to as "young men" or "young women," indicating that society recognizes a maturity of behavior not found during the early years of adolescence.

CHARACTERISTICS OF ADOLESCENCE

Certain attitudes and behavior patterns are characteristic of adolescence; these are discussed below.

Adolescence Is a Transitional Period

The adolescent, whose body is now more like that of an adult than that of a child, must adjust to a more mature status and to more mature levels of behavior. As Sorenson has pointed out, adolescence is an "intermission between earlier freedoms . . . and subsequent responsibilities and commitments . . . a last hesitation before . . . serious commitments concerning work and love" (118).

During any transitional period, the individual's status is vague, and he is confused about the roles he is expected to play. The adolescent is neither a child nor an adult. If he behaves like a child, he is told to "act his age," and yet he may also be reproved when he attempts to behave like an adult. This ambiguous status presents a dilemma for the teen-ager that contributes greatly to the adolescent "identity crisis," or the problem of ego-identity. As Erikson has explained (38):

The identity the adolescent seeks to clarify is who he is, what his role in society is to be. Is he a child or is he an adult? Does he have it in him to be someday a husband and father? . . . Can he feel self-confident in spite of the fact that his race or religious or national background makes him a person some people look down upon? Overall, will he be a success or a failure?

Erikson has further explained how this search for identity affects the adolescent's behavior (38):

In their search for a new sense of continuity and sameness, adolescents have to refight many of the battles of earlier years, even though to do so they must artificially appoint perfectly well-meaning people to play the roles of adversaries; and they are ever ready to install lasting idols and ideals as guardians of a final identity. The integration now taking place in the form of ego identity is more than the sum of childhood identifications.

Adolescence Is a Period of Change

The rate of change in attitudes and behavior during adolescence parallels the rate of physical change. During early adolescence, when physical changes are rapid, changes in attitudes and behavior are also rapid. As physical changes slow down, so do attitudinal and behavioral changes. Tanner has emphasized the impact of these changes (124):

For the majority of young persons, the years from twelve to sixteen are the most eventful ones of their lives so far as their growth and development is concerned. Admittedly during fetal life and the first year or two after birth developments occurred still faster, and a sympathetic environment was probably even more crucial, but the subject himself was not the fascinated, or horrified, spectator that watches the developments, or lack of developments, of adolescence.

There are four almost universal concomitants of the changes that occur during adolescence. The first is heightened emotionality, the intensity of which depends on the rate at which the physical and psychological changes are taking place.

Second, the rapid changes which accompany sexual maturing make the young adolescent unsure of himself, of his capacities, and of his interests. He has strong feelings of instability, which may be intensified by the ambiguous treatment he receives from both parents and teachers. As Luchins has pointed out, the young adolescent must "learn to dance in harmony with many different tunes while still attempting to maintain some degree of harmony with himself" (79).

Third, changes in the adolescent's body, his interests, and the role the social group now expects him to play create new problems for him. To the young adolescent, these may seem more numerous and less easily solved than any he has had to face before. Until he has solved his problems to his satisfaction, he will be preoccupied with them and with himself. Furthermore, he will suffer from feelings of inadequacy and inferiority, which in many cases he will try to hide by a cocky, self-assured attitude.

Fourth, as the adolescent's interests and behavior patterns change, so do his values. What was important to him as a child seems less important to him now that he is a near-adult. For example, the boy no longer thinks that a careless and slovenly appearance or crude and raucous speech is sex-appropriate. Instead, he accepts the more mature value of a neat appearance and more adult, restrained ways of expressing himself.

Adolescence Is a Dreaded Age

Acceptance of the cultural stereotype of the teen-ager as a sloppy, unreliable, irresponsible individual who is inclined toward destructiveness and antisocial behavior leads adults who must guide and supervise the lives of young adolescents to dread this responsibility and to be unsympathetic in their attitudes toward, and treatment of, normal adolescent behavior (4). The belief on the adolescent's part that adults have a poor opinion of him makes the transition to adulthood difficult for him, leads to much friction with his parents, and places a barrier between him and his parents which prevents him from turning to them for help in solving his problems.

Adolescence Is a Time of Unrealism

The unrealistically high aspirations the young adolescent has for himself, for his family, and for his friends are in part responsible for some of the heightened emotionality of early adolescence. The more unrealistic his aspiration, the more angry, hurt, and disappointed he will be when he feels that others have let him down or that he has not lived up to the goals he set for himself.

With increased social and personal experiences and with increased ability to think rationally, the older adolescent sees himself, his family and friends, and life in general in a more realistic way. As a result, he is happier and suffers less from disillusionment or disappointment than he did when he was younger.

Adolescence Is the
Threshold of Adulthood

As the adolescent approaches legal maturity, he is anxious to create the impression that he is no longer a teen-ager, but rather is on the threshold of adulthood. Dressing and acting like an adult, he finds, are not always enough, and he may then concentrate on behavior that is associated with adult status—smoking, drinking, and engaging in sex, for example.

DEVELOPMENTAL TASKS
OF ADOLESCENCE

All the developmental tasks of adolescence are focused on overcoming childish attitudes and behavior patterns and preparing for adulthood. See page 13 for a list of these tasks.

The developmental tasks of adolescence require a major change in the child's habitual attitudes and patterns of behavior. Consequently, few boys and girls can be expected to master them during the years of early adolescence. This is especially true of late maturers. The most that can be hoped is that the young adolescent will lay foundations on which to build adult attitudes and behavior patterns.

To the adolescent, smoking is a symbol of maturity. (Suzanne Szasz)

A brief survey of the important developmental tasks of adolescence will serve to illustrate the extent of the changes that must be made.

It may be difficult for the adolescent to accept his physique if, from earliest childhood, he has had a glamorized concept of what he wanted to look like when he grew up. It takes time to revise this concept and to learn ways to improve his appearance so that it will be more in harmony with his earlier ideals.

Acceptance of the adult-approved sex role is not too difficult for boys; they have been encouraged in this direction since early childhood. But for girls, who as children were permitted or even encouraged to play an egalitarian role, learning what the adult-approved feminine role is and accepting it is often a major task requiring many years of adjustment.

Because of the antagonism toward members of the opposite sex that often develops during late childhood and puberty, learning new relationships with members of the opposite sex actually means starting from scratch to discover what they are like and how to get along with them. Even developing new, more mature relationships with age-mates of the same sex may not be easy.

Achieving emotional independence from parents and other adults would seem, for the independence-conscious adolescent, to be an easy developmental task. However, emotional independence is not the same as independence of behavior. Many adolescents who want to be independent want and need the security that emotional dependence on their parents or some other adults gives. This is especially true for adolescents whose status in the peer group is insecure or who lack a close tie with a member of the peer group.

Economic independence cannot be achieved until the individual chooses an occupation and prepares for it. If he selects an occupation that requires a long period of training, there can be no assurance of economic independence until he reaches adulthood. Even then, he may have to remain economically dependent for several years until his training has been completed.

Schools and colleges put emphasis on developing intellectual skills and concepts necessary for civic competence. However, few adolescents are able to use these skills and concepts in practical situations. Those who are active in the extracurricular affairs of their schools and colleges get such practice, but those who are not active in this way—because they must take after-school jobs or because they are not accepted by their peers—are deprived of this opportunity.

Schools and colleges also try to build values that are in harmony with those held by adults; parents contribute to this development. When, however, the adult-fostered values clash with peer values, the adolescent must choose the latter if he wants the peer acceptance on which his social life depends.

Closely related to the problem of developing values in harmony with those of the adult world the adolescent is about to enter is the task of developing socially responsible behavior. Most adolescents want to be accepted by their peers, but they often gain this acceptance at the expense of behavior that adults consider socially responsible. If, for example, it is the "thing to do" to cheat or to help a friend during an examination, the adolescent must choose between adult and peer standards of socially responsible behavior.

The trend toward earlier marriages has made preparation for marriage one of the most important developmental tasks of the adolescent years. While the gradual relaxing of social taboos on sexual behavior has gone a long way toward preparing adolescents of today for the sexual aspects of marriage, they receive little preparation—at home, in school, or in college—for the other aspects of marriage and even less preparation for the duties and responsibilities of family life. This lack of preparation is responsible for one of the major pieces of "unfinished business" which the adolescent carries into adulthood.

PHYSICAL CHANGES DURING ADOLESCENCE

Growth is far from complete when puberty ends, nor is it entirely complete at the end of early adolescence. However, there is a slackening of the pace of growth, and there is more marked internal than external development. This cannot be so readily observed or identified as growth in height and weight or the development of the secondary sex characteristics. Box 8-1 gives the important external and internal bodily changes that take place during adolescence and the ages at which these changes normally occur.

As is true at all ages, there are individual differences in these changes. Sex differences are especially apparent. Even though boys start their growth spurt later than girls, their growth continues longer, with the result that, at maturity, they are taller than girls. Because boys' muscles grow larger than girls' muscles, at all ages after puberty boys surpass girls in strength, and this superiority increases with age.

Individual differences are also influenced by age of maturing. Late maturers tend to have slightly broader shoulders than those who mature early. The legs of early-maturing boys and girls tend to be stocky; those of late maturers tend to be more slender. Figure 8-1 shows the effects of age of maturing on body proportions when growth is completed.

As physical changes slow down, the awkwardness of puberty and early adolescence generally disappears. The older adolescent gains control of his enlarged body and learns how to use it as successfully as he did when he was younger. He also is motivated to use his newly acquired strength, which further helps him overcome any awkwardness that appeared earlier.

Because strength follows growth in

Box 8-1. BODY CHANGES DURING ADOLESCENCE

External Changes

Height
The average girl reaches her mature height between the ages of seventeen and eighteen and the average boy, a year or so later.

Weight
Weight changes follow a timetable similar to that for height changes, with weight now distributed over areas of the body where previously there was little or no fat.

Body Proportions
The various parts of the body gradually come into proportion. For example, the trunk broadens and lengthens, and thus the limbs no longer seem too long.

Sex Organs
Both male and female sex organs reach their mature size in late adolescence, but are not mature in function until several years later.

Secondary Sex Characteristics
The major secondary sex characteristics are at a mature level of development by late adolescence.

Internal Changes

Digestive System
The stomach becomes longer and less tubular, the intestines grow in length and circumference, the muscles in the stomach and intestinal walls become thicker and stronger, the liver increases in weight, and the esophagus becomes longer.

Circulatory System
The heart grows rapidly during adolescence; by the age of seventeen or eighteen, it is twelve times as heavy as it was at birth. The length and thickness of the walls of the blood vessels increase and reach a mature level when the heart does.

Respiratory System
The lung capacity of girls is almost at a mature level at age seventeen; boys reach this level several years later.

Endocrine System
The increased activity of the gonads at puberty results in a temporary imbalance of the whole endocrine system in early adolescence. The sex glands develop rapidly and become functional, though they do not reach their mature size until late adolescence or early adulthood.

Body Tissues
The skeleton stops growing at an average age of eighteen. Tissues, other than bone, continue to develop after the bones have reached their mature size.

---

muscle size, boys generally show their greatest increase in strength after age fourteen, while girls show improvement up to this age and then lag, owing more to changes in interests than to lack of capacity. Girls generally attain their maximum strength at about seventeen, while boys do not attain their maximum strength until they are twenty-one or twenty-two.

"STORM AND STRESS"

Traditionally, adolescence has been thought of as a period of "storm and stress"—a time of heightened emotional tension resulting from the physical and glandular changes that are taking place. While it is true that growth continues through the early years of adolescence, it does so at a progressively slower rate. What growth is taking place is primarily a completion of the pattern already set at puberty. It is necessary, therefore, to look for other explanations of the emotional tension so characteristic of this age.

The explanations are to be found in the social conditions that surround the adolescent of today. Adolescent emotionality can be attributed mainly to the fact that the individual comes under social pressures and faces new conditions for which he received little if any preparation during childhood.

Not all adolescents, by any means, go

through a period of exaggerated storm and stress. True, most of them do experience emotional instability from time to time, which is a logical consequence of the necessity of making adjustments to new patterns of behavior and to new social expectations. For example, problems related to romance are very real at this time. While the romance is moving along smoothly, the adolescent is happy, but he becomes despondent when things begin to go wrong. With the end of his schooling in sight, the adolescent also begins to worry about his future.

While adolescent emotions are often intense, uncontrolled, and seemingly irrational, there is generally an improvement in emotional behavior with each passing year. Fourteen-year-olds, Gesell et al. have reported, are often irritable, are easily excited, and "explode" emotionally instead of trying to control their feelings. Sixteen-year-olds, by contrast, say they "don't believe in worrying." Thus the storm and stress of this period lessens as early adolescence draws to a close (45).

The emotional patterns of adolescence, while similar to those of childhood (see Box 5-3), differ in the stimuli that give rise to the emotions and, even more important, in the degree of control the individual exercises over the expression of his emotions. For example, being treated "like a child" or being treated "unfairly" is more likely to make the adolescent angry than anything else. Instead of having temper tantrums, however, the adolescent expresses his anger by being sulky, refusing to speak, or loudly criticizing those who anger him. The adolescent also becomes envious of those whose material possessions are superior to his. However, while he may complain and feel sorry for himself, as a child does, he is likely to take a part-time job, or even drop out of school to be able to work full time, to get the things he wants.

Emotional Maturity

The individual has achieved maturity in this area of his development if, by the end of adolescence, he does not "blow up" emo-

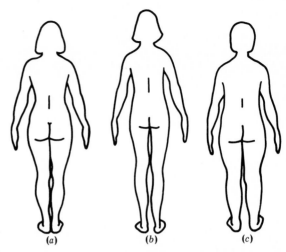

Figure 8-1 Three eighteen-year-old girls, who matured at different ages and at different rates. (*a*) Accelerated growth; (*b*) retarded growth; (*c*) irregular growth. (Adapted from N. Bayley. Individual patterns of development. *Child Develpm.*, 1956, **27**, 45–74. Used by permission.)

tionally when others are present, but waits for a convenient time and place to let off emotional steam in a socially acceptable manner. He assesses a situation critically before responding to it emotionally instead of reacting to it unthinkingly, as the child or immature person does. This results in his ignoring many stimuli that would have caused an emotional outburst when he was younger. Finally, the emotionally mature adolescent is stable in his emotional responses and does not swing from one reaction or mood to another, as he did earlier.

To achieve emotional maturity, the adolescent must learn to get a perspective on situations which otherwise would lead to emotional reactions. He can do this best by discussing his problems with others. His willingness to disclose his attitudes, feelings, and personal problems is influenced partly by how secure he feels in his social relationships, partly by how much he likes the "target person," and how much the target person is willing to disclose to him.

SOCIAL CHANGES
DURING ADOLESCENCE

One of the most difficult developmental tasks of adolescence relates to social adjustments. These adjustments must be made to members of the opposite sex in a relationship that never existed before and to adults outside the family and school environments.

To achieve the goal of adult patterns of socialization, the adolescent must make many new adjustments, the most important—and, in many respects, the most difficult—of which are those he must make to the increased influence of the peer group, changes in social behavior, new social groupings, new values in friendship selection, new values in social acceptance and rejection, and new values in the selection of leaders.

Increased Peer-Group Influence

The adolescent spends most of his time outside the home with members of the peer group, and they have a greater influence on his attitudes, interests, values, and behavior than his family has. If his friends experiment with alcohol or drugs, for example, he is likely to do the same. Horrocks and Benimoff have explained peer-group influence in this way (56):

The peer group is the adolescent's real world, providing him a stage upon which to try out himself and others. It is in the peer group that he continues to formulate and revise his concept of self; it is here that he is evaluated by others who are presumably his equals and who are unable to impose upon him the adult world sanctions from which he is typically struggling to free himself. The peer group offers the adolescent a world in which he may socialize in a climate where the values that count are those that are set, not by adults, but by others his own age. Thus, it is in the society of his peers that the adolescent finds support for his efforts at emancipation and it is there that he can find a world that enables

him to assume leadership if his worth as a person is such that he can assert leadership. In addition, of course, the peer group is the major recreational outlet of the teenager. For all these reasons it would seem of vital importance to the adolescent that his peer group contain a certain number of friends who can accept him and upon whom he can depend.

Changes in Social Behavior

Of all the changes that take place in social attitudes and behavior, the most pronounced is in the area of heterosexual relationships. In a short period of time, the adolescent makes the radical shift from disliking members of the opposite sex to preferring their companionship to that of members of his own sex. Social activities, whether with members of the same sex or with the opposite sex, usually reach their peak during the high school years.

As a result of broader opportunities for social participation, the older adolescent's *social insight* improves. He is now able to judge both members of the opposite sex and members of his own sex better than he could when he was younger. As a result, he makes better adjustments in social situations and quarrels less than he did earlier.

The greater the social participation, the greater the adolescent's *social competency*, as seen in his ability to dance, carry on conversations, play the sports and games that are popular with individuals of his age, and behave correctly in different social situations. As a result, he gains a self-confidence which is expressed in poise and ease in social situations.

New Social Groupings

The gangs of childhood gradually break up at puberty and during early adolescence as the individual's interests shift from the strenuous play activities of childhood to the less strenuous and more formal social activities of adolescence. In their place come new social groupings. The social groupings of

"The peer group is the adolescent's real world." (Bob S. Smith from Rapho Guillumette)

boys are, as a rule, larger and more loosely knit, whereas those of girls are smaller and more sharply defined.

The most common social groupings during adolescence are described in Box 8-2. Crowds tend to disintegrate in late adolescence and are replaced by loosely associated groups of couples. This is especially true of adolescents who go to work at the completion of high school. At work they are in contact with people of all ages, most of whom have friends and families of their own outside their jobs. Unless the noncollege older adolescent has friends from his school days who live and work near enough to make frequent contacts possible, he may find himself limited to a few friends connected with his work and out of touch with any group large enough to form a crowd.

New Values in Selection of Friends

The adolescent no longer selects his friends on the basis of their ready availability at school or in his neighborhood, as he did during childhood, nor is enjoyment of the same activities still such an important factor in friendship selection. The adolescent wants as friends those whose interests and values are similar to his, who understand him and make him feel secure, and in whom he can confide. See Figure 8-2. As Joseph has explained, most adolescents claim that they want as a friend "someone to be trusted, someone to talk to, someone who is dependable" (63). Because of these changed values, the adolescent's childhood friends will not necessarily be his friends in adolescence.

Nor is the adolescent interested only in friends of his own sex. Interest in friends of the opposite sex becomes increasingly stronger, and by the end of adolescence there is often a preference for friends of the opposite sex, though both boys and girls continue to have a few intimate friends of their own sex with whom they associate constantly.

To the young adolescent, popularity means having a large number of friends. As he grows older, the kind of friends he has

Box 8-2. ADOLESCENT SOCIAL GROUPINGS

Close Friends

The adolescent usually has two or three close friends, or confidants. They are of the same sex as he and have similar interests and abilities. Close friends have a marked influence on one another, though they may quarrel occasionally.

Cliques

Cliques are usually made up of groups of close friends. At first they consist of members of the same sex, but later include both boys and girls.

Crowds

Crowds, made up of cliques and groups of close friends, develop as interest in parties and dating grows. Because crowds are large, there is less congeniality of interest among the members and thus a greater social distance between them.

Organized Groups

Adult-directed youth groups are established by schools and community organizations to meet the social needs of adolescents who belong to no cliques or crowds. Many adolescents who join such groups feel regimented and lose interest in them by the time they are sixteen or seventeen.

Gangs

Adolescents who belong to no cliques or crowds and who gain little satisfaction from organized groups may join a gang. Gang members are usually of the same sex, and their main interest is to compensate for peer rejection through anti-social behavior.

---

becomes more important than the number. His values regarding the "right" kind of friends are likely to change from one year to another, depending on the values of the group with which he is identified.

Because he knows what he wants in his friends, the adolescent insists upon the right to select them without adult interference. This often leads to two consequences that interfere with the stability of his friendships. First, as a result of his inexperience (especially with members of the opposite sex), he may choose friends who turn out to be less congenial than he thought at first. Quarreling may ensue, and the friendships are broken.

Second, as in other areas of his life, the adolescent tends to be unrealistic concerning the standards he sets up for his friends. He may then become critical of them and try to reform them, which also leads to quarreling and the breaking off of friendships. In time, the adolescent tends to become more realistic about others and as a result is less critical and more acceptant of his friends.

New Values in Social Acceptance

Just as the adolescent has new values concerning friends, so he has new values concerning acceptable or unacceptable mem-

Figure 8-2 Self-disclosure to friends becomes an important value used in the selection of friends during adolescence. (Adapted from W. H. Rivenbark. Self-disclosure patterns among adolescents. *Psychol. Rep.,* 1971, **28,** 35–42. Used by permission.)

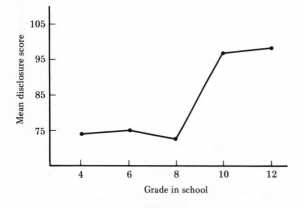

bers of one of the adolescent peer groups. These are based largely on peer-group values, and he discovers that he is judged by the same standards by which he judges others.

No one trait or characteristic pattern of behavior will guarantee acceptance during adolescence. Instead, acceptance depends upon a constellation of traits and behavior patterns—the *acceptance syndrome*—all of which make the individual fun to be with and add to the prestige of the clique or crowd with which he is identified. Similarly, no one trait or behavior pattern alienates the adolescent from his peers. Instead, there is a grouping of traits—the *alienation syndrome*—that makes others dislike him and reject him. Some of the common elements of the acceptance and alienation syndromes in adolescence are given in Box 8-3.

New Values in Selection of Leaders

The adolescent feels that his leaders represent him in the eyes of society, and he therefore wants leaders of superior ability whom others, as well as the group, will admire and respect and who will in turn reflect favorably on him. Because there are so many different kinds of groups in adolescence—athletic, social, intellectual, religious, and class or community groups—the leader of one group will not necessarily have the ability to be the leader of another. Leadership is now a function of the situation, as it is in adult life.

In general, however, adolescents expect their leaders to have certain qualities. While a good physique, in and of itself, does not make an adolescent a leader, it gives him prestige and at the same time contributes favorably to his self-concept. Usually a

---

Box 8-3. CONDITIONS CONTRIBUTING TO ACCEPTANCE AND REJECTION IN ADOLESCENCE

Acceptance Syndrome

A favorable first impression as a result of an attractive appearance, poise, and cheerfulness, for example

A reputation as a good sport and one who is fun to be with

Appearance that conforms to that of peers

Social behavior characterized by cooperativeness, responsibility, resourcefulness, interest in others, tact, and good manners

Maturity, especially in terms of emotional control and willingness to conform to rules and regulations

Personality traits that contribute to good social adjustments, such as truthfulness, sincerity, unselfishness, and extroversion

A socioeconomic status that is equal to, or slightly above, that of the other group members and a good relationship with family members

Geographic proximity to the group which permits frequent contacts and participation in group activities

Alienation Syndrome

An unfavorable first impression as a result of an unattractive appearance or an aloof, self-centered attitude

A reputation as a poor sport

Appearance that does not conform to group standards of physical attractiveness or grooming

Social behavior characterized by showing off, teasing and bullying others, bossiness, uncooperativeness, and lack of tact

Lack of maturity, especially in the areas of emotional control, poise, self-confidence, and tact

Personality traits that irritate others, such as selfishness, stubbornness, resentfulness, nervousness and irritability

A socioeconomic status below that of the group and poor relationships with family members

Geographic isolation from the peer group or inability to participate in group activities due to family responsibilities or a part-time job

leader is in excellent health and thus is energetic and eager to do things, both of which contribute to the quality of initiative.

The clothes-conscious adolescent expects his leaders to be attractive and well groomed. The characteristic leader of young adolescents will also be slightly above average in intelligence, academic achievement, and level of maturity.

As a rule, leaders in adolescent social activities come from families of higher socioeconomic status than nonleaders. This not only gives them prestige in the eyes of their peers but also makes possible better dressing and grooming, the possession of social know-how, opportunities for entertaining, and participation in group activities.

Because a leader is characteristically a more active participant in social life than a nonleader, he develops *social insight* and *self-insight*. He can judge himself realistically and can size up the interests and wishes of the group he leads. The leader is not "self-bound" in the sense that he is concerned with his personal interests and problems; instead, he directs his energies outward and concerns himself with the interests and problems of the group.

Perhaps the most important single factor that contributes to leadership is personality. Leaders have been found to be more responsible, more extroverted, more energetic, more resourceful, and more able to take initiative than nonleaders. They are emotionally stable, well-adjusted, happy individuals with few neurotic tendencies (82, 90).

SOME ADOLESCENT INTERESTS

The adolescent's interests will depend upon his sex, his intelligence, the environment in which he lives, the opportunities he has had for developing interests, the prestige value of different interests, what his peers are interested in, his status in the social group, his innate abilities, the interests of his family, and many other factors.

Since girls are expected to behave in a feminine way and boys in a masculine way, it is not surprising that girls' interests during adolescence are very different from boys'.

As adolescence progresses, many of the interests that were carried over from the childhood years wane and are replaced by interests of a mature sort. Because of the greater responsibilities of the older adolescent and the consequent decrease in time to spend as he may wish, he is forced to limit the range of his interests. This is especially true of recreational interests.

Furthermore, with experience he acquires a different sense of values. This is reflected in a shift of emphasis on different interests. Interests that were of major importance to him in early adolescence, such as his clothes and appearance, become less important as he grows older, while interest in a career, which in early adolescence was secondary to interests related to his life at the moment, now becomes one of the dominant interests of his life. Experience also helps the older adolescent to evaluate his interests more critically and to know which are important to him. As a result of this critical evaluation, he stabilizes his interests.

Certain adolescent interests are fairly universal in the American culture of today, though they may vary from one part of the country to another and with the different social classes within each area of the country. All young adolescents possess these interests to a greater or lesser extent, and they all have certain specific interests that fall within the different categories of interests, the most important of which are recreational interests, social interests, personal interests, vocational interests, interest in school, and religious interests.

Recreational Interests

As adolescence progresses, there is a breaking away from recreations that require much expenditure of energy and the development of a preference for recreations in which the adolescent is a passive spectator.

In early adolescence, there is a carryover of some of the play activities of the early years and the introduction of new and more mature forms of recreation. Gradually, the childish forms of play disappear, and when early adolescence comes to a close, the individual's recreational pattern is much the same as it will be during the latter part of adolescence and the early years of adulthood.

Because of the pressures of schoolwork, home duties, extracurricular activities, and after-school or weekend jobs, most adoles-

cents have far less time for recreation than they did when they were younger. As a result, they select the kinds of activities that they enjoy most or in which they excel. This limits the number of their activities.

The number of recreations the adolescent engages in is also greatly influenced by how popular he is. Because many of the recreations of adolescents require participants from the peer group, the adolescent who does not belong to a clique and who has few friends is forced to concentrate on solitary forms of recreation. Box 8-4 describes the

---

Box 8-4. RECREATIONAL INTERESTS OF ADOLESCENTS

Games and Sports
Organized games and sports lose their appeal as adolescence progresses, and the adolescent begins to prefer spectator sports. Games requiring intellectual skill, such as card games, increase in popularity.

Relaxing
Adolescents enjoy relaxing and talking with their friends. They often eat while gossiping and exchanging jokes, and older adolescents may smoke, drink, or take drugs.

Traveling
The adolescent enjoys traveling during vacations and may want to go further and further away from home. Parental affluence and youth hostels make travel possible for many adolescents.

Hobbies
Unpopular adolescents are more interested in hobbies than popular ones. Many pursue useful hobbies; girls may make their own clothes, and boys may enjoy repairing radios, bicycles, or cars, for example.

Dancing
Although many boys have little interest in dancing, they, like girls, try to become good dancers because it is an important part of dating.

Reading
Because adolescents have limited time for recreational reading, they tend to prefer magazines to books. As adolescence progresses, comic books and comic strips lose some of their appeal, and newspapers gain in popularity.

Movies
Going to the movies is a favorite clique activity and later a popular dating activity. Girls prefer romantic movies, while boys like those dealing with adventure.

Radio and Records
Adolescents enjoy listening to the radio while studying or engaging in solitary forms of amusement. Programs of popular music are the favorites. They also enjoy listening to records.

Television
Television watching loses some of its appeal as adolescence progresses, partly because the adolescent becomes increasingly critical of the programs and partly because he cannot study or read and watch television simultaneously.

Daydreaming
In a typical daydream, the adolescent sees himself as a conquering hero gaining prestige in the eyes of the peer group. Daydreaming is a popular recreation among *all* adolescents when they are bored or lonely.

favorite recreations of adolescents. Compare these with the play activities of early and late childhood.

Social Interests

The adolescent's social interests will depend partly on what opportunities he has to develop them and partly on how popular he is with members of the peer group. An adolescent whose family's socioeconomic status is low, for example, will have fewer opportunities to develop an interest in parties and dancing than adolescents from more favorable home backgrounds. Similarly, an adolescent who is unpopular will have a limited repertoire of social interests. However, certain social interests are almost universal among American adolescents of today, seven of which are described in Box 8-5.

Personal Interests

Interest in themselves is the strongest interest young adolescents have, partly because they realize that their social acceptance is markedly influenced by their general appearance and partly because they know the social group judges them in terms of their material possessions, independence, and school and social affiliations, as well as the amount of spending money they have. These are "status symbols" that will enhance the young adolescent's prestige in the eyes of his peers and hence increase his chances for greater social acceptance.

Interest in *appearance* covers not only clothes but also personal adornment, grooming, and attractive physical features. Cross and Cross have explained why the adolescent's appearance is so important to him:

Box 8-5. COMMON SOCIAL INTERESTS OF ADOLESCENTS

Parties
Interest in parties with members of the opposite sex first manifests itself at about age thirteen or fourteen. Girls enjoy parties more than boys throughout adolescence.

Drinking
Drinking on dates or at parties becomes increasingly more popular as adolescence progresses. Girls rarely drink with members of their own sex, as boys do.

Drugs
While far from universal, the use of drugs is a popular clique and party activity, beginning in early adolescence. Many adolescents try drugs because it is the "thing to do," although few become addicts.

Conversations
All adolescents derive a sense of security from getting together with a group of peers and talking about the things that interest or disturb them. Such get-togethers provide an opportunity to blow off emotional steam and get a new perspective on their problems.

Helping Others
The young adolescent is sincerely interested in trying to help people he feels have been misunderstood, mistreated, or oppressed. This interest wanes as adolescence progresses and the adolescent feels there is nothing he can do to right the wrongs he sees or that his attempts to help are unappreciated.

World Affairs
The adolescent often develops an interest in government, politics, and world affairs. He expresses this interest mainly through reading and discussions with his peers, teachers, and parents.

Criticism and Reform
Almost all young adolescents, but especially girls, become critical and attempt to reform their parents, peers, schools, and communities. Their criticisms are generally destructive rather than constructive, and their suggestions for reform are usually impractical.

"Beauty and physical attractiveness are of great practical importance for human beings. Social acceptance, popularity, mate selection, and careers are all affected by an individual's physical attractiveness" (28).

Because the adolescent's happiness and self-confidence depend largely upon his contemporaries' attitudes toward his *clothes*, he is anxious to conform to what the group approves of in the matter of dress. As Ryan has pointed out, "One of the primary requirements of clothing for the young adolescent is that their clothing meets the approval of the peer group" (108).

While boys claim not to be interested in clothes, grooming, or appearance, their behavior indicates that their interest is greater than they will admit. Like girls, they recognize that appearance plays an important role in social acceptance. This interest is heightened when they reach the end of their schooling and prepare to enter the world of work. They realize that an attractive appearance facilitates their getting and holding a job.

A strong desire for *independence* develops in early adolescence and reaches a peak as this period draws to a close. This leads to many clashes with parents and other adults in authority. Because girls are expected to conform more to parental wishes than boys are, they rebel more than boys against home restraints. Much of the radicalism of young adolescents can be traced to their attempts to think and act independently. If, however, adult authority is relaxed gradually so that the adolescent can see himself reaching his goal, there is far less friction between him and his parents or others in authority than when he sees no improvement in his status.

Money, every adolescent sooner or later discovers, is the key to independence. As long as parents pay the adolescent's bills and give him spending money, they can control his behavior. When, on the other hand, he has money he has earned, he can enjoy independence. Interest in money therefore becomes an important element in interest in independence. This interest centers mainly on how to earn the most money possible, regardless of the kind of work done.

Educational Interests

Typically, the young adolescent complains about school in general and about restrictions, homework, required courses, the food served in the school cafeteria, and the way the school is run. He is critical of his teachers and the way they teach. This is the "thing to do." The young adolescent who wants to be popular with his peers must avoid creating the impression that he is a "brain." This is even more true of girls than of boys because less prestige is associated with girls' scholastic achievements. However, in spite of their stated attitudes, most adolescents get along well both academically and socially and actually like school.

The older adolescent's attitude toward education and his interest in college or preparing for a profession are greatly influenced by his vocational interests. If he is aspiring to an occupation which requires education beyond high school, he will regard education as a stepping-stone. He will be interested in courses which he feels will be

The older adolescent often regards education as a stepping-stone. (Lynn McLaren from Rapho Guillumette)

useful to him in his chosen field of work. As is true of the younger adolescent, the older adolescent considers success in sports and social life as important as academic work as a stepping-stone to future success. Many factors influence the younger and older adolescent's attitude toward education; the most important of these are given in Box 8-6.

Vocational Interests

Boys and girls of high school age begin to think seriously about their futures. Boys are usually more seriously concerned about an occupation than girls, many of whom regard a job as just a stopgap until marriage.

Boys typically want glamorous and exciting jobs, regardless of the ability required or the chances that such jobs will be available for them. They also want jobs

Box 8-6. FACTORS INFLUENCING ADOLESCENT ATTITUDES TOWARD EDUCATION

Peer attitudes—whether they are college-oriented or work-oriented.

Parental attitudes—whether parents consider education a stepping-stone to upward social mobility or only a necessity because it is required by law.

Grades, which indicate academic success or failure.

The relevance or practical value of various courses. See Figure 8-3.

Attitudes toward teachers, administrators, and academic and disciplinary policies.

Success in extracurricular activities.

Degree of social acceptance among classmates.

with high prestige, even if they pay less than those with lower prestige. Many boys from low-status families hope to achieve higher social status through their occupations. Girls, as a rule, show a preference for occupations with greater security and less demand on their time. In their vocational choices, they usually stress service to others, such as teaching or nursing.

By late adolescence, interest in a life career has often become a source of great concern. The adolescent is concerned about what he would like to do or what he is capable of doing. The more he hears or talks about different lines of work, the less sure he is of what he would like to do, and he is also concerned about how he can get the kind of job he wants. The older adolescent has a growing realization of how much it costs to live, and he also knows what a young person can expect to earn; thus he approaches the choice of his career with a more practical and realistic attitude than he had when he was younger.

During childhood and early adolescence, for example, he judged different lines of work, such as law or medicine, in terms of stereotypes presented in the mass media; as a near-adult, he judges them in terms of his abilities and of the time and money required

Figure 8-3 For many adolescents, interest in school subjects is influenced by how relevant they perceive the subjects to be. (George Clark. "The Neighbors," Chicago Tribune–New York News Syndicate, Dec. 6, 1965. Used by permission.)

"I can guess YOUR question, Bivins. How can the study of ancient conquests help you make a buck?"

for training. While prestige is still an important factor in vocational selection, the older adolescent is more concerned about the autonomy, authority, and security the occupation will give him.

Because their attitudes toward vocations have gradually become more realistic, most adolescents change their minds often about their future occupations. They are in an "exploratory stage" and may take after-school or summer jobs in fields they think might interest them as a lifetime career. This experience gives them more information on which to base their final decisions.

Religious Interests

Contrary to popular opinion, adolescents of today are interested in religion and feel that it plays an important role in their lives.

They talk about religion, take courses in it in college, visit churches of different denominations, and join various religious cults.

On the other hand, adolescents now attend church, Sunday school, and church social events far less than adolescents of previous generations, suggesting that many of them are disillusioned with organized religion, but not uninterested in religion per se. As Jones has explained, "There is more a decrease in enthusiasm and in positive feelings *for* the church than an increase in antagonism *against* it." He says further that the change in interest in religion in adolescence reflects not a lack of belief but "a disillusionment with the church establishment and the use of its beliefs and preachments in the solution of current social, civic and economic problems" (62).

The changes in religious interest during adolescence are even more radical than the changes in vocational interests. Like childhood vocational interests, childhood concepts of religion are basically unrealistic, and the adolescent may become critical of his earlier beliefs. The pattern of changes in religious interest and their effect on behavior are given in Box 8-7.

CHANGES IN MORALITY

One of the important developmental tasks the adolescent must master is learning what the group expects of him and then being willing to mold his behavior to conform to these expectations without the constant guidance, supervision, proddings, and threats of punishment he experienced when he was a child. He is expected to replace the specific moral concepts of childhood with general moral principles and to formulate these into a moral code which will act as a guide to his behavior. Equally important, he must now exercise control over his behavior, a responsibility that was formerly assumed by parents and teachers.

Adolescents have reached what Piaget has called the *stage of formal operations* in cognitive ability. They are now capable of

---

Box 8-7. PATTERN OF CHANGES IN RELIGIOUS INTERESTS

Period of Religious Awakening
When the adolescent prepares to join his family's church, his interest in religion is heightened, and he may either become extremely enthusiastic about it or grow skeptical of his religious beliefs when he compares them with those of his friends.

Period of Religious Doubt
As a result of a critical examination of their childhood religious beliefs, adolescents often become skeptical of religious forms, such as prayer and formal church rituals, and later begin to doubt religious content, such as teachings about the nature of God, and life after death. For some adolescents, doubt leads to a lessening of all religious observances, while others attempt to find a religious faith that meets their needs better than that of their family.

Period of Religious Reconstruction
This period is characterized by a decreased interest in formal religion because it does not meet the adolescent's needs; changed beliefs, especially those concerning the appearance of God and life after death; and a decrease in prejudice against those of different faiths.

considering all possible ways of solving a particular problem and can reason on the basis of hypotheses or propositions. Thus they can look at their problems from several points of view and can take many factors into account when solving them (99).

Even with the best foundations, the three major tasks in achieving adult morality — replacing specific concepts with general moral concepts, formulating these newly developed concepts into a moral code as a guideline for behavior, and assuming control over one's own behavior — are difficult for many adolescents. Some fail to make the shift to adult morality during adolescence and must finish this task in early adulthood. Others not only fail to make the shift but also build a moral code on socially unacceptable moral concepts.

Changes in Moral Concepts

Two conditions make the replacement of specific moral concepts with generalized concepts of right and wrong more difficult than it should be. The first is lack of guidance in learning how to generalize specific concepts. Believing that the adolescent has already learned the major principles of right and wrong, parents and teachers frequently put little emphasis on teaching him to see the relationship between the specific principles he learned earlier and the general principles that are essential to control over behavior in adult life. Only in new areas of behavior, such as relationships with members of the opposite sex, do adults feel that there is any real need for further moral training.

The second condition that makes the replacement of specific moral concepts with generalized ones difficult has to do with the kind of discipline the adolescent is subjected to at home and in school. Because parents and teachers assume that he knows what is right, their major emphasis in discipline is on punishment for what they regard as intentional misbehavior. Little emphasis is placed on explaining to the adolescent why certain things are right and others wrong, and even less is placed on rewarding him for doing the right thing.

Building a Moral Code

The adolescent will no longer unquestioningly accept a moral code handed down to him by his parents, his teachers, or even his contemporaries, as he did when he was a child. He now wants to build his own moral code on the basis of concepts of right and wrong which he has changed and modified to meet his more mature level of development and which he has supplemented with laws and rules learned from parents and teachers. Some adolescents even supplement their moral codes with knowledge derived from their religious training.

Building a moral code is difficult for the adolescent because of the inconsistencies in standards of right and wrong he encounters in his daily life. These confuse him and impede his progress in building a moral code that is satisfactory to him and will lead to socially approved behavior. He discovers, for example, that peers of different socioeconomic, racial, or religious backgrounds have different codes of right and wrong; that his parents' and teachers' codes are stricter than those of his contemporaries; and that in spite of the breaking down of the traditional sex-approved roles, there is still a "double standard" (138).

While older children, for example, may condemn lying on moral grounds, many adolescents feel that "social lies," or lies told to avoid hurting other people's feelings, are sometimes justified. Much the same sort of confusion is apparent in high school and college students' attitudes toward cheating. Many feel that since it is so widespread, their contemporaries must condone it, and they also claim that it is justified when they are pressured to get good grades in order to be accepted by a college and thus succeed socially and economically in later life. As the adolescent's interest in members of the opposite sex increases, he discovers that certain patterns of behavior are not only approved but even applauded for boys, while they are harshly condemned for girls.

Inner Control of Behavior

Because parents and teachers cannot watch the adolescent as closely as they used to, he must now assume responsibility for control over his own behavior. While it was formerly believed that fear—either of punishment or of social disapproval—was the best deterrent to wrongdoing, today it is recognized that "outer-controlled" sources of motivation are effective only when there is a possibility that others will find out about the individual's misbehavior and punish him for it. Studies of juvenile delinquents have revealed not only that punishment is not a deterrent to willful wrongdoing but also that it is often a contributing factor to it. There is also evidence that fear of being shamed loses its effectiveness as a deterrent to misbehavior when there is little likelihood that others will know of the misbehavior or if the individual feels he will be able to rationalize his action or project the blame on others and thus avoid punishment or social disapproval (1, 134).

The only effective way in which an individual can control his behavior is through the development of a conscience—an inner force that makes external controls unnecessary. When he learns to associate pleasant emotions with group-approved behavior and unpleasant emotions with group-disapproved behavior, he will have the necessary motivation to behave in accordance with group standards. The individual feels guilty when he realizes that his behavior is falling below social expectations, while shame is aroused only when he is aware of others' unfavorable judgments of his behavior. Behavior controlled by guilt is thus inner-controlled, while that controlled by shame is outer-controlled (9, 98). In the morally mature individual, both guilt and shame are present though guilt plays a more important role than shame does in controlling the individual's behavior in the absence of external controls.

SEX INTERESTS AND SEX BEHAVIOR

To master the important developmental tasks of forming new and more mature relationships with members of the opposite sex and of playing the approved role for one's sex, the young adolescent must acquire more complete and more mature concepts of sex than he had as a child. The motivation to do so comes partly from social pressures and partly from his interest in sex.

Because of his growing interest in sex, the adolescent seeks more and more information about it. Few adolescents feel that they can learn all they want to know about sex from their parents (see Figure 8-4), and they take advantage of whatever sources of information are available to them—sex hygiene courses in school or college, discussions with their friends, books on sex, or experimentation through masturbation, pet-

Figure 8-4 Few adolescents feel that the sex information from parents is adequate. (George Clark. "The Neighbors," Chicago Tribune–New York News Syndicate, Oct. 22, 1971. Used by permission.)

"Well, so much for the birds and the bees, Mom. Now how about teen-age boys?"

ting, necking, or intercourse. By the end of adolescence, most boys and girls have enough information about sex to satisfy their curiosity.

Development of Heterosexuality

Now that he is sexually mature, the adolescent takes a different kind of interest in members of the opposite sex. The new interest that develops during the early part of adolescence is romantic in nature and is accompanied by a strong desire to win the approval of members of the opposite sex.

Development of interest in members of the opposite sex—heterosexuality—follows a predictable pattern. However, there are variations in ages at which the adolescent reaches different stages in this development, partly because of differences in age of sexual maturing and partly because of differences in opportunities to develop this interest. Interest in members of the opposite sex is also markedly influenced by patterns of interest among the adolescent's friends. If they are interested in activities involving members of both sexes, he must be also if he

is to retain his status in the peer group. The stages of heterosexual development are given in Box 8-8.

New social attitudes toward sex, the ready availability of contraceptive devices, and the legalization of abortion in many states have resulted in a great increase in sexual experimentation among adolescents. They often kiss or pet on the first date, and intercourse is common among couples who are going steady. Furthermore, since adolescents begin to date and go steady earlier today than in the past, they engage in the different forms of sexual intimacy at a younger age.

With the trend toward coeducational dormitories in many colleges and universities, the relaxing of restrictions on visiting hours in segregated dormitories and of requirements for residence in campus dormitories, and the widespread practice among adolescents of traveling together in unchaperoned groups composed of members of both sexes, living together in a premarital relationship is becoming an accepted pattern among college students. This is also true of older adolescents who go to work after com-

---

Box 8-8. STAGES OF HETEROSEXUAL DEVELOPMENT

Crush and Hero-Worship Stage
The adolescent often centers his affection first on an older member of his own sex and then on a member of the opposite sex. If he has personal contacts with the admired person, he is said to have a "crush"; if the person is admired from afar, it is "hero worship." This stage rarely lasts more than a year or two.

"Puppy-Love" Stage
Puppy love, or a transitory feeling of affection between a boy and girl, often occurs in adolescence. It precedes the more serious dating and going-steady stages.

Dating Stage
Dating often begins as early as age thirteen or four-

teen. At first adolescents "play the field" rather than dating only one person.

Going-steady Stage
After playing the field for a year or two, many boys and girls limit their dating to one individual. Going steady may involve no plans for the future, or the couple may be considering marriage, although no formal announcement is made.

Early Marriage
Adolescents who marry while still in high school or shortly after graduation are usually dependent on their families for at least part of their support. Many early marriages are the result of the girl's having become pregnant.

pleting high school and live apart from their parents in order to enjoy a freedom they would not otherwise have. There is also a growing trend toward communal living, patterned after the life-style of the so-called Hippie culture.

Approved Sex Roles

Learning to play approved sex roles is even more difficult than learning to get along with age-mates of the opposite sex. This is easier for boys than for girls. First, since early childhood boys have been made aware of sexually appropriate behavior and have been encouraged, prodded, or even shamed into conforming to the approved standards. Second, boys discover with each passing year that the male role carries far more prestige than the female role.

Girls, by contrast, often reach adolescence with blurred concepts of the female role, though their concepts of the male role are clearer and better defined. This is because, as children, they were permitted to look, act, and feel much as boys without constant proddings to be "feminine." Even when they learn what society expects of them, their motivation to mold their behavior in accordance with the traditional female role is weak because they realize that this role is far less prestigious than the male role and even less prestigious than the role they played as children.

If they rebel against the traditional female role, they may be rejected not only by members of the opposite sex but also by other girls. Before early adolescence is over, most girls accept, often reluctantly, the stereotype of the female role as a model for their own behavior and pretend to be completely "feminine," even though they prefer an egalitarian role that combines features of both the male and the female roles. This is a price they are willing to pay, temporarily at least, for social acceptance.

Because the Women's Liberation movement has concentrated on achieving equality for women in the business and professional fields and in marriage, it has had little im-

pact, to date, on younger adolescents' attitudes toward sex roles. However, the influence of this movement is beginning to be felt among older adolescents who go to college or begin training for business or a career, or who marry or go to work at the completion of high school. Older adolescent girls no longer meekly accept or pretend to accept the traditional female sex role. Instead, they expect, demand, and achieve a more egalitarian role, whether in school, at work, or in their own homes.

FAMILY RELATIONSHIPS DURING ADOLESCENCE

The relationships of the young adolescent with the members of his family deteriorate as adolescence progresses. The fault lies on both sides. Parents far too often refuse to modify their concept of their child's abilities as he grows older. As a result, they treat him much as they did when he was younger. In spite of this, they expect him to "act his age," especially when it comes to assuming responsibilities.

Even more important is the so-called "generation gap" between the adolescent and his parents. This gap is partly the result of the radical changes in values and standards of behavior that normally occur in any rapidly changing culture, like the American culture of today, and partly the result of the fact that young people now have greater educational, social, and cultural opportunities than their parents did when they were adolescents. Thus it is more of a "cultural gap," not due entirely to differences in chronological age.

In no area is this generation gap more apparent than in sexual mores. As was pointed out earlier, sexual behavior that is condoned today among adolescents would have been strongly condemned by their parents at that age.

Parents cannot be blamed for all the friction that develops between them and their adolescent children. No one is more irresponsible, more difficult to live with, more unpredictable, or more exasperating than a young adolescent, with the possible exception of a preadolescent. Parents find it difficult to accept the adolescent's objections to duties and to the restraints they feel are necessary, and they may be impatient with his failure to assume responsibilities they feel are appropriate for his age. These sources of irritation generally reach their peak between fourteen and fifteen years, after which there is an improvement in parent-child relationships.

Equally important, many adolescents feel that their parents do not "understand them" and that their standards of behavior are old-fashioned. This is due more to the cultural gap, explained above, than to differences in age.

Improvements in adolescent-parent relationships result, first, when parents begin to realize that their sons and daughters are no longer children. As a result, they give them more privileges, while at the same time expecting more in the way of work and assumption of responsibilities. Second, parent-adolescent relationships are eased when parents try to understand the adolescent and the new cultural values of his peer group—even if they do not wholeheartedly approve of them—and recognize that he is living in a different world from the one in which they grew up. When parents make these adjustments, the parent-adolescent relationship generally becomes more relaxed, and the home a pleasanter place in which to live.

Much the same pattern occurs in the adolescent's relationships with his siblings, grandparents, and other relatives. During early adolescence, these relationships are frictional, just as relationships with parents are. The older adolescent now accepts his siblings, who were frequently a nuisance to him when he was younger, in a calmer and more philosophical manner. He can understand the behavior of younger siblings better than he could earlier, and his newly acquired poise and self-confidence make him less easily embarrassed or upset by their

behavior. Often the older adolescent develops a parental attitude toward his younger siblings, and this eliminates much of the friction that previously existed in the home. Older siblings are treated more casually, and less envy is shown toward them than was the case earlier.

The older adolescent even accepts grandparents and older relatives more graciously than he did several years earlier. This difference in attitude may be a result of his more mature concept of old age, although it is far more likely to be due to the fact that his grandparents and other relatives treat him more like an adult than they formerly did and no longer criticize his appearance or behavior.

Although the sources of friction between the adolescent and members of his family are myriad, certain ones are almost universal in American families of today. These are given in Box 8-9.

As a rule, the adolescent's relationships with family members of the female sex are less favorable than those with male family members. While it is true that mothers tend to be more lenient with their sons than their daughters, this is one of the few exceptions to the rule. Because girls are more restricted by their mothers than by their fathers, mother-daughter friction is often intense, at least until the latter part of adolescence. Grandfathers and other male relatives assume little control over the adolescent's behavior, believing that it is his parents' responsibility. Grandmothers and other female relatives, however, tend to be more outspoken in their criticisms. Also, both boys and girls in adolescence have a more frictional relationship with a stepmother than with a stepfather.

The frictional relationship that existed between siblings of different sexes during childhood gives way to a friendly and even cooperative relationship during adolescence. Girls discover that their brothers can be counted on to bring their friends to parties, and boys discover that their sisters can supply them with dates. On the other hand,

---

Box 8-9. COMMON AREAS OF FAMILY FRICTION DURING ADOLESCENCE

Standards of Behavior
The adolescent often considers his parents' standards of behavior old-fashioned and feels that they do not understand him.

Methods of Discipline
If the adolescent regards the methods used as "unfair" or "childish," he may become rebellious.

Hypercritical Attitudes
Family members resent an adolescent's hypercritical attitude toward them and the general pattern of family life. See Figure 8-5.

"Latchkey" Problems
The adolescent's new, more active social life may result in his breaking family rules concerning times to return home or the people he associates with. See Figure 8-6.

Immature Behavior
Parents may develop punitive attitudes if the adolescent neglects his schoolwork, shuns responsibilities, or spends his money foolishly, for example.

Relationships with Siblings
The adolescent may be scornful of younger siblings and resentful of older ones, leading to friction with them as well as with parents, whom they may accuse of "playing favorites."

Rebellion against Relatives
Parents and relatives become angry if the adolescent openly expresses his feeling that family gatherings are "boring" or if he rejects relatives' suggestions or advice.

Feeling Victimized
The adolescent may become resentful if he has fewer status symbols—clothes and possessions, for example—than his peers have, if he must assume many household responsibilities, or if a stepparent comes into the home. This antagonizes parents and adds to an already-strained parent-adolescent relationship.

---

the friendly relationships of same-sex siblings during childhood often deteriorate in adolescence; an older girl may criticize her younger sister's appearance and behavior, for example, and younger siblings tend to resent the privileges their older siblings are granted (45).

PERSONALITY CHANGES DURING ADOLESCENCE

By early adolescence, both boys and girls are well aware of their good and bad traits, and they appraise these in terms of similar traits in their friends. They are also well aware of the role personality plays in social relationships and thus are strongly motivated to improve their personalities—by reading books or articles on the subject, for example—in the hope of increasing their social acceptance.

The older adolescent is also aware of what constitutes a pleasing personality. He knows what traits are admired by peers of his own sex as well as by those of the opposite sex. Although different traits are admired as adolescence progresses and although admired traits differ somewhat from one social group to another, the adolescent knows what the group with which he is identified admires.

Many adolescents use group standards as the basis for their concept of an "ideal" personality against which they assess their own personalities. Few feel that they measure up to this ideal, and those who do not may want to change their personalities.

This is a difficult, often impossible task. First, the personality pattern, established

"I don't cook this right! I don't bake that right! Why don't you get out and do your protesting in the street like other kids!"

Figure 8-5 Parental reactions to adolescent criticism. (M. O. Lichty. "Grin and Bear It," Publishers-Hall Syndicate, Nov. 11, 1966. Used by permission.)

during childhood, has begun to stabilize and take the form it will maintain with few modifications during the remaining years of life. True, there will be changes with age, but these will be more *quantitative* than qualitative, in that desirable traits will be strengthened, and undesirable traits will be weakened (3, 16, 66).

Second, many of the conditions in the adolescent's life that are responsible for molding his personality pattern are not within his control since they are a product of the environment in which he lives and thus will continue to affect his self-concept—the core of his personality pattern—as long as his environment remains stable. If he changes his environment, however—as when he goes away to school or college or goes to a new place to work or live—environmental changes may bring about personality changes. Adolescents who go away to col-

lege, for example, usually show greater social and emotional maturity and greater tolerance than those who remain under the parental roof (111, 133). On the other hand, even in a different environment the adolescent tends to seek people who treat him in a manner congruent with his self-concept and to avoid those who do not. This reinforces the already-established self-concept and the characteristic patterns of adjustment to life.

Even when the adolescent's environment does not change, some of the conditions contributing to an unfavorable self-concept will automatically change as group values change. When, for example, high value is placed on social acceptance, the adolescent who is not popular will feel inadequate. Later, as the closely knit peer groups begin to break up and less value is placed on popularity, he will view himself from a different frame of reference and thus will feel

Figure 8-6 Family friction often arises over the adolescent's choice of friends. (M. O. Lichty. "Grin and Bear It," Publishers-Hall Syndicate, July 7, 1966. Used by permission.)

"Well, if you intend keeping it, you're going to have to feed it and take care of it yourself!"

more adequate. This feeling of adequacy will be greatly increased if the older adolescent goes steady, is pinned, or gets married earlier than other members of the peer group or if he earns money, which enables him to have the autonomy and status symbols which his peers are unable to have.

Many conditions in the adolescent's life are responsible for molding his personality pattern through their influence on the self-concept. Some of these are similar to those present during childhood, but many are the product of the physical and psychological changes which occur during adolescence. The most important of these are given in Box 8-10.

Consequences of Attempts to Improve Personality

How successful the adolescent will be in his attempts to improve his personality depends on many factors. First, he must set an ideal that is realistic and attainable *for him*. Otherwise, he will inevitably experience failure and, along with it, feelings of inadequacy, inferiority, and even martyrdom if he projects the blame for his failure on others.

Second, he must make a realistic assessment of his strengths and weaknesses. A marked discrepancy between his actual personality and his ego-ideal will lead to anxiety, uneasiness, unhappiness, and the tendency to use defensive reactions.

Third, the adolescent must have a stable self-concept. The self-concept usually becomes increasingly more stable as adolescence progresses, and this gives the adolescent a sense of inner continuity and enables him to see himself in a consistent manner, rather than one way now and a different way later. This also increases his self-esteem and results in fewer feelings of inadequacy.

Box 8-10. CONDITIONS INFLUENCING THE ADOLESCENT'S SELF-CONCEPT

Age of Maturing
Early maturers, who are treated as near-adults, develop favorable self-concepts and thus make good adjustments. Late maturers, who are treated like children, feel misunderstood and martyred and thus are predisposed to maladjusted behavior.

Appearance
Being different in appearance makes the adolescent feel inferior, even if the difference adds to his physical attractiveness. Any physical defect is a source of embarrassment which leads to feelings of inferiority.

Sex-Appropriateness
Sex-appropriate appearance, interests, and behavior help the adolescent to achieve a favorable self-concept.

Names and Nicknames
The adolescent will be sensitive and embarrassed if the group judges his name unfavorably or if he has a nickname that implies ridicule.

Family Relationships
An adolescent who has a very close relationship with a family member will identify with this person and want to develop a similar personality pattern. If this person is of the same sex, the adolescent will be helped to develop a sex-appropriate self-concept.

Peers
Peers influence the adolescent's personality pattern in two ways. First, his self-concept is a reflection of what he believes his peers' concept of him is, and second, he comes under peer pressures to develop personality traits approved by the group.

Level of Aspiration
If the adolescent has unrealistically high levels of aspiration, he will experience failure. This will lead to feelings of inadequacy and anxiety and to defensive reactions in which he blames others for his failure. The adolescent who is realistic about his abilities will gain greater self-confidence with each success and, with it, a better self-concept.

Fourth, and most important of all, the adolescent must be reasonably well satisfied with his achievements and anxious to make improvements in any area in which he feels deficient. Self-acceptance leads to behavior that makes others like and accept the adolescent, and this in turn reinforces the favorable behavior and thus the feelings of self-acceptance. The adolescent's attitude toward himself therefore determines how well adjusted and happy he will be.

HAZARDS OF ADOLESCENCE

Physical hazards are now less numerous and less important than psychological hazards, although they do exist. However, they are significant primarily because of their psychological repercussions. Overweight per se, for example, would have relatively little effect on the adolescent's behavior and thus on his social adjustments, but it is a hazard because it can result in unfavorable peer attitudes.

Physical Hazards

Mortality as a result of illness is far less common during adolescence than in earlier years, although deaths due to automobile accidents and suicide increase (92). Adolescents are generally in good health, but they often discover they can avoid unpleasant situations by "not feeling well." Girls, for example, often use their menstrual periods as an excuse for not going to school (106).

Physical defects that can be corrected, such as crooked teeth, poor eyesight, or hearing loss, rarely prevent adolescents from doing what their peers do. However, they may become psychological hazards in the case of the adolescent who must wear glasses or a hearing aid, for example. Physical defects which prevent the adolescent from doing what his peers do, such as chronic asthma and obesity, are physical as well as psychological hazards.

As a result of muscle growth during early adolescence, strength increases. Because girls' muscles do not develop as much as boys' do, girls have less strength and tend to feel inadequate when they participate with boys in such sports as swimming and tennis, a feeling that contributes to their growing sense of inferiority.

Clumsiness and awkwardness are more serious during adolescence than at any other time in the life span. If the adolescent's skills and motor development are not on a par with those of his friends, he cannot take part in the games and sports that play such an important role in his social life. This has a serious impact on his social adjustments as well as on his self-concept.

Psychological Hazards

The major psychological hazards of adolescence center around the failure to make the psychological transitions to maturity that constitute the important developmental tasks of adolescence. In most cases adolescents fail to make these transitions not because they want to remain immature but because they encounter obstacles in their attempts to achieve mature patterns of behavior. For example, an adolescent who did not establish good foundations earlier will be unable to master the developmental tasks of adolescence. As Eisenberg has explained (36):

Optimal development in adolescence depends on successful accomplishment of the developmental tasks in infancy and childhood. Thus, clinical experience has indicated that adolescence is likely to be particularly stormy, prolonged, and sometimes poorly resolved if it follows a childhood marked by severe deficit.

Late maturers have less time in which to master the developmental tasks of adolescence than early maturers and those who mature at the average age. Many late maturers have barely completed the puberty changes when adolescence is drawing to a close, and thus they often have inadequate foundations on which to build more mature patterns of behavior. Even more serious, they were treated as children at the time their contemporaries were being treated as near-adults, and they may have developed feelings of inadequacy about their abilities to assume the rights, privileges, and responsibilities that go with adulthood.

An adolescent who goes to work after completing high school or dropping out of school undergoes a drastic role change almost overnight. He must assume an adult role earlier than his contemporaries who continue their education, and he is deprived of the opportunity to make a slow transition into adulthood during the latter part of adolescence.

A prolonged state of dependency is also handicapping to the adolescent, as when he continues his education into early adulthood. As Blos has pointed out, "Living in the twilight of an arrested transition renders the adolescent self-conscious and ashamed" (16). Because girls, as a rule, are more apt to be forced into a state of prolonged dependency than boys, they are especially handicapped in making the transition into adulthood.

It is important for the adolescent to show signs of maturity—to develop more adult interests, for example, and to control the overt expressions of his emotions. His level of maturity is also indicated by his social behavior; his use of money; his attitudes toward religion, education, and his future vocation; and his sexual and moral behavior. His performance in these areas determines whether his personal and social adjustments will be judged as mature or immature.

In the area of social behavior, for example, immaturity is shown in a preference for childish patterns of social groupings and social activities with peers of the same sex and in a lack of acceptance by peer groups, which in turn deprives the adolescent of the opportunity to learn more mature patterns of social behavior. Young adolescents, who are unsure of themselves and of their status

From student to employee: a drastic role change. (Suzanne Szasz)

in the peer group, tend to overconform; a persistence of this into late adolescence, however, suggests immaturity. Other common indications of immaturity in the area of social behavior include discrimination against those of different racial, religious, or socioeconomic backgrounds; attempts to reform those with different standards of appearance and behavior; and attempts on the part of the adolescent to draw attention to himself by wearing conspicuous clothes, using unconventional speech, bragging and boasting, and making jokes at the expense of others.

Immaturity is especially apparent in the area of sexual development because the adjustment from antagonism toward members of the opposite sex, characteristic of puberty, to the development of feelings of affection for them is a radical one. The adolescent who does not date either because he is unattractive to members of the opposite sex or because he has a childish dislike for them is regarded as immature by his contemporaries, and this cuts him off from social contacts with them. Rejection of the socially approved sex role, a continued preoccupation with sex, premarital pregnancy, and early marriage are also regarded as indications of immaturity. Rejection of the approved sex role, especially by girls, is also a potential source of trouble in marriage.

In few areas is immaturity more hazardous to good personal and social adjustments than in that of morality. The adolescent who establishes unrealistically high standards of behavior for himself feels guilty and ashamed when his behavior falls short of these standards. The adolescent who sets unreasonably high standards for others will become quarrelsome and disillusioned, and this can lead to the breaking of strong emotional ties with family members and peers.

Social adjustments are also damaged by willful defiance of rules and laws. Few adolescents are ignorant of the rules and laws by which they are expected to abide, and few are incapable of learning what is right and what is wrong. On the other hand, many are willing to sacrifice their standards and the standards of their parents if they feel this will guarantee acceptance by their peers. Many adolescents justify acts they know are wrong by claiming that "everyone" shoplifts, cheats, or uses drugs (12, 46).

Moral immaturity is also evident in juvenile delinquents from affluent families, as contrasted with the many adolescents who grow up in unfavorable environments that normally might produce antisocial attitudes and yet who are law-abiding in their behavior. They are "insulated" against delinquency in that they do not succumb to the temptation to behave in an antisocial way, regardless of how strong this temptation may be.

Poor family relationships are psychological hazards at any age, but especially so during adolescence because at this time boys and girls are typically unsure of themselves and depend on their families for a feeling of security. Even more important, they need guidance and help in mastering the developmental tasks of adolescence. When family relationships are marked by friction, the adolescent's feelings of insecurity are likely to be prolonged, and he will be deprived of the opportunity to develop poise and more mature patterns of behavior.

Furthermore, the adolescent whose family relationships are unfavorable may also develop poor relationships with people outside the home. While all relationships, whether in adulthood or in childhood, are sometimes strained, a person who consistently has difficulty getting along with others is regarded as immature and unpleasant to be with. This militates against good social adjustments.

Effects of Immaturity The adolescent who knows that his attitudes and behavior are viewed by the social group as immature and who realizes that others consider him incapable of handling the adult role successfully may develop an inferiority complex. Even if he has not set unrealistically high standards for himself, there will still be a gap between what he wants to be and what he thinks he is—a reflection of what he believes others think of him. If this gap is small, he will experience some self-dissatisfaction, but if it is wide, the adolescent may consider himself worthless and may even contemplate or attempt suicide.

Even when self-rejection is not overtly expressed, it is evidenced in ways that may be regarded as danger signals of maladjustment—indications that the individual is dissatisfied with himself and has a self-rejectant attitude. Box 8-11 lists some of the common danger signals of maladjustment in adolescence.

The self-rejectant person soon becomes maladjusted and unhappy. The adolescent who experiences these feelings finds himself playing the role of a social isolate. As a result, he misses out on the good times his contemporaries are enjoying, and he finds

> **Box 8-11. COMMON DANGER SIGNALS OF ADOLESCENT MALADJUSTMENT**
>
> Irresponsibility as shown in neglect of studies, for example, in favor of having a good time and winning social approval
>
> An overly aggressive, cocksure attitude
>
> Feelings of insecurity, which cause the adolescent to conform to group standards in a slavishly conventional manner
>
> Homesickness when away from familiar surroundings
>
> Feelings of martyrdom
>
> Excessive daydreaming to compensate for the lack of satisfaction the adolescent derives from his daily life
>
> Regression to earlier levels of behavior in an attempt to win favor and recognition
>
> Use of defense mechanisms such as rationalization, projection, fantasizing, and displacement

little compensation for these losses in his relationships with the members of his family. Although most adolescents experience unhappiness in some degree, the poorly adjusted not only experience unhappiness in more pronounced forms but also experience it more often.

HAPPINESS IN ADOLESCENCE

Because few adults separate early adolescence from late adolescence in their minds, they tend to remember *all* adolescence as a generally unhappy age. In addition, publicity given to adolescent suicides in recent years, especially among college students, has tended to strengthen the belief that this is an unhappy period in the life span.

Adolescents who are poorly adjusted, especially those who have been making poor adjustments since childhood, tend to be the most unhappy and the most persistently unhappy throughout the years of early adolescence. Their unhappiness comes more from personal than from environmental causes: They have unrealistically high levels of aspiration for themselves, and when their achievements fall below their expectations, they become dissatisfied with themselves and become self-rejectant in their attitudes. Although all adolescents tend to be unrealistic during the early years of adolescence, those who are poorly adjusted are not only more unrealistic than average but also less likely to modify their aspirations.

If, however, adolescents are able to solve the problems that face them with reasonable success and to feel increasingly confident of their abilities to cope with these problems without adult help, periods of unhappiness gradually become less frequent and less intense. By the time they reach the senior year in high school and look and act more like adults than like children, happiness should gradually outweigh unhappiness, and the stress and discontent that characterized early adolescence should have largely disappeared.

The greater happiness that is characteristic of late adolescence is due, in part, to the fact that the older adolescent is granted a status more in keeping with his level of development than was true during early adolescence. He is given more independence and consequently suffers from fewer frustrations; he is more realistic about his capacities and sets goals more within his reach; he uses sustained and definitely directed efforts to attain these goals; and he has built up a degree of self-confidence based on knowledge of past successes which counteracts some of the feelings of inadequacy that plagued him when he was younger.

When the adolescent's needs for acceptance, affection, and achievement are met to his satisfaction, he will be happy. Meeting these needs may be dependent on his environment or on himself. If the system of controls and outlets provided by the adolescent's environment are such that they permit him to satisfy his needs, he will be happy, *provided* his needs are realistic in the sense that he has the capacities necessary to meet them.

Chapter Highlights

1 Adolescence is usually subdivided into early adolescence, which extends roughly from ages thirteen to sixteen or seventeen, and late adolescence, which extends from then until age eighteen. The young adolescent is usually referred to as a "teen-ager," while the older adolescent is considered a "young man" or a "young woman."

2 Because adolescence is a transitional period, it is characterized by problems and feelings of instability. The developmental tasks of adolescence center on making the transition to adulthood.

3 The physical changes begun during puberty are completed during the early part of adolescence.

4 Adolescence is usually a period of heightened emotionality, "storm and stress." Only when the individual achieves control over his emotions is he regarded as emotionally mature.

5 There are marked changes in the adolescent's social interests and behavior, as shown by increased peer-group influence, new patterns of social groupings, new values in the selection of friends and leaders, and characteristics that lead to social acceptance or rejection.

6 The adolescent develops new interests related to recreation, social activities, his appearance, independence, religion, education, and his future vocation.

7 One of the major developmental tasks of adolescence is that of achieving control over behavior so that it will conform to standards approved by the social group. The adolescent who fails to achieve this control will be guilty of misdemeanors or may become a juvenile delinquent if he violates laws.

8 The adolescent's interest in members of the opposite sex develops in a fairly predictable pattern, and he learns to play the socially approved sex role.

9 Family relationships, which began to deteriorate during childhood, normally reach a low point in early adolescence and then begin to improve as parents, siblings, grandparents, and other relatives treat the adolescent as an adult or a near-adult.

10 Awareness of the role personality plays in social relationships motivates the adolescent to try to improve his personality. When he cannot do so because environmental conditions are unfavorable or because his aspirations are unrealistic, he becomes self-rejectant. This often leads to personality maladjustments, such as irresponsibility, feelings of insecurity, regression, or the use of defense or escape mechanisms.

11 Physical hazards during adolescence are less numerous and less serious than psychological hazards, which are mainly the result of poor foundations laid earlier. The adolescent may behave immaturely or show signs of maladjusted behavior.

12 Happiness normally increases as adolescence progresses and as the adolescent's personal and social adjustments improve, an improvement that paves the way for the three basic essentials of happiness at any age—acceptance, affection, and achievement.

Bibliography

1 Adelson, J., Green, B., & O'Neil, B. Growth of the idea of law in adolescence. *Adolescence,* 1969, **1,** 327–332.

2 Adinolfi, A. A. Characteristics of highly accepted, highly rejected and relatively unknown university freshmen. *J. counsel. Psychol.,* 1970, **17,** 456–465.

3 Allport, G. W. Crises in normal personality development. *Teachers Coll. Rec.,* 1964, **66,** 235–241.

4 Anthony, J. The reactions of adults to adolescents and their behavior. In G. Caplan & S. Lebovici (Eds.), *Adolescence: Psychosocial perspectives.* New York: Basic Books, 1969. Pp. 52–78.

5 Astin, H. S., & Myint, T. Career development of young women during the post-high school years. *J. counsel. Psychol.,* 1971, **18,** 369–393.

6 Ausubel, D. The peer group and adolescent conformity. *Delta,* 1971, **9,** 50–64.

7 Bakan, D. Adolescence in America: From idea to social fact. *Daedalus,* 1971, **100,** 979–995.

8 Baltes, B., & Nesselroade, J. R. Cultural change and adolescent personality development. *Develpm. Psychol.,* 1972, **7,** 244–256.

9 Bartemeier, L. H. Character formation. *Bull. Menninger Clin.,* 1969, **33,** 346–351.

10 Bauer, N. J. Differences in personality traits among most preferred and least preferred students in grades 10, 11, and 12. *J. educ. Res.,* 1971, **65,** 65–70.

11 Bealer, R. C., & Willets, F. C. The religious interests of American high school youth: A survey of recent research. *Relig. Educ.,* 1967, **62,** 435–444.

12 Berry, G. W. Personality patterns and delinquency. *Brit. J. educ. Psychol.,* 1971, **41,** 221–222.

13 Berscheid, E., Dion, K., Walster, E., & Walster, G. W. Physical attractiveness and dating choice: A test of the matching hypothesis. *J. exp. soc. Psychol.,* 1971, **7,** 173–189.

14 Biller, H. B., & Liebman, D. A. Body build, sex-role preference and sex-role adoption in junior high school boys. *J. genet. Psychol.,* 1971, **118,** 81–86.

15 Bledsoe, J. C., & Wiggins, R. G. Congruence of adolescents' self-concepts and parents' perceptions of adolescents' self-concepts. *J. Psychol.,* 1973, **83,** 131–136.

16 Blos, P. The child analyst looks at the young adolescent. *Daedalus,* 1971, **100,** 961–978.

17 Boshier, R. The effect of academic failure on self-concept and maladjustment indices. *J. educ. Res.,* 1972, **65,** 347–351.

18 Brosin, H. W. Adolescent crises. *N.Y. State J. Med.,* 1967, **67,** 2003–2011.

19 Burke, P. J. Task and social-emotional leadership role performance. *Sociometry,* 1971, **14,** 22–40.

20 Cameron, P. The words college students use and what they talk about. *J. commun. Disord.,* 1970, **3,** 36–46.

21 Cameron, P. The generation gap: Beliefs about sexuality and self-reported sexuality. In W. R. Looft (Ed.), *Developmental psychology: A book of readings.* Hinsdale, Ill.: Dryden Press, 1972. Pp. 479–484.

22 Caplan, G., & Lebovici, S. (Eds.). *Adolescence: Psychosocial perspectives.* New York: Basic Books, 1969.

23 Clifford, E. Body satisfaction in adolescence. *Percept. mot. Skills,* 1971, **33,** 119–125.

24 Coleman, J. S. *The adolescent society.* New York: Free Press, 1961.

25 Collins, J. K., & Thomas, N. T. Age and susceptibility to same sex peer pressure. *Brit. J. educ. Psychol.,* 1972, **42,** 83–85.

26 Constantinople, A. Some correlates of average level of happiness among college students. *Develpm. Psychol.,* 1970, **2,** 447.

27 Cottle, T. J. Of youth and the time of generations. In W. R. Looft (Ed.), *Developmental psychology: A book of readings.* Hinsdale, Ill.: Dryden Press, 1972. Pp. 196–210.

28 Cross, J. F., & Cross, J. Age, sex, race and the perception of facial beauty. *Develpm. Psychol.,* 1971, **5,** 433–439.

29 DeBord, L. W. Adolescent religious participation: An examination of sib-structure and church attendance. *Adolescence,* 1969, **4,** 557–570.

30 Deitz, G. E. The influence of social class, sex, and delinquency-nondelinquency on adolescent values. *J. genet. Psychol.,* 1972, **121,** 119–126.

31 DeLissovoy, V. High school marriages: A longitudinal study. *J. Marriage & Family,* 1973, **35,** 245–255.

32 Devereux, E. C. The role of peer-group experience in moral development. In P. H. Hill (Ed.), *Minnesota symposia on child psychology.* Vol. 4. Minneapolis: University of Minnesota Press, 1970. Pp. 94–140.

33 Diedrich, R. C., & Jackson, P. W. Satisfied and dissatisfied students. *Personnel Guid. J.,* 1969, **47,** 641–648.

34 Douvan, E., & Adelson, J. American dating patterns. In D. Rogers (Ed.), *Issues in adolescent psychology.* New York: Appleton Century Crofts, 1969. Pp. 386–395.

35 Dunphy, D. C. The social structure of the urban adolescent peer groups. *Sociometry,* 1963, **26,** 230–246.

36 Eisenberg, L. A developmental approach to adolescence. *Children,* 1965, **12,** 131–135.

37 Elkind, D. Egocentrism in adolescence. *Child Develpm.,* 1967, **38,** 1025–1034.

38 Erikson, E. H. *Identity: Youth and crisis.* New York: Norton, 1968.

39 Faltermayer, E. Youth after the revolution. *Fortune,* March 1973, 145–158.

40 Feshbach, N., & Sones, G. Sex differences in adolescent reactions toward newcomers. *Develpm. Psychol.,* 1971, **4,** 381–386.

41 Floyd, H. H., & South, D. R. Dilemma of youth: The choice of parents or peers as a frame of reference for behavior. *J. Marriage & Family,* 1972, **34,** 627–634.

42 Freud, A. Adolescence as a developmental disturbance. In G. Caplan & S. Lebovici (Eds.), *Adolescence: Psychosocial perspectives.* New York: Basic Books, 1969. Pp. 5–10.

43 Friedenberg, E. Z. The generation gap. *Ann. Amer. Acad. pol. soc. Sci.,* 1969, **382,** 32–42.

44 Garai, J. E., & Scheinfeld, A. Sex differences in mental and behavioral traits. *Genet. Psychol. Monogr.,* 1968, **77,** 169–299.

45 Gesell, A., Ilg, F. L., & Ames, L. B. *Youth: The years from ten to sixteen.* New York: Harper & Row, 1956.

46 Goldberg, L., & Guilford, J. S. Delinquent values: It's fun to break the rules. *Proc. Annu. Convent APA.* 1972, **7**(1), 237–238.

47 Good, E. H., & Kelley, E. A. Teenage boys' perceptions of the role clothing plays in the occupational world. *J. Home Econ.,* 1971, **63,** 332–336.

48 Gordon, C. Social characteristics of early adolescence. *Daedalus,* 1971, **100,** 931–960.

49 Grinder, R. E. The concept of adolescence in the genetic psychology of G. Stanley Hall. *Child Develpm.,* 1969, **40,** 355–369.

50 Gurel, L. M., Wilbur, J. C., & Gurel, L. Personality correlates of adolescent clothing styles. *J. Home Econ.,* 1972, **64**(3), 42–47.

51 Hambleton, K. B., Roach, M. E., & Ehle, K. Teenage appearance: Conformity, preferences, and self-concepts. *J. Home Econ.,* 1972, **64**(2), 29–33.

52 Hechinger, G., & Hechinger, F. M. *Teen-age tyranny.* New York: Morrow, 1963.

53 Heise, D. R., & Roberts, E. P. M. The development of role knowledge. *Genet. Psychol. Monogr.,* 1970, **82,** 83–115.

54 Hess, A. L., & Bradshaw, H. L. Positiveness of self-concept and ideal self as a function of age. *J. genet. Psychol.,* 1970, **117,** 57–67.

55 Hollender, J. W. Development of vocational decisions during adolescence. *J. counsel. Psychol.,* 1971, **18,** 244–248.

56 Horrocks, J. E., & Benimoff, M. Stability of adolescents' nominee status, over a one-year period, as a friend by their peers. *Adolescence,* 1966, **1,** 224–229.

57 Horrocks, J. E., & Weinberg, S. A. Psychological needs and their development during adolescence. *J. Psychol.,* 1970, **74,** 51–69.

58 Hurlock, E. B. American adolescents of today: A new species. *Adolescence,* 1966, **1,** 7–21.

59 Hurlock, E. B. The adolescent reformer. *Adolescence,* 1968, **3,** 272–306.

60 Irish, D. P. Sibling interactions: A neglected aspect of family life research. *Soc. Forces,* 1964, **42,** 279–288.

61 Jones, M. C. Psychological correlates of somatic development. *Child Develpm.,* 1965, **36,** 899–911.

62 Jones, V. Attitudes of college students and their changes: A 37-year study. *Genet. Psychol. Monogr.,* 1970, **81,** 3–80.

63 Joseph, T. P. Adolescents from the view of the members of an informal adolescent group. *Genet. Psychol. Monogr.,* 1969, **79,** 3–88.

64 Josselyn, I. M. *Adolescence.* New York: Harper & Row, 1971.

65 Kagan, J. A conception of early adolescence. *Daedalus,* 1971, **100,** 997–1012.

66 Kagan, J., & Moss, H. A. *Birth to maturity: A study in psychological development.* New York: Wiley, 1962.

67 Kang, T. S. Name and group identification. *J. soc. Psychol.,* 1972, **86,** 159–160.

68 Kelley, R. K. The premarital sexual revolution: Comments on research. *Family Coordinator,* 1972, **21,** 334–336.

69 Keniston, K. Student activism, moral development, and morality. In W. R. Looft (Ed.), *Developmental psychology: A book of readings.* Hinsdale, Ill.: Dryden Press, 1972. Pp. 437–456.

70 Kreitler, H., & Kreitler, S. Unhappy memories of "the happy past." Studies in cognitive dissonance. *Brit. J. Psychol.,* 1968, **59,** 157–166.

71 Krogman, W. M. Growth of head, face, trunk, and limbs in Philadelphia white and Negro children in elementary and high school. *Monogr. Soc. Res. Child Develpm.,* 1970, **35**(3).

72 Kugelmass, I. N. *Adolescent immaturity: Prevention and treatment.* Springfield, Ill.: Charles C Thomas, 1973.

73 Landsbaum, J. B., & Willis, R. H. Conformity in early and late adolescence. *Develpm. Psychol.,* 1971, **4,** 334–337.

74 LaVoie, J. C. Punishment and adolescent self-control. *Develpm. Psychol.,* 1973, **8,** 16–24.

75 Lee, L. C. The concomitant development of cognitive and moral modes of thought: A test of selected deductions from Piaget's theory. *Genet. Psychol. Monogr.,* 1971, **83,** 93–146.

76 Lerner, R. M., & Korn, S. J. The development of body-build stereotypes in males. *Child Develpm.,* 1972, **43,** 908–920.

77 Littrell, M. B., & Eicher, J. B. Clothing opinions and the social acceptance process among adolescents. *Adolescence,* 1973, **8,** 197–212.

78 Looft, W. R. Egocentrism and social interaction in adolescence. *Adolescence,* 1971, **6,** 485–494.

79 Luchins, A. S. On the theories and problems of adolescence. *J. genet. Psychol.,* 1954, **85,** 47–63.

80 Meredith, H. V. Body size of contemporary youth in different parts of the world. *Monogr. Soc. Res. Child Develpm.,* 1969, **34**(7).

81 Miller, N., Campbell, D. T., Twedt, H., & O'Connell, E. J. Similarity, contrast, and complementarity in friendship choice. *J. Pers. soc. Psychol.,* 1966, **3,** 3–12.

82 Mitchell, T. R. Leader complexity and leadership style. *J. Pers. soc. Psychol.,* 1970, **16,** 166–174.

83 Monge, R. H. Developmental trends in factors of adolescent self-concept. *Develpm. Psychol.,* 1973, **8,** 382–393.

84 Monks, F. Future time perspective in adolescents. *Hum. Develpm.,* 1968, **11,** 107–123.

85 Muuss, R. E. (Ed.) *Adolescent behavior and society: A book of readings.* New York: Random House, 1971.

86 Nawas, M. M. Change in efficiency of ego functioning and complexity from adolescence to young adulthood. *Develpm. Psychol.,* 1971, **4,** 412–415.

87 Neale, D. C., Gill, N., & Tismer, W. Relationship between attitudes toward school subjects and school achievement. *J. educ. Res.,* 1970, **63,** 232–237.

88 Nelson, E. A., & Rosenbaum, E. Language patterns within the youth subculture: Development of slang vocabularies. *Merrill-Palmer Quart.,* 1972, **18,** 273–285.

89 Nelson, M. O. The concept of God and feelings toward parents. *J. indiv. Psychol.,* 1971, **22,** 46–49.

90 Nelson, P. D. Similarities and differences among leaders and followers. *J. soc. Psychol.,* 1964, **63,** 161–167.

91 Nemy, E. Adolescents today: Are they more disturbed? *The New York Times,* Feb. 20, 1970.

92 Nemy, E. Suicide now no. 2 cause of deaths among young. *The New York Times,* Apr. 16, 1973.

93 Neugarten, B. L., & Weinstein, K. K. The changing American grandparent. *J. Marriage & Family,* 1964, **26,** 199–204.

94 Noe, F. An instrumental conception of leisure for the adolescent. *Adolescence,* 1969, **4,** 385–400.

95 Norton, D. L. The rites of passage from dependency to autonomy. *School Review,* 1970, **79,** 19–41.

96 Offer, D., & Offer, J. L. Profiles of normal adolescent girls. *Arch. gen. Psychiat.,* 1968, **19,** 513–522.

97 Paulson, M. J., Lin, T. T., & Hanssen, C. Family harmony: An etiologic factor in alienation. *Child Develpm.,* 1972, **43,** 591–603.

98 Peck, R. F., & Havighurst, R. J. *The psychology of character development.* New York: Wiley, 1962.

99 Piaget, J. The intellectual development of the adolescent. In G. Caplan & S. Lebovici (Eds.), *Adolescence: Psychosocial perspectives.* New York: Basic Books, 1969. Pp. 22–26.

100 Pierce, R. A. Need similarity and complementarity as determinants of friendship choice. *J. Psychol.,* 1970, **76,** 231–238.

101 Pressey, S. L., & Kuhlen, R. G. *Psychological development through the life span.* New York: Harper & Row, 1957.

102 Raymond, B. J., & Unger, R. K. "The apparel oft proclaims the man": Cooperation with deviant and conventional youths. *J. soc. Psychol.,* 1972, **87,** 75–82.

103 Reiss, I. L. Premarital sex as deviant behavior: An application of current approaches to deviance. *Amer. sociol. Rev.,* 1970, **35,** 78–87.

104 Rivenbark, W. H. Self-disclosure patterns among adolescents. *Psychol. Rep.,* 1971, **28,** 35–42.

105 Rode, A. Perceptions of parental behavior among alienated adolescents. *Adolescence,* 1971, **6,** 19–38.

106 Rogers, K. D., & Reese, G. Health studies: Presumably normal high school students. II. Absence from school. *Amer. J. Dis. Children,* 1965, **109,** 9–27.

107 Rubin, I., & Kirkendall, L. A. *Sex in the adolescent years.* New York: Association Press, 1968.

108 Ryan, M. S. *Clothing: A study in human behavior.* New York: Holt, 1966.

109 Rybak, W. Note on crushes and hero-worship of adolescents. *Psychiat. Quart. Suppl.,* 1969, **39,** 48–53.

110 Sappenfield, B. R. Perception of self as related to perception of the ideal personality. *Percept. mot. Skills,* 1970, **31,** 975–978.

111 Schmidt, M. R. Personality change in college women. *J. coll. student Personnel,* 1970, **11,** 414–418.

112 Schonfeld, W. A. The adolescent in contemporary American psychiatry. *Int. J. Psychiat.,* 1968, **5,** 470–478.

113 Sebald, H. *Adolescence: A sociological analysis.* New York: Appleton Century Crofts, 1968.

114 Simon, W., & Gagnon, J. H. On psychosexual development. In W. R. Looft (Ed.), *Developmental psychology: A book of readings.* Hinsdale, Ill.: Dryden Press, 1972. Pp. 456–478.

115 Skorepa, C. A., Horrocks, J. E., & Thompson, G. G. A study of friendship fluctuations of college students. *J. genet. Psychol.,* 1963, **102,** 151–157.

116 Smigel, E. O., & Seiden, R. The decline and fall of the double standard. *Ann. Amer. Acad. pol. soc. Sci.,* 1968, **376,** 6–17.

117 Snyder, E. E. A longitudinal analysis of social participation in high school and early adulthood voluntary associational participation. *Adolescence,* 1970, **5,** 79–88.

118 Sorenson, R. Youth's need for challenge and place in society. *Children,* 1962, **9,** 131–138.

119 Southworth, J. A., & Morningstar, M. E. Persistence of occupational choice and personality congruence. *J. counsel. Psychol.,* 1970, **17,** 409–412.

120 Sterrett, J. E., & Bollman, S. R. Factors related to adolescents' expectations of marital roles. *Family Coordinator,* 1970, **19,** 353–356.

121 Sudia, C., & Rea, J. H. Teenagers discuss their restrictions. *Children,* 1971, **18,** 232–236.

122 Sullivan, E. V., McCullough, G., & Stager, M. A developmental study of the relationship between conceptual, ego and moral development. *Child Develpm.,* 1970, **41,** 399–411.

123 Sutton-Smith, B. Play preference and play behavior: A validity study. *Psychol. Rep.,* 1965, **16,** 65–66.

124 Tanner, J. M. Sequence, tempo, and individual variation in the growth and development of boys and girls aged twelve to sixteen. *Daedalus,* 1971, **100,** 907–930.

125 Tapp, J. L., & Kohlberg, L. Developing senses of law and legal justice. *J. soc. Issues,* 1971, **27**(2), 65–91.

126 Thompson, G. G., & Gardner, E. F. Adolescents' perceptions of happy-successful living. *J. genet. Psychol.,* 1969, **115,** 107–120.

127 Thornburg, H. D. Peers: Three distinct groups. *Adolescence,* 1971, **6,** 59–76.

128 *U.S. News & World Report* article. We're reaping a harvest of permissiveness. *U.S. News & World Report,* Sept. 27, 1971, 22.

129 *U.S. News & World Report* article. 18-year-old adults: Their unexpected problems. *U.S. News & World Report,* Aug. 20, 1973, 40–42.

130 Wagner, H. Adolescent problems resulting from the lengthened educational period. *Adolescence,* 1970, **5,** 339–346.

131 Wagner, H. The increasing importance of the peer group during adolescence. *Adolescence,* 1971, **6,** 53–58.

132 Wallace, J. L., & Leonard, T. H. Factors affecting vocational and educational decision making of high school girls. *J. Home Econ.,* 1971, **63,** 241–245.

133 Waterman, A. S., & Waterman, C. K. A longitudinal study of changes in ego identity status during the freshman year at college. *Develpm. Psychol.,* 1971, **5,** 167–173.

134 Wax, D. E. Social class, race and juvenile delinquency: A review of the literature. *Child Psychol. Hum. Develpm.,* 1972, **3,** 36–49.

135 Weiner, I. B. *Psychological disturbances in adolescence.* New York: Wiley, 1970.

136 Wiebe, B., & Williams, J. D. Self-disclosure to parents by high school seniors. *Psychol. Rep.,* 1972, **31,** 690.

137 Windholz, G. Discrepancy of self and ideal-self and frequency of daydreams reported by male subjects. *Psychol. Rep.,* 1968, **23,** 1121–1122.

138 Winick, C. The Beige Epoch: Depolarization of sex roles in America. *Ann. Amer. Acad. pol. soc. Sci.,* 1968, **376,** 18–24.

139 Zube, M. J. Changing concepts of morality. *Soc. Forces,* 1972, **50,** 385–393.

CHAPTER | NINE

EARLY ADULTHOOD
Personal and Social Adjustments

The term adult comes from the same Latin verb as the term adolescence—*adolescere*—which means "to grow to maturity." However, it derives from the past participle of that verb—*adultus*—which means "grown to full size and strength" or "matured." An adult is, therefore, an individual who has completed his growth and is ready to assume his status in society along with other adults. Adulthood is legally reached in the American culture today at the age of eighteen, and with the gradual increase in longevity, it is by far the longest period in the total life span.

During the long period of adulthood certain physical and psychological changes occur at predictable times. Like childhood and adolescence—also long periods during which certain physical and psychological changes occur at predictable times—adulthood is customarily subdivided on the basis of the times at which these changes take place and the adjustment problems and cultural pressures and expectancies stemming from them. The subdivisions of adulthood are given in Box 9-1. These subdivisions are not rigid and indicate only the ages at which the average man or woman can be expected to begin to show some changes in appearance, bodily functions, interests, attitudes, or behavior and at which certain environmental pressures in our culture give rise to adjustment problems which few men or women escape.

```
┌─────────────────────────────────────────┐
│ Box 9-1.  SUBDIVISIONS OF ADULTHOOD      │
│                                          │
│ Early Adulthood                          │
│ Early adulthood extends from age eighteen to │
│ approximately age forty, when the physical and │
│ psychological changes which accompany the │
│ beginning of the loss of reproductive capacity ap- │
│ pear.                                    │
│                                          │
│ Middle Adulthood (Middle Age)            │
│ Middle adulthood, or middle age, begins at forty │
│ and extends to age sixty, when both physical and │
│ psychological decline become apparent in the │
│ average person.                          │
│                                          │
│ Late Adulthood (Old Age)                 │
│ Late adulthood—senescence, or old age—begins │
│ at sixty and extends to death.  While physical and │
│ psychological decline speed up at this time, mod- │
│ ern medical techniques, as well as careful attention │
│ to clothing and grooming, enable many men and │
│ women to look, act, and feel much as they did │
│ when they were younger.                  │
└─────────────────────────────────────────┘
```

CHARACTERISTICS OF EARLY ADULTHOOD

Early adulthood is a period of adjustments to new patterns of life and new social expectations. The young adult is expected to play new roles, such as that of spouse, parent, and breadwinner, and to develop new attitudes, interests, and values in keeping with these new roles. These adjustments make early adulthood a distinctive period in the life span, the most important characteristics of which are described below.

Early Adulthood Is the "Reproductive Age"

Parenthood is one of the most important roles in the lives of most young adults. Those who were married during the latter years of adolescence concentrate on the role of parenthood during their twenties and early thirties; many become grandparents before early adulthood ends. Those who do not marry until they complete their education or get started in their careers spend the major part of early adulthood playing the role of parents. This is especially true of those who have large families.

Early Adulthood Is the "Settling-down Age"

It has been said that childhood and adolescence are the periods of "growing up" and that adulthood is the time for "settling down." As he settles down, the individual develops a pattern of behavior which will be characteristically his for the remainder of his life. Any need to change this pattern, in middle or old age, will be difficult and emotionally disturbing for him. The average adult has established his life pattern by his mid-thirties, although many do so before this time.

Early Adulthood Is a "Problem Age"

The early adult years present many new problems, different in their major aspects from the problems experienced in the earlier years of life. From the beginning of adulthood until the early or mid-thirties, the average American of today is preoccupied with problems related to adjustments in the different major areas of his life. These adjustments will not all be made at the same time, nor will their final forms be accepted simultaneously (see Figure 9-1).

The young adult is often markedly preoccupied with an area in which he is making an adjustment. When the adjustment has been satisfactorily made, his attention shifts to another area. It is difficult, for example, for a young adult to deal with the choice of a career and a mate simultaneously. Adjustment to marriage and parenthood makes it difficult for the individual to adjust to work if he marries when still a student. He therefore solves one problem and then turns his attention to another.

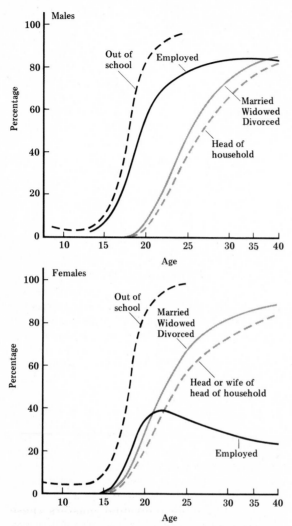

Figure 9-1 Pattern of male and female adjustments in different areas during the early years of adulthood. (Adapted from F. K. Stuttleworth. The adolescent years. *Monogr. Soc. Res. Child Develpm.*, 1949, **14** (1). Used by permission.)

Early Adulthood Is a Period of Emotional Tension

While the individual is trying to get the lay of the new land in which he finds himself, he is likely to be upset emotionally. By the early or mid-thirties, however, he should have solved these problems well enough so that he is generally emotionally stable and calm. Emotional tension is often expressed in worries. What the young adult worries about, however, will depend on what adjustment problems he is facing at the time and how much success or failure he is experiencing in meeting these problems.

Early Adulthood Is a Period of Social Isolation

With the end of formal education and the entrance into the adult life pattern of work and marriage, associations with the peer groups of adolescence wane and, with them, opportunities for social contacts outside the home. As a result, for the first time since babyhood, the individual is likely to experience social isolation, or what Erikson has referred to as an "isolation crisis" (40).

Many young adults, having become accustomed throughout childhood and adolescence to depend on peers for companionship, experience loneliness when responsibilities at home or at work isolate them from groups of their peers. Those who were most popular during their school and college days and who devoted much of their time to peer activities find the adjustment to social isolation in adulthood especially difficult. Whether the loneliness that comes from this isolation will be temporary or persistent depends on how quickly and how satisfactorily the young adult can establish new social contacts to replace those of his school and college days.

Isolation is intensified in the case of young adults with a competitive spirit and a strong desire to rise on the vocational ladder. To achieve success, they must compete with others—thus replacing the friendliness of adolescence with the competitiveness of the successful adult—and they must also devote most of their energy to their work, which leaves them little time for the socialization that leads to close relationships. As a result, they become self-centered, and this contributes to the loneliness that isolation brings (40).

Early Adulthood Is a Time of Value Changes

Many of the values developed during childhood and adolescence are revised in adulthood as the individual's social contacts with people of different ages broaden and as he considers his values from a more mature standpoint. Changes in values are usually toward more conservative and traditional views than toward new, more radical ones, as was true during adolescence.

Adults who assume the role of parenthood not only change their values earlier and more radically than those who are unmarried or childless but also shift to more conservative and traditional values. For example, the individual who approve of premarital intercourse when he was an adolescent may now strongly condemn such behavior in his own children (5, 67).

Similarly, the adult who used to consider school a necessary evil may now recognize the value of education as a stepping-stone to social and vocational success and to personal fulfillment. Many adults who dropped out of school or college decide to finish their education, and some find studying so stimulating that they continue to take courses even after receiving a high school or college diploma (129).

Early Adulthood Is a Creative Age

No longer shackled by the restrictions placed on his behavior by parents and teachers, the young adult is free to be himself and to do what he wants to do. What form creativity will take in adulthood depends upon the individual's interests and abilities and the activities that give him the greatest personal satisfaction. Some find a creative outlet in hobbies, while others choose a vocation in which they can express their creativity.

The individual's creative achievements often do not reach their peak until middle age. This is due to the fact that creativity is more often discouraged than encouraged in the early years of life. Thus it is during early adulthood that he must not only discover where his creative interests and talents lie but also develop his capacities, which in many cases remained dormant while the pattern of his life was prescribed by parents and teachers. As he approaches middle age, however, he should have overcome these obstacles sufficiently to achieve the maximum of which he is capable.

DEVELOPMENTAL TASKS OF EARLY ADULTHOOD

Social expectations for the young adult in our culture are clearly defined and familiar to him even before he reaches legal maturity. Perhaps at no other age in life does he know as clearly and distinctly what society expects of him. The developmental tasks of early adulthood (see page 13) center around these social expectations and include selecting a mate, learning to live with a marriage partner, starting a family, rearing children, managing a home, getting started in an occupation, taking on civic responsibility, and finding a congenial social group (48).

How well the individual masters these developmental tasks during early adulthood will influence the degree of his success when he reaches the peak during middle age—whether this peak relates to work, social recognition, or family living—and it will determine how happy he will be then as well as during the closing years of his life.

Success in mastering the developmental tasks of early adulthood is greatly influenced by the kind of foundations laid earlier. However, certain conditions in adult life facilitate the mastery of these tasks, the most important of which are given in Box 9-2.

Box 9-2. AIDS TO MASTERY OF DEVELOPMENTAL TASKS

Physical Efficiency
The peak of physical efficiency is generally reached in the mid-twenties, after which there is a slow and gradual decline into the early forties. Thus during the period when adjustment problems are the most numerous and difficult, the individual is physically able to meet and solve them.

Motor Abilities
The individual reaches the peak of his strength between the ages of twenty and thirty. Maximum speed of response comes between twenty and twenty-five years, after which decline begins at a slow rate. In learning new motor skills, the adult in his early twenties is superior to the one who is

approaching middle age. Furthermore, the young adult can count on his ability to perform in a given situation, which he could not do in adolescence when rapid and uneven growth often caused him to be awkward and clumsy.

Mental Abilities
The most important mental abilities needed for learning and for adjustment to new situations, such as recall of previously learned material, reasoning by analogy, and creative thinking, reach their peak during the twenties and then begin a slow and gradual decline. Even though the young adult may not learn quite as fast as he did earlier, the quality of his learning does not deteriorate.

CHANGES IN INTERESTS

Typically, the individual carries over into the adult years many of the interests he acquired during adolescence or even during childhood. Interests change during the adult years, however; some are no longer appropriate to the adult role, and others do not provide the satisfaction they did earlier. Box 9-3 gives some of the major reasons for changes in interests during early adulthood.

Changes in interests occur most rapidly during adolescence, which is also a period of rapid physical and psychological changes.

Box 9-3. CONDITIONS RESPONSIBLE FOR INTEREST CHANGES IN ADULTHOOD

Changes in Life Pattern
The young adult must reassess his old interests in terms of the time, energy, money, and companionship they entail to see whether they fit into his new life pattern and can give him as much satisfaction as they did earlier.

Changes in Values
The new values the individual acquires influence his already-existing interests or lead to new ones.

Sex-Role Changes
The pattern of adult women's lives differs markedly from that of adult men's lives, with the result that sex differences in interests become greater than they were earlier.

Changes from Single to Married Status
Because their life patterns differ, unmarried adults develop different interests from those of married adults of the same age level.

Changes in Preferences
Likes and dislikes, which have a profound influence on interests, tend to become stronger with age, and this leads to increased stability of interests in adulthood.

Changes in Cultural and Environmental Pressures
Because at every age interests are influenced by pressures from the social group, as social-group values change, so do interests.

As these physical and psychological changes slow down, so do interest changes. As Strong has pointed out, at "twenty-five years the adult is largely what he is going to be and even at twenty years he has acquired pretty much the interests he will have throughout life" (122).

The adult tends to narrow down the range of his interests, rather than change them entirely, and as a result he has fewer interests as he approaches middle age than he did during the years of early maturity. As duties and responsibilities change, there is normally a shift of emphasis on already-existing interests rather than the establishment of new ones. Most individuals do not acquire new interests as they grow older unless their environments change or they have the opportunity to develop new interests and a strong desire to do so.

Although the range of interests among young adults is extremely wide, certain interests may be regarded as typical for young adults in the American culture of today. The most important and common of these are discussed below.

Physical Appearance

By adulthood, most men and women have learned to accept their physiques and to make the most of them. Although their physical appearance may not be to their liking, they have learned that little can be done to alter it but that much can be done to improve it. As a result, the adult's major concern with his appearance is in improving it, and this leads to interest in beauty aids and in dieting and exercise. The adult's interest in his looks begins to wane during the late twenties, but it revives at the first signs of aging and becomes stronger as these signs appear with greater frequency and severity.

The first indication of aging that the young adult is confronted with is usually gain in weight. Men, as a whole, are less concerned about weight gain than women. However, these attitudes vary according to socioeconomic status. As Packard has pointed out (100):

As you go up the class scale, you find an increasing number of fat men. Among women, the opposite is true. You rarely see a really plump woman on the streets of the well-to-do suburbs surrounding New York. The slim figure is more of a preoccupation with women of the two upper classes. As you go down the scale, the married women take plumpness more calmly.

In addition to gaining weight, other signs of aging, such as sagging chins, gray hairs, and protruding abdomens, become problems for the young adult. Some accept these signs of aging without attempting to correct them. Most, however, recognize the important role appearance plays in business, social, professional, and even family life, and they try to correct the problem—by dieting, for example—and they also use clothes and beauty aids to camouflage the telltale signs of aging.

Clothes and Personal Adornment

Interest in clothing and personal adornment remains strong during early adulthood, as it was in adolescence. Because the young adult knows that appearance is important to success in all areas of his life, he frequently spends more time and money on clothing and grooming than he can afford. Box 9-4 gives some of the important roles played by clothes in the personal and social adjustments of young adults.

Interest in clothes does not lag as adulthood progresses, but remains strong or may even increase in intensity if the individual becomes aware that attractive, expensive clothing will help him succeed in an area that is important to him.

Symbols of Maturity

The young adult feels the need to impress upon his parents and other adults the fact that he is no longer an adolescent, but a full-fledged adult with the accompanying rights, privileges, and responsibilities. This arouses an interest in symbols of maturity.

As is true of all status symbols, symbols of maturity must be apparent to others in order to have an impact. Thus young adults

For many young adults, the most important status symbol is a home of their own. (Suzanne Szasz)

are interested in such symbols of maturity as adult styles of grooming and dress, patterns of speech and behavior that proclaim adult status, autonomy in all areas of life, and a name that suggests adult status, rather than a pet name used by family members or a nickname given by members of the peer group. Once the individual has established himself as an adult through his vocation or through marriage, his need for symbols of maturity wanes, and there is a decreased interest in these symbols.

Material Possessions

Because the individual's clothes, home, cars, and other possessions are indications of his social and economic status, the typical young man of today is eager to rise as fast as possible in the business world in the hope of acquiring material possessions that will proclaim high status.

While an automobile is a major status symbol for the adolescent, a home is the most important material possession of the young adult. Although a home may be important to older people mainly in terms of comfort, to the young adult it means prestige in the eyes of others. Packard has explained this as follows (100):

One reason the home is replacing the automobile as a favored way for demonstrating status is that a home can be a showcase for "culture." In a home you can display antiques, old glassware, leather-bound books, classical records, paintings. These are things a car can't do.

Money

The young adult is interested in money because of what it can do for him *now*, rather than in the future. He believes that if he can have and do the things that other young adults he wants to be identified with have and do, this will increase his chances for acceptance and solidify the acceptance he has already achieved.

Some of the problems relating to money that young adults face come from lack of knowledge of how to use money wisely or from values they have carried over from the peer-group standards of adolescence. As adolescents, they were concerned primarily with earning enough money for their needs or getting enough from their parents. They showed little interest in the management of the family finances and little desire to learn about the costs involved in family living.

Furthermore, as adolescents or even as young adults living with their families before marriage, they had little training in the use of money. Parents may advise younger adolescents on the use of their allowances, but older adolescents usually have complete freedom to use their money as they wish. As a result, they are ill prepared, as young adults, to budget the income they have to live on, and they frequently buy on credit or use installment plans, thus putting themselves in a position where they are always in debt.

Religion

By the time the individual reaches adulthood, either he has resolved his religious doubts and formulated a philosophy of life, based on religion, that is satisfactory to him or he has rejected religion as having little or nothing to offer him. In either case, he is less interested in religion than he was

---

Box 9-5. FACTORS INFLUENCING RELIGIOUS INTEREST IN EARLY ADULTHOOD

Sex
Women tend to be more interested in religion than men and to take a more active part in religious observances and church affairs.

Social Class
Members of the middle class are, as a group, more interested in religion than those of the upper and lower classes; they participate more in church functions of all kinds, and they assume leadership roles in different church organizations. Adults who are anxious to improve their social status in the community are more active in religious organizations than those adults who are satisfied with their status.

Place of Residence
Adults who live in rural and suburban areas tend to show a greater interest in religion than those who live in urban areas.

Family Background
Adults who were brought up in homes where religion played an important role and who became affiliated with a church tend to continue to show a greater interest in religion than those whose early religious experiences were less important to them.

Religious Interests of Friends
Adults are more likely to be interested in religion if their neighbors and friends are active in religious organizations than if their friends have little religious interest.

Spouses of Different Faiths
Husbands and wives of different faiths tend to be less active in religious affairs than those of the same faith.

Concern about Death
Adults who are concerned about death or who have a morbid preoccupation with death tend to be far more interested in religion than those whose attitude is more realistic.

Personality Pattern
The more authoritarian the personality pattern of the adult, the more preoccupied he is with religion per se and the more intolerant he is of other religions. The better adjusted he is, the more tolerant he is of other religions and the more he participates in religious activities.

when he was younger. That is why Peacocke has called the early twenties the "least religious period of life" (105). This lack of interest is shown by a decrease in church attendance and by an indifference to other religious observances.

When the responsibilities of parenthood are assumed, there is generally a return to religion, or at least a *show* of interest in it. Parents of young children often feel that it is their duty and responsibility not only to teach their children the fundamentals of their own faith and to see that they receive proper religious instruction in Sunday school but also to set a good example for them. Consequently, they may revive religious practices which were observed in their own homes, even if these are somewhat modified to fit into the pattern of life today. Regular attendance at church is now part of the parents' life, and they begin to take an active part in some of the church organizations. This does not, however, necessarily mean that they have experienced another period of religious awakening, as happens in early adolescence.

Many factors determine the strength and form of expression of religious interest among young adults, the most common of which are given in Box 9-5.

RECREATION IN EARLY ADULTHOOD

Young adults in the United States today have more leisure time than their parents or grandparents did and more than adults in most other cultures. This is due partly to the shorter workweek and partly to mechanization, which has made running a home less time- and energy-consuming than it formerly was. Furthermore, members of all social classes have more money to spend on recreation today than in the past.

In spite of these opportunities, many young adults do not find their recreational activities satisfactory. One of their major adjustment problems involves learning how to use their free time in an enjoyable way. There are several major reasons why recreation presents a major adjustment problem for young adults. First, while they were in school or college, various forms of recreation were readily available to them, at no cost or at only a minimum cost, and they had many friends with whom to engage in these activities. Second, parents and teachers encouraged them to participate in the readily available forms of recreation as an important part of school and college life. And third, schools and colleges provided them with guidance and supervision in recreation so that they learned how to use their leisure time in a way that gave them satisfaction.

Many factors influence the pattern of adult forms of recreation. Some of the most important of these factors are given in Box 9-6.

An analysis of the different kinds of recreational interests of American men and women today will show that they are in large part home- or neighborhood-centered and that they differ markedly from the recreational interests of adolescents. Many of these changes in interest are the result of necessity; for example, while the children are still young, many of the family's recreational activities are centered around them. Even when the children reach adolescence, the parents' recreation is largely family-centered.

Talking

Talking, especially with those whose interests are similar, is a popular pastime of both men and women. It is especially popular among married women whose household responsibilities keep them in the home for the major part of the day. Much of this talking must be done over the telephone because of the restrictions that children place on the young woman's activities. Men, by contrast, do much of their talking to friends outside the home, at work or at meeting places such as bars or recreation centers.

Box 9-6. FACTORS INFLUENCING ADULT RECREATION

Time

In spite of a shorter workweek, most young adults find that they have less time for recreation than they had as adolescents because of work or family responsibilities, obligations to community organizations, or the necessity of taking a second job so that they can acquire the status symbols they consider important. They engage in those forms of recreation which give them the greatest satisfaction or which are most practical from the point of view of time and money.

Marital Status

Young unmarried men and women not only have more time and money for different forms of recreation than those who are married but also spend more of their recreational time outside the home. In large families, much of the family-centered recreation is also home-centered—watching television and playing games with family members, for example.

Socioeconomic Status

Middle-class adults have more time for recreation, engage in a wider variety of recreational activities, spend more of their recreational time as spectators, and devote more of their recreational time to activities related to their work, such as reading, than those of the lower classes. Recreational activities of middle-class families are generally home-oriented, while those of lower-class adults involve commercial entertainments outside the home.

Sex

Regardless of marital status, young men and women must make radical changes in their recreational activities. Most of the recreational activities of women with children must be home-centered, for example. Figure 9-2 shows how women's recreational activities in early adulthood are affected by their roles as wives and mothers.

Most young adults talk mainly about personal, day-to-day concerns relating to their families, their work, and social matters. Gossiping about friends and neighbors is common among women, while men are more apt to tell jokes or discuss politics. In discussions with members of the opposite sex, women try to talk about matters of interest to men, while few men try to adapt their conversations to women's interests.

Dancing

Dancing, which is one of the most popular forms of recreation in adolescence, is engaged in only infrequently during early adulthood. Home and business responsibilities are assumed, and young adults have fewer opportunities to dance than they did during their high school and college days. Many adults, of all socioeconomic groups, dance only infrequently during their early twenties and even less during their thirties. Thus the quality of their dancing deteriorates, and they derive less satisfaction from it than they did during adolescence.

Sports and Games

Active participation in sports and athletic events of all sorts decreases during the adult years, not because adults are in poorer health or are less interested in sports, but because they have less time and money to invest in these activities than they did when they were in school or college. Participation reaches a low point as the adult approaches middle age. This is more true of members of the lower socioeconomic groups than of the middle and upper classes, who have more places such as clubs and recreation centers available to them (100).

Because they have fewer opportunities for active participation in sports, adults show their interest in this form of recreation

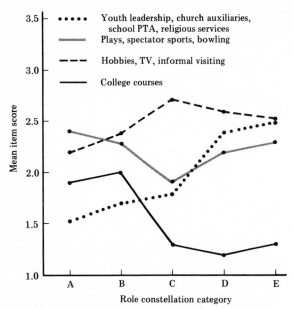

A—Single, working full time

B—Married, living with husband, childless, working at least ½ time

C—Married, living with husband, preschool children only, not working

D—Married, living with husband, preschool and school-age children, not working

E—Married, living with husband, school-age children only, not working

Figure 9-2 The pattern of female recreational activity is markedly influenced by the role the woman plays in life. (Adapted from S. S. Angrist. Role constellation as a variable in women's leisure activities. *Soc. Forces,* 1967, **45,** 423–431. Used by permission.)

by reading and talking about sports, attending athletic contests, listening to sports events on the radio, or watching them on television. This passive participation in sports increases as adults approach middle age.

Interest in games of strategy and games of chance, which began during adolescence, increases during adulthood. Games of strategy, where winning is dependent on the skill of the player—bridge, for example—appeal more to adults of the middle and upper socioeconomic groups. Games of chance, where winning depends on luck rather than

skill, appeal more to members of the lower socioeconomic groups. Women enjoy bingo, while men like poker, though these games are by no means limited to members of one sex or one social class.

Entertaining

Limited budgets and parental responsibilities restrict the amount of entertaining young adults do. Entertaining relatives is far more common among young married adults than entertaining friends and neighbors. Even unmarried adults do relatively little entertaining, and what little they do is more often done outside the home.

Entertainment of friends and neighbors is usually informal. During the summer months, picnics or backyard barbecues, which children also attend, are the favorite forms of entertainment. Home entertainment may also include card parties, where simple refreshments are served, or small dinner or cocktail parties.

Hobbies

Many adults do not pursue hobbies until their financial position is such that they have the necessary leisure time. Others who find their work boring and frustrating take up hobbies as a form of compensation. Men and women of high intelligence have more hobbies than those of lesser abilities. As a rule, men who are vocationally the most successful pursue more hobbies than those who are less successful.

Adult hobbies are, for the most part, of a constructive nature. They include such activities as cooking, gardening, painting, sewing, knitting, crocheting, making and repairing furniture, taking pictures and developing films, playing an instrument, and collecting things. Most of these hobbies can be carried out in the home and do not require the companionship or help of others. In a survey of a large number of adults, Bliven found that constructive hobbies and gardening were most common. According to him (15):

When a typical sample was checked as to their most recent activities, it was found that after the omnipresent television, watched by three-fifths of the total, some two-fifths just "visited" with friends or relatives, and one-third worked around the house and garden. Many, of course, did two, or all three, of these things.

Amusements

While amusements—activities in which the individual is a passive participant—are enjoyed by people of all ages, they grow in popularity during adulthood. Some of the amusements that the individual enjoyed when he was younger, such as going to the movies, become less appealing as he grows older, while his interest in others grows stronger. Box 9-7 gives the most popular amusements among adults in the American culture of today.

SOCIAL INTERESTS AND ACTIVITIES

Early adulthood is frequently a lonely time for men as well as for women. Young unmarried men often find themselves at loose ends during their leisure time. Their friends of earlier years and their business associates, as is true of the unmarried woman, are occupied with family activities or with courtship. As a result, young men miss the kind of social life they enjoyed during adolescence, when there was always a congenial group to talk to or do things with.

Even the young married adult is lonely at times and misses the companionship he enjoyed during the adolescent years. Tied down with the care of young children, limited by a budget that will permit little beyond the necessities of life, and often living in a community away from family and former friends, the married adult may be as lonely as the unmarried one and in a less favorable position to solve the problem of his loneliness.

Havighurst has explained that loneliness during early adulthood occurs because this is a "relatively unorganized period in life which marks the transition from an age-graded to a social-status-graded society" (48). No longer can the individual count on readily available companionship, as he could during his school or college days. Now he must make his own way, form his own

---

Box 9-7. POPULAR AMUSEMENTS AMONG YOUNG ADULTS

Reading
Because of his many responsibilities, the young adult has limited time for reading and thus becomes more selective about what he reads. Young adults spend more time reading newspapers and magazines than books.

Listening to Music
Young adults listen to records and to music on the radio, often as a way of relieving feelings of boredom or loneliness. Some prefer popular music, a carry-over from adolescence, while others may develop a taste for classical music.

Movies
Young unmarried adults often go to the movies on dates, as they did in adolescence. Married adults go to the movies less frequently, especially if they have children, in which case they must either hire baby-sitters or limit their choice of movies to those which are suitable for children.

Radio
Many women listen to the radio while doing housework, and men may listen as they drive to and from work. The radio provides both news and entertainment.

Television
Television watching, especially in the evenings, is a favorite amusement of adults with children. The larger the family and the lower the income, the more time is spent watching television.

friendships, and establish himself through his own efforts. As he reaches the thirties, the adult, whether married or single, has usually made adjustments to these changes and has established a satisfactory and relatively stable social life for himself.

Of the many changes in social interests and activities the young adult must make, the ones described below are the most common and the most difficult. The pattern of interests established now is radically different from that of the adolescent years.

Changes in Social Participation

Participation in social activities, so important to the adolescent because of its prestige value, must, of necessity, be limited during early adulthood. During adolescence, social activities took place mainly outside the home, while the social life of young adults is for the most part centered in the home, with members of the family replacing friends as companions.

Because the pattern of life is not the same for all adults, the amount of their social participation, as well as the form it will take, varies greatly. On the whole, there is more participation in social activities outside the home as adults approach middle age, during the mid- to late thirties, than there is during the early or even the late twenties. Furthermore, the pattern of social participation and the amount of such participation differs for married adults and those who are unmarried. The most important factors influencing social participation in early adulthood are listed in Box 9-8.

Box 9-8. FACTORS INFLUENCING SOCIAL PARTICIPATION IN EARLY ADULTHOOD

Social Mobility
The more anxious the adult is to improve his social status, the more he tries to become affiliated with the community organizations that will help him rise on the social ladder.

Length of Residence in the Community
Many young adults who must move to a new community become active participants in community organizations as a way of meeting people and forming friendships.

Social Class
Upper- and middle-class adults belong to more community organizations, are more active in these organizations, and assume more leadership roles in them than lower-class adults. They also have more intimate friends, entertain and visit more, and spend less time with relatives than do members of the lower classes.

Environment
The social life of young adults living in cities may center more around relatives than that of young adults who live in rural and suburban areas, where there is more "neighborliness" and social participation.

Sex
Married men are freer to engage in social activities outside the home than married women who often must limit their social participation to the home or immediate neighborhood. Unmarried women, however, are often more active in community life than men.

Age of Sexual Maturing
Men who matured early are more active in community affairs and more often play leadership roles than men who matured late. Women who were early maturers continue to be socially active in adulthood if circumstances in their lives permit this.

Birth Order
Firstborns, many of whom suffer from feelings of insecurity, tend to be "joiners" and are more active in community affairs than those who were born later.

Changes in Friendships

The craving for popularity and for a large number of friends, which started to wane during the latter part of adolescence, wanes still further during early adulthood. This is especially true of married men and women, who have each other for companionship and whose lives center around home and family responsibilities. Even unmarried adults, however, are more selective in their choice of friends than they were earlier. As a result, the individual has fewer but more intimate friends than he did when he was younger.

As is true at every age, friends in adulthood are selected on the basis of congeniality. The adult finds people whose interests and values are similar to his more congenial than those whose interests are different or who do not use the same values in judging people and behavior. As Packard has emphasized, "For better or worse, most people feel more at ease with their own kind" (100).

Changes in Social Groupings

The same degrees of friendship that existed in adolescence continue into adulthood. The adult has a small group of intimate friends or confidants; frequently these are old friends, unless his interests have changed so much that he no longer finds his old friends congenial.

How many intimate friends the adult has depends also on how much he is willing to disclose to them about his interests, problems, and aspirations. Many adults are reticent about discussing their personal affairs with outsiders as they grow older, partly because they want to create a favorable impression of themselves and partly because they do not want to run the risk of having their personal affairs discussed with others.

In addition to his intimate friends, the adult knows a number of people whom he sees fairly infrequently, as at parties or other social gatherings. On the outer rim of the friendship circle are many acquaint-

Most young adults have fewer but more intimate friends than they had during adolescence. (Suzanne Szasz)

ances whom the individual knows only slightly and with whom he comes in contact infrequently.

By the late thirties or mid-forties, most men and women have a circle of friends as large as they want. Because their interests are stabilized by this time, they are less likely to change friends than they were when they were younger. This results in a tightly knit social group, similar to the cliques of early adolescence, which is difficult for outsiders to penetrate. One of the problems of occupational mobility (to be discussed later in this chapter) is the difficulty of establishing new and close friendships when the family must move to a new community or to a new neighborhood in the old community.

Change in Value
Placed on Popularity

Popularity, so important to the adolescent, becomes increasingly less important as the adult approaches middle age. A few congenial friends mean more to him than a large group with whom he has less in common.

Social acceptance or the lack of it affects the adult much as it does the adolescent, but to a lesser extent. The more he is accepted by a group with which he would like to be identified, the more he conforms to group pressures. When he enjoys somewhat less than complete acceptance but sees the possibility of improving this situation, there will be a high degree of adherence to group standards. If, on the other hand, his acceptance is low, he has little motivation to conform to group standards except in public, and then only to forestall the possibility of complete rejection.

Changes in Leadership Status

Adults achieve their leadership status in different ways. Some are elected to an office in a business or community organization, while others are appointed. Some are

informal leaders in the community but are influential in that others look up to them and try to follow their patterns of behavior. Some who are elected or appointed to an office in community organizations are not perceived as influential and thus may have less influence in community life than the informal leaders.

Studies of persistence of leadership have revealed that in most cases, "once a leader, always a leader." The experience gained from leadership status in school, the prestige associated with leadership, and the self-confidence that being a leader engenders in the individual all contribute to his success in adult life.

However, whether he will continue to be a leader in adulthood depends largely on his ability and willingness to adapt himself to the wishes of the group. Most leaders have learned adaptability. As a result, they are flexible enough to adjust to groups of many different structures. This is especially true of very bright individuals who, during high school and college, participated in many extracurricular activities and played roles of leadership in these activities.

Studies of men and women who hold executive positions in business and industry and who play leadership roles in community affairs have shown that they have many of the qualities necessary for leadership in adolescence, as well as others not essential at that time. In addition, some of the qualities considered important in adolescent leaders,

---

Box 9-9. QUALITIES OF ADULT LEADERS

A high socioeconomic status
A higher level of education than the majority of the group
A realistic self-concept
Realistic goals
A high frustration tolerance
The ability to express hostility tactfully
The ability to accept success or failure gracefully
The ability and willingness to accept authority

There are fewer women than men leaders in every area of adult life. (Suzanne Szasz)

such as success in sports, are less important now. Box 9-9 gives some of the characteristic qualities of adult leaders.

Because of the prestige that accompanies leadership, a leader in one area may find himself in leadership roles in areas where his abilities and training are limited. As Marak has pointed out, "A leader's authority extends to many areas not justified by his abilities, after the group members develop conceptions of him as a rewarding person" (75).

The more leadership roles the individual plays, the more confident he becomes of his ability as a leader and the more leadership skills he acquires. Lack of self-confidence and lack of leadership skills, on the other hand, are fundamentally responsible for the fact that there are fewer women leaders in every area of adult life than one would expect on the basis of the number of women participating in these areas. Even those women who played leadership roles as girls are often prevented from doing so in business, industry, or community affairs because

their home responsibilities limit the time they can devote to such activities.

SOCIAL MOBILITY

Most Americans would like to have a better education and a better social and economic status than their families. They want this not only for themselves but also for their children. This desire is especially strong among young adults who discovered during adolescence that those who were most popular and held most of the leadership roles came from the higher socioeconomic groups.

Because men and women in American society today usually achieve their highest economic and social status in middle adulthood, from thirty years of age on, the young adult is motivated to do all he can to rise above his present status as rapidly as possible. The most important factors leading to upward social mobility are given in Box 9-10.

Box 9-10. CONDITIONS FACILITATING UP-WARD SOCIAL MOBILITY

A high level of education, which lays the foundation for success in business or a profession and brings the individual into contact with higher-status people

Marriage to a higher-status person

Family "pull" in the vocational world

Acceptance and adoption of the customs, values, and symbols of a higher-status group

Money, either inherited or earned, with which to buy a better home in a better neighborhood and other material possessions that proclaim high status

Transfer of membership to a higher-status church

Active participation in prestigious community affairs

Firstborn children, especially boys, are the most likely to be given opportunities to rise above the status of their families. As Altus has pointed out, firstborns are given "greater opportunities for education which makes rise on the social ladder possible" (2).

SEX-ROLE ADJUSTMENTS

Sex-role adjustments during early adulthood are extremely difficult. Long before adolescence is over, boys and girls are well aware of the approved adult sex roles, but this does not necessarily lead to acceptance. Many adolescent girls want to play the role of wife and mother when they reach adulthood, but they do not want to be wives and mothers in the traditional sense—being subordinate to their husbands, devoting most of their time to their homes and children, and having few or no outside interests. Their reason for wanting to avoid playing the traditional female role has been explained by Arnott and Bengtson (4):

The role of "homemaker" is undervalued in the United States, where occupation is the key to the assignment of role status, and achievement and monetary value tend to pro-vide the criteria for social ranking. In contemporary America, women tend to absorb the same values as the men with whom they are educated, and to use these men as reference persons in comparing role rewards. Educated women in the "homemaker only" role may feel a sense of "relative deprivation" in the distribution of social status. A "home-maker-plus" role (such as the addition of employment to home duties) may promise greater social recognition.

The hope of today's young woman for an egalitarian marriage is based not on wishful thinking but on the realization that there have been marked changes in the adult pattern of living. For example, wives often work until their husbands finish their education or become established in business, or they take jobs in order to acquire various status symbols that the family would otherwise be unable to afford. Most important of all, young women are aware of the breakdown of the "double standard," not only in sexual and moral behavior, but also in social, business, and professional life. As Blood has pointed out, "The old symmetry of male-dominated, female-serviced family life is being altered by a new symmetry" (17).

In every culture, certain patterns of behavior are approved for men, and others for women. While sex roles in most cultures are rigidly prescribed, those in the American culture of today are less strictly defined than in the past. In fact, the traditional concepts are gradually being modified or even replaced by new, more egalitarian ones—concepts that stress similar behavior patterns for members of the two sexes. These egalitarian concepts have found acceptance among all social groups, even those which formerly held firmly to traditional concepts of the male and female roles. The traditional and egalitarian concepts of adult sex roles are given in Box 9-11.

In cultures where sex roles are rigidly prescribed, it is relatively easy for the individual to accept and adjust to the approved role for his sex because he has been trained

---

Box 9-11. CONCEPTS OF ADULT SEX ROLES

Traditional Concepts
Traditional concepts of sex roles emphasize a prescribed pattern of behavior, regardless of individual interests or abilities. They emphasize masculine supremacy and intolerance toward any trait that hints of femininity or any work that is considered "woman's work."

Men
Outside the home the man holds positions of authority and prestige in the social and business worlds; in the home he is the wage earner, decision maker, adviser and disciplinarian of the children, and model of masculinity for his sons.

Women
Both in the home and outside, the role of the woman is other-oriented in that she gains fulfillment by serving others. She is not expected to work outside the home except in cases of financial necessity, and then she does only work that serves others, such as nursing, teaching, or secretarial work.

Egalitarian Concepts
Egalitarian concepts of sex roles emphasize individuality and the egalitarian status of men and women. Roles should lead to personal fulfillment and not be considered appropriate for only one sex.

Men
In the home and outside, the man works with the woman in a companionship relationship. He does not feel "henpecked" if he treats his wife as an equal, nor does he feel ashamed if she has a more prestigious or remunerative job than he does.

Women
Both in the home and outside, the woman is able to actualize her own potentials. She does not feel guilty about using her abilities and training to give her satisfaction, even if this requires employing someone else to take care of the home and children.

---

from earliest childhood to play this role and has never been given the opportunity to play any other roles. This is not true of young American adults today. Even after they learn what the approved role for their sex is, they must accept it, and usually they must learn how to play it—a learning that is complicated by the necessity of breaking habitual patterns of behavior developed in childhood and replacing them with new patterns in adulthood.

Many young women recognize the low prestige associated with the traditional role of wife and mother, and consequently they have little motivation to learn this role. When they become wives and mothers, they see little opportunity for escape from this role into one they previously found more satisfying and personally rewarding. Conflict between what they would like to do and what they know they must do further weakens their motivation to play the traditionally prescribed sex role.

PERSONAL AND SOCIAL HAZARDS OF EARLY ADULTHOOD

The major personal and social hazards of early adulthood stem from a failure to master some or most of the important developmental tasks for that age, making the individual seem immature as compared with other young adults. Up to age thirty, it is quite common for both men and women to be immature in certain areas of their behavior, while at the same time showing marked maturity in others. Gradually, with new achievements and new expectations from the social group, much of the immaturity that characterized behavior in the early part of this period disappears, resulting in more even development on a more mature level.

Mastering developmental tasks is difficult at any age, and this difficulty is increased when stumbling blocks impede the individual's progress. The most common stumbling blocks to the mastery of the devel-

The egalitarian concept of sex roles holds that a role should not be considered appropriate for only one sex. (Josephus Daniels from Rapho Guillumette)

opmental tasks of early adulthood are given in Box 9-12.

The person who has difficulty mastering the developmental tasks of adulthood finds it hard to cope with the problems that characteristically arise during this period. If he is not coping satisfactorily with these problems by the time he reaches his thirties, the individual feels unhappy and inadequate. In reporting on the studies of Rogers at the University of London, Schmeck has pointed out (112):

From these studies it appears that a particularly high risk period for divorce, unhappy extramarital affairs and other crises of personal life comes when man and wife are in their thirties. The studies also show that the young executive or professional man may suddenly see himself as not on a ladder leading upward but on a treadmill leading to nothing but old age and death. The result is sometimes a severe dislocation of career, sometimes, instead, it is a sudden rash of accidents or even attempted suicide.

Failure to master the developmental tasks of early adulthood, resulting in a failure to come up to social expectations in different areas of behavior, affects the individual's personal and social adjustments. For example, the young adult who clings to youthful interests and fails to develop more mature ones is judged by others as immature, leading to feelings of unhappiness. Similarly, much of the discontent experienced by young adults is due to the fact that they have fewer material possessions than they want or than their friends and neighbors have—an attitude that is a carryover from adolescence. This is especially true of young adults who married in their teens or while they were still students and dependent on their parents or on scholarships for support. Herrmann has explained how seriously this can affect their adjustments to marriage (52):

The optimistic expectations of teenagers about their first home after marriage and the high priority assigned to car ownership both appear to be potential sources of financial problems for teenagers entering marriage . . . these expectations and attitudes are almost certain to be carried over into marriage and are almost equally certain to become stumbling blocks for young couples.

Religious Hazards

The most difficult problem related to religion in early adulthood occurs in mixed marriages when in-laws pressure the couple to adopt one or the other faith. Even when the young adult has little interest in religion, he resents being forced to accept another faith, he objects to having the religious training of his children dictated by grandparents on either side, and he resents

---

Box 9-12. STUMBLING BLOCKS TO MASTERY OF DEVELOPMENTAL TASKS OF EARLY ADULTHOOD

Inadequate Foundations
The more unfinished business, in the form of un-mastered earlier developmental tasks, the individual carries into adulthood, the longer and harder his adjustment to adulthood will be.

Physical Handicaps
Poor health or physical defects that prevent the individual from doing what others of his age can do make mastery of the developmental tasks of adulthood difficult or impossible.

Discontinuities in Training
When training received at home or in school has little or no relationship to the individual's pattern of life in adulthood, he will be ill prepared to meet the demands of adult life.

Overprotectiveness
The adult who was overprotected during childhood and adolescence may find adjustment to adult life

extremely difficult. Many parents continue to over-protect their grown sons and daughters.

Prolongation of Peer-Group Influence
The longer the young adult continues his education, the longer peer-group influences will prevail and the more the individual will continue in behavior that conforms to peer-group values. Because he has become accustomed to behaving as an adolescent, learning to behave as an adult is more difficult than it otherwise would be.

Unrealistic Aspirations
The adult who was extremely successful athletically, academically, or socially in high school or college is likely to have unrealistic concepts of his abilities and expect to be equally successful in the adult world. Parental aspirations during adolescence often add to the adjustment problems of adulthood.

---

the implication that his religion is inferior to that of his mate—an implication inherent in the insistence that the change be made.

Furthermore, he has to contend with the pressures of his own parents, to whom adherence to the family faith may also be important. Adjustment problems in religion often complicate marital adjustments and are at the basis of "in-law" problems, one of the most difficult problems in the area of marital adjustments, as will be explained in the following chapter.

Social Hazards

Several conditions can make it difficult for the young adult to master the developmental task of finding a congenial social group. Women who are tied down by home responsibilities may have neither the time nor the money for the social activities they formerly enjoyed and may be unable to find satisfactory substitutes. This results in un-

happiness and discontentment which often affects their marital satisfaction. This is true of men as well as women; see Figure 9-3. Even when they have the time and money for social activities, some adults find it difficult to establish warm, friendly relationships with the people with whom they come in contact. This may be due to lack of congeniality, resulting from differences in interests and values, but more often it is due to the competitive spirit many young adults develop in their hopes of climbing the vocational ladder–a spirit which becomes habitual and carries over into their social relationships (40).

The adult who was accustomed to playing a leadership role in adolescence now finds it difficult to play the role of follower, should circumstances require this. A man who was a leader in his school and college days because he was a "football hero," for example, becomes frustrated when leadership roles in business, industry, or commu-

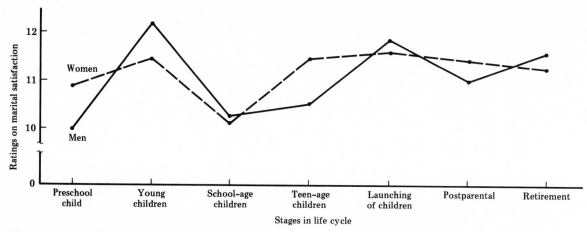

Figure 9-3 Satisfaction with social activities affects marital satisfaction among both men and women. (Adapted from W. R. Burr. Satisfaction with various aspects of marriage over the life cycle: A random middle class sample. *J. Marriage & Family,* 1970, **32,** 29–37. Used by permission.)

nity affairs go to men who have a higher socioeconomic status or more prestige in the community than he has.

Social mobility presents some of the most serious hazards in the area of social adjustments. The socially mobile person faces far more social dilemmas than the relatively immobile one because he must adjust to new social groups with new values and standards of behavior. Families that are upwardly mobile move to better neighborhoods, give up old associations and values, choose between associations with members of two classes, join new social organizations, and give up most of the social life they enjoyed with former neighbors. This increases the loneliness that is characteristic of early adulthood and may lead to depression.

Equally serious, social mobility often causes stress in the family, not only between husband and wife, but between parents and children as well. The husband will be critical of his wife if he feels that she is not presenting a favorable image to the new neighbors. Also, parents who are anxious to have their children become associated with the "better" group in their new neighborhood may become aggressive and punitive in their treatment of them.

Individuals who are forced to move downward in the social hierarchy find that they have little in common with the members of the social class with which they are now identified. As a result, they tend to isolate themselves. Furthermore, their former friends and neighbors are likely to drop them because they no longer live in the same neighborhood or can afford the social activities they formerly engaged in.

Sex-Role Hazards

Because of the conflict concerning approved sex roles today, adherence to either traditional or egalitarian concepts presents hazards. Adherence to traditional concepts of sex roles has a marked influence on a young adult's personal adjustments. For example, a man may go to any lengths to prove to himself and others that he is typically masculine. He may overtax his strength, disregarding warning signals of poor health in the belief that it is unmasculine to worry about one's health, or he may devalue feminine characteristics to the point where he tries constantly to assert his superiority in his relationships with women.

Women, as a result of being looked upon

and treated as inferior to men, often develop a typical "minority-group complex"—an emotionally toned belief in their own inferiority, not unlike that experienced by members of minority religious or racial groups.

In addition, married women often feel "trapped" in a situation they had not anticipated and from which they see little hope of escape. If the wife and mother finds that those for whom she has sacrificed her personal interests do not appreciate her efforts; if she finds the work she must do dull, lonely, confining, and below her abilities and training; and if she finds the romance she had associated with the role of a married woman lacking, she becomes disillusioned and resentful. See Figure 9-4.

This unfavorable attitude is exaggerated by the "lazy-husband syndrome." The wife feels resentful when she sees her husband taking it easy and enjoying himself while she works more or less continuously from morning to night, seven days a week. The lazy-husband syndrome has been described this way (93):

The picture is one of a husband who has had a "long" eight hour day at his air-conditioned office and who comes home, calls for a drink, plops exhausted into a chair with the newspaper or in front of the television set, gets up to eat his dinner an hour later, complains that the meat is not well done, pecks his wife on the cheek and goes out with the bowling team, has a beer, comes home, watches some more television, and plops into bed. Meanwhile, his wife, who has been working all day, gets the meal, tries to discipline the children so Daddy can rest, feeds the infant, serves the meal, does the dishes, feeds the dog, bathes the kids, puts them to bed, puts a load of washing through, does some ironing, watches TV for an hour (while darning). . . . This goes on day after day. The husband is happy but the woman becomes vaguely unhappy, tense and fatigued.

Even unmarried women, who do not have to divide their time and energies

Figure 9-4 For many women, the role of "only a housewife" leads to disillusionment and resentment. (Lou Erickson. *The Atlanta Journal and Constitution,* Jan. 28, 1974. Used by permission.)

between family and career and who do not suffer from the feeling of being trapped, often find barriers to advancement in their chosen fields of work. They find that men, less able than they, often receive larger salaries and are given positions with greater prestige and responsibility, mainly because the policy of the organization for which they work favors men.

The most important developmental tasks of early adulthood involve adjustments to marriage and parenthood and to a vocation. These are discussed in detail in the following chapter. Sex roles are fundamentally important in both areas. If adults are to make successful adjustments to marriage and parenthood, they must play roles that are mutually satisfying to both spouses, and they must derive satisfaction from playing these roles. In addition, if they are to derive satisfaction from their roles as parents, they must select roles that both parents agree are best for their children, and they must feel confident of their abilities to play these roles successfully.

Sex-role adjustment is fundamental to

vocational adjustment, just as it is to marital adjustment. For example, a man cannot be satisfied with a "masculine" vocation that he selected because of parental or social pressure when his real interest is in a vocation that is regarded as "feminine." Work dissatisfaction is not limited to the job; it soon becomes generalized and colors every area of the individual's life.

Women, accustomed during their school and college days to playing egalitarian roles with their male peers, find it hard to adjust to the treatment they receive in industry, business, and the professions. Playing a subordinate role as an adult, after playing an egalitarian or near-egalitarian role during the formative years, makes adjustment to their vocational roles far more difficult than it would be if they had played subordinate roles earlier.

Chapter Highlights

1 Early adulthood extends from age eighteen until approximately age forty, when the physical and psychological changes that accompany the beginning of the loss of the reproductive capacity start to appear.

2 Early adulthood is the "reproductive age" and the "settling-down" age. It is also a time of many personal, social, and vocational problems leading to emotional tension; a time of social isolation and loneliness; a time of value changes; and a time when the individual ordinarily approaches the peak of his achievement and creativity.

3 To become personally and socially well adjusted, the individual must master the developmental tasks of adulthood. For the most part, these are continuations of the developmental tasks of adolescence.

4 As the adult's role in life changes, he acquires new interests or puts greater emphasis on those acquired earlier, especially interests in appearance, clothes, symbols of maturity, material possessions, money, and religion.

5 Even though young adults have more leisure time today than in the past, their opportunities for recreation are often limited by environmental or economic obstacles. Thus they usually concentrate on such recreational activities as entertaining friends and relatives, watching television, pursuing hobbies that can be carried out alone, and reading.

6 Social activities, so important during adolescence, must often be limited during early adulthood because of family obligations, economic pressures, or conditions arising from social mobility.

7 The young adult wants a smaller number of friends whose interests and values are similar to his, rather than many friends, as he did in adolescence.

8 As changes in friendship values occur, there are changes in social groupings and in the value attached to popularity.

9 Leaders in adult vocational or social life are generally those who played leadership roles in adolescence.

10 Social mobility, more common in early adulthood than later, is facilitated by such factors as a high level of education, money, family "pull" in the vocational world, and participation in prestigious community affairs.

11 Sex-role adjustments are especially difficult for women during early adulthood if their roles during their school and college years were similar to those of boys.

12 The major personal and social hazards of early adulthood stem from a failure to master the most important developmental tasks for this age level. Such failure can be the result of inadequate foundations, overprotection during childhood and adolescence, prolongation of peer-group influences, and unrealistic aspirations.

Bibliography

1 Adams, B. N. Occupational position, mobility, and the kin of orientation. *Amer. sociol. Rev.,* 1967, **32,** 364–377.

2 Altus, W. D. Birth order and its sequelae. *Science,* 1966, **151,** 44–49.

3 Angrist, S. S. The study of sex roles. *J. soc. Issues,* 1969, **25**(1), 215–232.

4 Arnott, C., & Bengtson, F. L. "Only a homemaker": Distributive justice and role choice among married women. *Sociol. soc. Res.,* 1970, **54,** 495–507.

5 Arsenian, S. Change in evaluative attitudes during twenty-five years. *J. appl. Psychol.,* 1970, **54,** 302–304.

6 Babchuk, N. Primary friends and kin: Study of the associations of middle class couples. *Soc. Forces,* 1965, **43,** 485–493.

7 Babchuk, N., Crockett, H. J., & Ballweg, J. A. Change in religious affiliation and family stability. *Soc. Forces,* 1967, **45,** 551–555.

8 Balswick, J. O., & Peek, C. W. The inexpressive male: A tragedy of American society. *Family Coordinator,* 1971, **20,** 363–368.

9 Barrett, C. L., & Noble, H. Mothers' anxieties versus the effects of long distance move on children. *J. Marriage & Family,* 1973, **35,** 181–188.

10 Baumrind, D. From each according to her ability. *School Review,* 1972, **80,** 161–197.

11 Bayley, N. Research in child development: A longitudinal perspective. *Merrill-Palmer Quart.,* 1965, **11,** 183–208.

12 Becker, H. S. Personal changes in adult life. *Sociometry,* 1964, **27,** 40–53.

13 Bischof, L. J. *Adult psychology.* New York: Harper & Row, 1969.

14 Blank, L., Sugerman, A. A., & Roosa, L. Body concern, body image and nudity. *Psychol. Rep.,* 1968, **23,** 963–968.

15 Bliven, B. Using our leisure time is no easy job. *The New York Times,* Apr. 26, 1964.

16 Block, J. H. Conceptions of sex role: Some cross-cultural and longitudinal perspectives. *Amer. Psychologist,* 1973, **28,** 512–526.

17 Blood, R. C. Long-range causes and consequences of the employment of married women. *J. Marriage & Family,* 1965, **27,** 43–47.

18 Booth, A. Sex and social participation. *Amer. sociol. Rev.,* 1972, **37,** 183–193.

19 Brogan, C. L. Changing perspectives on the role of women. *Smith Coll. Stud. soc. Wk.,* 1972, **42,** 155–173.

20 Broverman, I. K. Sex-role stereotypes: A current appraisal. *J. soc. Issues,* 1972, **28**(2), 59–78.

21 Brown, F. Changes in sexual identification and role over a decade and their implications. *J. Psychol.,* 1971, **77,** 229–251.

22 Burr, W. R. Satisfaction with various aspects of marriage over the life cycle: A random middle class sample. *J. Marriage & Family,* 1970, **32,** 29–37.

23 Butler, E. W., McAllister, R. J., & Kaiser, E. J. The effects of voluntary and involuntary residential mobility on males and females. *J. Marriage & Family,* 1973, **35,** 219–227.

24 Calderone, M. S. New roles for women. *School Review,* 1972, **80,** 275–279.

25 Cantril, H. A study of aspirations. *Scient. American,* 1963, **208**(2), 41–45.

26 Chafe, W. H. *The American woman: Her changing social, economic and political roles, 1920–1970.* New York: Oxford University Press, 1972.

27 Clifford, C., & Cohn, T. S. The relationship between leadership and personality attributes perceived by followers. *J. soc. Psychol.,* 1964, **64,** 57–64.

28 Cline, V. B., & Richards, J. N. A factor-analytic study of religious belief and behavior. *J. Pers. soc. Psychol.,* 1965, **1,** 569–578.

29 Compton, N. H. Body perception in relation to anxiety among women. *Percept. mot. Skills,* 1969, **28,** 215–218.

30 Dahlstrom, E. (Ed.) *The changing social roles of men and women.* Boston: Beacon Press, 1971.

31 Darden, E. Masculinity-femininity body rankings by males and females. *J. Psychol.,* 1972, **80,** 205–212.

32 DeFleur, M. L. Mass communication and social change. *Soc. Forces,* 1966, **44,** 314–326.

33 Deutsch, D. Woman's role: An Adlerian view. *J. indiv. Psychol.,* 1970, **26,** 122–123.

34 Donald, M. N., & Havighurst, R. J. The meaning of leisure. *Soc. Forces,* 1959, **37,** 355–360.

35 Dunkelberger, C. J., & Tyler, L. E. Interest stability and personality traits. *J. counsel. Psychol.,* 1961, **8,** 70–74.

36 Eisdorfer, C., & Lawton, M. P. (Eds.) *The psychology of adult development and aging.* Washington: APA, 1973.

37 Elder, G. H. Achievement motivation and intelligence in occupational mobility: A longitudinal analysis. *Sociometry,* 1968, **31,** 327–354.

38 Elder, G. H. Role orientations, marital age and life patterns in adulthood. *Merrill-Palmer Quart.,* 1972, **18,** 3–24.

39 Ellis, R. A., & Lane, W. C. Social mobility and career orientation. *Sociol. soc. Res.,* 1966, **50,** 280–296.

40 Erikson, E. H. *Identity: Youth and crisis.* New York: Norton, 1968.

41 Evans, O. Married, working, 30 years old: Is there room for a child? *The New York Times,* June 6, 1973.

42 Feibleman, J. H. The leisurely attitude. *Humanitas,* 1972, **8,** 279–285.

43 Goode, E. Social class and church participation. *Amer. J. Sociol.,* 1966, **72,** 102–111.

44 Gording, E. J., & Match, E. Personality changes of certain contact lens patients. *J. Amer. Optom. Ass.,* 1968, **39,** 266–269.

45 Gould, R. L. The phases of adult life: A study in developmental psychology. *Amer. J. Psychiat.,* 1972, **129,** 521–531.

46 Hamid, P. N. Some effects of dress cues on observational accuracy, a perceptual estimate, and impression formation. *J. soc. Psychol.,* 1972, **86,** 279–289.

47 Harrell-Bond, B. E. Conjugal role behavior. *Hum. Relat.,* 1969, **22,** 77–91.

48 Havighurst, R. J. *Human development and education.* New York: Longmans, 1953.

49 Havighurst, R. J., & Feigenbaum, K. Leisure and life style. *Amer. J. Sociol.,* 1959, **64,** 396–404.

50 Hawkins, L. F. Urbanization, families, and the church. *Family Coordinator,* 1969, **18,** 49–53.

51 Helson, R. Personality characteristics and developmental history of creative college women. *Genet. Psychol. Monogr.,* 1967, **76,** 205–256.

52 Herrmann, R. O. Expectations and attitudes as a source of financial problems in teen-age marriages. *J. Marriage & Family,* 1965, **27,** 89–91.

53 Ivancevich, J. M., & Donnelly, J. H. Leader influence and performance. *Personnel Psychol.,* 1970, **23,** 539–549.

54 Jackson, E. F., Fox, W. S., & Crockett, H. J. Religion and occupational achievement. *Amer. sociol. Rev.,* 1970, **35,** 48–63.

55 Jarvick, L. E., Eisdorfer, C., & Blum, J. E. (Eds.) *Intellectual functioning in adults: Psychological and biological influences.* New York: Springer, 1973.

56 Jenkin, N., & Vroegh, K. Contemporary concepts of masculinity and femininity. *Psychol. Rep.,* 1969, **25,** 679–697.

57 Jones, M. C. Personality antecedents and correlates of drinking patterns in women. *J. consult. clin. Psychol.,* 1971, **36,** 61–69.

58 Jones, S. B. Geographic mobility as seen by the wife and mother. *J. Marriage & Family,* 1973, **35,** 210–218.

59 Kagan, J. The emergence of sex differences. *School Review,* 1972, **80,** 216–227.

60 Kahn, M. H., & Rudestam, K. E. The relationship between liking and perceived self-disclosure in small groups. *J. Psychol.,* 1971, **78,** 81–85.

61 Kaplan, H. B. Social class and self-derogation: A conditional relationship. *Sociometry,* 1971, **34,** 41–64.

62 Keller, S. The future role of women. *Ann. Amer. Acad. pol. soc. Sci.,* 1973, **408,** 1–12.

63 Koppe, W. A. The psychological meanings of housing and furnishings. *Marriage fam. Living,* 1955, **17,** 129–132.

64 Kurtz, R. M. Sex differences and variations in body attitudes. *J. consult. clin. Psychol.,* 1969, **33,** 625–629.

65 Lambert, S. Reactions to a stranger as a function of style of dress. *Percept. mot. Skills,* 1972, **35,** 711–712.

66 Landers, D. M. Sibling-sex-status and ordinal position effects on females' sport participation and interests. *J. soc. Psychol.,* 1970, **80,** 247–248.

67 Laney, J. T. The new morality and the religious communities. *Ann. Amer. Acad. pol. soc. Sci.,* 1970, **387,** 14–31.

68 Laumann, E. O., & House, J. S. Living room styles and social attributes: The patterning of material artifacts in a modern urban community. *Sociol. soc. Res.,* 1970, **54,** 321–342.

69 Lerner, R. M. The development of stereotyped expectancies of body build—behavior relations. *Child Develpm.,* 1969, **40,** 137–141

70 Lester, D., & Kam, E. G. Effect of a friend dying upon attitudes toward death. *J. soc. Psychol.,* 1971, **83,** 149–150.

71 Lewis, M. Parents and children: Sex-role development. *School Review,* 1972, **80,** 229–240.

72 Lipman-Blumen, J. How ideology shapes women's lives. *Scient. American,* 1972, **226**(1)**,** 34–42.

73 Luft, J. Monetary value and the perception of persons. *J. soc. Psychol.,* 1957, **46,** 245–251.

74 Manz, W., & Lueck, H. E. Influence of wearing glasses on personality ratings: Cross cultural validation of an old experiment. *Percept. mot. Skills,* 1968, **27,** 704.

75 Marak, G. E. The evolution of leadership structure. *Sociometry,* 1964, **27,** 174–182.

76 Martin, P. C., & Vincent, E. L. *Human development.* New York: Ronald Press, 1960.

77 Martineau, P. Adulthood in the adolescent perspective. *Adolescence,* 1966, **1,** 272–280.

78 McAllister, D. J., Butler, E. W., & Kaiser, E. J. The adaptation of women to residential mobility. *J. Marriage & Family,* 1973, **35,** 197–204.

79 McClusky, H. Y., & Jensen, G. The psychology of adults. *Rev. educ. Res.,* 1959, **29,** 246–255.

80 McGahan, P. The neighbor role and neighboring in a highly urban area. *Sociol. Quart.,* 1972, **13,** 397–408.

81 Mehrabian, A., & Diamond, S. G. Effects of furniture arrangement, props, and personality on social interaction. *J. Pers. soc. Psychol.,* 1971, **20,** 18–30.

82 Mettee, D. R., Hrelec, E. S., & Wilkens, P. C. Humor as an interpersonal asset and liability. *J. soc. Psychol.,* 1971, **85,** 51–64.

83 Meyer, H. D. The adult cycle. *Ann. Amer. Acad. pol. soc. Sci.,* 1957, **313,** 58–67.

84 Miller, A. R., & Stewart, R. A. Perception of female physiques. *Percept. mot. Skills,* 1968, **27,** 721–722.

85 Mintz, N. L. Effects of esthetic surroundings. II. Prolonged and repeated experiences in a "beautiful" and "ugly" room. *J. Psychol.,* 1956, **41,** 459–466.

86 Minuchin, P. The schooling of tomorrow's women. *School Review,* 1972, **80,** 199–208.

87 Money, J., & Ehrhardt, A. A. *Man and woman, boy and girl.* Baltimore: Johns Hopkins Press, 1973.

88 Mussen, P. H. Long-term consequents of masculinity of interests in adolescence. *J. consult. Psychol.,* 1962, **26,** 435–440.

89 Neisser, E. G. Emotional and social values attached to money. *Marriage fam. Living,* 1960, **22,** 132–139.

90 Nelson, P. D. Similarities and differences among leaders and followers. *J. soc. Psychol.,* 1964, **63,** 161–167.

91 Neugarten, B. L. Education and the life cycle. *School Review,* 1972, **80,** 209–216.

92 Neugarten, B. L. Continuities and discontinuities of psychological issues into adult life. In D. C. Charles & W. R. Looft (Eds.), *Readings in psychological development through life.* New York: Holt, 1973. Pp. 348–355.

93 *New York Times* article. Variety of causes cited for a mother's fatigue. *The New York Times,* Dec. 21, 1964.

94 *New York Times* article. Many converts called nominal. *The New York Times,* July 19, 1965.

95 *New York Times* article. Lazy husbands said to fatigue wives. *The New York Times,* Apr. 3, 1966.

96 *New York Times* article. Leisure use called factor in marriage. *The New York Times,* May 11, 1966.

97 *New York Times* article. Women's rights: A vote for equal status and equal burdens. *The New York Times,* Mar. 26, 1972.

98 *New York Times* article. Moving is linked with depression. *The New York Times,* Oct. 1, 1972.

99 *New York Times* article. If you feel worthless doing family chores. *The New York Times,* Mar. 29, 1973.

100 Packard, V. *The status seekers.* New York: Pocket Books, 1961.

101 Packard, V. *A nation of strangers.* New York, McKay, 1972.

102 Paige, K. E. Women learn to sing the menstrual blues. *Psychology Today,* 1973, **7**(4), 41–46.

103 Parker, E. *The seven ages of woman.* Baltimore: Johns Hopkins Press, 1960.

104 Patterson, C. H. Are ethics different in different settings? *Personnel Guid. J.,* 1971, **50,** 254–259.

105 Peacocke, A. R. The Christian faith in a scientific era. *Relig. Educ.,* 1963, **58,** 372–376.

106 Phillips, D. L. Social participation and happiness. *Amer. J. Sociol.,* 1967, **72,** 479–488.

107 Poloma, M. M., & Garland, T. N. The married professional women: A study in the tolerance of domestication. *J. Marriage & Family,* 1971, **33,** 531–540.

108 Pressey, S. L., & Kuhlen, R. G. *Psychological development through the life span.* New York: Harper & Row, 1957.

109 Rogers, D. L., Hefferman, W. D., & Warner, W. K. Benefits and role performance in voluntary organizations: An exploration of social exchange. *Sociol. Quart.,* 1972, **13,** 183–196.

110 Rosenberg, B. G., & Sutton-Smith, B. Family interaction effects on masculinity-femininity. *J. Pers. soc. Psychol.,* 1968, **8,** 117–120.

111 Ryan, M. S. *Clothing: A study in human behavior.* New York: Holt, 1966.

112 Schmeck, H. M. Mid-life viewed as crisis period. *The New York Times,* Nov. 20, 1972.

113 Schmitz-Scherzer, R., & Strödel, I. Age-dependency of leisure-time activities. *Hum. Develpm.,* 1971, **14,** 47–50.

114 Searls, L. G. Leisure role emphasis of college graduate homemakers. *J. Marriage & Family,* 1966, **28,** 77–82.

115 Segal, D. R., Segal, M. W., & Knoke, D. Status inconsistency and self-evaluation. *Sociometry,* 1970, **33,** 347–357.

116 Seward, G. H., & Williamson, R. C. (Eds.) *Sex roles in changing society.* New York: Random House, 1970.

117 Shainess, N. Is there a separate feminine psychology? *N.Y. State J. Med.,* 1970, **70,** 307–309.

118 Sherman, J. A. *On the psychology of women: A survey of empirical studies.* Springfield, Ill.: Charles C Thomas, 1971.

119 Southern, M. L., & Plant, W. T. Personality characteristics of very bright adults. *J. soc. Psychol.,* 1968, **75,** 119–126.

120 Stacey, B. Some psychological consequences of intergeneration mobility. *Hum. Relat.,* 1967, **20,** 3–12.

121 Steinmann, A., & Fox, D. R. Male-female perceptions of the female role in the United States. *J. Psychol.,* 1966, **64,** 265–276.

122 Strong, E. K. Satisfactions and interests. *Amer. Psychologist,* 1958, **13,** 449–456.

123 Sutton-Smith, B., Roberts, J. M., & Kozelka, R. M. Game involvement in adults. *J. soc. Psychol.,* 1963, **60,** 15–30.

124 *Time* article. The new woman, 1972. *Time,* Mar. 20, 1972, 25–94.

125 Tonks, C. M., Rack, P. H., & Rose, N. J. Attempted suicide and the menstrual cycle. *J. psychosom. Res.,* 1968, **11,** 319–323.

126 *U.S. News & World Report* article. Woman's changing role in America. *U.S. News & World Report,* Sept. 8, 1969, 44–46.

127 *U.S. News & World Report* article. 44 million young adults: A new wave of buyers. *U.S. News & World Report,* Jan. 17, 1972, 16–19.

128 *U.S. News & World Report* article. Leisure boom: Biggest ever and still growing. *U.S. News & World Report,* Apr. 17, 1972, 42–46.

129 *U.S. News & World Report* article. Big surge in education: Back to school for millions of adults. *U.S. News & World Report,* Apr. 2, 1973, 73–74.

130 Vogel, S. R., Broverman, I. K., Broverman, D. M., Clarkson, F. E., & Rosenkrantz, P. S. Maternal employment and perception of sex roles among college students. *Develpm. Psychol.,* 1970, **3,** 384–391.

131 Wicker, A. W., & Mehler, A. Assimilation of new members in a large and a small church. *J. appl. Psychol.,* 1971, **55,** 151–156.

132 Windham, G. O. Formal participation of migrant housewives in an urban community. *Sociol. soc. Res.,* 1963, **47,** 201–209.

133 Winick, C. The Beige Epoch: Depolarization of sex roles in America. *Ann. Amer. Acad. pol. soc. Sci.,* 1968, **376,** 18–24.

CHAPTER TEN

EARLY ADULTHOOD
Vocational and Family Adjustments

Among the developmental tasks of early adulthood, those relating to occupation and family life are the most numerous, the most important, and the most difficult to master. Even though the adult has had some work experience, has married, and has become a parent, he must now make major adjustment to these new roles.

The other developmental tasks of adulthood—finding a congenial social group, adjusting to changes in recreation necessitated by adult patterns of living, and taking on civic responsibilities, as described in the preceding chapter—are easier for the adult to master because he acquired a background of training and experience in these areas during childhood and adolescence. Thus these adjustments are mainly revisions of

patterns of behavior that have already been established.

In the case of the adjustments to be described in this chapter, the adult has less of a foundation on which to build. As a result, these adjustments are more difficult and require a longer time, and the end results are often far from satisfactory.

By far the most important aspect of the problem is the fact that the adult's success or failure in making these adjustments will affect the areas of his life most closely related to his prestige in the eyes of others, his concept of himself as an individual, and his own happiness and that of every member of his family. For these reasons they can correctly be considered the major adjustments of adulthood.

VOCATIONAL ADJUSTMENTS

To the average adult man, happiness depends largely on a satisfactory vocational adjustment. In speaking of the importance of vocations, Abramovitz has said, "Religion apart, no aspect of human affairs has such pervasive and penetrating consequences as does the way a society makes its living—and how large a living it makes" (1). This is also true of the individual because his whole pattern of life is influenced by how much he earns and how he earns it.

Because an increasing number of women, both single and married, now work, women today must also make vocational adjustments. These are likely to present an even more serious problem for women than for men because most women can find employment only in low-paying jobs and in lines of work which hold little prestige and require limited ability and training.

Some women adjust to the frustrations and resentments that are inevitable when occupational doors are shut to them or opened only slightly to comply with laws against discrimination. Many do this by wishing for their husbands the success they would have liked to achieve. Such women may have higher ambitions for their husbands than their husbands have for themselves (119).

Selection of a Vocation

Vocational adjustment becomes increasingly difficult for each successive generation of young adults. Much of this difficulty can be traced to the problems the young adult encounters in selecting a vocation. Box 10-1 gives the most common factors making vocational choice difficult.

Many young adults who have had little training for a particular line of work in high school or college go through a period during which they try out one job after another. Even though the individual's first vocational choice may have little relation to his mother's or father's occupation, his final

---

Box 10-1. FACTORS MAKING VOCATIONAL CHOICE DIFFICULT

The ever-increasing number of different kinds of work from which to choose

Rapid changes in work skills due to increased use of automation

Long and costly preparation, which makes job shifts impossible

Unfavorable stereotypes of some occupations

A desire for a job that will give the individual a sense of identity, rather than one that makes him feel like a cog in a large machine

The individual's ignorance of his own capacities due to lack of job experience or vocational guidance

Unrealistic vocational aims carried over from adolescence

Unrealistic vocational values, especially concerning prestige and autonomy

---

choice of a job is usually in the general occupational group of his parents.

Stability of Vocational Selection

Both men and women often change jobs or even lines of work during their twenties and sometimes their thirties. How stable the individual's vocational selection will be depends on two factors: job experience and vocational values.

The adult who has had *job experience* can make a far more satisfactory vocational choice than one who lacks such experience. Also, when the individual chooses a vocation that has some relation to his interests, as reflected in his choice of subjects in high school or college, he is usually more satisfied with his decision and thus less likely to change jobs.

Vocational values are an even more important factor in vocational stability than job experience. As Friedman and Havighurst have pointed out, work has different meanings for different people, whatever their occupations. It may be a source of prestige and social recognition, a basis for self-respect and a sense of worth, an opportunity for social participation, a way of being of service to others, a source of intrinsic enjoyment or of creative self-expression, or merely a way of earning a living (33).

Both men and women tend to change their vocational values as a result of experience. As they grow older, adults attach more value to independence than to interesting work or a high salary.

Stability of vocational choice has been found to increase with age. Those who change jobs do so either because their interests have changed or because they want a job with more prestige. Job changes within an occupation are more frequent than occupational changes. Professional workers change jobs least, while those in unskilled or the higher white-collar occupations change most. Skilled workers find it increasingly hard to change their occupations because of the difficulty of acquiring new skills (60). Individuals who are successful in their careers tend to be stable in their vocational choices. When such individuals do change jobs, they usually stay within their original general vocational category, and the change is the result of the individual's mature appraisal of his talents and predispositions, based on experience (120).

Women tend to be less stable in their vocational choices than men, mainly because married women, who constitute a large proportion of the female labor force, often must adapt their vocational interests to their home responsibilities or to changes in their husbands' jobs (127).

Adjustment to Work

When the adult has made a vocational selection, he must then adjust to the work itself, to the hours, to his coworkers and superiors, to the environment in which the work is done, and to the restrictions that the work imposes on his personal life. The conditions affecting the adjustments of men and women differ in some respects and are discussed separately below.

Men's Adjustments If the job allows the adult to play the role he wants to play, he will be satisfied and make good adjustments to his work. If, for example, he wants to play the role of leader, he will be satisfied with his work if he is in a position of authority over others.

The adult who is forced, because of limited education and training, to do work that is below his level of ability will derive little satisfaction from it or from the social group with which he is associated because of his work. This dissatisfaction soon spreads to all areas of the individual's life and has an adverse effect on his personal and social adjustments.

Adult men expect to be paid more each year than they were the year before and to be slightly higher up on the vocational ladder. If they see that they are advancing, they are satisfied, or at least partially satisfied.

Even climbing the vocational ladder does not necessarily guarantee good adjustments on the part of the worker. This is especially true if he thinks that his advancement is due to "pull" rather than to ability. This makes him feel inadequate for the work he is now expected to do. Sometimes a man can advance occupationally only if he moves to another community, in which case the entire family must make adjustments.

Women's Adjustments Women are often unable to find jobs suited to their abilities. This results in frustrations which militate against good adjustment to the work and to coworkers or superiors.

The working wife has additional problems. She may have to neglect many of the homemaking duties or rely on the children or outside help to assist her. The recreational activities of the family usually must be curtailed, and the mother is often too busy or too tired when she returns from work to take an active part in her children's interests. They resent this, and the home life may be far from satisfactory for the

The tasks of vocational selection and vocational adjustment are often more difficult for women. (Martha McMillan Roberts from Rapho Guillumette)

whole family. This adds to the adjustment problems arising from the work itself, as will be discussed at length later in the chapter.

Appraisal of Vocational Adjustment

How successfully the young adult adjusts to his chosen vocation can be judged by two criteria: his achievements on the job and the degree of satisfaction he and his family derive from his work and the socioeconomic status associated with it.

Achievements The desire to "get ahead" and be successful, so strong in adolescence, carries over into early adulthood. This motivates the young adult to put forth tremendous effort, often at the expense of his health, his family, and other interests. Thus he usually reaches the peak of his vocational achievement during the mid- to late thirties, as a result of initiative, ambition, and hard work.

The individual who has not made a satisfactory adjustment to his work or who has not shown at least reasonable success in it by the time he reaches middle age is not likely to do so as he grows older. By middle age, the drive for success is often replaced by a desire for security. For many adults, having a safe job now means more than climbing higher on the vocational ladder.

Relatively few men, and even fewer women, realize their vocational aspirations or even their vocational potentials. Adults may fail in this regard because of an environmental obstacle or a personal obstacle such as limited training, inadequate motivation to make the most of their training and abilities, unrealistically high aspirations, or fear of success. A person may fear vocational success because he feels inadequate to assume heavy job responsibilities. For example, a man who gets a job through "pull" may realize that he does not have the ability to handle the job successfully, and he may rationalize his poor achievements or project the blame on others when he does not do well.

Women's fear of success is far more

often the result of a feeling that success will be damaging to their image and may even lead to social rejection. Horner has explained the young woman's fear of success in this way (47):

Most highly competent and otherwise achievement motivated young women, when faced with a conflict between their feminine image and expressing their competencies or developing their abilities and interests adjust their behavior to their internalized sex-role stereotypes. . . . Among women, the anticipation of success, especially against a male competitor, poses a threat to the sense of femininity and self-esteem and serves as a potential basis for becoming socially rejected — in other words, the anticipation of *success is anxiety producing and as such inhibits otherwise positive achievement motivation and behavior. In order to feel or appear more feminine, women, especially those high in fear of success, disguise their abilities and withdraw from the mainstream of thought, activism, and achievement in our society.*

Satisfaction The degree of satisfaction the individual derives from his work is an even better index of his adjustment than his achievements are. There are, however, age cycles in vocational satisfaction for both men and women. In their early twenties, most individuals are glad to have a job, even if it is not entirely to their liking, because it gives them the independence they want and makes marriage possible. With the con-

---

Box 10-2. CONDITIONS INFLUENCING OCCUPATIONAL SATISFACTION

Opportunity to Choose Work
An adult who can choose a job in the area in which he is interested and can use his abilities and training is usually better satisfied than the one who must take what is available.

Vocational Expectations
The adult who expects his work to give him the autonomy he did not have when he was younger and to rise rapidly on the vocational ladder will become discouraged and dissatisfied with his job if his expectations are not met.

Degree of Career Orientation
A career-oriented worker is willing to work up to his capacities, to try to improve his skills, and to make personal sacrifices in terms of time and effort in the hope of achieving success.

Vocational Security
A reasonable amount of job security will contribute to the worker's satisfaction, while uncertainty — if he fears that he may be put out of work because of automation or that he may be fired, for example — makes him feel that he is "sitting on top of a volcano."

Opportunities for Advancement
The worker who sees a possibility of advancement will be far more satisfied than one who knows he is in a "dead-end" job.

Stereotypes about Jobs
A worker may be dissatisfied with his job if it is regarded unfavorably by the social group.

Nature of the Work
Work that is challenging or satisfies some need of the worker leads to satisfaction, while automated or highly routinized work leads to boredom and dissatisfaction.

Working Conditions
A reasonable amount of autonomy, the chance for congenial associations with coworkers, lack of discrimination, fair treatment and consideration from superiors, and liberal fringe benefits add to the worker's job satisfaction.

Attitudes of Significant People
The worker's satisfaction is increased when family members are proud of his job and satisfied with the salary he receives and when members of the social group regard the job favorably.

fidence of youth, they believe it will be just a matter of time until they are promoted to a better job or find one that is more to their taste. Dissatisfaction begins to set in during the mid-twenties if the individual has not risen as rapidly as he had hoped. If family responsibilities make it impossible for him to change jobs, this dissatisfaction increases. This period of unrest and dissatisfaction lasts generally until the early or mid-thirties, after which there is generally an increase in satisfaction resulting from greater achievement and better financial rewards. Most individuals in their thirties like their work, but they do not "love" it. They enjoy the social contacts work gives them, the feeling of being a part of the world of action, and the satisfaction they derive from achievement.

Within every age group, there are variations in the vocational satisfaction men and women experience. Box 10-2 gives the most important factors influencing the degree of satisfaction the worker derives from his job.

The degree of satisfaction the young adult derives from his job has a marked influence on the quality and quantity of his work. Satisfaction increases his motivation to do what he is capable of doing and to learn more about the work so that he can perform it more efficiently. It also increases his ego-involvement in his work, and this further increases his motivation.

Workers who are satisfied with their jobs become dedicated to their work and loyal to their organization. As a result, they play an important role in keeping worker morale at a high level. From the personal point of view, job satisfaction contributes to the worker's self-satisfaction, and this, in turn contributes to his happiness.

MARITAL ADJUSTMENTS

Although marital adjustment is difficult everywhere, certain factors in the American culture of today make it particularly hard. The most important of these are given in Box 10-3.

During the first year or two of marriage, the couple normally must make major adjustments to each other, to members of their families, and to their friends. This is often a very stormy period. People who marry during their thirties or in middle age frequently require a longer time for adjustment, and the end result is usually not as satisfactory as in the case of those who marry earlier.

Of the many adjustment problems in marriage, the most common and the most important for marital happiness are adjustments to a mate, sexual adjustments, adjustments to economic conditions, and in-law adjustments.

Adjustments to a Mate

Interpersonal relationships play as important a role in marriage as in friendships and business relationships. However, in the case of marriage, the interpersonal relationships are far more difficult to adjust to than in social or business life because they are complicated by factors not usually present in any other area of the individual's life.

The more experience in interpersonal relationships both the man and the woman have had in the past, the greater social insight they have developed, and the greater their willingness to cooperate with others, the better they will be able to adjust to each other in marriage.

Far more important to good marital adjustment is the ability of husband and wife to relate emotionally to each other and to give and receive love. Men who were trained during childhood to control the expression of their emotions—with the possible exception of anger—may have learned not to show affection, just as they learned not to show fear. They may also rebuff expressions of affection from others and thus seem cold and aloof to their wives—an attitude they regard as masculine.

While women have not usually been subjected to similar training, many who felt rejected by family and peers during childhood

---

Box 10-3. CONDITIONS CONTRIBUTING TO DIFFICULTY IN MARITAL ADJUSTMENT

Limited Preparation for Marriage
Although sexual adjustments may be easier now than in the past because of more readily available sex information in the home, schools, and colleges, most couples have received little preparation in the areas of domestic skills, child rearing, getting along with in-laws, and money management.

Roles in Marriage
The trend toward changes in marital roles for both men and women and the different concepts of these roles held by different social classes and religious groups make adjustment problems in marriage more difficult now than in the past, when these roles were more rigidly prescribed.

Early Marriage
Early marriage and early parenthood deprive the young couple of the opportunity to have many of the experiences that their unmarried contemporaries have and to become economically independent before they assume the responsibilities of marriage and parenthood.

Mixed Marriage
Adjustments to parenthood and to in-laws—which are important to marital happiness—are much more difficult in the case of mixed marriages.

Shortened Courtships
The courtship period is shorter now than in the past, and thus the couple has less time to solve many of the problems related to adjustment before they are actually married.

Romantic Concepts of Marriage
Many adults have a romantic concept of marriage developed in adolescence. Overly optimistic expectations of what marriage will bring often lead to disenchantment, which increases the difficulties of adjusting to the duties and responsibilities of marriage. See Figure 10-1.

Lack of Identity
If an individual feels that his family, friends, and associates treat him as "Jane's husband," for example, he may resent the loss of his identity as an individual, which he strove hard to achieve and valued highly before marriage.

---

have learned not to show affection for others as a defense against possible rejection of that affection. A husband and wife who have the habit of not expressing affection will have difficulty establishing a warm and close relationship because each interprets the other's behavior as an indication of "not caring."

Adults who were popular throughout childhood and adolescence have acquired the ability to adjust to others and the social insight necessary to make adjustments. They have also learned to give and receive affection from their peers and to show that they enjoy being with them and value their friendship. These experiences go a long way toward making marital adjustments easier. However, other factors contribute to the ease or difficulty with which the adult adjusts to a mate in marriage; the most common of these are given in Box 10-4.

Sexual Adjustments

Sexual adjustment is unquestionably one of the most difficult adjustments to marriage, and it is the one most likely to lead to marital discord and unhappiness if it is not satisfactorily achieved. Usually the couple has had less preliminary experience related to this adjustment than to the others, and they may be unable to make it easily and with a minimum of emotional tension. Many factors influence sexual adjustments to marriage, the most important of which are given in Box 10-5. See Figure 12-2, which shows satisfaction with sex at different times during adulthood.

Financial Adjustments

Money or lack of it will have a profound influence on the adult's adjustment to marriage. Today, as a result of premarital ex-

Figure 10-1 Disillusionment with marriage is often the result of an overly romantic concept of marriage. (Adapted from *The Saturday Evening Post,* Oct. 1, 1960. Used by permission.)

Box 10-4. FACTORS INFLUENCING ADJUSTMENT TO A MATE

Concept of an Ideal Mate
In choosing a marriage partner, both men and women are guided to some extent by a concept of an ideal mate built up during adolescence. The more the individual must readjust his ideal to fit reality, the more difficult his adjustment to his mate will be.

Fulfillment of Needs
If good adjustments are to be made, a mate must fulfill needs stemming from early experiences. If the adult needs recognition, a sense of achievement, and social status to be happy, his mate must help him meet these needs.

Similarity of Backgrounds
The more similar the backgrounds of husband and wife, the easier the adjustment. However, even when their backgrounds are similar, each adult has acquired a unique outlook on life, and the more these outlooks differ, the more difficult the adjustment will be.

Common Interests
Mutual interests in things the couple can do or enjoy together lead to better adjustments than mutual interests that are not easily shared.

Similarity of Values
Well-adjusted couples have more similar values than those who are poorly adjusted. Similar backgrounds are likely to produce similar values.

Role Concepts
Each mate has a definite concept of the role a husband and wife should play, and each expects the other to play that role. When role expectations are not fulfilled, conflict and poor adjustment result.

Change in Life Pattern
Adjustment to a mate means reorganizing the pattern of living, revamping friendships and social activities, and changing occupational requirements, especially for the wife. These adjustments are often accompanied by emotional conflicts.

Box 10-5. FACTORS INFLUENCING SEXUAL ADJUSTMENTS

Attitudes toward Sex

The individual's attitudes toward sex are greatly influenced by the way he received sex information during childhood and adolescence. Once unfavorable attitudes are developed, it is difficult to eradicate them completely.

Past Sexual Experiences

The way adults and peers reacted to masturbation, petting, and premarital intercourse when the individual was younger and the way he felt about them himself affect his attitude toward sex. If a woman's earlier experiences with petting were unpleasant, for example, this may have colored her attitude toward sex unfavorably.

Sexual Desire

Sexual desire develops earlier in men than in women and tends to be persistent, while that of

women is periodic, fluctuating during the menstrual cycle. These variations affect interest in, and enjoyment of, sex, which in turn affects sexual adjustments.

Early Marital Sexual Experiences

The belief that sexual relations produce states of ecstasy unparalleled by any other experience causes many young adults to be so disillusioned at the beginning of their married lives that later sexual adjustments are difficult or even impossible to make.

Attitudes toward Use of Contraceptives

There will be less friction and emotional conflict if husband and wife agree concerning the use of contraceptives than if they feel differently about this matter.

---

perience in the business world, many wives resent not having control of the money needed to run a home, and they find it difficult to adjust to living on their husband's earnings after having been accustomed to spending their own money as they wish.

Many men also find financial adjustments very difficult, particularly if the wife worked after they were married and then must stop with the arrival of the first child. Not only is their total income reduced, but the husband's earnings must now cover a wider area of expenses.

The couple's financial situation can pose a threat to their marital adjustments in two important areas. First, friction may develop if the wife expects her husband to share the work load. During the early years of marriage, when expensive laborsaving devices and domestic help are most needed, the family usually cannot afford such luxuries, and the wife may want her husband to help share the burden of running the home. This frequently causes friction, especially when the man considers homemaking "woman's work." If the wife resents the "lazy-hus-

band syndrome," discussed in the preceding chapter, marital adjustments can be adversely affected.

The second common threat that the couple's financial situation poses to good marital adjustments comes from a desire to have material possessions as a stepping-stone to upward social mobility and a symbol of the family's success. If a husband is unable to provide his wife and family with the material possessions they want, they may feel resentful of him, and a frictional attitude develops. Many wives, faced with this problem, take jobs to provide the family with such possessions. Many husbands object to this because they feel that others will think they are unable to provide for their families as well as husbands of nonworking wives do.

In-Law Adjustments

With marriage, the adult acquires a whole new set of relatives—his in-laws. These are people of different ages, different interests, and often markedly different cultural backgrounds, and the adult must learn to adjust to them. Furthermore, they may try to exercise some control over his life, as they do with those to whom they are directly related.

In-law adjustments have been made more difficult by a number of factors which are of recent origin and which members of past generations, for the most part, were not forced to cope with. These are listed in Box 10-6.

In-law trouble is especially serious during the early years of marriage and is one of the most important causes of marital breakup during the first year. It is more serious in families where there are no children or only a few children than in large families, where in-law help is often welcome. It is also more common in middle- and upper-class groups than in lower-class groups, where the traditional concept of an enlarged family, with relatives as the chief source of companionship, is more widely held.

Certain factors have been found to contribute to good in-law adjustments. These include approval of the marriage by the parents of both spouses, opportunities for

In-law trouble is especially serious during the early years of marriage. (Suzanne Szasz)

Box 10-6. FACTORS INFLUENCING IN-LAW ADJUSTMENTS

Stereotypes
The widely accepted stereotype of the "typical mother-in-law" can lead to unfavorable mental sets even before marriage. Unfavorable stereotypes about the elderly—that they are bossy and interfering—can add to in-law problems.

Desire for Independence
Young married adults tend to resent advice and guidance from their parents, even if they must accept financial aid, and they especially resent such interference from in-laws.

Family Cohesiveness
Marital adjustments are complicated when one spouse devotes more time to relatives than the other spouse wants to, when a spouse is influenced by family advice, or when a relative comes for an extended visit or lives with the family permanently.

Social Mobility
A young adult who has risen above his family's status or that of his in-laws may want to keep them in the background. Many parents and relatives resent this, and hostile relationships with the young couple as well as marital friction may result.

Care of Elderly Relatives
Caring for elderly relatives is an especially complicating factor in marital adjustments today because of present unfavorable attitudes toward older people and the belief that young people should be independent of relatives, especially when there are children in the family.

the parents to meet and become acquainted before the marriage, and friendliness on the part of both families when they meet. In-law problems are also eased if the marriage is between persons of the same religion; if the couple has taken a course in marriage, especially the wife; if relationships between the grandparents and grandchildren are good; if the in-laws have similar patterns of social activities; if the in-laws as well as the young couple are happily married; and if husband and wife accept each other's family as their own.

ADJUSTMENT TO PARENTHOOD

As LeMasters has pointed out, "Parenthood—not marriage—marks the final transition to maturity and adult responsibility." For many young adults, as he further explains, the birth of a child is a "crisis"— "sharp and decisive changes must be made for which old patterns are inadequate" (62). The family is temporarily upset, and all family members are under varying degrees of stress.

Although the arrival of every child in the family is a crisis, the arrival of the firstborn is generally the most upsetting, partly because both parents may feel inadequate for the parental role, partly because they have highly romanticized concepts of parenthood, and partly because of the personal, social, and economic privations that parenthood brings. Mothers with professional training and experience often suffer extremely severe crisis shock because they must give up a role that was highly important to them in favor of one for which they feel inadequate.

Many fathers show a general disenchantment with the parental role by becoming less sexually responsive to their wives, worrying about economic pressures, or developing feelings of resentment at being "tied down" or excluded from the mother-child relationship. These unfavorable reactions color the father's attitudes toward fatherhood and toward his wife.

The most important factors influencing adjustment to parenthood are given in Box 10-7. Some affect women more, while others have a greater influence on men.

ASSESSMENT OF MARITAL ADJUSTMENT

No one specific pattern of living is favorable to marital adjustment. The success of a marriage depends on whether it provides satisfaction for the whole family, not just one or two of the members. For ex-

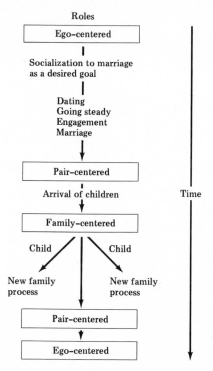

Figure 10-2 Role changes are inevitable with marriage, parenthood, and the growing up and departure of one's children. (Adapted from S. Clavan. The family process: A sociological model. *Family Coordinator,* 1969, **18**, 312–17. Used by permission.)

Box 10-7. FACTORS INFLUENCING ADJUSTMENT TO PARENTHOOD

Attitudes toward Pregnancy

The woman's attitude toward parenthood is colored by her physical and emotional condition during pregnancy. In most cases, if her attitude has been unfavorable, it improves after the baby's birth.

Attitudes toward Parenthood

Adults adjust better to parenthood if they want children because they feel they are essential to a happy marriage, rather than because of family or social pressures.

Age of Parents

Young parents tend to take their parental responsibilities lightly and not allow them to interfere too much with their other interests and pleasures. Older parents tend to be more anxious and concerned. Thus younger parents often make better adjustments.

Sex of Children

Adults' attitudes toward parenthood are more favorable if they have a child or children of the sex they prefer.

Number of Children

When adults have the number of children they consider "ideal," their adjustment to parenthood will be better than if they have more or fewer children than they want.

Parental Expectations

If parents have a "dream-child" concept, their adjustment to parenthood will be affected by how well the child measures up to this ideal.

Feelings of Parental Adequacy

Conflicts about child-training methods lead to confusion and to feelings of anxiety about doing the job well. This has an unfavorable effect on the adult's adjustment to parenthood.

Attitudes toward Changed Roles

Parenthood means that both the man and the woman must learn to play family-centered rather than pair-centered roles. See Figure 10-2. How the individual reacts to this role change will have a profound influence on his adjustment to parenthood.

The Child's Temperament

A child who is easy to manage and who is responsive and affectionate makes parents feel rewarded for their time and effort.

---

ample, a man who needs to succeed in his career in order to be happy but who feels that family duties and responsibilities are keeping him from achieving success will be dissatisfied with his marriage, and the marriage will suffer.

Marital adjustments are easier at some periods during the individual's married life than at others. As Paris and Luckey have pointed out, "There are identifiable periods in the lives of most married people that may be less happy than others" (88). The most readily identifiable periods are the first few years of marriage, when the couple must make adjustments to their new roles as spouses and parents; the period when the children reach the "troublesome teens" and tend to rebel against parental authority; and the "empty-nest" period, which requires readjustment to a childless home and loss of the parental role. Figure 10-3 shows parental satisfaction at different stages in the life cycle.

A spouse's ordinal position in his own family is an important factor in marital adjustment because it has resulted in his learning to play certain roles that he now transfers to the marital situation. The more similar the new situation is to the old one, the better his adjustment to it will be. Both men and women who were reared in homes with siblings make better adjustments to

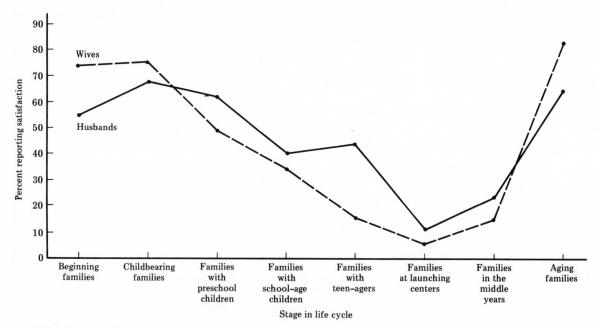

Figure 10-3 Parental satisfaction at different stages in the life cycle. (Adapted from B. C. Rollins & H. Feldman. Martial satisfaction over the family life cycle. *J. Marriage & Family,* 1970, **32,** 20–28. Used by permission.)

Box 10-8. CRITERIA OF SUCCESSFUL MARITAL ADJUSTMENT

Happiness of Husband and Wife

A husband and wife who are happy together derive satisfaction from the roles they play. They also have a mature and stable love for each other, have made good sexual adjustments, and have accepted the parental role.

Good Parent-Child Relationships

Good parent-child relationships reflect successful marital adjustment and contribute to it. If parent-child relationships are poor, the home climate will be marked by friction, which makes marital adjustment difficult.

Good Adjustment of Children

Children who are well adjusted, well liked by their peers, successful in school, and happy are proof of their parents' good adjustment to marriage and parental roles.

Ability to Deal Satisfactorily with Disagreements

Disagreements between family members, which are inevitable, generally end in one of three ways: There is a temporary truce with no solution, one person gives in for the sake of peace, or all family members try to understand the others' point of view. In the long run, only the latter leads to satisfactory adjustments though the first two help to reduce the tension that friction gives rise to.

"Togetherness"

When marital adjustments are successful, the family enjoys spending time together. If good family relationships are built up during the early, formative years, the individual will retain close ties with his family after he grows up, marries, and establishes a home of his own.

marriage than those who were only children.

For men, the best position is that of the oldest brother with younger sisters; for women, the best position is that of a younger sister with older brothers. Should the husband be the younger brother of older sisters, and the wife the older sister of younger brothers, there is likely to be a frictional marital relationship; the wife will try to "boss" her husband as she did her younger brothers. When both spouses were the oldest children in their homes, there is likely to be a highly frictional relationship, with each trying to dominate the other (39).

The success of a marriage is reflected in a number of interpersonal relationships and behavior patterns. The most important of these are given in Box 10-8.

ADJUSTMENT TO REMAINING SINGLE

The individual who does not marry is likely to be unhappy, lonely, and thwarted in his normal desires for sex, parenthood, affection from an admired member of the opposite sex, and the prestige that marriage and family living provide. In many communities there is no place for the bachelor or single woman except as an extra man at a dinner party or a baby-sitter for married relatives. There are many reasons why people remain single. The most common are given in Box 10-9.

In a culture in which marriage is the normal pattern for adult life, most adults want to marry and come under strong pressures from parents and peers to do so. Furthermore, early adulthood is a lonely time during which radical adjustments must be made in every area of life, and many adults feel that marriage will help them make these adjustments.

During their twenties, the goal of most unmarried women, whether working or not, is marriage. If they have not married by age thirty, they tend to shift their goals and

---

Box 10-9. REASONS WHY PEOPLE REMAIN SINGLE

An unattractive or sex-inappropriate appearance

An incapacitating physical defect or prolonged illness

Lack of success in the search for a mate

Unwillingness to assume the responsibilities of marriage and parenthood

A desire to pursue a career that requires working long and irregular hours or much traveling

Residence in a community where the sex ratio is unbalanced

Lack of opportunity to meet eligible members of the opposite sex

Responsibilities for aging parents or younger siblings

Disillusionment as a result of unhappy earlier family experiences or unhappy marital experiences of friends

Homosexuality

---

values and find a new life oriented toward work.

Thirty is thus a critical age for an unmarried woman, and her life may be characterized by stress as she approaches it. This reaches a peak at thirty and then gradually decreases as she makes adjustments to new goals and a new pattern of living. The desire for marriage and a family decreases after thirty as the woman realizes that she is not likely to achieve these goals.

Not all unmarried women, by any means, are willing to resign themselves to being single, nor are they all willing to allow themselves to be lonely because of lack of companionship with members of the opposite sex. They may become active in church and community-service or social organizations, where they will come in contact with members of both sexes; they may join clubs where members of both sexes engage in various sports or social activities; or they may spend their vacations at places where they are likely to meet eligible men.

It is usually easier for a man to adjust to

A sign of the times: One response to the worries and needs of "singles." (Esaias Baitel from Rapho Guillumette)

being single than for a woman. A single man is in great social demand and has little time to feel lonely. Furthermore, unless he is single because of responsibilities for family members, he is usually financially able to pursue a pattern of life that is to his liking.

Finding a satisfactory outlet for the sex drive, which is especially strong during early adulthood, is the most difficult problem the unmarried person faces. The unmarried man usually finds sexual gratification either by engaging in autoerotic practices or by having intercourse with women of his acquaintance or with prostitutes. Although women, like men, engage in autoerotic practices, they have less opportunity for sexual encounters, which are still not condoned for

women in all segments of society, and they must always face the possibility of pregnancy.

HAZARDS OF VOCATIONAL AND MARITAL ADJUSTMENTS DURING EARLY ADULTHOOD

Vocational and marital adjustments are particularly hazardous during the early years of adulthood. The young adult has fewer foundations on which to build in making adjustments in these areas than in other areas of his life, and he receives little guidance and help, as he did when making adjustments during childhood and adolescence.

Society has recognized these difficulties, and attempts have been made to eliminate some of the potential hazards of vocational and marital adjustments.

For example, the growing trend toward introducing vocational guidance in the schools, often as early as the elementary school years, is based on the belief that the individual will make a better vocational adjustment if he goes into a line of work which fits his needs and abilities and for which he has been at least partly trained while in school or college than if he enters the work world with no such preparation. Similarly, courses in family living and sex education, while far from universal in schools and colleges, are designed to ease the transition into marriage and parenthood.

Even this preparation has been found to be so far from adequate that many community agencies have been set up to provide vocational counseling and advice for dissatisfied workers, and many businesses and industries are attempting to cope with the causes of persistent worker dissatisfaction, especially boredom. Others are encouraging the more able among their dissatisfied workers to return to school or college, at night or on weekends, to prepare for jobs that are better suited to their abilities and will thus give them more satisfaction. Still other agencies are providing day care for the children of working mothers, thus enabling them to take full-time jobs and perhaps rise on the vocational ladder.

Because marital adjustments are even more serious and far-reaching in their effects on the adult's personal and social life than vocational adjustments, marriage clinics and private marriage counselors are widely available today even in small communities. Since some of the most serious marital hazards are the result of poor parent-child relationships, widespread attempts are being made to help parents cope with child-rearing problems and thus improve their marital relationships.

Even though marital and vocational adjustments are closely interrelated and influence each other, the hazards associated with each are distinct and will be discussed separately.

Vocational Hazards

The most common vocational hazard is job dissatisfaction. Although workers at all levels—white-collar, blue-collar, and professional—may become dissatisfied with their jobs, women and members of minority racial and religious groups are more apt to experience job dissatisfaction because they are subjected to discrimination and may feel they have little hope of advancing, regardless of the quality of their work (123,131).

The most common causes of job dissatisfaction are boredom, lack of autonomy, lack

"This is the part of the job I hate . . . doing the work!"

Figure 10-4 An antiwork attitude is a common vocational hazard in adulthood. (George Clark. "The Neighbors," Chicago Tribune–New York News Syndicate, Apr. 11, 1973. Used by permission.)

of congeniality with coworkers, restrictions on free time, a job that makes the worker feel like a cog in a big machine, slow advancement up the vocational ladder, and an antiwork attitude carried over from childhood and adolescence. See Figure 10-4. Job dissatisfaction is especially common among those who feel their job is below their abilities.

Job dissatisfaction is expressed in many ways, the most common of which are given in Box 10-10.

Besides affecting the worker's performance at his present job, dissatisfaction with work has many serious long-term consequences. First, motivation is lowered to the point where the worker becomes a habitual underachiever, working constantly below his capacities. As a result, he will be overshadowed when he competes with other, better-motivated workers who will exert more effort in their attempt to succeed. When women become underachievers be-

---

Box 10-10. COMMON EXPRESSIONS OF JOB DISSATISFACTION

A lowering of the worker's motivation resulting in underachievement

Complaining about all aspects of the job

Careless, slipshod work

Accident proneness

Lack of loyalty to the employer or company

Excessive absenteeism

Frequent job changes

cause they fear success, as Horner has pointed out, a high price is "paid by the individual in negative and interpersonal consequences and by the society in a loss of valuable human and economic resources" (47).

A second long-term consequence of job dissatisfaction is that the worker may verbalize his complaints and gain a reputation as a "griper" or a "troublemaker"—a reputation he may carry from one job to another.

A third consequence of job dissatisfaction is that it may color the worker's whole attitude toward work and toward those who have authority over him in the organization for which he works. Much of the aggressive hostility of workers that makes them "strike-prone" stems from the habitual dissatisfaction they experience in their work.

Many adults try to compensate for job dissatisfaction by pursuing an avocation that does give them satisfaction or by enjoying a happy home life and realizing that they are providing well for their families. A man may become active in community organizations, for example, or he may engage in a creative activity, such as painting or writing.

A less common vocational hazard is unemployment, the severity of which depends on three conditions. First, if unemployment is voluntary, the effects will be far less severe than if it is involuntary. For example, an adult who gives up his job in order to find a better one is less affected by unemployment than a worker who is fired.

Second, the length of unemployment determines how severe a psychological hazard it will be. If it lasts a relatively short time, the worker is far less seriously affected than if it is prolonged to the point where his whole standard of living must be radically revised and he thinks of himself as no longer employable.

The third and most important factor is what the worker believes to be the cause of his unemployment. Some workers tend to regard unemployment as their own fault, to think of themselves as failures, and to de-

velop defensive attitudes which militate against good adjustments to any jobs they may obtain in the future. Other workers place the blame on an antagonistic supervisor, for example. A worker who does not take the blame personally escapes many of the psychological effects that interfere with subsequent vocational adjustments.

Marital Hazards

Marital hazards center around the many conditions that contribute to poor marital adjustments, which are in turn a hazard to good personal and social adjustments. As Renne has explained: "Relations with the spouse are so central a feature of an individual's social and emotional life that an unhappy marriage may impair the capacity of both partners for satisfactory relations with their children and others outside the family" (97).

Adjustment to a Mate Good adjustment to a mate may be difficult when husband and wife have different racial, religious, or social backgrounds and thus have different interests, values, and frames of reference. This usually leads either to lack of communication or to quarreling, both of which are hazardous to good marital relationships. An equally serious obstacle to good marital adjustment is a highly romanticized concept of a mate built up before marriage—a concept that may have to be radically changed afterward. This is a more common hazard of first marriages than of subsequent ones because the individual has learned to be more realistic about a mate.

Competitiveness A more common and perhaps a more serious marital hazard is the competitive spirit many young adults develop in their attempts to achieve vocational success. While the competitive spirit is more characteristic of men than of women, women who hope to be successful in their social lives likewise learn to compete with others. This can make it difficult for them to establish warm, intimate relationships, which are even more essential to good adjustment to a mate—particularly sexual adjustments—than to good adjustment to friends. Erikson has said that young adulthood is characterized by "a crisis of intimacy vs. isolation" (28).

Sexual Adjustments Poor sexual adjustments, which are more hazardous during the early years of marriage than later, can result when either husband or wife has an unfavorable attitude toward sex because of earlier, unpleasant sexual experiences; when one spouse—usually the husband—attaches greater importance to sex than the other; when the wife is overly aggressive, which may result in the husband's impotence; or when the couple have unrealistic expectations about the role sex should play in marriage. As Bischof has explained, "As the adjusted adult husband and wife well know, marriage is not one long sexual orgy, but marriage is mortgages, PTA meetings, parental pressures, and the like" (9). Thus many adults find that their satisfaction with the sexual aspect of marriage declines during the time when parenthood plays a dominant role in their lives (12). This affects not only their relationships with each other but also their relationships with their children, and the home climate may deteriorate.

The individual whose sexual adjustments to his mate are unsatisfactory may engage in autoerotic practices, homosexuality, or extramarital relationships. While all may give temporary satisfaction, they might be hazardous in the long run. Autoerotic practices and homosexuality may lead to guilt and shame, while the individual who has extramarital relationships lives in constant fear of discovery, which he knows will further strain the marital relationship, possibly to the point of separation or divorce.

Economic Status An economic status below the expectations of either or both mates is a hazard to good marital adjust-ments, especially when the family is large and money worries are constant. Marital adjustments are also threatened when the woman has chosen her husband because she believed he could help her rise above her status. As Elder has explained (25):

A woman's prospect for social ascent through marriage is dependent on her access to men of higher status and on the exchange value of her personal resources for marriage. . . . One of the oldest forms of exchange in hypergamous marriage involves the woman's attractiveness and the man's higher social status or potential status.

This is a potential hazard to good marital adjustment not only because the woman's hopes may not be realized but also because she selected her husband without considering other areas important to good marital adjustment.

Role Changes As was pointed out earlier, the birth of a child is often a time of crisis in marriage. While this role change to the parental may be more difficult and therefore more traumatic than other marital role changes, it is by no means the only one that must be made.

The most hazardous role changes involve the woman's relegation of major decision making to her husband and her assumption of the role of housewife if she held a responsible position in the business or professional world before marriage. However, it is her attitude toward these role changes that determines how successfully she adjusts to marriage. If, for example, she enjoys the role of housewife and mother, giving up a career will not be hazardous to marital adjustment, and she may find volunteer work in the community a satisfactory substitute for her career, especially if she feels that it will contribute to upward social mobility.

Men must also make role changes in marriage. How great these role changes are will depend partly on the man's concept of a

The mother must devote more time to her children than to her husband. (Bob Combs from Rapho Guillumette)

husband's role and partly on the particular family situation—if the wife is overburdened with household responsibilities, for example, or must take a job to supplement the family income.

Relationships with In-Laws Poor relationships with in-laws may affect any family member, but since the woman's life is more family-centered than the man's, any friction with in-laws affects her more than it does her husband and thus is more hazardous to her marital adjustment than to his.

While any marriage can be threatened by poor in-law relationships, mixed marriages are most hazardous in this respect. Regardless of whether husband and wife come from different religious, racial, or socioeconomic backgrounds, there is usually opposition to the marriage on the part of parents and other family members on one or both sides.

Parenthood The role change to parenthood can and does represent a major hazard to

marital adjustment even when children are planned, although it is far more hazardous in the case of unwanted pregnancies, either before or after marriage. In discussing the hazardous nature of marital relationships following a premarital pregnancy, Dame et al. have explained: "Premarital pregnancy imposes additional strains, both emotional and realistic, upon a marriage at a time when the couple has many adjustments to make. Therefore it constitutes a severe hazard unless both partners have considerable ego strength" (19).

Parenthood is especially hazardous at certain times during a marriage (12,101). As may be seen in Figure 10-3, parental satisfaction drops sharply as children grow older, reaching its lowest point when they are in their teens and when they begin to leave home. The slight sex difference that has been reported is in favor of men, especially when children reach their teens and tend to be more critical of their mothers than of their fathers.

Parenthood involves several common potential hazards to good marital adjustment. First, the mother must devote more time to her children than to her husband, and the marital relationship will be strained if he resents this. Second, clashes over child-training methods—with one parent blaming the other for being too strict, while the other retaliates with accusations of overpermissiveness—will further strain the marital relationship.

Third, parents who have more children than they wanted and who are overworked and overburdened financially become disenchanted with marriage and with their relationships to each other.

Not having a child or children of the desired sex is a fourth common hazard to good marital relationships. The husband may blame his wife for not giving him the son he wanted, for example, or he may feel that not having a son is an indication of his lack of virility—a belief that can contribute to impotence.

Fifth, an older child or adolescent who becomes hypercritical of his parents can cause a good deal of friction in the home, which can seriously damage marital relationships. Figure 10-5 shows how readily a mother can become irritated by a child's criticism and attempts at reform.

Hazards of Remaining Single

The stronger a woman's desire to marry, the more hazardous remaining single will be for her. This is due in part to the unfavorable stereotype of the unmarried woman and in part to a feeling of inadequacy at not being able to attract a member of the opposite sex and of being "out of things" when her friends talk about their families.

Except for occasional periods of loneliness, remaining single is not hazardous for men. Most men are able to marry if they wish, and their eligibility increases with each passing year as they become vocationally more successful. Even those who have financial obligations for aging parents are usually able to support a family of their own as well as take care of their parents.

"You know, Mom, if you took vitamins like the lady in the commercial, you'd never be tired."

Figure 10-5 The hypercritical attitude and attempts at reform by a child or adolescent often have a damaging effect on family and marital adjustments. (George Clark. "The Neighbors," Chicago Tribune–New York News Syndicate, Mar. 30, 1973. Used by permission.)

DIVORCE AND REMARRIAGE

Divorce is the culmination of poor marital adjustment and comes only when husband and wife have been unable to find any other solution to their problems. Many unhappy marriages do not end in divorce, however, because of religious, moral, economic, or other reasons, and many marriages end in annulment, desertion, or informal or legal separation. Approximately two million married people are separated, either temporarily or permanently, every year, and one-fifth to one-sixth of all couples living together claim that they are unhappy. The peak year for separation is the first year of marriage, and for divorce, the third year (35,122).

Many conditions affect the stability of marital life and may lead to divorce. The most important of these are given in Box

Box 10-11. CONDITIONS AFFECTING STABILITY OF MARRIAGE

Number of Children
There are more divorces among childless couples and those with few children than among couples with big families, mainly because the former can manage better after divorce than the latter.

Social Class
Desertion is more common among the lower social classes, and divorce among the upper-middle and upper classes.

Similarity of Background
Divorce is much more common among couples who have different cultural, racial, religious, or socioeconomic backgrounds than among those whose backgrounds are more similar. This is especially true of couples with different religious backgrounds.

Time of Marriage
The divorce rate is very high among couples who marry early. There are three reasons for this: First, young people know that it will be relatively easy for them to remarry; second, those who marry early are likely to be plagued by financial problems, which make marital adjustment difficult; and third, young people often have overly romantic concepts of marriage, which inevitably lead to disenchantment.

Reason for Marriage
Those who are forced to marry because of pregnancy have a higher-than-average divorce rate.

Time at Which the Couple Become Parents
The shorter the interval between marriage and the birth of the first child, the higher the divorce rate. Couples who become parents early have not had time to adjust to marriage, which complicates their adjustment to parenthood.

Economic Status
The lower the economic status of the family, the higher the rate of desertion and divorce. This is true of couples of all ages.

Parental Model
Marital success or failure tends to run in families. Children of happily married parents are far less likely to be divorced than children of unhappily married or divorced parents.

Ordinal Position in Childhood Family
Men who were only children have the highest divorce rate, while women who were only children have the lowest. This can be attributed to the fact that only boys tend to be spoiled, while only girls learn to assume responsibilities. Firstborn men, who also assumed responsibilities when they were young, have a low divorce rate; firstborn women, who may have been domineering toward younger siblings, have a high divorce rate.

Maintenance of Identity
The individual who can maintain his identity as a person after marriage and who has opportunities for self-actualization is far less likely to be divorced than one whose life is completely submerged in that of his spouse.

10-11. No one of these conditions alone is likely to lead to desertion, separation, or divorce, however; instead, a constellation of causes is far more apt to be responsible. Furthermore, although all these conditions contribute to poor marital adjustment, they are not the actual cause of divorce. It has been found, for example, that there are slightly more divorces in families where the wife works than in families where she is a full-time homemaker. However, when such a marriage ends in divorce, it may not be the

wife's working but rather the low economic status of the family that caused the marital unhappiness (43,85).

It has also been found that the cause of divorce varies from one period in marriage to another. Drinking, for example, is the cause of only 9 percent of divorces during the first year of marriage, as contrasted with 43 percent after twenty-five years of marriage. Similarly, adultery is rarely given as the cause for separation in the first year of marriage, but is the cause for one-third of the separations in the eleven- to fifteen-year period (44,122). Those who marry because the woman has become pregnant are much more likely to seek a divorce early in marriage than later.

Certain people who have made poor personal adjustments seem to be "divorce-prone." Many poorly adjusted adults feel that marriage will be the solution to their emotional problems. It rarely is. Not only do they become more poorly adjusted with the assumption of new responsibilities, but they also create such an unhealthy atmosphere in the home that divorce may be the only solution.

Effects of Marital Disruptions

The traumatic effect of divorce is usually greater than that of death because of the bitterness and emotional tensions preceding it and because of social attitudes toward divorce. These complicate postdivorce adjustment.

Because of changed social attitudes toward remarriage after divorce, many adults try to solve their adjustment problems by marrying soon again. Approximately three-fourths of those who are divorced remarry within five years (122). For those who do not remarry and for those who remarry only after a longer interval, divorce often adds economic strains to the other adjustment problems. This is especially true of women who must work and hire someone else to care for the home and children.

As Landis has pointed out, divorce necessitates certain adjustments on the part of every family member (59):

*Adjustment to the knowledge that divorce will
    take place.*
Adjustment to the divorce itself.
*Adjustment to the use by one parent of the
    child against the other parent.*
Adjustment to peer group attitudes.
Adjustment to changed feelings.
Adjustment to living with one parent.

Adjustment to remarriage.
Adjustment to implications of family failure.

The effects of family disorganization, whether the result of separation, desertion, divorce, or death, are especially serious in the case of the children. The child whose parents are not living together or are remarried is embarrassed because he is "different." This is very damaging to his self-concept. Children are hurt most by divorce when their loyalties are divided and when they suffer from anxiety because of the uncertainties that divorce brings to their lives. Children of parents who are "emotionally divorced," even though living together under the same roof, suffer even more than those whose parents are legally divorced. As Goode has pointed out, "Almost every serious researcher in American family life has suggested that the effects of continued home conflict might be more serious for the children than the divorce itself" (36).

Remarriage

That remarriages are not as successful as first marriages is shown by the high divorce rate among those who remarry. This suggests that individuals are conditioned toward instability after divorce. Widows often have more stable remarriages than divorced women (17,36).

While remarriage may provide two parents and a home for the children, both the stepparent and the stepchildren find their roles exceedingly difficult. How successfully a child adjusts to a stepparent will be greatly influenced by his age at the time of the remarriage. Older children have already made adjustments to one pattern of life and are resistant to change, especially if they have developed an unfavorable attitude toward the stepparent for some reason. The younger child, however, may welcome a stepparent who brings greater stability to his life.

A child of any age who has been accustomed to the affection and attention of a parent may resent the transference of some of this to the stepparent. This resentment will be increased if the stepparent tries to assign him new roles. Furthermore, many children are embarrassed about having stepparents because of unfavorable peer attitudes toward them. All this complicates the problems of adjustment to the new pattern of family life, especially if the stepparent has never been a parent before.

SUCCESS OF ADJUSTMENT TO ADULTHOOD

Successful adjustment to adult life can be measured in terms of achievements, satisfaction, and personal adjustments as reflected in the individual's personality. All these are interrelated.

Achievement

Adulthood is a time of achievement. The individual usually reaches the peak of his achievement between the ages of thirty and thirty-nine; thirty-five is often called the "crisis year" (50). The age at which the adult reaches his peak depends on the area in which he attains distinction. The peak of performance in athletic abilities comes in the mid-twenties, though it varies somewhat for different types of activity. Those who are involved in science, mathematics, music, writing, philosophy, or inventing usually reach their peak during their thirties (22,61).

Satisfaction

The degree to which the individual is successful in adjusting to the important problems he faces in adult life will determine the degree of his satisfaction, which in turn affects his happiness.

During their twenties, young adults are apt to be somewhat pessimistic about the future, and many are dissatisfied and unhappy. However, as they approach the thirties, they become more optimistic and more realistic and thus are happier. In fact, this is one of the happiest periods in the life span (11,72).

Personal Adjustments

The success with which the individual adjusts to the problems of adult life has an effect on his self-concept. The more successfully he adjusts, the more favorable his self-concept will be and the more self-confidence, assurance, and poise he will have. Feelings of inadequacy, on the other hand, are the usual accompaniment of failures in adjustment.

By the time the individual reaches early adulthood, his personality pattern is fairly well established. As Thorndike has said (114):

A person's nature at 12 is prophetic of his nature in adult years. . . . The child to whom approval is more cherished than mastery is likely to become a man who seeks applause rather than power, and similarly throughout.

Thus the individual's personality pattern influences the kind of adjustments he makes to adult life, rather than the reverse. While there is unquestionably a cause-and-effect relationship working both ways, it is stronger in the direction of the personality's influence on adjustments. There is substantial evidence that adults who make good adjustments have integrated personality patterns in which the core is a stable, realistic self-concept, whereas those who make poor adjustments have poorly integrated personality patterns with unstable, unrealistic self-concepts (21,32,134).

Middle age in the American culture of today is an especially difficult time in the life span. How well the individual adjusts to it will depend on the foundations he laid earlier and on the adjustments he has made to the roles and social expectations of adult society. Good mental health, acquired in adulthood, will go a long way toward easing the adjustments to the new roles and new social expectations of middle age.

Chapter Highlights

1 The developmental tasks of early adulthood relating to vocational and family adjustments are the most numerous, the most difficult to master, and the most important.

2 Vocational adjustments in adulthood involve selecting a vocation, becoming vocationally stable, and adjusting to work. The individual's vocational adjustment can be assessed by his achievements and by the satisfaction he derives from his work.

3 Marital adjustment involves adjustment to a mate, sexual adjustment, adjustment to economic conditions, in-law adjustments, and adjustment to parenthood.

4 Marital adjustment can be assessed by the happiness of the husband and wife, the quality of parent-child relationships, the adjustments the children make, the methods used to settle disagreements, and the degree to which the family enjoys being together.

5 It is more difficult for women to adjust to remaining single than for men because fewer women are single by choice.

6 The vocational and marital hazards of early adulthood result mainly because the individual has fewer foundations on which to build in these areas than in others and because he receives little guidance and help in making these adjustments.

7 The most common vocational hazard of early adulthood is job dissatisfaction. This dissatisfaction is expressed in underachievement, complaining, careless, slipshod work, accident proneness, absenteeism, job shifting, and lack of loyalty to employer.

8 Unemployment in early adulthood is a less common vocational hazard for men than for women and minority-group members.

9 The most common marital hazards in early adulthood are in the areas of adjustment to a mate, sexual adjustments, role changes, and economic conditions below the individual's expectations.

10 Adjustments to in-laws and to parenthood are hazardous for many young adults, partly because they are inadequately prepared in these areas and partly because they have unrealistic expectations.

11 Divorce and remarriage are greater marital hazards today than in the past, though their frequency varies markedly. Their effects on children are especially serious.

12 The individual's adjustment to adulthood can best be assessed by his achievements, the satisfaction he derives from the pattern of his life, and the effect his adjustment has on his personality.

Bibliography

1 Abramovitz, M. Growing up in an affluent society. In E. Ginzberg (Ed.), *The nation's children.* Vol. 1. *The family and social change.* New York: Columbia University Press, 1960. Pp. 158–169.

2 Arasteh, J. D. Parenthood: Some antecedents and consequences. A preliminary survey of the mental health literature. *J. genet. Psychol.,* 1971, **118**, 179–202.

3 Armstrong, T. B. Job content and context factors related to satisfaction for different occupational levels. *J. appl. Psychol.,* 1971, **55**, 57–65.

4 Baker, L. G. The personal and social adjustment of the never-married woman. *J. Marriage & Family,* 1968, **30**, 473–479.

5 Balchin, N. Satisfaction in work. *Occup. Psychol.,* 1970, **44**, 165–173.

6 Balswick, J. O., & Peek, C. W. The inexpressive male: A tragedy of American society. *Family Coordinator,* 1971, **20**, 363–368.

7 Becker, H. S., & Strauss, A. L. Careers, personality and adult socialization. In B. L. Neugarten (Ed.), *Middle age and aging: A reader in social psychology.* Chicago: University of Chicago Press, 1968. Pp. 311–320.

8 Besanceney, P. H. *Interfaith marriages: Who and why.* New Haven, Conn.: College & University Press, 1970.

9 Bischof, L. J. *Adult psychology.* New York: Harper & Row, 1969.

10 Blood, R. O. Kinship interaction and marital solidarity. *Merrill-Palmer Quart.,* 1969, **15**, 171–184.

11 Bortner, R. W., & Hultsch, D. F. Personal time perspective in adulthood. *Develpm. Psychol.,* 1972, **7**, 98–103.

12 Burr, W. R. Satisfaction with various aspects of marriage over the life cycle: A random middle-class sample. *J. Marriage & Family,* 1970, **32**, 29–37.

13 Cameron, P. Stereotypes about generational fun and happiness vs. self-appraised fun and happiness. *Gerontologist,* 1972, **12**, 120–123, 190.

14 Chen, R. The dilemma of divorce: Disaster or remedy. *Family Coordinator,* 1968, **17**, 251–254.

15 Christensen, H. T. Children in the family: Relationship of number and spacing to marital success. *J. Marriage & Family,* 1968, **30,** 283–289.

16 Clavan, S. The family process: A sociological model. *Family Coordinator,* 1969, **18,** 312–317.

17 Clayton, P. N. Meeting the needs of the single-parent family. *Family Coordinator,* 1971, **20,** 327–336.

18 Cooper, A. J. "Neurosis" and disorders of sexual potency in the male. *J. psychosom. Res.,* 1968, **12,** 141–144.

19 Dame, N. G., Finck, G. H., Mayos, R. G., Reiner, R. S., & Smith, B. O. Conflicts in marriage following premarital pregnancy. *Amer. J. Orthopsychiat.,* 1966, **36,** 468–475.

20 DeJong, P. Y., Brawer, M. J., & Robin, S. S. Patterns of female intergenerational occupational mobility: A comparison with male patterns of intergenerational occupational mobility. *Amer. sociol. Rev.,* 1971, **36,** 1033–1042.

21 Denmark, F., & Guttentag, M. The effect of college attendance on mature women: Changes in self-concept and evaluation of student role. *J. soc. Psychol.,* 1966, **69,** 155–158.

22 Dennis, W. Creative productivity between the ages of 20 and 80 years. *J. Gerontol.,* 1966, **21,** 1–8.

23 Devor, G. M. Children as agents in socializing parents. *Family Coordinator,* 1970, **19,** 208–212.

24 Duberman, L. Step-kin relationships. *J. Marriage & Family,* 1973, **35,** 283–292.

25 Elder, G. H. Appearance and education in marriage mobility. *Amer. sociol. Rev.,* 1969, **34,** 519–533.

26 Elder, G. H. Role orientations, marital age, and life patterns in adulthood. *Merrill-Palmer Quart.,* 1972, **18,** 3–24.

27 Emmerich. W. The parental role: A functional-cognitive approach. *Monogr. Soc. Res. Child Develpm.,* 1969, **34**(8).

28 Erikson, E. H. Identity and the life cycle: Selected papers. *Psychol. Issues Monogr.,* Vol. 1, No. 1. New York: International Universities Press, 1967.

29 Fast, I., & Cain, A. C. The stepparent role: Potential for disturbances in family functioning. *Amer. J. Orthopsychiat.,* 1966, **36,** 485–491.

30 Figley, C. R. Child density and the marital relationship. *J. Marriage & Family,* 1973, **35,** 272–282.

31 Fillenbaum, G. G. On the relation between attitude to work and attitude to retirement. *J. Gerontol.,* 1971, **26,** 240–248.

32 Freedman, M. B., & Bereiter, C. A longitudinal study of personality development in college alumnae. *Merrill-Palmer Quart.,* 1963, **9,** 295–302.

33 Friedman, E. A., & Havighurst, R. J. *The meaning of work and retirement.* Chicago: University of Chicago Press, 1954.

34 Gebhard, P. H. Factors in marital orgasm. *J. soc. Issues,* 1966, **22**(2), 88–95.

35 Glick, P. C., & Norton, A. J. Frequency, duration and probability of marriage and divorce. *J. Marriage & Family,* 1971, **33,** 307–317.

36 Goode, W. J. *The family.* Englewood Cliffs, N. J.: Prentice-Hall, 1964.

37 Guion, R. M., & Landy, F. J. The meaning of work and the motivation to work. *Organiz. Behav. Hum. Perform.,* 1972, **7,** 308–339.

38 Hagstrom. W. O., & Hadden, J. K. Sentiment and kinship terminology in American society. *J. Marriage & Family,* 1965, **27,** 324–332.

39 Hall, E. Ordinal position and success in engagement and marriage. *J. indiv. Psychol.,* 1965, **21,** 154–158.

40 Hauser, R. M., & Featherman, D. L. Trends in the occupational mobility of U.S. men, 1962–1970. *Amer. sociol. Rev.,* 1973, **38,** 302–310.

41 Helson, R. The changing image of the career woman. *J. soc. Issues,* 1972, **28**(2), 33–46.

42 Hernes, G. The process of entry into first marriage. *Amer. sociol. Rev.,* 1972, **37,** 173–182.

43 Herrmann, R. O. Expectations and attitudes as a source of financial problems in teen-age marriages. *J. Marriage & Family,* 1965, **27,** 89–91.

44 Hicks, M. W., & Platt, M. Marital happiness and stability: A review of the research in the sixties. *J. Marriage & Family,* 1970, **32,** 553–574.

45 Hoffman, L. W. Early childhood experiences and women's achievement motives. *J. soc. Issues,* 1972, **28**(2), 129–155.

46 Holden, G. S. Scholastic aptitude and the relative persistence of vocational choice. *Personnel Guid. J.,* 1961, **40,** 36–41.

47 Horner, M. S. Toward an understanding of achievement-related conflicts in women. *J. soc. Issues,* 1972, **28**(2), 157–175.

48 Hunt, M. M. *The world of the formerly married.* New York: McGraw-Hill, 1966.

49 Jacoby, A. P. Transition to parenthood: A reassessment. *J. Marriage & Family,* 1969, **31,** 720–727.

50 Jaques, F. Death and the mid-life crisis. *Int. J. Psycho-Anal.,* 1965, **46,** 502–514.

51 Johansson, C. B., & Campbell, D. P. Stability of the Strong Vocational Interest Blank for men. *J. appl. Psychol.,* 1971, **55,** 34–36.

52 Kaley, M. M. Attitudes toward the dual role of the married professional woman. *Amer. Psychologist,* 1971, **26,** 301–306.

53 Karp, E. S., Jackson, J. H., & Lester, D. Ideal-self fulfillment in mate selection: A corollary to the complementary need theory of mate selection. *J. Marriage & Family,* 1970, **32,** 269–272.

54 Kerckhoff, A. C. Two dimensions of husband-wife interaction. *Sociol. Rev.,* 1972, **13,** 49–60.

55 Klemesrud, J. The stepmother: Coping with a new family and a bad image. *The New York Times,* Apr. 12, 1971.

56 Klemesrud, J. Jewish-Gentile marriages: As number grows, so does debate. *The New York Times,* June 25, 1973.

57 Kuhweide, K., Lueck, H. E., & Timaeus, E. Occupational prestige: A cross-cultural comparison. *Percept. mot. Skills,* 1968, **27,** 154.

58 Kunz, P. R. Romantic love and reciprocity. *Family Coordinator,* 1969, **18,** 111–116.

59 Landis, J. T. Social correlates of divorce or nondivorce among the unhappy married. *Marriage fam. Living,* 1963, **25,** 178–180.

60 Lau, A. W., & Abrahams, N. M. Stability of vocational interests within nonprofessional occupations. *J. appl. Psychol.,* 1971, **55,** 143–150.

61 Lehman, H. C. The psychologist's most creative years. *Amer. Psychologist,* 1966, **21,** 363–369.

62 LeMasters, E. E. Parenthood as a crisis. *Marriage fam. Living,* 1957, **19,** 352–355.

63 Lopata, H. Z. The life cycle of the social role of the housewife. *Sociol. soc. Res.,* 1966, **51,** 5–22.

64 Lott, B. E. Who wants the children? Some relationships among attitudes toward children, parents, and the liberation of women. *Amer. Psychologist*, 1973, **28**, 573–582.

65 Luckey, E. B. Number of years married as related to personality perception and marital satisfaction. *J. Marriage & Family*, 1966, **28**, 44–48.

66 Luckey, E. B., & Bain, J. K. Children: A factor in marital satisfaction. *J. Marriage & Family*, 1970, **32**, 43–44.

67 Mace, C. A. Satisfaction in work. *Occup. Psychol.*, 1970, **44**, 175–185.

68 Marsh, R. M. The explanation of occupational prestige hierarchies. *Soc. Forces*, 1971, **50**, 214–222.

69 Masters, W. H., & Johnson, V. E. *Human sexual response*. Boston: Little, Brown, 1965.

70 McIntyre, W. G., & Payne, D. C. The relationship of family functioning to school achievement. *Family Coordinator*, 1971, **20**, 265–268.

71 Meikle, S., & Gerritse, R. A comparison of husband-wife responses to pregnancy. *J. Psychol.*, 1973, **83**, 17–23.

72 Meltzer, H. Age and sex differences in workers' perceptions of happiness for self and others. *J. genet. Psychol.*, 1964, **105**, 1–11.

73 Meyerowitz, J. H. Satisfaction during pregnancy. *J. Marriage & Family*, 1970, **32**, 38–42.

74 Monahan, T. P. Are interracial marriages really less stable? *Soc. Forces*, 1970, **48**, 461–473.

75 Murray, J. B. The generation gap. *J. genet. Psychol.*, 1971, **118**, 71–80.

76 Murstein, B. I. Physical attractiveness and marital choice. *J. Pers. soc. Psychol.*, 1972, **22**, 8–12.

77 Neugarten, B. L. Education and the life cycle. *School Review*, 1972, **80**, 209–216.

78 Neugarten, B. L., & Moore, J. W. The changing age-status system. In B. L. Neugarten (Ed.), *Middle age and aging: A reader in social psychology*. Chicago: University of Chicago Press, 1968. Pp. 5–21.

79 Neugarten, B. L., & Weingarten, E. K. The changing American grandparent. *J. Marriage & Family*, 1964, **26**, 199–204.

80 *New York Times* article. Money, schooling said to help prevent divorce. *The New York Times*, Sept. 22, 1972.

81 *New York Times* article. If you feel worthless doing family chores. *The New York Times*, Mar. 29, 1973.

82 *New York Times* article. Employes respond to responsibility. *The New York Times*, June 12, 1973.

83 Nye, F. I., Carlson, J., & Garrett, G. Family size, interaction, affect and stress. *J. Marriage & Family*, 1970, **32**, 216–226.

84 Orden, S. R., & Bradburn, N. M. Working wives and marriage happiness. *Amer. J. Sociol.*, 1969, **74**, 392–407.

85 Orpen, C. Intrinsic and extrinsic factors in job satisfaction: An experimental investigation into the role of "method factors." *Psychology*, 1972, **9**, 16–18.

86 Osofsky, J. D., & O'Connell, E. J. Parent-child interaction: Daughters' effects on mothers' and fathers' behavior. *Develpm. Psychol.*, 1972, **7**, 157–168.

87 Packard, V. *The status seekers*. New York: Pocket Books, 1961.

88 Paris, B. L., & Luckey, E. B. A longitudinal study of marital satisfaction. *Sociol. soc. Res.*, 1966, **50**, 212–222.

89 Parker, E. *The seven ages of woman*. Baltimore: Johns Hopkins Press, 1960.

90 Propper, A. M. The relationship of maternal employment to adolescent roles, activities, and parental relations. *J. Marriage & Family*, 1972, **34**, 417–421.

91 Rallings, E. M. Problems of communication in family living. *Family Coordinator*, 1969, **18**, 289–291.

92 Ramsdell, M. J. The trauma of TV's troubled soap families. *Family Coordinator*, 1973, **22**, 299–304.

93 Rappaport, A. F., Payne, D., & Steinmann, A. Perceptual differences between married and single college women for the concepts of self, ideal woman, and man's ideal woman. *J. Marriage & Family*, 1970, **32**, 441–442.

94 Reeves, J. W. What is occupational success? *Occup. Psychol.*, 1970, **44**, 213–217.

95 Reevy, W. R. Petting experience and marital success: A review and statement. *J. sex Res.*, 1972, **8**, 48–60.

96 Reiss, I. L. The sexual renaissance: A summary and analysis. *J. soc. Issues*, 1966, **22**(2), 123–137.

97 Renne, K. S. Correlates of dissatisfaction in marriage. *J. Marriage & Family*, 1970, **32**, 54–67.

98 Rensberger, B. Impotence: Casualties of the liberated woman. *The New York Times*, Mar. 26, 1972.

99 Rico-Velasco, J., & Mynko, L. Suicide and marital status: A changing relationship? *J. Marriage & Family*, 1973, **35**, 239–244.

100 Ridley, C. A. Exploring the impact of work satisfaction and involvement on marital interaction when both partners are employed. *J. Marriage & Family*, 1973, **35**, 229–237.

101 Rollins, B. C., & Feldman, H. Marital satisfaction over the family life cycle. *J. Marriage & Family*, 1970, **32**, 20–28.

102 Rose, V. L., & Price-Bonham, S. Divorce adjustment: A woman's problem. *Family Coordinator*, 1973, **22**, 291–297.

103 Ryder, R. G., Kafka, J. S., & Olson, D. H. Separating and joining influences in courtship and early marriage. *Amer. J. Orthopsychiat.*, 1971, **41**, 450–464.

104 Salpukas, A. Can a worker find happiness in a dull job? *The New York Times*, Dec. 24, 1972.

105 Scherz, F. H. Maturational crises and parent-child interaction. *Soc. Casewk.*, 1971, **52**, 362–369.

106 Scott, R. D. Job expectancy: An important factor in labor turnover. *Personnel Psychol.*, 1972, **51**, 360–363.

107 Sherman, J. A. *On the psychology of women: A survey of empirical studies*. Springfield, Ill.: Charles C Thomas, 1971.

108 Simonetti, S. H., & Weitz, J. Job satisfaction: Some cross-cultural effects. *Personnel Psychol.*, 1972, **25**, 107–118.

109 Smardan, L. E., & Margosian, A. H. Marriage in magazines. *Family Coordinator*, 1973, **22**, 177–182.

110· Spanier, G. B. Romanticism and marital adjustment. *J. Marriage & Family*, 1972, **34**, 481–487.

111 Sprey, J. On the management of conflict in families. *J. Marriage & Family*, 1971, **33**, 722–731.

112 Starcevich, M. M. Job factor importance for job satisfaction and dissatisfaction across different occupational levels. *J. appl. Psychol.*, 1972, **56**, 467–471.

113 Stuart, I. R., & Abt, L. E. (Eds.) *Children of separation and divorce*. New York: Grossman Publishers, 1972.

114 Thorndike, E. L. Note on the shifts of interest with age. *J. appl. Psychol.*, 1949, **33**, 55.

115 *Time* article. The new woman, 1972. *Time,* Mar. 20, 1972, 25–94.

116 Toppen, J. T. Underemployment: Economic or psychological? *Psychol. Rep.,* 1971, **28,** 111–122.

117 Troll, L. E. Is parent-child conflict what we mean by the generation gap? *Family Coordinator,* 1972, **21,** 347–349.

118 Tulkin, S. R., & Cohler, B. J. Child bearing attitudes and mother-child interaction in the first year of life. *Merrill-Palmer Quart.,* 1973, **19,** 95–106.

119 Turner, R. H. Some aspects of women's ambition. *Amer. J. Sociol.,* 1964, **70,** 271–285.

120 Tyler, L. E. The antecedents of two varieties of vocational interests. *Genet. Psychol. Monogr.,* 1964, **70,** 177–227.

121 Udry, J. R. Sex and family life. *Ann. Amer. Acad. pol. soc. Sci.,* 1968, **376,** 25–35.

122 *U.S. News & World Report* article. Who stays married longer? *U.S. News & World Report,* Oct. 30, 1972, 39.

123 *U.S. News & World Report* article. "Blue-collar blues": Just a catch phrase, or a real threat? *U.S. News & World Report,* Dec. 25, 1972, 55–58.

124 *U.S. News & World Report* article. Latest moves to fight boredom on the job. *U.S. News & World Report,* Dec. 25, 1972, 52–54.

125 *U.S. News & World Report* article. Progress in role of women is steady and it is sure. *U.S. News & World Report,* May 14, 1973, 66–69.

126 Veevers, J. E. Voluntary childlessness: A neglected area of family study. *Family Coordinator,* 1973, **22,** 199–205.

127 Wagman, M. Interests and values of career and home-making oriented women. *Personnel Guid. J.,* 1966, **44,** 794–801.

128 Walters, J., & Stinnett, N. Parent-child relationships: A decade review of research. *J. Marriage & Family,* 1971, **33,** 70–111.

129 Wanous, J. P., & Lawler, E. E. Measurement and meaning of job satisfaction. *J. appl. Psychol.,* 1972, **56,** 95–105.

130 Waters, L. K., & Roach, D. Relationship between job attitudes and two forms of withdrawal from the work situation. *J. appl. Psychol.,* 1971, **55,** 92–94.

131 Weintraub, E. The real cause of workers' discontent. *The New York Times,* Jan. 21, 1973.

132 Wernimont, P. F. A systems view of job satisfaction. *J. appl. Psychol.,* 1972, **56,** 173–176.

133 Wild, R., & Kempner, T. Influence of community and plant characteristics on job attitudes of manual workers. *J. appl. Psychol.,* 1972, **56,** 106–113.

134 Williams, W. H., & Loeb, M. B. The adult's social life space and successful aging: Some suggestions for a conceptual framework. In B. L. Neugarten (Ed.), *Middle age and aging: A reader in social psychology.* Chicago: University of Chicago Press, 1968. Pp. 379–381.

135 Yarrow, M. R., Waxler, C. Z., & Scott, P. M. Child effects on adult behavior. *Develpm. Psychol.,* 1971, **5,** 300–311.

136 Zytowski, D. G. Toward a theory of career development for women. *Personnel Guid. J.,* 1969, **47,** 660–664.

CHAPTER | ELEVEN

MIDDLE AGE
Personal and Social Adjustments

Middle age is generally considered to extend from age forty to age sixty. The onset is marked by physical and mental changes, as is the end. At sixty, there is usually a decline in physical vigor, often accompanied by a lessening of mental alertness. Although many adults experience these changes later now than in the past, the traditional boundary lines are still recognized. The increasing trend toward voluntary or involuntary retirement at age sixty rather than age sixty-five also justifies considering sixty to be the boundary line between middle and old age.

Because middle age is a long period in the life span, it is customarily subdivided into *early middle age*, which extends from age forty to age fifty, and *advanced middle age*, which extends from age fifty to age sixty. During advanced middle age, physical and psychological changes that first began during the early forties become far more apparent.

Individuals differ in the ages at which the physical changes marking off middle age from early adulthood at one end, and old age at the other end, occur. As Brozek has pointed out, "Humans vary, as apples do; some ripen in July, others in October" (15).

There are two different philosophies about how a person should adjust to middle age: the philosophy that he should try to stay young and active and the philosophy that he should grow old gracefully, deliberately slowing down and taking life comfortably—the "rocking-chair" philosophy. People of the middle class tend to adhere to the former, and those of the lower classes, to the latter; members of the upper class are evenly divided between the two. Women, on the whole, are more likely to adopt the rocking-chair philosophy than men (31,85).

CHARACTERISTICS OF MIDDLE AGE

Fried has said that "Life is not the same at forty-five as at twenty-five; nor are we the same kind of people" (32). Like every period in the life span, middle age has associated with it certain characteristics that make it distinctive. Seven of the most important of these are discussed below.

Middle Age Is a Dreaded Period

Next to old age, middle age is the most dreaded period in the life span and the one the adult will not admit he has reached until the calendar and the mirror force him to do

Figure 11-1 Many middle-aged people become nostalgic about their younger years. (Adapted from the cover drawing by Amos Sewell, *The Saturday Evening Post*, Jan. 26, 1957. Used by permission.)

so. As Desmond has pointed out, "Americans slump into middle age grudgingly, sadly and with a tinge of fear" (24).

The many unfavorable stereotypes of the middle-aged person, the traditional beliefs concerning the physical and mental deterioration which is believed to accompany the cessation of the adult's reproductive life, and the emphasis on the importance of youth in our culture, as compared with the reverence for age found in many other cultures, all influence the adult's attitudes unfavorably as he approaches this period in his life. Most adults dread middle age and become nostalgic about their younger years as it draws closer. See Figure 11-1.

Middle Age Is a Time of Transition

Just as puberty is a period of transition from childhood to adolescence and then to adulthood, so middle age is a time when the individual leaves behind the physical and behavioral characteristics of adulthood and enters into a period in life when new physical and behavioral characteristics will prevail. As Muelder has pointed out, "Men undergo a change in virility and women a change in fertility" (72).

Sooner or later, every adult must make adjustments to the physical changes that come with middle age and must realize that the behavioral patterns of his younger years have to be radically revised. Adjustment to changed roles is even more difficult than adjustment to changed physical conditions. Figure 10-2 shows the pattern of role changes in adult life. Men must adjust to the changes that impending retirement and their changed physical condition necessitate in their work, while women must adjust to exchanging the role of housewife for that of a worker in business or industry or of an "isolate" in a formerly busy home.

Radical adjustments to changed roles and changed patterns of life, when accompanied by physical changes, tend to disrupt the individual's physical and psychological homeostasis. Marmor (63) has divided the common sources of stress in middle age leading to disequilibrium into four categories; these are explained in Box 11-1. Most women experience a disruption in homeostasis during their forties, when normally they go through the menopause and their last children leave home, thus forcing them to make radical readjustments in the pattern of their entire lives. For men, by contrast, the climacteric comes later—generally in the fifties—as does the imminence of retirement with its necessary role changes.

Middle Age Is a "Dangerous Age"

The most common way to interpret "dangerous age" is in terms of the male who wants to have a last fling in life, especially in his sex life, before old age catches up with him. As Archer has pointed out (4):

To those around him, it may seem that the mid-life man is pursuing a diffuse, almost promiscuous sampling of new activities and experiences. The period may be dramatized by episodic escapes into extramarital relationships, or by a form of alcoholism. For some men, the crisis of the mid-life decade can end in a relatively permanent disruption and constriction of their lives.

Middle age can be and is dangerous in other respects also. It is a time when individuals break down physically as a result of overwork, overworry, or careless living. The incidence of mental illness rises rapidly in middle age among both men and women, and it is also a peak age for suicides, especially among men. These matters will be discussed later.

The threats to good adjustment that make middle age dangerous are intensified by sex differences in the time when upsets in physical and psychological homeostasis occur. As Muelder has pointed out, middle age is a time when there is an "unfortunate synchronization of woman's change in life and man's middle-aged revolt" (72). This not only strains the husband-wife relationship, sometimes leading to separation or divorce, but also predisposes both men and women to physical and mental illness, alcoholism, use of narcotics, and suicide.

Middle Age Is an "Awkward Age"

Just as the adolescent is neither a child nor an adult, so the middle-aged person is no longer "young," nor is he yet "old." As Franzblau has put it, he "stands between the younger 'Rebel Generation' and the 'Senior Citizen Generation'—both of which are continuously in the spotlight," and suffers from the discomforts and embarrassments associated with both age groups (30).

Feeling that he has no recognized place in society, the middle-aged person tries to be as inconspicuous as possible. A *Time* magazine report has said that the middle-aged population in the American culture of today is "cloaked in a conspiracy of silence. It is a generation that dares not, or prefers not, to speak its name—middle age" (105).

The middle-aged person's desire to be inconspicuous is reflected in his clothing. Most middle-aged people try to dress as conservatively as possible and yet adhere to the prevailing styles. This conservatism rules their choice of material possessions, such as homes and cars, and their patterns of behavior—whether it is the way they entertain or the way they dance (72). The more

If the middle-aged individual has a strong desire to succeed, he will usually reach the peak of his achievements during these years. (Bruce Roberts from Rapho Guillumette)

sixties, when he is regarded as "too old" and usually must relinquish his job to a younger and more vigorous person. Earnings normally reach a peak during middle age. See Figure 11-2.

Middle age is the period when leadership in business, industry, and community organizations is the reward for achievement. Most organizations, especially the older ones, elect presidents who are in their fifties and older. The fifties are also the years when individuals are granted recognition from the various professional societies (56).

Because leadership roles are generally held by middle-aged persons, they regard themselves as the "command generation." As *Time* has explained (105):

Middle-aged men and women, while they by no means regard themselves as being in command of all they survey, nevertheless recognize that they constitute the powerful age group vis-a-vis other age groups; that they are the norm-bearers and the decision-makers; and they live in a society which, while it may be oriented towards youth, is controlled by the middle-aged.

Neugarten has explained this attitude on the part of middle-aged people: "The successful middle-aged person often describes himself as no longer 'driven' but as now the 'driver'—in short, 'in command' " (73).

inconspicuous they are, the less out of place they feel in a society that worships youth.

Middle Age Is a Time of Achievement

Middle age, according to Erikson, is a crisis age in which either "generativity" or "stagnation" will dominate. The person will either become more and more successful or will stand still and accomplish nothing more (28). If he has a strong drive to succeed, he will reach his peak at this age and reap the benefits of the years of preparation and hard work that preceded it. Middle age should be a time not only for financial and social success but also for authority and prestige. Normally a man reaches his peak between forty and fifty years, after which he rests on his laurels and enjoys the benefits of his hard-won success until he reaches the early

Middle Age Is a Time of Evaluation

Since middle age is the time when the individual normally reaches his peak of achievement, it is also a time when he evaluates his accomplishments in light of his earlier aspirations and the expectations of others, especially family members and friends. As Archer has pointed out, "It is in the twenties that we commit ourselves to an occupation and to a marriage. During the late thirties and early forties, it is common for men to review those early commitments" (4).

As a result of this self-evaluation,

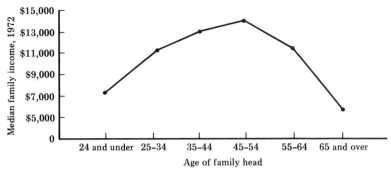

Figure 11-2 Earnings normally reach their peak during middle age. (U.S. Bureau of the Census statistics for 1972.)

Archer has further pointed out, "The mid-years seem to require the development of a different, generally more realistic sense of who one is. . . . In growing up, everyone nurtures fantasies or illusions about what one is, and what one will do. A major task of the mid-life decade involves coming to terms with those fantasies and illusions" (4).

Middle Age Is a Time of Boredom

Many, if not most, middle-aged men and women experience boredom during the late thirties and forties. Men become bored with the daily routine of work and with a family life that offers little excitement. Women, who have spent most of adulthood caring for the home and raising children, wonder what they will do for the next twenty or thirty years (48). The unmarried woman who has devoted her life to a job or career is bored for the same reasons men are. Archer has explained the boredom men experience in this way (4):

By the time you are 40, everyone—including you—knows that you can do whatever you are doing. And at that point some men get bored. Some begin looking for new territory. In most men, however, this impulse is checked by the sense that one has passed the last chance to change directions, to choose new goals.

At no age is boredom conducive to happiness or even contentment, and consequently middle age is often one of the unhappy periods of life. In a study of pleasant and unpleasant memories over a span of years, adults rated middle age, especially the years from forty to forty-nine, as the least pleasant (68). See Figure 1-6.

DEVELOPMENTAL TASKS OF MIDDLE AGE

Certain problems of adjustment are characteristic of middle age in today's culture. Some of these problems are more difficult for men, and others are more difficult for women. The major problems that American men and women must meet and adjust to satisfactorily during middle age involve the developmental tasks for this period. Havighurst (38) has divided these tasks into four major categories, which are given in Box 11-2. The first two of these categories will be discussed in this chapter, and the second two in the following chapter.

Like the developmental tasks of other periods, those of middle age are not all mastered at the same time or in the same way by all people. Some are more likely to be mastered during the early years of middle age, and some in the latter part of the period. This, however, will vary for different individuals.

Box 11-2. DEVELOPMENTAL TASKS OF MIDDLE AGE

Tasks Relating to Physical Changes
These include the acceptance of, and adjustment to, the physical changes that normally occur during middle age.

Tasks Relating to Changed Interests
The middle-aged person often assumes civic and social responsibilities and develops an interest in adult-oriented leisure-time activities in place of family-oriented activities, which prevailed during early adulthood.

Tasks Relating to Vocational Adjustments
These tasks revolve around establishing and maintaining a relatively stable standard of living.

Tasks Relating to Family Life
The important tasks in this category include relating oneself to one's spouse as a person, adjusting to aging parents, and assisting teen-age children to become responsible and happy adults.

The age at which middle-aged people married, the time when they became parents, and the number of children they have all influence the age at which they must adjust to the developmental tasks relating to family life, to civic and social responsibilities, and to adult leisure-time activities. Those who married when they were still in their teens may have no children at home when they reach middle age. Consequently, they can take a more active part in civic and social life; their leisure-time activities can be adult- rather than family-oriented; and they are free to spend more time together than they were able to do when there were children living at home.

Most of the developmental tasks of middle age prepare the individual for successful adjustment to old age; thus the mastery of these tasks is important for success and happiness not only in middle age but also in the latter years of life.

ADJUSTMENTS TO PHYSICAL CHANGES

One of the most difficult adjustments middle-aged men and women must make is to changed appearance. They must recognize that the body is not functioning as adequately as it formerly did and may even be "wearing out" in certain vital areas. They must accept the fact that their reproductive capacity is waning or coming to an end and that they may be losing some of their sex drive and sexual attractiveness. Like the pubescent child who has a childhood ideal of what he wants to look like when he grows up and who must adjust to the reality of his appearance, the middle-aged person must adjust to changes which he dislikes and which, even worse, are telltale signs of aging.

The adjustment to physical changes is made doubly hard by the fact that the individual's own unfavorable attitudes are intensified by unfavorable social attitudes toward the normal changes that come with advancing years. The most important physical changes to which the middle-aged person must adjust are discussed below.

Changes in Appearance

Having known, since early adolescence, the important role appearance plays in social judgments, social acceptance, and leadership, the middle-aged person rebels against threats to the status he fears he may lose as his appearance deteriorates. For the man, there is the added handicap of competition with younger, more vigorous, and more energetic men who tend to judge his capacity to hold down his job in terms of his appearance. For both men and women, there is the ever-present fear that their middle-aged looks will militate against their ability to hold their spouses or to attract members of the opposite sex. Figure 11-3 shows how middle-aged people react to the attitude of members of the social group toward their appearance.

As a general rule, men in our culture show signs of aging sooner than women. This may be explained by the fact that women, who know how much their attractiveness to members of the opposite sex depends on their physical appearance, quickly cover up the signs of middle age.

The signs of aging also tend to be more apparent among members of some socioeconomic groups than others. In general, men and women of the higher socioeconomic groups appear younger than their years, while those of the lower socioeconomic groups look older than they actually are. This may be explained partially by the fact that those of the more favored groups work less, expend less energy, and are better nourished than those who must earn their living by hard manual work. Furthermore, those who come from the less well-to-do groups are unable to afford the beauty aids and clothing that cover up the telltale signs of aging.

The most obvious — and, to most men and women, the most troublesome — telltale signs of aging are given in Box 11-3.

Changes in Sensory Abilities

Gradual deterioration of sensory abilities begins in middle age. The most troublesome and the most marked changes are in the eyes and ears. The degenerative and functional changes in the eye result in a decrease in pupil size, acuity, and glare resistance and in a tendency toward glaucoma, cataracts, and tumors. Most middle-aged people suffer from presbyopia, or farsightedness, which is a gradual loss of accommodative power of the eye resulting from a decrease in the elasticity of the lens. Between the ages of forty and fifty, the accommodative power of the lens is usually insufficient for close work, and the individual must wear glasses.

Hearing is likely to be impaired, with the result that the individual must listen more attentively than he formerly did. Sensitivity to high pitches is lost first, followed by

"All this started on a bus when two young soldiers offered him their seats!"

Figure 11-3 A person's recognition of others' attitudes toward his middle-aged appearance often causes him to have an unfavorable attitude toward himself. (George Clark. "The Neighbors." Chicago Tribune–New York News Syndicate, Apr. 20, 1967. Used by permission.)

progressive losses down the pitch scale. Because of hearing loss, many middle-aged people start to talk very loudly, and often in a monotone. The sense of smell grows weaker in men because of the increase in hair in the nose, and this affects the sense of taste.

Changes in Physiological Functioning

The changes in the exterior of the body are paralleled by changes in the internal organs and in their functioning. These changes are, for the most part, the direct or indirect result of changes in the body tissues. Like old rubber bands, the walls of the arteries become brittle as middle age progresses, and this leads to circulatory difficulties. Increase in blood pressure, especially among those who are overweight, may lead to heart complications.

Box 11-3. TELLTALE SIGNS OF AGING

Weight Gain
During middle age, fat accumulates mainly around the abdomen and on the hips.

Loss and Graying of Hair
The middle-aged man's hairline begins to recede, the hair becomes thinner, and baldness on the top of the head is very common. Hair in the nose, ears, and eyelashes becomes stiffer, while facial hair grows more slowly and is less luxuriant. Women's hair becomes thinner, and there is an increase of hair on the upper lip and chin. Both men and women have a predominance of gray hair by fifty, and some have white hair before middle age ends.

Skin Changes
The skin on the face, neck, arms, and hands becomes coarser and wrinkled. Bags appear under the eyes, and dark circles become more permanent and pronounced. Bluish-red discolorations often appear around the ankles and on the mid-calf.

Body Sag
The shoulders become rounded, and there is a general sagging of the body which makes the abdomen appear prominent and causes the person to look shorter.

Muscle Changes
Most middle-aged people's muscles become soft and flabby in the areas of the chin, upper arms, and abdomen.

Joint Problems
Some middle-aged people develop problems in their joints and limbs that cause them to walk with difficulty and to handle things with an awkwardness rarely found in younger adults.

Changes in Teeth
The teeth become yellowed and must often be replaced with partial or complete dentures.

Changes in Eyes
The eyes look less bright than they did when the individual was younger, and there is a tendency for mucous to accumulate in the corners of the eyes.

There is increasing sluggishness in the functioning of most of the glands of the body. The pores and skin glands rid the skin of waste materials more slowly, with the result that there is an increase in body odors. The different glands connected with the digestive process likewise function more slowly, with a consequent increase in the number and severity of digestive disorders.

To add to this problem, many middle-aged men and women wear dentures, which increase the difficulty of chewing. In addition, few individuals revise their eating habits in accordance with the slowing down of their activities, and this likewise adds a burden to the functioning of the digestive system. Constipation is very common in middle age.

Changes in Health

Middle age is characterized by a general decline in physical fitness and some deterioration of health is common. Beginning in the mid-forties, there is an increase in disability and invalidism, which progresses rapidly from then on (96). This trend is shown in Figure 11-4.

Common health problems in middle age include the tendency to fatigue easily; buzzing or ringing in the ears; muscular pains; skin sensitivity; general aches and pains; gastrointestinal complaints such as constipation, acid stomach, and belching; loss of appetite; and insomnia.

How middle age affects the individual's health depends on many factors, such as

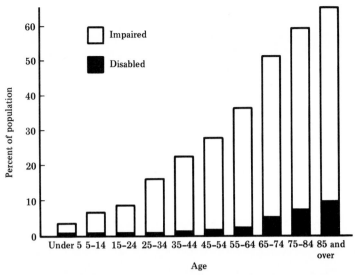

Figure 11-4 Disability and invalidism increase with advancing age. (Adapted from N. W. Shock. *Trends in gerontology.* (2nd ed.) Stanford, Calif.: Stanford University Press, 1959. Used by permission.)

heredity, his past health history, the emotional stresses of his life, and his willingness to adjust his pattern of living to his changed physical condition. For example, aggressive, ambitious men may be able to avoid health problems during early adulthood, but after forty they are more likely to have heart attacks than men who have a relatively calm outlook and less taxing jobs (78).

Sexual Changes

By far the most difficult physical adjustment men and women must make in middle age is to changes in their sexual capacity. Women go through the *menopause,* or *change of life,* at which time the menstrual periods cease, and they lose their childbearing ability. Men experience the *male climacteric.*

Both the menopause and the male climacteric are surrounded by mystery for most men and women, and there are many traditional beliefs which heighten the dread people feel as they approach the period in life when these physical changes occur. The

years during which the woman goes through the menopause, for example, are often referred to as "critical" (33).

Far more is known today about the causes and effects of the sexual changes that occur during middle age than in the past. Furthermore, there is growing evidence that these changes are a normal part of the life pattern and also that marked psychological changes during middle age are more the result of emotional stress than of physical disturbances. This is true of men as well as of women (4,54).

Sexual Changes in Women   General bodily and emotional changes occur at the time of the menopause but are not necessarily caused by it or related to it. Cessation of menstruation is therefore only one aspect of the menopause.

The average age for cessation of the menstrual flow is around forty-five years, though this varies widely among women, depending on hereditary endowment, general health conditions, and variations in climate.

Box 11-4. THE MENOPAUSAL SYNDROME

Cessation of Menstruation

The woman may experience a sudden cessation of menstruation; regular periods with a gradual diminution of the menstrual flow; increased irregularity, with the periods coming further and further apart; or shorter cycles with profuse flow.

Generalized Atrophy of the Reproductive System

There is a generalized atrophy of the genital tract, with the result that neither mature ova nor the ovarian hormones, estrogen and progestin, are produced.

Decline in Feminine Appearance

As production of the ovarian hormones ceases, the typically feminine secondary sex characteristics become less pronounced. Facial hair becomes coarser, the voice deepens, the curves of the body flatten out, the breasts appear flabby, and pubic and axillary hair become scantier.

Physical Discomforts

The most common physical discomforts experienced during the menopause are flushes, involving the head, neck, and upper thorax; sweating that accompanies or immediately follows the flush; hot flashes, typified by tingling over the entire body; headaches; fatigue; nervousness and irritability; heart palpitations; restlessness; and frigidity.

Weight Gain

Just as many pubescent children go through a "fat" period, many women gain weight during the menopause. Like the fat acquired during puberty, it is concentrated mainly around the abdomen and hips, making the woman seem heavier than she actually is.

Knobbiness

The joints, especially those of the fingers, often become painful with the decline in ovarian functioning. This causes them to become thickened, or "knobby."

Personality Changes

Many women experience personality changes during the menopause. They become depressed, hostile, and self-critical and have wide mood swings. With the restoration of endocrine balance as the menopause ends, these changes normally disappear.

Early puberty usually means late menopause, and vice versa. Loss of the childbearing function is not an overnight phenomenon, any more than the development of this function at puberty is. It takes several years for the reproductive apparatus to cease its normal functioning, the rate depending on the rate of decline of ovarian functioning. The menopause is regarded as officially over when there has been no menstruation for a year.

During the period when the endocrine interactional system is becoming adjusted to lessened ovarian functioning, certain physical symptoms normally occur. These are the result of the estrogen deprivation which comes from the decline in the functioning of the ovaries. In addition, other symptoms are due partly to estrogen deprivation but are mainly the result of environmental stress and thus are psychological in origin. The physical and psychological characteristics of the menopausal syndrome are given in Box 11-4.

Sexual Changes in Men The male climacteric is very different from the menopause. It comes later, usually during the sixties or seventies, and progresses at a very slow rate. With the general aging of the entire body comes a very gradual weakening of the male sexual and reproductive powers. It is hard to determine exactly when hormonal imbalance begins in men because there is no definite indication of this change, as occurs in the female with the cessation of menstruation. Testosterone secretion may begin to decline in men at any age, but the magnitude of the deficiency increases with advancing years.

While the climacteric in men actually comes during the period of old age, rather than during the middle years of life, many men in their forties or fifties have symptoms similar to those which women develop during the menopause. These occur in the absence of any demonstrable organic change and thus are emotional or social rather than physical in origin. They are the result of business, social, or family pressures, and the fact that they are not relieved by testosterone therapy may be regarded as proof of their psychological origin (4,54).

However, there is evidence that men experience a climacteric syndrome during middle age, just as women do. As Lear has said, "The male climacteric syndrome is a cluster of physiologic, constitutional and psychological symptoms occurring in some men aged approximately 45 to 60, associated with hormonal changes and often closely resembling the female climacteric syndrome" (54).

The major characteristics of the male climacteric are given in Box 11-5. Compare these with the characteristics of the menopausal syndrome, listed in Box 11-4.

ASSESSMENT OF ADJUSTMENT TO PHYSICAL CHANGES

Adjustments to physical changes are generally made gradually and reluctantly, but once the individual accepts these changes, he makes better adjustments to his

---

Box 11-5. THE MALE CLIMACTERIC SYNDROME

Decline in Functioning of the Sex Organs
After fifty, there is a gradual decline in gonadal activity, although men in their seventies and eighties occasionally father children.

Decline in Sexual Desire
A decline in sexual desire parallels the decline in sex-organ functioning. This is due partly to the decline in gonadal functioning and partly to psychological causes, such as unfavorable marital relationships or business, economic, or family worries.

Decline in Masculine Appearance
With the decline in gonadal activity, the man loses some of his typically masculine characteristics and takes on some that are more feminine. The voice, for example, becomes somewhat higher in pitch, there is less hair on the face and body, and the body becomes slightly more rounded, especially the abdomen and hips.

Anxiety about Virility
The man whose appearance and behavior seem less masculine may become concerned about his virility. This often leads to impotence.

Physical Discomforts
Many middle-aged men complain of depression, anxiety, irritability, tingling sensations in their extremities, headaches, insomnia, digestive disturbances, nervousness, flushes, fatigue, and many minor aches and pains.

Decline in Strength and Endurance
This decline is due in part to poor health and in part to gonadal deficiency. Because of the high social value placed on strength and endurance, men may feel they are losing their virility when decline in these areas sets in.

Personality Changes
Concern about loss of virility causes some middle-aged men to behave almost like the adolescent who is "sowing his wild oats." This can be a dangerous period for men, during which they may have extramarital affairs, engage in other behavior that leads to the breakup of the family, or cease caring about their business responsibilities.

role as a middle-aged person. Middle-aged people make adjustments more quickly and less reluctantly if they can camouflage some of the signs of aging.

Revolt against the loss of youth, as it becomes apparent in loss of physical and sexual vigor, often develops into a *generalized* revolt against work, the spouse, friends, and former pleasures. A middle-aged individual who reacts this way has not been willing to accept the inevitable changes that accompany aging and, as a result, has made poor adjustments to them.

By far the most difficult adjustment men and women must make is to changes in sexual functioning. This adjustment is much harder for women than for men, and fewer of them make it successfully. While many girls have difficulty adjusting during puberty, a larger number of women experience stress and strain in their attempts to adjust to the change in the pattern of life that comes with the menopause.

How successfully the woman makes the adjustment is influenced greatly by her past experiences, especially her willingness to accept the feminine sex role. Those who made poor adjustments have psychological reactions to the menopause that are similar to those experienced during puberty, especially a tendency to overeat.

While most women are prepared for the physical changes that come with the menopause, few are prepared for the psychological changes that occur at this time, some of which are unrelated to the menopause, such as those involving changes in life roles. Unfortunately, these changes usually coincide with the menopause, and this intensifies the difficulties the woman experiences in adjusting to the physical changes.

How well men adjust to the climacteric is likewise influenced by previous experiences and the success of adjustments in other areas. Men who are successful in business, who enjoy high prestige in the community, and who are well adjusted to their families accept the changes in appearance, the lessened physical strength, and the beginning of the waning of sexual desire as a normal part of aging and adjust philosophically to it.

ADJUSTMENT TO MENTAL CHANGES

There is a traditional belief that as physical abilities decline, so do mental abilities. As was pointed out earlier, scientific interest in middle age is of such recent origin that few longitudinal studies have been made; however, there is evidence that this traditional belief is not valid (6). Terman and Oden's study of a group of individuals followed from pre-school years to middle life has shown that mental decline does not set in during middle age among those with high intellectual abilities (101).

A more recent study, reported by Kangas and Bradway, has indicated that intelligence may even increase slightly in middle age, especially among those of higher intellectual levels. While this study was made on only a small group—forty-eight subjects—they were tested over a span of years: at the preschool level, during junior high school and young adulthood, and finally when they were between thirty-nine and forty-four years of age. No follow-up into the latter part of middle age has been done because the subjects are not yet old enough (50).

Like members of the Terman and Oden group, those with higher IQs showed less intellectual change than those with lower IQs. Men showed a slight gain in IQ scores as they grew older, while women showed a slight decline. Because men must be mentally more alert in order to compete vocationally than women must be in order to carry out their roles as homemakers, these findings suggest that use of mental abilities is an important factor in determining whether there will be mental decline in middle age.

That many men and women are anxious to remain mentally alert is evidenced by the growing interest in cultural pursuits as a form of recreation and by the increasing numbers who are completing their education or supplementing the education they received during their school and college years. This will be discussed later in connection with recreational interests.

ADJUSTMENT TO CHANGED INTERESTS

While there are changes in interests during middle age, they are far less marked than the changes that occurred during the earlier years of life. As Ryan has pointed out, "Whatever the chronological age, the interests, attitudes, and habits of earlier years will remain fundamentally the same" (91).

The changes in interests that take place now are the result of changes in duties and responsibilities, in health, and in roles in life. Men's concentration on vocational advancement plays an important role in narrowing down the range of interests they had when they were younger. The more successful the man, the more time and attention he must give to his vocation and the less time he has to devote to other activities.

Women experience far more pronounced role changes in middle age than men, and consequently there are more marked changes in their interests. The woman who played the role of mother during her earlier years of adulthood finds, when she faces the child-free days of middle age, that she has the time to pursue interests and activities she was forced to forgo earlier. Furthermore, because her husband spends more time and energy on his occupation than he did earlier, she must develop new interests to replace those she formerly shared with him.

New interests may be established in middle age, but the individual is more likely to cling to the old ones he found satisfying unless there are changes in his environment and pattern of life and unless he has opportunities to develop new interests or a strong motivation to do so.

Box 11-6. CHARACTERISTIC CHANGES IN INTERESTS IN MIDDLE AGE

Interests are more commonly narrowed down with advancing age than expanded.

There is a shift in emphasis on already-present interests—the middle-aged person now chooses clothes that will make him look younger, for example—and a shift toward interests that are more solitary in nature, such as hobbies.

The middle-aged person develops an increased interest in cultural pursuits, such as reading, painting, and attending lectures.

There is a lessening of sex differences in interests. Men are less interested in sports, for example, and increasingly interested in more feminine activities, such as reading or attending concerts.

There is increased interest in activities leading to self-improvement, such as attending lectures and taking courses, and a decreased interest in activities that are purely for enjoyment, such as dancing and playing cards.

This tendency to cling to old interests rather than establish new ones is frequently interpreted as indicative of the mental rigidity popularly associated with middle-aged and elderly people. There is little evidence from studies of middle-aged people that such is the case. Rather, the evidence points more in the direction of *values*. Middle-aged people know from experience what gives them satisfaction, and they see little reason to change just for the sake of change (24).

The characteristic changes in interests during middle age are given in Box 11-6.

The most common interests of middle-aged men and women in the American culture of today are discussed below.

Appearance and Clothes

Interest in appearance, which begins to wane after marriage and especially during the early years of parenthood, intensifies when the external physical changes which accompany advancing age become noticeable. Both men and women use diets, exercise, cosmetics, or clothing either to reverse those changes or to hide them, and as

Diet, exercise, cosmetics, and well-selected clothing help middle-aged people—especially the more affluent ones—to delay or conceal the signs of aging. (Ray Ellis from Rapho Guillumette)

a result, many middle-aged men and women look younger than they are.

Middle-aged people are well aware that clothes are important to their image. As Douty has pointed out, "Clothing may not be consciously perceived but its effect can be just as strong as though it were" (26). Men recognize the importance of clothing and grooming to business success. As they advance toward the peak of achievement in middle age, they become far more clothes-conscious than they were when they were younger and their status in the business world was lower. Women, by contrast, are less clothes-conscious in middle age than in early adulthood, though they, like men, recognize the importance of clothes and grooming to success in both the business and social worlds.

Money

Unless his wife, children, or relatives make heavy demands on him, the middle-aged man is less concerned about how much money he earns than he was when he was younger. Stability of work, job satisfaction, and prestige are more important to him than earnings. And because most men in the skilled-artisan field, in business, and in professional fields are reaching the peak of their achievement during middle age, many of the money worries they had when they were younger are lessened.

For those in the unskilled and semi-skilled groups, employment is less stable as the worker becomes middle-aged; in addition, the slowing down of the middle-aged worker's speed as well as the difficulties he has in learning new techniques often force him to accept jobs at wages below those of his earlier peak years. For him, money becomes a source of real concern.

Poor health, debts carried over from earlier years, or economic responsibilities for elderly relatives tend to heighten money worries for middle-aged men of all occupational groups, except those whose incomes are more than adequate to meet their needs. And with worry comes a focusing of attention on money.

The middle-aged woman is often more interested in money than the middle-aged man. Not only will money provide her with many of the material possessions she wants, such as clothes, a car, and a home that will compare favorably with those of her friends or come up to her own standards, but it also means security to her. Worry about financial security in case of the death or illness of the breadwinner or if there should be a divorce plagues many middle-aged women of today. This concern heightens their interest in money.

In middle age there is usually a change in attitude toward the use of money. As a result of having budgeted their incomes to meet family needs and because they realize the necessity for having money put aside in case of emergencies and for their old age, many adults regard extravagance as wrong. This attitude strengthens as the person grows older and is more the result of a different value system than of conservatism, which is typically associated with advancing age (19).

Status Symbols

Because middle-aged people like to think of themselves as the "command generation"—the group that exercises the most power—they want certain material possessions that will proclaim their status to others. As Packard has pointed out, "The status arises from the evaluations many people have in the backs of their heads as to the social worth of such things—address, home, etc.—as status symbols" (82).

Although most middle-aged people have known since adolescence how important a role status symbols play in the judgments others make of them, many were unable to afford these status symbols earlier, when the family income was smaller and the children were a heavy drain on the family budget. When the financial strains of early adulthood lessen, middle-aged people become keenly interested in status symbols.

While any material possession of value can be used as a status symbol, a home, a car, and clothing are most valuable because they are most visible. A home is generally considered the most important status symbol because others are impressed more by its cost than by the cost of a car or clothing. If it has a "proper" address, its status-symbol value is enhanced. Furthermore, it offers opportunities for the use of other status symbols such as expensive furnishings, antiques, and art objects.

The more anxious the individual is to move up the social ladder, the more important status symbols become. When a socially mobile individual moves to a new neighborhood or a new community, neighbors and business associates appraise him on the basis of status symbols before accepting or rejecting him. The more status

symbols he has, especially visible ones, the better his chance of gaining acceptance.

Religion

Middle-aged men and women show a greater interest in church and church-related activities than they did when they were younger, though this interest may be for reasons other than religious ones. For example, many middle-aged people, especially women, who have more free time and fewer family responsibilities find that religious activities fill their needs, whether religious or social. Increased interest in religion may also develop after the death of a family member or a close friend.

Many middle-aged men and women find that religion is a much greater source of comfort and happiness than it was during their younger years. On the whole, middle-aged people are less worried by religious questions, less dogmatic in their beliefs, less sure that there is only one true religion, and more skeptical about the devil and hell and about miracles than college students. They are not religiously disturbed at this time in their lives, and they are more tolerant in their attitudes toward other religions than they were when they were younger (45,88).

Community Affairs

Middle-aged men and women, who feel that they are in command of community life as well as their homes and businesses, also regard middle age as a time for service. The middle-aged man is well established in his work, and the average woman's home responsibilities have decreased. Thus they can devote more time to community affairs; they may serve on committees, on church or professional boards, or in leadership roles in different community organizations, for example. In addition, most middle-aged people can now afford to belong to various clubs and lodges.

The middle-aged person may participate in different formal community groups in order to enjoy himself, to be of service to the community, to help others, or to advance culturally or professionally. For example, he may serve on the school board, be active in the church or Red Cross, or participate in recreational activities at a branch of the YMCA or a lodge.

Recreation

One of the major developmental tasks of middle age is learning how to use leisure time in a satisfying way. This is an especially difficult task because the individual now has more leisure time than he did in early adulthood and because there is an ever-increasing number of recreational activities open to the middle-aged person.

Four important changes in recreational interests occur during middle age. First, interest in strenuous recreation wanes rapidly and the individual prefers quieter activities. Second, there is a shift from interest in recreational activities involving large groups to those involving only several people. When middle-aged people do participate in activities involving groups, it is usually in connection with a community organization such as a club, a lodge, or a civic or church group. Third, recreational activities of middle age tend to be adult-oriented rather than family-oriented, like those of early adulthood. And fourth, there is a narrowing down of recreational interests in middle age. The middle-aged person tends to concentrate on the activities

---

Box 11-7. POPULAR RECREATIONAL ACTIVITIES OF THE MIDDLE-AGED

Sports
The middle-aged person spends increasingly more time watching sporting events than participating in them. The sports he does engage in are the less strenuous ones—fishing, boating, swimming, golf, and bowling.

Reading
The middle-aged person spends more time reading newspapers and magazines than books and is more selective about what he reads than he was earlier He may prefer reading about world events, for example, than about crime or sex.

Movies
Movies are less popular in middle age than earlier, partly because many movies are slanted to the interests of adolescents and young adults and partly because the middle-aged couple got out of the habit of moviegoing when their children were young.

Radio and Television
Many middle-aged women listen to the radio while doing housework, and many men listen while driving to and from work. Many prefer news or discussion programs, rather than programs of popular

music, as they did earlier. Middle-aged people also enjoy television, but may have become more selective about their viewing.

Entertaining
Middle-aged people have more time and money for entertaining than they did earlier. Middle-aged friends of the same sex also like to get together informally to talk or play cards, for example.

Taking Trips
Now that they have fewer parental responsibilities and increased income, middle-aged people are able to take more trips to visit friends or relatives or to sightsee.

Hobbies
The hobbies of middle-aged people are mainly of a constructive nature—gardening, sewing, painting, cooking, and woodworking, for example

Taking Courses
Middle-aged people take courses for enjoyment rather than for vocational advancement. They like the intellectual stimulation, the social contacts, and the opportunity to get away from the home that adult education provides.

that give him the greatest pleasure and to abandon those which he finds less satisfying but may have engaged in for the sake of his children, for example.

Certain forms of recreation are universally popular among middle-aged American men and women today. These are shown in Box 11-7. Note how many of them fall into the category of "amusements," which require minimum effort.

There are more marked sex differences in recreational interests in middle age than there were in the earlier years of adulthood. Men of all social classes concentrate more of their recreational time on sports than women do, especially as spectators at athletic contests; they enjoy fishing and boating, and they may spend some of their time gardening, doing carpentry, and making home repairs.

Women, on the other hand, have a greater interest in formal and informal associations with other people than men have, they devote more time to reading than men do, and the manual tasks they undertake are more artistic than utilitarian in nature.

However, the middle-aged woman's recreational interests are greatly influenced by her role in the household. If she still has children at home, her recreational activities will be home-centered. If the children are grown and are living away from home, her activities will be more community-centered (2,80). Refer to Figure 9-2 for a graphic illustration of role constellation as a variable in women's leisure-time activities.

SOCIAL ADJUSTMENTS

Middle age often brings with it a renewed interest in social life. As the couple's family responsibilities decrease and as their economic status improves, they are better able to engage in social activities than they were during early adulthood, when family responsibilities and adjustment to work made an active social life difficult. Many middle-aged people, but especially women, find that an active social life alleviates the loneliness they experience when their children are grown and have homes of their own.

This session combines two types of recreation that are popular in middle age—hobbies and adult-education courses. (Suzanne Szasz)

Middle-aged people enjoy entertaining friends at dinners or parties, although much of the social life of middle age centers around gathering of members of the same sex. These activities reach their peak in the late forties and early fifties and then begin to decline as the individual approaches the sixties. A decrease in energy at this time puts a stop to a too active social life. Furthermore, as the individual looks ahead to retirement and decreased income, entertaining and active participation in community organizations lose much of their appeal (43,62,87).

As a result, the middle-aged person tends to spend most of his time with his family, intimate friends, and his children's newly established families. Figure 11-5 shows the pattern of participation in civic organizations during adulthood. This pattern is markedly influenced by the social-class status of the individual. Those of higher status are more active during middle age than those of lower status, most of whom belong to few community groups, rarely attend meetings, and have few friends except their close neighbors. Most

of their social contacts are with family members. As Packard has said, they are "socially isolated" (82).

There are also sex differences in social activities during middle age. Men have more friends and acquaintances than women, but women have a more affectionate and a closer relationship with their friends than men have. Men belong to more community organizations than women, but women devote more time and effort to the activities of the organizations with which they are affiliated than men do. Women have more social contacts with family members and relatives than with outsiders, while the reverse is true of men (12,74).

ASSESSMENT OF SOCIAL ADJUSTMENTS IN MIDDLE AGE

Social adjustments at every age are determined by two factors: how adequately the individual plays the social role that is expected of him and how much personal satisfaction he derives from playing this role. One of the important developmental tasks of

Figure 11-5 The pattern of participation in civic organizations during adulthood. (Adapted from S. L. Pressey & R. G. Kuhlen. *Psychological development through the life span.* New York: Harper & Row, 1957. Used by permission.)

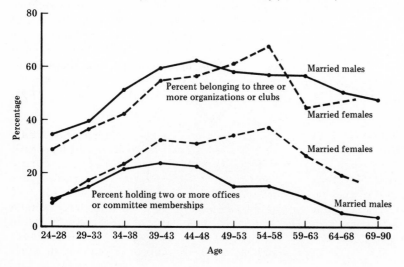

middle age is to achieve civic and social responsibility. How successfully the middle-aged person masters this task will affect not only his social adjustments but also his personal adjustments and his happiness.

However, the success with which the middle-aged individual masters this developmental task may be determined by physical or social factors over which he has little or no control. Poor health or a physical disability, for example, may prevent him from engaging in social or civic activities that he would otherwise enjoy.

Certain factors are conducive to good social functioning in middle age. The most important of these are reasonably good health, which enables the individual to participate in group activities; a strong liking for social activities, which motivates him to put forth the effort needed to take part in them; the previous acquisition of social skills; an absence of circumstances that limit the individual's ability to function as the social group expects him to, such as reduced income or impaired health; and a social status that has enabled him to form friendships in the desired social group and become affiliated with community organizations.

On the whole, middle-aged people make better social adjustments than younger ones because they must depend more on people outside the home for companionship than they did earlier. Thus they derive greater satisfaction from their social activities.

A study of patterns of social relationships among middle-aged couples has revealed that close-knit social networks are most common when the husband and wife have grown up and lived in the same area. Loose social networks, by contrast, are more common among those who have moved from place to place, especially upwardly mobile middle-class couples (108).

Because the middle-aged person derives more satisfaction from social contacts where there is a close personal relationship than from the greater social distance that characterizes acquaintanceships, he prefers the former to the latter.

PERSONAL AND SOCIAL HAZARDS OF MIDDLE AGE

The major personal and social hazards of middle age stem from the tendency of many men and women to accept the cultural stereotype of the middle-aged person as fat, forty, and balding. It has been reported, for example, that many men and women between the ages of thirty and sixty consider themselves "middle-aged" (106).

Because of a lack of scientific information about middle age, cultural stereotypes and many traditional beliefs about middle age have persisted and can have serious effects on the attitudes of middle-aged persons and of members of the social group toward them.

Personal Hazards

Acceptance of traditional beliefs about middle age has a profound influence on attitudes toward the physical changes that come with advancing age. The menopause, for example, is often referred to as a "critical" period, and this can heighten a woman's dread of it. As Parker has said (85):

This [term] carries the implication of danger — that woman is on the brink of disaster, that her health, her happiness, and her very life is in jeopardy. It further implies that this is not merely a time of crisis that can be met forthwith and dissolved, but rather years when she must feel her way along a narrow ledge of safety, at any moment of which by one false step she might fall into the abyss of a mental breakdown or serious physical illness.

Because men commonly associate hair on the head, face, body, arms, and legs with virility, the thinning of the hair during middle age is likely to be a source of great concern to them. Even the beginning of baldness disturbs them because they believe that it is indicative of a decline in their sexual powers. In reality, *anxiety about virility* is one of the chief causes of such decline, and the balding middle-aged man who worries about his sexual powers merely accelerates the rate of their decline (27,64).

Many middle-aged people, particularly men, are in constant rebellion against the restrictions age places on their usual patterns of behavior. A man may refuse to adhere to a diet his doctor prescribes or to restrict his activities for the sake of his health. Like the pubescent child, the middle-aged adult rebels against restrictions on his behavior, but for a different reason. His rebellion stems from a recognition of the value that society attaches to youth and thus he is rebelling against restrictions that mean he is growing old. This may bring on middle-aged ailments of minor or major seriousness. As Steincrohn has pointed out (99):

If you relax more often, if you slow up, don't believe that you will grow old prematurely. The grim reaper won't swish his scythe at you and cut you off long before you reach the 70s and 80s. On the contrary, the reaper seems to have patience for the relaxers and is impatient with the overdoers.

Women who make the poorest adjustments to middle age are those who have attached a great deal of importance to a youthful appearance and masculine admiration. When they are forced to recognize that they are no longer as attractive as they once were and that they cannot attract and hold masculine attention, they may openly rebel against middle age.

When adjustment to middle age is poor, as shown by constant rebellion against the physical changes that inevitably come with aging, interest in clothing is intensified, and the individual concentrates mainly on selecting clothes which will make him look younger than he is. Bright colors, extreme styles, and a large wardrobe become as important to the middle-aged man or woman who is trying to defy age as to the adolescent.

Rebellion against middle age is often heightened by magazine articles, television advertisements, and so on, that stress what the middle-aged person can and should do to camouflage the telltale signs of aging. Ryan, however, has suggested that these changes in appearance are not necessarily unattractive. According to her (91):

Some of these changes may make the individual more, rather than less, attractive. Often the first and most obvious change is in the color of the hair which usually turns to gray and then to white. This frequently is a positive factor: many people are more attractive with white hair. Also, as individuals grow older, the face becomes more lined and wrinkled. This, again, is not necessarily a detriment. These lines may give a pleasing character to a face which was bland and uninteresting with the smoothness of youth.

The second important hazard to good personal adjustment in middle age involves the necessity for changing roles. Changing roles is never easy, especially after one has played certain prescribed roles over a period of time and has learned to derive satisfaction from them. Furthermore, too much success in one role is likely to lead to rigidity and may make adjustment to another role difficult. Also, a person who has played a narrow range of roles is likely to be less flexible than one who has played a wider range and has learned to derive satisfaction from different roles. The person who has played many roles finds it easier to shift to a new one. To make a good adjustment to new roles, the individual must, as Havighurst has explained, "withdraw emotional capital from one role and invest it in another one" (39).

A third hazard to good personal adjustment in middle age comes from the necessity for changing interests as physical strength and endurance decrease and as health deteriorates. Unless the individual can develop new interests to replace those he must give up or unless he has developed enough interests in his earlier years to be able to abandon some of them without feeling their loss too seriously, he is likely to become bored and wonder how he can spend his leisure time.

Like the adolescent who becomes bored when he has too few interests and activities to fill his time, the middle-aged person is likely to try to "stir up some excitement." Usually he does this by seeking out extramarital relationships. While these may be temporarily satisfying, they are likely to lead to feelings of guilt and shame and to serious problems with the spouse and other family members if the individual is discovered. This will be discussed in more detail in the following chapter.

A woman's increased interest in status symbols, which is characteristic of middle age, can be a hazard to her good personal adjustment if the family cannot afford the things she wants, in which case she may go to work to earn money for them herself. This often leads to friction with the husband, who feels that it reflects poorly on his ability to provide for his family as other men do.

Middle-aged people who have unrealistic aspirations concerning their achievements—often carried over from their adolescence—face a fourth serious hazard to good personal adjustments when they realize that they have fallen short of their goals and that time is fast running out.

While this hazard is more likely to have a direct effect on men than on women, women are indirectly affected when their husbands fail to achieve the financial and vocational success they had expected. Even

---

Box 11-8. CONDITIONS MILITATING AGAINST GOOD SOCIAL ADJUSTMENTS IN MIDDLE AGE

The "Rocking-Chair" Philosophy
The person who subscribes to the philosophy that an aging person should be inactive and remain on the sidelines contributes little to the enjoyment of others in social situations.

Unattractive Appearance
The middle-aged person who allows his appearance to deteriorate and makes little or no effort to improve it is more likely to be ignored or rejected than one whose clothing and grooming make him look more youthful and attractive.

Lack of Social Skills
The person who never learned proper social skills in adolescence or who allowed his social skills to become rusty during early adulthood, because of vocational or household pressures, feels ill at ease in social situations and either withdraws from them or plays an onlooker role.

Preference for Family Contacts
The individual who has found family members more congenial than outsiders and family social activities more enjoyable than community activities will not be motivated to broaden his social horizons in middle age to include outsiders and community activities.

Desire for Popularity
Some middle-aged men and women, especially those who married early and were deprived of the social experiences their unmarried contemporaries enjoyed, now want an active social life as evidence of their popularity. This can be dangerous if the individual, in his effort to achieve the goal of popularity, breaks up the established pattern of his family life, seeks adventure and excitement outside the home, and neglects his work.

Social Mobility
A socially mobile person who finds it difficult to break into the close-knit social networks of the middle-aged must play the role of involuntary isolate or affiliate himself with any group that will accept him, regardless of congeniality of interests.

though women who work tend to have more realistic aspirations than men, as was explained in Chapter 10, they may also realize that they have not reached their goals and that time is running short.

Failure to reach any goal can lead to feelings of inferiority and inadequacy, feelings that tend to become generalized and result in a failure complex. The individual who develops such a complex has a defeatist attitude toward everything he undertakes, and as a result, his achievements fall even further below his aspirations.

Social Hazards

Social adjustments in middle age are less affected by traditional beliefs and stereotypes than personal adjustments. However, social adjustments are affected to some extent by traditional beliefs such as "you can't teach an old dog new tricks"—the new "tricks" being new social skills—or "Once a leader, always a leader." For example, a middle-aged person who was not a leader in school or college may feel that he has no hope now of achieving leadership roles in either the vocational or the social world.

The other important conditions that influence social adjustments in middle age are given in Box 11-8.

Making poor social adjustments in middle age is hazardous because, with advancing age, most men and women must rely more and more on the companionship of outsiders, as their spouses become ill or die and as their grown children become increasingly preoccupied with their own lives. Middle-aged persons who do not master the important developmental task of achieving adult civic and social responsibility are likely to be lonely and unhappy in their old age and may find that it is too late then to make good social adjustments.

Chapter Highlights

1 Middle age is commonly subdivided into early middle age, which extends from age forty to age fifty, and advanced middle age, which extends from age fifty to age sixty.

2 Middle age is a dreaded period, a time of transition, a "dangerous" age, an "awkward" age, a time of achievement, a time of evaluation, and a time of boredom.

3 The developmental tasks of middle age are related to physical changes, changed interests, vocational adjustments, and changes in family life.

4 Adjustments to physical changes in middle age include adjustments to changes in appearance, in sensory abilities, in physiological functioning, in health, and in sexual drive and behavior.

5 Of all the physical changes that occur in middle age, the menopause and the male climacteric are the most traumatic and also the most difficult to adjust to.

6 The middle-aged person's adjustment to physical changes can best be assessed by the effect of these changes on his self-concept.

7 Contrary to popular belief, intellectual abilities do not decrease in middle age, but may even increase slightly, especially among those of high intelligence.

8 Changes in interests during middle age are due primarily to role changes resulting from social expectations or from physical changes or reduced income.

9 The middle-aged person's interests most commonly change in the areas of appearance and clothes, money, status symbols, religion, community affairs, and recreational activities.

10 Because there is often a renewed interest in social life during middle age, adjustment to a changed pattern of social life becomes a major developmental task for many middle-aged people.

11 The major personal hazards of middle age come from acceptance of the cultural stereotypes about middle age, from rebellion against the restrictions age places on the individual's usual pattern of behavior, and from the necessity for changing roles.

12 The major social hazards of middle age are

conditions that militate against good social adjustments, such as an unattractive appearance, a lack of social skills, social mobility, and a preference for family contacts.

Bibliography

1 Amundsen, D. W., & Diers, C. J. The age of menopause in classical Greece and Rome. *Hum. Biol.,* 1970, **42,** 79–86.

2 Angrist, S. S. Rôle constellation as a variable in women's leisure activities. *Soc. Forces,* 1967, **45,** 423–431.

3 Applebaum, S. B., & Kavinoky, N. R. *Understanding your menopause.* New York: Public Affairs Pamphlets, 1965, No. 243.

4 Archer, D. The male change of life. *Yale Alumni Mag.,* March 1968, 33–35.

5 Babchuk, N., Crockett, H. J., & Ballweg, J. A. Change in religious affiliation and family stability. *Soc. Forces,* 1967, **45,** 551–555.

6 Bayley, N. Research in child development: A longitudinal perspective. *Merrill-Palmer Quart.,* 1965, **11,** 183–208.

7 Bellini, G. Plastic surgery: Why? When? Where? How? *Harper's Bazaar,* August 1973, 59, 88.

8 Benedek, T. Climacterium: A developmental phase. *Psychoanal. Quart.,* 1950, **19,** 1–27.

9 Bergler, E. *The revolt of the middle-aged man.* New York: Wyn, 1954.

10 Bischof, L. J. *Adult psychology:* New York: Harper & Row, 1969.

11 Bliven, B. Using our leisure is no easy job. *The New York Times,* Apr. 26, 1964.

12 Booth, A. Sex and social participation. *Amer. sociol. Rev.,* 1972, **37,** 183–193.

13 Brayshaw, A. J. Middle-age marriage: Idealism, realism and the search for meaning. *Marriage fam. Living,* 1962, **24,** 358–364.

14 Brozan, N. Middle age needn't be like dark ages. *The New York Times,* Mar. 29, 1973.

15 Brozek, J. Personality changes with age: An item analysis of the Minnesota Multiphasic Personality Inventory. *J. Gerontol.,* 1955, **10,** 194–206.

16 Bruch, H. Developmental obesity and schizophrenia. *Psychiatry,* 1958, **21,** 65–70.

17 Cavan, R. S. Adjustment problems of older women. *Marriage fam. Living,* 1952, **14,** 16–18.

18 Cavan, R. S. Unemployment: Crises of the common man. *Marriage fam. Living,* 1959, **21,** 139–146.

19 Christenson, R. M. The old values are the best values. *The New York Times,* June 3, 1972.

20 Clavan, S. The family process: A sociological model. *Family Coordinator,* 1969, **18,** 312–317.

21 Conley, V. L. Common skin worries. *Today's Hlth.,* January 1957, 31–32.

22 Denney, N. W., & Lennon, M. L. Classification: A comparison of middle and old age. *Develpm. Psychol.,* 1972, **7,** 210–213.

23 Dennis, W. Creative productivity between the ages of 20 and 80 years. In B. L. Neugarten (Ed.), *Middle age and aging: A reader in social psychology.* Chicago: University of Chicago Press, 1968. Pp. 106–114.

24 Desmond, T. C. America's unknown middle-agers. *The New York Times,* July 29, 1956.

25 Donald, M. N., & Havighurst, R. J. The meaning of leisure. *Soc. Forces,* 1959, **37,** 355–360.

26 Douty, H. I. Influence of clothing on perception of persons. *J. Home Econ.,* 1963, **55,** 197–202.

27 Eisdorfer, C., & Lawton, M. P. (Eds.) *The psychology of adult development and aging.* Washington: APA, 1973.

28 Erikson, E. H. Identity and the life cycle: Selected papers. *Psychol. Issues Monogr.,* Vol. 1, No. 1. New York: International Universities Press, 1967.

29 Feibleman, J. K. The leisurely attitude. *Humanitas,* 1972, **8,** 279–285.

30 Franzblau, R. N. *The middle generation.* New York: Holt, 1971.

31 Frenkel-Brunswik, E. Adjustments and reorientation in the course of the life span. In B. L. Neugarten (Ed.), *Middle age and aging: A reader in social psychology.* Chicago: University of Chicago Press, 1968. Pp. 77–84.

32 Fried, B. *The middle-age crisis.* New York: Harper & Row, 1967.

33 *Geriatric Focus* article. A new look at the "crisis" of middle age. *Geriatric Focus,* 1970, **9**(1), 7–9.

34 Goldzieher, M., & Goldzieher, J. W. The male climacteric and the postclimacteric state. *Geriatrics,* 1953, **8,** 1–10.

35 Greenblatt, R. B. Metabolic and psychosomatic disorders in menopausal women. *Geriatrics,* 1955, **10,** 165–169.

36 Greenblatt, R. B. Treatment of menopausal symptoms. *Geriatrics,* 1957, **12,** 452–453.

37 *Harper's Bazaar* article. The menopause that refreshes. *Harper's Bazaar,* August 1973, 87, 134.

38 Havighurst, R. J. *Human development and education.* New York: Longmans, 1953.

39 Havighurst, R. J. Flexibility and the social roles of the retired. *Amer. J. Sociol.,* 1954, **59,** 309–311.

40 Havighurst, R. J. The leisure activities of the middle-aged. *Amer. J. Sociol.,* 1957, **63,** 152–162.

41 Havighurst, R. J. The social competence of middle-aged people. *Genet. Psychol. Monogr.,* 1957, **56,** 297–375.

42 Havighurst, R. J. Body, self, and society. *Sociol. soc. Res.,* 1965, **49,** 261–267.

43 Havighurst, R. J., & Feigenbaum, K. Leisure and life style. In B. L. Neugarten (Ed.), *Middle age and aging: A reader in social psychology.* Chicago: University of Chicago Press, 1968. Pp. 347–353.

44 Havighurst, R. J., Neugarten, B. L., & Tobin, S. S. Disengagement and patterns of aging. In B. L. Neugarten (Ed.), *Middle age and aging: A reader in social psychology.* Chicago: University of Chicago Press, 1968. Pp. 161–172.

45 Hawkins, L. F. Urbanization, families and the church. *Family Coordinator,* 1969, **18,** 49–53.

46 Heilbaum, A. A., Eskridge, J. B., & Payne, R. W. The influence of pituitary factors on the menopausal vasomotor instability. *J. Gerontol.,* 1956, **11,** 58–60.

47 Hess, E., Roth, R. B., & Kaminsky, A. F. Is there a male climacteric? *Geriatrics,* 1955, **10,** 170–173.

48 Jacoby, S. What do I do for the next 29 years? *The New York Times,* June 17, 1973.

49 Johnson, W. M. *The years after fifty.* College Park, Md.: McGrath Publishing, 1970.

50 Kangas, J., & Bradway, K. Intelligence at middle age: A thirty-eight-year follow-up. *Develpm. Psychol.,* 1971, **5,** 333–337.

51 Kuhlen, R. G. Developmental changes in motivation during the adult years. In B. L. Neugarten (Ed.), *Middle age and aging: A reader in social psychology.* Chicago: University of Chicago Press, 1968. Pp. 115–136.

52 Landau, R. L. The concept of the male climacteric. *Med. Clin. N. Amer.,* 1951, **35,** 279–288.

53 Laumann, E. O., & House, J. S. Living room styles and social attributes: The patterning of material artifacts in a modern urban community. *Sociol. soc. Res.,* 1970, **54,** 321–342.

54 Lear, M. W. Is there a male menopause? *The New York Times,* Jan. 28, 1973.

55 Lehman, H. C. *Age and achievement.* Princeton, N.J.: Princeton University Press, 1953.

56 Lehman, H. C. Ages at time of first election of presidents of professional organizations. *Scient. Mon., N.Y.,* 1955, **80,** 293–298.

57 Lehman, H. C. The most creative years of engineers and other technologists. *J. genet. Psychol.,* 1966, **108,** 263–277.

58 Lehman, H. C. The psychologist's most creative years. *Amer. Psychologist,* 1966, **21,** 363–369.

59 Lehman, H. C. The creative production rates of present versus past generations of scientists. In B. L. Neugarten (Ed.), *Middle age and aging: A reader in social psychology.* Chicago: University of Chicago Press, 1968. Pp. 99–105.

60 LeShan, E. *The wonderful crisis of middle age.* New York: McKay, 1973.

61 Lester, D., & Kam, E. G. Effect of a friend dying upon attitudes toward death. *J. soc. Psychol.,* 1971, **83,** 149–150.

62 Lopata, H. Z. The life cycle of the social role of the housewife. *Sociol. soc. Res.,* 1966, **51,** 5–22.

63 Marmor, J. The crisis of middle age: *Amer. J. Orthopsychiat.,* 1967, **37,** 336–337.

64 Masters, W. H., & Johnson, V. E. *Human sexual response.* Boston: Little, Brown, 1966.

65 *McCall's* article. The empty days. *McCall's,* September 1965, 78–81, 140–146.

66 McGhie, A., & Russell, S. M. The subjective assessment of normal sleep patterns. *J. ment. Sci.,* 1962, **108,** 642–654.

67 Mehrabian, A., & Diamond, S. G. Effects of furniture arrangement, props and personality on social interaction. *J. Pers. soc. Psychol.,* 1971, **20,** 18–30.

68 Meltzer, H., & Ludwig, D. Age differences in memory optimism and pessimism in workers. *J. genet. Psychol.,* 1967, **110,** 17–30.

69 Meyer, H. D. The adult cycle. *Ann. Amer. Acad. pol. soc. Sci.,* 1957, **313,** 58–67.

70 Moore, J. W. Patterns of women's participation in voluntary associations. *Amer. J. Sociol.,* 1961, **66,** 592–598.

71 Morgan, R. F. The adult growth examination: Preliminary comparisons of physical aging in adults by sex and race. *Percept. mot. Skills,* 1968, **27,** 595–599.

72 Muelder, W. G. Middle age: Its problems and challenge. *Pastoral Psychol.,* 1958, **9**(88), 9–13.

73 Neugarten, B. L. The awareness of middle age. In B. L. Neugarten (Ed.), *Middle age and aging: A reader in social psychology.* Chicago: University of Chicago Press, 1968. Pp. 93–98.

74 Neugarten, B. L. (Ed.) *Middle age and aging: A reader in social psychology.* Chicago: University of Chicago Press, 1968.

75 Neugarten, B. L., & Gutmann, D. L. Age-sex roles and personality in middle age: A thematic apperception study. In B. L. Neugarten (Ed.), *Middle age and aging: A reader in social psychology.* Chicago: University of Chicago Press, 1968. Pp. 58–71.

76 Neugarten, B. L., & Kraines, R. J. "Menopausal symptoms" in women of various ages. *Psychosom. Med.,* 1965, **27,** 266–273.

77 Neugarten, B. L., Wood, V., Kraines, R. J., & Loomis, B. Women's attitudes toward the menopause. In D. C. Charles and W. R. Looft (Eds.), *Readings in psychology through life.* New York: Holt, 1973. Pp. 380–390.

78 *New York Times* article. "Go-getters" called more susceptible to heart attacks. *The New York Times,* Jan. 8, 1966.

79 *New York Times* article. Woman begins to find her place—and it's not in the kitchen. *The New York Times,* Feb. 16, 1966.

80 *New York Times* article. Leisure use called factor in marriage. *The New York Times,* May 11, 1966.

81 Novak, E. R. The menopause. *J. Amer. Med. Ass.,* 1954, **156,** 575–578.

82 Packard, V. *The status seekers.* New York: Pocket Books, 1961.

83 Packard, V. *The pyramid climbers.* New York: McGraw-Hill, 1962.

84 Packard, V. *A nation of strangers.* New York: McKay, 1972.

85 Parker, E. *The seven ages of woman.* Baltimore: Johns Hopkins Press, 1960.

86 Peck, R. C. Psychological developments in the second half of life. In B. L. Neugarten (Ed.), *Middle age and aging: A reader in social psychology.* Chicago: University of Chicago Press, 1968. Pp. 88–92.

87 Phillips, D. L. Social participation and happiness. *Amer. J. Sociol.,* 1967, **72,** 479–488.

88 Pressey, S. L., & Kuhlen, R. G. *Psychological development through the life span.* New York: Harper & Row, 1957.

89 Rickles, N. K. The discarded generation: The woman past fifty. *Geriatrics,* 1968, **23,** 112–116.

90 Rosencranz, M. L. Social and psychological approaches to clothing research. *J. Home Econ.,* 1965, **57,** 26–29.

91 Ryan, M. S. *Clothing: A study in human behavior.* New York: Holt, 1966.

92 Schmitz-Scherzer, R., & Strödel, I. Age-dependency of leisure-time activities. *Hum. Develpm.,* 1971, **14,** 47–50.

93 Sessoms, A. D. An analysis of selected variables affecting outdoor recreation patterns. *Soc. Forces,* 1963, **42,** 112–115.

94 Shanas, E., Townsend, P., Wedderburn, D., Friis, H., Milhøj, P., & Stehouwer, J. The psychology of health. In B. L. Neugarten (Ed.), *Middle age and aging: A reader in social psychology.* Chicago: University of Chicago Press, 1968. Pp. 212–219.

95 Sherman, J. A. *On the psychology of women: A survey of empirical studies.* Springfield, Ill.: Charles C Thomas, 1971.

96 Shock, N. W. *Trends in gerontology.* (2nd ed.) Stanford, Calif.: Stanford University Press, 1959.

97 Simon, A. W. *The new years: A new middle age.* New York: Knopf, 1968.

98 Slotkin, J. S. Life course in middle age. *Soc. Forces,* 1954, **33,** 171–177.

99 Steincrohn, P. J. Exercise after 40? Forget it! In C. B. Vedder (Ed.), *Problems of the middle-aged.* Springfield, Ill.: Charles C Thomas, 1965. Pp. 18–24.

100 Strong, E. K. Permanence of interest scores over 22 years. *J. appl. Psychol.,* 1951, **35,** 89–91.

101 Terman, L. M., & Oden, M. H. *The gifted group at mid-life: Thirty-five years' follow-up of the superior child.* Vol. 5. Stanford, Calif.: Stanford University Press, 1959.

102 Thompson, L. J. Stresses in middle life from the psychiatrist's viewpoint. In C. B. Vedder (Ed.), *Problems of the middle-aged.* Springfield, Ill.: Charles C Thomas, 1965. Pp. 116–120.

103 *Time* article. The springs of youth. *Time,* Apr. 16, 1965, 73.

104 *Time* article. Pills to keep women young. *Time,* Apr. 1, 1966, 50.

105 *Time* article. The command generation. *Time,* July 29, 1966, 50–54.

106 Tuckman, J., & Lorge, I. Classification of the self as young, middle-aged, or old. *Geriatrics,* 1954, **9,** 534–536.

107 Udry, J. R. Structural correlates of feminine beauty preferences in Britain and the United States: A comparison. *Sociol. soc. Res.,* 1965, **49,** 330–342.

108 Udry, J. R., & Hall, M. Marital role segregation and social networks in middle-class, middle-aged couples. *J. Marriage & Family,* 1965, **27,** 392–395.

109 *U.S. News & World Report* article. Advice to businessmen on health and retirement. *U.S. News & World Report,* Mar. 7, 1966, 62–67.

110 *U.S. News & World Report* article. Effects of shift in population. *U.S. News & World Report,* Mar. 7, 1966, 50–52.

111 *U.S. News & World Report* article. Leisure boom: Biggest ever and still growing. *U.S. News & World Report,* Apr. 17, 1972, 42–45.

112 *U.S. News & World Report* article. Big surge in education: Back to school for millions of adults. *U.S. News & World Report,* Apr. 2, 1973, 73–74.

113 Vahanian, G. Ethic of leisure. *Humanitas,* 1972, **8,** 347–365.

114 Vedder, C. B. (Ed.) *Problems of the middle-aged.* Springfield, Ill.: Charles C Thomas, 1965.

115 Werner, A. A. Sex behavior and problems of the climacteric. In M. Fishbein and E. W. Burgess (Eds.), *Successful marriage.* (Rev. ed.) Garden City, N.Y.: Doubleday, 1955. Pp. 475–490.

116 Winokur, G. Depression in the menopause. *Amer. J. Psychiat.,* 1973, **130,** 92–93.

117 Zatlin, C. E., Storandt, M., & Botwinick, J. Personality and values of women continuing their education after thirty-five years. *J. Gerontol.,* 1973, **28,** 216–221.

CHAPTER TWELVE

MIDDLE AGE
Vocational and Family Adjustments

Adjustments that center around work and the family are even more difficult in middle age than personal and social adjustments, discussed in the preceding chapter. Establishing and maintaining a comfortable standard of living, for example, has become increasingly difficult in recent years. As a result of increased use of automation and because of the trend toward the merging of small companies with larger ones, many middle-aged persons are thrown out of work. They may find that the jobs for which their training and experience have fitted them no longer exist and that they lack the training and experience for jobs that do exist; thus they are forced into the ranks of the unemployed.

Adjustments to changed patterns of family life are equally difficult. It is never easy to adjust to playing the role of adviser to grown or nearly grown children after many years of caring for them and supervising their activities. These difficulties are intensified and prolonged when parents must subsidize a child's early marriage or extended education.

Many middle-aged men and women find it difficult to relate to their spouses as persons, as they did during the days of courtship and early marriage, after having played the role of coparent for many years while their children were growing up. Perhaps the most difficult adjustment of all relates to the care of aged parents after years of freedom from responsibility for them. For many men, adjustment problems arising in relation to work are the most serious, while for women, those involving family relationships are the hardest to cope with.

In addition to these areas of adjustment, the middle-aged person is faced with a totally new problem, that of adjusting to impending old age. Like all adjustments for which the individual has had no previous experience, this one is often difficult and gives rise to strong emotional tension.

VOCATIONAL ADJUSTMENTS

The vocational adjustments of middle-aged men and women today are complicated by a number of new conditions in the working environment. Some of the most important changes affecting vocational adjustments in middle age are given in Box 12-1.

In the past, as has been pointed out before, relatively few people lived to middle age, and even fewer were vocationally active during this entire period. Furthermore, changes in vocational patterns and in working conditions took place at a much slower rate than they do now. Thus relatively few workers were affected by such changes, and those who were affected suffered only slightly.

All this has changed, especially since World War II, when many of today's middle-

---

Box 12-1. CHANGED WORKING CONDITIONS THAT AFFECT MIDDLE-AGED WORKERS

Unfavorable Social Attitudes
While older workers used to be respected for the skills they had acquired through years of experience, today the tendency is to regard them as too old to learn new skills or keep pace with modern demands, as uncooperative in their relations with coworkers, and as subject to absenteeism and accidents because of failing health.

Hiring Policies
Because of the widespread belief that maximum productivity can be achieved by hiring and training younger workers and because employers want to spend the minimum amount for retirement pensions, middle-aged workers have greater difficulty getting jobs than younger ones, although this varies for different kinds of work. Thus changing jobs becomes increasingly more hazardous with each passing year.

Increased Use of Automation
Automated work requires a higher level of intelligence and greater speed than work that is not automated, and this has an adverse effect on middle-aged people who have low levels of intelligence or are in poor health.

Group Work
Training in the home, neighborhood, and school puts more stress on social adjustments now than in the past; thus younger workers can get along

better with their superiors and coworkers than middle-aged workers can.

Role of the Wife
As the man becomes more successful, the wife must act as a sounding board for his business problems, she must be an asset to him at social functions related to his work, and she must become active in community affairs.

Compulsory Retirement
With compulsory retirement now coming in the early to mid-sixties, the chances of promotion after fifty are slim, and the chances of getting a new job are even slimmer, except at a lower level and with lower pay.

Dominance of Big Business
Many small organizations are now being taken over by larger ones. A middle-aged worker whose company merges with another may find that he has no place in the new organization or that his job is on a lower level than before.

Relocation
With the consolidation of small businesses into big corporations, many workers are forced to relocate as factories and offices are moved near the parent company. The middle-aged worker who must move in order to keep his job may have more difficulty adjusting to a new location than a younger worker.

aged workers were entering the labor force. Even more important, many more middle-aged workers are affected by these changes in working conditions now than in the past. According to U.S. Department of Labor reports, there were 33.7 million middle-aged men and women working in 1972; it is estimated that by 1990, there will be 45.9 million (113).

Sex Differences in Vocational Adjustment

Now that ever-increasing numbers of women are entering the work world during middle age, vocational adjustment problems are no longer experienced mainly by men. Women have many of the same problems men do and also many that are unique to them.

Normally, the height of vocational success for men comes during the forties and early fifties. Not only does the worker reach the peak of his status in the organization at this time, but his income reaches its peak also.

However, many middle-aged men who have achieved status vocationally are still dissatisfied with their work. Vocational instability in the early forties stems from a number of causes, the most important of which are the general restlessness characteristic of this period of life; the ending of responsibility for the support of the children, which frees the worker from a burden he has carried for many years; and the realization that if he wants to change jobs, he must do it now or never.

As the number of middle-aged women in business and industry increases, so do their adjustment problems. One of the major problems involves full equality with men in terms of hiring, promotion, and salary. Most women, regardless of their training and ability, find it more difficult to get jobs and to be promoted than men. This is true in all except "women's fields," such as elementary school teaching, nursing, and beauty culture, where women encounter less

competition from men than in other lines of work.

Because of these conditions, not only do many middle-aged women derive less satisfaction from their work than they would otherwise, but they also have less desire to remain in the same job or to get another job as middle age advances.

Factors Influencing Vocational Adjustment in Middle Age

Good vocational adjustment in early adulthood will not necessarily guarantee good adjustment in middle age because the conditions contributing to good adjustment at one age often differ from those which contribute to good adjustment at another. Box 12-2 gives some of the conditions that influence the vocational adjustments of middle-aged men and women.

Assessment of Vocational Adjustment

Vocational adjustment in middle age, like that in early adulthood, can be assessed in terms of the success the individual achieves in his work and the degree of satisfaction he derives from it. Unless both these conditions are taken into consideration, an assessment of his adjustment will not be accurate.

Achievements Many middle-aged workers enjoy a degree of success that gives them the income, the prestige, the authority, and the autonomy they had hoped for. Others, also trained and experienced, find themselves in less rewarding jobs below their capacities. Still others may be successful in that they have made the most of their abilities and training, but regard themselves as failures because they have not achieved the success they had hoped for when they were younger. This lack of satisfaction with their achievements makes them discontented with their jobs and with themselves as workers.

Women, far more often than men, fail to achieve the vocational success they are ca-

---

Box 12-2. CONDITIONS INFLUENCING VOCATIONAL ADJUSTMENTS IN MIDDLE AGE

Satisfaction with Work
The middle-aged person who likes his work will make far better vocational adjustments than one who has stayed at a job he dislikes because of earlier family responsibilities and who now feels "trapped."

Opportunities for Promotion
Each year, as the worker approaches the age of compulsory retirement, his chances of promotion grow slighter, and he is more likely to be pushed aside to make way for a younger worker. This has an adverse effect on his vocational adjustments.

Vocational Expectations
As retirement becomes imminent, the middle-aged worker assesses his achievements in light of his earlier aspirations; this assessment has a profound effect on his vocational adjustments.

Increased Use of Automation
Certain aspects of automation militate against good vocational adjustment on the part of the middle-aged worker, such as boredom and lack of pride in his work; the possibility of losing his job to a younger worker; increased speed required on the job, which makes older workers nervous; and unwillingness to retrain because of the imminence of retirement.

Attitude of Spouse
If the wife is dissatisfied with her husband's status at work, his pay, or the fact that she is left alone now that the children are grown, he may become dissatisfied too. Women whose husbands object to their working may also experience job dissatisfaction.

Attitude toward a Big Company
The worker who takes pride in being associated with a big, prestigious company will make better adjustments to his work than one who regards himself as merely a little cog in a big machine.

Attitude toward Coworkers
The middle-aged worker who resents the treatment he receives from his superiors or his subordinates and who regards younger workers as shiftless and careless will have a less favorable attitude toward his work than one who is on friendlier terms with his coworkers.

Relocation
How the worker feels about moving to another community in order to keep his present job or be promoted to a better one will have a profound influence on his vocational adjustments.

---

pable of during middle age. This is just as true of women who have worked continuously since they finished their education as of women who left their jobs after they were married and then returned to work after their home and parental duties diminished. This failure is due not to lack of ability and training but to prejudice against women in positions of responsibility.

Satisfaction Among industrial workers, the forties are the "critical age" for job satisfaction. This age comes slightly later for workers in business and the professions. By the end of the fifties and early sixties, there is a sharp drop in vocational satisfaction (93). This is shown in Figure 12-1.

About five years before the compulsory retirement age, whether it is sixty, sixty-two, or sixty-five, there is usually a sharp drop in the satisfaction the worker experiences. (See Figure 12-1.) The reason for this drop is that the worker now feels he has little chance for advancement, no matter how hard he may work or how faithfully he may report to his job.

Job satisfaction also wanes as middle age progresses because the worker begins to feel the pressure of work more as a result of his general slowing down and his increased tendency toward fatigue, which are natural accompaniments of aging. In addition, he resents the attitudes of younger workers who can do the work more easily than he and

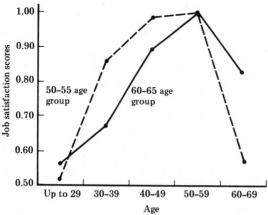

Figure 12-1 Job satisfaction reaches its peak in the mid-fifties and then declines abruptly. (Adapted from S. D. Saleh & J. L. Otis. Age and level of job satisfaction. *Personnel Psychol.,* 1964, **17**, 425–430. Used by permission.)

who often seem to be counting the days until he retires and they can take his place. None of these conditions leads to job satisfaction.

Middle-aged women, even more than men, fail to derive the satisfaction they should from their work. And, like men, their dissatisfaction increases with each passing year until they welcome the compulsory re-

---

Box 12-3. CONDITIONS CONTRIBUTING TO VOCATIONAL SATISFACTION IN MIDDLE AGE

Achievement or near achievement of a vocational goal set earlier

Satisfaction on the part of family members, especially the spouse, with the worker's vocational achievements

Opportunities for self-actualization on the job

Congenial relationships with coworkers

Satisfaction with treatment from management and direct superiors

Satisfaction with the provisions made by management for illness, vacations, disability, retirement, and other fringe benefits

Feelings of security about the job

Not being forced to relocate to hold a job, advance in it, or get a new job

---

tirement age. Their dissatisfaction is due to many of the same factors that cause dissatisfaction in men, but it is intensified by their resentment at not being given equal opportunities for advancement when their abilities justify it. Members of minority groups, both men and women, also experience job dissatisfaction for this reason.

The most important conditions leading to vocational satisfaction in middle age are given in Box 12-3. When satisfaction is high, the worker will do all he possibly can to keep his work up to previous standards, even though he may have to press himself to do so; he will be loyal to his employers and not take unnecessary time off from work; he will try to bolster the morale of his coworkers; and he will not complain, even when things are not to his liking.

ADJUSTMENT TO CHANGED FAMILY PATTERNS

The pattern of family life undergoes marked changes during the period of middle age. As Cavan has pointed out, "The most obvious change is the withdrawal of . . . children from the family, leaving husband and wife as the family unit" (21). This change is usually more difficult for the woman to adjust to than for the man, primarily because her life is centered around the home and family members. During the "shrinking circle stage," as Lopata has called it, the middle-aged housewife no longer derives all her satisfaction and prestige from her roles as wife and mother, and the replacements she finds for these roles, whether as a worker outside the home or as a participant in community activities are rarely as satisfying to her (53).

Adjustment to changed family patterns in middle age is often complicated by a number of factors that are either directly or indirectly related to family life. The most important of these are given in Box 12-4.

Some of these factors affect men and women differently, and some are more important early in middle age than later. For example, because the woman has had to

---

Box 12-4. CONDITIONS COMPLICATING ADJUSTMENT TO CHANGED FAMILY PATTERNS IN MIDDLE AGE

Physical Changes

The physical and psychological disturbances that accompany the menopause and the male climacteric often intensify the other adjustment problems of middle age which, in turn, heighten these physical and psychological disturbances.

Loss of Parental Role

Like all habits, that of centering one's life around one's home and children is hard to break. Middle-aged people who are able to occupy their time with activities they find satisfying will be able to adjust to the loss of the parental role.

Lack of Preparation

While most middle-aged people are prepared for the physical changes that accompany middle age, few are prepared for the role changes that take place in both their family and vocational lives. Adjustment problems are greatly intensified if role changes and physical changes occur simultaneously.

Feelings of Failure

The middle-aged person whose marriage has not turned out as he had hoped or whose children have not come up to his expectations often blames himself and feels that he is a failure.

Feelings of Uselessness

The more child-centered the home was earlier, the more useless the middle-aged person will feel when parental responsibilities diminish or come to an end.

Disenchantment with Marriage

Disenchantment with marriage is often caused or intensified by unforeseen changes in the marital situation, such as the husband's loss of a job or lack of success or the failure of children to come up to parental expectations.

Care of Elderly Relatives

Most middle-aged people resent having to care for an elderly relative because they do not want to be tied down, as they were when their children were young, and because they fear that strained relationships with the spouse or adolescent children will result.

---

center her interests mainly around the home, her habit of being family-oriented is more firmly fixed than her husband's and is more difficult to break in middle age. Also, the impact of the menopause occurs earlier and more suddenly than the impact of the male climacteric, and women must make a more radical adjustment to the physical and psychological changes that accompany loss of the reproductive function.

While both men and women must make role changes as their children grow up and leave home, these changes are easier for men to make than for women, partly because the father's role is far less time- and energy-consuming than the mother's and partly because men can compensate for radical changes in family life by deriving added sat-

isfaction from their work, which most women cannot do. Finally, men and women become disenchanted with marriage for different reasons. The man may be disenchanted with his marriage if he feels that his lack of vocational success is the result of the strains of family life or the unfavorable attitudes of family members toward his work. A woman is more likely to become disenchanted with marriage if she feels useless now that her maternal responsibilities have lessened or are over or if she feels that her husband is more concerned about his work than about his home and family. Thus in the case of both men and women during middle age, disenchantment with marriage is due more to conditions within the family than to the relationship between husband and wife, though this tends to intensify the effects of changed family patterns.

Some of the adjustment problems that middle-aged men and women must face in their family lives are individual in nature, while others are more or less universal and a product of the culture in which the person lives. The most important of these are discussed below.

Adjustment to Changed Roles

When the children reach maturity and leave home, either to marry or to pursue a career, parents must face the adjustment problems of a period which is almost as long today as the whole period during which the children were living at home. This means a change of roles for both parents and a branching out from the family, which is especially difficult for the woman. Refer to Figure 10-2 for a graphic illustration of the pattern of role changes that middle-aged men and women must make when their parental responsibilities are over.

The difficulties of adjusting to the departure of children from the home and to the role changes that this necessitates are increased for parents who have few outside interests and have built their lives around their children. Overly protective and possessive parents are especially prone to make their children the center of their lives.

As their married children become increasingly involved in their own families, it becomes clear to parents that they feel more love and concern for their children than their children feel for them. This intensifies the parents' adjustment problems, especially those of the mother.

Adjustment to Spouse

With the ending of parental responsibilities, the husband and wife once again become dependent upon each other for companionship. Whether they will adjust successfully to this changed pattern of family relationships is greatly influenced by how well adjusted they were when parental roles took precedence over husband-wife roles.

Only when husband and wife can establish a close relationship, similar to the one they had during the early years of marriage, can they find happiness in marriage during middle age. Establishing such a relationship is often difficult and, even more important, may take time, as husbands and wives adjust to their new roles (89). Marital satisfaction reaches a low point when children are leaving home and when role changes must be made. As these role changes are made, marital satisfaction increases.

Sexual Adjustments

Sex is as important to marital satisfaction during middle age as it is in early adulthood (18). See Figure 12-2. Women, it has been found, can enjoy coitus without orgasm more during middle age than they could during the early years of marriage (117).

While poor sexual adjustment does not necessarily lead to marital unhappiness and divorce, it has been found to be an important contributing factor to the disenchantment with marriage that so often occurs during middle age (26,80). Thus poor sexual adjustment is a serious interference with good marital adjustment.

One of the major causes of poor sexual adjustment in middle age is differences in the sex drive at this time. Studies of the pattern of development of the sex drive have shown that the male's sex drive is stronger in adolescence and reaches its peak earlier than the female's sex drive. The woman's sex drive and interest in sex, by contrast, become stronger as she approaches middle age. The fact that husband and wife are at different stages of development of the sex drive during middle age, combined with differences in interest in sexual behavior, may result in marital discord (55,79).

Poor sexual adjustments also result

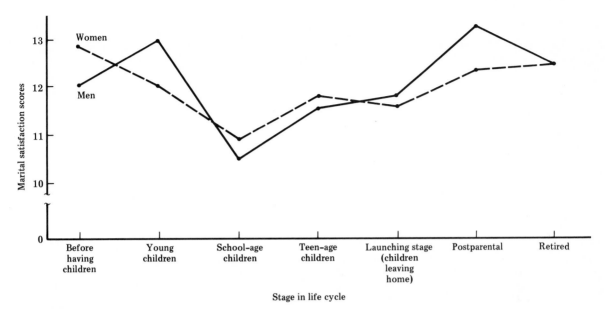

Figure 12-2 Sexual satisfaction is as important to good marital adjustment in middle age as it is during early adulthood. The graph shows how this phase of marital satisfaction varied for a sample of couples at various stages of their married life. (Adapted from W. R. Burr. Satisfaction with various aspects of marriage over the life cycle: A random middle-class sample. *J. Marriage & Family,* 1970, **32,** 29–37. Used by permission.)

when the man becomes concerned about the loss of his sexual vigor. He may develop feelings of inadequacy or go to the opposite extreme and have sexual relations with younger women to prove to himself that he is still virile (55,79).

During the forties and early fifties, many women lose their earlier inhibitions and develop more interest in sex. Because this occurs at the time when the man's interest in sex is declining, middle-aged women may be sexually unsatisfied and unhappy.

Some middle-aged women, knowing that it is their last chance, decide to have a child. This often complicates their adjustments to their husbands, who may not want a baby now that they have won freedom from their parental responsibilities or who may be embarrassed at having a baby the age of their grandchildren.

The middle-aged woman who derives

little satisfaction from intercourse or who feels that it is no longer interesting to her husband or a necessary part of marriage may take the initiative in stopping it. This intensifies an already-existing belief that she is no longer needed or wanted, a belief that neither adds to her happiness nor contributes to good adjustments with her husband.

In spite of the difficulties involved in sexual adjustment during middle age, there is evidence that many middle-aged men and women make satisfactory sexual adjustments, which contributes to their marital satisfaction (18). As may be seen in Figure 12-2, after a drop in satisfaction with sex during early adulthood, when the children are young, satisfaction increases as they grow up and begin to leave home. A woman's decline in satisfaction from sex during middle age is due primarily to the attitudes and behavior of her husband. By contrast, a man's lessening of satisfaction with sex is due primarily to conditions within himself (79).

Adjustments to In-Laws

Two new kinds of in-law adjustments may have to be made during middle age: adjustments to the care of aging parents and adjustments to children's spouses (11). The most important difficulties middle-aged people experience in adjusting to their children's spouses are given in Box 12-5.

Although the second in-law adjustment problem that may arise during middle age—that of caring for aged parents—is less common now than in the past, it is far more complicated today because the typical pattern of family life is that of the nuclear family—parents and children. The most important conditions influencing the middle-aged person's adjustment to the problem of

The "fun-seeking" grandparental role is characterized by informality and playfulness; the grandparent tries to be a "pal" to the grandchild. (Suzanne Szasz)

Box 12-5. CONDITIONS CONTRIBUTING TO DIFFICULTIES IN ADJUSTING TO CHILDREN'S SPOUSES

The expectation on the part of the middle-aged couple that they will continue to have the same relationship with their children that existed before marriage and that their relationship with a son- or daughter-in-law will be the same as their relationship with their own children

The necessity for married children to live with their parents or in-laws

The tendency of the middle-aged couple to offer too much advice to a son- or daughter-in-law

Dissimilarity of sociocultural background of in-laws, leading to criticisms and strained relationships

Elopement, which leads to parental embarrassment and resentment

Residential propinquity, which encourages frequent contacts and parental overprotectiveness and interference

Psychological dependency of a married daughter on her parents, which may make her husband resent them

A lack of grandchildren, which may be a disappointment to the middle-aged parents and which may also give the married children more independence and thus cause them to neglect their parents, which adds to parental resentment

---

caring for elderly parents are given in Box 12-6.

Middle-aged persons who carry this burden are often deprived of opportunities to develop new interests and engage in social activities outside the home to take the place of the child-centered activities of early adulthood. While caring for an elderly parent may help fill the gap created when children leave home, the satisfaction derived from this companionship may be far from adequate and may even intensify parental loneliness.

Adjustment to Grandparenthood

With the present trend toward early marriage, many men and women today become grandparents before middle age ends.

Box 12-6. CONDITIONS AFFECTING ADJUSTMENT TO CARE OF AGING PARENTS

Role Reversal

The elderly parent does not find it easy to relinquish the authority and autonomy he enjoyed in his or her own home, even to a grown child, especially not to an in-law.

Place of Residence

The adjustment to care of elderly parents is eased if the parents can remain in their own home and receive only financial aid from their children, rather than moving in with them or living in a home for the aged.

Degree of Responsibility

Many middle-aged people become resentful if the care of elderly parents represents a heavy financial burden or greatly restricts their activities.

Relationship of Aging Parent to Middle-aged Person

Although both husbands and wives are more resentful about caring for an in-law than a parent, the wife is especially resentful because she has the major responsibility for this care.

Role Played by Elderly Parent

When the elderly parent is physically able to help with household chores and does not disrupt the family routine, the adjustment will be far better than if he expects to be waited on and interferes in the lives of other family members.

Sex of Elderly Parent

Regardless of whose home the elderly parent lives in, men cause less work and interfere less than women.

Earlier Experiences with Elderly Parent

Middle-aged people whose earlier experiences with their parents or in-laws have been favorable make far better adjustments to the care of these elderly relatives than those whose earlier experiences have been unfavorable.

Attitude toward Elderly Parent

The middle-aged person's adjustment to the care of an elderly relative depends greatly on his attitude toward him, which may range from loathing to love, depending partly on earlier experiences and partly on the behavior of the elderly person now.

In fact, some become greatgrandparents during this period.

Grandparents now play a less important role in the lives of their children and grandchildren than in the past. Not only do families live further apart today, but younger people now have less respect for the elderly. Thus the middle-aged person of today has fewer contacts with his grandchildren and less influence over them than was true in past generations.

However, the relationships of grandparents with their grown children and their grandchildren depend on the role they play in their grandchildren's lives. Neugarten and Weinstein have distinguished five roles that the modern grandparent can play (66). These are listed in Box 12-7.

Most American grandparents of today prefer a "pleasure without responsibility"

relationship with their grandchildren. The older the grandchildren are, the more trying the grandparents find them after a short time, and thus they prefer shorter contacts with them and fewer responsibilities (66). This is illustrated in Figure 12-3.

ADJUSTMENT TO BEING SINGLE

By middle age, most unmarried men and women have adjusted to being single and are reasonably happy with the pattern of life they have established for themselves. Some, however, have not made a satisfactory adjustment to being single and decide to marry during middle age.

Most women are realistic enough to know that after they pass forty, their chances for marriage grow slimmer every

---

Box 12-7. ROLES PLAYED BY TODAY'S GRANDPARENTS

The Formal Role

The grandparents follow a "hands-off" policy as far as care and discipline are concerned, although they may enjoy providing treats for special occasions.

The Fun-seeking Role

The grandparents enjoy an informal, playful relationship with their grandchildren, but do not want to assume any responsibility for them.

The Surrogate-Parent Role

The grandparents assume responsibility for the care of grandchildren in the event of divorce or the death of a parent, if the mother must work outside the home, or when the parents want to take a short vacation from the children. Usually the grandmother is more active in this role.

The "Reservoir of Family Wisdom" Role

The grandparents dispense special knowledge to the grandchildren or teach them certain skills. The grandfather is usually more active in this role.

The Distant-Figure Role

The grandparents appear only on special occasions and have fleeting and infrequent contacts with their grandchildren. This role is especially common when grandparents are geographically or socially remote.

Figure 12-3 For many middle-aged people, the grandparent role is often more trying than pleasurable. (M. O. Lichty. "Grin and Bear It," Publishers-Hall Syndicate, Nov. 14, 1972. Used by permission.)

"They got some idea that asking us to sit with our grandchildren makes us feel 'needed' . . . All I get is a feeling of being 'used'! . . ."

year. This is far more true in the case of single women than of widows or divorcees. After forty-five, it has been reported, the single woman's chances of marriage are 9 out of 100, as compared with 50 out of 100 for divorcees and 18 out of 100 for widows (94,115). Knowing how slim her chances of marriage are, the middle-aged single woman adjusts her life pattern accordingly and often centers her life around her work.

Most men who are single in middle age are so by preference. They find it socially advantageous to be bachelors, and they know they can marry whenever they no longer derive satisfaction from being single. Furthermore, if they have high aspirations for vocational success, they may prefer to devote their time and energy to working and getting ahead.

Just as marriage creates many problems for men and women in middle age, so does being single. Furthermore, single women, like those who are married, tend to have more difficult problems during middle age than men do. The most complex problems that single men and women must cope with during middle age, are discussed below.

Problems of Women Problems related to employment and vocational advancement are even more serious for the middle-aged woman than for the man. If she should lose her job, she has even less chance of finding another one than a middle-aged man in the same position. Also, women who hold their jobs through middle age are far less often promoted to positions of prestige and responsibility than men, and they must face an earlier retirement age in most companies.

As a result of these practices, working is not always a satisfactory substitute for marriage, with the security it normally brings. Worries about economic security and frustrations arising from the realization that promotion will be denied her more because of her sex than because of lack of ability make middle age a less happy period for women than early adulthood, when job security was taken for granted and there was always the possibility of marriage.

To add to her adjustment problems, it is usually the single woman in a family who is expected to assume the responsibility of caring for an elderly parent. This often creates a financial burden in addition to the physical and emotional burden of caring for an elderly person while holding down a job.

Assuming responsibilities for the care of an aging parent generally means that the middle-aged single woman must limit her social life. As a result, she often cuts herself off from social contacts and activities in community organizations so drastically that when the care of the parent ends with the parent's death, she finds herself far lonelier than the middle-aged widow or divorcée, who may have her children or friends she acquired during the years of her marriage to fall back on for companionship.

Problems of Men The single man is usually in a more favorable position in middle age than the single woman. Because he has not had the responsibilities of a family through the early adult years, he has been able to devote as much time as he wished to his work, and he has been free to move to areas where greater opportunities were available. Although success in the bus-

iness world depends on hard work and a willingness to adapt oneself to new situations, the middle-aged man is usually better rewarded for his past efforts than the middle-aged woman who has followed the same pattern of hard work and personal sacrifice in earlier years, and he is more likely to be promoted. The middle-aged bachelor is therefore generally at the peak of his career, and he has little reason to be concerned about unemployment.

Furthermore, a single man is not handicapped by the problems of caring for elderly parents unless no other family members can assume the responsibility. When he must take on this burden, he usually provides financial aid rather than sacrificing his time and efforts to take care of their needs. Consequently, he is free to lead the kind of life he wants, and he has relatively few of the adjustment problems that the middle-aged single woman must face.

ADJUSTMENT TO LOSS OF A SPOUSE

The loss of a spouse, whether as a result of death or divorce, presents many adjustment problems for the middle-aged man or woman, but especially for the woman. The middle-aged woman whose husband dies or who is divorced experiences extreme feelings of loneliness. This is intensified by frustrations of the normal sexual desires, which are far from dormant. A person who loses a spouse and remains alone for ten or more years generally makes satisfactory adjustments to being single, although he may tend to be lonely and to find the single state unsatisfactory.

Loss of a spouse as a result of divorce affects middle-aged people very differently, depending primarily upon who wanted the divorce. A woman whose husband divorced her to marry someone else will have very different reactions from those of a woman who found her marriage intolerable and initiated the divorce herself. This will be discussed in more detail later in connection with the hazards of middle age.

The man whose wife dies or who is divorced experiences a disruption in his pattern of living unless a relative can manage the home for him. A woman who is widowed or divorced in middle age often must give up her home, go to work, and live very differently from the way she did when her husband was alive or before her divorce. The woman alone also encounters social complications which men do not face. She may be reluctant to go out by herself, and the problem of entertaining is likewise awkward.

For the divorced woman, the social complications are even greater. Not only may she be excluded from social activities, but, even worse, she often loses old friends. While some will remain her friends, many will ostracize her or rally around her husband. As Goode has explained (67):

The divorcee is often anathema to married couples because she embodies tensions they may be feeling but are trying to overlook. Wives, suspicious of her motives, misinterpret her most casual gestures toward their husbands. Husbands, meanwhile, assume she is in a perpetual state of tumescence.

Perhaps the most serious problem that loss of a spouse in middle age presents to women stems from the fact that their chances for remarriage become slimmer as they grow older. And since women can expect to live longer than men, this means a long period of loneliness complicated by financial and social problems.

ADJUSTMENT TO APPROACHING OLD AGE

In recent years, many business and industrial organizations have come to realize that they have an obligation to help their employees adjust to the problems of retirement since they are largely responsible for creating these problems. At first, the main emphasis was on an adequate income after retirement, but it soon became apparent that preparation for old age should take into account other, more difficult problems as well.

As a result, some large corporations now provide lectures and individual counseling for employees who will soon reach the retirement age. Thus many laymen have become aware of what psychologists have stressed for a number of years, namely, that a person adjusts more quickly and easily to a problem if he is prepared ahead of time for it.

Middle-aged people who have unfavorable attitudes toward old age literally shut their eyes and ears to anything relating to it. It has been reported, for example, that middle-aged people show little or no interest in watching television programs about the problems of the aged (2).

Because middle-aged men and women so often dread old age as a result of their acceptance of the unfavorable stereotypes about it, they are often inadequately prepared to make the necessary adjustments to this age. Thus many adults find old age one of the most unsatisfactory periods of life.

Most of the problems of old age, it has been found, originate in middle age or even earlier (114). Therefore, if the individual is to adjust successfully to it, he must make preparations earlier in life for the problems that are most likely to arise during old age. The most important areas of preparation for old age are given in Box 12-8.

VOCATIONAL AND MARITAL HAZARDS OF MIDDLE AGE

Vocational and marital adjustments during middle age are the most difficult to make and thus the most hazardous. Satisfactory adjustments in these areas are even more important to happiness in middle age than satisfactory personal and social adjustments, and failure to make good adjustments in these areas is at the basis of much

---

Box 12-8. AREAS OF PREPARATION FOR OLD AGE

Health

Preparation for old age should include health measures that will prevent or mitigate the effects of the chronic and debilitating diseases of old age.

Retirement

The older person who has prepared for retirement or for loss of the parental role by acquiring new interests and engaging in new activities makes better adjustments to old age than the one who has made no such preparation.

Use of Leisure Time

The middle-aged person should pursue hobbies and acquire interests that will be satisfactory during old age, when he must give up his more strenuous leisure-time activities.

Role Changes

The middle-aged person must prepare for the role changes which are inevitable in old age, whether in business, in the home, or in community activities. It is especially important that he learn gradually to relinquish leadership roles and play the role of follower and to be content with this change.

Life Patterns

Middle-aged people should recognize that circumstances in old age may force them to move from their homes and change their life patterns. Those who are unprepared to make such changes—necessitated by poor health or reduced income, for example—will be unable to adjust to a new pattern of life and will be unhappy.

---

of the dissatisfaction that middle-aged people experience. Members of both sexes are faced with these hazards, though the effects they have on them may be slightly different.

Vocational Hazards

While many vocational hazards of middle age are similar to those of early adulthood, the following are particularly characteristic of this period.

First, failure to have reached a goal set earlier is an ego-deflating experience for the middle-aged person because he knows that this is the peak time for achievements and that he is unlikely to attain his goals in old age. His reaction to such a failure will affect his attitude toward himself and the kind of personal and social adjustments he makes now and also when he reaches old age. In discussing the effects of failure to achieve a goal set earlier, Bischof has pointed out (11):

Middle age is a "time of truth." Dreams and aspirations may have carried the man well through his 20s, 30s, and into his 40s. . . .

When a man gets to be 50 or so he settles his brains, if he is wise, to the realities of life. He must learn to cooperate with the inevitable. Whatever it was he had in his younger days that gave him the confidence to plan or to dream may not have been adequate for the advancement he sought in his occupation. Many men when faced with this time of truth may seek solace in at least one of two ways; compensation or rationalization.

Not all men and women cling to their early aspirations. Some revise them because they have become more realistic, while others do so because their values have changed. Whatever motivates this revision, it is important because it eliminates the potential hazard stemming from failure to come up to earlier aspirations and expectations. In a forty-year follow-up of Terman's "gifted group," Oden pointed out that some of the "C men"—those least successful vocationally—fell below their expectations because of value changes as they grew older. As she pointed out, "It should not be overlooked that a few of the C men have deliberately chosen not to seek 'success,' expressing a preference for a less competitive way of life with greater opportunity for personal happiness and freedom from pressure to pursue their avocational interests" (72).

The second vocational hazard that middle-aged people face is a decline in creativity, even though their level of productivity may remain the same or even improve (11,31). A decline in vocational creativity makes the middle-aged person less satisfied with his achievements, and he no longer is acclaimed for his creativity, as he was earlier. This decline may be due not to a lessening of mental abilities or to mental rigidity, as is widely believed, but rather to the fact that the middle-aged person has less time for creative work than he did before as a result of the added responsibilities and pressures that come with success. As has

The middle-aged craftsman who takes pride in his work is less likely than other middle-aged workers to feel bored by or trapped in his job. (Steinway & Sons)

already been pointed out, those who were successful earlier are usually assigned leadership roles when they reach middle age, and this leaves them little free time for the mental "play" essential to creativity (11).

While boredom—a third vocational hazard in middle age—is also a hazard during early adulthood, it affects the middle-aged worker more because his chances of finding a more stimulating job grow slimmer with each passing year. Boredom is especially common among industrial workers, who find that automation is increasingly replacing individual workmanship. As Packard has pointed out (75):

The repetitious arm movement he makes hour after hour is excruciatingly boring. His father, he recalls, was poor, but a craftsman who was proud of the barrels he made. Here the machine has all the brains, all the reason for pride. Perhaps the rules also forbid him to talk to workers nearby, or to get a drink of water except at the break period.

The fourth vocational hazard facing the middle-aged worker of today involves the tendency toward "bigness" in business, industry, and the professions. A middle-aged person who has been accustomed to working in a friendly, informal atmosphere may derive less satisfaction from working in a large, impersonal organization.

The fifth vocational hazard of middle age is a feeling of being "trapped." While a younger worker who is dissatisfied or bored with his job knows that he can always get another one, many middle-aged men and women feel that they must stay in a line of work they dislike because it is too late to train for another one. As one middle-aged man, when interviewed about his attitudes toward his work, put it (106):

Sure I feel trapped. Why shouldn't I? Twenty-five years ago, a dopey 18-year-old college kid made up his mind that I was going to be a dentist. So now here I am, a dentist. I'm stuck. What I want to know is: who told that kid he could decide what I was going to do with the rest of my life?

The sixth vocational hazard of middle age—unemployment—is always very serious, though more so in times of economic recession than in times of prosperity. Teen-age workers or young adults who lose their jobs or give them up can count on getting another job in a relatively short time. However, finding a new job becomes increasingly difficult with each passing year, and the period of unemployment grows increasingly longer (85). This is illustrated in Figure 12-4.

Three groups of middle-aged workers are especially vulnerable to unemployment: those with low IQs, women, and men of minority groups. As Anman has pointed out, the main problem for those with low IQs is that with the increased use of automation, ". . . we are eliminating the 80 IQ jobs but haven't yet determined what to do with the 80 IQ jobless" (3).

Even during periods of prosperity, women and men of minority groups are more subject to unemployment than men who are not minority-group members, and they are far more likely to be laid off during periods of economic recession or depression. Middle-aged women who want to reenter the business world after their children are grown up and who try to prepare for this by learning new skills or brushing up on old ones often find that the available jobs go to younger women (36).

Unemployment is a serious psychological hazard for any worker, regardless of age, sex, race, or minority-group status. Those who have been unemployed for a long time often develop feelings of inadequacy and of being unwanted, which result in either overaggressiveness or extreme passivity, both of which are handicaps to possible future employment.

Unfavorable attitudes toward one's job—the seventh vocational hazard of middle age—can have detrimental effects on both the worker's achievements and his per-

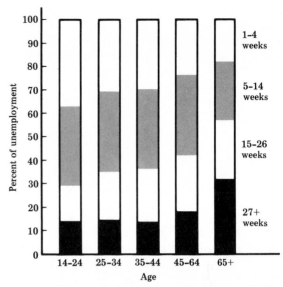

Figure 12-4 For the working population as a whole, the period of unemployment increases with each passing year. (From the *Report of the President's Council on Aging,* 1961.)

sonal adjustments. Like the student who dislikes school or college, the dissatisfied worker becomes an underachiever and a complainer who can undermine the morale of those around him. If he is dissatisfied because he feels trapped in a job he dislikes or because he thinks that his race, sex, or some other condition over which he has no control is blocking his path to success, he will develop feelings of martyrdom, which will intensify his unfavorable attitude. This militates against his holding the job he already has and makes getting and holding a new job far more difficult than it otherwise might be.

Marital Hazards

Although some of the marital hazards of middle age are similar to those of early adulthood, most stem from changes in the pattern of family life that occur at this time and thus are unique to middle age. Furthermore, marital hazards are often more serious now than they were in early adulthood because the chances of establishing good adjustments grow slimmer as time passes and as the children leave home, lowering the adult's motivation to provide a happy family atmosphere.

While marital hazards have a greater direct impact on middle-aged women than on middle-aged men, since the woman's life has been centered around her home and family for many years, they have an important indirect effect on the man's vocational life. As has been pointed out before, not only do the attitudes of different family members, especially those of the wife, influence the man's attitude toward his work and thus his vocational adjustments, but his adjustment to his family life also affects the quality of his work and his dedication to it. A man whose family life is stressful and unhappy, for example, finds it difficult to give his wholehearted attention to his work and may become a vocational underachiever. Also, because competing with other workers requires more concentrated effort in middle age than earlier, the middle-aged man whose home life is unhappy is doubly disadvantaged in this respect.

A number of hazards to the good personal and social adjustments of middle-aged men and women develop from conditions within their marriage. The most important of these are discussed below.

Role Changes As has been pointed out earlier, role changes are a serious hazard for the woman. When the children leave home, she finds herself in much the same position that the typical man does at retirement—unemployed. Few women, however, receive preparation for this, as many men now do from their employers. As one woman has put it, "Freshman have their advisers to help them to adjust to the changes that college life brings, but who helps the parent emeritus?" (116).

While most mothers want their children to be independent when they are developmentally ready, to have homes and families of their own, and to be successful in their work, many put roadblocks in their children's paths when the time actually comes for them to be on their own. Instead of gladly relinquishing the burden they have carried for so many years, many mothers cling to it because they fear that their lives will now seem empty and futile. For such women, the ending of the parental role is a traumatic experience, and neurotic difficulties are often the aftermath (33,76).

Opposition to a Child's Marriage Another serious problem arises when a child marries someone of whom his middle-aged parents do not approve. They will oppose the marriage, which militates against their making satisfactory adjustments to the child's departure from the home. This opposition also generally creates a barrier between them and their child, with the result that their contacts with the child after marriage are few and their relationships with the child's family are unfavorable.

Inability to Establish Satisfactory Relationships with the Spouse as a Person One of the important developmental tasks of middle age is that of establishing satisfactory relationships with a spouse. This is especially difficult for the woman because of the problems she faces in making satisfactory adjustments to the new role she must play now that the children have left home. This hazard to good marital adjustment affects men as well, however.

While many men and women do make this adjustment successfully and are even happier in their marriages than they were during the child-rearing years, for others it is a hazardous transition. The most important attitudes on the part of husband and wife that militate against the establishment of good relationships are given in Box 12-9. Many of these unfavorable attitudes have developed over the years, and by middle age they are often so deep-rooted that they are impossible to eradicate.

Box 12-9. ATTITUDES MILITATING AGAINST THE ESTABLISHMENT OF GOOD RELATIONSHIPS WITH A SPOUSE

Husband's Attitudes

Dissatisfaction with sexual adjustments

If he is successful vocationally, the feeling that his wife has not kept pace with him in his upward climb

If he is unsuccessful vocationally, the feeling that his wife has been of no help and may even have handicapped him

The feeling that he and his wife have little in common because she has refused to be interested in the things that are important to him

A critical attitude toward his wife's management of the home and the family finances and a belief that her child-training methods have been too permissive

Dissatisfaction with his wife's appearance

The feeling that his wife dominates him and treats him like a child

Wife's Attitudes

Dissatisfaction with sexual adjustments

Disillusionment with her husband because of his lack of success

The feeling of being a slave to the home or to an elderly relative

The belief that her husband was stingy about money for clothes and recreation when the children were young

The belief that her husband does not appreciate the time and effort she has devoted to homemaking

The feeling that her husband is more interested in his career than in her

The feeling that her husband spends too much time and money on members of his own family

The suspicions that he is involved with another woman

Sexual Adjustments Failure to achieve a good relationship with the spouse inevitably has an adverse effect on sexual relationships during middle age. This is a hazard to good marital adjustments and contributes greatly to disenchantment with marriage during this period.

A woman who is disenchanted with her marriage may try to compensate for this by devoting her time and energies to helping her grown children, by becoming active in community affairs, or by having an extramarital relationship with a man who she feels appreciates her more than her husband does.

The middle-aged man whose sexual life is unsatisfactory may likewise turn to extramarital affairs, or he may feel guilty because he has failed to give his wife sexual gratification. As Clark and Wallin have explained (26):

Women's lack of sexual gratification has repercussions for their husbands as well as for themselves. In a culture that stresses the equality of marital partners and the right of both to sexual enjoyment, it is to be expected that husbands will tend to suffer some guilt in urging an activity they know is not pleasurable to their wives. Added to the guilt, and accentuating it, may be feelings of inadequacy engendered in husbands by the thought that the fault is or could be theirs.

A serious hazard to good sexual adjustments during middle age is the unfavorable attitude of younger members of the family—especially teen-agers—toward sexual behavior on the part of their parents. As McKain has said, "Most children have never thought of their parents in the role of husband and wife. Instead, they have seen them only as mother and father—a self-sacrificing, asexual, and narrow role" (57).

The awareness that their children have such attitudes tends to make middle-aged parents self-conscious about their sexual behavior or to regard it as something to be

The three-generational household has good things to offer, but it also poses problems for the marital adjustment of middle-aged couples. (Suzanne Szasz)

ashamed of "at their age." This is unquestionably hazardous to good sexual adjustments.

Caring for an Elderly Parent Caring for an elderly parent in their homes is a serious hazard to good marital adjustments for many middle-aged couples because it interferes with their adjustment to each other after the children begin to leave home. It also interferes with good sexual adjustments. As Komarovsky has said, having an elderly relative in one's home requires the "combined virtues of a diplomat, statesman, and saint"—attributes that few middle-aged people have (48). To complicate the situation, the elderly relative is usually the mother of one of the spouses. If she does not want to change her role from that of head of a household to that of a dependent, she may try to dominate, as she did in her own home. This leads to friction with all family members and results in a generally stressful home climate.

Divorce and Remarriage Unquestionably, the most serious marital hazard of middle

age is divorce or the threat of one. In contrast to younger people, who usually seek a divorce because of sexual incompatibility, parental interference, or disenchantment with marriage and parenthood, most middle-aged people want to be divorced because the husband or wife has been unfaithful, because they feel their spouse has become irresponsible or is constantly nagging, or because they no longer have anything in common (12,80,91).

Because divorce in middle age is "major surgery" for both men and women, they do not rush into it impulsively, as young adults often do (106). However, there is evidence that divorce in middle age is the result of conditions that have worsened and persisted over the years until they finally became intolerable. Dame et al. have said (30):

One factor in the ultimate breakdown of some of the marriages was "grudges" which had been cherished on both sides for many years. Several husbands were preoccupied with unanswered questions about possible sexual activity of their wives either before or after the marriage. . . . Many of the wives held

*grudges about their suffering during preg-
nancies and their husbands' attitudes toward
them at that time. . . . The actual turning
point for the wife depends on many
factors—release from the confining care of
small children, the end of a shared endeavor
(such as building and furnishing a home), a
sense that life is slipping by or encouragement from another woman.*

Remarriage in middle age is likely to be
hazardous, especially when it follows divorce. Such marriages are more likely to
end in divorce than those of younger people
who remarry after having been divorced
(67,71). While financial problems plague
younger adults who remarry following divorce, problems of adjustment to each other
and to a new pattern of living are more likely
to interfere with the success of remarriage
in middle age. It is always difficult for
middle-aged people to change their roles and
follow new patterns of living (88,94).

ASSESSMENT OF ADJUSTMENT TO MIDDLE AGE

Middle age should be a time of "payoff"
and of newfound freedom, not only from
the cares and responsibilities of the home,
but also from economic problems and
worries. It should also be a time for rede-
fining oneself as a person, rather than as
just "Mother" or "Father," and it should be
a time of contentment and satisfaction
derived from a feeling that the years have
been well spent. As Hervey Allen pointed
out many years ago in *Anthony Adverse*,
"The only time you really live is from 30 to
60. The young are slaves of dreams: the old,
servants of regrets. Only the middle-aged
have all their five senses in the keeping of
their wits" (1).

For far too many people, unfortunately,
middle age is a time of regrets, of disappointments, and of general unhappiness. They
may be plagued by financial problems, vocational worries, career failures, or marital dif-

ficulties of long standing which flare up into
serious problems at this age. Even worse,
middle-aged people often feel that they are
failures and that it is now too late to achieve
all they had hoped to. As Erikson has
pointed out, "In middle life and beyond we
begin to see not so much what we wanted to
do but what we actually have done" (35).

The high suicide rate among middle-
aged people is evidence that this is far too
often a time of poor adjustment (107). In
one study it was found that the suicide rate
starts to climb between the ages of thirty-six
and forty years, reaching its peak between
forty and sixty years. It then declines in
the sixties, only to rise again at seventy.
Suicide is more common among men than
among women, and money problems are the
major cause (43). Rates of suicide at different ages are shown in Figure 12-5.

Four criteria can be used in determining
how well the middle-aged man or woman has
adjusted to this period in the life span: (1)
his achievements, (2) his emotional states, (3)
the effects of this adjustment on his personality, and (4) how happy or unhappy he is.

Achievements

The closer the middle-aged person has
come to achieving the goals he set for himself earlier, the better satisfied and hence
the better adjusted he will be. Even when
the middle-aged person has been as successful as could reasonably be expected, considering his abilities and training, he often
feels that he has been a failure because he
has clung to aspirations developed in youth
or even in childhood. As Whitman has explained (118):

*Many middle-aged men and women feel like
failures when they aren't failures at all.
They are merely using the wrong tape measure. They look at themselves in their 40s
and 50s and take their measures by the standards of childhood dreams and ambitions.
These standards are as ill-fitting to their
present stature as the trousers or the dresses*

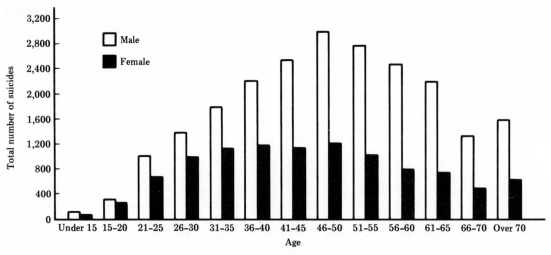

Figure 12-5 The suicide rate is highest among middle-aged persons. From data based on the Medical Examiner's records for New York City over a 30-year period. (Adapted from J. Hirsch. *Suicide. Ment. Hyg., N.Y.,* 1959, **43,** 516–525. Used by permission.)

they wore when they were youngsters. Childhood dreams are wonderful for children: but when we keep clinging to them in our middle years, they can make failures of us all. This is not because the childhood dreams are wrong—it is rather that we misunderstand their function. . . . *Somewhere in the middle years we must let go of the dream. We must, in our maturity, recognize the dream for what it really is: a childhood spur to get us on our way, a goad.*

Because many middle-aged people are not realistic about their potentials, they become discouraged when their achievements fall below their expectations. This discouragement, in turn, lowers their motivation, with the result that they do less than they are capable of doing.

Emotional States

An important criterion of adjustment to middle age is how stressful the individual is. As Billig and Adams have pointed out, "There has been an increasing awareness that middle age can bring anxiety and in-

security" (10). Stress, they explain, may be shown in many ways, the most common of which are conflicts with members of the family and a tendency to make great demands on them; excessive demands by the middle-aged person on those who work under him; a glorification of youthful patterns of behavior, especially as evidenced in sexual relations with younger people; and intense anxieties.

Middle-aged men and women have also been found to worry more than younger people (83). There is also evidence that emotional stress is more common during the early part of middle age than it is during the latter part. This can be explained by the fact that during the forties, changes in living patterns, role changes, and changes in self-concepts resulting from physical and role changes generally come upon men and women suddenly. Although changes are always difficult and thus are generally accompanied by stress, they are especially disturbing and emotion-provoking for those who have not made adequate provision for them (83).

By the mid-fifties, most individuals are

fairly well adjusted to middle age and are no longer upset by it. They have adjusted their roles, their interests, and their activities in accordance with the physical and psychological changes they have undergone. Life then moves along smoothly until the onset of old age (10). As worries subside during the latter part of middle age, the individual is calmer and, thus, happier.

Effects on Personality

The way in which physical and role changes affect the middle-aged person's self-concept is a good criterion of how well he is adjusting to middle age. When he is making satisfactory adjustments, his self-concept will be positive; he will feel that he is still a useful member of society and that he can still make worthwhile contributions, whether they be familial, social, or vocational. By contrast, the poorly adjusted individual develops a negative self-concept, characterized by feelings of worthlessness and uselessness.

Personality disorganization in middle age is related to poor social and emotional adjustment, much of which stems from poor adjustment in the earlier years. There is little evidence to indicate that middle age, per se, is responsible for the mental illnesses that occur at this time. On the other hand, there is adequate evidence that those who break under the strain of adjustments in middle age have a history of unresolved problems which have interfered with good adjustments. The stresses of middle age then prove to be too much for them to cope with, and mental illness severe enough to require institutionalization may set in (6,29,65).

Happiness

Happiness in middle age, as at all ages, comes when the individual's needs and desires *at that time* are satisfied. The person who is well adjusted, in the sense that he is able to satisfy his needs and desires quickly and adequately within the controls and outlets provided by the cultural group with which he is identified, will be far happier than the one who has been unable or unwilling to make the adjustments essential to satisfy them.

Success in a chosen vocation, which brings with it prestige, financial rewards, and improved social status for the family, goes a long way toward making middle age a satisfying period of life for men and helps to compensate for the lack of satisfaction they may derive from other areas of their lives. For women, whose lives have usually been centered around the home, satisfaction in middle age depends mainly on the success with which they are able to adjust to the changes they must make in the homemaking role. These adjustments are easier if the husband is successful vocationally and the woman is able to enjoy her newfound freedom, rather than being forced to go to work herself (90). Figure 12-6 shows how markedly the degree of satisfaction experienced by middle-aged men and women varies (42). Note that women tend to be better satisfied than men and that they derive greater satisfaction from their marital relations and their children than from their occupations and leisure-time and social activities. Note also that they are reasonably well satisfied with their self-concepts, further suggesting that they are able to make the good adjustment that is essential to happiness.

To be happy in middle age, as at all ages, the person must be realistic and realize that life has its problems as well as its rewards. If the rewards are adequate to compensate for the problems, the scale will be balanced in favor of happiness. As Levine has pointed out (52):

What the mind loses in alertness, it makes up for it in the assurance of reflective thinking. If the muscles grow sensitive to fatigue, they learn to respond more selectively to stimuli. If the bodily functions show signs of impairment, they flash intermittently the amber

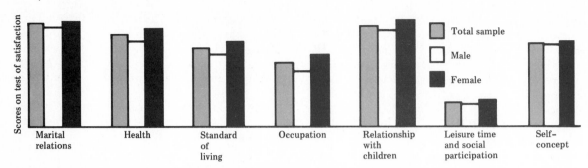

Figure 12-6 The degree of satisfaction middle-aged men and women derive from different areas of their lives varies markedly. (Adapted from M. P. Hayes & N. Stinnett. Life satisfaction of middle-aged husbands and wives. *J. Home Econ.*, 1971, **63**, 669–674. Used by permission.)

lights of caution. And if the fires of passion are being damped, one comes to prize the release from their tyrannical domination.

Chapter Highlights

1 Adjustments centering around work and the family are even more difficult during middle age than during early adulthood because many conditions over which the individual has little or no control arise to interfere with these adjustments.

2 Vocational adjustments during middle age are complicated by increased use of automation, problems arising from the merging of small companies with larger ones, group work, the necessity for the wife to play a role in her husband's climb up the vocational ladder, and unfavorable social attitudes toward older workers, which affect hiring policies.

3 Vocational adjustments in middle age are far more difficult for women than for men, partly because of unfavorable social attitudes toward them and partly because they have less work experience, as a result of having devoted the years of early adulthood to child rearing.

4 The most important conditions contributing to vocational satisfaction in middle age are the worker's satisfaction with the work itself, his opportunities for promotion, the attitude of his spouse, his ability to adjust to automation and group work, and his attitudes toward co-workers, toward working in a large organiza-

tion, and toward the necessity of relocating in order to keep his present job or be promoted to a better one.

5 How well the worker makes vocational adjustments during middle age can be determined by his achievements and by the degree of satisfaction he derives from his work.

6 The most important conditions complicating adjustment to family life in middle age are physical changes which interfere with adjustment to other changes; the difficulty of changing a habitual pattern of life; lack of preparation for the changes in family life that occur during middle age; feelings of failure or of uselessness; disenchantment with marriage; and problems arising from the necessity of caring for elderly relatives.

7 The major adjustments to family life that the middle-aged person must make are in the areas of changed family roles; new relationships with the spouse, necessitated by these changed roles; sexual relationships; relationships with in-laws, especially the children's spouses; caring for aged parents; and problems of grandparenthood.

8 By middle age, most unmarried men and women have made reasonably good adjustments to being single and are happy with the pattern of life they have established for themselves.

9 Loss of a spouse, whether due to death or divorce, disrupts the pattern of life for middle-aged men and women, and many try to adjust to this change by remarrying.

10 Some of the adjustment problems of old age can be minimized by proper preparation during middle age, especially in the areas of health, retirement, use of leisure time, and plans for family living.

11 The seven common vocational hazards that middle-aged men and women face are failure to reach goals they set for themselves earlier; a decline in creativity; the difficulty of shifting to a job that would be more to their liking; a feeling of being trapped in a job they dislike; unemployment, which becomes increasingly serious as the person grows older; and an unfavorable attitude toward the job. The common marital hazards of middle age include changing one's accustomed role in the family, the inability to establish favorable relationships with the spouse as a person, poor sexual adjustments, caring for an elderly parent in the home, divorce, and remarriage following divorce.

12 The four criteria used to assess the individual's adjustment to middle age are his achievements, his emotional states, the effect of physical and role changes on his self-concept, and how satisfied and happy he is with the pattern of his life.

Bibliography

1 Allen, H. *Anthony Adverse.* New York: Farrar & Rinehart, 1933.

2 Anderson, J. E. Aging and educational television: A preliminary survey. *J. Gerontol.,* 1962, **17,** 447–449.

3 Anman, F. A. Retraining: How much of an answer to technological unemployment? *Personnel J.,* 1962, **41,** 505–507.

4 Axelson, L. J. Personal adjustment in the postparental period. *Marriage fam. Living,* 1960, **22,** 66–68.

5 Bayley, N. Research in child development: A longitudinal perspective. *Merrill-Palmer Quart.,* 1965, **11,** 183–208.

6 Becker, H. S. Personal change in adult life. In B. L. Neugarten (Ed.), *Middle age and aging: A reader in social psychology.* Chicago: University of Chicago Press, 1968. Pp. 148–156.

7 Belbin, E., & Belbin, R. M. New careers in middle age. In B. L. Neugarten (Ed.), *Middle age and aging: A reader in social psychology.* Chicago: University of Chicago Press, 1968. Pp. 341–346.

8 Bernard, J. Marital stability and patterns of status variables. *J. Marriage & Family,* 1966, **28,** 421–448.

9 Bernard, J. No news but new ideas. In P. Bohannon (Ed.), *Divorce and after.* Garden City, N.Y.: Doubleday, 1970. Pp. 3–29.

10 Billig, O., & Adams, R. W. Emotional conflicts of the middle-aged man. In C. B. Vedder (Ed.), *Problems of the middle-aged.* Springfield, Ill.: Charles C Thomas, 1965. Pp. 121–133.

11 Bischof, L. J. *Adult psychology.* New York: Harper & Row, 1969.

12 Bohannon, P. (Ed.) *Divorce and after.* Garden City, N.Y.: Doubleday, 1970.

13 Bossard, J. H. S., & Boll, E. S. Marital unhappiness in the life cycle. *Marriage fam. Living,* 1955, **17,** 10–14.

14 Bowerman, C. E., & Kinch, J. W. Changes in family and peer orientation of children between the fourth and tenth grades. *Soc. Forces,* 1959, **37,** 206–211.

15 Brayshaw, A. J. Middle-aged marriage: Idealism, realism, and the search for meaning. *Marriage fam. Living,* 1962, **24,** 358–364.

16 Brozan, N. Middle age needn't be like dark ages. *The New York Times,* Mar. 29, 1973.

17 Brozek, J. Personality of young and middle-aged normal men: An analysis of a psychosomatic inventory. *J. Gerontol.,* 1962, **7,** 410–418.

18 Burr, W. R. Satisfaction with various aspects of marriage over the life cycle: A random middle-class sample. *J. Marriage & Family,* 1970, **32,** 29–37.

19 Cameron, P. Stereotypes about generational fun and happiness vs. self-appraised fun and happiness. *Gerontologist,* 1972, **12,** 120–123, 190.

20 Cavan, R. S. Family tensions between the old and the middle-aged. In C. B. Vedder (Ed.), *Problems of the middle-aged.* Springfield, Ill.: Charles C Thomas, 1965. Pp. 82–91.

21 Cavan, R. S. *The American family.* (4th ed.) New York: Crowell-Collier, 1969.

22 Chen, R. The dilemma of divorce: Disaster or remedy. *Family Coordinator,* 1968, **17,** 251–254.

23 Chilman, C. S. Families in development at mid-stage of the family life cycle. *Family Coordinator,* 1968, **17,** 297–312.

24 Christenson, C. V., & Gagnon, J. H. Sexual behavior in a group of older women. *J. Gerontol.,* 1965, **20,** 351–356.

25 Christrup, H. A preretirement program that works. *J. Home Econ.,* 1973, **65**(4), 20–22.

26 Clark, A. L., & Wallin, P. Women's sexual responsiveness and the duration and quality of their marriages. *Amer. J. Sociol.,* 1965, **71,** 187–196.

27 Clavan, S. The family process: A sociological model. *Family Coordinator,* 1969, **18,** 312–317.

28 Clayton, P. J., Halikas, J. A., & Maurice, W. L. The depression of widowhood. *Brit. J. Psychiat.,* 1972, **120,** 71–77.

29 Crisp, A. H., & Priest, R. G. Psychoneurotic profiles in middle age. *Brit. J. Psychiat.,* 1971, **119,** 385–392.

30 Dame, N. G., Finck, G. H., Reiner, B. S., & Smith, B. O. The effect on the marital relationship of the wife's search for identity. *Family Life Coordinator,* 1965, **14,** 133–136.

31 Dennis, W. Creative productivity between the ages of twenty and eighty years. In D. C. Charles & W. R. Looft (Eds.), *Readings in psychological development through life.* New York: Holt, 1973. Pp. 283–295.

32 Desmond, T. C. America's unknown middle-agers. *The New York Times,* July 29, 1956.

33 Deutscher, I. The quality of postparental life. In B. L. Neugarten (Ed.), *Middle age and aging: A reader in social psy-*

chology. Chicago: University of Chicago Press, 1968. Pp. 263–268.

34 Eisdorfer, C., & Lawton, M. P. (Eds.) *The psychology of adult development and aging.* Washington: APA, 1973.

35 Erikson, E. H. Identity and the life cycle: Selected papers. *Psychol. Issues Monogr.,* Vol. 1, No. 1. New York: International Universities Press, 1967.

36 Evans, O. They got their degrees—often the hard way—and then what? *The New York Times,* July 16, 1972.

37 Franzblau, R. N. *The middle generation.* New York: Holt, 1971.

38 Frenkel-Brunswik, E. Adjustments and reorientation in the course of the life span. In B. L. Neugarten (Ed.), *Middle age and aging: A reader in social psychology.* Chicago: University of Chicago Press, 1968. Pp. 77–84.

39 Fried, B. *The middle-age crisis.* New York: Harper & Row, 1967.

40 Gebhard, P. Postmarital coitus among widows and divorcees. In P. Bohannon (Ed.), *Divorce and after.* Garden City, N.Y.: Doubleday, 1970. Pp. 89–106.

41 *Harper's Bazaar* article. Childbirth after 40: New freedom from risk. *Harper's Bazaar,* August 1973, 32, 57, 86.

42 Hayes, M. P., & Stinnett, N. Life satisfaction of middle-aged husbands and wives. *J. Home Econ.,* 1971, **63,** 669–674.

43 Hirsch, J. Suicide. *Ment. Hyg., N.Y.,* 1959, **43,** 516–525.

44 Jacoby, S. What do I do for the next 20 years? *The New York Times,* June 17, 1973.

45 Johnson, W. M. *The years after fifty.* College Park, Md.: McGrath Publishing, 1970.

46 Kahana, E., & Kahana, B. Theoretical and research perspectives on grandparenthood. *Aging & hum. Develpm.,* 1971, **2,** 261–268.

47 Kalish, R. A. Of children and grandfathers: A speculative study on dependency. *Gerontologist,* 1967, **7,** 65–69, 79.

48 Komarovsky, M. Functional analysis of sex roles. *Amer. sociol. Rev.,* 1950, **15,** 508–516.

49 Lazerwitz, B., & Rowitz, L. The three-generation hypothesis. *Amer. J. Sociol.,* 1964, **69,** 529–538.

50 Lehman, H. C. *Age and achievement.* Princeton, N.J.: Princeton University Press, 1953.

51 LeShan, E. *The wonderful crisis of middle age.* New York: McKay, 1973.

52 Levine, A. J. A sound approach to middle age. In C. B. Vedder (Ed.), *Problems of the middle-aged.* Springfield, Ill.: Charles C Thomas, 1965. Pp. 40–43.

53 Lopata, H. Z. The life cycle of the social role of the housewife. *Sociol. soc. Res.,* 1966, **51,** 5–22.

54 Marmor, J. The crisis of middle age. *Amer. J. Orthopsychiat.,* 1967, **37,** 336–337.

55 Masters, W. H., & Johnson, V. E. *Human sexual response.* Boston: Little, Brown, 1966.

56 *McCall's* article. The empty days. *McCall's,* September 1965, 80–81, 140–146.

57 McKain, W. C. A new look at older marriage. *Family Coordinator,* 1972, **21,** 61–69.

58 Meltzer, H. Attitudes of workers before and after 40. *Geriatrics,* 1965, **20,** 425–432.

59 Miller, A. A. Reactions of friends to divorce. In P. Bohannon (Ed.), *Divorce and after.* Garden City, N.Y.: Doubleday, 1970. Pp. 63–86.

60 Monk, A. Factors in the preparation for retirement by middle-aged adults. *Gerontologist,* 1971, **11,** 348–351.

61 Morgan, M. I. The middle life and the aging family. *Family Coordinator,* 1969, **18,** 296–298.

62 Neugarten, B. L. Adult personality: Toward a psychology of the life cycle. In B. L. Neugarten (Ed.), *Middle age and aging: A reader in social psychology.* Chicago: University of Chicago Press, 1968. Pp. 137–147.

63 Neugarten, B. L. (Ed.) *Middle age and aging: A reader in social psychology.* Chicago: University of Chicago Press, 1968.

64 Neugarten, B. L., & Garron, D. C. Attitudes of middle-aged persons toward growing older. In C. B. Vedder (Ed.), *Problems of the middle-aged.* Springfield, Ill.: Charles C Thomas, 1965. Pp. 12–17.

65 Neugarten, B. L., Havighurst, R. J., & Tobin, S. S. Personality and patterns of aging. In B. L. Neugarten (Ed.), *Middle age and aging: A reader in social psychology.* Chicago: University of Chicago Press, 1968. Pp. 173–177.

66 Neugarten, B. L., & Weinstein, K. K. The changing American grandparent. *J. Marriage & Family,* 1964, **26,** 199–204.

67 *Newsweek* article. The divorced woman—American style. *Newsweek,* Feb. 13, 1967, 64–70.

68 *New York Times* article. What business demands from its workers' wives. *The New York Times,* Dec. 7, 1964.

69 *New York Times* article. Study profiles top executives. *The New York Times,* July 18, 1965.

70 *New York Times* article. Woman begins to find her place—and it's not in the kitchen. *The New York Times,* Feb. 16, 1966.

71 *New York Times* article. Divorce rise laid to "20-year-slump." *The New York Times,* Dec. 9, 1970.

72 Oden, M. H. The fulfillment of promise: 40-year follow-up of the Terman Gifted Group. *Genet. Psychol. Monogr.,* 1968, **77,** 3–93.

73 Ogle, J. Sex begins at forty. *Harper's Bazaar,* August 1973, 86–87.

74 Packard, V. *The status seekers.* New York: Pocket Books, 1961.

75 Packard, V. *The pyramid climbers.* New York: McGraw-Hill, 1962.

76 Parker, E. *The seven ages of woman.* Baltimore: Johns Hopkins Press, 1960.

77 Parkes, C. M. The first year of bereavement: A longitudinal study of the reaction of London widows to the death of their husbands. *Psychiatry,* 1970, **33,** 444–476.

78 Peterson, J. A. *Married love in the middle years.* New York: Association Press, 1968.

79 Pfeiffer, E., Verwoerdt, A., & Davis, G. C. Sexual behavior in middle life. *Amer. J. Psychiat.,* 1972, **128,** 1262–1267.

80 Pineo, P. C. Disenchantment in the later years of marriage. In B. L. Neugarten (Ed.), *Middle age and aging: A reader in social psychology.* Chicago: University of Chicago Press, 1968. Pp. 258–262.

81 Poe, W. D. *The old person in your home.* New York: Scribner, 1969.

82 Powers, E. A. The effect of the wife's employment on

household tasks among postparental couples: A research note. *Aging & hum. Develpm.,* 1971, **2,** 284–287.

83 Pressey, S. L., & Kuhlen, R. G. *Psychological development though the life span.* New York: Harper & Row, 1957.

84 Reiss, I. L. The sexual renaissance: A summary and analysis. *J. soc. Issues,* 1966, **22**(2), 123–137.

85 *Report of the President's Council on Aging.* Washington: GPO, 1961.

86 Rickles, N. K. The discarded generation: The woman past fifty. *Geriatrics,* 1968, **23,** 112–116.

87 Rico-Venasco, J., & Mynko, L. Suicide and marital status: A changing relationship? *J. Marriage & Family,* 1973, **35,** 239–244.

88 Rollin, B. The American way of marriage: Remarriage. *Look,* 1971, **35,** 62, 64–67.

89 Rollins, B. C., & Feldman, H. Marital satisfaction over the family life cycle. *J. Marriage & Family,* 1970, **32,** 20–28.

90 Rose, A. M. Factors associated with the life satisfaction of middle-class, middle-aged persons. In C. B. Vedder (Ed.), *Problems of the middle-aged.* Springfield, Ill.: Charles C Thomas, 1965. Pp. 59–67.

91 Rose, V. L., & Price-Bonham, S. Divorce adjustment: A woman's problem? *Family Coordinator,* 1973, **22,** 291–297.

92 Ross, A. M., & Ross, J. N. Employment problems of older workers. In C. B. Vedder (Ed.), *Problems of the middle-aged.* Springfield, Ill.: Charles C Thomas, 1965. Pp. 68–74.

93 Saleh, S. D., & Otis, J. L. Age and level of job satisfaction. *Personnel Psychol.,* 1964, **17,** 425–430.

94 Schlesinger, B. Remarriage: An inventory of findings. *Family Coordinator,* 1968, **17,** 248–250.

95 Silverman, P. R. The widow as a care giver in a program of preventive intervention with other widows. *Ment. Hyg., N.Y.,* 1970, **54,** 540–547.

96 Simon, A. W. *The new years: A new middle age.* New York: Knopf, 1968.

97 Somerville, R. M. The future of family relationships in the middle and older years: Clues in fiction. *Family Coordinator,* 1972, **21,** 487–498.

98 Spence, D., & Lonner, T. The "empty nest": A transition within motherhood. *Family Coordinator,* 1971, **20,** 369–375.

99 Steincrohn, P. J. Exercise after 40? Forget it. In C. B. Vedder (Ed.), *Problems of the middle-aged.* Springfield, Ill.: Charles C Thomas, 1965. Pp. 18–24.

100 Stone, F. B., & Rowley, V. N. Children's behavior problems and mother's age. *J. Psychol.,* 1966, **63,** 229–233.

101 Streib, G. F. Intergenerational relations: Perspectives of the two generations on the older parent. *J. Marriage & Family,* 1965, **27,** 469–476.

102 Sussman, M. B., & Burchinal, L. Kin family networks: Un-

heralded structure in current conceptualizations of family functioning. In B. L. Neugarten (Ed.), *Middle age and aging: A reader in social psychology.* Chicago: University of Chicago Press, 1968. Pp. 247–254.

103 Terman, L. M., & Oden, M. H. *The gifted group at mid-life: Thirty-five years' follow-up of the superior child.* Vol. 5. Stanford, Calif.: Stanford University Press, 1959.

104 Terrien, F. W. Turn backward, oh time. In C. B. Vedder (Ed.), *Problems of the middle-aged.* Springfield, Ill.: Charles C Thomas, 1965. Pp. 29–39.

105 Thompson, L. J. Stresses in middle life from the psychiatrist's viewpoint. In C. B. Vedder (Ed.), *Problems of the middle-aged.* Springfield, Ill.: Charles C Thomas, 1965. Pp. 116–120.

106 *Time* article. The command generation. *Time,* July 29, 1966, 50–54.

107 *Time* article. On suicide. *Time,* Nov. 25, 1966, 48–49.

108 *Time* article. People. *Time,* Oct. 2, 1972, 42.

109 Townsend, P. The emergence of the four-generation family in industrial society. In B. L. Neugarten (Ed.), *Middle age and aging: A reader in social psychology.* Chicago: University of Chicago Press, 1968. Pp. 255–257.

110 Tuckman, J. College students' judgment of the passage of time over the life span. *J. genet. Psychol.,* 1965, **107,** 43–48.

111 *U.S. News & World Report* article. Advice to businessmen on health and retirement. *U.S. News & World Report,* Mar. 7, 1966, 62–67.

112 *U.S. News & World Report* article. How women's role in the U.S. is changing. *U.S. News & World Report,* May 30, 1966, 58–60.

113 *U.S. News & World Report* article. When nation will have 113 million workers. *U.S. News & World Report,* Apr. 30, 1973, 60–62.

114 Vedder, C. B. (Ed.) *Problems of the middle-aged.* Springfield, Ill.: Charles C Thomas, 1965.

115 *Vital Statistics of the U.S., 1961: Divorce.* Washington: U.S. Department of Health, Education, and Welfare, 1965, Vol. 3, Secs. 3, 4, 7.

116 Wade, B. Freshmen have advisers, but who helps the parent emeritus? *The New York Times,* Sept. 24, 1972.

117 Wallin, P., & Clark, A. L. A study of orgasm, as a condition of women's enjoyment of coitus in the middle years of marriage. *Hum. Biol.,* 1963, **35,** 131–139.

118 Whitman, H. Let go of the dream. In C. B. Vedder (Ed.), *Problems of the middle-aged.* Springfield, Ill.: Charles C Thomas, 1965. Pp. 199–202.

119 Zatlin, C. E., Storandt, M., & Botwinick, J. Personality and values of women continuing their education after thirty-five years. *J. Gerontol.,* 1973, **28,** 216–221.

CHAPTER | THIRTEEN

OLD AGE
Personal and Social Adjustments

Old age is the closing period in the life span. As Henry and Cumming have pointed out, it is a "period of moving away from some previous and more desirable period—'the prime of life' or 'the years of usefulness'" (53). As the individual moves away from the earlier periods of his life, he looks back on them, often regretfully, and tends to live in the present, ignoring the future as much as possible.

As has been stressed repeatedly, the individual is never static: instead, he constantly changes. During the early part of life the changes are evolutional in that they lead to maturity of structure and functioning. In the latter part of life they are mainly involutional, involving a regression to earlier stages. These changes are the natural accompaniment of what we commonly refer to as *aging*, and they affect physical as well as mental structures and functioning.

Age sixty is usually considered the dividing line between middle and old age. However, it is recognized that chronological age is a poor criterion to use in marking off the beginning of old age because there are such marked differences among individuals in the age at which aging actually begins.

Because of better living conditions and better health care, most men and women today do not show the mental and physical signs of aging until the mid-sixties or even the early seventies. For that reason, there is a gradual trend toward using sixty-five—the age of compulsory retirement in many businesses—to mark the beginning of old age.

Old age is usually subdivided into *early*

old age, which extends from age sixty to age seventy, and *advanced old age*, which begins at seventy and extends to the end of life.

CHARACTERISTICS OF OLD AGE

Like every other period in the life span, old age is characterized by certain physical and psychological changes, and the effect of these changes on the individual determines, to a large extent, whether he will make good or poor personal and social adjustments. The characteristics of old age, however, are far more likely to lead to poor adjustments than to good ones and to unhappiness rather than to happiness. That is why old age is even more dreaded in the American culture of today than middle age.

Old Age Is a Period of Decline

The period during old age when physical and mental decline is slow and gradual and when compensations can be made for it is known as *senescence*. The individual may become senescent in his fifties or not until his early or late sixties, depending upon the rate of this decline.

The term *senility* is used to refer to the period during old age when a more or less complete physical breakdown takes place and when there is mental disorganization. The individual who becomes eccentric, careless, absentminded, socially withdrawn, and poorly adjusted is usually described as *senile*. Senility may come as early as the fifties, or it may never occur because the individual dies before deterioration sets in.

Decline comes partly from physical and partly from psychological factors. The *physical* cause of decline is a change in the body cells due not to a specific disease but to the aging process. Decline may also have *psychological* causes. Unfavorable attitudes toward oneself, other people, work, and life in general can lead to senility, just as changes in the brain tissue can. Individuals who have no sustaining interests after retirement are likely to become depressed and

disorganized. As a result, they go downhill both physically and mentally and may soon die. How the individual copes with the strains and stresses of living will also affect the rate of his decline.

Motivation likewise plays a very important role in decline. The individual who has little motivation to learn new things or to keep up to date in appearance, attitudes, or patterns of behavior will deteriorate much faster than one whose motivation to ward off aging is stronger. The new leisure time, which comes with retirement or with the lessening of household responsibilities, often brings boredom which lowers the individual's motivation.

There Are Individual Differences in the Effects of Aging

Individual differences in the effects of aging have been recognized for many centuries. Cicero, for example, in his *De Senectute*, stressed this in his reference to the popular belief that aging makes people difficult to live with. According to him, "As it is not every wine, so it is not every disposition that grows sour with age" (73). Today, even more than in the past, it is recognized that aging affects different people differently. Thus it is impossible to classify anyone as a "typically" old person or any trait as "typical" of old age. People age differently because they have different hereditary endowments, different socioeconomic and educational backgrounds, and different patterns of living. These differences are apparent among members of the same sex, but they are even more apparent when men and women are compared because aging takes place at different rates for the two sexes.

As differences increase with age, they predispose individuals to react differently to the same situation. For example, some men think of retirement as a blessing, while others regard it as a curse.

As a general rule, physical aging precedes mental aging, though sometimes the reverse is true, especially when the individual is concerned about growing old and

Individuals who have no sustaining interests after retirement are likely to become depressed and disorganized. (Robert Hauser from Rapho Guillumette)

lets go mentally when the first signs of physical aging appear.

Aging Requires Role Changes

Just as middle-aged people must learn to play new roles, so must the elderly. Refer to Figure 10-2 for a graphic illustration of the role changes that must be made in old age. In the American culture of today, where efficiency, strength, speed, and physical attractiveness are highly valued, elderly people are often regarded as useless. Because they cannot compete with young people in the areas where highly valued traits are needed, the social attitude toward them is unfavorable.

Furthermore, it is expected that old people will play a decreasingly active role in social and community affairs, as they do in the business and professional worlds. As a result, there is a marked reduction in the number of roles the elderly person is able to play, and there are changes in some of the remaining roles. While these changes are due in part to the individual's preferences, they are due mainly to social pressures.

Because of unfavorable social attitudes, few rewards are associated with old-age roles, no matter how successfully they are carried out. Feeling useless and unwanted, elderly people develop feelings of inferiority and resentment—feelings that are not conducive to good personal or social adjustments. As Busse and Pfeiffer have pointed out, "It is difficult to maintain a positive identity when one's usual props for such an identity, such as one's social and occupational roles, have been taken away" (17).

There Are Many Stereotypes of the Aged

Role changes among the aged are markedly influenced by the cultural stereotypes of old people, which in turn have led to unfavorable social attitudes toward them. There are three main sources of stereotypes about old age. First, folklore and fairy tales, handed down from one generation to another, tend to depict the aged unfavorably. Although it is true that some of these picture old people as kindly and understanding, many depict them as wicked and cruel, especially women.

Second, the elderly are often characterized unfavorably in literature as well as in the mass media. Shakespeare, for example, makes 132 references to the physical and behavioral changes accompanying old age (119). In describing senility, he writes:

> Last scene of all,
> That ends this strange eventful history,
> Is second childishness, and mere oblivion,
> Sans teeth, sans eyes, sans taste, sans everything.

Shakespeare also writes of the elderly person's appearance:

> His youthful hose, well saved, a world too wide
> For his shrunk shank; and his manly voice,
> Turning again toward childish treble, pipes
> And whistles in his sound.

One of the few cheerful literary references to old age is provided by Browning:

> Grow old along with me!
> The best is yet to be,
> The last of life, for which the first was made.

Third, stereotypes have been reinforced by scientific studies of the aged. Because the subjects in most of these studies, as was emphasized earlier, have been persons in institutions whose physical and mental decline was primarily responsible for their institutionalization, it is not surprising that the results of these studies support the popular stereotype. And yet studies of representative samplings of noninstitutionalized elderly people have provided little evidence to justify this stereotype.

The common stereotype of the aged individual is that of a person who is worn out physically and mentally; who is unproductive, accident-prone, crotchety, and hard to live with; and who, because his useful days are over, should be pushed aside to make way for younger people. As Chown and Heron have pointed out, this unfavorable stereotype makes it "difficult for anyone to see **aging** as anything but a 'negative phase'" (24).

Equally important, the person's own concept of old age, which was built up in the early years of life and is based more on the prevailing cultural stereotype than on personal experiences with the elderly, affects his attitudes not only toward elderly people but also toward himself as he grows older. This contributes to his dread of old age.

The Aged Have a Minority-Group Status

In spite of the fact that the number of old people in America today is growing, they occupy a minority-group status—a status which excludes them to some extent from interaction with other groups in the population and which gives them little or no power. This minority-group status is primarily the result of the unfavorable social attitudes toward the aged that have been fostered by the unfavorable stereotype of them. As Rosow (103) pointed out:

Their second-rate citizenship is no accident, no minor misfunctioning of our institutions and values. It is inherent in the nature of our society. Underlying the practical immediacies of health and income, the deeper human problems of old people boil down to two central issues: (1) How will we share the fruits of our abundance with them, and by what principles? (2) How can we integrate them into our society on a basis of dignity and respect? Or, simply put, how can we redeem their second-class citizenship?

This "second-class citizenship" puts the elderly on the defensive and has a marked effect on their personal and social adjustments. It makes the latter years of life far from "golden" for most people, and it causes them to be victimized by some members of the majority group. As Langer has stressed (70):

If the aged are victimized in general, they are also victimized in particular. Their illness, loneliness, and terrors make the aged easy prey to a growing army of charlatans in whom their vulnerability arouses instincts not of sympathy but of greed. An ingenious array of frauds, from quack medicines to uninhabitable homesites, and from dancing lessons to fake furnace repairs has been revealed.

Figure 13-1 Many older women regard beauty aids as a way to regain their youthful attractiveness. (Dan Tobin. "The Little Woman." King Features Syndicate, Oct. 22, 1973. Used by permission.)

"I keep hoping Herbert will look at me and say, 'How beautiful,' but all he ever says is 'how much?'"

The Desire for Rejuvenation Is Widespread in Old Age

The minority-group status accorded to most elderly persons has naturally given rise to a desire to remain young as long as possible and to be rejuvenated when the signs of aging appear. See Figure 13-1. Among the ancients, elixirs or potions, alchemy, witchcraft, and sorcery were used to achieve these ends. Later, there were searches for "fountains of youth" that were believed to have the magical powers of turning the aged into young men and women.

Today, medicine is taking over the task of trying to ward off old age. Because a deficiency of sex hormones plays such an important role in aging, attempts have been made to rejuvenate aging people by means of sex-hormone therapy. Recent experiments have shown that it is impossible to make aging people young again (16, 45, 93). The administration of hormones can, however, build up the individual's health and vigor and thus slow down the rate of aging. As Scheinfeld has commented, the "Ponce de Leons remain as far from their Fountain of Youth as ever" (108).

DEVELOPMENTAL TASKS OF OLD AGE

For the most part, the developmental tasks of old age relate more to the individual's personal life than to the lives of others. (See page 13 for a list of these tasks.) The old person is expected to adjust to decreasing strength and to gradually failing health. This often means marked revisions in the roles he has played in the home and outside. He is also expected to find activities to replace the work that consumed the major part of his time when he was younger.

Meeting social and civic obligations is difficult for many older people as their health fails and as their income is reduced by retirement. As a result, they are often forced to become socially inactive. Failing health and reduced income likewise require the establishment of new living arrangements which are often radically different from those of the earlier years of adulthood.

Sooner or later, most old people must adjust to the death of a spouse. This is far more likely to be a problem for women than for men. Because the death of a spouse often means reduced income and hazards associated with living alone, it may necessitate changes in living arrangement.

As grown children become increasingly involved in their own vocational and family affairs, the elderly can count less and less on their companionship. This means that they must establish affiliations with members of their own age group if they are to avoid the loneliness that plagues the elderly when their contacts with the larger social group are cut off because of retirement and because they gradually reduce their contacts with community organizations.

Although most older people learned during childhood and adolescence to get along with their age-mates successfully, during most of their adult lives they have had to be affiliated with individuals of all age groups. Regressing to this earlier pattern of social life is often difficult because it means that the individual must now become affiliated with a group that is largely rejected by society. Having known since childhood and adolescence that affiliation with a rejected group brings little prestige, old people have little motivation to become involved with such a group.

Certain problems of adjustment resulting from these developmental tasks are unique to old age. The most common of these are given in Box 13-1.

ADJUSTMENT TO PHYSICAL CHANGES

While it is unquestionably true that physical changes do occur with aging and that these changes are, for the most part, in the direction of deterioration, individual dif-

To avoid loneliness, the elderly must reestablish affiliations with their own age group—a task they sometimes resist because they recognize that as a group they are largely rejected by society. (Allan L. Price from Rapho Guillumette)

```
Box 13-1.  PROBLEMS UNIQUE TO OLD AGE
Physical helplessness, which necessitates depen-
    dency on others
Economic insecurity severe enough to necessitate
    a complete change in pattern of living
Establishing living conditions in accordance with
    changes in economic or physical conditions
Making new friends to replace those who have
    died or moved away or who are invalided
Developing new activities to occupy increased lei-
    sure time
Learning to treat grown children as adults
```

ferences are so marked that no two people of the same age are necessarily at the same state of deterioration. Furthermore, within the same individual there are variations in the rate of aging of different parts of the body. The organs of reproduction, for example, age sooner than the other organs. The major physical changes that occur during old age are discussed below.

Changes in Appearance

Bischof has said that aging means "proceeding from bifocals to trifocals and dentures to death" (8). This suggests that the most obvious signs of aging are changes in the face. Even though women can use cosmetics to cover up some of the telltale signs of aging on the face, many cannot be camouflaged, as changes in other areas of the body can.

The hands also give away a person's age. Like the face, they change more with aging than the rest of the body, and these changes are also less subject to camouflage.

Box 13-2 gives the changes in appearance that normally occur during old age. While not all old people show all these signs of aging, nor do all of them appear simultaneously, sooner or later they will become apparent in the individual if he lives long enough.

Internal Changes

Although internal changes are not as readily observable as external ones, they are nevertheless as pronounced and as widespread. Changes in the skeleton are due to hardening of the bones, deposits of mineral salts, and modifications of the internal structure of the bones. As a result of these changes, the bones become brittle and are subject to fractures and breaks, which are increasingly slow to heal as age progresses.

Changes in the nervous system are especially marked in the case of the brain. In old age, there is a loss in brain weight, the lateral ventricles tend to be dilated, and the ribbon of cortical tissue is narrowed.

Central nervous system changes come early in the aging period; they are reflected first in a decrease in the speed of learning and later in a decline in intellectual powers.

The viscera go through a marked transformation with advancing age. Atrophy is particularly marked in the spleen, liver, testes, heart, lungs, pancreas, and kidneys. Perhaps the most marked change of all is in the heart. In the early years of life, the heart is positioned more nearly in the center of the chest than it is in advanced age. It increases in bulk with age and continues to grow even after the body has ceased to do so. Therefore, the ratio of heart weight to body weight decreases gradually with age. As a result of an increase in fibrous tissue from deposits of fat and calcium and because of changes in the quality of the elastic tissue, the valves gradually become less soft and pliable. The gastrointestinal tract, the urinary tract, and the smooth-muscle organs generally are the least and last affected by aging.

Changes in Physiological Functions

There are also changes in the functioning of the organs. Regulation of body temperature is influenced by impairment of the regulatory devices. Old people cannot

---

Box 13-2. COMMON CHANGES IN APPEARANCE DURING OLD AGE

Head Region

The nose elongates.

The mouth changes shape as a result of tooth loss or the necessity of wearing dentures.

The eyes seem dull and lusterless and often have a watery look.

A double or triple chin develops.

The cheeks become pendulous, wrinkled, and baggy.

The skin becomes wrinkled and dry, and dark spots, moles, or warts may appear.

The hair on the head becomes thin and turns gray or white, and tough, bristly hair appears in the nose, ears, and eyebrows.

Trunk Region

The shoulders stoop and thus seem smaller.

The abdomen bulges and droops.

The hips seem flabbier and broader than they did earlier.

The waistline broadens, giving the trunk a sacklike appearance.

The woman's breasts become flabby and droop.

Limbs

The upper arm becomes flabby and heavy, while the lower arm seems to shrink in diameter.

The legs become flabby and the veins prominent, especially around the ankles.

The hands become scrawny, and the veins on the back of the hand are prominent.

The feet become larger as a result of sagging muscles, and corns, bunions, and callouses often appear.

The nails of the hands and feet become thick, tough, and brittle.

---

tolerate extremes of temperature, either hot or cold, because of the decreased vascularity of the skin. Reduced metabolic rate and lessened muscular vigor also make regulation of body temperature difficult.

When an old person becomes short of breath as a result of unusual exertion, it takes longer to restore breathing and heart action to normal than it did when he was younger. Pulse rate and oxygen consumption are more varied among the elderly than among younger people. Elevated blood pressure due to the increased rigidity of the walls of the aorta and central arteries is quite common in old age. Elderly people excrete less urine, and there is less creatine in their urine than in that of younger adults.

In old age, there is a decline in the amount of sleep needed and in the quality of sleep. By age sixty or seventy the daily amount is reduced an hour or two, and brief periods of rest and sleep generally replace the longer periods of sleep of the younger person. Most old people suffer from insomnia, especially women.

Digestive changes are perhaps the most marked of the changes in the regulatory functions. Difficulties in eating are due partly to loss of teeth, which is fairly universal in old age, and also to the fact that the senses of smell and taste become less acute, making even the best food seem somewhat tasteless.

Gradual atrophy of the glands lining the walls of the stomach and bowels results in a decrease in the ferments and juices that aid in digestion. Thus the old person needs more fluids to lubricate and to dissolve food elements.

Strength and the ability to work decrease as muscular flabbiness and general weakness make it more difficult for the old person to use his muscles. The ability to do strenuous work for a short period of time diminishes with age, while the ability to withstand a long, steady grind increases. It also takes the older person longer to recover from physical fatigue and from fatigue caused by continued mental work or nervous strain. As a result, most old people learn to

Among the elderly, more men than women are "hard of hearing." (Hella Hammid from Rapho Guillumette)

cut down on any work that requires either strength or speed.

Sensory Changes

All the sense organs function less efficiently in old age than they did when the individual was younger. However, because sensory changes are slow and gradual in most cases, the individual has an opportunity to make adequate adjustments to them. Furthermore, glasses and hearing aids can almost completely compensate for impaired vision or hearing loss.

The eyes and ears, which are the most useful of all the sense organs, are also the most seriously affected by old age, although changes occur in the functioning of all the sense organs. Box 13-3 gives the changes in sensory functioning in old age.

Sexual Changes

The male climacteric comes later than the menopause and requires more time. Generally there is a decline in sexual potency during the sixties, which continues as age advances. Like the menopause, it is accompanied by a decline in gonadal func-

tioning, which is responsible for the changes that occur during the climacteric.

The male climacteric has two common effects on the aging man. First, there is a waning of the secondary sex characteristics. The voice, for example, becomes higher in pitch; the hair on the face and body becomes less luxuriant; and the heavy musculature gives way to a general flabbiness. In general, older men are less "masculine" than they were in the prime of life, just as women are less "feminine" after the menopausal changes have taken place.

Second, the male climacteric affects sexual functioning. However, even though sexual potency has declined, there is not necessarily a decline in sexual desire or in the ability to have intercourse. There is evidence that cultural influences are more important in the waning of the sex drive than physical changes. Cultural influences produce anxieties, which in turn affect attitudes toward sex and sexual behavior. Men and women often refrain from continuing sexual relations in old age or from remarrying because of unfavorable social attitudes toward sex among older people and because of doubts about their sexual capacities. To avoid having their pride hurt, men especially are likely to refrain from sexual activity as they grow older (25, 80).

The strength of the sex drive in old age will depend largely upon the individual's general health and the kind of sexual adjustments he made earlier in life. Those who made poor sexual adjustments when they were younger have been found to lose the sex drive earlier than those who made better adjustments (25, 80).

CHANGES IN MOTOR ABILITIES

Most old people are aware that they move more slowly and are less well coordinated in movements than they were when they were younger. These changes in motor abilities are due partly to physical causes and partly to psychological causes.

The physical causes of changes in motor

Box 13-3. CHANGES IN SENSORY FUNCTIONING IN OLD AGE

Vision

There is a consistent decline in the ability to see at low levels of illumination and a decline in color sensitivity. Most old people suffer from presbyopia—farsightedness—which is due to the diminishing elasticity of the lenses.

Hearing

Old people lose the ability to hear extremely high tones, as a result of atrophy of the nerve and end organs in the basal turn of the cochlea, although most can hear tones below high C as well as younger people. Men tend to experience greater hearing loss in old age than women.

Taste

Marked changes in taste in old age are due to atrophy of the taste buds in the tongue and the inner surface of the cheeks. This atrophy becomes progressively more widespread with advancing age.

Smell

The sense of smell becomes less acute with age, partly as a result of the atrophy of cells in the nose and partly because of the increased hairiness of the nostrils.

Touch

As the skin becomes drier and harder, the sense of touch becomes less and less acute.

Sensitivity to Pain

The decline in the sensitivity to pain occurs at different rates in different parts of the body. There is a greater decline, for example, in the forehead and arms than in the legs.

---

abilities in old age include a decrease in strength and energy, which is a normal accompaniment of the physical changes that take place with age; lack of muscular tone; stiffness of the joints; and tremors of the hands, forearms, head, and lower jaw.

The psychological causes of changes in motor abilities stem from the individual's awareness that he is "slipping" and from feelings of inferiority he experiences when he compares himself with younger people in terms of strength, skills, and speed. Emotional tension stemming from these psychological causes may hasten the changes in motor abilities or decrease the individual's motivation to do what he is capable of doing. However, even under the most favorable conditions and with the strongest motivation, few individuals can hope that their motor abilities will continue at the same level they reached when they were younger.

While all motor abilities decline to some extent with advancing age, some decline more rapidly and earlier than others. The changes in motor abilities that have the most important effect on personal and social adjustments are given in Box 13-4.

CHANGES IN MENTAL ABILITIES

As is true of all other areas of decline, there are marked individual variations in mental decline. There is no one age at which the decline begins and no specific pattern of decline that is characteristic of all old people.

In general, those of higher intellectual levels experience relatively less decrease in mental efficiency than those of lower levels. Studies of gifted individuals carried out over a long period of time, for example, have provided evidence that mental decline sets in later than is popularly believed (4, 89).

In the past it was assumed that mental deterioration inevitably accompanied physical deterioration. That physical decline does contribute to mental decline has been shown by the fact that sex-hormone treatment of elderly women can result in improve-

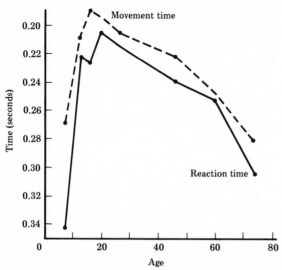

Figure 13-2 Speed of reaction and of movement decline sharply as age advances. (Adapted from J. Hodgkins. Influence of age on the speed of reaction and movement in females. *J. Gerontol.*, 1962, **17,** 385–389. Used by permission.)

ment in the ability to think, to learn new material, to memorize, and to remember and in increased willingness to expend intellectual energy (20). On the other hand, some pathological conditions, such as hypertension, lead to intellectual loss with aging, although, as Wilkie and Eisdorfer have emphasized, such loss is not part of the "'normal' aging process" (122).

Lack of environmental stimulation also affects the rate of mental decline. In mental as in motor learning, continuation of practice through the years slows down the rate of decline. Those who continue to work as they reach the latter years of life, for example, have more normal brain functioning and do better on intelligence tests than those who are idle. In reviewing the studies made of intellectual changes in the aged, Eisdorfer has concluded (37):

Patterns of response may in large measure be influenced by socially and psychologically mediated interaction with the environment.

Box 13-4. COMMON CHANGES IN MOTOR ABILITIES IN OLD AGE

Strength
Decline in strength is most pronounced in the flexor muscles of the forearms and in the muscles which raise the body. Elderly people tire quickly and require a longer time to recover from fatigue than younger people.

Speed
Decrease in speed with aging is shown in tests of reaction time and skilled movements, such as handwriting. It is especially marked after age sixty as may be seen in Figure 13-2.

Learning New Skills
Even when the individual believes that learning a new skill will benefit him personally, he learns more slowly than a younger person, and the end result is less satisfactory.

Awkwardness
Old people tend to become awkward and clumsy, which causes them to spill and drop things, to trip and fall, and to do things in a careless, untidy manner. The breakdown in motor skills proceeds in inverse order to that in which the skills were learned, with the earliest-learned skills being retained longest.

These in turn may lead to physiological changes which make the effort of responding to new situations more difficult.

It is important to recognize that the mental decline associated with old age may not be as great as popularly supposed or as reported in earlier studies. As has been pointed out, there is a growing belief that what is assumed to be a decline in mental ability may be the result of discrepancies in the choice of groups at different age levels for comparisons and of the differences between education now and at the time the elderly groups were schoolchildren. Schaie et al. have emphasized the importance of this (107):

Conventional cross-sectional studies confound historical (generational) with individual (ontogenetic) change components. Since such designs sample individuals differing not only in age but also in terms of generation-related environmental backgrounds, the resulting age differences provide most inappropriate evidence for ontogenetic change.

Other conditions may account, to some extent, for the apparent mental decline that accompanies age. Most old people, for example, are not familiar with testing, are not sympathetic toward it, and refuse to be tested. This biases the samplings used for studies and usually means that institutionalized persons must be used for studies of old-age groups, thus giving an unfair sampling of the old-age population and an inaccurate picture of how mental abilities are affected by aging.

In addition, since it is known that speed of action slows down with advancing age, tests of mental ability that emphasize the time element are unfair to older subjects. As Lorge has pointed out, in measuring mental decline, the "power to cope with mental tasks must be considered freed from the influence of other factors or traits that may obscure it. In my opinion, speed obscures sheer mental power in older adults" (78).

The only way to measure the amount of decline precisely is to have an accurate record of the individual's abilities at their peak and then to determine from this standard the percentage of decline that sets in at different ages. To date, as has been stressed earlier, few studies have been made using the longitudinal method; most have been made using samples from different age levels—the cross-sectional method. One longitudinal study reported decline to be far less than is popularly believed (11). See Figure 13-3.

Just as there are differences in the rate of mental decline among different individuals of the same chronological age, so there are also differences within the same individual in the rate of decline of different

Figure 13-3 Changes in test scores for different mental abilities between the ages of sixty-four and eighty-four years. (Adapted from J. E. Blum, J. L. Fosshage, & L. F. Jarvik. Intellectual changes and sex differences in octogenarians: A twenty-five year longitudinal study of aging. *Develpm. Psychol.,* 1972, **7,** 178–187. Used by permission.)

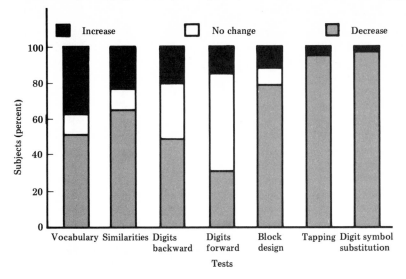

Box 13-5. MENTAL CHANGES IN OLD AGE

Learning
Older people are more cautious about learning, need more time to integrate their responses, are less capable of dealing with new material that cannot readily be integrated with earlier experiences, and are less accurate than younger people.

Reasoning
There is a general reduction in the speed with which the individual reaches a conclusion in both inductive and deductive reasoning. This is partly the result of the tendency to become increasingly cautious with age.

Creativity
Older people tend to lack the capacity for, or interest in, creative thinking. Thus significant creative achievements are less common among older people than among younger ones.

Memory
Old people tend to have poor recent memories but better remote memories. This may be due partly to the fact that they are not always strongly motivated to remember things and partly to lack of attentiveness.

Recall
Recall is affected more by age than recognition. Many older people use cues, especially visual, auditory, and kinesthetic ones, to aid their ability to recall.

Reminiscing
The tendency to reminisce about the past becomes increasingly more marked with advancing age. How much the individual reminisces depends mainly on how pleasant or unpleasant he finds his living conditions now.

Vocabulary
Deterioration in vocabulary is very slight in old age because the elderly person constantly uses words, most of which he learned in childhood or adolescence.

Mental Rigidity
The mental rigidity that sometimes sets in during middle age often becomes more pronounced as the person grows older, partly because he learns more slowly and with more difficulty than he did earlier and partly because he believes that old values and ways of doing things are better than new ones.

---

mental abilities. Even when the element of speed is eliminated and the tests are given as power tests to measure different mental abilities, declines of varying degrees have been found. This is illustrated in Figure 13-3. In summarizing the results of their studies, Schaie et al. have reported (107):

In abilities heavily dependent upon educational and acculturation output systems (such as Verbal Meaning, Reasoning, Numbers, etc.) there was a negligible amount of genuine longitudinal change. The strong cross-sectional age decrements reported in the conventional literature for these abilities simply are a consequence of whatever cultural change factors produce higher and higher intellectual performance in successive generations. . . . Abilities mediated by formal education systems should not show any pronounced aging decrements.

An analysis of different mental abilities, as measured by tests, has revealed the characteristic changes that occur with advancing age and the apparent reasons for these changes. These are given in Box 13-5.

CHANGES IN INTERESTS

A number of conditions are responsible for changes in interests during old age; the most important of these are given in Box 13-6. There is a close correlation between the number and kind of interests the individual has and the success of his adjust-

---

Box 13-6. CONDITIONS AFFECTING CHANGE OF INTERESTS IN OLD AGE

Health
Changes in health and energy are reflected in an increased interest in sedentary pursuits and a decreased interest in activities requiring strength and energy.

Social Status
Older people of the higher social groups usually have a wider range of interests than those of the lower groups. Many of these are carry-overs of interests developed earlier in life.

Economic Status
The older person who has inadequate money to meet his needs may have to give up many interests

that are important to him and concentrate on ones that he can afford, regardless of whether they are meaningful to him or meet his needs.

Sex
Women have more interests in old age, just as they do throughout adulthood. Men who are retired often find it difficult to cultivate interests to occupy their time.

Values
Older people may come to value social contacts rather than hobbies as a compensation for the loneliness that retirement or loss of a spouse brings.

---

ment to old age, which in turn determines how happy or unhappy he will be.

It is important to recognize, however, that adjustments are markedly affected by whether the change in interests is voluntary or involuntary. If the elderly person wants to change his interests because of his health or his financial situation, for example, he will be better satisfied than if he must give up activities he enjoys because of unfavorable attitudes on the part of the social group or for health or economic reasons.

Like the interests of people at every age level, those of the elderly differ markedly. However, certain interests may be regarded as typical of old age: personal interests, recreational interests, social interests, religious interests, and interest in death. These are discussed below.

Personal Interests

Personal interests in old age include interest in self, interest in appearance, interest in clothes, and interest in money.

Interest in Self People become increasingly more preoccupied with themselves as

they grow older. They may become egocentric and self-centered to the point where they think more about themselves than about others and have little regard for others' interests and wishes.

Even when they are in good physical condition, older people are often preoccupied with their health and with the bodily processes. They tend to complain about their health and to exaggerate any ailment they may have. They also show their preoccupation with themselves by talking endlessly about their pasts, expecting to be waited on, and wanting to be the center of attention. This self-centeredness contributes to the unfavorable social attitude toward old people that is so prevalent today. Younger people, who are aware of the social expectation of cooperativeness and unselfishness, often find the self-centeredness of old people completely contradictory to their standards of socially acceptable behavior.

Interest in Appearance Although some old people are as concerned about their appearance as they were when they were younger, most show little interest in how they look. They may cease to care about their clothes or become careless about grooming. While few are dirty and slovenly in appearance, most elderly people do not take the time and trouble to make the most of their looks or to camouflage the telltale signs of physical aging as well as they could.

The more socially active the elderly person is, the more incentive he has to be careful about his looks. Socially withdrawn elderly people have little motivation to keep up their appearance.

Old men, as a rule, are more interested in their appearance than old women are. This is in direct contrast to the situation earlier and may be explained by the fact that women who are distressed by their looks in old age often adopt an "I don't care" attitude toward their appearance. It may also be explained partly by habit. Older men have become accustomed to being careful about their grooming because it is important to them in their work, and this habit often persists even into retirement.

Interest in Clothes Interest in clothes in old age depends to some extent upon how socially active the individual is but more upon how willing he is to accept the fact that he is growing old and must adjust to it. Some elderly people continue to wear styles they wore earlier and refuse to dress according to the current fashion, even when this means that they must have their garments made to order.

Other older people, by contrast, are very fashion-conscious and may choose clothes that are designed for those young enough to be their children or even their grandchildren. They are rebelling against old age and are trying to convince themselves and others that they are younger than they really are.

Limited incomes prevent many elderly people from having as great an interest in their clothes and appearance as they might otherwise have. They simply do not have enough money to buy new clothes except when it is absolutely necessary. Lack of in-come also contributes to the elderly person's social withdrawal. If he cannot afford to be well dressed, he may shun social and community activities for fear that he will be embarrassed by his shabby and out-of-date appearance. This is especially true of women because styles in women's clothing change faster than styles in men's clothing.

Older people's interest in clothing is also affected by the difficulty they have finding ready-made clothes that are stylish and yet fit their aging figures. When short skirts are in vogue, for example, it is hard for an older woman to find a ready-made dress, skirt, or coat of a length that she considers appropriate for her age. Also, clothing intended for elderly women is often poorly designed, uninteresting, and made in prints or colors that are unflattering to the older woman's skin and hair. The problem of finding ready-made clothes that are becoming affects elderly men also, but less than it affects women.

Interest in Money Interest in money, which starts to wane during middle age, generally is revived and becomes more intense as old age progresses. Retirement or unemployment may leave the elderly person with a greatly reduced income or with no income at all unless he is eligible for social security benefits. This focuses his attention on money and stimulates his interest in how he can get more money or make ends meet with what he has.

The elderly person whose income is drastically reduced is interested in money not because he wants to buy more material possessions, as the adolescent or young adult does, but because he wants to maintain his independence—to live where and how he wishes—without relying on charity or relatives. In order to maintain their pattern of life, many older people are forced to cut down their expenditures for clothes and grooming aids, for social contacts and recreation, and for membership in different community organizations.

Recreational Interests

Elderly men and women tend to remain interested in the recreational activities they enjoyed in early adulthood, and they change these interests only when necessary. The changes in recreational interests that do occur consist mainly of a gradual narrowing down of interests, rather than a radical change in the pattern of interests, and a shift toward more sedentary forms of recreation.

Although an older person seldom cultivates a new recreational interest, he may devote his time to an activity which interested him when he was younger but which he had to put aside because of the pressures of work and family life or for economic reasons. For example, a woman who enjoyed painting when she was young but who had to give it up during the busy years

Elderly men and women tend to continue the recreational patterns they formed in early childhood, changing them only when failing health or some other obstacle forces them to. (Geoffrey Gove from Rapho Guillumette)

Box 13-7. CONDITIONS RESPONSIBLE FOR CHANGES IN RECREATIONAL ACTIVITIES

Health

As health gradually fails and as physical disabilities such as poor eyesight set in, the individual acquires an interest in recreational activities that require a minimum of strength and energy and can be enjoyed in the home.

Economic Status

Reduced income after retirement may force the individual to cut down on or eliminate recreational activities, such as moviegoing, that cost money. This is especially true of older people in the lower socioeconomic groups.

Education

The more formal education a person has, the more intellectual recreational activities, such as reading, he cultivates. Because these require little energy, they can be enjoyed in old age. Those with limited education must often depend mainly on television for recreation.

Sex

Women tend to cultivate a wide range of recreational interests throughout life, many of which are sedentary in nature and thus can be carried into old age. Men, by contrast, tend to limit their recreational interest to sports, which they must give up when their health fails. Thus they have a paucity of recreational interests in old age and may depend mainly on television.

Living Conditions

Elderly persons who live in a home for the aged have recreations provided for them that are suited to their physical and mental abilities. Those who live in their own homes or with a married child have fewer opportunities for recreation, especially if their economic status is poor or if failing health or transportation problems prevent them from participating in community-sponsored recreational activities.

of homemaking and child rearing, may become interested in it again in old age.

Changes in recreational activities in old age are inevitable. However, most of these changes are made as a result of necessity, not choice. As one woman, over seventy, put it, "I am holding on to life with both hands, but I feel that as life goes on society pries loose one finger after another" (126). The most important factors affecting the recreational patterns of the elderly are given in Box 13-7.

Common recreational interests of older people include reading, writing letters, listening to the radio, watching television, visiting friends and relatives, sewing, embroidering, gardening, traveling, playing cards, going to the theater or movies, and taking part in the activities of civic, political, or religious organizations. In general, the number and variety of activities the individual engages in declines with advancing age, even though an interest in them may persist.

Social Interests

With advancing age, old people suffer increasing social losses, or social disengagement. Social disengagement, as Birren has explained, involves four elements of "load shedding": less involvement with other people, a reduction in the variety of social roles played, a greater use of mental ability, and less participation in physical activity (7).

Social disengagement in old age is commonly expressed in a narrowing down of the sources of social contact and a decline in social participation. For most older people this means a radical change in the pattern of social life they established during early adulthood and carried on, with only minor changes, through middle age.

Social disengagement may be voluntary or involuntary. In the case of voluntary social disengagement, the individual may withdraw from social activities because they no longer meet his needs. As the elderly person's interest in himself increases, his interest in others decreases until his social interests are limited to his immediate family. The more socially isolated the elderly person is, the more ingrown he becomes and the fewer opportunities he has to keep up to date. As a result, he becomes boring to others which further adds to his social isolation.

Involuntary social disengagement comes when the elderly person wants and needs social contacts but is deprived of the opportunity to have them because of conditions over which he has little or no control. When many of his contemporaries have died or have moved away or are physically unable to do things with him, for example, he no longer has the companionship he formerly enjoyed. As one elderly woman put it, "All my friends have either gone to heaven or Miami" (17).

The elderly person may also lack the

Box 13-8. SOURCES OF SOCIAL CONTACT AFFECTED BY AGING

Close, Personal Friendships
Close, personal friendships with members of the same sex, many of which date back to adolescence or the early years of marriage, often end when one of the friends dies or moves away, and it is unlikely that the old person will be able to establish another such relationship.

Friendship Cliques
These cliques are made up of couples who banded together when they were younger because of mutual interests stemming from the husbands' business associations or because of the wives' mutual interests in their families or community organizations. As men retire and women's home and community activities dwindle, the members have little left in common and gradually drift apart.

Formal Groups or Clubs
As leadership roles in formal groups and clubs are taken over by younger members and as the activities are planned mainly around their interests, older people feel unwanted in these organizations and discontinue their membership in them.

strength or the means of transportation to see his friends. If his income is limited, he may not be able to participate in church or community activities, and he often finds it difficult or impossible to keep up with the pace set by his younger relatives or friends. As a result, he is no longer welcome in many groups containing younger members. In discussing attitudes toward older people in social situations, Kalish has said (59):

We Americans like to invest our efforts, money, time, and emotional involvements in people who will pay off. Society is contrived so that older people are very unlikely to pay off. Since they will probably not be productive in the ways we wish, they will not be able to be independent as they were when they were younger, they will be less meaningful, and they have limited futures.

Sources of Social Contact   Three sources of social contact are seriously affected by aging; these are given in Box 13-8. Once these sources of social contact are broken, they are rarely mended or replaced.

Women, as a rule, retain their friendships longer than men, mainly because their friends come from their neighborhoods, while men's friends are largely work associates who live in scattered areas of the community and who are not brought together by their common interest in work after retirement. Thus many retired men are forced to rely mainly on their wives for companionship and to play "homebody" roles, which they find damaging to their masculine egos. Only when the man has a group of intimate friends, many of whom are his contemporaries and have been his friends since childhood, can he rely to any extent upon social contacts outside the home. Even then, these contacts may be infrequent because of problems relating to health or transportation, for example.

As a result of the shrinkage of sources of social contact in old age, the family circle constitutes the nucleus of the older person's social life. The older he is, the more he must rely upon members of his family for companionship.

One of the advantages of institutional living for the elderly person is that it provides him with opportunities for social contacts with contemporaries, which he usually does not have if he lives in his own home or with relatives. Social contacts with contemporaries are greatly advantageous to elderly people, even though many of them resist making such an adjustment. The elderly person's contemporaries have interests in common with his; he does not have to make radical adjustments in his pattern of behavior when he is with them; he moves physically and mentally at a tempo similar to theirs; he knows he is certain of acceptance because his friendship will help to eliminate their loneliness; and he has an opportunity for prestige, based on his past accomplishments, which he would not have in a group of younger people. The social advantages of institutional living for the elderly will be discussed further in the following chapter.

Social Participation   With advancing age, participation in social activities declines and its scope narrows. As may be seen in Figure 11-5, the number of married men and women who belong to three or more clubs or community organizations begins to drop after the age of sixty, while the number holding two or more offices or committee memberships declines even more steeply. There is also less attendance at the meetings of community organizations and different social functions.

While declining health is generally believed to be the main reason for the decline in social participation, this is not always the case. Other reasons are as important and sometimes even more important. The extent of the individual's participation when he was younger will, for example, have a marked influence on his participation in old age. Studies of social participation at different ages have shown that those who are active in adolescence and early adulthood continue to be active in middle and old age, except when such obstacles as poor health, economic privations, or family responsibilities prevent them from being so (49, 58). As King and Howell have pointed out, "The community role at 15–25 years of age seems to reflect the image of the late adult community role" (67).

At every age, socioeconomic status plays an important role in the amount of participation in community and social organizations. Members of the upper groups dominate the organized life of the community and supply it with leadership. Because members of the lower groups usually did not belong to these organizations when they were younger, they hesitate to join them when they are older.

Not only do members of the lower socioeconomic groups belong to fewer social organizations and take a less active part in them, but they also have fewer friends outside the family than members of the middle and upper groups. This led Rose to conclude that "Old age is generally likely to have a greater deleterious effect on the social relations of the lower class than of the middle class" (101).

Because many community organizations are occupation-oriented, as is true of the different business clubs and trade unions, older people who are retired usually no longer belong to these organizations. Thus their participation is limited mainly to the nonoccupationally oriented organizations. This partly accounts for the fact that elderly people tend to discontinue their membership in community organizations or to become less active in them.

A change in the individual's status, due either to loss of a spouse or to retirement, is likely to affect his friendships and social participation. For example, fewer men and women are widowered or widowed during their sixties than during their seventies, and thus the social life of people in their sixties is usually dominated by the married. During the seventies, by contrast, more are widowed or widowered, and most men are re-

tired. As a result, men and women in their seventies whose spouses have died have more opportunities for friendships and social activities.

The same principle holds true in the case of retirement. A man or woman who retires earlier than others of his age group or than his friends is deviant in the sense that he does not fit into the social life dominated by those who still work. After the majority of his friends retire, he finds that they have more time for socialization and more interests in common with him.

Religious Interests

Although it is popularly believed that old people turn to religion as life draws to a close, there is little evidence to support this view. Although an old person may become more religious as death approaches or if he is seriously disabled, the average elderly person does not necessarily turn to religion.

An analysis of research studies relating to attitudes toward religion and religious practices in old age has provided some evidence of greater interest in religion with advancing age and some evidence of declining interest. Instead of a turn to or away from religion in old age, most people carry on the religious beliefs and habits formed earlier in life (41, 90). As Covalt (30) has pointed out:

The attitude of most older people about religion is probably most often that with which they grew up or which they have accepted as they achieved intellectual maturity. Patterns of worship and of church attendance have remained much the same or have been modified by circumstances which, to the individual, are logical modifications.

However, certain changes in religious interests and attitudes are typical of older people in the American culture of today. The most common of these changes and the effects they have on personal and social adjustments during old age are given in Box 13-9.

There is evidence that the *quality* of church membership plays a more important role in the individual's adjustments in old age than membership per se. Those who joined voluntarily when they were younger and who have been active participants tend to be better adjusted in old age than are those whose interest and activity in religious organizations have been limited. Religion, as Moberg has explained, is only one factor in the adjustment to old age, but it is an important one (83).

The relationship between church attendance and personal adjustment in old age may be affected more by the social experiences the church offers than by the religious experiences. The church offers opportunities for social life and companionship, thus satisfying the older person's need to belong and to feel useful, and it minimizes feelings of loneliness. In addition, religion alleviates anxieties about death and the afterlife. As Moberg has pointed out, "A sense of serenity and decreased fear of death tend to accompany conservative religious beliefs" (83).

Whatever the reasons for interest in religion, attendance at church, and participation in religious organizations, there is evidence that these contribute to good adjustment in old age (47, 48, 83). There is also evidence, as Covalt has pointed out, that "The religious have a reference group that gives them support and security: the nonreligious are more likely to lack such social support" (30).

Interest in Death

During childhood, adolescence, and—to a lesser extent—early adulthood, interest in death revolves more around life after death than on what causes a person to die. As a result of religious training in the home, Sunday school, church, or synagogue, many young people have distinct concepts of heaven or hell and about the afterlife.

As the person grows old, he often becomes less interested in life after death and more concerned about death per se and about his own death. This is especially true of elderly people whose physical or mental condition has begun to deteriorate. When the elderly person's health fails, he often concentrates his attention on death and becomes preoccupied with it. This is in direct contrast to younger people, to whom death seems very far away and is of little concern.

When interest in death shifts from interest in the afterlife to interest in the individual's own death, it is usually concentrated on three questions, discussed below. Even when these questions dominate the elderly person's interest in death, he may still fear it because of uncertainty about whether there is an afterlife and what it will be like.

The first question about death that is of profound interest to many elderly people is: When will I die? While they know that no one can predict this with any degree of accuracy—not even the ablest doctors or life insurance actuaries—they try to estimate approximately how much longer they have to live on the basis of the longevity of family members and the present state of their health.

Even elderly people who have no fear of death may want to know how much time they have left because of what they regard as "unfinished business" in their lives—a trip they had always planned to take or a project they want to complete, for example. Many older people want their doctors to be frank about impending death so that they can tend to this unfinished business or settle their affairs.

The second question about death that concerns many elderly people is: What is likely to cause my death? While statistics show that heart disease, cancer, strokes, and accidents are the most common causes of death among the elderly, many die from other causes.

Interest in the question of what will lead to the individual's death centers around four major areas of concern. First, he wonders whether he can do anything to ward off his death, even for a short time. For example, if he knows that he is in danger of having a stroke because of high blood pressure, he may try to lower it by relaxing, by losing weight, and by taking proper medication.

The individual's second concern about what will cause his death stems from his desire to take care of unfinished business, as discussed above. Knowing what the probable cause of his death will be gives him some idea of the time remaining to him, since some diseases progress more rapidly than others.

Financial considerations are the individual's third concern relating to the question of what will cause his death. If he has reason to suspect that he may die as a result of a heart attack, for example, which comes quickly and is not likely to involve a long period of invalidism, he may have an "eat, drink, and be merry" philosophy about his money, as opposed to a person who believes that his death will be a slow and lingering process and will involve great medical expenses for him and his family.

Fourth, the individual wants to know what the cause of his death will be because this determines whether his last days will be debilitating and painful or whether he has a good chance of remaining mentally alert and physically active until the end.

The third question about death that most elderly people ask is: What can I do to die as I wish to die? In the past, many men and women accepted the belief that death is a matter of "God's will" and that the individual should have no voice in the matter.

Today there is a growing tendency, fostered by those who believe in euthanasia and backed by the theories of some members of the medical, psychological, psychiatric, and legal professions, as well as by some members of the clergy, that the individual should have some say about how he will die and even when he will die. Proponents of euthanasia, or "mercy killing," believe that those who are suffering from a painful, incurable disease or who are hopelessly injured should be put to death or allowed to die peacefully, by doing nothing to prolong their lives, such as performing surgery or giving artificial respiration or blood transfusions. However, such solutions to the problem of the hopelessly ill or injured person are the subject of heated legal, religious, and medical debate.

The elderly person who believes that he has the right to determine the manner of his death is urged to make a "living will," in which he spells out his wishes in this matter. A living will differs from a traditional will in three major respects. First, it contains information about how the individual wishes to die and about what he wants done with his body, rather than information about what he wants done with his material possessions; second, its contents are always known to the next of kin before his death so that they will be able to carry out his wishes; and third, a living will is not a legal document, as a traditional will is.

The elderly person who believes that he has the right to die in dignity and peace and to be spared a long, debilitating illness that may sap the energies and financial resources of family members sometimes believes that he is justified in taking his own life while he is still physically and mentally able to do so, *after* a careful and accurate medical diagnosis has shown that there is no hope of recovery. Even if his earlier moral and religious training has emphasized the wrongful nature of suicide, his personal belief that he has a right to determine the time and manner of his death may be strong enough to counteract any feelings of guilt he may have about committing such an act.

HAZARDS TO PERSONAL AND SOCIAL ADJUSTMENT IN OLD AGE

At few times during the life span are there as many potentially serious hazards to good personal and social adjustment as there are in old age. This is due partly to the older person's physical and mental decline, which makes him more vulnerable to potential hazards than he was earlier, and partly to lack of recognition of these potential hazards on the part of the social group. The result is that few attempts are made to warn the individual about these hazards or to prepare him for them as he grows older. For example, elderly people are seldom prepared for the hazard of accidents, which are so common in old age, nor are they taught how to avoid them. Similarly, few are given help in learning how to use their increased amount of leisure time in ways that are compatible with their declining strength and energy and their decreased incomes.

During the past decade or so, doctors have become increasingly active in their campaign to encourage middle-aged or even younger patients to take off weight in order to avoid the potential danger of heart trouble as they grow older. Unfortunately, many middle-aged people fail to follow such advice or even to recognize that they may avoid trouble in the future if they change their pattern of living gradually, rather than having to change it abruptly and rad-

ically later on, when it may be too late to repair the damage done earlier.

Just as there is no conclusive evidence that preparation for retirement always guarantees good adjustment to it, so there is no justification for believing that preparation for old age will always lead to good personal and social adjustments during this period. However, there is ample evidence that the person who is prepared for the personal and social changes that take place during old age is better able to adjust to them than one who has received no such preparation.

In the following discussion of the physical and psychological hazards of old age, it should be apparent how important a role preparation can play and how greatly increased the hazards are when preparation is minimized or completely absent.

Physical Hazards

All the common hazards to physical well-being at earlier ages not only are more common during old age but also affect a larger proportion of individuals. The causes and effects of these hazards are given in Box 13-10.

In addition to real physical hazards, there are imaginary ones. Many older people suffer from imaginary illness and concentrate on any ache or pain they may have, thus exaggerating it out of all proportion. Talking about aches, pains, medicine, and doctors is a favorite pastime of many old people. It serves as a means of attracting attention to themselves and of winning sympathy from others (34).

Many old people learn to cope with their physical ailments, while others do not. Some complain and feel sorry for themselves, and this may destroy any motivation they otherwise might have had to cope with their physical condition successfully. Still others make practical use of their disorders as a way of controlling others. (See Figure 13-4.) As Kassel has pointed out, "Their disabilities have become status symbols, a means whereby they can obtain attention and control their families" (60).

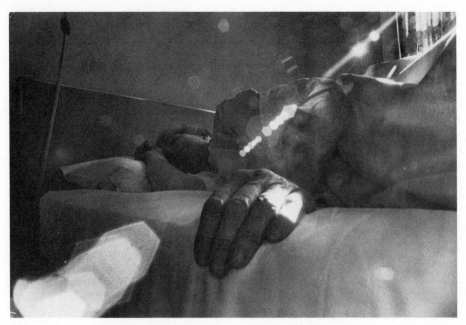

Illness and pain: common afflictions in old age. (Mottke Weissman)

Figure 13-4 Some elderly people make practical use of their disabilities to gain attention and to control the actions of others.

An often-overlooked hazard associated with the impaired physical condition of the older person is the financial drain it represents. Even Medicare, Medicaid, and health insurance policies often do not cover all expenses, such as the cost of hiring someone to take care of the household or the cost of expensive dental work.

These health costs often prevent the elderly person from doing things he would like to do, such as joining a club or visiting a relative or friend. He may even have to cut down on expenditures for clothing and grooming aids, both of which, as was pointed out earlier, are essential morale builders for the elderly.

Grown children or other relatives may become resentful if they must bear the burden of the elderly person's health costs, and this will jeopardize his major source of social contact. Furthermore, the older person may become extremely money-conscious and cut down on expenses unneces-

---

Box 13-10. COMMON PHYSICAL HAZARDS OF OLD AGE

Diseases and Physical Handicaps

Elderly people are most commonly afflicted by circulatory disturbances, metabolic disorders, involutional mental disorders, disorders of the joints, tumors (both benign and malignant), heart disease, rheumatism, arthritis, visual and hearing impairments, hypertension, gait disorders, and mental and nervous conditions. Figure 11-4 shows the marked increase in physical disability with age.

Malnutrition

Malnutrition in old age is due more to psychological than to economic causes. The most common psychological causes are lack of appetite resulting from anxiety and depression, not wanting to eat alone, and food aversions stemming from earlier prejudices. Even when their food intake is not deficient qualitatively or quantitatively, many older people do not get the full value from their food because of malabsorption resulting from digestive or intestinal disturbances or failure of the endocrine system to function as it formerly did.

Dental Disorders

Sooner or later, most elderly people lose some or all of their teeth. Those who must wear dentures often have difficulty in chewing foods that are rich in proteins, such as meat, and may concentrate on those high in carbohydrates. Chewing difficulties also encourage the swallowing of larger and coarser food masses, which may lead to digestive disorders. Ill-fitting dentures or the absence of teeth often causes lisping and slurring, which interferes with the older person's speech and causes him embarrassment.

Sexual Deprivation

Sexual deprivation or unfavorable attitudes toward sex in old age affect the old person in much the same way that emotional deprivation affects the young child. Happily married elderly people are healthier and live longer than those who never married or who have lost a spouse.

Accidents

Older people are generally more accident-prone than younger ones. Even when the accidents they have are not fatal, they frequently leave the individual disabled for life. Falls, which may be due to environmental obstacles or to dizziness, giddiness, weakness, or defective vision, are the most common accidents among older women, while older men are most commonly involved in motor-vehicle accidents, either as a driver or as a pedestrian.

---

sarily because he fears greater future expenditures for illness or disability. This can be a hazard to good social adjustments if it cuts the elderly person off from social contacts he would otherwise have (66).

Psychological Hazards

The psychological hazards of old age are often the result of acceptance of traditional beliefs and cultural stereotypes concerning older people. This acceptance is hazardous because it encourages the individual to feel inadequate and inferior; even worse, it tends to stifle his motivation to do what he is capable of doing. For example, the elderly person who believes that he is too old to learn new skills will be at a disadvantage if he tries to seek full- or part-time work after retirement or to pursue a new hobby to fill his time. Similarly, if the older person accepts the belief that the elderly should withdraw from life, his health will be impaired because of lack of exercise, and he will also be encouraged to reminisce about his past, which others find boring and which sets up roadblocks to good social adjustments.

A second psychological hazard stems from the feelings of inferiority and inadequacy that come with the physical changes of aging. The loss of an attractive, sex-appropriate appearance may lead the aging individual to feel that he will be rejected by society, since he has known from adolescence how important appearance is to social acceptance.

The necessity for establishing a different, more appropriate pattern of life in old age also presents a psychological hazard to elderly people, who may no longer need a large home, for example, now that their children are grown. Many older people cling to their homes and cherished possessions and to the life-style associated with them. Streib has explained why giving up homes and cherished possessions is so traumatic to older people (113):

Part of our depression at the loss of possessions is due to our feeling that we must now go without certain goods that we expected the possessions to bring in their train. Yet in every case there remains, over and above this, a sense of the shrinkage of our personality, a partial conversion of ourselves to nothingness, which is a psychological phenomenon by itself.

Elderly people also realize that they are becoming somewhat forgetful, that they have difficulty learning new names or facts, and that they cannot hold up under pressure as well as they used to. They may come to think that they are "slipping" mentally, and this encourages them in their belief that they are too old to learn anything new. Instead of adjusting their activities to conform to their mental state, they withdraw from *all* activities that might involve competition with younger people, and thus they experience all the problems, described earlier, that social disengagement brings.

Older people of today, who grew up in a more work-oriented society, may feel guilty about doing nothing after retirement or after their home responsibilities have diminished. They want to do something useful and thus may shy away from many community-planned activities for older citizens, even though they want the companionship these activities would provide.

Many old people are also unable to afford leisure-time activities they consider worthwhile, such as attending lectures or concerts or participating in various community activities. If they must rely on television for entertainment, they often find that the majority of the programs are youth-oriented and do not offer opportunities for self-improvement or cultural advancement.

Elderly people's need to feel useful, as well as their social needs, often can be met by volunteer work in hospitals, for example. Volunteer work, it is claimed, is a suitable substitute for the retired person's former occupation because it presents a personal challenge for the individual, thus generating self-respect, while at the same time winning him social approval and esteem.

Elderly men, on the whole, tend to be less willing to engage in volunteer community work than women. This is partly because they have become accustomed to being paid for their services and thus resist "working" for nothing and partly because they associate volunteer work with the feminine role. The cultural stereotype of the volunteer as a dilettante who dabbles in this work to kill time has a strong influence on the attitudes of those who have lived a work-oriented life and who shun any substitute that does not conform to their earlier-developed values.

Chapter Highlights

1 Certain characteristics of old age make it a distinctive period in the life span. It is a period of physical and mental decline, though there are marked individual differences in the speed and pattern of decline, and it requires role changes. There are many unfavorable stereotypes of the aged that are responsible for their minority-group status, which has lead to a widespread desire for rejuvenation.

2 The developmental tasks of old age relate mainly to the individual's personal life and to his adjustments to the changes, both physical and mental, that aging brings and the effects

these changes have on the pattern of his life.

3 The major physical changes accompanying aging include changes in appearance, in the different internal organs and their functioning, in sensitivities, and in sexual potency.

4 Changes in motor abilities in old age are due partly to physical causes, such as a decrease in energy, and partly to psychological causes, especially emotional tension. These changes result in decreased strength and speed, in difficulties in learning new skills, and in increased awkwardness.

5 Decline in mental abilities with aging comes at different rates in such areas as learning, memory, recall, and creativity.

6 Conditions responsible for changes in interests in old age include health, social and economic status, sex, and values.

7 The personal interests of the elderly person are concentrated on self, appearance, clothes, and money, while his recreational interests center mainly around amusements which require a minimum of strength and energy.

8 Social disengagement, which is characteristic of the elderly and may be voluntary or involuntary, is reflected in a narrowing of social contacts and of opportunities for social participation.

9 Interest in religion in old age does not necessarily increase, as is popularly believed; the older person's interest in death, however, assumes a new pattern.

10 Hazards to personal and social adjustments in old age are due partly to the physical and mental changes that characteristically occur at this time and partly to lack of preparation for these changes and their effect on the pattern of the individual's life.

11 The common physical hazards of old age include diseases, physical handicaps, malnutrition, dental disorders, sexual deprivation, and accidents.

12 The psychological hazards of old age stem mainly from acceptance of traditional beliefs and cultural stereotypes concerning old people. These encourage the individual to feel inferior and inadequate and may destroy his motivation to do what he is capable of doing.

Bibliography

1 Adams, D. L. Correlates of satisfaction among the elderly. *Gerontologist,* 1971, **11,** 64–68.

2 Back, K. W. Transition to aging and the self-image. *Aging & hum. Develpm.,* 1971, **2,** 296–304.

3 Barrett, J. H. *Gerontological psychology.* Springfield, Ill.: Charles C Thomas, 1972.

4 Bayley, N. Research in child development: A longitudinal perspective. *Merrill-Palmer Quart.,* 1965, **11,** 183–208.

5 Bell, B. D. The family life cycle, primary relationships and social participation patterns. *Gerontologist,* 1973, **13,** 78–81.

6 Berkowitz, B., & Green, R. F. Changes in intellect with age. V. Differential changes as functions of time interval and original score. *J. genet. Psychol.,* 1965, **107,** 179–192.

7 Birren, J. E. *The psychology of aging.* Englewood Cliffs, N.J.: Prentice-Hall, 1964.

8 Bischof, L. J. *Adult psychology.* New York: Harper & Row, 1969.

9 Blank, M. L. Recent research findings on practice with the aging. *Soc. Casewk.,* 1971, **52,** 382–389.

10 Bliven, B. Using our leisure is no easy job. *The New York Times,* Apr. 26, 1964.

11 Blum, J. E., Fosshage, J. L., & Jarvik, L. F. Intellectual changes and sex differences in octogenarians: A twenty-five year longitudinal study of aging. *Develpm. Psychol.,* 1972, **7,** 178–187.

12 Botwinick, J. *Aging and behavior.* New York: Springer, 1973.

13 Boyarsky, R. E., & Eisdorfer, C. Forgetting in older persons. *J. Gerontol.,* 1972, **27,** 254–258.

14 Bradway, K. P., & Thompson, C. W. Intelligence at adulthood: A 25-year follow-up. *J. educ. Psychol.,* 1962, **53,** 1–16.

15 Bultena, G. L., & Oyler, R. Effects of health on disengagement and morale. *Aging & hum. Develpm.,* 1971, **2,** 142–148.

16 Busse, E. W. Theories of aging. In E. W. Busse & E. Pfeiffer (Eds.), *Behavior and adaptation in late life.* Boston: Little, Brown, 1969. Pp. 11–32.

17 Busse, E. W., & Pfeiffer, E. Functional psychiatric disorders in old age. In E. W. Busse & E. Pfeiffer (Eds.), *Behavior and adaptation in late life.* Boston: Little, Brown, 1969. Pp. 183–235.

18 Butler, R. N. Crises and characteristics of later life. *Amer. J. Orthopsychiat.,* 1967, **37,** 337–338.

19 Butler, R. N. Age: The life review. *Psychology Today,* 1971, **5**(7), 49–51, 89.

20 Caldwell, B. M., & Watson, R. I. An evaluation of sex hormone replacement in aged women. *J. genet. Psychol.,* 1954, **85,** 181–200.

21 Cameron, P. Stereotypes about generational fun and happiness vs. self-appraised fun and happiness. *Gerontologist,* 1972, **12,** 120–123, 190.

22 Cameron, P., Stewart, L., & Biber, H. Consciousness of death across the life span. *J. Gerontol.,* 1973, **28,** 92–95.

23 Chevotarev, D. Fight against old age. *Gerontologist,* 1971, **11,** 359–361.

24 Chown, S. M., & Heron, A. Psychological aspects of ageing in man. *Annu. Rev. Psychol.,* 1965, **16,** 417–450.

25 Christenson, C. V., & Gagnon, J. H. Sexual behavior in a group of older women. *J. Gerontol.,* 1965, **20,** 351–356.

26 Clavan, S. The family process: A sociological model. *Family Coordinator,* 1969, **18,** 312–317.

27 Coppinger, N. W., & Nehrke, M. F. Discrimination learning and the transfer of training in the aged. *J. genet. Psychol.,* 1972, **120,** 93–102.

28 Corso, J. F. Sensory processes and age effects in normal adults. *J. Gerontol.,* 1971, **26,** 90–105.

29 Costa, P., & Kastenbaum, R. Some aspects of memories and ambitions in centenarians. In D. C. Charles & W. R. Looft (Eds.), *Readings in psychological development through life.* New York: Holt, 1973. Pp. 408–420.

30 Covalt, N. K. The meaning of religion to older people. In C. B. Vedder & A. S. Lefkowitz (Eds.), *Problems of the aged.* Springfield, Ill.: Charles C Thomas, 1965. Pp. 215–224.

31 Crawford, M. P. Retirement and disengagement. *Hum. Relat.,* 1971, **24,** 255–278.

32 Cryns, A. G., & Monk, A. Attitudes of the aged toward the young: A multivariate study of intergenerational perception. *J. Gerontol.,* 1972, **27,** 107–112.

33 Cutler, S. J. Voluntary association participation and life satisfaction: A cautionary research note. *J. Gerontol.,* 1973, **28,** 96–100.

34 Dovenmuehle, R. H., Busse, E. W., & Newman, G. Physical problems of older people. In E. B. Palmore (Ed.), *Normal aging.* Durham, N.C.: Duke University Press, 1970. Pp. 29–39.

35 Durfak, J. A. Relationship between attitudes toward life and death among elderly women. *Develpm. Psychol.,* 1973, **8,** 146.

36 Dye, D., Goodman, M., Roth, M., Blex, N., & Jensen, K. The older adult volunteer compared to the nonvolunteer. *Gerontologist,* 1973, **13,** 215–218.

37 Eisdorfer, C. Attitudes toward old people: A re-analysis of the Item-Validity of the Stereotype Scale. *J. Gerontol.,* 1966, **21,** 455–462.

38 Eisdorfer, C., & Lawton, M. P. *The psychology of adult development.* Washington: APA, 1973.

39 Erikson, E. H. Identity and the life cycle: Selected papers. *Psychol. Issues Monogr.,* Vol. 1., No. 1. New York: International Universities Press, 1967.

40 Felstein, I. *Later life: Geriatrics today and tomorrow.* Baltimore: Penguin, 1969.

41 *Geriatric Focus* article. Church attendance may decline with age but religious interest and concern increases. *Geriatric Focus,* 1965, **4**(11), 2–3.

42 *Geriatric Focus* article. Over-65 accident toll is highest in nation. *Geriatric Focus,* 1969, **8**(10), 1–5.

43 *Geriatric Focus* article. Old age seen negatively by old as well as young. *Geriatric Focus,* 1970, **9**(10), 1, 11–13.

44 *Geriatric Focus* article. Free time poses problems to elderly in our society. *Geriatric Focus,* 1971, **10**(2), 1, 9–10.

45 *Geriatric Focus* article. Implantation of synthetic sex hormones. *Geriatric Focus,* 1971, **10**(2), 1, 5.

46 Gilbert, J. C. Thirty-five-year follow-up study of intellectual functioning. *J. Gerontol.,* 1973, **28,** 68–72.

47 Glock, C. Y. *American piety.* Berkeley: University of California Press, 1968.

48 Guinan, St. M. Aging and religious life. *Gerontologist,* 1972, **12,** 21.

49 Havighurst, R. J. The leisure activities of the middle aged. *Amer. J. Sociol.,* 1957, **63,** 152–162.

50 Havighurst, R. J., & Albrecht, R. *Older people.* New York: Longmans, 1953.

51 Havighurst, R. J., & Glasser, R. An exploratory study of reminiscence. *J. Gerontol.,* 1972, **27,** 245–253.

52 Havighurst, R. J., Neugarten, B. L., & Tobin, S. S. Disengagement and patterns of aging. In B. L. Neugarten (Ed.), *Middle age and aging: A reader in social psychology.* Chicago: University of Chicago Press, 1968. Pp. 161–172.

53 Henry, W. E., & Cumming, E. Personality development in adulthood and old age. *J. proj. Tech.,* 1959, **23,** 383–390.

54 Hodgkins, J. Influence of age on the speed of reaction and movement in females. *J. Gerontol.,* 1962, **17,** 385–389.

55 Horwitt, M. K. Nutritional problems in the aged. In C. B. Vedder & A. S. Lefkowitz (Eds.), *Problems of the aged.* Springfield, Ill.: Charles C Thomas, 1965. Pp. 172–178.

56 Jeffers, F. C., & Verwoerdt, A. How the old face death. In E. W. Busse & E. Pfeiffer (Eds.), *Behavior and adaptation in late life.* Boston: Little, Brown, 1969. Pp. 163–181.

57 Johnson, W. M. *The years after fifty.* College Park, Md.: McGrath Publishing, 1970.

58 Jones, M. C. Psychological correlates of somatic development. *Child Develpm.,* 1965, **36,** 899–911.

59 Kalish, R. A. Of social values and dying: A defense of disengagement. *Family Coordinator,* 1972, **21,** 81–94.

60 Kassel, V. Polygyny after 60. *Geriatrics,* 1966, **21,** 214–218.

61 Kastenbaum, R. (Ed.) *New thoughts on old age.* New York: Springer, 1964.

62 Kastenbaum, R. The foreshortened life perspective. In W. R. Looft (Ed.), *Developmental psychology: A book of readings.* Hinsdale, Ill.: Dryden Press, 1972. Pp. 485–493.

63 Kastenbaum, R., & Aisenberg, R. *The psychology of death.* New York: Springer, 1973.

64 Kastenbaum, R., & Durkee, N. Young people view old age. In R. Kastenbaum (Ed.), *New thoughts on old age.* New York: Springer, 1964. Pp. 237–249.

65 Kent, D. P. Social and cultural factors influencing the mental health of the aged. *Amer. J. Orthopsychiat.,* 1966, **36,** 680–685.

66 Kent, D. P., & Matson, M. B. The impact of health on the aged family. *Family Coordinator,* 1972, **21,** 29–36.

67 King, C. E., & Howell, W. H. Role characteristics of flexible and inflexible retired persons. *Sociol. soc. Res.,* 1964, **49,** 153–165.

68 Koller, M. R. *Social gerontology.* New York: Random House, 1972.

69 Kuypers, J. A. Changeability of life-style and personality in old age. *Gerontologist,* 1972, **12,** 336–342.

70 Langer, E. Growing old in America: Frauds, quackery swindle the aged and compound their troubles. *Science,* 1963, **140,** 470–472.

71 Leaf, A. Getting old. *Scient. American,* 1973, **229**(3), 45–52.

72 Lehman, H. C. *Age and achievement.* Princeton, N.J.: Princeton University Press, 1953.

73 Leon, E. F. Cicero on geriatrics. *Gerontologist,* 1963, **3,** 128–130.

74 Lester, D., & Kam, E. G. Effect of a friend dying upon attitudes toward death. *J. soc. Psychol.,* 1971, **83,** 149–150.

75 Lewis, C. N. Reminiscing and self-concept in old age. *J. Gerontol.,* 1971, **26,** 240–243.

76 Linn, M. W. Perceptions of childhood: Present functioning and past events. *J. Gerontol.,* 1973, **28,** 202–206.

77 Lopata, H. Z. The life cycle of the social role of housewife. *Sociol. soc. Res.,* 1966, **51,** 5–22.

78 Lorge, I. Gerontology (later maturity). *Annu. Rev. Psychol.,* 1956, **7,** 349–364.

79 Maddox, G. L. Fact and artifact: Evidence bearing on disengagement theory. In E. B. Palmore (Ed.), *Normal aging.* Durham, N.C.: Duke University Press, 1970. Pp. 318–328.

80 Masters, W. H., & Johnson, V. E. *Human sexual response.* Boston: Little, Brown, 1966.

81 Meltzer, H., & Ludwig, D. Age differences in memory optimism and pessimism in workers. *J. genet. Psychol.,* 1967, **110,** 17–30.

82 Miller, S. J. The social dilemma of the aging leisure participant. In B. L. Neugarten (Ed.), *Middle age and aging: A reader in social psychology.* Chicago: University of Chicago Press, 1968. Pp. 366–374.

83 Moberg, D. O. Religiosity in old age. In B. L. Neugarten (Ed.), *Middle age and aging: A reader in social psychology.* Chicago: University of Chicago Press, 1968. Pp. 497–508.

84 Morgan, A. F. Nutrition in the aging. *Gerontologist,* 1962, **2,** 77–84.

85 Nehrke, M. F. Age and sex differences in discrimination learning and transfer of training. *J. Gerontol.,* 1973, **28,** 320–327.

86 Neugarten, B. L. Grow old with me! The best is yet to be. *Psychology Today,* 1971, **5**(7), 45–46, 79–81.

87 *New York Times* article. Hard facts about nation's elderly show latter years are not golden for most. *The New York Times,* May 3, 1965.

88 Nutthall, R. L., & Fozard, J. L. Age, socioeconomic status and human abilities. *Aging & hum. Develpm.,* 1970, **1,** 161–169.

89 Owens, W. A. Age and mental abilities: A longitudinal study. In D. C. Charles & W. R. Looft (Eds.), *Readings in psychological development through life.* New York: Holt, 1973. Pp. 243–254.

90 Packard, V. *The status seekers.* New York: Pocket Books, 1961.

91 Palmore, E. B. (Ed.) *Normal aging.* Durham, N.C.: Duke University Press, 1970.

92 Pǎrizková, J., & Eiselt, E. A further study on changes in somatic characteristics and body composition of old men followed longitudinally for 8–10 years. *Hum. Biol.,* 1971, **43,** 318–326.

93 Parker, E. *The seven ages of woman.* Baltimore: Johns Hopkins Press, 1960.

94 Peck, R. C. Psychological development in the second half of life. In B. L. Neugarten (Ed.), *Middle age and aging: A reader in social psychology.* Chicago: University of Chicago Press, 1968. Pp. 88–92.

95 Peterson, D. A. Financial adequacy in retirement: Perceptions of older Americans. *Gerontologist,* 1972, **12,** 379–383.

96 Plutchik, R., Weiner, M. B., & Conte, H. Studies in body image. I. Body worries and body discomforts. *J. Gerontol.,* 1971, **26,** 344–350.

97 Pressey, S. L. Not all decline! *Gerontologist,* 1966, **6,** 3–4.

98 Reimanis, G., & Green, R. F. Imminence of death and intellectual decrement in the aging. *Develpm. Psychol.,* 1971, **5,** 270–272.

99 Riley, M. W., Johnson, M., & Foner, A. *Aging and society.* Vol. 3. *A sociology of age stratification.* New York: Russell Sage, 1972.

100 Robin, E. P. Discontinuities in attitudes and behaviors of older age groups. *Gerontologist,* 1971, **11,** 79–84.

101 Rose, A. M. Class differences among the elderly: A research report. *Sociol. soc. Res.,* 1966, **50,** 356–360.

102 Rosencranz, H. A., & Pihlblad, C. T. Measuring the health of the elderly. *J. Gerontol.,* 1970, **25,** 129–133.

103 Rosow, I. The social context and the aging self. *Gerontologist,* 1972, **13,** 82–87.

104 Ryan, M. S. *Clothing: A study in human behavior.* New York: Holt, 1966.

105 Savage, R. D., Britton, P. G., George, S., O'Connor, D., & Hall, E. H. A developmental investigation of intellectual functioning in the community aged. *J. genet. Psychol.,* 1972, **121,** 163–167.

106 Schaie, K. W. Age changes and age differences. In W. R. Looft (Ed.), *Developmental psychology: A book of readings.* Hinsdale, Ill.: Dryden Press, 1972. Pp. 60–67.

107 Schaie, K. W., Labouvie, G. V., & Buech, B. U. Generational and cohort-specific differences in adult cognitive functioning: A fourteen-year study of independent samples. *Develpm. Psychol.,* 1973, **9,** 151–161.

108 Scheinfeld, A. *Your heredity and environment.* Philadelphia: Lippincott, 1965.

109 Sherwood, S. Gerontology and the sociology of food and eating. *Aging & hum. Develpm.,* 1970, **1,** 61–85.

110 Sinex, F. M. Health and nutrition. *Gerontologist,* 1972, **12,** 21–28.

111 Smith, M. E. Delayed recall of previously memorized material after fifty years. In D. C. Charles & W. R. Looft (Eds.), *Readings in psychological development through life.* New York: Holt, 1973. Pp. 158–159.

112 Storch, P. A., Looft, W. R., & Hooper, F. H. Interrelationships among Piagetian tasks and traditional measures of cognitive abilities in mature and aged adults. *J. Gerontol.,* 1972, **27,** 461–465.

113 Streib, G. F. Are the aged a minority group? In B. L. Neugarten (Ed.), *Middle age and aging: A reader in social psychology.* Chicago: University of Chicago Press, 1968. Pp. 35–46.

114 Taub, H. A. Memory span, practice, and aging. *J. Gerontol.,* 1973, **28,** 335–338.

115 Tibbitts, C. (Ed.) *Handbook of social gerontology: Societal aspects of aging.* Chicago: University of Chicago Press, 1960.

116 *Time* article. The old in the country of the young. *Time,* Aug. 3, 1970, 49–54.

117 Trembly, D., & O'Connor, J. Growth and decline of natural and acquired intellectual characteristics. *J. Gerontol.,* 1968, **21,** 9–12.

118 Twente, E. E. *Never too old.* San Francisco: Jossey-Bass, 1970.

119 Vest, W. E. William Shakespeare, gerontologist. *Geriatrics,* 1954, **9,** 80–82.

120 Wallach, M. A., & Green, L. R. On age and the subjective speed of time. In B. L. Neugarten (Ed.), *Middle age and aging: A reader in social psychology.* Chicago: University of Chicago Press, 1968. Pp. 481–485.

121 White, K. L. Life and death and medicine. *Scient. American,* 1973, **229**(3), 23–33.

122 Wilkie, F., & Eisdorfer, C. Intelligence and blood pressure in the aged. *Science,* 1971, **172,** 959–962.

123 Wingrove, C. R., & Alston, J. P. Age, aging, and church attendance. *Gerontologist,* 1971, **11,** 356–358.

124 Wood, V. Age-appropriate behavior for older people. *Gerontologist,* 1971, **11,** 74–78.

125 Youmans, E. G. Age stratification and value orientations. *Int. J. Aging & hum Develpm.,* 1973, **4,** 53–65.

126 Zborowski, M. Aging and recreation. *J. Gerontol.,* 1962, **17,** 302–309.

CHAPTER | FOURTEEN

OLD AGE
Vocational and Family
Adjustments

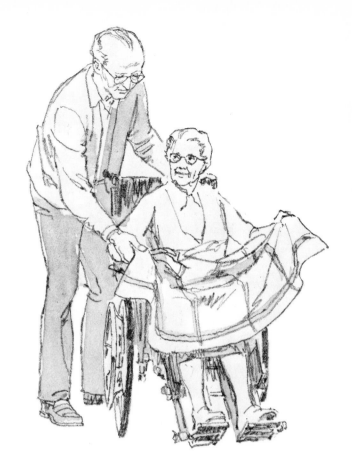

Two of the most difficult developmental tasks of old age relate to areas which are especially important for all adults—work and family life. The elderly person faces adjustment problems in these areas which are similar in some respects to those he faced earlier but which are unique in many ways. Not only must he adjust to his working conditions, but he must also adjust to the realization that his usefulness is lessened as he grows older and that his status in the work group decreases. Furthermore, he has the problem of adjusting to retirement when the time comes.

In the family, older men and women must adjust to depending on each other for companionship; to the lack of contact with, and influence over, their children; and often to the loss of a spouse. Unmarried elderly people often face adjustment problems that are more serious than the ones confronting those who are married or who have lost a spouse.

Vocational and family adjustments in old age are complicated by economic factors which play a far more important role now than they did earlier. Although government aid, in the form of social security, old-age benefits, and Medicare, and the gradual spread of retirement benefits from business and industry alleviate the elderly person's financial problems to some extent, they by no means solve them. This is especially true during periods of spiraling inflation.

VOCATIONAL ADJUSTMENTS
IN OLD AGE

Older men are more interested in steady work than in advancement which they realize is not likely to be forthcoming. As a result, they are more satisfied with their jobs than younger men. Even knowing that retirement is imminent does not affect their attitudes toward their work if they enjoy what they are doing and are anxious to work.

Even women who did not work during early adulthood, when they were preoccupied with housework and child care, often return to work during middle age and find it a satisfactory compensation for diminished home and family responsibilities. However, they tend to be less satisfied with their jobs than men, primarily because the only jobs available to middle-aged women who reenter the labor force are even less interesting and less challenging than those available to middle-aged men who shift to another job during middle age. As a result, older women are less satisfied with the jobs they have and are less disturbed at the thought of retirement than older men.

At all ages, people have different reasons for wanting to work. However, as Havighurst has pointed out, attitudes to-

---

Box 14-1. WORK ATTITUDES OF OLDER WORKERS

Society-maintaining Work Attitudes
The worker whose attitude is society-maintaining has little or no interest in his work per se and gains little personal satisfaction from it. His main interest is in his paycheck, and he often regards his job as a heavy and unpleasant burden and looks forward to retirement.

Ego-involving Work Attitudes
The individual who finds his work ego-involving derives great personal satisfaction from it. Work is the basis of self-respect and a sense of worth for some workers; others find that it is a means of gaining prestige, a locus of social participation, or a source of intrinsic enjoyment or creative self-expression, as well as a way of making time pass in a pleasant, routine manner. Because his work means so much to a worker with such an attitude, he may become preoccupied with it to the exclusion of other interests and dread the time when he will be forced to retire.

---

ward work, which are at the basis of a desire to work, fall roughly into two categories; these are explained in Box 14-1 (45).

A worker can have either of these two attitudes toward any job. If he has a society-maintaining attitude toward his work, his leisure time will be more important to him than his time on the job. If, on the other hand, he regards it as ego-involving, the time he spends at work will take on greater significance for him, and leisure time will decrease in significance.

The prevailing cultural attitude toward work also influences the older worker's attitude toward it. Those who grew up when the cultural attitude toward work was more favorable than it is today have a very different attitude toward work than young people now. This colors their attitude toward their own work and increases the difficulties they have adjusting to not being able to get employment if they are physically able to work. For the work-oriented older person, having a job that gives him status and

For the work-oriented older person, it is important to have a job that provides both status and feelings of usefulness. (Ray Ellis from Rapho Guillumette)

makes him feel useful is essential to good mental health. Remunerative work is essential to good adjustment for such individuals; as was pointed out in the preceding chapter, they may regard volunteer work with disdain.

Vocational Opportunities

Unfortunately, there are very few job opportunities for older people who want to work and are able to do so. The most important reasons for this are given in Box 14-2.

After middle age, vocational opportunities decrease rapidly. For the most part, older workers are in dead-end, monotonous jobs which are far below the level of their ability or which they do not find satisfying; relatively few are in highly skilled positions or have jobs involving responsibility. In business and industry, only the worst jobs are usually available to the older worker.

On the whole, older workers are overrepresented at the bottom of the earning scale and underrepresented at the top of the earning scale. Thus it is not surprising that they often derive little satisfaction from their jobs.

Appraisal of Older Workers

Studies of the advantages and disadvantages of hiring older workers reveal that these differ according to the kind of work to be done. Some jobs are more appropriate for older workers, and some for younger workers. Jobs in which judgment and experience are required or in which quality is

---

Box 14-2. CONDITIONS LIMITING EMPLOYMENT OPPORTUNITIES FOR OLDER WORKERS

Compulsory Retirement
Most industries, businesses, and governmental bureaus and agencies require men to retire at ages sixty-two to sixty-five, and many force women to retire at sixty. There is a rapidly growing tendency toward even earlier retirement.

Hiring Policies
When the personnel departments of business and industry are in the hands of younger people, the older worker's difficulties in finding employment are greatly increased.

Pension Plans
There is a close correlation between the existence of a pension plan in business and industry and the failure to make use of workers over sixty-five years of age.

Social Attitudes
The widespread belief that older workers are accident-prone, that they are too slow to keep pace with younger workers, and that retraining them to use modern techniques is too costly militates against employing older workers.

Fluctuations in Business Cycles
When business conditions are poor, older workers are generally the first to be laid off and are then replaced by younger workers when the situation improves.

Kind of Work
The period of employment of workers in executive positions is limited by retirement policies. Skilled, semiskilled, and unskilled workers find that their strength and speed decrease with age and that their usefulness to their employers also decreases as a result. Only a person who owns his own business or who is in a profession can continue to work as long and as much as he wishes.

Sex
Women generally find it more difficult to hold their jobs or to get new ones as they grow older than men do. Part-time work in offices or stores and domestic work are among the few vocational opportunities open to older women.

more important than speed are more appropriate for older workers. Even in work where speed and ability to adjust to new tasks are essential, as in skilled, unskilled, and clerical work, the older worker usually compensates for loss of speed and difficulties of adjustment by his steadiness and ability to work without supervision (7, 23).

The older worker, because of his experience, tends to do things with less wasted motion than the younger, less-experienced worker. This compensates for his slower work pace. He is also less inclined to be preoccupied with problems related to his personal life than the younger worker, whose interests are centered around his romances or his family. He is less restless and less likely to be dissatisfied with his job or to want to change jobs than the younger worker. While the volume of his work may be less than that of the younger worker, the quality is generally higher, and he spoils less material. He makes fewer mistakes, partly because his judgment is better and partly because he works at a slower pace.

There is greater conscientiousness among older workers because of their more mature attitudes and their desire to keep their jobs. As a result, they are generally more dependable. Absenteeism, due to illness or disinclination to work, is highest among younger workers, especially those under twenty years of age, while older workers are far less prone to absenteeism.

Disabling illnesses and injuries, popularly believed to make older workers less desirable employment risks, are far less frequent among them than is thought and are less frequent among older workers than among younger ones. Even workers up to seventy-four years of age are affected by chronic disabilities in only about half the cases, and these are not serious enough to militate against their working abilities.

Accident proneness is likewise far less common among older workers than is popularly believed. The argument that older workers get along less well with coworkers than those who are younger has likewise

been found not to be true. While some older workers unquestionably make poorer adjustments to their fellow workers than others do, the percentage who have such difficulty is not appreciably greater than the percentage of younger workers who have trouble getting along with coworkers. In summary, as Pressey has emphasized, the "values of older workers have actually been adequately demonstrated; the big need, now, is to develop adjustments to meet the needs of the older, and agencies to foster opportunities for them" (92).

ADJUSTMENT TO RETIREMENT

Until recently, retirement was a problem that affected relatively few workers. Today, however, with the widespread acceptance of compulsory-retirement policies and the growing tendency for men and women to live longer than ever before, retirement is becoming one of the major social problems of our culture. Each year, the gap between the total life span and the span of the working life for men and women is widened. As a result, the length of the retirement period grows longer and longer for more people. Figure 14-1 shows the increase in leisure time and the decrease in work time from 1855 to 2000.

To the younger person, whose days are so often overly crowded with duties and responsibilities, the years of retirement or semiretirement seem like a golden period of life. By middle age, thoughts of retirement grow increasingly strong, not only because the individual finds the burden of work becoming heavier and heavier as his strength and energy diminish, but also because he realizes that he is waging a losing battle in his competition with younger workers.

When retirement actually comes, however, it may seem far less desirable than it did earlier. For most elderly people, there is a marked difference between the expectations before retirement and the realities of retirement.

Certain conditions facilitate adjustment to retirement. First, the person who retires voluntarily will adjust better than one who is forced to retire, especially if he wants to continue to work. Second, poor health at the time of retirement facilitates the adjustment, while good health is likely to militate against it. Third, most workers find that tapering off is better than abruptly ending patterns of work and living established many years earlier.

A fourth factor in adjustment is pretirement planning. The individual who has developed an interest in substitute activities which are meaningful to him and which provide many of the satisfactions he formerly derived from his work will not find adjustment to retirement emotionally disturbing. As Back has pointed out, "The more retirement is looked on as a change to a new status, and the less it is perceived as the giving up of a prized status, the better the transition will be accomplished" (6).

Because one of the most difficult aspects of retirement is that of severing social ties at work, a fifth aid to good adjustment to retirement is the provision for social contacts. Those who spend their retirement years in homes for the aged have more opportunities for social contacts and recreational activities than those who remain in their own homes or live with relatives. However, unless such institutions provide opportunities for activities that will promote a feeling of usefulness, they will not contribute to good adjustment to retirement.

Sixth, because changing a pattern of living becomes increasingly difficult with each passing year, the less change retirement necessitates, the better the individual will adjust to it. It has been reported that those who can stay in their community and who have enough money to live just about as they lived before retirement make the best adjustment to it. (14, 39).

Women, as a whole, adjust more easily to retirement than men. The role change is not as radical for them because they have always played the domestic role, whether

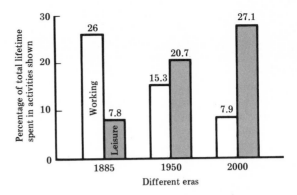

Figure 14-1 Increase in leisure time and decrease in work time—actual and projected. (Adapted from J. W. Still. Boredom: The psychological disease of aging. *Geriatrics,* 1957, **12,** 557–560. Used by permission.)

they were married or single, throughout their working lives, in addition to their vocational role. Furthermore, because few have held executive positions, they do not feel that they have suddenly lost all their power and prestige. Men, on the other hand, have less readily available means of deriving satisfaction to replace that which their work provided, and as a result, they adjust less well to the role change necessitated by retirement.

ADJUSTMENTS TO CHANGES IN FAMILY LIFE

The pattern of family life, established in early adulthood, starts to change with the onset of middle age. These changes are often made more pronounced by retirement, with the accompanying reduced income, or by the death of a spouse.

Of the many adjustments centering around family relationships that the elderly person must make, the most important involve relationship with a spouse, changes in sexual behavior, relationships with offspring, parental dependency, and relationships with grandchildren.

Relationship with a Spouse

With the role change from a worker to a retiree, the man spends much more of his time at home than he ever did before. If his relationship with his wife is good, this will contribute to the happiness of both. When their relationship is strained, however, the friction is increased by constant contacts.

Because many retired men feel lost and do not know what to do with their free time, they tend to be depressed and unhappy. They may show their feelings by being critical, faultfinding, and irritable in their treatment of their wives. Many of them resent any suggestion that they assume some of the household responsibilities on the grounds that that is "woman's work."

How well husbands and wives will adjust to each other in old age when retirement forces them together more than at any previous time in their marriage will depend largely on how many interests they have in common. This, in turn, will depend largely on how compatible they have been earlier, especially in middle age, when their children left home and thus freed them from parental responsibilities and child-oriented recreation.

Middle- and upper-class adults, on the whole, spend more of their leisure time with spouses and have more recreational interests in common with them than those of the lower-class groups. Because they have developed a pattern of "togetherness" in their recreational activities, it is easier for them to apply this pattern to all areas of their lives when the husband's retirement forces him to spend the major part of his time in the home.

Changes in Sexual Behavior

In old age, compatibility with the spouse influences the kind of sexual behavior the individual engages in. While it is popularly believed that impotence and loss of interest in sex are natural accompaniments of old age, there is evidence that changes in sexual behavior are due more to antagonistic relationships and incompatibility than to physical causes.

There is also evidence that many middle-aged women, freed from the fear of pregnancy, develop a new interest in sex. This interest, when uninhibited by unfavorable attitudes, continues into old age. While it is true that both men and women experience a diminishing of their sexual powers that parallels the decline in other bodily functions, there is a much stronger interest in sex and a greater desire for sexual activity in old age than is popularly believed to exist. Today, it is recognized that the sexual needs of the elderly are too widespread to be considered pathological (36, 74).

Studies of the sexual behavior of elderly people have revealed that men and women in their sixties, and even seventies, have intercourse, though it is spaced further apart than in the earlier years, and the man's preliminary orgastic phase is longer (82, 89). Decline in sexual activity with advancing age is illustrated in Figure 14-2.

When the individual is in reasonably good health, there is diminishing of sexual activity, rather than a sudden cessation of it. As Rubin has pointed out, there is "no automatic cut off to sexuality at any age" (99). Those who terminate sexual intercourse in old age usually do so because of the physical illness of one of the spouses or because the husband experiences difficulties in achieving orgasm, which affects his desire to continue coitus.

Many factors other than physical ones have a marked influence on the sexual behavior of elderly people. The most important of these are given in Box 14-3.

Studies of sexual interests and activities in old age have revealed marked sex differences. As men grow older, they are sexually *interested* more than sexually active. For women, by contrast, interest and activity remain static, but at a much lower level than in men (89, 99). As Masters and Johnson have commented, "There is no time limit drawn by the advancing years to female sexuality" (74).

In old age, as at other ages, sexual activity has a marked influence on marital adjustments, which in turn affect sexual activity. However, it is not the quantity or quality of sexual activity per se that influences marital adjustments, but whether the sexual activity meets the needs of both partners. When an elderly woman finds that coitus does not meet her sexual needs, she may seek substitute sources of satisfaction in masturbation or erotic dreams and daydreams, and this will affect her attitude unfavorably.

The psychological effects of unfavorable social attitudes toward sexual behavior in old age are far more serious than is generally recognized. Guilt feelings, emotional stress due to thwarted sexual desires, and feelings of inadequacy may lead to impotence. As a result, there is a decrease in the frequency of coitus and an increase in other sexual outlets. This is especially damaging psychologically to elderly men for whom

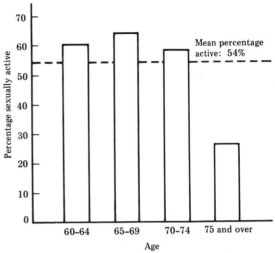

Figure 14-2 There is a decline in sexual activity with advancing age. (Adapted from G. Newman & C. R. Nichols. Sexual activities and attitudes in older persons. In E. B. Palmore (Ed.), *Normal aging.* Durham, N.C.: Duke University Press, 1970. Pp. 277–281. Used by permission.)

Box 14-3. PSYCHOLOGICAL FACTORS AFFECTING SEXUAL BEHAVIOR IN OLD AGE

Pattern of Earlier Sexual Behavior
People who derived enjoyment from sexual behavior and were sexually active during the earlier years of their marriage continue to be sexually more active in old age than those who were less active earlier.

Compatibility of Spouses
When there is a close bond between husband and wife built on mutual interests and respect, the desire for intercourse is much stronger than when a frictional relationship exists.

Social Attitudes
Unfavorable social attitudes toward sex in old age make many elderly men and women feel that interest in sexual matters not only is "not nice" but may even be perverted.

Marital Status
Married people are more likely to continue sexual activity into old age. Those who are single or

divorced or whose spouses have died usually do not have a strong-enough sex drive to make them seek partners.

Preoccupation with Outside Problems
When either spouse is preoccupied with financial, family, or other problems, it tends to weaken his sexual desire. If he eats or drinks excessively in order to escape from these problems, his sexual desire is further weakened.

Overfamiliarity
Being together too much over a long period of time tends to deaden a couple's sexual desire in old age.

Impotence
Many men who find themselves impotent on one occasion, regardless of the condition that gave rise to it, withdraw from further sexual activity to avoid the ego-shattering experience of repeated episodes of sexual inadequacy.

potency is a symbol of their masculinity.

Diminishing sexual power can have a serious effect on marital adjustments during old age. If the man believes that his growing impotence is the result of his wife's lack of sexual responsiveness and if she, in turn, blames him for not satisfying her sexual needs, their relationship will be strained, particularly if they are already experiencing difficulties in adjustment as a result of a lack of common interests and boredom on the husband's part stemming from his retirement.

Relationships with Offspring

Elderly people in America today can count less on their grown children for companionship and help than was true in the past. For the most part, their relationships with their offspring are far less satisfactory than many believed possible, even during

middle age, when these relationships may have begun to deteriorate. Figure 14-3 shows the drop in parental satisfaction that occurs during old age; this drop is more pronounced for men than for women.

When parents are willing to shift their attitudes toward their children to suit the children's age and developmental level, the chances are that the parent-child relationship will be a wholesome one as the years go on, and that the elderly person will find much satisfaction in the companionship of sons and daughters. However, parents who have been unwilling over the years to adjust their attitudes to meet the changing needs of growing children are likely to face a lonely old age. The strain in the parent-child relationship which began in adolescence is more likely to grow worse rather than better as time goes on.

For the most part, elderly women are more absorbed in their relationship with

Figure 14-3 Parents' satisfaction with their children at different stages of their married life. (Adapted from W. R. Burr. Satisfaction with various aspects of marriage over the life cycle: A random middle-class sample. *J. Marriage & Family,* 1970, **32,** 29–37. Used by permission.)

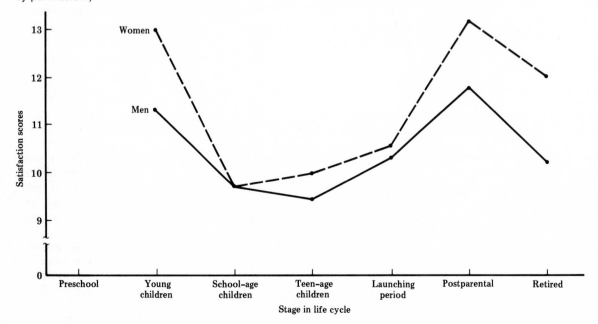

their children than elderly men are. This is a continuation of the parent-child relationship that started at the time of the child's birth. Because women have a closer relationship with their grown children than men have, there is usually more friction between women and their children than between men and their children. If the parent-child relationship has been satisfactory up to the age of fifty or fifty-five, it is unlikely that new alienations will develop after that.

Parental Dependency

Role reversals, as has been stressed before, are very difficult for older people to make successfully. One role reversal that is especially difficult is that of becoming dependent on grown children. Many elderly people, even when they depend on their children for financial support and companionship, are unable or unwilling to relinquish their role of authority over their children and continue to treat them as they did when they were young. Grown children resent this, especially when they are supporting their parents and taking care of their physical and social needs.

Elderly parents who are happily married and have interests of their own are emotionally less dependent on their children than those whose marriages are unhappy or who have failed to develop interests to occupy the time formerly devoted to parental roles. Financial dependency on their children is a bitter pill for most parents to swallow. This is especially true of men, who have played the role of provider for the major part of their lives. Those who accept the role of financial dependency without resistance have usually come from countries where the cultural background differs from that which prevails in America today.

Relationships with Grandchildren

By the time men and women reach old age, their grandchildren may be teen-agers or young adults. In this case, they are no longer called upon to help with their care. How much they see them and the kind of contacts they have with them will depend partly on how close they live to their grandchildren and partly on how well they get along with them when they are together.

If the grandparents live far away from the grandchildren, as is often the case today, they will have only occasional contacts with them, unless the grandparents go to live in the parents' homes. Even then, the grandchildren eventually go away to college or establish homes of their own and thus many have fewer contacts with the grandparents than they did when they were younger.

As a result of rapidly changing values, attitudes, patterns of dress and behavior, and moral standards, grandparents often find that there is a gap between them and their grandchildren that is too great to bridge. They disapprove of their grandchildren, and the grandchildren in turn regard them as old-fashioned.

When grandparents verbalize their disapproval of their grandchildren, a frictional relationship develops not only between them and the grandchildren but also between them and their own children, whom the grandparents may criticize for not having brought the grandchildren up properly. This frictional relationship is much more likely to develop if grandparents live under the same roof with their grandchildren than if their contacts with them are only occasional and brief.

When conflicts do develop between parents and grandparents about the grandchildren's behavior, they more often involve the mother and the grandmother rather than the father and the grandfather. Grandfathers, on the whole, have fewer and more remote contacts with grandchildren than grandmothers do, and they are far less likely to be called on for help in an emergency. As a result, grandmothers generally are more interested and absorbed in the lives of their grandchildren than grandfathers are. While the grandfather may be proud of the achievements of his grandchildren and feel that they reflect favorably on the family, grandmothers' reactions are usually more personal and more emotionally toned.

Assessment of Adjustment to Changes in Family Life

Those adults who feel generally happily married find that their marriages become more satisfying to them as they grow older. With time, mutual interests are developed; the children grow up and leave home, thus drawing the partners closer together; illness or retirement on the part of the husband may make the wife feel useful again, as she did when the children were young; and the death of demanding and dominating parents-in-law may remove a source of friction between husband and wife.

The older person's satisfaction with his marriage is increased if his children are suc-

People who feel their marriage is generally happy find that it becomes more satisfying as they grow older. (Hella Hammid from Rapho Guillumette)

cessful and happily married and if he has a good relationship with his grandchildren, even if his contacts with them are infrequent.

Studies of marital happiness in old age have revealed that most older people feel that their marriages have been very satisfactory, that their lives are calmer now that their parental responsibilities are over, and that they have a new freedom to do as they please. Refer to Figure 10-3, which shows how the curve of satisfaction with the present stage in the family life cycle rises during old age. This is true for husbands as well as wives. As Stinnett et al. have commented, this suggests that "progressive marital disenchantment over the life cycle may be a myth" (107).

ADJUSTMENT TO LOSS OF A SPOUSE

Loss of a spouse in old age may be due to death or divorce, though it is far more likely to be due to the former. Because it is customary for women to marry men their own age or older than they and because men, on the average, die sooner than women, widowhood in old age is far more common than widowerhood.

People in their sixties and seventies do get divorces, but far less frequently than younger people. No matter how unsatisfactory marriage may be to elderly people, most of them do not contemplate ending it in a divorce court. When they do decide to get a divorce in old age, it is generally not a new decision, but rather something they have contemplated since the early days of marriage but have put off for their children's sake or for economic reasons.

It has been estimated that 50 percent of sixty-year-old women are widows, while 85 percent of women age eighty-five are widows. There are no statistics available concerning the number of men of comparable ages who are widowers, but there is reason to believe that because widowers at every age remarry more than widows do, the percentages would be far less. Thus widow-hood is a greater problem than widowerhood during old age.

Adjustment to the death of a spouse or to divorce is difficult for men and women in old age because at this time *all* adjustments are increasingly difficult to make. When a man's wife dies shortly after he retires, this greatly increases his difficulties in adjusting to retirement. Furthermore, because old age is a period during which interests narrow, especially social interests, the elderly person who is left alone cannot compensate for this by developing new interests as readily as he could earlier.

The widow usually has the additional problem of a greatly decreased income, which frequently necessitates giving up interests which she might otherwise have retained and which would provide her with opportunities for social contacts. Decreased income often means moving into new, smaller, and less desirable living quarters; going to live with a married child; or living in an institution, all of which require adjustment and further complicate adjustment to the loneliness which widowhood brings.

For the widower, the economic problem is far less serious than the problem of loneliness. Even though he may not always have been satisfied with his marriage, he still could count on his wife to provide companionship and to take care of his physical needs and manage the home. Furthermore, men are more reluctant than women about becoming dependent on their grown children and living in their homes, unless it is an absolute necessity. They also resist going to homes for the aged, partly because it implies loss of independence and partly because they do not like to be surrounded by people who are a constant reminder of their own advancing age. Therefore, they often solve the loneliness and dependency problems of widowerhood by remarrying.

Elderly people, especially women, often try to solve the problem of loneliness in old age by getting a pet, usually a dog or a cat. While a pet undoubtedly provides some of the companionship the lonely person craves, he should also attempt to establish social contacts, although this becomes more difficult with each passing year (65).

ADJUSTMENT TO REMARRIAGE

One of the ways older people solve the problem of loneliness after the loss of a spouse is by remarrying. However, adjusting to a new spouse, to a new set of relatives, to a new pattern of life, and sometimes to a new community or a new home in the same community is far from easy. And, as is true of younger people's marriage, it is the woman rather than the man who is expected to make most of the adjustments.

The adjustment problem of remarriage is often complicated by age differences, which militate against congeniality of interests and similarity of values at any age. Older men, it has been reported, usually select younger women when they remarry. Up to middle age, women usually marry older men or men of approximately the same age. After that, a reverse trend appears, and the tendency for older women to marry younger men increases with age. Often the man in a second or later marriage is fifteen to twenty years younger than the woman (38, 75). While both men and women in the later years of their lives do marry individuals of approximately their own age, the number of those who marry people younger than they has been reported by Bossard to be "surprisingly large" (10).

While some remarriages in old age do not work out satisfactorily for those involved or for the other members of their families, remarriage late in life is reported to be usually very successful. Certain conditions have been found to contribute to good adjustment to remarriage in old age; the most important of these are given in Box 14-4.

While remarriage is a common solution among elderly people for the problems of loneliness or sexual deprivation, some try to

---

Box 14-4. CONDITIONS CONTRIBUTING TO ADJUSTMENT TO REMARRIAGE IN OLD AGE

A happy first marriage

Knowing what traits and behavior patterns to look for in a potential mate

A desire to marry because of love and a need for companionship, rather than for reasons of convenience or financial support

An interest in continuing sexual behavior

A similarity of educational and social backgrounds

Adequate income

Approval of the marriage by offspring and friends

Reasonably good health and a lack of disabling physical condition on the part of both spouses

---

solve these problems by living together without marrying. Unlike young people, who usually live together to determine whether they are compatible before actually marrying, older people are more often motivated by practical financial considerations.

For example, if a woman's inheritance from her dead spouse is in the form of a trust fund that will end if she remarries or if her social security or other sources of income will cease with her remarriage, it might be impossible for her to marry a retired man and live on his social security and pension benefits. However, if the couple's combined incomes would make a comfortable life-style possible, they may accept living together without marriage as a solution to their problems.

Older couples who live together face the possibility of the strong disapproval of grown children, relatives, friends, and neighbors. Some cope with this problem by moving to another community, where new friends and neighbors will not know of their marital status, while others remain in their home community, ignoring the attitudes of others and maintaining that the enjoyment and satisfaction they derive from their chosen life-style more than compensates for its disadvantages.

ADJUSTMENT TO BEING SINGLE IN OLD AGE

The popular belief that an old person who has never married will face an unhappy, lonely old age is not borne out by real experiences. The single man has learned over the years to develop interests and become involved in activities to compensate for the lack of companionship of a family of his own. As a result, he is less likely to face a lonely old age than the man who married, whose interests centered around his home and family, and who now, in old age, may find himself without his wife and children.

The modern single woman builds up a life of her own, just as a man does. As a result, she has much to keep her happy and occupied in old age. Even though she is retired, she usually has the benefit of a pension or social security, in addition to what she has saved, to enable her to live and do much as she pleases. And because she never had to devote her leisure time to a family, she has had an opportunity to establish many interests which will keep her from being lonely when she reaches retirement age.

LIVING ARRANGEMENTS FOR THE ELDERLY

Patterns of living vary much more in old age than in middle age, when the pattern is well standardized. Five patterns are common among the elderly today: a married couple living alone; a person living alone in his own home; two or more members of the same generation living together in a nonmarital relationship, such as brothers and sisters or friends; a widow or widower living with a married child and perhaps grandchildren; and an elderly person living in a home for the aged or in a club or hotel. Which pattern of living the elderly individual selects will depend upon a number of conditions; the most important of these are given in Box 14-5.

Box 14-5. CONDITIONS INFLUENCING CHOICE OF LIVING ARRANGEMENTS IN OLD AGE

Economic Status

If they are financially able to do so, most elderly people continue to live in their homes or move to smaller, more convenient homes of their own in a comparable neighborhood. If his economic status deteriorates, the elderly person is forced to move into less desirable living quarters or into the home of a married child.

Marital Status

When both spouses are living, their living arrangements are usually determined by their economic status and their health. Single men and women, as a rule, live with family members or friends, in clubs, or in institutions for the aged.

Health

When the elderly person's health makes it impossible for him to maintain his home, he must live with a relative or friend or in an institution.

Sex

Widows generally live in their own homes or with a married child, while widowers are more likely to live in a club, a hotel, or an institution for the elderly.

Children

If they have children, elderly people live either near one of them in a home of their own or with a married child. Those who are childless usually live in institutions if they have lost a spouse or are unable to maintain their own homes.

Desire for Companionship

The elderly person whose health is good, and who wants companionship may move either to a home of his own near a married child or relative or to a retirement community, where he can count on social contacts with contemporaries. If his health is poor, he may prefer living in a home for the aged, where he can have contacts with his contemporaries, rather than living with a married child, which limits his opportunities for such contacts.

The needs and wants of elderly people vary greatly, and thus not all of them will find the same living arrangements suitable. However, almost all elderly people have certain physical and psychological needs that must be met by their living arrangements if these arrangements are to promote health and happiness. These are given in Box 14-6.

When health, economic status, or other conditions make it impossible for an elderly person to live in his own home and when there is no member of the family who can or will offer him a place to live, he must take up residence in an institution for the aged—either a retirement home where living quarters are similar to those of a club or hotel, or a nursing home, where his physical needs can be taken care of by trained personnel and where he can be hospitalized if he should require this.

How well elderly people adjust to institutional living depends upon three conditions. First, if the person enters an institution voluntarily instead of being forced to by circumstances, he will be happier and have a stronger motivation to adjust to the radical changes that institutional living brings. Second, the more accustomed the individual is to being with other people and to taking part in community activities, the more he will enjoy the social contacts and recreational opportunities provided by such institutions.

Third, and perhaps most important, the elderly person will adjust better to living in an institution if it is close enough to where he lived before so that family members and friends can keep up their former contacts with him. Moving to an institution that is far away from the elderly person's former

The elderly person is more likely to make a good adjustment to life in a retirement home or nursing home if he enters the institution by choice. (Hella Hammid from Rapho Guillumette)

home is usually a traumatic experience and militates against good adjustment to institutional living and to happiness in old age.

Regardless of where elderly people live, it is important that they feel they are still a part of the family and not cut off from contacts with their children and relatives. As his friends die or become unable to provide him with companionship, the elderly person depends increasingly on his family. As Brody and Spark have emphasized, "The importance of 'family' to the child has been universally accepted. The need of the aged person for 'family' is no less vital. . . . The lack of family, for the infant and aged alike, can be a major deprivation" (12). They further point out that if the individual is deprived of contacts with his family in old age, when he is subjected to the "insults of aging," such as death of a spouse, retire-

ment, and decreasing physical and mental capacities, he will be less able to cope with this deprivation successfully than he was earlier. For that reason, they claim, "as his dependence increases, those on whom he is dependent hopefully should be able to accept the additional demands" (12).

GEOGRAPHIC MOBILITY IN OLD AGE

Because the individual must often move from the home where he has lived for the major part of his adult life in order to find suitable living quarters for his old age, there is much mobility among the elderly. An elderly person may move from place to place for ten or fifteen years until he finally finds living quarters that meet his needs, whether it is in the home of a grown child, in an

Box 14-6. PHYSICAL AND PSYCHOLOGICAL NEEDS IN LIVING ARRANGEMENTS

Physical Needs

The house temperature should be comparatively even from floor to ceiling because poor circulation makes the elderly person especially sensitive to chilling.

The elderly person needs large windows to ensure plenty of light because of the gradual impairment of his vision.

Provisions should be made for the safety of the elderly person. He should have to climb few steps, and floors should be unwaxed.

There should be adequate space for indoor and outdoor recreation, a condition best met in multiple housing developments or homes for the aged.

Noise should be controlled, especially during the night. This can be done by locating the elderly person's sleeping quarters in a quiet part of the house.

The elderly person should have laborsaving devices, especially for cooking and cleaning.

The living quarters should be on one floor to avoid possible falls on steps.

Psychological Needs

The elderly person should have at least one small room of his own so that he can have an opportunity for privacy. The living arrangements should include space for sedentary recreations, such as reading and television watching.

There should be provision for storage of cherished possessions.

The elderly person should live close to stores and community organizations so that he can be independent in his activities, and he should also be near relatives and friends so that frequent contacts are possible.

institution, or in a retirement community.

There are many reasons for mobility in old age. Among the most important are changes in economic conditions following retirement, failing health, loneliness, a desire to be close to members of the family, and changes in marital status. Widows and widowers, for example, are more likely to move and move more often than those whose spouses are still alive.

In recent years, there has been a migration of elderly people to more favorable climates, especially to Florida, Arizona, and California. As a result, these states have had a proportionally greater increase in the number of older residents than other areas of the country. While this migration is not as great as is popularly believed, it is a trend. As Havighurst and Albrecht have pointed out, "The trickle of people from thousands of towns and cities becomes a fairly large stream when seen at the receiving end of the migration in Florida, Arizona, or California" (46).

There are many reasons for this new trend toward migration to "paradises for the aged." The most important of these reasons are a warmer climate, which is favorable for those in poor health and which eliminates the possibility of being cut off from social contacts during the winter months; the breakdown of three-generation family units; improved transportation; inflationary pressures, which make lower living costs necessary; and opportunities for contact with those of the same age group and with similar interests.

In addition to migrating to warmer areas, many first-generation Americans return to their former homelands when they retire, and others who have enjoyed travel abroad during their adult years decide to retire to a foreign country, where until recently they could live better on their retirement pensions and social security than they could here. With rampant inflation in most foreign countries and with the devaluation of the dollar, however, this trend has been reversed, and many elderly people are finding that they cannot live as well abroad as they can in their own country. Thus they are gradually returning.

VOCATIONAL AND FAMILY-LIFE HAZARDS OF OLD AGE

Because of the importance of work and family to the older person, anything that prevents good adjustments in these areas is a potential hazard. Vocational and family-life hazards increase as his social horizons narrow and as his interests become concentrated on his work and his family.

While hazards are associated with every age, as has been pointed out repeatedly, the difference between the hazards of old age and those of the younger ages is that the elderly individual has little or no control over the conditions that are primarily responsible for these hazards. The younger person, for example, who feels that marriage is not complete without children in the home can control the situation by having children of his own or by adopting them. The elderly person, by contrast, cannot control what his children do, where they will live, or how they will treat him. Nor are social pressures or feelings of filial obligation always strong enough to make a grown child offer the elderly person a place in his home, should poor health or economic necessity make it impossible for him to continue to live in his own home.

Because the conditions that give rise to the vocational and family-life hazards of old age are usually beyond the individual's control and because adjustments in these areas are even more important to satisfaction and happiness in old age than personal and so-

cial adjustments, they may be regarded as the major hazards of this period.

Vocational Hazards

How important a role vocational hazards will play in the older person's adjustments is greatly influenced by his attitude toward work. As was pointed out earlier, the majority of old people in America today grew up during a time when work was more highly valued as a source of personal satisfaction and social esteem than it is now, and therefore many old people today place an extremely high value on work. Thus anything that prevents an older person who *wants to work* from doing so may be regarded as hazardous to his self-esteem and may even lead to feelings of uselessness and martyrdom.

There are three reasons why older people may be prevented from working. First, there is a lack of vocational opportunities for the older worker. Few industrial and business organizations will employ older workers, and even when they are hired, they are most likely to be laid off when business conditions are poor and are least likely to be called back when conditions improve. This is especially true of women and blacks.

Second, unemployment becomes more serious as the individual grows older. Not only is it harder for the older worker to get another job than it is for a younger one, but the effects on his personality are far more serious and far-reaching. The younger worker knows that his chances of obtaining future employment are good, even if he must take a temporary setback in wages. The older worker, however, has a far less hopeful outlook. He knows that most business and industrial organizations have a strict policy against hiring older workers and that if he is lucky enough to get a job, it is likely to be far below his capacities, the pay will be much less than he formerly received, and the job may be only temporary or on a part-time basis. Box 14-7 shows the most common con-

<table>
<tr><td>

Box 14-7. CONDITIONS CONTRIBUTING TO THE SERIOUSNESS OF UNEMPLOYMENT IN OLD AGE

Kind of Work
As a general rule, workers who are at either the top or the bottom of the business or industrial ladder are in the least favorable position when it comes to getting a new job.

A New Job
It is more difficult for a worker who has left his job or has been released from it to find a new job with a different organization than for one who merely wants to shift to another job in the same organization because he finds his work too taxing.

Necessity for Retraining
When getting a new job requires retraining, older workers are at a distinct disadvantage, not only because they are believed to be too old to learn, but also because employers feel that they will not be useful to the organization long enough to justify the time and expense involved in retraining.

Minority-Group Status
Fewer job opportunities are open to members of minority groups, and thus unemployment lasts longer for them.

</td></tr>
</table>

feeling of uselessness. Should he get work, it is likely to be on a lower grade than the work he previously did, and this is humiliating to him (58, 92).

The third condition creating difficulties for the older person who wants to work is the necessity of retiring at a certain age. The individual who resists retirement and who thus refuses to prepare himself psychologically for it by becoming involved in new interests and activities to replace those related to work will make poorer adjustments than one who is better prepared for the changes that retirement brings. Even worse, an older person who believes that the organization cannot get along without him and will eventually call him back into service will have little motivation to try to adjust to retirement. See Figure 14-4. This unfavor-

Figure 14-4 The person who believes that his work group cannot get along without him makes poor adjustments to retirement. (Dale McFeatters, "Strictly Business," Publishers-Hall Syndicate, Feb. 22, 1973. Used by permission.)

"Ever since he retired he's been waiting for the company to call him back to straighten it out."

ditions contributing to the seriousness of unemployment in old age.

Because unemployment lasts longer for older workers than for younger workers (see Figure 12-4), it causes them more psychological damage. Studies of the mental effects of unemployment on older workers have revealed how serious they are. Measures of the mental efficiency and attitudes of employed and unemployed older people have shown that those who engage in regular, gainful occupation are, on the whole, mentally superior to those who are unemployed. Lack of practice, lack of motivation, and unfavorable attitudes are important contributing factors to the deterioration that comes with unemployment. Being unable to get work contributes to the older person's

able attitude prolongs the adjustment period and, in some cases, causes the individual to be less well adjusted a year or more after he retires than he was at the time of his retirement.

Even when he is prepared for retirement, the older person faces an "identity crisis" not unlike the one he faced in adolescence, when he was treated sometimes as a child and other times as an adult (32). The identity crisis that comes with retirement results from the necessity of making radical role changes—from that of a worker to that of a person of leisure. Furthermore, suddenly changing the habits and patterns established over a lifetime is often very traumatic for the elderly person. Monk has explained why this is so (77):

Retirement entails a loss of status and prestige, a "roleless" situation where appropriate, or at least clearly defined, social positions and role expectations are notoriously absent. . . . Once a person is unable to perform his occupational roles, his former claims to prestige, competence, and social position are no longer valid, thus precipitating the likelihood of an identity breakdown.

An unfavorable attitude toward retirement affects the individual's health, often causing physical decline and premature death. As Horwitz has pointed out, "'Retirement shock' is the new sickness of the aged" (51). The effects of retirement shock are most serious immediately after retirement, when the individual must adjust to changes in routine and to the breaking off of social relationships. It is especially serious for men who lose their wives at this time.

Family-Life Hazards

When the elderly person's work life comes to an end, he focuses his interests and attention on his home and family life. This is true not only of retired men but also of women who went to work after their children were grown. Because of this concen-

tration of interest and attention, conditions which were previously only minor hazards become major hazards, threatening the individual's physical as well as his psychological well-being.

Because the pattern of family life differs greatly for different people throughout the life span, the changes in this pattern that old age brings will also differ greatly. However, four family-life hazards are especially common in old age.

First, the change in the pattern of family life in old age may result in sexual deprivation at a time when the sex drive is far from dormant. Elderly people who are sexually deprived may engage in substitute forms of sexual expression, some of which met their needs earlier. Most of these are frowned on by others and may lead to unfavorable social and self-judgments. The most common substitute sources of sexual satisfaction during old age are given in Box 14-8.

Box 14-8. SUBSTITUTE SOURCES OF SEXUAL SATISFACTION IN OLD AGE

Masturbation
There is evidence that masturbation is widely practiced by elderly men and women who have few if any other sexual outlets, particularly those who are becoming senile.

Erotic Dreams and Daydreams
Erotic dreams and daydreams are a common substitute source of sexual satisfaction among elderly women who are widowed or divorced and also among those who are married but whose husbands are unable, because of failing health or impotence, to engage in sexual activities.

Sexual Recrudescence
Elderly men may be sexually attracted to young girls or women, and some want to marry girls young enough to be their granddaughters. Occasionally they may rape children or adults. Older women may play with dolls, assume a mothering role with someone else's child, or become infatuated with a man young enough to be their grandson.

"Then how come I never see anybody?"

Figure 14-5 Few escape loneliness in old age. (Lou Erickson. *The Atlanta Journal,* Sept. 11, 1973. Used by permission.)

The second almost universal family-life hazard to good adjustment in old age is loneliness. See Figure 14-5. Even when grown children live nearby, the elderly person's contacts with them may be only occasional, and he can count on their companionship far less than was the case when the three-generation household was more common.

One of the most common causes of loneliness in old age is loss of a spouse. While many elderly people acknowledge the possibility of the death of a spouse and make plans for it, relatively few realize the problems involved and are prepared to meet them or to adjust to the loneliness that it brings. Women, as a group, are generally better prepared psychologically for the death of a spouse than men. Heyman and Gianturco have explained the reason for this (50):

The elderly widow seems psychologically prepared to accept the death of the spouse through death rehearsal and lessening of social pressures, and she adjusts by maintaining a high rate of social activities. Religious convictions appear to be particularly important sources of strength.

The third major family-life hazard in old age involves the living arrangements of the elderly person, which may be physically or psychologically hazardous or both. Physically, it may be hazardous for the older person to remain in the home he has occupied since the early years of marriage because it is likely to be too large for him to take care of without overtaxing his strength. It may also be psychologically hazardous to good adjustment by being a constant reminder of happier times or by requiring such a large portion of the elderly person's income to maintain that he must cut down in other areas, such as clothes or participation in community activities.

If the elderly person moves to a place

Loss of a spouse is one of the most common causes of loneliness in old age. (Inger Abrahamsen McCabe from Rapho Guillumette)

that is better suited to his needs, the physical hazards may be reduced, but the psychological hazards may increase. If his health or his financial situation forces him to live with a married child or in an institution, he may resist the change and thus make a poor adjustment to his new environment. Moving to an area where climatic conditions are more favorable may likewise reduce the physical hazards but increase the psychological hazards if the elderly person feels lonely without his family and friends.

Another common psychological hazard that results when the elderly person moves, even if he stays in the same community, is not being able to keep all his cherished possessions with him. If he goes to live in a smaller home of his own, in the home of a married child or a relative, or in an institution, he may have to give up the furniture, pictures, china, and other material posses-

sions which served as status symbols for many years. He may also have to give up hobbies, such as gardening, if his new home does not provide the opportunity for such pursuits. This may leave him with a feeling of uselessness and will complicate the adjustments he must make to his new living arrangements.

The fourth major family-life hazard in old age, and unquestionably one of the most serious, is the necessity for making role changes. As has been stressed repeatedly, role changes are always difficult and emotion-provoking, and they become increasingly more difficult with each passing year. The more radical the change and the less prestige there is associated with the new role, the more the individual will resist making the change and the more disturbed he will be if circumstances force him to make it.

The man or woman who has been accustomed to playing the role of head of the household or of family breadwinner will find it difficult to live as a dependent in the home of a grown child. Similarly, the man who has achieved a position of prestige and responsibility in the vocational world will find it very difficult to become his wife's "helper" when he retires, a role which implies lack of authority and masculinity. See Figure 14-6. This militates against good adjustment not only to retirement but also to family life. In time it may have a profoundly unfavorable effect on his self-concept, thus leading to poor personal and social adjustments.

ASSESSMENT OF ADJUSTMENTS TO OLD AGE

How successfully or unsuccessfully the individual will adjust to the problems arising from the physical and mental changes that accompany old age and from the changes in status that occur at this time will be influenced by many factors, some of which are beyond his control. The most important of these are given in Box 14-9.

The kind of adjustment the elderly person makes can be assessed on the basis of his behavior patterns, his emotional states, his personality, and the degree to which he is happy or unhappy. These are discussed below.

Quality of Behavior Patterns

As was pointed out earlier, there are two different and contrasting theories of successful aging: the activity theory and the disengagement theory. According to the *activity theory*, the individual should maintain the attitudes and activities of middle age as long as possible and then find substitutes for the activities he must give up—substitutes for work when he is forced to retire, substitutes for the clubs and associations he must give up, and substitutes for friends and relatives he loses through death.

"It's so nice now that Henry's retired. We're doing together all the things I'd planned."

Figure 14-6 With retirement, many men find themselves drawn into the role of their wives' helpers. (George Clark. "The Neighbors." Chicago Tribune–New York News Syndicate, Nov. 14, 1966. Used by permission.)

According to the *disengagement theory*, the individual curtails, either voluntarily or involuntarily, his involvement in the activities of middle age. He cuts down his direct contacts with people, he feels carefree, he is less influenced by the opinions of others, and he does the things that are important to him. As Henry and Cumming have pointed out, "He displays behavior characteristic of one who has withdrawn his investment from the world around him and reinvested it in himself" (49). However, it is important to note that disengagement does not come all at one time. Instead, it is a gradual process.

Studies of well-adjusted and poorly adjusted old people have shown that those whom others consider well-adjusted have traits one would expect in a person who has followed the activity theory, while those who seem poorly adjusted have characteristics associated with the disengagement theory.

Box 14-9. FACTORS INFLUENCING ADJUSTMENT TO OLD AGE

Preparation for Old Age
Those who have not prepared themselves psychologically or economically for the changes that old age inevitably brings often find adjusting to these changes a traumatic experience.

Earlier Experiences
The difficulties experienced in adjusting to old age are often the result of earlier learning of certain forms of adjustment that are not appropriate to this period of the life span.

Satisfaction of Needs
To be well adjusted in old age, the individual must be able to satisfy his personal needs and live up to the expectations of others within the framework of life provided for him.

Social Attitudes
One of the greatest handicaps to good adjustment in old age is society's unfavorable attitude toward the elderly.

Personal Attitudes
A resistant attitude is a serious obstacle to successful adjustment in old age.

Method of Adjustment
Rational methods include accepting the limitations of age, developing new interests, learning to give up one's children, and not dwelling on the past; *irrational* methods include denying the changes that come with age and trying to continue as before, becoming preoccupied with the pleasures and triumphs of bygone days, and wanting to be dependent on others for bodily care.

Health Conditions
Chronic illness is a greater handicap to adjustment than temporary illnesses, even though the latter may be more severe while they last than the former.

Living Conditions
When an elderly person is forced to live in a place that makes him feel inferior, inadequate, and resentful, this has an unfavorable effect on the kind of adjustment he makes to old age.

Economic Conditions
It is especially difficult for the elderly person to adjust to financial problems because he knows that he will have no opportunity to solve them, as he could when he was younger.

The characteristics of well-adjusted and poorly adjusted elderly people are summarized in Box 14-10.

In general, there is evidence that those who made good adjustments when they were younger will make good adjustments when they are old. As Cicero pointed out in his *De Senectute,* "Those with simple desires and good dispositions find old age easy to take. Those who do not show wisdom and virtue in their youth are prone to attribute to old age those infirmities which are actually produced by former irregularities." How the individual meets the stresses of adolescence and adjusts to them will influence his adjustment to old age because patterns of adult attitudes and behavior are set then.

The cultural milieu in which the individual lived during the formative years of his life will also affect the kind of adjust-

ment he makes to old age. Because this is a youth-conscious country in which social attitudes toward old age are often negative and unfavorable, it is difficult for an individual who has grown up here to accept old age gracefully. Although the old person is a "senior citizen," he has none of the prestige associated with this status that elderly people have in countries where they are respected because of their wisdom and experience.

Changes in Emotional Behavior

Studies of elderly people have shown that they tend to be apathetic in their affective life. They are less responsive than they were when they were younger and show less enthusiasm. Typically, their emotional responses are more specific, less varied, and

---

Box 14-10. CHARACTERISTICS OF GOOD AND POOR ADJUSTMENT IN OLD AGE

Good Adjustment

Strong and varied interests

Economic independence, which makes independence in living possible

Many social contacts with people of all ages, not just the elderly

The enjoyment of work which is pleasant and useful but not overtaxing

Participation in community organizations

The ability to maintain a comfortable home without exerting too much physical effort

The ability to enjoy present activities without regretting the past

A minimum of worry about self or others

Poor Adjustment

Little interest in the world of today or the individual's role in it

Withdrawal into the world of fantasy

Constant reminiscing

Constant worry, encouraged by idleness

A lack of drive, leading to low productivity in all areas

The attitude that the only activities available are "make-work" activities

Loneliness due to poor family relationships and lack of interest in contemporaries

Involuntary geographic isolation

Involuntary residence in an institution or with a grown child

---

less appropriate to the occasion than those of younger people. It is not unusual for the elderly person to show signs of regression in his emotional behavior, such as negativism, temper tantrums, and excitability characteristic of a child (26, 62).

Many elderly people have little capacity to express warm and spontaneous feelings toward others. They become "miserly" with their affections in that they are afraid to express positive feelings toward others because they have discovered, from past experience, that it is unlikely that such feelings will be returned and their efforts will then have been fruitless. The more self-bound the individual becomes, the more passive he is emotionally.

While the old person's affective emotions are, on the whole, less intense than they were earlier, his resistant emotions may become very strong. The old person is likely to be irritable, quarrelsome, crotchety, and contrary. Fears and worries, disappointments and disillusions, and feelings of persecution are far more common than the pleasanter emotional states.

Recovery from emotional experiences also takes longer as the individual grows older. While the child or adult may find a release for his emotional energy in play or

Involuntary institutionalization—being made to live in a nursing home, for example—can have a devastating effect on an elderly person's physical and psychological health. (Mottke Weissman)

work, the elderly person usually has no such outlet and may remain anxious and depressed for a long time.

Personality Changes

It is popularly believed that *all* old people, regardless of the personality patterns they had when they were younger, develop into ogrelike creatures who are mean, stingy, quarrelsome, demanding, selfish, self-centered, egotistical, and generally impossible to live with. Furthermore, it is popularly believed that if old people live long enough, their personalities will become childish in the closing years of life, requiring them to be treated like children.

As long ago as Plato's time, it was recognized that the individual's personality prior to old age influences his reactions to old age, which in turn determine how much change will take place in his personality when he becomes old. This point of view has been substantiated by modern studies of personality, which emphasize that although changes in personality do occur, they are *quantitative* rather than qualitative: the fundamental pattern of personality, set earlier in life, becomes more set with advancing years (3, 106).

Although the individual may, for example, become more rigid in his thinking, more conservative in his actions, more prejudiced in his attitudes toward others, more opinionated, and more self-centered with age, these are not new personality traits that developed as he became elderly; they are exaggerations of lifelong traits that have become more pronounced with the pressures of old age. When pressures are too severe for the individual to adjust to and personality breakdown occurs, there is still evidence that the predominant traits developed earlier will be dominant in the pattern the breakdown takes.

Changes in personality during old age come from changes in the core of the personality pattern, the individual's *concept of self*. How much this self-concept changes and in what direction the change occurs will determine the quality and quantity of change in the personality pattern.

Changes in the self-concept in old age are due to the individual's subjective awareness of aging, which is often accentuated by his acceptance of the cultural stereotypes concerning old age, and also to his recognition of others' attitudes toward him and of the treatment he receives from them because of his age.

When the individual becomes aware of the physical and psychological changes that are taking place in him, he thinks of himself as "old." As a result he is likely to think and behave as an old person is supposed to and thus develop a personality pattern that conforms to social expectations.

The treatment that the elderly person receives from members of the social group because of his age also contributes to changes in his self-concept. In spite of the fact that the number of old people is increasing rapidly, they still constitute a "minority group" in our culture. They suffer from subordination to the younger members of society, and they are discriminated against and made to feel unwanted, as all minority-group members are. Because of their minority-group status, many old people develop personality traits that are typical of members of minority groups, such as hypersensitivity, self-hatred, feelings of insecurity and uncertainty, quarrelsomeness, apathy, regression, introversion, anxiety, overdependency, and defensiveness (80).

It is important to recognize that *not all* older people develop "minority-group" personality patterns. Even those who do develop such patterns do not develop all the traits characteristic of such patterns or in equal strength. Personality differences occur in old age as in every other period of life. However, those who are institutionalized, especially when against their wishes, have poorer attitudes toward themselves and more marked characteristics of the minority-group personality than those who live outside institutions.

A radical change in the self-concept at any age and for any reason is likely to lead to a breakdown in the personality structure of minor or major severity. Advancing age and its pressures bring an increase in personality breakdowns and in the number of individuals committed to mental institutions (2).

In the milder forms, these breakdowns consist of such disorders as disturbances of memory; falsifications of memory; faulty attention; disturbances of orientation concerning time, place, and person; suspiciousness; disturbances in the ethical domain; hallucinations and delusions—especially of persecution—and such common neuroses as anxiety, preoccupation with bodily functions, chronic fatigue, compulsion and hysterical disorders, neurotic depressions, and sex deviations (11, 16).

Personality breakdown of a more serious kind, as in mental disease, increases greatly with advancing age. After sixty-five, for example, there is a marked upward trend in serious emotional disorders. In the sixties, psychoses with cerebral arteriosclerosis and senile dementia predominate, and these increase steadily to the end of life. After seventy, senile psychoses are most prevalent (28).

There is evidence that most personality breakdowns in old age are not the result of brain damage but rather of social conditions which give rise to feelings of insecurity. These are especially serious when there is a history of poor adjustment. Many old people have shown similar maladaptive behavior under stress when they were younger. Then, under the pressure of problems relating to the death of a spouse or to retirement, for example, they experience a breakdown in the personallty pattern, which is already weakened by past experiences (11).

Happiness

According to Erikson, old age is characterized by either ego-integrity or despair (32). When the individual's achievements have come up to the standards he set for himself earlier, so that the gap between his real self and his ideal self is small, he experiences ego-integrity and is reasonably happy and satisfied with himself and his achievements.

On the other hand, the elderly person who feels that he has fallen far short of his earlier expectations experiences despair because he realizes that with each passing day his chances for attaining his goals grow slimmer and slimmer. This is one cause of suicide among men in old age. Refer to Figure 12-5, which shows suicide rates at different ages.

Even those who have been successful or reasonably successful may become dissatisfied in old age. As the sands of time run out, they too experience despair, though not to the same extent as those who believe themselves to be failures or near-failures. As Erikson has commented, "Despair is there for everyone, no matter how much he has accomplished" (32).

Happiness or unhappiness in old age is usually a carry-over of attitudes formed earlier as a result of the success or failure of past adjustments. At no other time in life do unsuccessful past adjustments make present adjustment as difficult as in old age, and the adjustments that must be made at this time are more than any the individual faced earlier. Thus unless the elderly person has made reasonably good adjustments in the past and has been able to maintain a high degree of ego-integrity, he has far less chance for happiness than he did earlier. Refer to Figure 1-5, which shows that, with the exception of early middle age, ratings for pleasant memories are lower in old age than at other periods in life.

However, it is important to recognize that people derive happiness from different things as they grow older. To the adolescent, for example, happiness means freedom from care and responsibility, popularity with members of both sexes, and engaging in enjoyable activities. Barrett has described what makes an elderly person happy (7):

The older person who is financially secure, able to utilize his free time constructively, happy in his social contacts and able to contribute services to others will find the later longevous period of life truly rewarding. He will retain a superior self-concept, remain highly motivated, rarely become neurotic or psychotic and live out his life happily. He will not suffer from psychosocial deprivation, nor will he become senescent. When one is adequately prepared for retirement, these may truly be the "golden years."

Because happiness does not have the same meaning for the elderly person that it did when he was younger, he cannot expect to experience the same kind or degree of happiness that he did earlier. However, what a person does is more important to his happiness in old age than what he is. In general, happy old people are more alert and ready to engage in new activities than unhappy old people. Because middle- and upper-class people tend, on the whole, to be more active in the life of their communities than those of the lower classes, middle-class people tend to be happier in old age than lower-class people. Regardless of social class, sex, or any other variable, however, certain conditions can be counted on to contribute to happiness in old age. These are given in Box 14-11.

Even though all these conditions contribute to happiness in old age, it is not essential that they all be present in order for the elderly person to be happy. Furthermore, because people have different needs, what brings happiness to one in old age may not bring happiness to another. On the other hand, because the pattern of life that brings happiness in old age is usually similar to the pattern that brought happiness earlier, an essential to happiness in the closing years of life is the opportunity to continue the life-style that previously led to happiness. Havighurst has stressed this point (44).

Persons with an active, achieving, and outward-directed life style will be best sat-

---

Box 14-11. CONDITIONS CONTRIBUTING TO HAPPINESS IN OLD AGE

A favorable attitude toward old age developed as a result of earlier pleasurable contacts with elderly people

Happy memories of childhood and adulthood

Freedom to pursue a desired life-style without outside interference

A realistic attitude toward, and acceptance of, the physical and psychological changes that aging inevitably brings

Acceptance of self and present living conditions even if these fall below expectations

An opportunity to establish a satisfying, socially acceptable pattern of life

Continued participation in interesting and meaningful activities

Acceptance by, and respect from, the social group

A feeling of satisfaction with present status and past achievements

---

isfied with a continuation of this style into old age with only slight diminution. Other persons with a passive, dependent, home-centered life style will be best satisfied with disengagement. . . . Undoubtedly there is a disengaging force operating on and within

(Mottke Weissman)

people as they pass 70 and 80. But they will still retain the personality-life style characteristics of their middle years.

Chapter Highlights

1 Vocational and family adjustments — the most difficult adjustments in old age — are complicated by economic factors.

2 Even though most older people, unless their health is poor, want to continue to work, few jobs are open to them, and the ones that are available are usually uninteresting or below the elderly person's level of ability and training.

3 Older workers can generally be said to have either society-maintaining attitudes toward their work (the worker's main interest is in his paycheck) or ego-involving attitudes (the worker derives great personal satisfaction from his work).

4 The quality of the older person's work and his attitudes toward work are better than is generally believed.

5 The most important conditions facilitating adjustment to retirement are wanting to retire rather than being forced to; poor health at the time of retirement; a tapering off of work rather than an abrupt ending; preretirement training; opportunities for social contacts after retirement; and a minimum amount of change in the individual's accustomed pattern of living.

6 The major family-life adjustments of old age are in the areas of changes in relationships with a spouse and with grown children; changes in sexual behavior; and dependency on grown children or other relatives.

7 The older person's adjustments to changes in family life can be assessed on the basis of the degree of satisfaction of all family members, the success of the children, and the amount of friction that exists between family members.

8 Adjustment to loss of a spouse, which is a far more common problem for women than for men in old age, depends greatly on the individual's economic status. Elderly people often solve the problems of this adjustment by remarrying.

9 The elderly person's living arrangements are influenced by his economic and marital status, his health, his sex, pressures from grown children, and his desire for companionship. Sometimes the elderly person must move to a different community or another part of the country in order to establish satisfactory living conditions.

10 The major vocational hazards in old age center around lack of vocational opportunities for those who want to work, unemployment, and compulsory retirement regardless of the individual's desire or ability to work.

11 Four common family-life hazards in old age that militate against good personal and social adjustments are the effect of physical and psychological changes on the individual's sexual adjustments; loneliness, especially among those who have lost a spouse; unsatisfactory living conditions; and the necessity to make role changes.

12 The individual's adjustment to old age can be assessed on the basis of the quality of his behavior patterns, changes in his emotional behavior, changes in his personality, and the degree of satisfaction or happiness he experiences.

Bibliography

1 Adams, D. L. Correlates of satisfaction among the elderly. *Gerontologist,* 1971, **11,** 64–68.

2 Allison, R. S. The varieties of brain syndrome in the aged. in M. P. Lawton & F. G. Lawton (Eds.), *Mental impairment in the aged.* Philadelphia: Philadelphia Geriatric Center, 1965. Pp. 1–66.

3 Allport, G. W. *Pattern and growth in personality.* New York: Holt, 1961.

4 Alston, J. P., & Dudley, C. J. Age, occupation and life satisfaction. *Gerontologist,* 1973, **13,** 58–61.

5 Alvarez, W. C. Retirement provides opportunity for new life style. *Geriatrics,* 1973, **28**(4), 70.

6 Back, K. W. The ambiguity of retirement. In E. W. Busse & E. Pfeiffer (Eds.), *Behavior and adaptation in late life.* Boston: Little, Brown, 1969. Pp. 93–114.

7 Barrett, J. H. *Gerontological psychology.* Springfield, Ill.: Charles C Thomas, 1972.

8 Birren, J. E. *The psychology of aging.* Englewood Cliffs, N.J.: Prentice-Hall, 1964.

9 Bock, E. W., & Webber, I. L. Suicide among the elderly: Isolating widowhood and mitigating alternatives. *J. Marriage & Family,* 1972, **34,** 24–31.

10 Bossard, J. H. S. Marrying late in life. *Soc. Forces,* 1951, **29,** 405–408.

11 Britton, J. H., & Britton, J. O. *Personality changes in aging.* New York: Springer, 1972.

12 Brody, E. M., & Spark, G. M. Institutionalization of the aged: A family crisis. *Family Process,* 1966, **5,** 76–90.

13 Brown, R. G. Family structure and social isolation of older persons. In E. B. Palmore (Ed.), *Normal aging.* Durham, N.C.: Duke University Press, 1970. Pp. 270–277.

14 Burck, G. That ever expanding pension balloon. *Fortune,* October 1971, 100–103, 130–134.

15 Burr, W. R. Satisfaction with various aspects of marriage over the life cycle: A random middle-class sample. *J. Marriage & Family,* 1970, **32,** 29–37.

16 Busse, E. W., Dovenmuehle, R. H., & Brown, R. G. Psychoneurotic reactions of the aged. In E. B. Palmore (Ed.), *Normal aging.* Durham, N. C.: Duke University Press, 1970. Pp. 75–83.

17 Busse, E. W., & Eisdorfer, C. Two thousand years of married life. In E. B. Palmore (Ed.), *Normal aging.* Durham, N.C.: Duke University Press, 1970. Pp. 266–269.

18 Busse, E. W., & Pfeiffer, E. (Eds.) *Behavior and adaptation in late life.* Boston: Little, Brown, 1969.

19 Cameron, P. Stereotypes about generational fun and happiness vs. self-appraised fun and happiness. *Gerontologist,* 1972, **12,** 120–123, 190.

20 Carp, F. M. Effects of improved housing on the lives of older people. In B. L. Neugarten (Ed.); *Middle age and aging: A reader in social psychology.* Chicago: University of Chicago Press, 1968. Pp. 409–416.

21 Chown, S. M., & Heron, A. Psychological aspects of ageing in man. *Annu. Rev. Psychol.,* 1965, **16,** 417–450.

22 Clayton, P. J., Halikas, J. A., & Maurice, W. L. The depression of widowhood. *Brit. J. Psychiat.,* 1972, **120,** 71–77.

23 Clemente, F., & Hendricks, J. A further look at the relationship between age and productivity. *Gerontologist,* 1973, **13,** 106–110.

24 Crumbaugh, J. C. Aging and adjustment: The applicability of logotherapy and the Purpose-in-Life Test. *Gerontologist,* 1972, **12,** 418–420.

25 Cryns, A. G., & Monk, A. Attitudes of the aged toward the young: A multivariate study of intergenerational perception. *J. Gerontol.,* 1972, **27,** 107–112.

26 Dean, L. R. Aging and the decline of affect. *J. Gerontol.,* 1962, **17,** 440–446.

27 Dennis, W. Creative productivity between the ages of twenty and eighty years. In D. C. Charles & W. R. Looft (Eds.), *Readings in psychological development through life.* New York: Holt, 1973. Pp. 283–295.

28 Dovenmuehle, R. H., Reckless, J. B., & Newman, G. Depressive reactions in the elderly. In E. B. Palmore (Ed.), *Normal aging.* Durham, N.C.: Duke University Press, 1970. Pp. 90–97.

29 Ehrlich, I. F. Life-styles among persons 70 years and older in age-segregated housing. *Gerontologist,* 1972, **12,** 27–31.

30 Eisdorfer, C., & Lawton, M. P. (Eds.) *The psychology of adult development and aging.* Washington: APA, 1973.

31 Epstein, L. A., & Murray, J. H. Employment and retirement. In B. L. Neugarten (Ed.), *Middle age and aging: A reader in social psychology.* Chicago: University of Chicago Press, 1968. Pp. 354–356.

32 Erikson, E. H. Identity and the life cycle: Selected papers. *Psychol. Issues Monogr.,* Vol. 1, No. 1. New York: International Universities Press, 1967.

33 Felstein, I. *Later life: Geriatrics today and tomorrow.* Baltimore: Penguin, 1969.

34 Fillenbaum, G. G. On the relation between attitude to work and attitude to retirement. *J. Gerontol.,* 1971, **26,** 244–248.

35 Foley, A. R. Preretirement planning in a changing society. *Amer. J. Psychiat.,* 1972, **128,** 877–881.

36 *Geriatric Focus* article. Menopause not end of sex. *Geriatric Focus,* 1966, **5**(5), 1, 6.

37 *Geriatric Focus* article. Correlates of high morale in community-based aged. *Geriatric Focus,* 1969, **8**(18), 1, 5.

38 *Geriatric Focus* article. Remarriage late in life usually very successful. *Geriatric Focus,* 1969, **8**(20), 1–5.

39 *Geriatric Focus* article. Retirement to age-segregated communities facilitates social adjustment of the elderly. *Geriatric Focus,* 1969, **8**(9), 2–3.

40 Goldfarb, A. I. Institutional care of the aged. In E. W. Busse & E. Pfeiffer (Eds.), *Behavior and adaptation in late life.* Boston: Little, Brown, 1969. Pp. 289–312.

41 Gordon, S. K. The phenomenon of depression in old age. *Gerontologist,* 1973, **13,** 100–105.

42 Gove, W. R. Sex, marital status, and mortality. *Amer. J. Sociol.,* 1973, **79,** 45–67.

43 Guion, R. M., & Landy, F. J. The meaning of work and the motivation to work. *Organiz. Behav. hum. Perform.,* 1972, **7,** 308–339.

44 Havighurst, R. J. Successful aging. *Gerontologist,* 1961, **1,** 8–13.

45 Havighurst, R. J. Body, self, and society. *Sociol. soc. Res.,* 1965, **49,** 261–267.

46 Havighurst, R. J., & Albrecht, R. *Older people.* New York: Longmans, 1953.

47 Havighurst, R. J., & Glasser, R. An exploratory study of reminiscence. *J. Gerontol.,* 1972, **27,** 245–253.

48 Heidbreder, E. M. Factors in retirement adjustment: White-collar/blue-collar experience. *Industr. Gerontol.,* 1972, **12,** 69–79.

49 Henry, W. E., & Cumming, E. Personality development in adulthood and old age. *J. proj. Tech.,* 1959, **23,** 383–390.

50 Heyman, D. K., & Gianturco, D. T. Long-term adaptation by the elderly to bereavement. *J. Gerontol.,* 1973, **28,** 359–362.

51 Horwitz, J. This is the age of the aged. *The New York Times,* May 16, 1965.

52 Jaeger, D., & Simmons, L. W. *The aged ill: Coping with problems in geriatric care.* New York: Appleton Century Crofts, 1970.

53 Johnson, W. M. *The years after fifty.* College Park, Md.: McGrath Publishing, 1970.

54 Kahana, B., & Kahana, E. Grandparenthood from the perspective of the developing grandchild. *Develpm. Psychol.,* 1970, **3,** 98–105.

55 Kalish, R. A. *The dependencies of old people.* Ann Arbor, Mich.: Institute of Gerontology, 1969, No. 6.

56 Kassel, V. Polygyny after 60. *Geriatrics,* 1966, **21,** 214–218.

57 Kastenbaum, R. (Ed.) *Contributions to the psychobiology of aging.* New York: Springer, 1965.

58 Kent, D. P. Social and cultural factors affecting the mental health of the aged. *Amer. J. Orthopsychiat.,* 1966, **36,** 680–685.

59 Kent, D. P. Planning facilities, programs, and services:

Government and nongovernment. *Gerontologist,* 1972, **12,** 36–48.

60 Kreps, J. M. Economics of retirement. In E. W. Busse & E. Pfeiffer (Eds.), *Behavior and adaptation in late life.* Boston: Little, Brown, 1969. Pp. 71–91.

61 Kuypers, J. A. Changeability of life-style and personality in old age. *Gerontologist,* 1972, **12,** 336–342.

62 Lakin, M., & Eisdorfer, C. Affective expression among the aged. In E. B. Palmore (Ed.), *Normal aging.* Durham, N. C.: Duke University Press, 1970. Pp. 243–250.

63 Lawton, G. *Aging successfully.* New York: Columbia University Press, 1951.

64 Lawton, M. P., & Bader, J. Wish for privacy by young and old. *J. Gerontol.,* 1970, **25,** 48–54.

65 Levinson, B. M. *Pets and human development.* Springfield, Ill.: Charles C Thomas, 1972.

66 Linn, M. W. Perceptions of childhood: Present functioning and past events. *J. Gerontol.,* 1973, **28,** 202–206.

67 Linn, M. W., & Gurel, L. Family attitude in nursing home placement. *Gerontologist,* 1972, **12,** 220–224.

68 Lopata, H. Z. The life cycle of the social role of housewife. *Sociol. soc. Res.,* 1966, **51,** 5–22.

69 Lopata, H. Z. *Widowhood in an American city.* Cambridge, Mass.: Schenkman, 1973.

70 Lowenthal, M. F. Social isolation and mental illness in old age. In B. L. Neugarten (Ed.), *Middle age and aging: A reader in social psychology.* Chicago: University of Chicago Press, 1968. Pp. 220–234.

71 Lynch, D. J. Future time perspective and impulsivities in old age. *J. genet. Psychol.,* 1971, **118,** 245–252.

72 Maddox, G. L. Disengagement theory: A critical evaluation. *Gerontologist,* 1964, **4,** 80–82.

73 Maddox, G. L. Retirement as a social event in the United States. In B. L. Neugarten (Ed.); *Middle age and aging: A reader in social psychology.* Chicago: University of Chicago Press, 1968. Pp. 357–365.

74 Masters, W. H., & Johnson, V. E. Human sexual response: The aging female and the aging male. In B. L. Neugarten (Ed.), *Middle age and aging: A reader in social psychology.* Chicago: University of Chicago Press, 1968. Pp. 269–279.

75 McKain, W. C. A new look at older marriage. *Family Coordinator,* 1972, **21,** 61–69.

76 Meltzer, H. Age differences in happiness and life adjustments of workers. *J. Gerontol.,* 1963, **18,** 66–70.

77 Monk, A. Factors in the preparation for retirement by middle-aged adults. *Gerontologist,* 1971, **11,** 348–351.

78 Montgomery, J. E. Magna Carta of the aged. *J. Home Econ.,* 1973, **65**(4), 6–13.

79 Morison, R. S. Dying. *Scient. American,* 1973, **229**(3), 55–62.

80 Neugarten, B. L. Adult personality: A developmental view. In D. C. Charles & W. R. Looft (Eds.), *Readings in psychological development through life.* New York: Holt, 1973. Pp. 356–366.

81 Neugarten, B. L., & Weinstein, K. K. The changing American grandparent. *J. Marriage & Family,* 1964, **26,** 199–204.

82 Newman, G., & Nichols, C. R. Sexual activities and attitudes in older persons. In E. B. Palmore (Ed.), *Normal aging.* Durham, N.C.: Duke University Press, 1970. Pp. 277–281.

83 *New York Times* article. One fear for women in 60's: To wake up with nothing to do. *The New York Times,* May 19, 1972.

84 *New York Times* article. Job survey finds aged work well. *The New York Times,* Sept. 22, 1972.

85 Paillat, P. M., & Bunch, M. E. Age, work, and automation. *Interdisciplinary Topics in Gerontology,* 1970, Vol. 6.

86 Palmore, E. B. Why do people retire? *Aging & hum. Develpm.,* 1971, **2,** 269–283.

87 Payne, S., Summers, D. A., & Stewart, T. R. Value differences across three generations. *Sociometry,* 1973, **36,** 20–30.

88 Peterson, D. A. Financial adequacy in retirement: Perceptions of older Americans. *Gerontologist,* 1972, **12,** 379–383.

89 Pfeiffer, E., Verwoerdt, A., & Wang, H-S. Sexual behavior in aged men and women. In E. B. Palmore (Ed.), *Normal aging* Durham, N.C.: Duke University Press, 1970. Pp. 299–303.

90 Pollman, A. W. Early retirement: A comparison of poor health to other retirement factors. *J. Gerontol.,* 1971, **26,** 41–45.

91 Powers, E. A., & Goudy, W. J. Examination of the meaning of work to older workers. *Aging & hum. Develpm.,* 1971, **2,** 38–45.

92 Pressey, S. L. Potentials of age: An exploratory field study. *Genet. Psychol. Monogr.,* 1957, **56,** 159–205.

93 Reichard, S., Livson, F., & Petersen, P. G. Adjustment to retirement. In B. L. Neugarten (Ed.), *Middle age and aging: A reader in social psychology.* Chicago: University of Chicago Press, 1968. Pp. 178–180.

94 Rollins, B. C., & Feldman, H. Marital satisfaction over the family life cycle. *J. Marriage & Family,* 1970, **32,** 20–28.

95 Rose, A. M. A current theoretical issue in social gerontology. In B. L. Neugarten (Ed.), *Middle age and aging: A reader in social psychology.* Chicago: University of Chicago Press, 1968. Pp. 184–189.

96 Rosow, I. Housing and local ties of the aged. In B. L. Neugarten (Ed.), *Middle age and aging: A reader in social psychology.* Chicago: University of Chicago Press, 1968. Pp. 382–389.

97 Rosow, I. *The social integration of the aged.* New York: Free Press, 1968.

98 Rowe, A. R. Scientists in retirement. *J. Gerontol.,* 1973, **28,** 345–350.

99 Rubin, I. The "sexless older years": A socially harmful stereotype. In D. C. Charles & W. R Looft (Eds.), *Readings in psychological development through life.* New York: Holt, 1973. Pp. 367–379.

100 Semple, R. B. New help for the 18,457,000 of us who are old. *The New York Times,* Feb. 5, 1967.

101 Shanas, E. Living arrangements and housing of old people. In E. W. Busse & E. Pfeiffer (Eds.), *Behavior and adaptation in late life.* Boston: Little, Brown, 1969. Pp. 129–149.

102 Sheppard, H. L. Employment and retirement: Roles and activities. *Gerontologist,* 1972, **12,** 29–35.

103 Sherman, S. R. Methodology in a study of residents of retirement housing. *J. Gerontol.,* 1973, **28,** 351–358.

104 Shock, N. W. *Trends in gerontology.* (2nd ed.) Stanford Calif.: Stanford University Press, 1957.

105 Silverman, P. R. Widowhood and preventive intervention. *Family Coordinator,* 1972, **21,** 95–102.

106 Slater, P. E., & Scarr, H. A. Personality in old age. *Genet. Psychol. Monogr.,* 1964, **70,** 229–269.

107 Stinnett, N., Carter, L. M., & Montgomery, J. E. Older persons' perceptions of their marriages. *J. Marriage & Family,* 1972, **34,** 665–670.

108 Streib, G. F. Older families and their troubles: Familial and social responses. *Family Coordinator,* 1972, **21,** 5–19.

109 Tanenbaum, D. E. Loneliness in the aged. *Ment. Hyg., N.Y.,* 1967, **51,** 91–99.

110 Thompson, G. B. Work versus leisure roles: An investigation of morale among employed and retired men. *J. Gerontol.,* 1973, **28,** 339–344.

111 Tibbits, C. (Ed.) *Handbook of social gerontology: Societal aspects of aging.* Chicago: University of Chicago Press, 1960.

112 *Time* article. The old in the country of the young. *Time,* Aug. 2, 1970, 49–54.

113 Troll, L. E. The family of later life: A decade review. *J. Marriage & Family,* 1971, **33,** 263–290.

114 Tuckman, J. Older people's judgment of the passage of time over the life span. *Geriatrics,* 1965, **20,** 136–140.

115 Twente, E. E. *Never too old.* San Francisco: Jossey-Bass, 1970.

116 Vedder, C. B., & Lefkowitz, A. S. (Eds.) *Problems of the aged.* Springfield, Ill.: Charles C Thomas, 1965.

117 Verwoerdt, A., Pfeiffer, E., & Wang, H-S. Sexual behavior in senescence. II. Patterns of sexual activity and interest. *Geriatrics,* 1969, **24,** 137–154.

118 Wake, S. B., & Sporakiwski, M. J. An intergenerational comparison of attitudes towards supporting aged parents. *J. Marriage & Family,* 1972, **34,** 42–48.

119 Wallin, J. E. W. The psychological, educational, and social problems of the aging as viewed by a mid-octogenarian. *J. genet. Psychol.,* 1962, **100,** 41–46.

120 Weiss, W. U., & Waldrop, R. S. Some characteristics of individuals who remain in an institution for the aged. *Develpm. Psychol.,* 1972, **6,** 182.

121 Williams, R. H., Tibbitts, C., & Donahue, W. *Process of aging: Social and psychological perspectives.* New York: Atherton Press, 1963.

122 Wolff, K. Personality type and reaction toward aging and death. *Geriatrics,* 1966, **21,** 189–192.

123 Wylie, M. L. Life satisfaction as a program impact criterion. *J. Gerontol.,* 1970, **25,** 36–40.

INDEX

INDEX